PUBLIC ECONOMICS

This new and up-to-date textbook provides a thorough treatment of all the central topics in public economics. Written in an accessible style and aimed squarely at senior undergraduate and graduate students, it will be invaluable to those teaching in the field and will also be a vital resource for professional economists.

The book is entirely self-contained and covers, in the first section, the competitive equilibrium theory and welfare economics that underpin the analysis of policy design. The second section then studies commodity taxation, income taxation, tax reform, the public economics of risk and corporation taxation within the context of the competitive economy.

In the third section, departures from the standard competitive assumptions and their implications for public economics are carefully considered. The final section provides an introduction to the overlapping generation economy before addressing intertemporal issues concerning social security and debt.

PUBLIC ECONOMICS

Gareth D. Myles
University of Exeter

Published by the Press Syndicate of the University of Cambridge
The Pitt Building, Trumpington Street, Cambridge CB2 1RP
40 West 20th Street, New York, NY 10011-4211, USA
10 Stamford Road, Oakleigh, Melbourne 3166, Australia

First published 1995

Printed in Great Britain at the University Press, Cambridge

A catalogue record for this book is available from the British Library

Library of Congress cataloguing in publication data

Myles, Gareth D.
    Public economics / Gareth D. Myles.
      p. cm.
    Includes bibliographical references.
    ISBN 0 521 49721 3 (hbk.).   ISBN 0 521 49769 8 (pbk.)
    1. Welfare economics. 2. Economic policy. 3. Taxation.
    4. Public welfare. 5. Social choice. 6. Equilibrium (Economics)
    I. Title.
    HB846.M95   1995
    336–dc20   94-44774
                                                   CIP

ISBN 0 521 49721 3 hardback
ISBN 0 521 49769 8 paperback

SE

To Tracy
to Georgina
and to Harriet
who's disappointed it has no pictures

CONTENTS

FIGURES

TABLES

PREFACE

This book provides a systematic treatment of the major themes in public economics. It is primarily theoretical although empirical results and simulation results are described where these illustrate the theoretical arguments. The merit of the theoretical approach is that it provides arguments and methods of reasoning that are not dependent on transitory institutional detail but can be applied in a wide variety of contexts. The unifying feature of the analysis is the employment of general equilibrium theory to provide a consistent foundation on which results are developed. The use of general equilibrium techniques reflects the author's belief that, since the secondary effects of policy can sometimes outweigh the direct effects, this is the only method that can provide defensible conclusions.

The book is written primarily for graduate students and economists from other fields wishing to learn about public economics. Although this means that some sections are advanced, and some of the proofs terse, there is much that can be profitably read by advanced undergraduates. In fact, the first three chapters could constitute a self-contained treatment of general equilibrium and welfare economics for such students. I have also attempted to structure the chapters so that the basic points are made early on in the simplest acceptable framework. For graduate students, the book should show them public economics as it appears in academic journals. If they wish really to understand the material and intend to contribute to its future development, then mastery of the methods of argument and the details of proofs is essential. After completing this book they should have moved some way towards achieving these objectives.

In writing the book I have benefited immeasurably from the assistance of my colleagues. From amongst these, special thanks are due to Martin Cripps and Norman Ireland from Warwick and Jean Fan, Ben Lockwood and David de Meza from Exeter. John Black provided invaluable assistance in reading, and correcting, the entire manuscript. I have also received very helpful comments on individual chapters from Sheng Cheng Hu, Stephen Jenkins, Kevin Roberts,

C.C. Yang and John Weymark. Vidar Christiansen provided encouragement when I was originally planning the text and acted as the final reader for Cambridge University Press. His efforts have improved the book considerably. Although I did not always agree with them (nor did they entirely agree amongst themselves), the anonymous referees of Cambridge University Press must also be thanked. Their comments helped provide the incentive to complete the text when it seemed that there was so much left to do and were significant in the direction it developed. Part of the material in chapter 6 on policy reform has its origins in joint work with Ravi Kanbur. In addition, some of the content of chapter 12 reflects my collaboration with Robin Naylor on the economics of tax evasion.

The book originally developed from a series of lectures on public economics first given to graduate students at the University of Warwick in 1988 and to the undergraduate lectures that I have been giving since 1987. Thanks are due to all the students whose comments contributed towards improvement of the early drafts; particular thanks are due to Luigi Franzoni, Umberto Galmirini and Guido Merzoni. Writing was started in earnest in 1991 and the outlines of chapters shown to Cambridge University Press in February 1992. Since that time Patrick McCartan of Cambridge University Press has been a source of continuing enthusiasm which has been of great help. The manuscript was completed at the University of Exeter in November 1994.

For the most part, I have typed the text but the task of converting some of the original lecture notes into typed text at the start of the project was undertaken by Lisa Hayes at Warwick and some of the bibliography was produced by Anita Long at Exeter.

Part I

FOUNDATIONS

1

INTRODUCTION

1 PUBLIC ECONOMICS

In the broadest interpretation, public economics is the study of economic policy, with particular emphasis upon taxation. The subject therefore encompasses topics as diverse as responses to market failure due to the existence of externalities and the determination of optimal social security policies. This characterisation reflects an extension of the scope of public economics from its initial emphasis upon the collection and disbursement of government revenues to its present concern with all aspects of government economic intervention. The intention of this book is to provide an introduction to the vast literature of public economics, emphasising the foundations upon which future research can be laid.

Public economics has a long history as a discipline within economics and many eminent economists have written on the subject. For example, Ricardo (1817) discussed the effects of public debt, the incidence of taxation in imperfectly competitive markets was analysed by Cournot (1838), Edgeworth (1925) considered the effects of taxation on multi-product firms and Pareto (1909) set out the foundations for making social decisions. The explanation for this interest in public economics is no doubt contained in the close connection of the analysis with policy and application, which are the ultimate inspiration of most economists. Exposing a theoretical construction to policy analysis also highlights its value and provides a test of its relevance. However, it is also true that before a good policy can be designed an adequate theory must be developed. One of the challenges of public economics is that much of the subject area is still in its infancy with considerable work still to be done.

Although a number of partitions could be used to break down the subject matter of public economics into convenient portions, the most instructive division is between that of determining the effects of alternative policies and that of determining the optimal policy. This division represents the distinction between the exercise in positive economics involved in calculating the change in equilibrium caused by the introduction of a policy and the normative exercise of evaluating, in terms of welfare, the outcome of policy. To achieve the first objective requires a theory that describes how economic agents choose their actions and how these actions are affected by changes in policy. The individual agents must then be combined to form an economy and a theory of equilibrium provided for this economy. The evaluation of policy, and the choice of optimal policy, necessitates the specification of an objective for the policy maker that is capable of providing a measure of the performance of each policy based on the relevant features of the equilibrium resulting from the policy. This evaluation process represents an application of normative economics. The success of public economics has largely followed from the systematic application of these methods.

The theory that is described in the following chapters has developed mainly since 1970 and has built upon developments in microeconomics, macroeconomics, general equilibrium theory and game theory. One of its characteristic features is the use of duality techniques to allow problems to be phrased in the manner most amenable to solution. These techniques permit optimisation exercises to be phrased in terms of the natural choice variables. In this context, the work of Diamond and Mirrlees (1971) was of fundamental importance in introducing these methods into public economics. The use of duality theory has also allowed many problems to be studied with great generality and has often overcome the need to impose restrictive sets of assumptions. A second characteristic feature is the consistent use of general equilibrium theory to provide a rigorous foundation for the policy analysis. A general equilibrium analysis of policy captures both the direct effects of policy and the secondary effects. As the latter may well outweigh the former, a convincing policy analysis cannot be conducted except within a general equilibrium context. These underlying methods of duality and general equilibrium provide the cohesion to what at first glance may appear to be a number of disparate topics.

An emerging trend in the public economics literature has been the use of numerical methods. These have taken the form of both simulations of economies in order to test their behaviour and the evaluation of policy proposals using empirical data. The latter technique indicates a promising convergence between theory and application and is clearly a direction in which the subject will continue to move. Although this book is primarily intended to be a text on the theory of public economics, numerical results are given prominence due to their obvious importance.

The dominant setting for the analysis of public economics is within the mixed economy so that individual decisions are respected but the government intervenes to affect these choices. The design of policy can then be interpreted as the manipulation of individual choices by the choice of policy parameters so as to arrive at an equilibrium preferred to that which would arise in the absence of policy. This makes the results of the studies applicable to most developed economies and concurs with the present ascendancy of such a form of economic organisation. To provide a benchmark from which to judge the outcome of the economy under alternative policies the perfectly controlled command economy with an omniscient planner is often employed. Naturally, this usage of the command economy implies no claim that such perfect control is possible, or even desirable.

2 MOTIVATION

The motivation for the study of public economics follows naturally from the observation that unregulated economic activity does not lead to a socially optimal outcome. At a very basic level, an economy could not function effectively if there were no contract laws since this would inhibit satisfactory exchange. In addition, although the anarchic equilibrium that would occur without contracts may be in the core of the economy, it need not be particularly stable (Bush and Mayer 1974). It must therefore be accepted that no economy could operate without law enforcement and that in order for organised economic activity to take place, there must be a clearly defined and enforced set of contract laws. These laws cannot be policed free of cost. There is also a need for the enforcement of more general criminal laws and for the provision of a means of defence for the nation. These are also costly activities.

Consequently, even the minimal requirements of the enforcement of contract and criminal laws and the provision of defence need the collection of revenue to provide the required finance. This is the case whether these services are provided by the state or by private-sector organisations. The coordination of the collection of revenue and the provision of services to ensure the attainment of efficient functioning of economic activity therefore provides a natural role for a central state in any economy that wishes to develop beyond the most rudimentary level. In addition, this reasoning also illustrates that to achieve even the most minimal level of efficiency and organisation of economic activity some unavoidable revenue requirements are generated and require financing.

Having determined that the organisation of economic activity must generate a revenue requirement, one aspect of the role of public economics is to determine how this revenue can be collected at the least cost to the economy. Although the concept of least cost has several possible interpretations, both positive and normative, under any interpretation the aim of the economic policy design would be that of finding an efficient means of revenue collection. Such design would involve the identification of feasible policy instruments from the set of possible policies, the choice of policy instruments to be imposed from amongst those that are feasible and the calculation of the optimal level of each instrument. The issue of efficiency in policy design is a continuing and central theme of public economics.

Moving beyond the basic requirements for organised economic activity, it is arguable that there are other situations where state intervention in the economy has the potential to increase welfare. Unlike the basic revenue requirements, however, there will always be a degree of contentiousness about further intervention motivated on these grounds. The situations where state intervention may be warranted can be divided into two categories: those that involve market failure and those that do not. With market failure, the argument for considering whether intervention would be beneficial is compelling. For example, if economic activity generates externalities, so that there is divergence between private and social costs and the competitive outcome is not efficient, it may be felt necessary for the state to intervene to limit the inefficiency that results. This latter point can also be extended to other cases of market failure such as those connected to the existence of public goods and of imperfect competition.

Where market failure does not occur, state intervention can be motivated by the observation that although an equilibrium may be efficient it need not be optimal according to the state's welfare criterion. Such a situation may arise if the equilibrium of the economy is characterised by widespread poverty and an inequitable distribution of income. In such circumstances, the level of economic welfare as viewed by the state may well be raised by a programme of income redistribution. Similar arguments can be applied to the provision of state education, social security programmes and compulsory pension schemes. It should be stressed that such potential increases are with respect to normative assessments of welfare, unlike the positive criteria lying behind the concept of economic efficiency.

In the cases of both market failure and welfare-motivated policies, policy intervention concerns more than just the efficient collection of revenue. The reasons for the failure of the economy to reach the optimal outcome have to be understood and a policy that can counteract these has to be designed. It must also be recognised that the actions of the state, and the feasible policies that it can choose, are often restricted by the same features of the economy that make the competitive outcome inefficient. In each case, policy intervention can only be justified by proving that the state can actually improve upon the market. That it can always do so should not be taken for granted. Extending the scope of public economics to address such issues provides the breadth to public economics.

3 EFFICIENCY VERSUS EQUITY

In conducting an economic policy the state will generally have two conflicting aims. On the one hand, it will aim to implement the policy with the minimum loss to society. The use of policy will cause a loss due to the resources used in the implementation process and from the economic distortions that the policy will cause. Minimising these losses is the efficiency aspect of policy design. Conversely, the state may also feel that it is desirable to intervene in the economy in order to attain a more equitable distribution of the economy's resources. This is often accompanied by a corresponding reduction in the degree of concern for the aggregate level of economic activity. This motivation represents the equity side of policy design.

Due to their distinct natures, it is inevitable that the aims of equity and efficiency regularly conflict. It is often the case that the efficient policy is highly inequitable whilst the equitable policy would introduce into the economy significant distortions and disincentives. Given this fact, the design of optimal policy can be seen as the process of reaching the correct trade-off between equity and efficiency objectives. This optimum trade-off will depend upon the concern for equity that is expressed in the objectives of the policy maker. In many analyses of policy problems, the resolution of the trade-off between equity and efficiency is the major determinant of the resulting policy programme, with aspects of the policy being attributable to one or the other. This distinction is often a helpful way in which to think about optimality problems and their solutions. It is worth stressing that the conflict between equity and efficiency does not always arise. For example, in some instances of uncertainty, such as the provision of social insurance discussed in chapter 7, the two aims of efficiency and equity may not be competing.

To illustrate this discussion, a simple example of the conflict between equity and efficiency can be found in the optimal taxation of commodities. Under assumptions that will be described later, it is efficient to tax goods with low elasticities of demand, as shown by the well-known inverse elasticity rule, since this introduces the least distortion into the pattern of demand. However, goods with low elasticities of demand tend to be necessities that are consumed disproportionately by less well-off households. Taxing these goods highly would then cause a proportionately greater reduction in the welfare of poor households. The proposed tax programme is therefore highly inequitable and equity criteria would shift the taxes on to goods consumed by higher-income groups. The Diamond–Mirrlees tax rule that is developed in chapter 4 shows how this conflict between efficiency and equity is resolved.

In this context, it is worth adding one final note concerned with modelling techniques. A standard simplification that will be employed on a number of occasions in this book is to work with one-consumer economies or with economies composed of a population of identical consumers. In such economies there can be no distributional issues, so the resulting policy recommendations are based only on considerations of efficiency. This generally leads to results that can be expressed much more clearly and precisely than would be possible if equity considerations were present, which is of considerable assistance when an issue is analysed for the first time. In considering the practical value of such results, the implications of introducing equity considerations must always be borne in mind.

4 INFORMATION

The role of information is central to public economics. The availability of information to private agents determines the nature of the equilibrium without policy intervention and the information set of the government determines feasible policy instruments. If information deficiencies, particularly asymmetric information between agents in the economy, lead the market outcome to be inefficient, the state can only improve the outcome if it is not subject to the same informational limitations.

As will be made clear in chapter 2, the first-best outcome could be sustained if the state levied lump-sum taxes that were contingent upon all economically relevant characteristics of the agents in the economy. Naturally, some of these characteristics will be private information and therefore not directly observable by the state. If the state cannot costlessly induce the agents to truthfully reveal these characteristics, then the lump-sum tax system that supports the first best cannot be implemented. Policy design then involves the optimal utilisation of the available information. The outcome that is achieved will necessarily be second best. This simple example demonstrates the essential consequences of informational restrictions and captures themes that will recur throughout the book.

Further examples are easily found. In the context of commodity taxation, limited information prevents commodity taxes being differentiated between consumers. It also results in the use of an income tax levied upon the observable income of households, rather than an ability tax on their unobservable earning potential. The optimal provision of public goods is also prevented by the fact that the government cannot observe consumers' willingness to pay for such goods. The outcome in each of these cases is described in the relevant chapters.

Although asymmetries of information are at the heart of most of the analysis that follows, their nature will rarely be made explicit. Instead, the nature of information will be implicit in the assumptions that describe the structure of the economies employed and the restrictions that are placed upon feasible policy instruments. In considering the results derived below, it will always be advantageous to reflect upon the nature of the informational restrictions involved and the consequences of their relaxation or strengthening.

5 METHODOLOGY

The method of analysis adopted within this book is invariably to consider policy within the context of a general equilibrium representation of the economy. In parts I to III of the book, the underlying framework is the Arrow–Debreu economy and its extensions. The overlapping generations economy employed in part IV is a particular infinite horizon version of the general formulation. The general equilibrium perspective is maintained wherever it is feasible to do so. This aim is not achieved in places such as when only partial equilibrium treatments are available in the existing literature, or when a general equilibrium treatment would only obscure the major issues.

A general equilibrium economy is undoubtedly the most appropriate framework to adopt since it is the only means by which all the repercussions of a policy may be captured. In contrast, concentration upon partial equilibrium can lead to important consequences of policy being overlooked, particularly if there are significant adjustments in markets other than those forming the focus of the analysis. However, partial equilibrium analysis is often useful as a means of obtaining preliminary insights into a problem, but its limitations should never be underestimated. Although most attention in the literature has been focused upon competitive economies, economies with market imperfections are now being widely used and policy analysis within such economies will also be considered.

Within a general equilibrium context, changes in policy, or alternative policies, can be viewed as resulting in different equilibria for the economy. To treat the question of optimality in policy choice, the equilibria for different policies are contrasted via some welfare measure. The optimal policy is then defined as the feasible policy yielding the greatest level of welfare. Since Pareto optimality generally provides too incomplete a ranking of states to be of use as a guide for policy, the welfare criterion that is used is typically a Bergson–Samuelson social welfare function. This procedure naturally invokes questions about the comparability of individual utilities and the formulation of welfare measures.

The analytical tools used in the book are generally fairly simple and the mathematics rarely uses anything more difficult than the theory of constrained maximisation and comparative statics analysis. There are exceptions to this rule. Separation arguments are used in chapters 2 and 9. Chapters 5 and 15 employ the maximum principle, chapter 7 employs a theorem of the alternative and chapter 13 touches upon non-linear dynamic systems. Dynamic programming is used in chapter 15. Since a self-contained treatment of general equilibrium analysis and welfare economics is given in chapter 2, the economics that is employed, but not otherwise introduced in the text, should be covered by any advanced undergraduate or graduate course in microeconomics and involves mainly standard duality results in producer and consumer theory. An excellent source of reference for this material is Varian (1992).

6 PREVIEW

Following the discussion of the methodology that will be employed, it is clear that a necessary starting point is a review of the competitive general equilibrium economy and the standard results of welfare economics. These represent the content of chapter 2. The chapter introduces the agents involved in the economy and characterises economic equilibrium. It also introduces a useful perspective from which to view Walras' law and formalises the notion of how policy changes are modelled. Emphasis is placed upon the institutional assumptions underlying the competitive equilibrium economy since much of the subject matter of public economics can be motivated by discomfort with the nature of the equilibrium of the competitive market or by the failure of one or more of the institutional assumptions. The Two Theorems of Welfare Economics are proved and a critical analysis of their scope and relevance is provided. This naturally leads into a discussion of the measurement of social welfare and the contrast between the implications for interpersonal comparability of ordinal and cardinal utility.

In practice, if economists are to be concerned about equity it is necessary to find measures that capture aspects of the distribution of welfare. Chapter 3 considers three topics that have been the subject of considerable interest. Alternative methods of constructing equivalence scales are reviewed as a prelude to developing measures of distribution. The measurement of poverty and of inequality are then used to illustrate the axiomatic approach to measurement, which specifies the properties that an index should have and then constructs the indices that have those properties, and the statistical approach which simply uses readily accessible formulae. These three introductory chapters constitute part I of the book.

Part II is concerned with the analysis of five topics of fundamental importance for public economics which are conducted within the competitive economy. Chapters 4 and 5 consider the characterisation of optimal commodity and income taxes respectively. Both of these chapters illustrate the resolution of the equity/efficiency trade-off in the design of policy and the consequences of government informational limitations. In addition to the theoretical analysis, the results of simulations and applications of the methods to data are considered. The numerical results are useful since the theoretical analysis leads only to characterisations of optimal taxes rather than to explicit solutions. Policy reform is the subject matter of chapter 6 and the link is drawn between the existence of improving reforms and non-optimality. The question of production efficiency along the reform path is also considered. Chapter 7 considers the public economics of risk. Finally, chapter 8 analyses the effects of corporate taxation and the issues that need to be taken into account in tax design.

The focus of part III is upon the consequences of relaxing certain of the institutional assumptions on which the competitive economy is based. Chapter 9 introduces public goods into the economy and contrasts the allocation that is achieved in the private provision equilibrium with the optimal allocation. Methods of financing public goods are also considered and this analysis has close parallels with the chapter on commodity taxation. Private provision and preference revelation are also addressed. The treatment of externalities in chapter 10 relaxes another of the institutional assumptions. It is shown why market failure can occur and reviews alternative policy schemes designed to improve efficiency. Imperfect competition and its consequences for commodity taxation are the subject of chapter 11. The measurement of welfare loss is discussed and a general equilibrium economy with imperfect competition is developed. Emphasis is given to the incidence of taxation and the determination of optimal taxes. A distinction is also drawn between the effects of specific and *ad valorem* taxes. Part III is completed by chapter 12 on tax evasion. Estimates of the size of the black economy are reviewed, the tax evasion decision is modelled and the effects of evasion on optimal taxes are determined.

Part IV concentrates upon intertemporal issues in public economics. The first chapter, 13, describes the overlapping generations economy that is the main analytical tool of this part. The relationship between the overlapping generations economy and the Arrow–Debreu economy is emphasised, as are the different efficiency properties of the two economies. The concept of the Golden rule is introduced for economies with production and capital accumulation. The chapter also touches upon the dynamic adjustment process of the economy. Chapter 14 analyses social security policy and relates this to the potential non-optimality of the competitive equilibrium. Both the motivation for the existence of social security programmes and the determination of the level of benefits are addressed. The interaction between debt and taxation is the subject of chapter 15. The effects of government debt and the issue of debt neutrality are considered. Ricardian equivalence is linked to the existence of gifts and bequests. The choice between the taxation of income and expenditure is also analysed.

7 PUBLIC-SECTOR INCOME AND EXPENDITURE

The public sector plays an important role in the mixed economies of the major industrialised countries. To show quite how important, this section presents some summary statistics concerning the size and structure of the public sector. Whilst there are some well-recognised issues concerning the appropriate definition of the public sector, these do not affect the validity of the broad sketch given here.

Figure 1.1 shows the pattern of public-sector total outlay as a percentage of nominal GNP over the period 1978–93 for seven of the major industrialised countries from North America, Europe and Asia. For these countries, public-sector expenditure falls in the range of 30–55 per cent of GNP with Japan and the United States having the smallest public sectors and Italy and France the largest. Even though the range is large, the public sector is significant in every case. Expenditure in Italy shows sustained growth through the period, as it does in the US but to a lesser extent. Other than these countries, the pattern is generally one of the public sector being a constant proportion of GNP. This relative stability over the recent past is in sharp contrast to the period of expansion of the public sector experienced by the industrialised countries from 1890 through to 1970.

The major implication of figure 1.1 is that it clearly justifies the claim that the

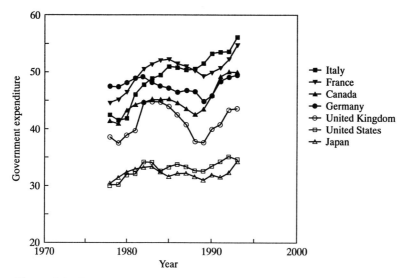

Figure 1.1   General government total outlay as a percentage of nominal GDP
Notes: Total outlay is current outlay plus net capital outlay. United States excludes
insurance outlays.
Source: OECD 1994a, *Economic Outlook*, 55.

public sector is significant in the economies of the industrialised countries and
the mixed economies of these countries are characterised by substantial
government involvement. They are far from being free market with minimal
government intervention. The size of the public sector alone is justification for
the study of how it should best choose its means of revenue collection and its
allocation of expenditure. It is also worth noting that data on expenditure
typically understate the full influence of the public sector upon the economy.
For instance, regulations such as employment laws or safety standards infringe
upon economic activity but without generating any measurable government
expenditure or income.

Figure 1.2 shows the proportion of Japanese government income derived
from various sources and the division of its expenditure. The chart for income
shows that direct taxation is the largest single component. Social security
contributions and indirect taxation are the next largest and make fairly similar
contributions to income. In terms of expenditure, social security spending is the
largest category followed by purchases of goods and services. Interest on public
debt is also a significant item of expenditure.

A similar breakdown of income and expenditure is reported for the United
Kingdom in figure 1.3. Contrasted to Japan, the UK shows greater reliance
upon indirect taxation, with indirect taxation generating slightly more revenue
than direct taxation. The relative size of social security contributions is also
much less than in Japan. The relative sizes of the expenditure items are very
similar, although the UK spends more on goods and services but less on

Division of income

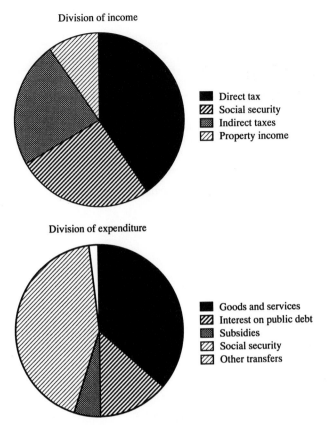

■ Direct tax
▨ Social security
▨ Indirect taxes
▨ Property income

Division of expenditure

■ Goods and services
▨ Interest on public debt
▨ Subsidies
▨ Social security
▨ Other transfers

Figure 1.2   Japanese government income and expenditure, 1991
Source: OECD 1993b, *Economic Survey of Japan*, November.

subsidies. The social security item in Japan is equivalent in relative size to the transfers in the UK.

Figures 1.2 and 1.3 demonstrate the importance of direct and indirect taxation in the collection of revenue for the UK and for Japan. Taken together, these generate 73 per cent of revenue in the UK and 63 per cent in Japan. The third item of income, social security contributions, are 17 per cent of income in the UK and 27 per cent in Japan. These figures support the prominence given to the design of commodity taxation in chapter 4, income taxation in chapter 5 and social security in chapter 14.

An alternative perspective on the relative importance of the three major categories of income is given in table 1.1. This shows receipts as a percentage of GDP for the US and as an average for other OECD countries. For the US, consumption taxes are relatively less important than as shown for Japan and the UK above and as against the average over OECD countries. However, consumption tax receipts still equal over 4 per cent of US GDP. Social security taxes raise twice the income of consumption taxes whilst income tax receipts

Table 1.1. *Comparison of tax yields*

	United States			Other OECD		
	1989	1990	1991	1989	1990	1991
Tax receipts (% GDP)						
Income tax	10.6	10.6	10.4	11.4	11.6	11.6
Social security tax	8.7	8.7	8.9	9.1	9.2	9.5
Consumption tax	4.2	4.2	4.4	11.1	11.0	11.2

Source: OECD, 1993a, Economic Survey of the United States, November.

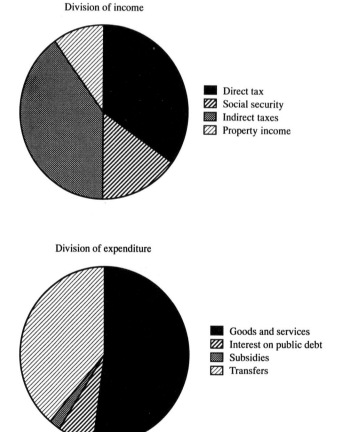

Figure 1.3   United Kingdom government income and expenditure, 1991
Notes: Property income includes the community charge. Current transfers include social security.
Source: OECD 1994, *Economic Survey of the United Kingdom*, July.

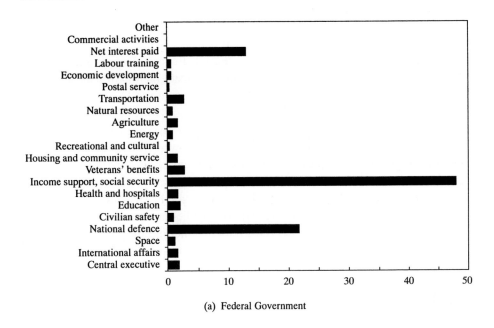

(a) Federal Government

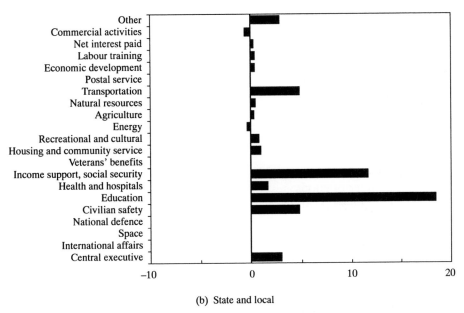

(b) State and local

Figure 1.4   US Federal and State expenditure by type and function, 1992
Note: Figures are percentage of total expenditure.
Source: Department of Commerce 1993, *Survey of Current Business*, 73, September,
tables 3.16 and 3.17.

represent one tenth of GDP. In contrast, the OECD average shows rather more equality between receipts from income and consumption taxes.

Figure 1.4a shows the expenditure of the US Federal Government broken down into type and function, expressed as a percentage of total expenditure. Similarly, figure 1.4b has the same breakdown for State and Local Government. These tables reveal that the major items of expenditure for Federal Government are income support and social security, and defence. In contrast, the major item for State and Local Government is education followed by income support and social security. Other than these, the most significant items are the net interest paid by the Federal Government and transportation and civilian safety paid for by State and Local Government. The items can be placed into separate categories representing the breakdown of public-sector objectives: defence expenditure is one of the minimal requirements; income support is evidence of concern for equity; and education represents provision of a public good to counter market failure.

Although brief, this review of statistics on the size and structure of public-sector income and expenditure has illustrated the significant extent of public-sector intervention in the mixed economies of the industrialised countries. The relative importance of alternative sources of revenue has been shown as has the range of expenditure.

8 NOTATION

There are many symbols that have a constant meaning through the text. The most important of these are listed below.

H	number of households
m	number of firms
n	number of goods
p_i	pre-tax price (of good i)
q_i	post-tax price
t_i	tax rate
R	government revenue requirement
G	public good supply
x^h	consumption plan (of household h)
X^h	consumption set
ℓ^h	level of labour supply (when distinguished from other commodities)
ω^h	initial endowment
I^h	lump-sum income
M^h	total income
Ω^h	wealth
T^h	lump-sum tax paid by h
α^h	marginal utility of income
β^h	social marginal utility of income

$U^h(\cdot)$	household utility function
$V^h(\cdot)$	indirect utility function
$E^h(\cdot)$	expenditure function
$W(\cdot)$	social welfare function
y^j	production plan (of firm j)
Y^j	production set
π^j	profit level
θ^h_j	share of h in j
X_i	aggregate demand (for good i)
Y_i	aggregate supply
Z_i	excess demand
$\mathscr{E}[\cdot]$	expectations operator
K_t	capital stock (in period t)
k_t	capital–labour ratio
r_t	interest rate
w_t	wage rate

In addition to these symbols, there are others which are more chapter specific.

The is one further notational convention that must be noted. Throughout the text round brackets proceeded by a symbol always represent functions so that $f(x)$ denotes the function f of x. In contrast, square brackets denote algebraic operations so that $f[x]$ is read f times x. The only exception to this rule is the expectations operator $\mathscr{E}[\cdot]$.

2

GENERAL EQUILIBRIUM AND WELFARE ECONOMICS

1 INTRODUCTION

The competitive general equilibrium economy described in this chapter has been developed over a considerable period of time and has been subjected to closer study than any other form of economy. The earliest formal construction is generally attributed to Walras (1874) and this was developed in the German literature of the 1930s. These developments reached maturity in the seminal contribution of Arrow and Debreu (1954) and in the monograph by Debreu (1959); hence its common title of the *Arrow–Debreu* economy. The importance of the Arrow–Debreu contribution was the demonstration that an equilibrium existed for the economy under reasonable assumptions and the formal elaboration of the welfare properties of equilibrium. This chapter provides an informal but self-contained introduction to the Arrow–Debreu general equilibrium economy. The discussion emphasises those aspects of the economy that are most relevant to the study of public economics. Technical aspects of the economy that are not strictly necessary for later analysis will be noted but, where there is no harm from doing so, will not be discussed in detail. Formal treatments of the issues dealt with here can be found in Arrow and Hahn (1971), Debreu (1959) and Hildenbrand and Kirman (1988).

The Arrow–Debreu economy is studied for two primary reasons. Firstly, it provides the analytical foundation for the economies analysed in later chapters which are often simplifications or modifications of the general framework. The focus of part III of the book will be on the consequences of relaxing the assumptions on which the Arrow–Debreu economy is based so the results of this chapter act as a benchmark from which to judge the effects of the relaxation. The second reason is that welfare properties of the economy, which are commonly known as the *Two Theorems of Welfare Economics*, are used as the basis for claims concerning the efficiency, and thus desirability, of the competitive outcome. These Theorems represent the formalisation of Smith's (1776) notion of the efficiency of the invisible hand of competition and play a central role in welfare economics. The First Theorem states that a competitive equilibrium is optimal, in a sense to be made precise below, and the Second Theorem that any optimum can be decentralised as a competitive equilibrium. An understanding of the economy is therefore a prerequisite for appreciating the content and limitations of these claims.

The Theorems provide the motivation for two alternative viewpoints upon economic policy. One viewpoint would be to take the Theorems as evidence that policy should always be attempting to move the economy as close to the competitive ideal as possible. In this interpretation, the Theorems are seen as prescriptive of what should be achieved. The alternative view is that the Two Theorems provide a description of what could be achieved if the economy were competitive and a demonstration of why it cannot, and possibly should not, be achieved in practice. The cannot refers to the assumptions of the economy that will not be met in practice and the should not to the distributional aspects of competitive equilibrium. The mainstream of public economics combines parts of both of these caricatured viewpoints. Many policy analyses take for granted the presumption that competitive behaviour should be advocated and encouraged when it leads to economic efficiency. However, its failings are also readily admitted and policies designed to correct for them. Indeed, much of public economics implicitly takes as its starting point the rejection of the practical value of the Second Theorem.

The chapter begins by introducing the assumptions that describe the underlying framework of the economy and this is followed by discussions of Walras' law, normalisations and the effect of policy, all being of particular relevance for the understanding of the techniques employed in public economics. A formal demonstration of the Two Theorems and a critical discussion of their content and implications is given. The criticism focuses upon the possibility of designing and employing optimal lump-sum taxes, the assumptions underlying the structure of the economy and on the limitations of the Pareto criterion. The discussion of the Two Theorems leads naturally into a number of other basic topics in welfare economics. The Pareto criterion is considered in detail and the role of interpersonal comparisons of utility and the possibility of making such comparisons are described. This is followed by a discussion of the formulation of social welfare functions and the relation of these to the permissible extent of interpersonal comparisons.

2 THE ARROW–DEBREU ECONOMY

This section introduces the constituent parts of the Arrow–Debreu economy, defines an equilibrium and sketches a proof of existence. The role of price normalisations and Walras' law are emphasised for their importance in public economics.

2.1 The institutional framework

The institutional framework consists of those assumptions that describe the basic structure of the economy. Included within this structure are the nature of the agents that constitute the active participants in the economy and the description of the trading environment. Such assumptions need to be distinguished from the technical assumptions (such as convexity and continuity) made upon preferences and technology in order to prove theorems about the economy.

There are two agents in the standard Arrow–Debreu economy: *consumers* (or *households*) and *producers* (or *firms*). A third agent, the *government*, will be included at a later stage. The households own initial endowments of goods and have shares in firms which yield dividend payments. They engage in trade to maximise their satisfaction or utility. Producers use inputs to produce outputs subject to the technological knowledge they have available. Their aim is to maximise profit, which is the difference between revenue and costs. All profits earned are distributed to shareholders.

It is assumed that all trade takes place at a given date. The possibility of making contracts at the trading date for delivery at future dates allows the introduction of time but the accounts for such contracts must be settled when the contract is formed. Uncertainty can also be introduced by allowing contracts to be written with delivery contingent upon the state of nature that arises, but this will not be done formally until risk is considered in chapter 7. More importantly, no trade is permitted to take place except at equilibrium prices.

The essential requirement that must be satisfied for the economy to be competitive is that all agents treat prices as parametric. That is, in determining their optimal action, the agents do not believe that their decision can affect the prices observed. Formally, this belief can only be consistent with reality when agents are infinitesimally small relative to the market (Aumann 1964). Since the economies that are considered below (with the exception of the overlapping generations economy of part IV) have a finite number of consumers, Aumann's conditions cannot be satisfied and competitive behaviour is imposed as an assumption. The competitive assumption implies that there is no monopoly power and hence no market distortions through price setting. Households and firms are all taken to act as independent units and to interact only via the price system. This ensures that there are no external effects and no public goods.

These assumptions provide the basic framework of the Arrow–Debreu economy. They should not be viewed as immutable concepts but rather as a starting point for the analysis. The eventual aim should be to choose the correct set of assumptions that capture the economic reality of the situation of interest. The analysis of part III shows how this can be done by introducing external effects, public goods and imperfect competition.

2.2 Commodities

The concept of a commodity is central to the economy and the flexibility in the definition of commodities gives the economy its breadth of interpretation. *Commodities* are simply defined as the set of goods that are available during the operation of the economy. The definition brings with it the implication that at the trading date all present and future commodities must be known to firms and households. This does not imply that all commodities are available for delivery at the trading date because some contracts may only be written for delivery at some future date. In this way, the economy can cope with the introduction of new products and is consistent with the observation that the set of available products tends to change over time.

It is assumed that there is a finite number n of commodities for which trades can take place. These commodities are indexed $i = 1, \ldots, n$. Each commodity is distinguished by its location and its time of availability. Thus bread available for delivery today is a different commodity from bread available for delivery tomorrow and bread available for delivery today in Coventry is a different commodity from bread available in Exeter. The list of commodities is intended to be exhaustive and, as already noted, includes all presently available commodities and all commodities that will be available for delivery at some specified future date. A quantity of some, or possibly all, of the commodities is held as an initial stock by each household; this is the household's initial endowment. The initial stock of a commodity is augmented by the productive activities of firms if it is an output and diminished if it is an input.

To each commodity is associated a price. For good i the price is denoted p_i. This price can be given two essentially identical interpretations. The first interpretation is that p_i is the number of units of numeraire that have to be surrendered in exchange for one unit of commodity i, where the numeraire is that good denoted as having unit price. The alternative interpretation is that p_i is the price in terms of some unit of account (i.e., money). The distinction between these definitions is that money may be a purely artificial construct, whereas the numeraire is one of the commodities. For the functioning of the economy, the interpretation does not actually matter. The structure of the household and firm decision problems that are described below make it clear that it is only relative prices, p_i/p_j, that determine choices. Since these ratios are independent of the interpretation of prices, the interpretation is irrelevant.

2.3 Consumers

Consumers are one type of economic agent in the economy. Each consumer brings to the economy an initial endowment of goods and also holds shareholdings in the firms. The consumers use the income from the sale of the endowment and from dividend payments to purchase their preferred choice of commodities. These commodities are then consumed.

The number of consumers is fixed and is given by H. This can either be interpreted as the number of individual consumers or as the broadest partition of the set of consumers into distinct consumption units. In terms of the economies used in public economics, the second interpretation is often adopted and, when it is, a consumption unit can be viewed as a household rather than as an individual. This is acceptable provided the household acts as if following a single objective. In this book the terms household and consumer are inter-changeable in parts I to III (with household invariably adopted) but are carefully distinguished in part IV.

Each of the H households, $h = 1, \ldots, H$ has a consumption set, X^h, that describes feasible consumption plans. This should be distinguished from the budget set, defined below, which describes affordable consumption plans. As an example of the kind of restriction that is embodied in the consumption set, twenty-four hours of work per day and no food would not be regarded as a feasible consumption plan and the consumption set would therefore not include this plan. The consumption set is assumed to be convex.

Each household, h, also has a utility function that represents its preferences. The adoption of utility functions to represent preferences is not restrictive since, as shown by Debreu (1954a), the conditions necessary for a functional represen-tation of preferences to exist are very weak. In fact, the required assumptions are that preferences are reflexive, transitive, complete and continuous. However, the comparability of utilities between households is more troublesome and is discussed later in the chapter. The utility function is assumed to be strictly quasi-concave, so the set $\{x^h : U^h(x^h) \geq U^h(\hat{x}^h), x^h \in X^h\}$ is strictly convex for any $\hat{x}^h \in X^h$. This assumption is equivalent to assuming the preference order is strictly convex.

The utility function of household h is written

$$U^h = U^h(x_1^h, \ldots, x_n^h), \tag{2.1}$$

where x_i^h is the consumption of good i by household h. If good i is supplied by the household, as would be various forms of labour services, then $x_i^h < 0$. Household h also has an initial allocation, or *endowment*, of the n goods given by the vector

$$\omega^h = (\omega_1^h, \ldots, \omega_n^h). \tag{2.2}$$

Included in this endowment is the stock of labour services that the household can supply. The household is assumed to liquidate this endowment and to use the resulting income to purchase desired commodities.

The shareholdings of household h in the m firms in the economy are denoted

$$\theta_1^h, \ldots, \theta_j^h, \ldots, \theta_m^h, \tag{2.3}$$

where each $\theta_j^h \geq 0$. Hence if firm j makes a profit of amount π^j, household h receives a dividend of size

$$\theta_j^h \pi^j, \tag{2.4}$$

from firm j. As all profits are distributed, it must also be true that the firm is fully owned by households. Across all households, the individual shares must therefore sum to 1, hence

$$\sum_{h=1}^{H} \theta_j^h = 1, \text{ all } j = 1, \ldots, m. \tag{2.5}$$

In the framework of the basic competitive economy there is no market for these shareholdings so they remain fixed at their initial values.

With these definitions it is now possible to describe the economic behaviour of the household. Each household h chooses a consumption vector

$$(x_1^h, \ldots, x_n^h), \tag{2.6}$$

to maximise their utility function $U^h(\cdot)$ subject to the budget constraint

$$\sum_{i=1}^{n} p_i x_i^h \leq \sum_{i=1}^{n} p_i \omega_i^h + \sum_{j=1}^{m} \theta_j^h \pi^j \tag{2.7}$$

and subject to the consumption vector being feasible in the sense that it belongs to the consumption set of h. The budget constraint simply requires that the value of expenditure is not more than the value of the endowment plus dividends received.

Under the maintained assumption of strict quasi-concavity of the utility function, the solution of the household's maximisation problem will result in a demand function for each good, i, from household h. The demand of household h for good i is written in the form

$$x_i^h = x_i^h(p, \omega^h, \theta^h, \pi), \tag{2.8}$$

where $p, \omega^h, \theta^h, \pi$ are the variables that the household takes as parametric. As already noted, if $x_i^h > 0$, good i is regarded as being consumed and if $x_i^h < 0$, good i is regarded as being supplied. The corresponding outcome when the assumption of strict quasi-concavity is relaxed will be discussed in section 2.8.

The important concept for the existence of equilibrium is the level of aggregate demand from the consumption sector which is calculated by summing the individual demands of households. Carrying out the summation, the aggregate demand for good i is given by

$$X_i = \sum_{h=1}^{H} x_i^h = X_i(p, \omega, \theta, \pi). \tag{2.9}$$

As individual demands may be negative, it is clearly possible for the aggregate demand for a good to be negative.

In this discussion of the household it has been implicit that a solution to the utility maximisation problem exists. Conditions that guarantee that this is permissible will be given in the discussion of the existence of equilibrium.

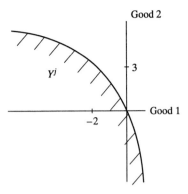

Figure 2.1 A typical production set

2.4 Producers

The producers in the economy are the firms that take inputs and turn them into outputs. Inputs may come from the initial endowments of households or they may be intermediate goods that are produced by other firms. Each firm is characterised by the technology that it has available and aims to maximise profits by their choice of a production plan.

The description of the individual firms begins with the production technology. Each firm, j, is described by its production set, Y^j, which represents the technology of the firm. This set describes feasible input–output combinations that are known to the firm. In other words, it is a list of all the alternative combinations of inputs and outputs of which the firm has knowledge. An example of a typical production set for a firm operating in an economy with two goods is illustrated in figure 2.1.

Figure 2.1 has adopted the standard convention in general equilibrium theory of measuring inputs as negative numbers and outputs as positive. The reasoning behind this convention is that the use of a unit of a good as an input represents a subtraction from the stock of that good available for consumption. In addition, when aggregation takes place across firms, the inputs of one firm will cancel with the output of another so that the aggregate represents net changes in the stock.

The important features of figure 2.1 that capture commonly made assumptions on the structure of production sets are that it is a strictly convex set and the origin and the negative orthant are included in the set. In addition, no strictly positive vector is in the production set. The inclusion of the origin captures the possibility of inactivity on the part of the firm; at some prices the firm may choose not to produce at all. Including the negative orthant can be interpreted as allowing the firms to freely dispose of inputs. Finally, a strictly positive vector would represent the production of outputs with no use of inputs. This cannot be permitted.

Consider the firm shown in figure 2.1 choosing the production plan described by the vector $y^j = (-2, 3)$. When faced with the price vector $p = (2, 2)$, the firm's level of profit, which is given by the inner product of the price vector and the production vector, is

$$\pi^j = py^j = (2, 2).(-2, 3) = 2. \qquad (2.10)$$

The representation of profit as an inner product is mathematically convenient and illustrates the value of the sign convention. In addition, dividing the inner product into positive and negative components shows that the positive part can be given the interpretation of sales revenue and the negative part becomes production costs.

More generally, in an n-good economy, each firm will choose a production plan y^j, where

$$y^j = (y_1^j, \ldots, y_n^j), \qquad (2.11)$$

to maximise profit subject to y^j being in the production set Y^j. It is assumed that the production set is strictly convex, this will be relaxed in section 2.8. The firm thus solves the maximisation problem

$$\max_{\{y^j\}} py^j \text{ subject to } y^j \in Y^j. \qquad (2.12)$$

The maximisation in (2.12) determines the firm's supply of each good, which will be negative if the good is an input and positive if an output, as a function of the price vector. Firm j's supply function for good i is

$$y_i^j = y_i^j(p). \qquad (2.13)$$

As noted in the discussion of household demand, it is the level of aggregate supply rather than individual firms' supply that is important for equilibrium existence questions. Aggregate supply is formed from the supply decisions of the individual firms by summing across the firms. This gives aggregate supply as

$$Y_i = \sum_{j=1}^{m} y_i^j(p) = Y_i(p). \qquad (2.14)$$

Note that if good i is an input for some firms and an output for others, the sign convention results in these being cancelled out so that $Y_i(p)$ represents net supply from the productive sector. The vector of aggregate supplies $Y(p)$ $= (Y_1(p), \ldots, Y_n(p))$ will have both positive and negative elements.

2.5 Equilibrium

The equilibrium of the economy occurs when demands and supplies are in balance. In such a state, each agent is able to carry out its planned action and has no reason for wanting to modify its plan. The equilibrium state is important because it is presumed to be the position that the economy will achieve. However, why the economy should actually reach the equilibrium is not entirely clear. It is sometimes argued that equilibrium is reached as the outcome of a dynamic adjustment process but such dynamics fit very uncomfortably with the static nature of the economy. This issue is still subject to debate. The procedure adopted here is to follow the tradition of focusing upon equilibrium both for the above reason and because of the lack of any satisfactory alternative.

To permit a precise definition of equilibrium, first observe that the level of profit of each firm can be written as a function of the price vector by using the supply function defined in (2.13) to write

$$\pi^j = py^j = py^j(p) = \pi^j(p). \tag{2.15}$$

Hence, using (2.15) and the fact that ω and θ are constant to eliminate them as arguments of the functions, aggregate demand (2.9) can be written

$$X_i = X_i(p, \pi(p)) = X_i(p). \tag{2.16}$$

Equation (2.16) expresses aggregate demand as a function of the price vector alone. Next, define the excess demand for good i, $Z_i(p)$, as the difference between demand and supply, or

$$Z_i(p) = X_i(p) - Y_i(p) - \sum_{h=1}^{H} \omega_i^h. \tag{2.17}$$

In reading (2.17) it should be recalled that the total supply of each good is the sum of the initial endowment and the additional net output of the firms. If $Y_i(p) < 0$ then the available quantity is less than the endowment due to some of good i being used in the production process.

A natural definition of equilibrium is that demand must equal supply, or supply is greater than demand and the price is zero. The second part of the definition reflects, for example, the possibility that the economy may be endowed with a quantity of a good for which no household or firm has any use. Phrasing this in terms of excess demand, equilibrium occurs when excess demand is zero or negative for all goods, with the price of a good being zero if its excess demand is negative. Stated formally, a set of equilibrium prices satisfies

$$Z_i(p) \leq 0, \ i = 1, \ldots, n \text{ and if } Z_i(p) < 0, \ p_i = 0. \tag{2.18}$$

The use of excess demand just provides a convenient representation of the equilibrium conditions.

The equilibrium is assumed to be found by adjustment of the price vector until (2.18) is satisfied. Any price vector that satisfies (2.18) is termed an equilibrium price vector or a set of equilibrium prices. The existence question is concerned with whether there is a solution to (2.18). However, even though it can be shown that an equilibrium price vector will always exist under fairly weak conditions, the question remains as to how such an equilibrium is reached since there is no notion of price formation in the description of the economy.

2.6 Walras' law

Walras' law provides a result that carries significant implications for the analysis of the general equilibrium economy. Two different statements of the law will be given, with the second having an important role in public economics.

Taking excess demand to be less than or equal to zero for the n goods provides n equations in (2.18) to be solved simultaneously. However, the content of Walras' law is that these n equations are not independent and that only $n-1$ actually need to be solved. To show this result, first note that as each household is satisfying their individual budget constraint and the firms are distributing their entire profit to shareholders, the value of each agent's demand is equal to, or less than, the value of their supply. Summing over all agents it must be true that the aggregate value of demand cannot be greater than the aggregate value of supply. Starting with the individual budget constraint

$$\sum_{i=1}^{n} p_i x_i^h \leq \sum_{j=1}^{m} \theta_j^h \pi^j + \sum_{i=1}^{n} p_i \omega_i^h, \tag{2.19}$$

summing over all households gives

$$\sum_{i=1}^{n} p_i X_i \leq \sum_{j=1}^{m} \sum_{h=1}^{H} \theta_j^h \pi^j + \sum_{h=1}^{H} \sum_{i=1}^{n} p_i \omega_i^h, \tag{2.20}$$

where the first term follows from the definition of aggregate demand. Now recalling (2.5) and (2.15), (2.20) can be written

$$\sum_{i=1}^{n} p_i X_i \leq \sum_{j=1}^{m} p_i y_i^j + \sum_{h=1}^{H} \sum_{i=1}^{n} p_i \omega_i^h. \tag{2.21}$$

Using the definition of aggregate supply in (2.14), (2.21) can be expressed as

$$\sum_{i=1}^{n} p_i X_i(p) \leq \sum_{i=1}^{n} p_i Y_i(p) + \sum_{i=1}^{n} p_i \sum_{h=1}^{H} \omega_i^h, \tag{2.22}$$

or

$$\sum_{i=1}^{n} p_i Z_i(p) \leq 0. \tag{2.23}$$

Equation (2.23) is the standard form of Walras' law. In words, Walras' law can be stated succinctly: the aggregate value of excess demand is non-positive. It should be noted that Walras' law holds for all price vectors, not just equilibrium prices. In the important case in which all households are non-satiated, so that they spend their entire income, there will be equality in (2.23) and the value of excess demand will be precisely zero.

Assuming non-satiation and returning to the equilibrium conditions (2.18), the equality form of Walras' law implies that if $n - 1$ markets have zero excess demand so must the nth. Hence there are only $n - 1$ independent equations in (2.18) since the value of any $n - 1$ implies the value of the nth. This may seem to imply that there are only $n - 1$ equations to determine the n prices so that an equilibrium price vector will generally not exist but, as it is only relative prices that determine trade patterns, it is only necessary to solve for $n - 1$ relative prices.

Walras' law does have another implication that has been exploited in public economics. The statement above can be modified to the following. If n markets are in equilibrium and all agents but one are satisfying their budget constraint, the remaining agent must also be satisfying his budget constraint. The consequence of this statement in an economy with a government is that if the n markets are in equilibrium and households are meeting their budget constraints, the government must also be meeting its budget constraint. When describing such an economy it is therefore optional to include the government budget constraint as an equation and to consider equilibrium on $n - 1$ markets or to specify equilibrium on n markets and leave the government budget constraint to be implicitly satisfied. Both of these approaches will be employed below.

2.7 Normalisations

It has already been noted that only relative prices matter in determining demands and supplies; this is clear from studying the household and firm maximisation problems. This observation implies that there is a degree of freedom in the measurement of prices since the scale of prices does not matter.

In proving the existence of equilibrium this freedom is invariably removed by restricting prices to a suitable compact set that is capable of capturing all feasible price ratios. The use of compactness provides a helpful restriction on the set that has to be searched to find an equilibrium price vector. The most commonly used compact sets are the simplex, so that the prices must satisfy $\sum_{i=1}^{n} p_i = 1$, or the unit sphere where the restriction $\sum_{i=1}^{n} p_i^2 = 1$ must be met.

When the Arrow–Debreu economy is used in public economics it is also necessary to choose a normalisation rule. Without such a rule, it is not possible to assign any real meaning to rates of taxation since some basis is needed from which to measure these. The normalisation rule that is normally adopted is to select a good as the numeraire and to set its price at unity and, often in addition to this, to fix its rate of tax at zero. Other prices and taxes are then measured relative to this. This procedure is used repeatedly below. Further discussion of normalisations is given in chapters 4 and 11.

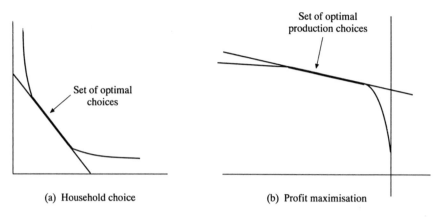

(a) Household choice   (b) Profit maximisation

Figure 2.2   Non-uniqueness of optimal choices

2.8 Relaxation of strict convexity

The assumption of strict convexity that has been made for preferences and production sets results in the optimal choice for the household or firm being unique at any given set of prices. As prices vary, so does the unique choice, but in a way that can be represented by a point-valued function. It is this observation that permitted the use of demand and supply functions in the development above. This section briefly explores the consequences of relaxing the assumption of strict convexity.

If the utility function is assumed instead to only be quasi-concave rather than strictly quasi-concave, which is equivalent to the underlying preferences being convex, this allows the possibility that the indifference curves may posses flat sections. For example, a household which regards two goods as perfect substitutes has indifference curves which are straight lines. Similarly, if a firm's production set is convex rather than strictly convex, its boundary may be flat at some points. The obvious example of this possibility is the constant returns to scale technology for which the boundary is flat along any ray from the origin.

Whenever preferences or production sets have flat sections there will exist price ratios at which the optimal choice will not be unique. This is illustrated in figures 2.2a and 2.2b. When such non-uniqueness arises the relationship between prices and the optimal choice must be described by a set-valued function or, as it is more commonly known in economics, by a correspondence.

It should be apparent from figure 2.2 that provided convexity is assumed, the set of optimal choices will be convex. Furthermore, the definition of continuity for point-valued functions can be generalised to a definition for set-valued functions. A correspondence $\varphi(x)$, $\varphi: x \to y$, y compact, is said to be *upper semi-continuous* at the point x^0 if $x^q \to x^0, y^q \in \varphi(x^q), y^q \to y^0$ implies $y^q \in \varphi(x^0)$. It is *lower semi-continuous* at the point x^0 if $x^q \to x^0, y^q \in \varphi(x^0)$ implies there is y^q such

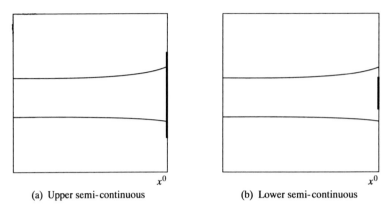

(a) Upper semi-continuous   (b) Lower semi-continuous

Figure 2.3   Semi-continuity

that $y^q \in \varphi(x^q)$, $y^q \to y^0$. A correspondence that is both upper and lower semi-continuous at x^0 is said to be *continuous*. The distinction between upper and lower semi-continuity is shown in figure 2.3. The bold lines and the area between them represent the graph of the correspondence. In figure 2.3a it can be seen how upper semi-continuity allows explosion of the graph at x^0 while lower semi-continuity in figure 2.3b permits implosion.

The relevance of semi-continuity is that if preferences are convex, and some further technical assumptions are satisfied, the resulting demand correspondence is upper semi-continuous. The aggregate demand correspondence is then upper semi-continuous as the sum of upper semi-continuous functions. Similarly, if the production set is convex then the supply correspondence, and the aggregate supply correspondence, are upper semi-continuous. Together, these result in upper semi-continuity of the excess demand correspondence. The interpretation of Walras' law is then that the value of any point in the image set of a price vector must have a non-positive value. This extension allows the important case of constant returns to scale to be accommodated in the analytical framework.

To minimise the level of technical knowledge required to read this text, there are very few places where correspondences are employed below. Instead, it is typically assumed that sufficient convexity is present to permit the employment of point-valued functions. It should be borne in mind, however, that almost all the results given can be extended to apply to correspondences and hence to incorporate constant returns to scale.

2.9 Existence of equilibrium

The existence of an equilibrium for the competitive economy has been the subject of a long literature which is elegantly summarised in Debreu (1980). A sufficient set of conditions for equilibrium to exist are:

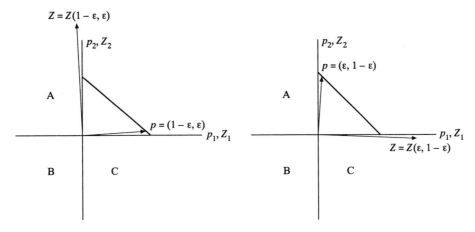

Figure 2.4   The existence of equilibrium

a) For each household preferences are continuous and convex, there is no point of satiation in the consumption set and their endowment is interior to the consumption set.
b) Each firm may choose to be inactive.
c) The aggregate production set is closed and convex, contains the negative orthant and satisfies irreversibility.

It should be noted that the conditions in (a) are sufficient to imply the existence of a utility function that represents the preferences. The role of these assumptions is to guarantee upper semi-continuity of the excess demand correspondence. Without such continuity, it would clearly not be possible to prove the existence of an equilibrium as a supply–demand diagram for a single market makes clear. The assumption of irreversibility states that if a production plan $y \neq 0$ is feasible then the plan $-y$ is not. This assumption is made to guarantee that the set of feasible production plans for the economy is bounded.

   A sketch of the existence argument for the two-good case can easily be given when it is assumed that excess demand is a continuous function of the price vector. To do this it is useful to restrict prices so that they sum to unity, hence $p_1 + p_2 = 1$, which demonstrates the use of the simplex in price normalisation. Any price vector must therefore end on the line joining $(1,0)$ to $(0,1)$.

   Now consider the price vector $(1,0)$ in figure 2.4. Along the horizontal axis of the figure are measured the price of good 1 and the quantity of good 1. The price and quantity of good 2 are measured on the vertical axis. Assume that preferences satisfy non-satiation so that the equality form of Walras' law can be used and that the excess demand for each good becomes unbounded as its price falls to zero. An investigation of the conditions that guarantee the second assumption is given in Arrow and Hahn (1971). With non-satiation, equality in the statement of Walras' law in (2.23) implies that p and Z must be orthogonal so that the angle between them is 90°. For p close to $(1,0)$ excess demand must then lie in quadrant A since the price of good 2 is close to zero and excess demand for it must be positive. Denote this excess demand vector by $Z(1-\varepsilon,\varepsilon)$.

Consider next a price vector $p=(\varepsilon,1-\varepsilon)$ close to $(0,1)$. By the same argument excess demand must lie in quadrant C since excess demand for good 1 must be positive. Denote this excess demand vector by $Z(\varepsilon,1-\varepsilon)$.

The argument is completed by considering the effect of continuously changing prices from $p=(1-\varepsilon,\varepsilon)$ to $p=(\varepsilon,1-\varepsilon)$, which is a rotation of the price vector upwards. It has already been assumed that the excess demand begins in A and ends in C and excess demand has also been assumed to be a continuous function of prices and to satisfy Walras' law. Putting these facts together, the excess demand vector must cross from quadrant A to C at some point in the rotation of p. As excess demand is continuous and cannot enter quadrant B, it follows that there must be at least one price vector for which excess demand is the zero vector. It is otherwise not possible for excess demand to move continuously from A to C.

The proofs of equilibrium in the n-good case given by Gale (1955) and Debreu (1959) are essentially extensions of this brief sketch of the argument which overlooks a number of technical difficulties. In addition a formal proof of the existence result requires the use of a fixed point theorem; a fact that was not apparent in the argument given.

2.10 Analysis of policy

It is helpful at this point to consider the general method of analysing policy in the competitive economy set out above. A policy is considered to affect the maximisation decisions of the economic agents and, by changing the solution to the maximisation, to affect their behaviour. The change in behaviour is then manifested by changes in demands and supplies and hence of the equilibrium.

To proceed formally, consider some set of L policy instruments whose values are denoted by the vector $\xi=(\xi_1,\ldots,\xi_L)$. These could be a list of tax rates or supplies of public goods or any other such policies. It will then follow that demands and supplies will depend upon the values of these policy instruments, so that excess demand can be written

$$Z=Z(p,\xi). \tag{2.24}$$

Equilibrium prices will therefore depend on ξ, as will the equilibrium quantities. Thus

$$p=p(\xi),\ X=X(\xi). \tag{2.25}$$

Two alternative policies ξ and ξ' will generate, via the equilibrium prices, two arrays of consumption levels

$$\{x^1(\xi),\ldots,x^H(\xi)\},\ \{x^1(\xi'),\ldots,x^H(\xi')\}. \tag{2.26}$$

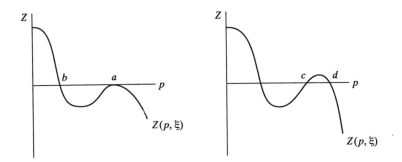

Figure 2.5   Continuity of equilibrium

These arrays can then be compared according to the chosen indicator of economic performance, be it a welfare measure or a statistic such as total output. Naturally the policy achieving the higher value on this indicator will be preferred and, out of any set of potential policies, that achieving the highest value will be the optimal policy.

This procedure invites two further questions. Firstly, assuming that individual households' and firms' decisions are continuously dependent upon the policy parameters, will it be the case that the equilibrium values will also be continuously dependent upon the policy? It is evident that the use and analysis of policy will be difficult if a small change in policy leads to a discrete jump in the equilibrium values. Fortunately, the answer to this question is that the equilibria are almost always continuous with respect to the policy parameters. The formal definition of almost always can be found in Mas-Collel (1980a), but advanced methods are needed to provide the formalisation.

Diagrammatically, the claim amounts to stating that equilibria such as a in figure 2.5, which is such that any small policy change that moves $Z(p, \xi)$ downwards switches the equilibrium to b, are exceptional and that b, c and d are the typical cases.

The exceptional nature of a can be judged by noting that slight modification of $Z(p)$ will either remove the equilibrium at a entirely or lead to two equilibria like c and d that are continuous in policy parameters. Therefore very few excess demand functions out of the set of possible excess demands can generate such equilibria and for practical purposes they can be ignored.

The second question is that of uniqueness of equilibrium: given any set of policy parameters can we be certain that there is a single equilibrium? Unfortunately the answer to this is invariably no. Very strong restrictions are required to ensure uniqueness, far stronger than can be justified by standard restrictions on preferences and technology. Such results as have been found involve restrictions on the Jacobian matrix of the excess demand function and are summarised in Arrow and Hahn (1971). The typical response to this difficulty is to simply assume uniqueness or at least not to worry about it. Although this is unsatisfactory, there is little alternative.

2.11 Core of the economy

The concept of the *core* of the economy is derived from considering economic activity as a cooperative game. This provides insights into the nature of the competitive economy. To introduce the concept, consider an exchange economy (so there is no production) consisting of H households. Each household has an initial endowment of the n goods. Rather than conduct bilateral exchanges, it is now assumed that the households form coalitions and allocate the total endowment of each coalition amongst the members of that coalition. A coalition can therefore be composed of between one and H households. At any time, a household can belong to only one coalition.

Given some allocation for the economy $\{x^1, \dots, x^H\}$, coalition S can *improve* upon this allocation if there is some allocation $\{\hat{x}^h\}$ for $h \in S$ such that

(i) $\displaystyle \sum_{h \in S} \hat{x}^h = \sum_{h \in S} \omega^h$;

(ii) $\hat{x}^h$ is preferred to x^h by all $h \in S$.

Condition (i) asserts that the allocation $\{\hat{x}^h\}$ is feasible for the coalition in the sense that they can meet the allocation from their initial endowment. If such a coalition exists, then the allocation $\{x^1, \dots, x^H\}$ would not be accepted by the members of the coalition. Instead, they would rather form the coalition and benefit from the improved allocation. This process of potential coalition formulation will continue indefinitely unless there exist some allocations which cannot be improved upon. The core of the economy is defined as the set of allocations which cannot be improved upon by any coalition.

The first issue that arises is whether there are any allocations that are in the core. That the core is non-empty is proved in the following theorem

Theorem 2.1

If $\{\tilde{x}^h\}$ is the equilibrium allocation for an Arrow–Debreu economy with endowments $\{\omega^h\}$ and $\tilde{p}$ the corresponding equilibrium price vector, then $\{\tilde{x}^h\}$ is in the core of the economy.

Proof

Assume that the claim is not true so that there exists some coalition S that can improve upon the allocation $\{\tilde{x}^h\}$ with allocation $\{\hat{x}^h\}$, $h \in S$. This implies, from (i) that $\displaystyle \sum_{h \in S} \hat{x}^h = \sum_{h \in S} \omega^h$. However, since $\{\tilde{x}^h\}$ were the optimal choices for the households in the economy at prices $\tilde{p}$, condition (ii) implies $\tilde{p}\hat{x}^h > \tilde{p}\omega^h$ for all $h \in S$. Summing this over $h \in S$ gives $\tilde{p} \displaystyle\sum_{h \in S} \hat{x}^h > \tilde{p} \sum_{h \in S} \omega^h$. This contradicts feasibility and proves the theorem.

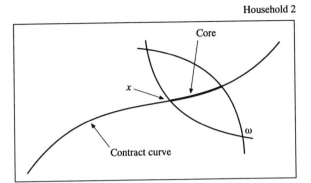

Figure 2.6   Core of the economy

This theorem shows that allocations achieved as competitive equilibria are in the core of the economy. That there generally exist allocations in the core that are not competitive equilibria can be seen in an Edgeworth box for a two-household, two-good economy. The core of such an economy is that part of the contract curve which is in the trading set and the competitive equilibria are generally a subset of this. This is shown in figure 2.6.

Introducing additional households into a two-household economy makes possible the formation of new coalitions and it is clear that some coalitions will be able to improve upon allocations that are in the core of the two-household economy. For instance, if the economy of figure 2.6 is enlarged by the addition of a second type 1 household and a second type 2 household, the coalition of two type 1s and one type 2 can improve upon the allocation labelled x. The limit of this process is described in the Debreu–Scarf core convergence theorem.

Theorem 2.2 (Debreu–Scarf)

Consider an exchange economy with m types of household and r households of each type. Assume the preferences of each type of household satisfy insatiability (given any consumption plan x^h there exists $\tilde{x}^h$ strictly preferred to x^h), strong convexity and continuity and that the endowment of each household is strictly positive. Then, if an allocation is in the core for all values of r, it is a competitive equilibrium allocation.

Proof

See Debreu and Scarf (1963).

Theorem 2.2 establishes that as the size of the economy increases by replication, the core of the economy shrinks to the set of competitive equilibria. This observation provides an additional motivation for considering the competitive equilibrium as the relevant outcome in a large economy. Although replication by increasing the number of each type of household may seem rather artificial, it is not actually necessary in order to derive the conclusion that the core converges to the set of competitive equilibria in the limit. As shown by Aumann (1964), for a continuum economy the core and the set of competitive equilibria are identical.

2.12 Net trades

When taxation is introduced into the competitive economy, it becomes necessary to be more careful about the actual trades that are carried out by households. The preceding analysis was conducted as if the household liquidated their entire endowment to obtain income and then purchased the consumption plan they desired. This was the essence of the budget constraint in (2.7). Without taxation, it is equivalent to think of the households as determining only *net trades* in commodities, which are the quantities of each commodity they will purchase over and above their initial endowment. For example, if a household is endowed with two units of each of the two available goods and wishes to enjoy the consumption plan (1,3), their net trade pattern will be $(-1,1)$ which will be feasible provided the cost of the plan $(-1,1)$ is less than or equal to zero. All the arguments given above can be recast in terms of net trades simply by subtracting the initial endowment from the demand functions determined in (2.8).

Now consider commodity taxation in a competitive economy with no production. Such taxes can only be levied upon the trades that are observed by the government. When levied they have the effect of driving a wedge between the selling price of a commodity, p, and the purchase price, q, with the difference $q-p$ being the commodity tax paid. If a household h were to liquidate their endowment it would be valued at $p\omega^h$ but would cost $q\omega^h$ to repurchase. If all taxes were positive, the value of the endowment would be less than its cost. It follows from this observation that it pays the household to minimise the number of purchases of commodities that are subject to positive taxes. For such commodities it is only the net trades that will be observed and taxed. In contrast, the household will attempt to maximise the supply of those commodities with negative taxes: the entire endowment will be sold at price p and some bought back at $q<p$. This distinction between selling prices and purchase prices introduces a kink into the budget constraint at the endowment point.

When firms are introduced, the situation becomes slightly more complex. Firms will always buy and sell at the prices p. If a household either buys from a firm or supplies a firm they will transact at the prices q. When $q>p$ the difference between the two is a tax on the household when buying from the firm and a subsidy to the household when supplying the firm. In contrast, in a transaction between households, the household supplying the good must receive price p and the household purchasing must pay price q. The actual budget constraint of a household then becomes dependent upon whether transactions are conducted with firms or with other households. To eliminate this difficulty, the economies studied in the following chapters implicitly assume that households only trade with firms so that they face prices q for all transactions. Although this is an important restriction, it does make the analysis considerably more tractable.

3 WELFARE PROPERTIES OF COMPETITIVE EQUILIBRIUM

Section 2 has described the structure of the competitive Arrow–Debreu economy and has characterised its equilibria. That the economy can be shown to possess an equilibrium under very weak assumptions can be judged as fairly remarkable. What is even more surprising is that this equilibrium also has certain features of efficiency; out of a system in which individual households and firms are all pursuing their independent objectives, a final state emerges that exhibits a considerable degree of cohesion.

The belief that the competitive equilibrium has certain properties of optimality appears to have been widely held for some considerable time prior to an actual demonstration of the fact. The first proof of the result is generally attributed to Barone (1935) and this line of analysis, involving the use of calculus to characterise optima, reached its final form in Lange (1942). This approach was, however, severely limited by its use of calculus and the assumptions of interior maxima and smoothness of functions. Employing convexity and separation theory permits a more formal and more general proof of the Two Theorems. The modern presentation began with the work of Arrow (1951a). Although of great generality, the model of Arrow worked with an aggregate production possibility set rather than with individual profit-maximising firms. Debreu (1951) presented similar results but with individual firms. The Theorems were presented in what has become their final form in Debreu (1954b). An excellent discussion of this line of work and its interpretation is contained in Koopmans (1957), and Takayama (1985) is a good source for further discussion.

3.1 Basic definitions

The first step is to give a formal definition of a Pareto optimum. For this it is necessary to define the concept of a feasible array of consumption vectors.

Feasibility

An array of consumption vectors $\{x^1,\ldots,x^h,\ldots,x^H\}$ is *feasible* if $x^h \in X^h$, all h, and there exists an array of production vectors $\{y^1,\ldots,y^j,\ldots,y^m\}$, each $y^j \in Y^j$, such that

$$x \le y + \omega, \tag{2.27}$$

where

$$x = \sum_{h=1}^{H} x^h, \omega = \sum_{h=1}^{H} \omega^h, y = \sum_{j=1}^{m} y^j. \tag{2.28}$$

This definition states that a given allocation of consumption bundles to households is feasible if it can be produced using the economy's fixed initial endowment and production technology.

Pareto optimality can now be defined.

Pareto optimality

A feasible consumption array $\{\hat{x}^h\}$ is *Pareto optimal* if there does not exist a feasible array $\{\bar{x}^h\}$ such that

$$U^h(\bar{x}^h) \geq U^h(\hat{x}^h), h = 1, \ldots, H, \tag{2.29}$$

with

$$U^h(\bar{x}^h) > U^h(\hat{x}^h), \text{ for at least one } h. \tag{2.30}$$

Therefore $\{\hat{x}^h\}$ is Pareto optimal if it is not possible to find an alternative feasible array which gives every household at least as much utility as $\{\hat{x}^h\}$ and gives strictly more utility to at least one household.

The competitive equilibrium described in section 2 can be given the following formal statement.

Competitive equilibrium (CE)

An array $[\hat{p}, \{\hat{x}^h\}, \{\hat{y}^j\}]$ is a competitive equilibrium if

$$\hat{x}^h \in X^h, \hat{p}\hat{x}^h \leq \hat{p}\omega^h + \sum_{j=1}^{m} \theta_j^h \hat{p}\hat{y}^j, h = 1, \ldots, H, \tag{2.31}$$

$$\hat{y}^j \in Y^j, j = 1, \ldots, m, \tag{2.32}$$

and

(i) $U^h(\hat{x}^h) \geq U^h(x^h)$ for all $x^h \in X^h$ such that $\hat{p}x^h \leq \hat{p}\omega^h + \sum_{j=1}^{m} \theta_j^h \hat{p}\hat{y}^j$,

(ii) $\hat{p}\hat{y}^j \geq \hat{p}y^j$, all $y^j \in Y^j$,

(iii) $\hat{x} \leq \hat{y} + \omega$.

Equations (2.31) and (2.32) require households' demands to be both affordable and in their consumption sets and firms' choices to be in their production sets. (i) implies that the equilibrium choices of households maximise utility, (ii) that firms maximise profits and (iii) that the equilibrium is feasible.

3.2 The First Theorem

To develop the First Theorem it is necessary to state a preliminary result. Let household h have locally non-satiated preferences and let $\hat{x}^h$ be their chosen consumption plan. Lemma 2.1 relating to the costs of preferred individual consumption plans can then be proved.

Lemma 2.1

Let $\hat{x}^h$ be a locally non-satiating choice for household h at prices $\hat{p}$. Then

(i) $U^h(x^h) > U^h(\hat{x}^h) \Rightarrow \hat{p}x^h > \hat{p}\hat{x}^h$,
(ii) $U^h(x^h) = U^h(\hat{x}^h) \Rightarrow \hat{p}x^h \geq \hat{p}\hat{x}^h$.

Proof

If (i) were false then clearly x^h would have satisfied the household's budget constraint and would have been chosen in preference to $\hat{x}^h$. To prove (ii) suppose $\hat{p}x^h < \hat{p}\hat{x}^h$. Since $\hat{x}^h$ is not a point of local satiation neither is x^h. There then exists $\tilde{x}^h$ at a distance of ε from x^h with $U^h(\tilde{x}^h) > U^h(x^h) = U^h(\hat{x}^h)$. The distance ε may be chosen small enough so that $\hat{p}\tilde{x}^h < \hat{p}\hat{x}^h$. This contradicts the assumption that $\hat{x}^h$ was the optimal choice.

With this background it is now possible to state and prove the First Theorem.

Theorem 2.3 (The First Theorem of Welfare Economics)

Let $[\hat{p}, \{\hat{x}^h\}, \{\hat{y}^j\}]$ be a competitive equilibrium with no household locally satiated at $\{\hat{x}^h\}$. Then $[\{\hat{x}^h\}, \{\hat{y}^j\}]$ is a Pareto optimum.

Proof

Suppose $[\{\hat{x}^h\}, \{\hat{y}^j\}]$ is not a Pareto optimum. Then there exists $[\{\bar{x}^h\}, \{\bar{y}^j\}]$ with $\bar{x}^h \in X^h$, $\bar{y}^j \in Y^j$ and

(i) $\bar{x} \leq \bar{y} + \omega$,
(ii) $U^h(\bar{x}^h) \geq U^h(\hat{x}^h)$ all h,
(iii) $U^h(\bar{x}^h) > U^h(\hat{x}^h)$ some h.

Given (ii) and (iii), (a) and (b) imply $\sum\limits_{h=1}^{H} \hat{p}\bar{x}^h > \sum\limits_{h=1}^{H} \hat{p}\hat{x}^h$. Under local non-satiation (iii) of CE gives $\hat{p}\hat{x} = \hat{p}\hat{y} + \hat{p}\omega$ so it follows that $\hat{p}\bar{x} > \hat{p}\hat{y} + \hat{p}\omega$. Profit maximisation ((ii) of CE) implies $\hat{p}\hat{y}^j \geq \hat{p}y^j$ all $y^j \in Y^j$ and, in particular, that $\hat{p}\hat{y}^j \geq \hat{p}\bar{y}^j$. Summing over j, $\hat{p}\hat{y} \geq \hat{p}\bar{y}$. Hence $\hat{p}\bar{x} > \hat{p}\bar{y} + \hat{p}\omega$ or $\hat{p}[\bar{x} - \bar{y} - \omega] > 0$. From this inequality it follows that $[\{\bar{x}^h\}, \{\bar{y}^j\}]$ is not feasible thus proving the theorem by contradiction.

To appreciate the generality of this theorem, it is worth reconsidering the assumptions that were required in its proof. When this is done it can be seen that all that was used, in addition to profit and utility maximisation, was the local non-satiation of preferences, which is a very mild restriction, the existence of the competitive equilibrium and finiteness of the number of goods and households. Therefore, being based on such weak assumptions, the result cannot easily be dismissed. The consequences of relaxing the assumption that the number of goods and households is finite are addressed by the overlapping generations

Household 2

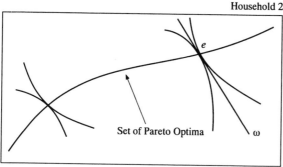

e

Set of Pareto Optima

ω

Household 1

Figure 2.7   The First Theorem

economy of chapter 13 which shows how Pareto optimality can fail when both are infinite.

For a two-household exchange economy, the First Theorem can be demonstrated by using an Edgeworth box diagram. In figure 2.7 the Pareto optima are given by the tangencies of the indifference curves and the locus of tangencies determines the contract curve. A competitive equilibrium is given by a price line through the initial endowment point, ω, which is tangential to both indifference curves at the same point. The common point of tangency results in household choices that lead to the equilibrium levels of demand. Such an equilibrium is indicated by point *e*. It is clear that there is no other point which is preferred by both households to point *e*. The equilibrium is therefore Pareto optimal. In addition, it should be noted that the set of Pareto optima for an exchange economy, given by the contract curve, generally consists of an infinite set of points.

The importance of the non-satiation assumption is shown in figure 2.8 in which household 1 has an area of satiation. Trading from ω, the equilibrium is at point *e* but this is not Pareto optimal since the satiated household would be equally satisfied with less consumption which would allow for an increase in the utility of the non-satiated household.

Household 2

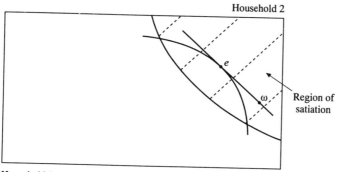

e

ω

Region of satiation

Household 1

Figure 2.8   The non-satiation assumption

Household 2

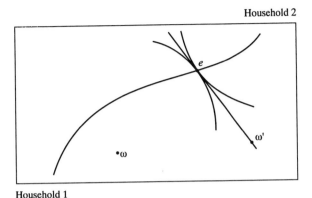

Household 1

Figure 2.9   The Second Theorem in an exchange economy

3.3 The Second Theorem

The Second Theorem is concerned with the converse of the First and its focus can be summarised as follows: given a Pareto optimum, can a competitive economy be constructed for which the Pareto optimum is a competitive equilibrium? In terms of an Edgeworth box, the same question can be formulated as asking whether it is possible to decentralise all points on the contract curve. Using the diagram, it can be seen that this is possible in an exchange economy if the households' indifference curves are convex. With convexity, the common tangent at a Pareto optimum provides the equilibrium prices. To decentralise the economy, a point on this price line is chosen as the initial endowment point.

This process is illustrated in figure 2.9 where the Pareto optimum e is decentralised by selecting ω' as the endowment point. Note that if the endowments of the households are initially given by ω and the equilibrium at e is to be decentralised, some transfer of endowment or, equivalently, of income will be necessary.

The Second Theorem is now stated formally and its proof given.

Theorem 2.4 (The Second Theorem of Welfare Economics)

Suppose that $[\{\hat{x}^h\}, \{\hat{y}^j\}]$ is a Pareto optimum such that at least one household is not satiated. Then, with: (a) convex preferences; (b) convex production sets; (c) the allocation $\hat{x}^h$ interior to the consumption set of h, for all h; and (d) continuity of preferences, there exists $\hat{p} \neq 0$ such that $[\hat{p}, \{\hat{x}^h\}, \{\hat{y}^j\}]$ is a competitive equilibrium.

Proof

Assume that household 1 is not satiated at the allocation $\{\hat{x}^h\}$ and define the sets $\bar{C}^h(\hat{x}^h) = \{x^h : U^h(x^h) > U^h(\hat{x}^h)\}$ and $C^h(\hat{x}^h) = \{x^h : U^h(x^h) \geq U^h(\hat{x}^h)\}$.   Given assumption (a), these sets are convex for all h. Now define the convex set Z by

$Z = \bar{C}^1(\hat{x}^1) + \sum_{h=2}^{H} C^h(\hat{x}^h)$ and the set W by $W = \left\{ w : w = \omega + \sum_{j=1}^{m} y^j, \in Y^j \right\}$. Since the individual production sets Y^j are convex, W, the set of feasible production plans for the economy, is also convex. In addition, as $\{\hat{x}^h\}$ is a Pareto optimum, it must not be feasible to produce a preferred consumption array, thus no member of W is in Z.

The separating hyperplane theorem implies that there exists a vector $\hat{p}$ such that $\hat{p}z \geq \hat{p}w$ for all z in Z and w in W. By definition any point in Z can be written $z = \sum_{h=1}^{H} x^h$ and any point in W as $w = \omega + \sum_{j=1}^{m} y^j$. Noting that feasibility implies $\omega \geq \sum_{h=1}^{H} x^h - \sum_{j=1}^{m} y^j, \hat{p}z \geq \hat{p}w$ is equivalent to

$$\hat{p}\left[\sum_{h=1}^{H} x^h - \sum_{h=1}^{H} \hat{x}^h \right] - \hat{p}\left[\sum_{j=1}^{m} y^j - \sum_{j=1}^{m} \hat{y}^j \right] \geq 0, \tag{2.33}$$

for all $x^1 \in \bar{C}^1(\hat{x}^1)$, $x^h \in C^h(\hat{x}^h)$, and $y^j \in Y^j$. Now as the inequality in (2.33) must hold for all x^1 such that $U^1(x^1) > U^1(\hat{x}^1)$, it must also hold in the limit for any x^1 with $U^1(x^1) = U^1(\hat{x}^1)$. Hence (2.33) holds for all $x^h \in C^h(\hat{x}^h)$, and $y^j \in Y^j$. Taking all but one of the x^h, y^j equal to $\hat{x}^h$, $\hat{y}^j$, then (2.33) shows that

$$\hat{p}x^h \geq \hat{p}\hat{x}^h, \text{ for all } x^h \in C^h(\hat{x}^h), \text{ for all } h, \tag{2.34}$$

$$\hat{p}y^j \geq \hat{p}\hat{y}^j, \text{ for all } y^j \in Y^j, \text{ all } j. \tag{2.35}$$

Inequality (2.35) shows that at the price system supporting the Pareto optimum each firm is maximising profit (consider (ii) of CE).

To show that households are maximising utility requires a demonstration that $\hat{p}x^h \geq \hat{p}\hat{x}^h$ implies there is no x^h with $\hat{p}x^h = \hat{p}\hat{x}^h$ and $U^h(x^h) > U^h(\hat{x}^h)$. Now assume that there is some x^h such that $\hat{p}x^h = \hat{p}\hat{x}^h$ and $U^h(x^h) > U^h(\hat{x}^h)$. From assumption (c) there also exists $\tilde{x}^h$ with $\hat{p}\tilde{x}^h < \hat{p}\hat{x}^h$ but (2.34) shows that $U^h(\tilde{x}^h) < U^h(\hat{x}^h)$. Now take a convex combination of and $\tilde{x}^h$ and x^h. As preferences are continuous from assumption (d), this convex combination can be made to satisfy

$$U^h(t\tilde{x}^h + [1-t]x^h) > U^h(\hat{x}^h), \tag{2.36}$$

and

$$\hat{p}[t\tilde{x}^h + [1-t]x^h] < \hat{p}\hat{x}^h, \tag{2.37}$$

by moving arbitrarily close to x^h. This contradicts $\hat{p}x^h \geq \hat{p}\hat{x}^h$, for all $x^h \in C^h(\hat{x}^h)$, all h. Hence the households must be maximising utility and the price vector decentralises the Pareto optimum.

Two points about the proof are worth noting. Theorem 2.4 implicitly assumes that the households are given sufficient income to purchase the optimal

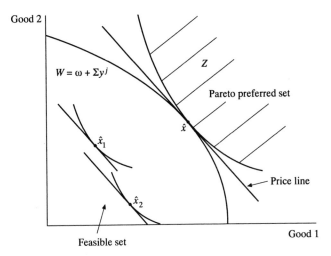

Figure 2.10   Proof of the Second Theorem

allocation. In fact, household h must receive an endowment that satisfies $\hat{p}\omega^h = \hat{p}\hat{x}^h$. Secondly the reasoning of the proof is based on the fact that a price vector that supports the sum of sets also supports the individual sets that form that sum. This is illustrated in figure 2.10.

Before proceeding further, it is worth emphasising that the proof of the Second Theorem required more assumptions than the proof of the First so there may be situations in which the First Theorem is applicable but the Second is not. For instance, an equilibrium may exist with some non-convexity in the production sets of the individual firms but the separation theorem can then not be applied which prevents the proof of the Second Theorem.

A moment's reflection is sufficient to realise the importance to economic policy of the Second Theorem. In designing policy, it is almost certain that a policy maker would wish to achieve a Pareto optimum, otherwise welfare could be increased at no cost. The theorem demonstrates that the objective of the policy maker can be achieved by making the economy competitive, selecting the equilibrium that is to be decentralised and providing each household with sufficient income to afford their allocation. The only policy instrument employed is a lump-sum redistribution of endowments to ensure that each household has the required income. If this approach could be applied in practice, then economic policy analysis reduces to the calculation and redistribution of the lump-sum taxes and the subject matter of public economics is completed.

4 A CRITICAL APPRAISAL

There are several viewpoints from which the Two Theorems can be criticised. Firstly, it is possible to question the practical value of the Second Theorem on

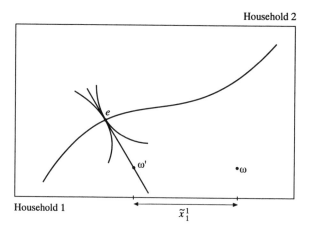

Figure 2.11 The use of lump-sum transfers

the basis of its requirement for lump-sum transfers in implementing the decentralisation. Secondly, it is possible to question the merit of Pareto optimality as a method of judging the acceptability of a given equilibrium. In addition it is also possible to consider the structure of the economy: is it an accurate representation of reality and what are the consequences for welfare economics of relaxing its assumptions?

This section will consider each of these issues. The use of lump-sum transfers will be taken up first since these are central to applications of the Second Theorem. This will be followed by an assessment of the structure of the economy and the implications of this for the subject matter of the subsequent chapters. The value of Pareto optimality as a criterion for social decision making is then considered.

4.1 Lump-sum transfers and taxes

The strong implications of the Second Theorem for policy design have already been noted. However, the practical value of the Second Theorem is dependent on the possibility of making the lump-sum transfers of endowments that it requires. Without recourse to such transfers, the decentralisation would not be possible.

The exchange economy illustrated in figure 2.11 makes clear the role and the nature of lump-sum transfers. The initial endowment point is denoted ω and the Pareto optimum at point e is to be decentralised. This requires the endowment point to be moved to a point on the budget line through e. Assume that the new endowment point ω' leaves the distribution of good 2 constant. This move can be supported by the transfer of $\tilde{x}_1^1$ units of good 1 from household 1 to household 2. Trading from ω' will lead to the competitive equilibrium at e as required.

Such a transfer of part of an endowment from one household to another is the most basic form of a lump-sum transfer. The lump-sum nature of the transfer is due to the fact that neither household can alter the size of the transfer by changes in their behaviour; there is simply no scope for such changes in the economy described. The transfer is an optimal transfer if the resulting equilibrium at e maximises the policy maker's objective function.

Although the lump-sum transfer above involved quantities of goods it can be reinterpreted to introduce lump-sum taxes. If at the equilibrium e the prices of the two goods are p_1 and p_2, then the value of the transfer in figure 2.11 is $p_1 \tilde{x}_1^1$. The notional income of household 1 prior to taxation is

$$M^1 = p_1 \omega_1^1 + p_2 \omega_2^1. \tag{2.38}$$

Now, rather than actually redistributing quantities of the goods, the government could tax household 1 an amount T^1, $T^1 = p_1 \tilde{x}_1^1$, which reduces their income to

$$\tilde{M}^1 = p_1 \omega_1^1 + p_2 \omega_2^1 - p_1 \tilde{x}_1^1, \tag{2.39}$$

and give household 2 an amount of income $T^2, = T^1$. If it is intended that the equilibrium be attained at e then T^1 is the optimal lump-sum tax on household 1 and $-T^1$ is the optimal tax on 2, as this pair of taxes ensures the households face the budget line through e.

The important point of this reinterpretation is that the tax scheme consisting of the taxes $\{T^1, -T^1\}$ is equivalent in its effect to the original transfer of endowment $\{-\tilde{x}_1^1, \tilde{x}_1^1\}$. This equivalence demonstrates that it is possible to view the transfers needed to achieve the decentralisation as taking the form of either real transfers of goods between households or as transfers of income in the form of lump-sum taxes. This description of lump-sum taxes can be easily generalised to an H household economy in which a chosen equilibrium would be decentralised by a vector of lump-sum taxes

$$(T^1, \ldots, T^H), \ \sum_{h=1}^{H} T^h = 0. \tag{2.40}$$

Since these taxes sum to zero, they represent a simple redistribution of resources.

Lump-sum taxes have a central role in public economics due to their efficiency in achieving distributional objectives. It should be clear from the discussion above that the economy's total endowment is not reduced by the application of the lump-sum taxes. This point applies to lump-sum taxes in general. As households cannot affect the level of the tax by changing their behaviour, lump-sum taxes do not lead to any inefficiency. There are no resources lost due to the imposition of lump-sum taxes and redistribution is achieved with no efficiency cost. Having identified the nature and value of optimal lump-sum taxes, the question of their applicability is now considered.

In practice, the endowment of most households is simply their future labour supply. Given this, it would be impossible to conduct lump-sum transfers of endowments as a quantity of future labour cannot be transferred from one household to another without the reintroduction of slavery. It is therefore possible to dismiss the idea of transferring quantities of goods, except in very particular and inconsequential cases, and to focus upon the design of optimal lump-sum taxes.

In order for a transfer, or tax, to be lump-sum the household involved must not be able to affect the size of the transfer by changing their behaviour. It is clear that lump-sum taxes can be used, for example, by taxing each household some fixed amount a lump-sum tax is imposed. Setting aside minor details, this was effectively the case of the UK poll tax. This example motivates the following important observation. The efficiency of lump-sum taxation rests partly on the fact that their imposition is costless but this was far from the case with the UK poll tax. In fact, the difficulties of actually collecting and maintaining information on the residential address of all households made the imposition of a uniform lump-sum tax prohibitively expensive. Therefore, although the structure of lump-sum taxes makes them appear deceptively simple to collect, this may not be the case in practice since the tax base, people, is highly mobile and evasive.

However, the costs of collection are only part of the issue. What is the primary concern here is the use of optimal lump-sum taxes. Optimality requires the tax to be based on all relevant economic characteristics, and households must not be able to alter these characteristics in response to the taxes. It may be possible to differentiate lump-sum taxes according to sex, age or eye colour for instance, but these are unlikely to be the relevant characteristics on which to base the tax. For the exchange economy examples, the characteristics were the endowments and preferences of the households. More generally they may be the expected future labour incomes of the households or the determinants of each household's human capital. Such characteristics are unlikely to be directly observable by the government and it must either rely on households honestly reporting their characteristics or the characteristics must be inferred from the actions of households. In the latter case, there is invariably scope for changes in market behaviour which implies the taxes are no longer lump sum. When reports are the sole source of information, unobserved characteristics cannot form a basis for taxation unless the tax scheme is such that there is an individual gain to truthful revelation.

As an example of the interaction between taxes and reporting, consider the following. Let the system of lump-sum taxes be based on the characteristic IQ level. If the level of tax was inversely related to IQ and if all households had to complete IQ tests, then the tax system would not be manipulated since the incentive would always be to maximise the score on the test. In contrast, if taxes were positively related to IQ, a testing procedure could easily be manipulated and the mean level of tested IQ would be expected to fall considerably. This indicates the potential for misrevelation of characteristics.

These ideas have been developed formally by Mirrlees (1986) who presents theorems on the (im)possibility of designing non-manipulable lump-sum tax schemes. The central theorem considers a population of households who each have the utility function

$$U^h = U^h(c_1 x_1^h, \ldots, c_n x_n^h). \tag{2.41}$$

The households vary, however, in the values of the constants $c = (c_1, \ldots, c_n)$ that appear in the utility function. The preferences of each household are fully described by their c vector. Since the cs are the only differentiating characteristic between households, any optimal set of lump-sum taxes must be based on these characteristics. Now assume that the government cannot observe the c vectors, that households only truly report their characteristics when they do not lose by doing so and that misrepresentation can only take place by a household claiming that the values of the characteristics are above their true values.

With this formulation, a tax policy $T = T(c)$ conditional on the characteristics can only be administered, in the sense that it generates truthful revelation from the households, if the final utility allocation $U^h = U^h(T(c)) = \tilde{U}^h(c)$ generated by the taxes is non-increasing in c. The following theorem shows that $\tilde{U}^h(c)$ will be increasing in c_i with the optimal tax policy if good i is normal. Since some goods must be normal, the optimal policy cannot be administered.

Theorem 2.5 (Mirrlees)

If the utility of each household is given by (2.41) and social welfare is defined as

$$W = \int U^h(c_1 x_1^h, \ldots, c_n x_n^h) \gamma(c_1, \ldots, c_n) dc_1, \ldots, dc_n, \tag{2.42}$$

where $\gamma(\cdot)$ is the distribution function of the cs, then with the optimal tax policy that maximises (2.42) given the economy's endowment, $\tilde{U}^h(c)$ is increasing in c_i if commodity i is always a normal good.

Proof

The optimum occurs when the marginal utility of income is identical for all households. If this were not the case, transfers of income would raise welfare. Inverting this reasoning, the marginal income required to obtain another unit of utility must be the same for all households. Corresponding to the utility function (2.41) is the expenditure function for h which takes the form

$$E^h = E^h \left(\frac{p_1}{c_1}, \ldots, \frac{p_n}{c_n}, U^h \right). \tag{2.43}$$

Optimality then implies

$$E_U^h = \Xi, \tag{2.44}$$

for some constant Ξ. Differentiating (2.44) with respect to c_i gives

$$E_{UU}^h \frac{\partial \tilde{U}_h}{\partial c_i} - E_{Ui}^h \frac{p_i}{c_i^2} = 0, \tag{2.45}$$

or, since $E_i^h = \chi_i^h \left(\dfrac{p_1}{c_1}, \ldots, \dfrac{p_n}{c_n}, U^h \right)$ where $\chi_i^h \left(\dfrac{p_1}{c_1}, \ldots, \dfrac{p_n}{c_n}, U^h \right)$ is the Hicksian or compensated demand for good i from h

$$E_{UU}^h \frac{\partial \tilde{U}_h}{\partial c_i} = \frac{p_i}{c_i} \frac{\partial \chi_i^h}{\partial U^h}. \tag{2.46}$$

With a concave utility function $E_{UU}^h > 0$ and the normality of good i implies $\dfrac{\partial \chi_i^h}{\partial U^h} > 0$. Therefore the normality of good i implies $\dfrac{\partial \tilde{U}^h}{\partial c_i} > 0$ at the optimum as was to be proved.

This theorem shows why optimal lump-sum taxes may not be feasible. The government cannot observe the relevant characteristics and relies on the households to reveal them. However, under the optimal tax policy it is not in the household's interest to truthfully reveal their characteristics. This theorem is dependent upon the precise assumptions made but it is indicative of the general results that emerge when policy relies on individual revelation of information.

The main points of the argument can now be summarised. To have any content the Second Theorem relies on the use of optimal lump-sum transfers but such transfers are unlikely to be available in practice or to satisfy all the criteria required of them. The taxes may be costly to collect and the characteristics upon which they should be levied may not be observable. When characteristics are not observable, households may have incentives to make false revelations. It is therefore best to treat the Second Theorem as being of considerable theoretical interest but of very limited practical relevance.

4.2 The institutional assumptions

Before considering the concept of Pareto optimality, some comments are now offered on the assumptions underlying the model and the consequences for the Two Theorems of their relaxation. The assumptions can be conveniently placed into two categories: those whose relaxation is possible without destroying the validity of the theorems and the others whose relaxation does so. Time and uncertainty belong to the former category, although when they are introduced the interpretation becomes less tenable. Public goods, externalities and mono-poly power, or imperfect competition generally, are firmly in the latter.

In the presence of time and uncertainty the existence of sufficient markets permits a re-interpretation of the economy and the proof of the Two Theorems proceeds as above. However, the passage of time introduces the questions of investment, savings and growth which cannot be addressed satisfactorily in the Arrow–Debreu economy. Fortunately a number of more appropriate structures are available. One of these, the overlapping generations economy, will be studied in chapter 13. Uncertainty introduces aspects such as the correct amount of risk taking and portfolio choice. This is an area of public economics that is being developed particularly with respect to the normative implications of uncertainty and the important aspects of this literature are reviewed in chapter 7.

Turning to externalities, public goods and monopoly power, since any one of these will remove the Pareto optimality of equilibrium, the Two Theorems are no longer applicable to any economy in which they are present. However, the theorems do show some properties of the state that could be achieved if the externality etc. could be eliminated. The failure of the Two Theorems in these cases can be viewed as providing the motivation for the analysis given in part III.

4.3 Pareto optimality

Even when all the criticisms noted above are set aside, the Two Theorems are still dependent upon the value of Pareto optimality as a welfare criterion. For this reason, and also because Pareto optimality is regularly encountered in public economics, it is worthwhile taking a closer look at Pareto optimality and considering its implications and deficiencies as a means of choosing between economic states. From this perspective it is possible to assess the usefulness of Pareto optimality as a criterion for guiding public policy.

The Pareto criterion was introduced by Pareto (1909) and given its name by Little (1950). The motivation for its use was that it provided a means of comparing economic states without requiring interpersonal comparisons of utility; an issue that will be returned to below. To begin the discussion, it is helpful to start with a restatement of Pareto optimality.

Consider a set of states, $S = \{s_1, s_2, \ldots\}$ and a set H, indexed $h = 1, \ldots, H$, of economic agents. Writing $\succ_h$ for the strict preference relation of household h and $\succeq_h$ for at least as good as, then state s_1 is Pareto preferred to state s_2 if

$$s_1 \succeq_h s_2 \text{ for all } h = 1, \ldots, H, \tag{2.47}$$

and

$$s_1 \succ_h s_2 \text{ for at least one } h. \tag{2.48}$$

A preference order is then induced on the set of states by (2.47) and (2.48). This preference order is denoted by $\succ_P$, hence

$$s_1 \succ_P s_2 \Leftrightarrow (2.47) \text{ and } (2.48). \tag{2.49}$$

In addition, define $\succeq_P$ by

$$s_1 \succeq_P s_2 \Leftrightarrow (2.47). \tag{2.50}$$

State s_1 is then defined as being Pareto optimal if there exists no other state that is Pareto preferred to s_1. Formally, s_1 is Pareto optimal if $\exists$ no $s_2 \in S$ such that $s_2 \succ_P s_1$. It is important to note that this general definition has been in terms of two *states* and that no utility concepts were involved. This demonstrates that Pareto optimality is a very broad concept and can be used for far more than assessing allocations of utility.

Now consider s_1 and s_2 to represent different allocations of a fixed stock of goods amongst the H agents. Then allocation s_1 is Pareto optimal if there exists no reallocation that is Pareto preferred to s_1. In other words, starting from s_1 it must be impossible to reallocate the fixed stock of goods in a manner which makes one household better off without making another worse off. Alternatively, s_1 and s_2 could represent two states with alternative political parties being in power. Then s_1 is Pareto preferred if no voter prefers party s_2 and at least one would strictly prefer party s_1.

With this background it is now possible to proceed to an assessment of Pareto optimality. By considering even the simplest examples, it is not difficult to see several deficiencies of the Pareto criterion. First consider the division of a cake between two people where both people like cake and their preferences satisfy non-satiation. In such circumstances every division of the cake is Pareto optimal, from the most inequitable to the most equitable. This claim follows from noting that, starting from any division, there are no changes in the distribution that satisfy (2.47) and (2.48). In other words, any reallocation that provides more to one household must take it away from the other. The latter point illustrates that situations exist in which the set of Pareto optima

$$\{s_i : s_i \in S \text{ and } \exists \text{ no } s_j \in S \text{ such that } s_j \succ_P s_i\}, \tag{2.51}$$

is infinite.

From this simple example it is possible to infer two deficiencies of Pareto optimality. Firstly, extreme allocations may be Pareto optimal and, consequently, although an equilibrium may be Pareto optimal there is no reason why anyone should advocate it as good in any other sense. Secondly, it is possible for there to be a multiplicity of Pareto-optimal allocations even for this very simple allocation problem. When the Pareto criterion does not provide a unique optimal allocation it is not of much assistance as a social rule for choosing an allocation.

The points made in the cake division example are also relevant when considering allocations in a two-household exchange economy. The contract curve in figure 2.12 gives the set of Pareto optima and there is generally an uncountable number of these optima, so the ordering $\succeq_P$ does not select a unique maximal element. In addition, the competitive equilibrium may be as the one illustrated in the bottom left corner. This is Pareto optimal but highly inequitable.

Another failing of Pareto optimality is that the ordering $\succeq_P$ need not provide a complete ranking of states in S. That is, there may be some pairs of states which are incomparable under the Pareto criterion. Incomparability arises if, in the move between two states s_1 and s_2, some agent gains and another agent loses. This is illustrated in figure 2.13 where allocations s_1 and s_2 cannot be compared although s_1 and s_3 and s_2 and s_3 can. Such gains and losses are invariably a feature of policy choices and much of policy analysis consists of weighing up the gains and losses. In this respect, the Pareto criterion is inadequate as a basis for policy choice.

Household 2

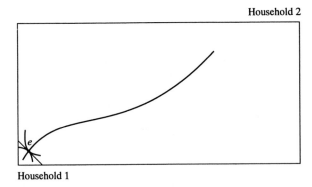

Household 1

Figure 2.12   Pareto optimal allocations

Household 2

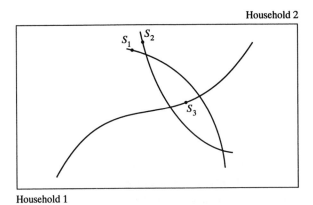

Household 1

Figure 2.13   Incompleteness of the Pareto ranking

To summarise these arguments, Pareto optimality does not embody any concept of justice and highly inequitable allocations may be optimal under the criterion. In many situations, the set of Pareto-optimal allocations is infinite and the criterion then provides little guidance for policy choice. Finally, the Pareto criterion may not provide a complete ordering of states so that some states will be incomparable under the criterion. The source of all these failings is that the Pareto criterion avoids making interpersonal comparisons whereas it is such comparisons that have to be made in most allocation decisions.

5 INTERPERSONAL COMPARISONS AND SOCIAL WELFARE

Pareto optimality was originally proposed as a means by which it was possible to analyse the consequences of alternative allocations without requiring interpersonal comparisons of welfare to be made and it is from this that the failures of Pareto optimality emerge. To make further progress it is necessary to consider the scope for comparability between the utility levels of different individuals. This section reviews alternative degrees of comparability and considers the problem of aggregating individual preferences into social preferences.

5.1 Interpersonal comparability

If sufficiently strong interpersonal comparisons are possible, statements such as 'the welfare loss of agent i in the new allocation is more than offset by the gain of agent j' would be permissible. Given the relative weights attached to individuals i and j in social preferences it would then be possible to make a judgement on whether the change was socially beneficial or not.

The first step in making such comparisons is the construction of a comparable utility index to measure i's and j's welfare. If, for example, i gains in the move from allocation $\{\bar{x}^h\}$ to allocation $\{\hat{x}^h\}$ and j loses, with other households unaffected, the aim is to weigh the gain $\hat{U}^i - \bar{U}^i$ against the loss $\bar{U}^j - \hat{U}^j$. Such comparisons run against the spirit of the Pareto criterion which, as already stated, was originally intended to replace such utility comparisons since these were felt to be making judgements that were scientifically untenable; a viewpoint expounded most strongly by Robbins (1932).

The issues motivating Robbins' denial of interpersonal comparability can best be understood by reviewing the development of utility theory. Nineteenth-century economists assumed that utility was something measurable and that it was naturally comparable between individuals. As such, it followed that the welfare of society could be inferred in some straightforward manner from the welfare levels of the individuals forming that society. Reasoning of this form provides the scientific basis for utilitarianism.

The notion of measurable and comparable utility began to be dispelled in the early twentieth century after the demonstrations by Hicks (1939) and others that the entire theory of the household could be based on ordinal non-comparable utility. In other words, since it was the household's preference ordering that determined consumption choices, utility was only relevant as a convenient functional representation of preferences, with no greater meaning attached to it, and that given a utility function representing the preference ordering, any increasing monotonic transformation of that utility function would also be an equally valid representation of preferences. Ordinality and non-comparability then became the accepted concepts. This acceptance left no scientific basis upon which to justify the comparability of different household's utility levels.

Ordinality means that if $x_1 \succ_h x_2$ then it is given a higher utility number but the actual relationships between the numbers assigned to different xs, for instance the size of the difference between any two, have no content. This, consequently, prevented welfare comparisons between people and created the necessity of developing concepts, such as Pareto optimality, that were free of interpersonal comparisons. However the weaknesses of these criteria soon became obvious and, following Scitovsky (1951), the trend since the 1960s has been to explore the consequences of readmitting interpersonal comparability into the analysis. Some economists, for instance Mirrlees (1971) and Ng (1985), have argued most strongly for this, although there is some divergence of opinion on the acceptable extent of comparability.

Between non-comparability and full comparability there are several interme-diate cases that vary as to precisely how comparable are the utility levels. For instance, the claim that one household has a higher level of utility than another requires rather less comparability than claiming it has 15 per cent more utility. Different degrees of comparability carry obvious implications for the welfare measures that can be based upon them.

The various degrees of comparability have been classified by Sen (1977) and Roberts (1980b). The starting point for the classification is a utility function U^h for each household h and the set Φ of admissible transformations of this utility function. That is, $\phi = (\phi^1, \ldots, \phi^H) \in \Phi$ if $\phi^h(U^h)$ is an equally valid utility function for h. Alternative degrees of measurability and comparability then appear as restrictions on the set Φ. The alternatives that have been considered in the literature, in increasing order of comparability, can now be stated as follows.

(i) Ordinality and non-comparability (ONC)
    $\phi \in \Phi$ is a list of H independent strictly monotonically increasing transformations.

This is the set of transformations that arises when utility is viewed only as the representation of preference in conditions of certainty. It implies that there can be no interpersonal comparability.

(ii) Cardinality and non-comparability (CNC)
    $\phi \in \Phi$ is a list of H independent strictly positive affine transformations: $\phi^h(U^h) = a^h + b^h U^h, b^h > 0$.

When there is uncertainty involved in the decision-making environment CNC can be justified by appeal to the von Neumann and Morgernstern (1953) utility representation theorem. Condition CNC demonstrates that cardinality, in itself, does not carry any implications for interpersonal comparisons.

(iii) Ordinality and level comparability (OLC)
    $\phi \in \Phi$ is a list of H identical strictly monotonically increasing transforma-tions: $\phi^h(U^h) = \phi(U^h)$, ϕ independent of h.

With OLC it is possible to rank the households in terms of their utility levels, so that one household can be seen as having more or less utility than another, but changes in utility levels cannot be compared across households. This degree of comparability formalises what is probably intended by claims that households have roughly similar preferences and can hence have their utility levels compared.

(iv) Cardinal unit comparability (CUC)
    $\phi \in \Phi$ is a list of H strictly positive affine transformations which differ only in their constants: $\phi^h(U^h) = a^h + bU^h, b > 0$.

Although CUC does not allow comparability of welfare levels, since the constant terms may differ, it does allow the comparability of gains and losses in utility. This follows from the restriction of the utilities to the same units of measurement.

(v) Cardinal full comparability (CFC)
$\phi \in \Phi$ is a list of H identical strictly positive affine transformations:
$\phi^h(U^h) = a + bU^h, b > 0$.

CFC represents the maximum degree of comparability that is possible without the introduction of a natural zero for utility since it allows comparison of both levels and gains and losses. If a zero is introduced, the set of transformations then becomes:

(vi) Cardinal ratio scale (CRS)
$\phi \in \Phi$ is a list of H identical strictly positive linear transformations:
$\phi^h(U^h) = bU^h, b > 0$.

Amongst these alternative degrees of comparability, only ONC and CNC are formally justified via representation theorems on preferences. Moving further down the list requires an increasing degree of pure faith that the procedure is justified. The next section relates the degree of comparability to permissible welfare criteria.

5.2 Social choice

In moving from individual to social preferences the basic problem is one of aggregation. From the individual preference relations must be constructed a social preference relation that satisfies certain attractive criteria. What aggregation procedures are possible depends critically on the level of comparability assumed.

The starting point for the literature on social choice was Arrow's (1950, 1951b) impossibility theorem. Arrow considered a set S of states and H individual preference orderings $\succeq_h$, $h = 1, \ldots, H$, over S and attempted to construct from these a social welfare function, F, that would determine the social ordering, $\succeq$, of S for any set of individual orderings, so $\succeq = F(\{\succeq_h\})$. An ordering is defined here as being complete, reflexive and transitive. Conditions that may be imposed upon such a social welfare function include the following.

Unrestricted domain (U): The domain of F includes all logically possibly H-tuples of individual orderings of S.

Independence of irrelevant alternatives (I): The restriction of $\succeq$ to the pair $\{s_1, s_2\}$, $s_i \in S$, $i = 1, 2$, is a function only of the restrictions of individual preferences to that pair $\succeq|_{\{s_1, s_2\}} = F(\{\succeq_h|_{\{s_1, s_2\}}\})$.

Weak Pareto principle (P): For any pair $\{s_1, s_2\}$ if $s_1 \succ_h s_2$ for all h, then $s_1 \succ s_2$.

Non-dictatorship (D): There must be no individual h such that for all individual preference orders, for each ordered pair s_1, s_2, $s_i \in S$, $i = 1$, 2, $s_1 \succ_h s_2$ implies $s_1 \succ s_2$.

From these conditions follows Arrow's impossibility theorem.

Theorem 2.6 (Arrow)

If H is finite and S has at least three elements then there is no social welfare function satisfying conditions U, I, P and D.

Proof

See Sen (1986).

The implication of this theorem is that a social welfare function does not exist that can aggregate the individual preference orderings without conflicting with one, or more, of the conditions U, I, P or D. At the heart of this non-existence result is the limited information contained in the individual preference orderings. This information is not sufficient for the social ordering to be constructed without violating one of the conditions. Following the first demonstrations of this theorem, attempts were made to derive possibility results by weakening the conditions U, I, P and D and relaxing the requirement of transitivity for the social ordering. None of these relaxations provided a convincing path out of the impossibility.

An alternative approach is to allow greater information about individual preferences, in particular to consider the consequences of alternative forms of interpersonal comparability. That admitting interpersonal comparability increases the scope for making consistent welfare judgements, and generates possibility theorems, has been demonstrated by Roberts (1980a, b) and Sen (1977). The formal method is to consider a social welfare functional that determines the social ordering over S for any given H-tuple of individual utility functions over S, that is $\succeq = F(\{U^h\})$. The conditions U, I, P and D can be translated into equivalent restrictions on the social welfare functional. The degree of interpersonal comparability then determines the permissible transformations of the individual utility functions. For example, with ONC the same ordering must be generated whatever monotonic transformations are applied to the individual utilities or $\succeq = F(\{U^h\}) = F(\{\phi^h(U^h)\})$ for any set of monotonic transformations $\{\phi^h\}$. Since ONC is equivalent to the information content in theorem 2.6, the translation of that theorem applies directly.

When further information is introduced, possibility theorems can be proved. Taking ordinal level comparability (OLC) first, since this is sufficient to permit the ranking of individuals in terms of utility levels, it also permits social welfare functionals that are defined as the welfare of the hth individual in the ranking for any h. One special example of such a welfare function is the Rawlsian or *max–min* given by

$$W = \min\{U^1(x^1), \ldots, U^H(x^H)\}. \tag{2.52}$$

With unit comparability it is possible to assess the gains and losses between individuals. Furthermore, once one set of the constants appearing in the utility function are specified, it is meaningful to consider the sum of utilities as a welfare criterion. Formally, CUC implies that the welfare functional

$$W = \sum_{h=1}^{H} a^h U^h, a^h > 0, \tag{2.53}$$

is permissible. If the welfare functional is also assumed to satisfy the condition of anonymity given by

Anonymity (A): if $\{\widetilde{U}^h\}$ is a re-ordering of the utility vector $\{U^h\}$, then

$$F(\{\widetilde{U}^h\}) = F(\{U^h\}),$$

the constants a^h in (2.53) cannot vary with h so that the welfare functional reduces to the standard utilitarian form

$$W = \sum_{h=1}^{H} U^h(x^h). \tag{2.54}$$

Full comparability leads to the class of welfare functionals determined by

$$W = \bar{U}(x) + g(U(x) - \bar{U}(x)), U(x) = (U^1(x^1), \ldots, U^H(x^H)), \bar{U}(x) = \sum_{h=1}^{H} \frac{U^h(x^h)}{H}, \tag{2.55}$$

where $g(\cdot)$ is homogeneous of degree 1. An example of such a welfare functional is

$$W = \bar{U}(x) + \gamma \min\{U^h(x) - \bar{U}(x)\}, \tag{2.56}$$

which is Utilitarian for $\gamma = 0$ and Rawlsian for $\gamma = 1$. Finally, CRS leads to

$$W = W(U(x)), \tag{2.57}$$

where $W(\cdot)$ is a homothetic function. When anonymity is also imposed, the social welfare functional becomes

$$W = \sum_{h=1}^{H} \frac{[U^h(x^h)]^{1-\upsilon}}{1-\upsilon}. \tag{2.58}$$

5.3 Bergson–Samuelson social welfare function

The Bergson–Samuleson social welfare function was first introduced into economics by Bergson (1938) since when there has been considerable controversy over its correct interpretation and its validity. The general Bergson–Samuelson social welfare function is defined as a function of the state $W = W(s_i)$, where $s_i \in S$, and is intended to represent the social preference ordering. If the social welfare function is *neutral* towards non-utility features of the states it is evaluating, so that only the utility levels of the individuals matter for social welfare, then the Bergson–Samuelson social welfare function takes the form

$$W = W(U^1(x^1), \ldots, U^H(x^H)). \tag{2.59}$$

There has been much discussion of the relationship between the social welfare function in the sense of Arrow and in the sense of Bergson–Samuelson. Samuelson (1977) asserts that a Bergson–Samuelson social welfare function can be constructed even when the utility levels are ordinal and non-comparable. If such a social welfare function is expected to hold for all possible preference orderings, then theorem 2.6 shows that it must violate one (or more) of U, I, P and D. One potential route out of this impasse was to suggest that the Bergson–Samuelson social welfare function needs to hold only for the given set of preference orders that characterise the economy under consideration. In this case, condition U is not applicable. This restriction to the given set of preferences represents the *single-profile* approach to social choice where the social ordering only has to satisfy the specified criteria for a single profile of preference orders. In contrast, the Arrow theorem is characteristic of the *multi-profile* approach where the ordering must be constructed for any possible set of preference orderings. Unfortunately, the restriction to single profiles does not avoid the impossibility result. As shown by Kemp and Ng (1976) and Roberts (1980c) the impossibility result remains intact when the requirements of the social ordering are translated to the single-profile context.

The use of a Bergson–Samuleson social welfare function therefore implies the adoption of comparability assumptions on individual utilities. Accepting this, the maximisation of a Bergson–Samuelson social welfare function is invariably adopted as the objective of policy in public economics. In such exercises it is usually assumed that the social welfare function satisfies the Pareto criterion

$$U^h(\hat{x}^h) \geq U^h(\tilde{x}^h), \text{ all } h \text{ implies } W(U^h(\hat{x}^h)) \geq W(U^h(\tilde{x}^h)) \tag{2.60}$$

and, when the social welfare function is differentiable, that

$$\frac{\partial W}{\partial U^h} \geq 0 \text{ and } \frac{\partial^2 W}{\partial U^{h2}} \leq 0. \tag{2.61}$$

The assumption on the second derivative is often strengthened to that of strict concavity or strict quasi-concavity. Unfortunately, as is discussed further in chapter 4, this does not always guarantee second-order conditions will be satisfied when the welfare function is used as the objective in a maximisation.

For a given value of $W(')$ it is possible to draw its level sets, typically called *social indifference curves*, as in Figure 2.14.

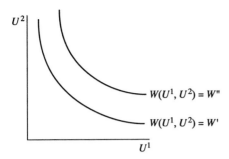

Figure 2.14   Social indifference curves

The convexity of these was the subject of discussion in the 1950s. Gorman (1959b) demonstrated the important result that convexity in itself does not require interpersonal comparability.

6 SUMMARY

The aim of this chapter was to introduce the Arrow–Debreu economy and to review a number of fundamental issues in welfare economics. This material underlies much of the analysis in the following chapters, providing both the analytical method and a baseline against which changes can be assessed.

The Two Theorems, which characterise the efficiency properties of the competitive economy, were described and proved. Although the Theorems have strong implications, it was argued that they both are limited in their value; the First Theorem due to the weakness of Pareto optimality and the Second because of its reliance upon lump-sum taxation. It was argued that criteria for judging between economic states that did not employ interpersonal comparisons were too weak to be of practical usefulness. If comparability is permitted, stronger criteria are possible.

There are two major conclusions to be drawn from the discussion. Firstly, the limitations of the Two Theorems provide a natural point of departure for the study of public economics. Secondly, if decisions about economic policy are to be taken on welfare grounds, it is necessary that interpersonal comparisons must be made.

3

TOPICS IN MEASUREMENT

1 INTRODUCTION

The previous chapter has reviewed the theory and concepts involved in the measurement of welfare and the motivations for adopting these approaches. The welfare judgements that emerged from that analysis were based unavoidably upon utility concepts and this basis is found by many to be objectionable. In response to this, alternative means of assessing the economic outcome that rely, in the main, on observable and measurable quantities are now discussed. At first sight these appear to be rather more tangible concepts than those of utility and social welfare. Most of what is said below applies equally to a range of economic indices far broader than just those considered here.

The chapter begins with a discussion of the definition of income which is the basic observable and measurable quantity from which indices of inequality and poverty are formed. Although there is little doubt about the meaning of income in a world of certainty, it is rather less well specified when there is uncertainty about the values of future variables. The distinctions between the available definitions of income are clarified and their relative merits noted. Data on household incomes, though, cannot be used directly in the construction of economic indices since the households will differ in their size and composition and, consequently, in their requirements. This observation motivates the consideration of equivalence scales, which are a means of adjusting observed household incomes to take account of household composition effects and to provide a set of comparable income measures.

This is followed by a review of the measurement of inequality. The link is drawn between statistical measures and their implied social welfare functions. This motivates the consideration of explicit welfare-based measures and axiom systems. A similar approach is taken to the measurement of poverty. It is worth noting at the outset that the major theme to emerge from the discussion is that the construction of a successful index requires the welfare assumptions on which it is based to be made explicit.

2 THE MEASUREMENT OF INCOME

Many of the indices that measure economic well being, including those of inequality and poverty, are formed from data on incomes on the grounds that income is the means to achieve welfare. Given this important role, it is necessary that the income statistics should provide accurate data. This will be achieved if there is precise collection of information, which is a topic that will not be pursued here, and the correct definition of what is to be measured is employed. It is the latter aspect that is the subject of this section.

In the static and deterministic economy of chapter 2 a household's income can be unambiguously defined. If the household enters the economy with a zero stock of goods and is given its endowment and list of shareholdings after entry, then its income, for any given price vector, is the value of the endowment plus dividend income. Defined in this way, income is the value of consumption that can be undertaken whilst leaving the household with the same stock of goods, which was zero, at the end of the economy as it had at the start of the economy. The definitions of income below will also try to apply this reasoning, but only in the deterministic setting can it be applied without difficulty of interpretation.

Fisher (1930) proposed the view that income was formed by the set of pleasurable experiences that the consumer enjoyed over the period in which income was to be measured. This was based on the view that neither the actual receipt of money nor the purchase of goods represented the end product of economic activity; it was actual consumption that played this role. The difficulty of this approach is that it leads to income as an unmeasurable and purely personal construct. As an approximation, Fisher suggested that the level of expenditure in the period, less the disutility of any labour performed, should be the measure of income since it is from expenditure that consumption results. Unfortunately, even this approximation cannot be directly calculated due to its inclusion of the disutility of labour.

An alternative definition provided by Hicks (1939) constitutes what is generally taken as the standard definition of income. In Hicks' words 'income is the maximum value which a man can consume during a week and still expect to be as well-off at the end of the week as he was at the beginning' (Hicks 1939, p. 172). This definition embodies both the consumption aspect emphasised by Fisher (1930) and reduces to the stock-of-goods measure in a static and certain environment. The difficulties of applying this definition follow from the inclusion of the word *expect* and from the consequent forward-looking nature of the definition. The definition does not make it clear whose expectations are referred to and how to resolve differences in expectations, nor does it show how the possibility of false expectations should be accommodated. A literal application of the definition would not count windfall gains as income, since by definition they are not expected, although they unarguably raise the potential level of consumption. For these reasons, the Hicks definition of income does not command universal acceptability.

In contrast, Simons (1938) adopts the position that a workable and calculable definition is preferable to one that is formally correct but non-operational. Simons' definition is backward looking, measuring income in retrospect. In full, the definition is that 'Personal income may be defined as the algebraic sum of (1) the market value of rights exercised in consumption and (2) the change in the value of the store of property rights between the beginning and end of the period in question' (Simons 1938, p. 50). This can easily be applied and does not involve expectations so removing some of the drawbacks of the Hicks formulation. As Simons required, it provides an operational definition.

These alternative definitions highlight the distinctions between *ex ante* and *ex post* measures of income. In practice, tax assessments adopt the backward-looking viewpoint and measure income as all relevant payments received over the stated period. The definition of income for the purposes of tax codes does not precisely satisfy any of the definitions given above. For instance, capital gains if not realised during the period in question are not usually measured as income. Such observations have motivated the concept of the *comprehensive income tax*, under which income from all sources would be treated equally. This would accord with the definitions of income given above. In practice, though, the ideal measure of income cannot be achieved so preventing the application of a truly comprehensive income tax. The systems that do arise can then be viewed as deriving from the resulting second-best problem. For the purposes of the following chapters, the fact that much of the analysis is conducted within certain environments eliminates the problems of definition. When uncertainty is explicitly introduced, care will be taken to highlight the measure of income adopted.

3 EQUIVALENCE SCALES

The income level of a household is often treated as a proxy for its level of welfare since, at the very least, income is the means to achieve welfare. The fact that households differ in make up and composition implies that if the welfare levels of two households are to be compared it will not generally be sufficient, taking environmental variables, etc. as constant, to simply compare their income levels. To make the issue concrete, a household of one adult with no children needs less income to achieve a given level of welfare than a household with two adults and two children. The question is then, of course, how much less income? Equivalence scales are a means of adjusting measured incomes into comparable quantities.

The typical causes of differentiation between households are the number of adults and the number and ages of their dependants; the relevant features of such differentiation are typically referred to as *demographic variables*. The

Table 3.1. *Minimum needs equivalence scales*

	Rowntree (1901)	Beveridge (1942)	US Poverty Scale (1942)
Single person	60	59	78
Couple	100	100	100
+ 1 child	124	122	123
+ 2 children	161	144	152
+ 4 children	222	188	208

Note: For the Beveridge scale, children are taken to be in the 5–9 age group.

general problem in designing equivalence scales is to achieve the adjustment of observed income to take account of demographic differences. The discussion begins with an approach based on identifying the minimum needs that a household requires in order to survive at some chosen level of welfare, typically a level on or just above that identified as implying poverty. This method represents more of an *expert judgement* of equivalent incomes than an application of economic theory. Following this, the methods of Engel and Rothbarth are considered, both of which employ restrictive assumptions on the underlying preferences of households. Relaxing these assumptions then leads into the Barten method and its generalisation.

3.1 Minimum needs

The calculation of equivalence scales based upon minimum needs can be traced back to at least Rowntree (1901). Such scales are calculated by determining the cost of an identified bundle of goods and services that are seen as representing the minimum needs for the household. The exact bundle will differ between households of varying size. In the work of Rowntree the set of goods included in the minimum needs were food, rent and rates, and household sundries.

There have been many studies since that of Rowntree employing this methodology and some illustrative numbers are given in table 3.1. In each case a household with zero children is assigned the index of 100 and other compositions are measured relative to this. Hence with the Beveridge scale, a single child is seen as requiring an increase in the income of a couple of 22 per cent in order for the same minimum level of consumption needs to be attained.

Table 3.1 demonstrates that these equivalence scales assume that there are returns to scale in household size so that, for example, a family of two adults does not require twice the income of a single person. The major shortcomings of this method of computing equivalence scales are that by focusing on the cost of obtaining a minimum level of consumption they are inappropriate for applying to incomes above the minimum level and, since they do not take account of optimisation by the households, they cannot be claimed to measure the true economic cost of demographic differences.

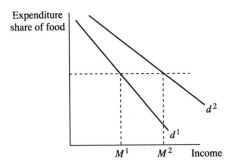

Figure 3.1   Construction of Engel scale

3.2 Engel and Rothbarth

The next two methods of computing equivalence scales both have a basis in the theory of household optimisation. They derive from the following observation: if the welfare level of a household can be judged by its consumption of some specific commodity, then equivalent incomes are those which lead different households to consume the same quantity of the commodity. The distinction between the two scales is in the commodities they select as relevant for the comparison.

3.2.1 Engel

The Engel (1895) approach to equivalence scales rests on the hypothesis that the welfare of a household can be measured by the proportion of its income that is spent on food. In particular, *Engel's law* asserts that the food share of expenditure falls as income, and hence welfare, rise. If this is accepted, equivalence scales can be constructed for demographically different households by calculating the income levels at which their expenditure share on food is equal. This is illustrated in figure 3.1 in which the expenditure share on food as a function of income is shown for two households with demographic characteristics d^1 and d^2. Using the Engel method, incomes M^1 and M^2 are equivalent and the equivalence scale is given by the ratio M^2/M^1.

There are two shortcomings to this approach. Firstly, although its content may be empirically true, this alone does not provide a basis for making welfare comparisons. Secondly, even if welfare conclusions can be inferred via Engel's law, it can be argued that the Engel method overestimates the cost of additional children for a household. Nicholson (1976) argues that a child is largely a food-consuming addition to a household. If, after the addition of a child, a household is compensated sufficiently to restore the share of food in its expenditure to its original level, this would represent overcompensation with respect to other commodities. Deaton and Muellbauer (1986) provide a formalisation of this argument.

The approach of Engel has been extended to the more general *iso-prop*

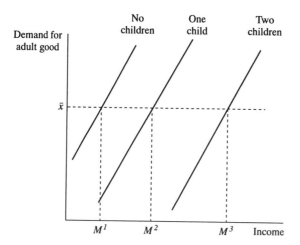

Figure 3.2 Rothbarth equivalence scale

method in which the expenditure shares of a basket of goods, rather than simply food, becomes the basis for the construction of scales. Seneca and Taussig (1971) employ a basket consisting of food, housing, clothing and transportation and find that this provides less compensation than the Engel method at low incomes but more compensation at high incomes. However, considering a basket of goods does not overcome the theoretical shortcomings of the Engel method.

3.2.2 Rothbarth

The procedure of Rothbarth (1943) selects for attention a set of goods that are consumed only by adults, termed *adult goods*, and such that the expenditure upon them can be treated as a measure of welfare. If these goods also have the property that changes in demographic characteristics only affect their demand via income effects, then the extra income required to keep their consumption constant when household composition changes can be used to construct an equivalence scale. Typical examples of such goods that have been used in practice are tobacco and alcohol.

For the chosen consumption level $\bar{x}$, the procedure is illustrated in figure 3.2 with three Engel curves representing different household compositions. On the basis that they generate the same level of demand as family composition changes, the Rothbarth procedure would assert that M^1, M^2 and M^3 are equivalent incomes and the equivalence scale would be constructed from their ratios.

There are a number of difficulties with this approach. It rests upon the hypotheses that consumption of adult goods accurately measures welfare and that they are affected only via income effects; theoretically both hypotheses are asserting separability between the utility from adult goods and that from goods which are affected by demographic characteristics. These hypotheses could be refuted by empirical evidence and, as noted by Cramer (1969), the typical adult goods, alcohol and tobacco, are empirically unresponsive to income effects. In addition, it is not clear that their demand is unaffected via changes in demographic characteristics. The evidence reported in Deaton, Ruiz-Castillo and Thomas (1989) supports these doubts about the method's validity. Furthermore, the ratios of M^1 to M^2 and M^3 will depend upon the level of demand chosen for the comparison except in the special case in which the Engel curves are straight lines through the origin, so that utility is homothetic, and the ratios may vary for different goods. This leads into a further aggregation problem of forming some total ratio out of the ratios for each good. These observations suggest that the formulation of equivalence scales should be more closely related to consumer preferences.

3.3 Prais and Houthakker

The approach to equivalence scales based on the Engel curve has been extended by Prais (1953) and Prais and Houthakker (1955) and investigated more recently by Muellbauer (1974) and McClements (1977). This method begins by specifying the Engel curve for good i as

$$\frac{x_i^h}{\tilde{a}_i} = x_i^h \left(\frac{M^h}{\tilde{a}_0} \right), \quad i = 1, \ldots, n, \tag{3.1}$$

where $\tilde{a}_i$, $i = 1, \ldots, n$, is a function of the vector of demographic characteristics $d = (d_1, \ldots, d_m)$ that describe the household. For example, d_1 could the number of children under 1 and d_2 the number between 1 and 3. The income deflator $\tilde{a}_0$ is then a function of the $\tilde{a}_i$. In this specification of the Engel curve, real income and the effective consumption level of each good are obtained by deflating by terms determined by household composition. This provides two channels through which household composition can affect demand.

From (3.1) the effect of a change in characteristic k of household composition upon demand can be expressed in elasticity terms as

$$\frac{d_k}{x_i^h} \frac{\partial x_i^h}{\partial d_k} = \frac{d_k}{\tilde{a}_i} \frac{\partial \tilde{a}_i}{\partial d_k} - \frac{M^h}{x_i^h} \frac{\partial x_i^h}{\partial M^h} \frac{d_k}{\tilde{a}_0} \frac{\partial \tilde{a}_0}{\partial d_k}. \tag{3.2}$$

The budget identity $\sum_{j=1}^{n} p_j \frac{\partial x_j^h}{\partial d_k} = 0$ and the condition that $\sum_{j=1}^{n} \frac{p_j x_j^h}{M^h} \frac{M^h}{x_j^h} \frac{\partial x_j^h}{\partial M^h} = 1$

imply $\frac{d_k}{\tilde{a}_0} \frac{\partial \tilde{a}_0}{\partial d_k} = \sum_{j=1}^{n} \frac{p_j x_j^h}{M^h} \frac{d_k}{\tilde{a}_j} \frac{\partial \tilde{a}_j}{\partial d_k}$. Substituting into (3.2) gives

$$\frac{d_k}{x_i^h} \frac{\partial x_i^h}{\partial d_k} = \frac{d_k}{\tilde{a}_i} \frac{\partial \tilde{a}_i}{\partial d_k} - \sum_{j=1}^{n} \left[\frac{M^h}{x_i^h} \frac{\partial x_i^h}{\partial M^h} \right] \frac{p_j x_j^h}{M^h} \frac{d_k}{\tilde{a}_j} \frac{\partial \tilde{a}_j}{\partial d_k}. \tag{3.3}$$

In principle, (3.3) provides a basis for empirically estimating the effects of household composition on demand elasticities. An example of an empirical application of (3.3), which forms the basis for the equivalence scales used by the Department of Social Security in the UK, can be found in McClements (1977).

3.4 Barten

Since the shortcomings of the methods discussed so far are due to their lack of a choice-theoretic foundation, the value of building equivalence scales from a basis in utility theory is clear. Although each of the methods so far can be interpreted in terms of the restrictions they place on preferences, see Muellbauer (1977) and Coulter *et al.* (1992), this was not explicit in their original motivation. The first attempt at making preference restrictions explicit can be attributed to Barten (1964) who approached the derivation via the direct utility function. Extensions of the method using duality can be found in Gorman (1978) and Muellbauer (1974).

It has been noted that some goods may not be consumed by children, the *adult goods* of Rothbarth, whilst children consume relatively large proportions of goods such as food. This observation motivates letting a household of type d be equivalent to $a^i(d)$ adults for the consumption of good i, $i=1,\ldots,n$. The household's utility is then

$$U^h = U^h \left(\frac{x_1^h}{a^1(d)}, \ldots, \frac{x_n^h}{a^n(d)} \right) = U^h(\hat{x}_1^h, \ldots, \hat{x}_n^h), \qquad (3.4)$$

where $\hat{x}_i^h = \dfrac{x_i^h}{a^i(d)}$. The behaviour of the household is determined by choosing the quantities $(\hat{x}_1^h, \ldots, \hat{x}_n^h)$ to maximise $U^h(\hat{x}_1^h, \ldots, \hat{x}_n^h)$ subject to the budget constraint $M^h = \sum_{i=1}^{m} \hat{p}_i \hat{x}_i^h$, where $\hat{p} = (\hat{p}_1, \ldots, \hat{p}_n)$ is the demographically adjusted price vector with $\hat{p}_i = a^i(d)p_i$. The form of this price vector and budget constraint motivates the observation that lies at the heart of this approach 'When you have a wife and a baby, a penny bun costs threepence' (Gorman 1978, p. 9).

Solving the maximisation gives the demand functions $\hat{x}_i^h = \hat{x}_i^h(\hat{p}, M^h)$ or $x_i^h = a^i(d)\hat{x}_i^h(p_1 a^1(d), \ldots, p_n a^n(d), M^h)$. The latter of these shows how a change in composition has two effects upon demand. It affects demand directly via the equivalence term $a^i(d)$ and indirectly via the equivalence terms affecting the demographically adjusted prices. This specification should be contrasted to (3.1). In elasticity form the effect of a change in demographic characteristic k upon demand for good i is

$$\frac{d_k}{x_i^h} \frac{\partial x_i^h}{\partial d_k} = \frac{\partial a^i}{\partial d_k} \frac{d_k}{a^i} + \sum_{j=1}^{n} \left[\frac{p_j}{x_i^h} a^i \frac{\partial \hat{x}_i^h}{\partial p_j} \right] \left[\frac{d_k}{a^j} \frac{\partial a^j}{\partial d_k} \right]. \qquad (3.5)$$

Equation (3.5) provides a basis for empirically estimating the effects of household composition on demand elasticities and an application can be found in Muellbauer (1977).

Contrasting (3.5) to (3.3) differences emerge only in the final term. If the Slutsky equation for the effect of a change in the price of good j on the demand for good i is multiplied by $\dfrac{p_j}{x_i^h}$ it becomes

$$\frac{p_j}{x_i^h}\frac{\partial x_i^h}{\partial p_j}=\frac{p_j}{x_i^h}\frac{\partial \chi_i^h}{\partial p_j}-\frac{M^h}{x_i^h}\frac{\partial x_i^h}{\partial M^h}\frac{p_j x_j^h}{M^h},\tag{3.6}$$

where χ_i^h is the compensated demand for good i from household h. The specifications in (3.3) and (3.5) can then be seen to be identical if $\dfrac{\partial \chi_i^h}{\partial p_j}=0$ so that the compensated demand for good i is independent of the price of good j. The two methods are therefore equivalent when the compensated demands are independent.

To construct the equivalence scale, the expenditure function dual to the utility function, $U^h(\hat{x}_1^h,\ldots,\hat{x}_n^h)$, can be defined by

$$E^h(\hat{p},U^h)=\min\{\hat{p}\hat{x}^h \text{ subject to } U^h(\hat{x}^h)\ge U^h\}.\tag{3.7}$$

Using the definition of demographically adjusted prices it follows that

$$E^h(\hat{p},U^h)=E^h(a^1(d)p_1,\ldots,a^n(d)p_n,U^h),\tag{3.8}$$

so the expenditure function captures all the demographic information via the equivalence terms $a^i(d)$. For some given level of welfare, $\bar{U}^h$, the equivalence scale for two-household compositions $\hat{d}$ and $\tilde{d}$ is given by

$$\frac{E^h(a^1(\hat{d})p_1,\ldots,a^n(\hat{d})p_n,\bar{U}^h)}{E^h(a^1(\tilde{d})p_1,\ldots,a^n(\tilde{d})p_n,\bar{U}^h)}.\tag{3.9}$$

If the specification in (3.4) is correct, (3.9) provides an *exact equivalence scale* in the sense that it measures the true economic cost of demographics. Its form also makes apparent how equivalence scales will generally be dependent upon the price level and the base level of welfare, $\bar{U}^h$, at which the comparison is made. Equivalence scales that are independent of the base level of utility will be considered in the next section.

For the two-good case, this procedure is illustrated in figure 3.3. The outward shift of the indifference curve is caused by the increase in the number of family members requiring an increase in household consumption to keep household utility constant. The extent to which the budget line has to be shifted outward determines the extra income required to compensate for the change in demographic characteristics.

The Barten approach provides a model of household welfare formation that is empirically implementable. The specification of utility chosen is a particularly precise one but has been rejected as inappropriate in some econometric tests, see Muellbauer (1977). In common with all the methods discussed so far, it also treats the demographic variables as lying outside the control of the household. In some circumstances this may be appropriate; the consequences of this assumption and the effect of relaxing it are considered in the next section.

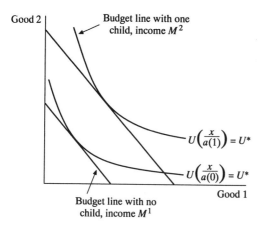

Figure 3.3   The Barten scale

3.5 General case

The preceding equivalence scales were constructed upon the implicit assumption that the demographic variables were exogenous and were not an object of choice by the household; in the terminology of Pollak and Wales (1979) they were *conditional* scales. If the demographic vector, or some components of it, affect utility directly rather than just through its interaction with consumption, an *unconditional* equivalence scale is required. To see the distinction, let utility take the form

$$U^h = \Phi(U(x^h, d), d). \tag{3.10}$$

An estimation procedure based upon observed market demand will only be able to infer information on the separable component $U(x^h, d)$ and will not uncover the function $\Phi(\cdot)$. Unfortunately, for welfare comparisons and for the construction of equivalence scales, the function $\Phi(\cdot)$ is required.

The relevance of the distinction between conditional and unconditional equivalence scales is critically dependent upon whether the demographic vector enters the utility function. If it does not, there is no distinction between the two and the previous approaches are valid. When it does, Blundell and Lewbel (1991) prove that demand data observed in a single price regime can provide no information on equivalence scales. There are three responses to this. The first is simply to use the demand data to construct cost functions relating to the component of utility $U(x^h, d)$ and use these to form cost of living indices for demographically different groups. These cannot be used to make welfare comparisons. An alternative procedure is to impose a convenient form upon the function $\Phi(\cdot)$ and proceed as if this were the correct form. Whether the imposed form is correct will not be testable. Finally, it may be possible to employ evidence other than demand data that sheds some light upon preferences over demographic variables. None of these alternatives provides an exact solution to the identification problem.

Given the utility function $U^h = \Phi(U(x^h, d), d)$, let the corresponding expenditure function be

$$E^h(p, d, U^h) = \min \{px^h \text{ subject to } \Phi(U(x^h, d), d) \geq U^h\}. \tag{3.11}$$

As in (3.9), the equivalence scale for two demographic compositions $\hat{d}$ and $\tilde{d}$ is defined by

$$\frac{E^h(p, \hat{d}, U^h)}{E^h(p, \tilde{d}, U^h)}. \tag{3.12}$$

A desirable property for an equivalence scale to possess is for it to be independent of the level of utility at which it is evaluated since this permits the same equivalence scale to be used to adjust all levels of income. If the equivalence scale satisfies this property, it is said to be *independent of base*. For the equivalence scale in (3.12) to be independent of the base level of utility, Lewbel (1989, 1991) has shown that the cost function must be of the form

$$E^h(p, d, U^h) = F(p, d)G(p, U^h). \tag{3.13}$$

The sufficiency of this condition can be seen by forming the ratio in (3.12) to obtain the equivalence scale

$$\frac{F(p, \hat{d})}{F(p, \tilde{d})}, \tag{3.14}$$

which is independent of the base level of utility. Two special cases arise from (3.13). If $G(p, U^h)$ is independent of p, hence $G(p, U^h) = G(U^h)$, the cost function represents homothetic preferences. When $F(\cdot)$ is independent of p the underlying utility function takes the form

$$U^h = U\left(\frac{x^h}{f(d)}\right), \tag{3.15}$$

which is a special case of the Barten model.

The main conclusion to be drawn from this analysis is that equivalence scales are only independent of the base level of utility if the cost function is separable between utility and demographic characteristics. Whether this is true in practice, and if it were many applications of equivalence scales would receive theoretical justification, is a matter of empirical testing. Evidence to date, namely that of Blundell and Lewbel (1991), rejects the independent of base assumption.

3.6 In practice

There have been many equivalence scales constructed (Buhmann *et al.* (1989) list thirty-four and their study is not comprehensive) and so it is necessary to find a simple means of summarising their content. Buhmann *et al.* (1989) suggest that an acceptable approximation of existing equivalence scales is to write equivalised incomes as

$$\tilde{M}^h = \frac{M^h}{[d^h]^\varepsilon},$$
(3.16)

where the demographic variable, d^h, now measures only the number of family members and the elasticity, ε, varies between 0 and 1. Four types of equivalence scales are then identified. *Expert statistical* scales are designed for statistical purposes such as counting the number above or below a given standard of living. Their typical value of ε is 0.75. *Expert programme* scales are designed to assist with welfare programmes and have a typical ε value of 0.55. Both these expert scales are constructed in the manner of the Beveridge scale where an outside judgement is made on needs. *Consumption* scales are based on observed expenditures and lead to an average ε value of 0.36. Finally, *subjective* scales, constructed on the basis of questionnaire evaluations of income, have the smallest ε of 0.25.

There is considerable variation in these scales which is linked to the means of construction and the purpose for which the scale is required. The expert statistical scales assign the largest increase in cost for increases in family size and give little weight to potential economies of scale in consumption. Conversely, the subjective scales find the greatest economies of scale but, being based on consumers' own perceptions of their welfare status, are not free from reporting bias.

In assessing these methods of constructing equivalence scales, it should be noted that the minimum needs and the Engel–Rothbarth approaches are straightforward but as a consequence are not without their faults. The exact measures capture precisely what the other two are attempting to approximate but correspondingly are more difficult to calculate. It should also be noted that by basing the exact measures upon utility analysis, they are subject to the difficulties concerning interpersonal comparability discussed in chapter 2 and dependent on the appropriateness of the utility maximisation assumption. Furthermore, there is also the difficulty of imposing a single, well-defined, utility function such as (3.10) as a representation of a household's preferences. The household utility function must represent the aggregation of the preferences of the individuals constituting the household but, although on a smaller scale, such aggregation is subject to the difficulties already noted for social preferences in chapter 2. This observation raises obvious questions about the interpretation of (3.10).

4 THE MEASUREMENT OF INEQUALITY

Given a set of income levels for the households in an economy, or a specified subgroup of an economy, adjusted by an appropriate equivalence scale, an obvious question for anyone who has any concern for distributive justice is to ask how equally distributed is income in that economy or subgroup. Income inequality may be of interest in its own right or it may be relevant because of its perceived consequences. In either case, in order to meaningfully discuss inequality, it must first be necessary to measure it.

There are many measures of inequality that can be employed and all have features to commend them. Broadly speaking, measures of inequality can be divided into three groups. The first group are those measures that can be termed *statistical* and, as such, are typically standard statistical indices applied to inequality. The *welfare measures* constitute the second group and take as their starting point an explicit formulation of social welfare from which the inequality measure is developed. This division does not imply that statistical measures have no welfare implications; in fact, a fundamental observation in the theory of inequality measurement was the recognition of their implicit welfare assumptions. The final category of measures can be termed *axiomatic*. These are derived by specifying properties that it is thought a satisfactory measure should possess and deriving all measures that satisfy those conditions.

After providing basic definitions, the most relevant of the statistical measures are noted. This is done both for completeness and because a number of these measures feature in the ensuing analysis. The connection between social welfare and statistical measures is then clarified and this is followed by discussion of explicitly welfare-based indices. The axiomatic derivation of inequality measures is then reviewed. As a final point, the discussion is given in terms of the measurement of income inequality. However, the measures that are described can be applied to the measurement of the inequality of any vector or distribution of observations, be it data on wages, wealth, welfare or even non-economic data such as weights. The only distinction between these applications are the properties that it may be desirable for the index to possess.

4.1 Basic definitions

Measures of income inequality can either be defined in terms of discrete or continuous distributions of income. Although the former is correct in an observational sense, the latter often allows simpler derivation of results and is a valid approximation for large populations. Most attention will be paid below to the discrete case but the continuous case will be used where appropriate.

With a discrete distribution of income, it is assumed that there are H households labelled $h = 1, \ldots, H$ with the labelling chosen so that their incomes, M^h, form a increasing sequence. Hence

$$M^1 \leq M^2 \leq M^3 \leq \ldots \leq M^H. \tag{3.17}$$

The mean income, μ, is defined by

$$\mu = \frac{1}{H} \sum_{h=1}^{H} M^h. \tag{3.18}$$

For a continuous distribution, the basic data is a density function for income. Denoting the density by $\gamma(M)$ and assuming the support of this function to be $[0,\bar{M}]$, where $\bar{M}$ is the maximum level of income, so that $\int_0^{\bar{M}} \gamma(M)dM=1$, the mean level of income is

$$\mu = \int_0^{\bar{M}} M\gamma(M)dM. \tag{3.19}$$

The basic task in inequality measurement is to assign a single number to the distribution $M^1,\ldots,M^H$ that describes the inequality of the distribution and permits alternative distributions to be ranked. Formalising this, given the set of incomes $M=\{M^1,\ldots,M^H\}$, an inequality measure is a function $I(M)$ such that if $I(\tilde{M})>I(\hat{M})$ then the income distribution $\tilde{M}$ is judged as having more inequality than distribution $\hat{M}$. Typically, a normalisation is adopted so that $I:\mathcal{R}_+^H \to [0,1]$ with a value of 0 representing complete equality and 1 maximum inequality. For continuous distributions, the inequality measure is defined as the functional I with $I:C[0,\bar{M}]\to[0,1]$, where $C[0,\bar{M}]$ represents the space of continuous density functions on $[0,\bar{M}]$. These definitions imply that the inequality measure has to provide a complete ranking of income distributions. Other than defining its range and domain, the form of the function $I(M)$ has not been restricted. This permits the maximum freedom in the choice of $I(M)$ and allows its form to be restricted only by considerations directly relevant to the measurement of income inequality.

Given an income vector $M=\{M^1,\ldots,M^H\}$, an index that assigns the same inequality to the vectors M and λM for any $\lambda>0$ is termed a *relative index*. Equivalently, $I(M)=I(\lambda M)$ so a relative index is homogeneous of degree 0 in M. This property is not entirely innocuous. Its acceptance leads to an interpretation of inequality as a relative concept in which a scaling up of all incomes leaves inequality unchanged. An alternative view would be that an addition of an equal amount to all incomes should leave inequality unchanged so that $I(M)=I(M+\delta)$ for all $\delta> -M^1$. The implications of these assumptions are investigated further below.

4.2 Statistical measures

The statistical measures of inequality that are presented represent only a selection from the many that exist. The selection is on the grounds of extent of use in practice or theoretical relevance; Sen (1973) and Cowell (1977) discuss further statistical measures.

4.2.1 The Lorenz curve

The Lorenz curve has played an important role in the measurement of inequality since its introduction by Lorenz (1905) and constitutes a helpful graphical device

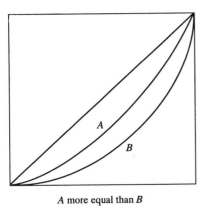

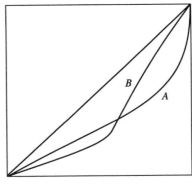

A more equal than B   A and B incomparable

Figure 3.4   Lorenz curves as an incomplete ranking

for presenting a summary of data on income distribution. Although not an inequality index as defined above, Lorenz curves are considered here because of their use in illustrating inequality and the central role they play in the motivation of other inequality indices.

The Lorenz curve is constructed by arranging the population in order of increasing income and then graphing the proportion of income going to each proportion of the population. If all households in the population had identical incomes the Lorenz curve would then be the diagonal connecting the points (0, 0) and (1, 1). If there is any degree of inequality, the ordering in which the households are taken ensures that the Lorenz curve lies below the diagonal since, for example, the poorest half of the population must have less than half the proportion of income. For a continuous income distribution, the coordinates (x, y) of the Lorenz curve are given by

$$\left(\int_0^m \gamma(M)dM, \frac{1}{\mu} \int_0^m M\gamma(M)dM \right),$$ (3.20)

as m varies from 0 to $\bar{M}$.

Although the Lorenz curve does not constitute an index of inequality in the sense of assigning a number to the distribution, it can still be employed to unambiguously rank some income distributions. As illustrated in figure 3.4, if the Lorenz curve for distribution B lies entirely outside that for distribution A, distribution B can be seen to be less equal. In particular, B could have been derived from A by transfers from poor to rich. In this case, A can be said to *Lorenz dominate B*. If the Lorenz curves representing distributions A and B cross, an unambiguous ranking of the two distributions cannot be derived from the Lorenz curve alone. The concept of *Lorenz domination* therefore provides only a partial ordering of income distributions.

A fundamental concept in the theory of inequality measurement is the *Pigou–Dalton Principle of Transfers* which was first formulated by Dalton (1920). The basis of this principle is that any transfer from a poor household to a rich one must increase inequality. The principle can be defined formally as follows.

Pigou–Dalton Principle of Transfers

The inequality index must decrease if there is a transfer of income from a richer household to a poorer household which preserves the ranking of the two households in the income distribution and leaves total income remaining unchanged.

Any inequality measure that satisfies the Principle is said to be *sensitive to transfers*. The Pigou–Dalton Principle is generally viewed as a condition that any acceptable measure of inequality should meet and is therefore adopted in most axiomatisations of inequality indices. Jenkins (1991) assesses the transfer sensitivity of a number of statistical inequality measures. For the Lorenz curve, a transfer of income from poor to rich moves the Lorenz curve further from the diagonal. The Lorenz curve therefore satisfies the Pigou–Dalton Principle.

4.2.2 The Gini coefficient

The Gini coefficient, attributed to Gini (1912), has been the subject of extensive attention in the literature on inequality measurement, finding both proponents and opponents. This interest has lead to a thorough understanding of the implications of its structure and to extensions of the basic index. The Gini coefficient has also seen considerable use in applied economics.

The basic Gini index, G, can be expressed in several alternative, but equivalent, ways. The first method of expressing the Gini is the most straightforward mathematically but in itself carries little obvious meaning. In this case, the Gini appears as the following affine function of a weighted sum of relative incomes

$$G = 1 + \frac{1}{H} - \frac{2}{H^2 \mu} \left[M^H + 2M^{H-1} + \ldots + [H-1]M^2 + HM^1 \right]. \tag{3.21}$$

The second formulation expresses the means by which the first was derived. The Gini index considers all possible pairs of incomes and out of each pair selects the minimum income level. Summing and normalising provides a formula equivalent to (3.21) but demonstrating more clearly the process involved

$$G = 1 + \frac{1}{H} - \frac{2}{H^2 \mu} \sum_{i=1}^{H} \sum_{j=1}^{H} \min\{M^i, M^j\}. \tag{3.22}$$

The final way of expressing the Gini coefficient exploits its relationship to the Lorenz curve. As illustrated in figure 3.5, the Gini index is equal to the area between the Lorenz curve and the line of equality as a proportion of the area of the triangle beneath the line of equality. If the area of the box is normalised at 1, the Gini coefficient is then twice the area between the Lorenz curve and the

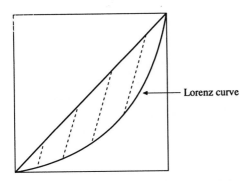

Figure 3.5   Relating Gini to Lorenz

equality line. Expressed in this way, it can be seen that the Gini coefficient can take values lying between 0 and 1. This definition of the Gini index makes it clear that the Gini can be used to rank distributions when the Lorenz curves cross since the relevant areas are always well defined. Since the measure is stronger than the Lorenz dominance criteria, it must contain some additional assumptions over and above those which are present in the Lorenz curve comparison. What this extra structure involves will be investigated below when statistical measures are related to social welfare.

The Gini index is a relative index of inequality so that it is independent of scale and it also satisfies the Pigou–Dalton criterion. This can be seen by considering a transfer from household i to household j of ΔM with the households chosen so that $M^i > M^j$. From the ranking of incomes this implies $j > i$. Then

$$\Delta G = \frac{-2}{H^2 \mu} [j - i] < 0, \tag{3.23}$$

as required. It is important to note that the effect of the transfer on the index depends only on the relative rankings of i and j in the income distribution. For example, a transfer from $i = 1$ to $j = 11$ counts as much as one from $i = 151$ to $j = 161$. It might be expected that an index should be more sensitive to transfers between households low in the income distribution but it is actually most sensitive to transfers around the modal income.

A final relevant property of the Gini index is that the Gini can incorporate the negative income observations which often arise in income data. Extensions of the Gini index are analysed in Donaldson and Weymark (1980) and Weymark (1979a).

4.2.3 Theil's entropy measure

The entropy measure of Theil (1967) is drawn from information theory and, in particular, the measurement of the average information content of a system of information. Although there is little apparent economic motivation in the construction of the entropy measure, it will appear below when decomposable inequality measures are discussed.

The definition of the (normalised) Theil entropy index, T, is given by

$$T = \frac{1}{\log H} \sum_{h=1}^{H} \frac{M^h}{H\mu} \left[\log \frac{M^h}{H\mu} - \log \frac{1}{H} \right] = \frac{1}{H \log H} \sum_{h=1}^{H} \frac{M^h}{\mu} \log \frac{M^h}{\mu}. \qquad (3.24)$$

In respect of the Pigou–Dalton criteria, the effect of an income transfer, $d\varepsilon$, between households i and j upon the entropy index is given by

$$\frac{dT}{d\varepsilon} = \frac{1}{H\mu \log H} \left[\log \frac{M^j}{M^i} \right] < 0, \qquad (3.25)$$

so that the entropy measure does satisfy the criteria. However, the change in the index now depends on the relative incomes of the two households involved in the transfer. Whether this form of sensitivity to transfers is the correct one is again open to question.

This concludes the review of the statistical measures of inequality. At a number of points in the discussion reference has been made to acceptable criteria for an inequality index to possess and to whether the properties of the indices, such as the manner in which they were affected by transfers, were satisfactory. Obviously, to judge whether criteria are acceptable or not requires the existence of some underlying notion of distributive justice or social welfare. Two questions then arise. Firstly, to what extent can income distributions be compared without the need for an explicit welfare function and, secondly, do the statistical measures of inequality have implied social welfare functions? The answers to these questions constitute the subject of the next section.

4.3 Statistical measures and welfare

One of the significant developments in the theory of inequality measurement was the clarification of the link between statistical measures and social welfare. There are two aspects involved in this link. The first concerns the extent to which income distributions can be ranked in terms of inequality without specifying a precise social welfare function and the link between such a ranking and the statistical measures. The essential work in this respect was undertaken by Atkinson (1970), Dasgupta *et al.* (1973) and Rothschild and Stiglitz (1973). The second aspect is rather more subtle and involves the construction of the social welfare function implied by an inequality measure. This line of enquiry is exemplified by the work of Blackorby and Donaldson (1978). Throughout this section it is assumed that the income distributions to be ranked have the same mean level of income.

To discuss the extent to which distributions can be ranked without specifying a precise welfare function it is necessary to introduce a number of definitions. A square matrix is said to be *bistochastic* if its entries are non-negative and each of its rows and columns sum to 1. A *permutation* matrix is a bistochastic matrix that has a single positive element in each row and each column. For example the matrix

$$\begin{bmatrix} 0.5 & 0.2 & 0.3 \\ 0.1 & 0.6 & 0.3 \\ 0.4 & 0.2 & 0.4 \end{bmatrix}, \tag{3.26}$$

is bistochastic and

$$\begin{bmatrix} 0 & 1 & 0 \\ 1 & 0 & 0 \\ 0 & 0 & 1 \end{bmatrix}, \tag{3.27}$$

is a permutation matrix. The permutation matrices form the extreme points of the set of bistochastic matrices.

The relevance of these concepts are that given a bistochastic matrix Q and an income vector M, the vector $\tilde{M} = QM$ represents an averaging of M, or equivalently, could be obtained from M by a series of transfers from rich to poor. If P is a permutation matrix, then $\hat{M} = PM$ is obtained from M by re-ordering the components of M.

Now consider a social welfare function

$$W = \tilde{W}(U^1(M^1), \dots, U^H(M^H)) = W(M^1, \dots, M^H), \tag{3.28}$$

where $W(\cdot)$ is increasing in its arguments. The welfare function is *symmetric* if

$$W(M) = W(PM), \tag{3.29}$$

for all permutation matrices P and *Schur-concave* (or S-concave) if

$$W(QM) \geq W(M). \tag{3.30}$$

The social welfare function is strictly S-concave if the inequality is strict for all bistochastic matrices which are not permutation matrices. The assumption of S-concavity is a natural one in the context of inequality since QM can obtained from M by transfers from rich to poor and a welfare function that is sensitive to distribution should increase with such transfers. Conversely, an inequality index is S-convex if $I(QM) \leq I(M)$.

The interconnections between these concepts and the inequality indices already discussed are summarised in the following lemma due to Kolm (1969) and Dasgupta *et al.* (1973).

Lemma 3.1

Given two income vectors $\hat{M} = (\hat{M}^1, \dots, \hat{M}^H)$ and $\tilde{M} = (\tilde{M}^1, \dots, \tilde{M}^H)$, with $\sum_{h=1}^{H} \hat{M}^h = \sum_{h=1}^{H} \tilde{M}^h$, which are ordered so that $\hat{M}^1 \leq \hat{M}^2 \leq \cdots \leq \hat{M}^H$ and $\tilde{M}^1 \leq \tilde{M}^2 \leq \cdots \leq \tilde{M}^H$, then the following four conditions are equivalent:

(i) there exists a bistochastic matrix Q (which is not a permutation matrix) such that $\tilde{M} = Q\hat{M}$;

(ii) $\sum_{h=1}^{k} \tilde{M}^h \geq \sum_{h=1}^{k} \hat{M}^h$ for all $k \leq H$ and $\sum_{h=1}^{H} \tilde{M}^h = \sum_{h=1}^{H} \hat{M}^h$;

(iii) $\tilde{M}$ can be obtained from $\hat{M}$ by sequence of transfers with all transfers moving income from richer to poorer households;

(iv) $W(\tilde{M}) > W(\hat{M})$ for all strictly S-concave functions $W(\cdot)$.

Proof

A formal proof of this lemma can be found in Berge (1963) but it should be clear from the previous discussion.

The interpretation of this lemma rests on the observation that (ii) is simply the statement that the Lorenz curve for distribution $\tilde{M}$ lies everywhere inside that for $\hat{M}$. The equivalence of this to (iv) then implies that all S-concave social welfare functions will assign greater welfare to the distribution that is ranked higher by the Lorenz criterion. Hence when a ranking can be derived by the Lorenz criterion, this ranking will be agreed by all S-concave welfare functions. To complete this discussion, it is noted that S-concavity is a weaker concept than quasi-concavity; hence any symmetric quasi-concave function is S-concave. Slightly different versions of this result can be found in Rothschild and Stiglitz (1973) and treatment of the continuous case in Atkinson (1970).

The converse of lemma 3.1 is that if the Lorenz curves for two distributions cross, then quasi-concave social welfare functions can be found that will rank the two distributions differently.

Put together, the lemma and its converse show that the Lorenz dominance criteria provide the most complete ranking of income distributions that is possible given only that social welfare is an S-concave function of incomes. To provide a complete ranking when Lorenz curves cross requires more restrictions to be placed upon the structure of the social welfare function. In addition, any index of inequality is necessarily stronger than Lorenz dominance and, when it can be derived from a social welfare function, is derived from a social welfare function that has more structure than simply satisfying S-concavity (and may not even satisfy that condition).

The preceding discussion has demonstrated that the statistical inequality indices may represent social welfare functions with restrictive properties. To formalise this link consider a social welfare function

$$w = W(M^1, \ldots, M^H) = W(M), \tag{3.31}$$

that is S-concave and increasing along rays, so that $W(\lambda M) > W(M)$, $\lambda > 1$. Corresponding to this social welfare function is its *transformation*, or distance, function $D(w, M)$ defined by

$$D(w, M) = \max_{\lambda} \left\{ \lambda > 0 : W\left(\frac{M}{\lambda}\right) \geq w \right\}. \tag{3.32}$$

The transformation function determines the maximum extent to which the income vector in a given situation can be reduced while social welfare remains on, or above, a target level. From its construction, it can be seen that $D(w, M)$ is homogeneous of degree 1 in M and strictly decreasing in w. The distance function is also an implicit representation of the social welfare function since solving

$$D(w, M) = 1, \tag{3.33}$$

generates the initial social welfare function.

Employing the transformation function, Blackorby and Donaldson (1978) suggest as an index of equality (the converse of an inequality index) the function $E(w, M)$ defined by

$$E(w, M) = \frac{D(w, M)}{D(w, \mu e)}, \tag{3.34}$$

where e is the vector $(1, \ldots, 1)$. The interpretation of (3.34) is that it measures the proportion that income can be reduced if it is distributed equally while remaining on the same level surface of the transformation function. If the social welfare function is homothetic then $D(w, M)$ can be written in the form $D(w, M) = \theta(w) \tilde{D}(M)$ and the index is independent of the base level of welfare or *reference-level-free*; in all other cases it will be dependent on its base. In addition, if social welfare is homothetic then

$$E(w, \tilde{M}) \geq E(w, \hat{M}) \Leftrightarrow W(\tilde{M}) \geq W(\hat{M}), \tag{3.35}$$

so that the index has normative significance. It can also be shown that $E(w, M)$ is homogeneous of degree zero in M and S-concave in M.

To construct a social welfare function from an equality measure, note that since $D(w, M)$ is homogeneous of degree 1 in M it follows that

$$D(w, \mu e) = \mu D(w, e) = \mu \psi(w). \tag{3.36}$$

Equation (3.34) can therefore be rearranged to give

$$D(w, M) = \psi(w) \mu E(w, M). \tag{3.37}$$

In (3.37), $\psi(w)$ implies the form of the transformation function and is essentially arbitrary except for the requirement that $D(w, M)$ must be decreasing in w. If $E(w, M)$ is S-concave in M, so is $D(w, M)$. A social welfare function can then be generated by solving $D(w, M) = \psi(w) \mu E(w, M) = 1$, with a social welfare function for each $\psi(w)$. For this constructed welfare function, the implied measure of equality is, of course, $E(w, M)$.

The connection of this result with statistical measures of inequality is given in theorem 3.1.

Theorem 3.1 (Blackorby and Donaldson)

If the index of equality is reference-level-free then the implied social welfare functions are homothetic. Conversely, if the social welfare function is homothetic then its measure of equality is reference-level-free.

Proof

A reference-level-free equality index can be written $E(w, M) \equiv \bar{E}(M)$ so that $D(w, M) = \psi(w)\bar{D}(M) = \psi(w)\mu\bar{E}(M)$. Solving around 1 gives $w = W(M) = f(\bar{D}(M))$ with $f = [1/\psi(w)]^{-1}$. Hence f is increasing in w and $\bar{D}(M)$ is homogeneous of degree 1. This implies $W(M)$ is homothetic.

If $W(M)$ is homothetic then $W(M) = \phi(\bar{W}(M))$ with $\bar{W}(M)$ homogeneous of degree 1. The transformation function for $W(M)$ is then defined by $D(w, M)$

$$= \max_\lambda \left\{ \lambda > 0: \phi\left(W\left(\frac{M}{\lambda}\right)\right) \geq w \right\} = \frac{1}{\phi^{-1}} \bar{W}(M) = \psi(M)\bar{W}(M) = \psi(M)\bar{D}(M)$$

where $\bar{D}(M) = \max_\lambda \left\{ \lambda > 0: \bar{W}\left(\frac{M}{\lambda}\right) > 1 \right\}$. $\bar{D}(M)$ is homogeneous of degree 1 so

that the index of equality can be written $E(w, M) = \dfrac{\psi(w)\bar{D}(M)}{\psi(w)\bar{D}(\mu e)} = \dfrac{\bar{D}(M)}{\mu} = \bar{E}(M)$

where the normalisation $\bar{D}(e) = 1$ has been employed. This proves the equality measure is reference-level-free.

The proof of theorem 3.1 provides the statement required for the construction of the social welfare functions underlying the statistical measures. It has been shown that for reference-level-free indices, which all the statistical indices given above are, the identity $\bar{D}(M) = \mu\bar{E}(M)$ holds. Given $\bar{E}(M)$ the transformation function can be calculated from this identity and then solved to give the social welfare function.

Blackorby and Donaldson show that the welfare functions corresponding to the Gini and Theil entropy inequality indices are given respectively by

$$W_G(M) = \frac{1}{H^2}\left[M^H + 3M^{H-1} + \ldots + [2H-1]M^H\right] \tag{3.38}$$

and

$$W_T(M) = \frac{1}{H \log H}\left[H\mu \log H\mu - \sum_{h=1}^{H} M^h \log M^h\right]. \tag{3.39}$$

The form of $W_G(M)$ is particularly interesting since it shows that the Gini coefficient is implied by a quasi-concave, but not strictly quasi-concave, and homothetic social welfare function. This observation clarifies a number of the issues raised in Newbery (1970) and Sheshinski (1972a) concerning the form that the social welfare function consistent with the Gini must take. In addition, it can be seen that neither of these functions is obviously superior to the other as a measure of social welfare.

This section has investigated the link between statistical measures of inequality and social welfare. The first lemma demonstrated that the Lorenz ranking is consistent with that produced by any S-concave social welfare function so that to proceed beyond the Lorenz criterion it is necessary to provide further restrictions upon the social welfare function. The statistical measures that can be related to social welfare functions have properties stronger than S-concavity. It was shown how equality measures could be constructed from a social welfare function and how the converse construction could also be achieved. The resulting forms of social welfare function for three of the statistical measures could then be seen to embody very particular, and not necessarily acceptable, assumptions.

4.3.1 Generalised Lorenz curves

The relation between the Lorenz curve and the ranking introduced by a social welfare function summarised by lemma 3.1 concerned only the ranking of income distributions with the same mean level of income. Analogous results for the ranking of income distributions with different means have been derived by Shorrocks (1983) using the generalised Lorenz curve.

Assume that the social welfare function is of the form (3.31), is S-concave and is non-decreasing in each income level so that $\frac{\partial W}{\partial M^h} \geq 0$, all h. Given two income distributions $\hat{M}$ and $\tilde{M}$, then it is clear that $W(\hat{M}) \geq W(\tilde{M})$ for any S-concave and non-decreasing social welfare function if the Lorenz curve of $\hat{M}$ lies inside that of $\tilde{M}$ and the mean of $\hat{M}$ is greater than that $\tilde{M}$. To proceed beyond these sufficient conditions, it is necessary to introduce the generalised Lorenz curve.

Generalised Lorenz curve

In the continuous case the coordinates of the generalised Lorenz curve are given by

$$\left(\int_0^m \gamma(M)dM, \int_0^m M\gamma(M)dM, \right) \text{ and in the discrete case by } \left(\frac{h}{H}, \frac{\sum_{i=1}^h M^i}{H} \right). \quad (3.40)$$

In the continuous case the generalised Lorenz curve is a continuous curve connecting $(0,0)$ to $(1,\mu)$. The same is true in the discrete case if the discrete points are connected by straight lines and the point for $h=1$ is connected to the origin.

Theorem 3.2 determines the relation between the ranking of income distributions with different means by the generalised Lorenz curve and by the social welfare function.

Theorem 3.2 (Shorrocks)

$W(\hat{M}) \geq W(\tilde{M})$ for all non-decreasing S-concave social welfare functions if and

only if $\dfrac{\sum\limits_{i=1}^{h} \hat{M}^i}{H} \geq \dfrac{\sum\limits_{i=1}^{h} \tilde{M}^i}{H}$ *so that the generalised Lorenz curve for* $\hat{M}$ *lies inside that for* $\tilde{M}$.

Proof

To prove the 'if' part, define $\tilde{\tilde{M}}$ by $\tilde{\tilde{M}}^h = \tilde{M}^h$ for $h = 1, \ldots, H-1$ and $\tilde{\tilde{M}}^H = \tilde{M}^H + H[\hat{\mu} - \tilde{\mu}]$. As the social welfare function is non-decreasing, $W(\tilde{\tilde{M}})$ $\geq W(\tilde{M})$. In addition, since $\hat{\mu} = \tilde{\tilde{\mu}}$ and $\dfrac{\sum\limits_{i=1}^{h} \hat{M}^i}{H} \geq \dfrac{\sum\limits_{i=1}^{h} \tilde{\tilde{M}}^i}{H}$ for all h, the Lorenz curve for $\hat{M}$ lies inside that for $\tilde{\tilde{M}}$ so $W(\hat{M}) \geq W(\tilde{\tilde{M}}) \geq W(\tilde{M})$.

To prove the 'only if' define $W_h(M) = \dfrac{\sum\limits_{i=1}^{h} M^i}{h}$, $h = 1, \ldots, H$, and note that $W_h(M)$ is S-concave and non-decreasing. Then $W_h(\hat{M}) \geq W_h(\tilde{M})$ for all h only if

$$\dfrac{\sum\limits_{i=1}^{h} \hat{M}^i}{H} \geq \dfrac{\sum\limits_{i=1}^{h} \tilde{M}^i}{H}.$$

This theorem demonstrates that a ranking of two income distributions with different means can only be unambiguous if the generalised Lorenz curves do not intersect. It also shows that even if the Lorenz curves for two distributions intersect, the condition on the generalised Lorenz curve may still be satisfied.

4.4 Welfare-theoretic indices

The discussion above has emphasised the unsatisfactory nature of the implicit welfare assumptions that are embodied in statistical measures of inequality. A response to this is to make the welfare judgements explicit by deriving the inequality measure from a specific social welfare function. One method of achieving this was discussed in the previous section; the present section considers the method of equally distributed equivalent incomes suggested by Dalton (1920), Kolm (1969) and Atkinson (1970). With this procedure, social concern for equity can be incorporated in the index by the choice of the utility of income function assigned to households and the function employed for aggregating household utilities into social welfare.

To simplify, assume social welfare can be represented by a utilitarian social welfare function

$$W = \sum_{h=1}^{H} U(M^h), \tag{3.41}$$

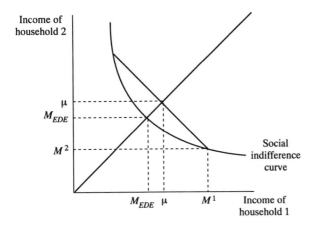

Figure 3.6   The equally distributed equivalent income

where the household utility of income function, $U(M)$, is increasing and strictly concave so that $U'(M) > 0$ and $U''(M) < 0$. Utility $U(M)$ can either be the true cardinal utility function representing households' preferences or it can be chosen by the state as its evaluation of the utility of income to each household. In this second interpretation, since social welfare is then obtained by adding the individual utilities, welfare judgements can be captured in the choice of $U(M)$. Increasing the concavity of the utility function effectively places a higher weight on low incomes.

Before specifying a useful form of $U(M^h)$, it is possible to derive the measure of inequality proposed by Kolm (1969) and Atkinson (1970). Define M_{EDE} as the solution to

$$\sum_{h=1}^{H} U(M^h) = HU(M_{EDE}).\tag{3.42}$$

M_{EDE} is called the *equally distributed equivalent* income and is that level of income that if given to all households would generate the same level of social welfare as the initial income distribution.

Using the definition of M_{EDE}, the Atkinson–Kolm index is given by

$$A = 1 - \frac{M_{EDE}}{\mu} = \frac{\mu - M_{EDE}}{\mu}.\tag{3.43}$$

The concavity of the household utility function guarantees that index A is non-negative. In addition, it is independent of the mean level of income and is therefore a relative index.

For a two-household economy the construction of M_{EDE} is illustrated in figure 3.6. The initial income distribution is given by M^1, M^2 and this determines the relevant indifference curve of the social welfare function. M_{EDE} is found by moving round this indifference curve to the line of equal incomes. It is clear that because of the concavity of the social indifference curve, M_{EDE} is less than the mean income, μ.

The flexibility of this index lies in the freedom of choice of the utility of income function and it is this function that determines the importance attached to inequality by the index. One form of utility function that was proposed by Atkinson (1970) is

$$U(M) = \frac{M^{1-\varepsilon}}{1-\varepsilon}, \ U'(M) = M^{-\varepsilon}, \varepsilon \neq 1. \tag{3.44}$$

This function is isoelastic and concave if $\varepsilon \geq 0$. At $\varepsilon = 1$ and $\varepsilon = 0$ the function takes the following form

$$\varepsilon = 1 \Rightarrow U(M) = \log M, \varepsilon = 0 \Rightarrow U(M) = M. \tag{3.45}$$

The welfare judgements of the policy maker are contained in the chosen value of ε since ε determines the degree of concavity of the utility function. Increasing ε makes the utility function more concave and reduces the importance given to high incomes in the determination of social welfare. Utility function (3.44) has found numerous uses in applications of public economics.

The Atkinson–Kolm index is an attempt to make explicit the welfare judgements that are contained within statistical measures of inequality. Although the derivation above worked with a utilitarian social welfare function, this is not essential and it can be seen that the definition of equally distributed equivalent income applies to any form of welfare function. Within this framework, however, there is considerable ambiguity as to the distinction between the form of social welfare and the form of individual utility. As noted, the utility of income function can either be the true function capturing households' preferences or it can be the state's evaluation of income to households. In the latter case, the distinction between individual utility and social welfare becomes arbitrary.

4.5 Axiomatic inequality measures

The aim of the axiomatic approach to inequality measurement is to derive the set of inequality indices that satisfy a chosen set of axioms. The axioms are chosen to capture what are viewed as the desirable properties for an index to possess and the set of derived indices will constitute all indices with those properties. As the number of independent axioms is increased, the set of indices that satisfy them will generally decrease. This is advantageous in focusing attention on a reduced set of alternative indices and in clarifying which properties indices that do not satisfy the axioms fail to possess.

A number of potential axioms have already been noted informally in the above discussion. The first of these, and the least questionable, is the axiom of symmetry. Letting the index of inequality, $I(M,H)$, depend on the income distribution, M, and population size, H, this axiom can be stated as

Axiom I1 (Symmetry)

$I(M, H) = I(PM, H)$ for all permutation matrices P.

This axiom has also been termed *anonymity* and requires that the inequality measure is not affected by the order in which households are labelled. The second axiom usually invoked relates to S-concavity of social welfare and the principle of transfers.

Axiom I2 (Transfer)

$I(QM, H) < I(M, H)$ for all bistochastic matrices which are not permutation matrices.

The direction of this inequality implies that the inequality measure is an S-convex function of incomes.

Axioms other than I1 and I2 do not meet with universal approval. This can either be on the grounds that they are not strictly necessary, which is the case for the decomposability axioms introduced below, or because there exists an alternative property to that expressed by the axiom which could be equally justified. Such is the case for the next axiom.

Axiom I3 (Relative)

$I(\lambda M, H) = I(M, H)$ for all $\lambda > 0$.

Axiom I3 captures the notion of inequality as a relative concept and states that a proportional increase in all incomes should leave inequality unchanged. This has been termed *rightist* by Kolm (1976). An alternative to axiom I3 is

Axiom I3′ (Absolute)

$I(M + \tau e, H) = I(M, H)$ for all τ such that $M + \tau e \geq 0$,

which has been termed *leftist*. An intermediate axiom between I3 and I3′, termed μ-invariance by Eichhorn (1988), is the following

Axiom I3″ (Intermediate)

$I(M + \tau[\mu M + [1 - \mu]e], H) = I(M, H)$ for all $0 < \mu < 1$ and $M + \tau[\mu M + [1 - \mu]e] \geq 0$.

Clearly, I3″ would reduce to I3 if $\mu = 1$ and to I3′ if $\mu = 0$.

Fields and Fei (1978) and Foster (1983) note that many of the standard statistical measures, including G, A and T, satisfy axioms I1–I3. This point was implicit in the previous discussion. For the alternative axioms I3′ and I3″,

Eichhorn (1988) classifies the set of functions that satisfy axioms I1, I2 and one of I3–I3″. This class of functions has the general form

$$I(M,H) = \phi\left(\frac{\mu M + [1-\mu]e}{\mu\alpha(M) + [1-\mu]}\right), \quad \alpha(M) = \frac{M^1 + M^2 + \ldots + M^H}{H}, \tag{3.46}$$

where $\phi(\cdot)$ is Schur-convex and satisfies $\phi(e) = 0$. An application of these alternative axioms can be found in Pfingsten (1986) where tax changes that are inequality neutral under the alternative criteria are identified.

A second aspect of inequality measurement that has been pursued via the axiomatic approach is that of decomposability. Let the population be divided into subgroups $1, \ldots, g, \ldots, G$ with the population in each being H^g. An inequality measure is decomposable if total inequality can be found by a weighted sum of the inequality within the subgroups and between the subgroups. Defining M_g as the income vector within group g, μ_g as the mean income of group g and e_g as the vector of 1s with H^g entries, decomposability is captured in the following axiom

Axiom I4 (Theil Decomposability)

$$I(M_1, \ldots, M_G, H) = \sum_{g=1}^{G} w_g^G I(M_g, H^g) + I(\mu_1 e_1, \ldots, \mu_G e_G, H), \quad w_g^G = \frac{\sum_{h=1}^{H^g} M^h}{\sum_{h=1}^{H} M^h}.$$

With this definition of decomposability, the weights are the ratio of the total income in subgroup g to total income in the population. The following theorem is proved in Foster (1983).

Theorem 3.3 (Foster)

An inequality index satisfies axioms I1, I2, I3 and I4 if and only if it is a positive multiple of T.

Proof

See Foster (1983).

The surprising conclusion of theorem 3.3 concerns the emergence of Theil's entropy index, T, as the unique index that satisfies decomposability as defined in I4. Although this index appears to have little economic motivation, it does receive convincing support from an axiomatic derivation. In contrast, other indices which appear more appealing on the surface fail to satisfy the required criteria. A more general result on decomposable indices is proved in Shorrocks (1984). Replacing I4 by

Axiom I4' (Decomposability)

A decomposable index satisfies $I(M_1, M_2) = A(I(M_1), \mu_1, H^1, I(M_2), \mu_2, H^2)$ where A is continuous and strictly increasing in $I(M_1)$ and $I(M_2)$.

Shorrocks proves the following theorem.

Theorem 3.4 (Shorrocks)

An inequality index $I(M)$ satisfies I1, I2, I3, I4' *and $I(\mu, \ldots, \mu) = 0$ if and only if there exists a parameter c and function $F(I(M), H)$, continuous and strictly increasing in I with $F(0, H)$, such that*

$$
F(I(M), H) = \begin{cases} \dfrac{1}{H} \dfrac{1}{c[c-1]} \sum_{h=1}^{H} \left[\left[\dfrac{M^h}{\mu} \right]^c - 1 \right] & \text{if } c \neq 0, 1, \\[3ex] \dfrac{1}{H} \sum_{h=1}^{H} \left[\dfrac{M^h}{\mu} \log \dfrac{M^h}{\mu} \right] & \text{if } c = 1, \\[3ex] \dfrac{1}{H} \sum_{h=1}^{H} \log \dfrac{M^h}{\mu} & \text{if } c = 0. \end{cases}
$$

Proof

See Shorrocks (1984).

The class of inequality measures identified in theorem 3.4 are termed *Generalised Entropy* indices and include the Theil index (4.28) as a special case. In essence, the theorem shows that once decomposability is imposed, the class of inequality measures reduces to the Generalised Entropy indices.

Further results on decomposable indices can be found in Bourguignon (1979) and Shorrocks (1980) who consider alternative definitions of decomposability, and Cowell and Kuga (1981). Pyatt (1985) provides a rather different set of axioms which characterise the Gini index.

4.6 Summary

The section began with an introduction to statistical measures of inequality which, at first sight, appeared to avoid the requirement for welfare analysis. Closer inspection of these indices indicated that each embodied implicit welfare assumptions and that their failings emphasised basic criteria that an index should satisfy. The first point was developed by considering the methodology of Blackorby and Donaldson (1978) for generating inequality measures from social welfare functions and constructing underlying social welfare functions from inequality measures. The examples given underline the belief that statistical measures can have unsatisfactory welfare implications. One response to this has been the suggestion that an explicit social welfare function should form the basis of the inequality measure and an example of this approach, the Kolm–Atkinson index, was described. The existence of basic criteria for an index to satisfy has been developed into the axiomatic approach to inequality. Some of the directions in which this can be taken were illustrated by the study of relative and absolute measures and decomposability. It was surprising to find that decomposability led back to one of the statistical measures.

5 THE MEASUREMENT OF POVERTY

The measurement of poverty involves many of the same issues as the measurement of inequality and it can be argued, as most notably in Lewis and Ulph (1988), that the two are simply different aspects of the same phenomenon. As with inequality, it is easy to appreciate at an abstract level what constitutes poverty and an increase in poverty but difficulties arise once an attempt is made to provide a quantitative representation.

The presentation of this section is somewhat similar to that on inequality. After discussing competing notions of poverty and introducing the necessary definitions, a number of standard poverty measures are discussed and the critical discussion of these leads naturally into an axiomatic approach. The major distinction between the measurement of inequality and poverty is that the latter necessitates the identification of those households in poverty as distinct from those which are not. Identification, which is discussed in detail in Sen (1979), is typically based on the idea of a level of income, termed the *poverty line*, above which a household is no longer in poverty. The poverty line is therefore of central importance in the measurement of poverty so that methods to define the poverty line and attempts to avoid some of its implications will both be discussed.

5.1 Relative or absolute?

Before measuring poverty, it is first necessary to define it. It is obvious that poverty refers to a situation involving a lack of income and consequent low level of consumption and welfare. What is not so clear is the standard against which the level of income should be judged. Two possibilities arise in this context: an absolute conception of poverty and a relative one. The distinction between these has implications for changes in the level of poverty over time and the success of policy in alleviating poverty.

5.1.1 Absolute poverty

The concept of *absolute poverty* assumes that there is some fixed minimum level of consumption (or similarly of income) that constitutes poverty and that is independent of time or place. Such a minimum level of consumption is often taken to be a diet that is sufficient to maintain health and provision of housing and clothing. From this view, if the incomes of all households rise, there will eventually be no poverty. Viewed as an absolute concept, it is possible for poverty to be eliminated.

Although a concept of absolute poverty was probably implicit in early studies of poverty, such as Rowntree (1901, 1941) and in the claims following Rowntree and Lavers (1951) that poverty was no longer a problem, the appropriateness of absolute poverty has since generally been rejected. In its place has been adopted the notion of relative poverty.

5.1.2 Relative poverty

The concept of *relative poverty* is not a recent one; it is only the usage of the concept that has been recently adopted. Its history can be traced back to at least Adam Smith (1776) who frames the definition of relative poverty as the lack of necessities, where necessities are defined as 'what ever the custom of the country renders it indecent for creditable people, even of the lowest order, to be without'. It is clear from this definition that relative poverty is defined in terms of the standards and norms of a given society at a given time. As the standard of living of the society rises and more goods are required to be decent, the income level required to be out of poverty must increase.

The notion of relative poverty has also been advocated more recently in Townsend's (1979) discussion of participation in society. This approach to poverty considers whether the household possesses sufficient resources to allow it to participate in the activities which are customary for the economy to which it belongs. The ability to participate is clearly a relative concept and this view captures much the same features as that of Smith. Relative poverty is also embodied in the measurement of poverty in the UK and EU.

The adoption of either an absolute or relative view of poverty does have implications for how the poverty line is determined for a particular economy at a particular time but is of most consequence for comparisons of poverty across time or across economies and in the properties that it is felt a satisfactory poverty measure should have. The latter aspect will become evident in the specification of axioms for poverty measures.

5.2 The poverty line

As already noted, the starting point for the measurement of poverty is to determine a poverty line. The poverty line is defined here as that level of income on or below which a household is defined as being in poverty. It should be noted that this definition is not universally agreed and the poverty line is often interpreted as the level of income just sufficient to move the household out of poverty. This procedure is somewhat arbitrary since it is difficult to accept such a precise cut-off between poverty and non-poverty. It is, however, now standard practice and is followed throughout almost all the literature.

In practice, poverty lines have often been determined by following the minimum needs approach that was discussed in connection with equivalence scales. As noted in Sawhill (1988), this is the case with the US poverty line that was set in 1965 and has been updated for inflation since. The practice in the UK has been to set the poverty line as the level of income which is 120 per cent or 140 per cent of the minimum supplementary benefit level (see Callan and Nolan 1991) but, since this level of benefit is itself determined by minimum needs, this amounts to a minimum needs poverty line. In addition, since the level of benefits have tended to rise with increases in average income, this embodies some aspects of relative poverty.

An alternative approach that has also been used is the Engel method of employing the proportion of income spent on food as an indicator of welfare with those in excess of a critical proportion being deemed as living in poverty. For examples of this approach see Rao (1981). Desai and Shah (1988) argue that poverty should be measured by the distance of a household's consumption experience from the norm.

Obviously, these do not exhaust the possible methods of defining the poverty line and debate about what constitutes the poverty line and how it changes over time cannot be avoided.

5.3 Standard measures

Prior to the recent interest in poverty measurement following the work of Sen (1976), the number of available poverty measures was rather limited. Effectively, the measurement of poverty would be based upon either the headcount ratio or some variant of the income gap ratio. These measures are now discussed both for their historical importance and because of the role they play in the development of later measures.

It is first necessary to introduce the following notation that is used extensively below. The poverty line is denoted by z, so that any income level below or equal to z represents poverty. For a typical household, h, $g^h \equiv z - M^h$, is the income shortfall of household h and measures the extent to which the household is below the poverty line. Given the poverty line z and an income distribution M, the number of households in poverty is given by $q = q(M, z)$. The dimensionality of the income distribution vector determines the size of the population, H, via the relation $H = H(M)$.

The headcount ratio measures the extent of poverty by counting the number of households whose incomes are not above the poverty line. Expressing this as a proportion of the population, the headcount ratio is defined by

$$\mathscr{E} = \frac{q}{H}.$$ (3.47)

This measure of poverty was used by Rowntree (1901) and has been used in many subsequent studies.

The major advantage of the headcount ratio is its simplicity of calculation. Its major disadvantage is that it pays no attention to how far the households fall below the poverty line and therefore gives no indication of how costly it would be to alleviate the observed poverty. In addition, a transfer from a poor household to one that is slightly richer does not change $\mathscr{E}$ if both households remain on the same side of the poverty line and will actually reduce it if the transfer takes the recipient's income above z.

The aggregate poverty gap and the income gap ratio both take account of how far below the poverty line are the incomes of the poor households. They are defined respectively by

$$\mathscr{V} = \sum_{h=1}^{q} g_h,$$
(3.48)

and

$$\mathscr{L} = \frac{1}{q(M,z)} \sum_{h=1}^{q} \frac{g^h}{z}.$$
(3.49)

Since both measures take account of income shortfalls, they do provide information on the expenditure needed to eliminate poverty but, because they give equal weight to all income shortfalls, they are not sensitive to transfers unless the transfer takes one of the households out of poverty.

5.4 Axiomatic approach

As with inequality measurement, these criticisms of the basic measures indicate the existence of beliefs about the properties that a poverty measure must have. Having noted this, an axiomatic approach follows naturally. Two alternative axiomatic developments will now be considered: the original derivation of Sen (1976) and the axiom system of Foster, Greer and Thorbecke (1984).

Denoting a poverty measure as a function $P(M;z)$, a basic set of axioms for poverty measurement begin with the focus axiom which restricts attention to the incomes of those in poverty.

Axiom P1 (Focus)

If income distribution $\hat{M}$ is obtained from $\tilde{M}$ by a change in incomes of households above the poverty line then $P(\tilde{M};z) = P(\hat{M};z)$.

The second axiom expresses the requirement that measured poverty must increase when the income level of any of the poor households falls. This axiom is termed monotonicity.

Axiom P2 (Monotonicity)

If income distribution $\hat{M}$ is obtained from $\tilde{M}$ by reducing the income of household h, $M^h < z$, and all other incomes remain unchanged then $P(\tilde{M}; z) < P(\hat{M}; z)$.

As discussed in connection with inequality, the level of poverty should not be affected by a re-labelling of the households. This property is captured by the symmetry axiom.

Axiom P3 (Symmetry)

If income distribution $\hat{M} = P\tilde{M}$ for some permutation matrix then $P(\tilde{M}; z) = P(\hat{M}; z)$.

These three axioms are perhaps the least contentious, although poverty measures that do not satisfy P1 have been considered, for example Beckerman (1979) employs the aggregate poverty gap as a proportion of aggregate income. They are, however, usually adopted as the basis of an axiomatic system. Defining a *regressive transfer* to be a transfer from a household to one with a higher income level, the fourth axiom relates to the effect of transfers upon measured poverty.

Axiom P4 (Transfer)

If income distribution $\hat{M}$ is obtained from $\tilde{M}$ by a regressive transfer among the poor households then $P(\tilde{M}; z) < P(\hat{M}; z)$.

This is the first form of the transfer axiom; an alternative will be introduced below.

Taken together, any poverty measure that satisfies these axioms must be a strictly decreasing and strictly S-convex function of the incomes of the poor households. Since the poverty measure is S-convex, it must also agree with the Lorenz criteria applied to incomes below the poverty line. It can be seen that neither the headcount ratio nor the income gap ratio satisfies the Lorenz dominance criterion of 4.2.1 and therefore do not satisfy axioms P1–P4. To proceed beyond the Lorenz criteria requires the addition of further axioms.

5.4.1 Sen measure

Let Γ denote the set of households with incomes on, or below, the poverty line; there are q of these. Sen (1976) proposes that the general form of a poverty measure should be given by a multiple of a weighted sum of income gaps

$$P(M; z) = A(M; z) \sum_{h \in \Gamma} g_h(M; z) v_h(M; z), \tag{3.50}$$

where the form of $A(M;z)$ and the weights $v_h(M;z)$ are determined by additional axioms.

To derive the form of Sen's measure, two additional axioms are imposed. The symmetry axiom permits the q households to be ranked with the household closest to the poverty line given rank of 1 and the poorest household, that furthest from the poverty line, given rank q. Let the rank of poor household h be given by $r_h(M;z)$. The next axiom is

Axiom P5 (Ranked deprivation)

The weight assigned to household h is given by their ranking amongst the poor: $v_h(M;z)=r_h(M;z)$.

The fifth of Sen's axioms is derived by arguing that when all the households in poverty have the same income, the level of poverty is measured by the product of the headcount ratio and the income gap ratio. This axiom acts much in the way of a normalisation to determine $A(M;z)$. Expressed as an axiom

Axiom P6 (Normalisation)

If M is such that $M^h=\bar{M}$, $h\in\Gamma$, then $P(M;z)=\mathscr{E}\mathscr{I}$.

From these axioms follows the Sen measure

$$\mathscr{S}=\frac{2}{[q+1]Hz}\sum_{h\in\Gamma}g_hr_h=E\left[I+[1-I]G_p\left[\frac{q}{q+1}\right]\right], \tag{3.51}$$

where G_p is the Gini index of income inequality amongst the households below the poverty line. Expressed in the latter form, this poverty measure can be seen as combining a measure of the shortfall of income of the poor with one of distribution of income between the poor.

The method of constructing this measure illustrates the alternative directions that could be taken. The general form given is not the only possibility and Takayama (1979) presents an example of an alternative form. Using the ranking of the poor as the weights is also restrictive; an alternative to this will be considered below. Finally, the normalisation axiom is also arbitrary and any number of other possibilities could be chosen. Although having many features in its favour, the poverty measure (3.51) cannot be assigned any particularly special value since any variation in the particular axioms chosen would lead to a different index and some of the axioms are not entirely compelling.

5.4.2 Decomposability

An important class of poverty measures that constitute an alternative to (3.51) have been derived on the basis of decomposability amongst subgroups. To motivate this discussion, consider the poverty measure given by

$$\mathscr{P}(M,z) = \frac{1}{Hz^2} \sum_{h \in \Gamma} g_h^2.$$ (3.52)

The measure given in (3.52) is an example of the general form of measure given by (3.50) but with the weights given by the income gap rather than by the ranking. Given the composition of (3.51) in terms of the Gini index, it is interesting to note that (3.52) can also be written

$$\mathscr{P}(M,z) = \mathscr{E}[\mathscr{L}^2 + (1 - \mathscr{L})^2 \mathscr{C}_p^2],$$ (3.53)

where $\mathscr{C}_p$ is the coefficient of variation of income amongst the poor. Hence (3.52) also captures poverty by combining total income shortfall and an index of distribution.

To allow the index to be decomposable amongst subgroups, aggregate measured poverty must rise if it increases for any subgroup. This requirement is captured by the following axiom.

Axiom P7 (Subgroup monotonicity)

If income distribution $\hat{M}$ is obtained from $\tilde{M}$ by increasing poverty in subgroup g without affecting either the number in poverty or incomes in other subgroups then $P(\hat{M}, z) > P(\tilde{M}, z)$.

An argument that can be levelled against the transfer axiom, P4, is that the effect of the transfer should be dependent upon the incomes of those involved in the transfer. For instance, a transfer away from the lowest income household should have more effect on measured poverty than a transfer away from a household closer to the poverty line. This interpretation of the transfer axiom is captured in axiom P4'.

Axiom P4' (Transfer sensitivity)

If a transfer $t > 0$ of income takes place from a poor household with income M^h to a poor household with income $M^h + d, d > 0$, then the magnitude of the increase in poverty must be smaller for larger M^h.

Although the poverty measure defined by (3.52) does not satisfy P4', its form suggests a class of measures that do. Consider the following extension of (3.52)

$$\mathscr{P}_\alpha(M;z) = \frac{1}{H} \sum_{h \in \Gamma} \left(\frac{g_h}{z}\right)^\alpha,$$ (3.54)

and note that $\mathscr{P}_0 = \mathscr{E}$, $\mathscr{P}_1 = \mathscr{E}\mathscr{L}$. As α increases, more concern is placed on the lower income level households which leads to the following proposition.

Theorem 3.5 (Foster, Greer, Thorbecke)

$\mathscr{P}_\alpha$ satisfies monotonicity, P3, for $\alpha > 0$, transfer, P4, for $\alpha > 1$ and transfer sensitivity, P4', for $\alpha > 2$. In addition, $\mathscr{P}_\alpha$ satisfies subgroup monotonicity, P7.

Proof

Obvious by inspection.

In applications to data, for instance to Kenya in Foster, Greer and Thorbecke (1984), $\mathscr{P}_\alpha$ measures have proved popular. However, the UK practice has been to remain with the headcount ratio, as has the US, despite its faults and the limited information it conveys. It is, however, statistically robust and corresponds to a concept of poverty based on minimum rights – on the latter see Atkinson (1987). There is therefore a growing difference between the first-best practice of economists and that of government.

5.5 Variable poverty line

The notion of the poverty line conveys a switch out of poverty as a household's income crosses the line. Two obvious difficulties exist with this notion. First, it is difficult to accept such a precise line between poverty and non-poverty. It would seem more natural for there to be a gradual move out of poverty as income increases. Secondly, the precision of the poverty line also leads to difficulty in determining where it should lie since the level of poverty may be critically dependent on the precise level chosen.

   These difficulties can be overcome by observing that often it is not the precise level of poverty that matters but changes in the level of poverty over time and across countries. In these instances the poverty value is not too important but only the rankings. This suggests the procedure of calculating poverty for a range of poverty lines (Atkinson 1987). If poverty is higher today for all poverty lines than it was yesterday, then it seems unambiguous that poverty has risen. In this sense, the poverty line may not actually be of critical importance for the uses to which poverty measurement is often put.

6 CONCLUSIONS

The chapter began with the aim of studying measures of the state of an economy which were intended to be independent of welfare criteria. To allow income levels to be comparable between households of different demographic composition equivalence scales need to be constructed. Although these have been computed upon the basis of minimum needs and observed expenditure on food, careful examination revealed deficiencies in such approaches. It was then shown that, if the household acts in accord with the theory of utility maximisation, exact comparisons could only be made by basing the scales upon a comparison of household expenditure functions and hence upon the underlying utility functions. A broadly similar conclusion was reached with measures of both inequality and poverty: statistical measures that appear welfare free are actually founded upon implicit assumptions concerning the form of the social welfare function. In any case, a close examination of the methodology led back to the need for welfare-theoretic constructions.

The response to this finding can either be to construct the required index directly from a specified utility or social welfare function, as in the Atkinson–Kolm inequality index for example, or to specify the properties that the measure must possess and derive the measure from these. This latter approach has gained popularity in the literature on inequality and poverty and has also led to some surprising conclusions. There remains further research to be undertaken, not least in refining the link between inequality and poverty.

Part II

ANALYSIS IN THE COMPETITIVE ECONOMY

4

COMMODITY TAXATION

1 INTRODUCTION

This chapter is the first to consider policy analysis and to arrive at characterisations of optimal policies. The ideas that it surveys have developed over a considerable period, beginning with the seminal contribution of Ramsey (1927). One important feature of this development is the gradual increase in generality and the recent move towards applying the theoretical analysis to data. This has moved the theory closer to practical application.

The initial literature on commodity taxation focused upon the following simple problem. There is a given level of government revenue to be raised which must be financed solely by taxes upon commodities: how should these taxes be set so as to minimise the cost to society of raising the required revenue? If a social welfare function is adopted to represent the state's preferences, the problem can be conveniently rephrased as that of choosing the commodity tax rates to maximise social welfare subject to the revenue constraint.

The first solution to this problem was given by Ramsey (1927) following its proposal to him by Pigou. This contribution appears to have been overlooked for the following forty years during which time the less general inverse elasticities rule became a standard feature of textbooks. The results of Ramsey were rediscovered by Samuelson (1986) in a 1951 memo to the US Treasury. The theory of commodity taxation was given its modern form by Diamond and Mirrlees (1971) in an analysis that made much use of the emerging duality methods and results in general equilibrium theory. Diamond and Mirrlees (1971) derived both single-household and many-household tax rules and proved the Production Efficiency lemma. Developments since the publication of Diamond and Mirrlees have been concerned with the practical implementation of the methods of that paper and in extensions of the basic economy away from the standard competitive framework with constant returns to scale.

It should be noted that there are close connections between the theory of commodity taxation and that of public-sector pricing. In both cases the government is choosing the set of consumer prices that maximise welfare subject to a constraint. Under the commodity taxation interpretation these prices are achieved by setting the level of tax to be included in each consumer price whereas with public-sector pricing the prices are chosen directly. However the choice of tax rate is equivalent to the choice of consumer price. In the context of public-sector pricing, the optimal prices are generally known as *Ramsey prices*. The constraint on the optimisation with commodity taxation requires the raising of a specified level of revenue. With public-sector pricing this can be reinterpreted as the need to raise a given level of revenue in excess of marginal cost. The tax rates of the commodity taxation problem then translate into the mark-up over marginal cost in the public-sector pricing interpretation.

The chapter begins by deriving the single-household Ramsey rule and providing an interpretation of this. It is then shown how the inverse elasticity rule follows as a special case. The extension to many consumers is made and the resolution of the equity/efficiency trade-off is emphasised. This is followed by a review of numerical calculations of optimal taxes based on empirical data. Three more specialised topics are then considered: generalising the production technology; the status of untaxed goods; and conditions guaranteeing the uniformity of taxes. A discussion of the Diamond–Mirrlees Production Efficiency lemma concludes the chapter.

2 METHODOLOGY

The analysis restricts the set of feasible policy instruments available to the government to commodity taxes. The use of optimal lump-sum taxes is assumed to be prevented by the arguments covered in chapter 2: the relevant characteristics for the determination of taxes are preferences and endowments but these are private information and will not be truthfully revealed under the optimal tax system. In contrast, the employment of commodity taxes requires only that the government is able to observe trades in commodities, which is a far weaker informational requirement. Although it may be possible for the government to levy a uniform lump-sum tax, and in a one-household economy such a tax would also be optimal, it is assumed for simplicity that such taxes cannot be employed. In an economy where the households are not identical, their introduction does not significantly modify the conclusions.

The standard methodology in optimal commodity tax theory has been to consider only linear taxes, either additive so that the post-tax price of good i is given by $p_i + t_i$ or multiplicative with post-tax price $p_i[1 + t_i]$. In the competitive framework of this chapter, the choice is immaterial. The analysis of income taxation in chapter 5 will present an analysis of non-linear taxation. A social welfare function is then maximised by choice of the tax rates and the first-order conditions for this maximisation are manipulated to provide a qualitative description of the optimal tax system. The qualitative description is then interpreted in terms of efficiency criteria and the concern for equity embodied in the social welfare function. Explicit formulae for taxes are rarely calculated and, indeed, can only be calculated for a number of uninteresting special cases. In response to this, numerical studies have been employed to provide concrete results.

There are two important points that need to be made here. Firstly, because of the normalisation rules employed, the actual values of tax rates can be argued to have little meaning. Instead, it is the real effect of the tax system upon the equilibrium quantities of each good that is relevant. This point is argued forcefully in Mirrlees (1976) where the index of discouragement is introduced to measure the effect of taxes. The standard procedure of deriving the tax rates will be followed in this chapter but the Mirrlees interpretation, which is introduced formally below, should always be borne in mind. Secondly, the discussion of net trades in 2.13 showed how a household's budget constraint could be non-linear in the presence of commodity taxation. To avoid this, the economies of this chapter assume that households trade only with firms.

3 THE RAMSEY RULE

The *Ramsey rule* is one of the oldest results in the theory of optimal taxation and is probably the oldest formally stated result. It is derived from an analysis of the simplest form of general equilibrium economy, that with a single household. The single household basis implies that there can be no equity considerations in the setting of tax rates so that the resulting tax rule describes an efficient tax system. As the Ramsey rule forms the basis for later results, its derivation is described in some detail.

3.1 The economy

The Ramsey rule is derived within the context of a competitive economy in which there are available n consumption goods and a single form of labour. Labour is the only input into production. In addition, each industry is assumed to produce a single output using a constant returns to scale technology. There is a single household or, equivalently, a population of identical households, whose preferences can be represented by an indirect utility function.

The assumptions on production imply that for each good i there is a coefficient c^i that describes the labour input necessary to produce one unit of that good. With a wage rate w, the competitive assumption ensures that the pre-tax price of good i is determined by

$$p_i = c^i w, \ i = 1, \ldots, n. \tag{4.1}$$

The normalisation rule that is adopted is to choose labour as the numeraire and to fix the wage rate at the constant value w. In conjunction with the production assumptions and condition (4.1), this normalisation rule provides a set of effectively fixed pre-tax, or *producer*, prices for the consumption goods. Labour is also untaxed; that this does not involve a further restriction on this system will be demonstrated in section 6.

Employing the competitive assumption again, post-tax or *consumer* prices are equal to the pre-tax prices plus the taxes. For good i the consumer price q_i is

$$q_i = p_i + t_i, \; i = 1, \ldots, n. \tag{4.2}$$

Writing x_i for the consumption level of good i, the tax rates on the n consumption goods must be chosen to raise the required revenue. Denoting the revenue requirement by R, the revenue constraint can be written

$$R = \sum_{i=1}^{n} t_i x_i. \tag{4.3}$$

To ensure that there is an economy-wide balance in supplies and demands, the formal interpretation of this constraint is that the revenue raised by the government is used to purchase a quantity of labour with value R. This labour is used by the state for some undefined purpose and does not produce any good that is traded in the economy. One example that satisfies this assumption would be the use of labour for defence purposes. The use of a revenue constraint, rather than a production constraint, has been discussed in 2.6 and will be discussed further below.

The preferences of the single household are represented by the indirect utility function

$$U = V(q_1, \ldots, q_n, w, I). \tag{4.4}$$

The form of (4.4) implies that the household consumes the goods produced and supplies the labour used in production and by the state. The assumption of constant returns to scale and competitive behaviour imply that the firms earn zero profits. The household therefore receives no profit income and lump-sum income, I, is zero.

3.2 Derivation

Employing the economy described above, the optimal tax problem can be summarised by the maximisation

$$\max_{\{t_1, \ldots, t_n\}} V(q_1, \ldots, q_n, w, I) \text{ subject to } R = \sum_{i=1}^{n} t_i x_i. \tag{4.5}$$

The Lagrangean corresponding to (4.5) is given by

$$\mathcal{L} = V(q_1, \ldots, q_n, w, I) + \lambda \left[\sum_{i=1}^{n} t_i x_i - R \right]. \tag{4.6}$$

From (4.6), the first-order necessary condition for the choice of tax rate on good k is

$$\frac{\partial \mathscr{L}}{\partial t_k} \equiv \frac{\partial V}{\partial t_k} + \lambda \left[x_k + \sum_{i=1}^{n} t_i \frac{\partial x_i}{\partial q_k} \right] = 0, \tag{4.7}$$

where the identities

$$\frac{\partial V}{\partial q_k} \equiv \frac{\partial V}{\partial t_k}, \frac{\partial x_i}{\partial q_k} \equiv \frac{\partial x_i}{\partial t_k}, \tag{4.8}$$

have been used. Equation (4.7) can be rearranged to give

$$\frac{\partial V}{\partial t_k} = -\lambda \left[x_k + \sum_{i=1}^{n} t_i \frac{\partial x_i}{\partial q_k} \right], \tag{4.9}$$

and a similar condition must hold for all n of the goods. The interpretation of (4.9) is that for all goods the utility cost of raising the tax rate on good k should stand in the same proportion to the marginal revenue raised by the tax rise. Expressed alternatively, additional tax revenue per unit of utility foregone should be the same regardless of which tax rate is changed to generate that extra revenue.

From Roy's identity it follows that

$$\frac{\partial V}{\partial q_k} = -\frac{\partial V}{\partial I} x_k = -\alpha x_k, \tag{4.10}$$

where I is the household's lump-sum income and α is their marginal utility of income. Lump-sum income, I, should be clearly distinguished from total income, M, used previously since total income includes both lump-sum income, income from the sale of endowment and labour income. Substituting (4.10) into (4.9)

$$\alpha x_k = \lambda \left[x_k + \sum_{i=1}^{n} t_i \frac{\partial x_i}{\partial q_k} \right]. \tag{4.11}$$

After rearrangement (4.11) becomes

$$\sum_{i=1}^{n} t_i \frac{\partial x_i}{\partial q_k} = -\left[\frac{\lambda - \alpha}{\lambda} \right] x_k. \tag{4.12}$$

The next step in the derivation is to employ the Slutsky equation to note that

$$\frac{\partial x_i}{\partial q_k} = S_{ik} - x_k \frac{\partial x_i}{\partial I}. \tag{4.13}$$

Substituting from (4.13) into (4.12) gives

$$\sum_{i=1}^{n} t_i \left[S_{ik} - x_k \frac{\partial x_i}{\partial I} \right] = -\left[\frac{\lambda - \alpha}{\lambda} \right] x_k. \tag{4.14}$$

or

$$\sum_{i=1}^{n} t_i S_{ik} = -\left[\frac{\lambda - \alpha}{\lambda}\right] x_k + \sum_{i=1}^{n} t_i x_k \frac{\partial x_i}{\partial I}. \tag{4.15}$$

The right-hand side of (4.15) is now simplified by extracting the common factor x_k which yields

$$\sum_{i=1}^{n} t_i S_{ik} = -\left[1 - \frac{\alpha}{\lambda} + \sum_{i=1}^{n} t_i \frac{\partial x_i}{\partial I}\right] x_k. \tag{4.16}$$

The symmetry of the Slutsky substitution matrix implies that $S_{ki} = S_{ik}$. This symmetry can be used to rearrange (4.16) to give the expression

$$\sum_{i=1}^{n} t_i S_{ik} = -\theta x_k, \theta = \left[1 - \frac{\alpha}{\lambda} + \sum_{i=1}^{n} t_i \frac{\partial x_i}{\partial I}\right]. \tag{4.17}$$

Equation (4.17) is the Ramsey rule describing a system of optimal commodity taxes and an equation of this form must hold for all goods, $k = 1, \ldots, n$. It is important to note that the value of θ is independent of the particular good chosen.

Finally, multiplying both sides of the Ramsey rule by t_k and summing over k gives

$$\sum_{k=1}^{n} \sum_{i=1}^{n} t_i t_k S_{ki} = -\theta R. \tag{4.18}$$

As the Slutsky matrix is negative semi-definite, the left-hand side of (4.18) is negative so that θ has the same sign as government revenue. Given the sign of θ, it is now possible to provide a descriptive interpretation of the Ramsey rule.

3.3 Interpretation

To provide an interpretation of the Ramsey rule the focus upon the typical good k is maintained. First note that, by definition of the substitution terms

$$S_{ki} = \frac{\partial \chi_k}{\partial q_i}, \tag{4.19}$$

where χ_k is the Hicksian or compensated demand for good k. Consequently, starting from a position with no taxes, and noting that t_i is then the change in the tax rate on good i

$$t_i S_{ki} = t_i \frac{\partial \chi_k}{\partial q_i}, \tag{4.20}$$

is a first-order approximation of the change in compensated demand for good k due to the introduction of the tax t_i, but with the property that the derivative is evaluated at the final set of prices and at the post-tax utility level. If the taxes are

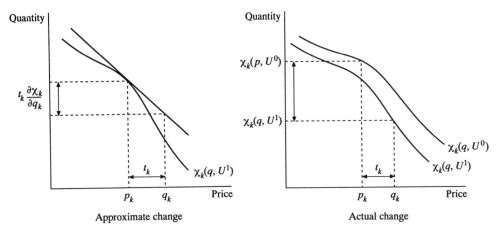

Figure 4.1   Interpretation of the Ramsey rule

small, this should be a good approximation. Extending this argument to the entire set of taxes, it follows that

$$\sum_{i=1}^{n} t_i S_{ki},$$
(4.21)

is an approximation to the total change in compensated demand for good k due to the introduction of the tax system from an initial no-tax position.

In considering the value of this interpretation, note that because both utility and prices change when the tax system is introduced, the actual change in demand is given by

$$\chi_k(p, U^0) - \chi_k(q, U^1),$$
(4.22)

where U^0 is the initial utility level prior to the introduction of commodity taxes and U^1 the final level after taxation. The structure of the approximation is illustrated in figure 4.1.

Putting these points together and recalling that if R is positive then so is θ, the Ramsey rule when written in the form

$$\frac{\sum_{i=1}^{n} t_i S_{ki}}{x_k} = -\theta, \ k = 1, \ldots, n,$$
(4.23)

can be interpreted as saying that the optimal tax system should be such that the compensated demand for each good is reduced in the same proportion relative to the pre-tax position. This is the standard interpretation of the Ramsey rule.

The importance of this observation is reinforced when it is set against the alternative, but completely unfounded, view that the optimal tax system should raise the prices of all goods by the same proportion in order to minimise the distortion caused by the tax system. What the Ramsey rule is approximately saying is that it is the distortion in terms of quantities that should be minimised. Since it is the level of consumption that actually determines welfare, it is not surprising that what happens to prices is unimportant; they only matter in so far as they determine demands. In addition, the importance of working in terms of quantities rather than prices is highlighted when it is recalled that prices can only be determined up to a normalising factor. This point is discussed further in section 6.

This emphasis upon quantities suggests defining

$$d_k = \frac{\sum_{i=1}^{n} t_i S_{ki}}{x_k},$$

(4.24)

where d_k, the proportional reduction in demand, is Mirrlees' (1976) *index of discouragement*. The Ramsey rule states that the tax system is optimal when the index of discouragement is equal for all goods.

3.4 Implications

The Ramsey rule only provides an implicit expression for the optimal tax rates and precise statements cannot be made without further restrictions. However, some general comments can be made. Accepting the approximation interpretation, this suggests that since the proportional reduction in compensated demand must be the same for all goods it can be expected that goods whose demand is unresponsive to price changes will bear higher taxes. Although broadly correct, this statement can only be truly justified when all cross-price effects are accounted for. One simple case that overcomes this difficulty is that in which there are no cross-price effects between the taxed goods; this limiting case will be considered in the next section.

Returning to the general case, goods that are unresponsive to price changes are typically necessities such as food and housing. Consequently, the implementation of a tax system based on the Ramsey rule would lead to taxes that would bear most heavily on necessities, with the lowest tax rates on luxuries. This interpretation has been demonstrated more formally by Deaton (1981) under the assumption of weak separability of preferences. Put into practice, this structure of taxation would involve low-income households paying disproportionately larger fractions of their incomes in taxes. The inequitable nature of this outcome is simply a reflection of the single-household assumption: the objective function of the maximisation does not care about equity and the solution reflects only efficiency criteria.

The equilibrium determined by the set of optimal taxes is second best compared to the outcome that would arise if the tax revenue had been collected via a lump-sum tax. This is because the commodity taxes lead to substitution effects which distort the household's optimal choices and lead to efficiency losses. Although unavoidable when commodity taxes are employed, these losses are minimised by the optimal set of taxes that satisfy the Ramsey rule.

Since the single-household framework is untenable as a description of reality and leads to an outcome that would be unacceptable on the most minimal of equity criteria, the value of the Ramsey rule is therefore primarily in providing a framework and a method of analysis that can easily be generalised to more relevant settings. Contrasting the Ramsey rule tax system with later results will also highlight the consequences of the introduction of equity considerations.

3.5 Inverse elasticities rule

The *inverse elasticities rule*, discussed in detail in Baumol and Bradford (1970), is derived by placing further restrictions on the economy used to derive the Ramsey rule. To be precise, it is assumed that there are no cross-price effects between the taxed goods so that the demand for each good is dependent only upon its own price and the wage rate. Invoking this assumption essentially turns the general equilibrium model into one of partial equilibrium as it removes all the interactions in demand and, as shown by Atkinson and Stiglitz (1980), the inverse elasticities rule can be derived from minimising the excess burden of taxation in a partial equilibrium framework. The independence of demands is clearly a strong assumption and it is therefore not surprising that a clear result can be derived.

To derive the inverse elasticity rule, equation (4.11) is taken as the starting point. Hence

$$\alpha x_k = \lambda \left[x_k + \sum_{i=1}^{n} t_i \frac{\partial x_i}{\partial q_k} \right]. \tag{4.25}$$

The assumption of independent demands implies that

$$\frac{\partial x_i}{\partial q_k} = 0 \text{ for } i \neq k. \tag{4.26}$$

Employing (4.26), equation (4.25) reduces to

$$\alpha x_k = \lambda \left[x_k + t_k \frac{\partial x_k}{\partial q_k} \right]. \tag{4.27}$$

Rearranging (4.27) and dividing by q_k, where by assumption $q_k = p_k + t_k$, gives

$$\frac{t_k}{p_k + t_k} = \left[\frac{\alpha - \lambda}{\lambda} \right] \left[\frac{x_k}{q_k} \frac{\partial q_k}{\partial x_k} \right]. \tag{4.28}$$

As

$$\frac{x_k}{q_k} \frac{\partial q_k}{\partial x_k} = \frac{1}{\varepsilon_k^d}, \tag{4.29}$$

where ε_k^d is the price elasticity of demand for good k, (4.28) can be written

$$
\frac{t_k}{p_k + t_k} = \left[\frac{\alpha - \lambda}{\lambda} \right] \frac{1}{\varepsilon_k^d}.
\tag{4.30}
$$

Equation (4.30) is the inverse elasticities rule. From inspection, it can be seen that this states that the proportional rates of tax should be inversely related to the price elasticity of demand of the good on which they are levied. Recalling the discussion in 3.4, this statement can be viewed as an extreme version of the general interpretation of the Ramsey rule. Its implication is clearly that necessities, which by definition have low elasticities of demand, should be highly taxed. In this case it is a clearly defined result and it is not necessary to be concerned with approximations. However the restrictiveness of the assumptions invoked to arrive at (4.30) should not be understated.

4 EXTENSION TO MANY HOUSEHOLDS

The objective of this section is to extend the single-household economy of the Ramsey rule to incorporate further, non-identical, households. This extension naturally introduces equity considerations into the determination of the optimal tax rates. The principal paper in this area is Diamond and Mirrlees (1971) in which was presented the first integrated analysis of this issue. Other important references are Diamond (1975) and Mirrlees (1975).

The variant of the Diamond–Mirrlees economy studied in this section is a restriction of the general case and simply involves extending that used to derive the Ramsey rule by adding further households. The restrictions on the production technology are retained, so that labour remains the only input into production and technology is constant returns to scale. The original Diamond–Mirrlees analysis, which permits greater generality of the production technology, will be described in section 6. It is worth noting that the restrictions do not significantly affect the form of the optimal tax structure.

4.1 The optimal tax rule

The economy is assumed to consist of H households. Each household h is described by an indirect utility function

$$
U^h = V^h(q_1, \ldots, q_n, w, I^h).
\tag{4.31}
$$

These functions vary amongst the households. If they did not, the economy would reduce to that of a single household since lump-sum incomes are all zero under the assumption of constant returns to scale. Labour remains the untaxed numeraire with wage rate w, and all households supply only the single form of labour service.

Writing $x_1^h, \ldots, x_n^h$ for the consumption demands from h, the revenue constraint is given by

$$R = \sum_{i=1}^{n} \sum_{h=1}^{H} t_i x_i^h. \tag{4.32}$$

Social welfare is determined by a Bergson–Samuelson social welfare function which is defined on the vector of indirect utilities

$$W = W(V^1(\cdot), \ldots, V^H(\cdot)). \tag{4.33}$$

Combining (4.32) and (4.33), the optimal set of commodity taxes solve the maximisation problem

$$\max_{\{t_1, \ldots, t_n\}} W(V^1(\cdot), \ldots, V^H(\cdot)) \text{ subject to } \sum_{i=1}^{n} \sum_{h=1}^{H} t_i x_i^h = R. \tag{4.34}$$

Two alternative presentations of the solution to (4.34) are now given. The first solution follows closely that of Diamond and Mirrlees (1971) and emphasises efficiency and equity aspects. The second solution parallels the Ramsey rule and has formed the basis for numerical implementation.

From the Lagrangean for the maximisation, the first-order condition for the choice of the tax rate on good k, is

$$\sum_{h=1}^{H} \frac{\partial W}{\partial V^h} \frac{\partial V^h}{\partial q_k} + \lambda \left[\sum_{h=1}^{H} x_k^h + \sum_{i=1}^{n} \sum_{h=1}^{H} t_i \frac{\partial x_i^h}{\partial q_k} \right] = 0. \tag{4.35}$$

Using Roy's identity the first term of (4.35) can be written

$$\sum_{h=1}^{H} \frac{\partial W}{\partial V^h} \frac{\partial V^h}{\partial q_k} = - \sum_{h=1}^{H} \frac{\partial W}{\partial V^h} \alpha^h x_k^h. \tag{4.36}$$

Now define

$$\beta^h = \frac{\partial W}{\partial V^h} \alpha^h. \tag{4.37}$$

β^h is formed as the composition of the effect of an increase in household h's utility on social welfare and the marginal utility of income for h. It can be interpreted as the increase in social welfare resulting from a marginal increase in the income of household h. Following Diamond and Mirrlees (1971), β^h is termed the *social marginal utility of income* for household h.

Employing the definition of β^h, (4.35) becomes

$$\sum_{h=1}^{H} \beta^h x_k^h = \lambda \left[\sum_{h=1}^{H} x_k^h + \sum_{i=1}^{n} \sum_{h=1}^{H} t_i \frac{\partial x_i^h}{\partial q_k} \right]. \tag{4.38}$$

Substituting from the Slutsky equation

$$\frac{\partial x_i^h}{\partial q_k} = S_{ik}^h - x_k^h \frac{\partial x_i^h}{\partial I^h}, \tag{4.39}$$

into (4.38) and rearranging gives the tax rule

$$\frac{\sum_{i=1}^{n} \sum_{h=1}^{H} t_i S_{ki}^h}{\sum_{h=1}^{H} x_k^h} = \frac{1}{\lambda} \frac{\sum_{h=1}^{H} \beta^h x_k^h}{\sum_{h=1}^{H} x_k^h} - 1 + \frac{\sum_{h=1}^{H} \left[\sum_{i=1}^{n} t_i \frac{\partial x_i^h}{\partial I^h} \right] x_k^h}{\sum_{h=1}^{H} x_k^h}. \tag{4.40}$$

In (4.40), the left-hand side has an equivalent interpretation to that of the Ramsey rule: it is approximately the proportional change in aggregate compensated demand for good k and is the generalisation of the discouragement index of (4.24). When a positive amount of revenue is to be raised, it is natural to assume that the level of demand will be reduced by the tax system, so that the left-hand side of (4.40) will be negative. As with the approximation involved with the interpretation of the Ramsey rule, this has two sources of error. Firstly, real incomes change in moving to the system of optimal taxes and, secondly, the gradients of the demand functions are unlikely to be constant.

The right-hand terms indicate that the reduction in demand should be smaller when: (i) demand for good k is concentrated amongst individuals with high values of β^h, these are the consumers regarded as socially important and (ii) demand is concentrated amongst those whose tax payments change considerably as income changes. The first of these points can be seen as reflecting equity criteria. An individual will have a high value of β^h when their personal marginal utility of income, α^h, is large and when their *social welfare weight* $\frac{\partial W}{\partial V^h}$ is also large. If the social welfare function is concave, both of these will be satisfied by low-utility households with low incomes. Hence the implication is that concern for such households will reduce the rates of tax levied on the goods they consume. The remaining term is related to the efficiency aspects of the tax system. If taxation were to be concentrated on goods consumed by those whose tax payments fell rapidly with reductions in income, then increased taxation, and consequently greater distortion, would be required to meet the revenue target.

The optimal tax rule (4.40) can be expressed in an alternative form that is closer to that of the standard Ramsey rule. To do this, (4.40) is rearranged to give

$$\sum_{i=1}^{n} \sum_{h=1}^{H} t_i S_{ik}^h = - \left[H \bar{x}_k - \frac{\sum_{h=1}^{H} \beta^h x_k^h}{\lambda} - \sum_{i=1}^{n} t_i \left[\sum_{h=1}^{H} \frac{\partial x_i^h}{\partial I^h} x_k^h \right] \right], \tag{4.41}$$

where

$$\bar{x}_k = \frac{\sum_{h=1}^{H} x_k^h}{H},$$ (4.42)

is the mean level of consumption of good k across the households.

Now define

$$b^h = \frac{\beta^h}{\lambda} + \sum_{i=1}^{n} t_i \frac{\partial x_i^h}{\partial I^h},$$ (4.43)

where b^h is Diamond's (1975) *net social marginal utility of income* measured in terms of government revenue. It is net in the sense that it measures both the gain in social welfare β^h due to an increase in income to h and the increase in tax payments of h due to this increase in income. From reviewing its definition, it can be seen that b^h involves both equity and efficiency effects. Using definition (4.43), equation (4.41) can be rearranged to give

$$\frac{\sum_{i=1}^{n} \sum_{h=1}^{H} t_i S_{ki}^h}{\sum_{h=1}^{H} x_k^h} = - \left[1 - \sum_{h=1}^{H} \frac{b^h}{H} \frac{x_k^h}{\bar{x}_k} \right].$$ (4.44)

Tax rule (4.44) shows that the reduction in aggregate compensated demand for the kth commodity due to the introduction of the tax system should be inversely related to the correlation between b^h and x_k^h. In other words, to the extent that the values of b^h reflect equity concerns, equity implies that goods consumed by those with high b^hs should be discouraged less or, effectively, they should have lower taxes. In general, the reduction in demand is smaller: (i) the more the good is consumed by individuals with a high b^h; (ii) the more the good is consumed by individuals with a high marginal propensity to consume taxed goods.

The two forms of the optimal commodity tax rule for a many-household economy in (4.40) and (4.44) illustrate aspects of the efficiency/equity trade-off by the manner in which the reduction in demand for a good is related to the social importance of the major consumers of that good and their general contribution to the tax revenue. The rules also demonstrate that the major feature of the Ramsey rule, the focus upon changes in quantities, is maintained in the general setting.

As with the Ramsey rule, the results do not give an explicit statement of the structure of taxes but only provide a characterisation of the consequences of the optimal system. This lack of clear results provides some of the motivation for the numerical studies reviewed in section 5. That section will also consider the information required to implement the optimal tax rule.

4.2 Reduction to the Ramsey rule

The tax rule given in the form of (4.44) is useful for discovering when the many-household rule actually collapses to the standard Ramsey rule. In such circumstances the equity criteria are eliminated. The two examples below illustrate that this can occur either because all households are given the same social valuation or because the tax system is unable to discriminate between households. The latter reason motivates an alternative interpretation of the tax problem as one of inferring the status of the households from the signals they provide in their choice of demands.

Example 1: $b^h = b$ all $h = 1, \ldots, H$.

In this case the bracketed term in (4.44) becomes

$$\left[1 - \sum_{h=1}^{H} \frac{b^h}{H} \frac{x_k^h}{\bar{x}_k}\right] = \left[1 - \frac{b}{\bar{x}_k} \sum_{h=1}^{H} \frac{x_k^h}{H}\right] = [1 - b]. \tag{4.45}$$

As (4.45) is independent of k, it implies that the proportional reduction in demand will be the same for all goods. Recalling the interpretation of b^h, this will occur if all households are valued equally and have the same propensity to pay tax or, most unlikely, the valuation and propensity sum to the same for all households. In either case, the equity considerations are effectively lost and the solution returns to that describing an efficient tax system. It must be emphasised that the value of b^h is endogenous to the system.

Example 2: $\dfrac{x_k^h}{\bar{x}_k}$ is the same for all k.

This condition implies that no good is consumed disproportionately by rich and poor, a situation that will arise whenever households have identical Engel curves and these are lines through the origin. When this occurs there is no method of subsidising high b^h people that doesn't also subsidise low b^h people since all households have the same expenditure patterns and pay the same proportion of income in tax. It should be noted that identical linear Engel curves aggregate perfectly hence the economy acts as if it were a single household. As above, it should be stressed that the value of $\dfrac{x_k^h}{\bar{x}_k}$ is determined endogenously.

  This result also highlights that the commodity tax problem can be viewed as one of signal extraction. From the purchases of each household the state is attempting to infer the household's preferences and endowment in order that it be taxed according to its circumstances. However, when the purchases carry no information, as in the case above, no signal can be extracted and redistribution fails. Without any redistributive aspect, the taxes must be chosen to meet efficiency criteria only.

An example of an economy that has these properties is one in which all households have identical Cobb–Douglas preferences and differ only in lump-sum incomes. It is not specified how these lump-sum incomes arise but they could be due to the operation of a non-uniform (but non-optimal) lump-sum subsidy system by the government. Assuming each household has the utility function $U^h = \Pi_{i=1}^n [x_i^h]^{\phi_i} - \ell$, where ℓ is labour supply and $\sum_{i=1}^n \phi_i = 1$, the demand for good k from household h is

$$x_k^h = \frac{\phi_k [I^h + w]}{q_k},$$ (4.46)

and

$$\bar{x}_k = \frac{1}{H} \sum_{h=1}^H \frac{\phi_k [I^h + w]}{q_k} = \frac{\phi_k}{q_k} \sum_{h=1}^H \frac{[I^h + w]}{H} = \frac{\phi_k}{q_k} [\bar{I} + w].$$ (4.47)

Thus calculating the ratio of the demand of household h to the mean level of demand provides the expression

$$\frac{x_k^h}{\bar{x}_k} = \frac{[I^h + w]}{[\bar{I} + w]}, \text{ all } k = 1, \ldots, n,$$ (4.48)

which clearly satisfies (ii).

4.3 A cautionary note

To this point the analysis has proceeded on the implicit assumption that the first-order conditions for the maximisations in (4.5) and (4.34) accurately characterise the solution. However this need not always be the case. It is a standard result that an indirect utility function representing convex preferences will be quasi-convex in prices. That is, the set of prices that lead to less than a specified level of utility is a convex set. In addition, with linearity in labour supply the indirect utility function may even be strictly convex, see Varian (1984). This poses difficulties for many maximisations in public economics.

For the Ramsey rule, the objective function was the household's indirect utility function and hence was quasi-convex. In the many-household economy, the objective was some concave function of the vector of indirect utility functions. Despite the concavity of social welfare in utility it need not be concave in the choice variables, the tax rates, due again to the quasi-convexity of indirect utilities. In addition, the set of tax rates that generate at least the required revenue may not be a convex set.

For these reasons the standard sufficiency conditions of quasi-concave programming cannot be appealed to so there is no guarantee that the first-order conditions actually describe a maximum. This problem occurs throughout public economics where many maximisations are ill-conditioned and has been explored extensively by Mirrlees (1986). It is often put to one side and it is simply assumed that the first-order conditions will correctly describe the optima.

Although unsatisfactory, there is typically little alternative to this. Some comfort can be taken in the present circumstances by appealing to the work of Diamond and Mirrlees (1971) who prove that their first-order conditions do represent the solution to the optimal commodity tax problem.

5 NUMERICAL RESULTS

Numerical analysis of optimal tax rates has become popular for two reasons. Firstly, the tax rules derived above suggest general observations about the structure of optimal taxes but they do not have precise implications. Numerical analysis can be seen as providing a check on the interpretations and a means of investigating them further. Secondly, the motive for the analysis is to provide practical policy recommendations. To do this, the tax rules must be capable of being applied to data and the values of the resulting optimal taxes calculated. Numerical studies in this context represent the development of a technology for carrying out this programme of work.

5.1 Applications

A series of papers by Ray (1986a), Murty and Ray (1987) and Srinivasan (1989) have presented progressively more refined estimates of optimal commodity taxes for the many-household economy based on data from the Indian National Sample Survey. To calculate the optimal tax rates, the first step is to specify the social welfare function. The procedure used for this is based on the work of Atkinson (1970), which was discussed in chapter 3, and involves adopting an additive social welfare function and defining a social utility of income function for each household. Together these give the social evaluation of income to the household.

Denote the aggregate expenditure of household h, which is assumed to be equal to income, by μ^h and let the social utility of income to h be given by

$$
U^h = \begin{cases} \dfrac{K[\mu^h]^{1-v}}{1-v} & v \neq 1 \\[2ex] K \log \mu^h & v = 1 \end{cases}
\tag{4.49}
$$

for some positive K. With the additive social welfare function $\dfrac{\partial W}{\partial V^h} = 1$ so the marginal social utility of income to h, β^h, is given by

$$
\beta^h = \frac{\partial U^h}{\partial \mu^h} = K[\mu^h]^{-v}.
\tag{4.50}
$$

The households are then ranked according to their expenditures, with the lowest expenditure household first in the ranking. Setting $\beta^1 = 1$ for the lowest expenditure household in the data set, it follows that

$$\beta^h = \left[\frac{\mu^1}{\mu^h}\right]^v.$$

(4.51)

Equation (4.51) implies that as μ^h increases relative to μ^1, β^h declines monotonically at rate v. Since a higher value of v reduces β^h relative to β^1 for all $h > 1$, v can be seen as the concern for equity as expressed in the social welfare function, with high values representing the greatest concern for equity.

The advantage of this method of defining the marginal social utilities is that the β^hs are fixed exogenously and can be determined by the observed expenditure levels in the data set. In addition, the concern for equity is clearly expressed and can be varied parametrically. However, it is important to note that (4.50) is imposing a very particular structure on the product of social preferences and individuals' utilities of income, a point that can be appreciated by reconsidering the definition in (4.37). Furthermore, it is denying the endogeneity of income and hence expenditure.

Given the specified structure of the β^hs, the optimal tax rates are determined from the equations

$$\sum_{h=1}^{H} \beta^h x_k^h = \lambda \left[\sum_{h=1}^{H} x_k^h + \sum_{i=1}^{n} \sum_{h=1}^{H} t_i \frac{\partial x_i^h}{\partial q_k} \right], \quad k = 1, \dots, n,$$

(4.52)

and

$$R = \sum_{i=1}^{n} \sum_{h=1}^{H} t_i x_i^h,$$

(4.53)

which were derived above as (4.38) and (4.32) respectively. To apply these equations to data, it is necessary to have knowledge of individual demands and the demand derivatives. To obtain these, a demand system is specified and then estimated for the data set. The demand functions estimated are then substituted together with the definition of β^h into (4.52) and (4.53). The resulting $n + 1$ equations are then solved for the n tax rates and the Lagrange multiplier.

The first paper to adopt this approach was Ray (1986a). In that paper the $n + 1$ equations in (4.52) and (4.53) were taken as simultaneous equations with the demand levels and demand derivatives held constant at their initial levels. This constancy implies that the tax rates given by solving the equations are not fully optimal but only optimal conditional upon the constant demands. A more advanced approach is given in Murty and Ray (1987) which incorporates the effects of the taxes on demand and uses an iterative procedure to solve for the optimum. The demand system used in Murty and Ray (1987) is based on the indirect utility function

$$V^h(\cdot) = \frac{\mu_h^\alpha - \sum_{i=1}^{n} \gamma_i p_i^{\alpha_1} w_h^{\alpha_2}}{\prod_{k=1}^{n} p_k^{\alpha\beta_k} w_h^{\alpha\beta_0}}.$$

(4.54)

Table 4.1. *Optimal tax rates*

Item	$\theta = 0.05$	$\theta = 0.1$
Cereals	-0.015	-0.089
Milk and milk products	-0.042	-0.011
Edible oils	0.359	0.342
Meat, fish and eggs	0.071	0.083
Sugar and tea	0.013	0.003
Other food	0.226	0.231
Clothing	0.038	0.014
Fuel and light	0.038	0.014
Other non-food	0.083	0.126

The form of this function permits the evaluation of various separability assumptions via the values of the estimated parameters. There is separability between goods and leisure in utility if α_2 and β are both zero and non-separability between different goods when α_1 differs from unity. The tax rates were calculated on the basis of the estimated values of the parameters γ_i, β_i, α_1 given in Ray (1986a), β_0 was set to zero and the value of α_2 was assumed.

Defining θ to be the wage as a proportion of expenditure, the value of which is imposed upon the analysis, a sample of the results of Murty and Ray (1987) are given in table 4.1 for $v = 2$ and $\alpha_2 = 0.025$.

Table 4.1 illustrates that redistribution takes place via these optimal taxes since cereals and milk products, both basic foodstuffs, are subsidised. Such redistribution is a reflection of the concern for equity embodied in a value of v of 2. In addition, the results are not too sensitive to the choice of θ which could not be estimated from the data set. However, the analysis is limited by the degree of aggregation that leads to the excessively general other non-food category.

Ray (1986b) also used this framework to analyse the redistributive impact of Indian commodity taxes. The method employed was to calculate the total payment of commodity tax, T^h, by household h relative to the expenditure μ^h of that household. The net gain from the tax system for h can then be defined by

$$-\frac{T^h}{\mu^h}. \tag{4.55}$$

The household is gaining from the tax system if $-\dfrac{T^h}{\mu^h}$ is positive since this implies a net subsidy is being received. Contrasting the gains of household h from the existing tax system with those of the optimal system then provides an indication of both the success of the existing system and the potential gains from the optimal system. For demand estimates based on a linear expenditure system, the calculations for the existing Indian tax system give the gains noted in table 4.2.

Table 4.2. *Redistribution of Indian commodity taxes*

Expenditure level	Rural $-T^h/\mu^h$	Urban $-T^h/\mu^h$
Rs. 20	0.105	0.220
Rs. 50	0.004	0.037

Table 4.3. *Optimal redistribution*

	$v=0.1$	$v=1.5$	$v=5$
$-T/\mu$	0.07	0.343	0.447

The expenditure levels of Rs. 20 and Rs. 50 place households with these incomes in the lower 30 per cent of the distribution. In this case there is a net gain to households at both income levels from the tax system with the lower expenditure householder making a proportionately greater gain.

From Ray (1986a) the redistributive impact of the optimal tax system for a household with expenditure level $\mu = 0.5\bar{\mu}$, where $\bar{\mu}$ is mean expenditure, is given in table 4.3. For $v = 1.5$ or more, it can be seen that the potential gains from the tax system, relative to the outcome that would occur in the absence of taxation, are quite substantial. Therefore it can be seen that with sufficient weight given to equity considerations the optimal set of commodity taxes can effect significant redistribution and that the existing Indian tax system does not attain these gains.

5.2 Further results

Atkinson and Stiglitz (1972) calculated the optimal tax rates satisfying the Ramsey rule for a single-household economy. Two demand systems were considered: the direct addilog with the parameters and data taken from Houthakker (1960); and the linear expenditure system calculated by Stone (1954). In both cases, additive separability in labour supply was assumed. The results support the interpretation of the Ramsey rule in 3.3: food and rent (necessities) bear the highest tax rates and durable goods (luxuries) the lowest and the optimal tax system is non-uniform. Deaton (1977) presents numerical results that rely on an aggregation argument and therefore fall somewhere between the single-household and a true many-household economy. The major finding of the analysis is that the tax rates move further from uniformity as the concern for equity increases.

A further calculation of optimal commodity taxes can be found in Ebrahimi and Heady (1988) which, following Deaton and Stern (1986), augments the standard analysis by including publicly observable demographic characteristics. The observability of the demographic variable, which is the number of children in the household, allows lump-sum tax payments to be based upon it and the tax system consists of commodity taxes, a lump-sum payment independent of demograhics and a child benefit, with the child benefit potentially variable according to the children's ages. The data for the calculation are taken from the 1981 UK Family Expenditure Survey and relate to 2,126 households with two adults but various numbers of children. The computational procedure is based on an algorithm for finding the fixed point of a mapping that was described in Heady and Mitra (1980). The results illustrate again that optimal taxes will be non-uniform. This remains true even with the considerable flexibility in the setting of lump-sum transfers permitted by the use of the lump-sum transfer and two distinct child benefits. The tax rates, the lump-sum transfer and the benefits are all large in value relative to the taxes and transfers seen in practice.

An alternative approach to computation is given in Harris and MacKinnon (1979) who develop an algorithm for solving the necessary conditions for optimal taxes. The algorithm finds the fixed point of a mapping and is applicable even when supply is a set-valued function of prices rather than a point-valued function. Although Harris and McKinnon present the results of some simulation experiments, their algorithm does not yet appear to have been applied to empirical data.

The results above indicate conclusively that the optimal tax rules can be operationalised, albeit in somewhat restricted settings. The numerical analyses all have small commodity groupings and none truly solves the problem in its full generality since producer prices are generally taken as fixed. However the results do show that progress is being made and illustrate a fruitful direction for future research.

6 GENERALISING THE PRODUCTION TECHNOLOGY

The economies analysed in sections 3 and 4 assumed that labour was the only input into production and that there were constant returns to scale. These assumptions were adopted to provide the simplest basis on which to develop the results. Both assumptions can be relaxed and this section briefly considers the consequences of so doing.

Retaining the assumption of constant returns but allowing all goods to be potential inputs into production alters the method of analysis but does not affect the structure of the results derived. The argument in this case, developed in Diamond and Mirrlees (1971), relies on the disconnection between households and firms. As there are constant returns to scale, all firms earn zero profits and households' incomes are derived solely from the sale of goods. All these sales take place at consumer prices, q. Hence households' actions are determined only by consumer prices. In contrast, firms transact at producer prices, p, and are not influenced in their decisions by the consumer price level. Effectively, the two sets of prices can be chosen separately and the difference between the two determines the tax rates.

Expressed formally, the government can face households with a price vector $(q_1, \ldots, q_n)$ which then entirely determines their actions. Aggregating the individual firms' production sets determines the economy's production possibility set. The choice of a producer price vector $(p_1, \ldots, p_n)$ then determines supply as the profit-maximising choice at these prices over all points in the aggregate production possibility set. Since constant returns to scale are assumed, profit maximisation determines a supply correspondence rather than a supply function. For the reasons noted in the discussion of the Second Theorem of Welfare Economics, it is not necessary to worry about the maximisation of individual firms. Summarising this discussion, the behaviour of the agents in the economy is described by

$$\textit{Households:} \quad \max_{\{x^h\}} U^h(x^h) \text{ subject to } \sum_{i=1}^{n} q_i x_i^h = \sum_{i=1}^{n} q_i \omega_i^h, \qquad (4.56)$$

with optimal choices

$$x_i^h = x_i^h(q_i), \; i = 1, \ldots, n, \; h = 1, \ldots, H, \qquad (4.57)$$

and

$$\textit{Production:} \quad \max_{\{y\}} py \text{ subject to } y \in Y, \qquad (4.58)$$

where Y is the aggregate production possibility set, with supply correspondence

$$y(p). \qquad (4.59)$$

Equations (4.57) and (4.59) capture the independence of household choices from the producer price vector and of the production choice from consumer prices.

From the maximisations (4.56) and (4.58) it should be noted that both demands and supplies are homogeneous of degree zero in the relevant price vectors. This implies

$$X_i(q) = X_i(\lambda q), \; \forall \lambda > 0, \; i = 1, \ldots, n, \qquad (4.60)$$

and

$$y(p) = y(\lambda p), \; \forall \lambda > 0. \qquad (4.61)$$

Given a set of producer and consumer prices, the tax rates are determined implicitly by the identity

$$t = q - p. \qquad (4.62)$$

However, the homogeneity in (4.60) and (4.61) implies that an equivalent tax system to that in (4.62) is given by

$$t' = \phi q - \rho p, \tag{4.63}$$

for any ϕ, $\rho > 0$. The equivalence of t and t' follows from noting that the prices supporting both tax systems elicit the same production choice and the same level of demand from consumers. In this sense, the values of the tax rates themselves are of limited interest since these are only determined up to the choice of the arbitrary constants ϕ, ρ.

This degree of freedom in the choice of tax rates is the basis upon which Mirrlees (1976) argues for considering the index of discouragement and its generalisations, which are defined in terms of quantities rather than prices, since it is the effect upon equilibrium quantities that is the real property of the tax system. It should be recalled that it was reasoning in terms of quantities that provided the basis for the interpretations of the tax rules given above. The indeterminacy in the values of the tax rates is usually resolved by adopting the standard normalisation rule of setting the tax on one of the goods to zero. This is effectively what was done with the wage rate above, which is why there was no loss of generality in using that assumption. There has been much confusion on this point, see particularly the remarks of Mirrlees (1976) which attempt to provide clarification and the discussion in section 7.

Returning now to the analysis of the more general economy, the optimal tax system is found by choosing the consumer price vector q to maximise welfare subject to there being some producer price vector p that will generate the appropriate level of supply from firms in order to match demand with supply, with demand being the sum of household and government demand. As this procedure guarantees that all markets are in equilibrium, the government budget constraint does not need explicit recognition; see chapter 2, section 6. Writing the production possibility set in implicit form as

$$F(X(q) + x^G) \leq 0, \tag{4.64}$$

where x^G is the fixed vector of government demands, the Diamond and Mirrlees formulation is summarised by the maximisation

$$\max_{\{q\}} W(V^1(\cdot), \ldots, V^H(\cdot)) \text{ subject to } F(X(q) + x^G) \leq 0. \tag{4.65}$$

With profit-maximising behaviour, producer prices can be determined by noting that they will be proportional to the normal to the production possibility set at the equilibrium point. Such a price vector will guarantee zero profit for the firms. Hence p is proportional to ∇F evaluated at $X(q) + x^G$. Although this problem appears distinct from that described in (4.34), it does have the same solution which is given by (4.40) or (4.44).

If the assumption of constant returns to scale is relaxed and decreasing returns are permitted, those firms with decreasing returns will earn positive profits. If profits are assumed to be taxed at a rate of 100 per cent then all firms' profits are returned to the government and the separation between households and firms remains. The optimal tax problem is then still described by (4.65), with suitable assumptions on the production possibility set, and the Diamond–Mirrlees results still apply. When profits are not taxed at 100 per cent, some profit income will accrue to households through their shareholdings in firms. Once this occurs, the separation between households and firms no longer applies.

To show the effect of profits, the simplest case is chosen and it is assumed that profits are entirely untaxed. Profits will then be distributed to households in accordance with the distribution of shareholdings and will modify the typical household's decision problem to

$$\max_{\{x^h\}} U^h(x^h) \text{ subject to } \sum_{i=1}^{n} q_i x_i^h = \sum_{i=1}^{n} q_i \omega_i^h + \sum_{j=1}^{m} \theta_j^h \pi^j. \tag{4.66}$$

Since the profit levels of the firms are determined by producer prices, as shown in (2.15), the solution of (4.66) is now dependent upon p so the household is affected by the level of producer prices. Household demands are therefore given by

$$x_i^h = x_i^h(q,\pi) = x_i^h(q,p), \ i=1,\dots,n, \ h=1,\dots,H, \tag{4.67}$$

since π must depend on p and q. As shown by Munk (1978), this dependence necessitates that a different solution procedure is employed.

To derive the single-household tax rule in this case, first let the aggregate production constraint be written in the form

$$F(y)=y_1-f(y_2,\dots,y_n)=0. \tag{4.68}$$

Profit maximisation subject to this constraint implies that

$$p_i = -p_1 \frac{\partial f}{\partial y_i}. \tag{4.69}$$

Using (4.67), the demands from the single household can be written

$$x_i = x_i(q,\pi), \tag{4.70}$$

where π is the aggregate level of profit given by $\pi = py$.

Now assume that the government demands a fixed vector x^G of commodities. Equilibrium occurs when demands equal supplies or

$$x + x^G = y + \omega. \tag{4.71}$$

From (4.71)

$$y = x + x^G - \omega. \tag{4.72}$$

Now using (4.69), (4.70), (4.72) and the definition of aggregate profit gives the equations

$$\pi = \sum_{i=1}^{n} p_i[x(q_1,\dots,q_n,\pi) + x^G - \omega], \tag{4.73}$$

$$p_i = -p_1 \frac{\partial f(x_2(q,\pi) + x_2^G - \omega_2, \dots, x_n(q,\pi) + x_n^G - \omega_n)}{\partial y_i}, \ i=2,\dots,n. \tag{4.74}$$

Normalising p_1 at unity, the n equations in (4.73) and (4.74) will be sufficient, when the conditions of the implicit function theorem are satisfied, to provides solutions

$$p_i = p_i(q), \ i = 2, \ldots, n, \ \pi = \pi(q) \tag{4.75}$$

for the producer prices and the profit level conditional upon the vector of consumer prices. Any consumer price vector, q, that satisfies the market equilibrium condition

$$x(q, \pi(q)) + x^G = y(p(q)) + \omega, \tag{4.76}$$

where $p(q)$ is the vector $(p_1, p_2(q), \ldots, p_n(q))$, is an admissible price vector. The set of admissible equilibrium consumer price vectors is denoted Q.

With this formulation, the optimal tax problem involves choosing the vector of consumer prices to solve the maximisation

$$\max_{\{q\}} V(q, \pi(q)) \text{ subject to } [q - p(q)]x(q, \pi(q)) = p(q)x^G \text{ and } q \in Q, \tag{4.77}$$

where the first constraint in (4.77) is the government budget constraint. Differentiating and using Roy's identity, the optimal tax rule is

$$\sum_{i=1}^{n} t_i \left[\frac{\partial x_i}{\partial q_k} + \frac{\partial x_i}{\partial \pi} \frac{\partial \pi}{\partial q_k} \right] = \frac{\lambda - \alpha}{\lambda} \left[-x_k + \frac{\partial \pi}{\partial q_k} \right], \ k = 1, \ldots, n. \tag{4.78}$$

Hence the reduction in demand is now related to the effect of consumer prices upon profits. Further analysis of this result can be found in Munk (1978).

7 UNTAXED GOODS

The role of normalisation procedures and of the *untaxed* good was discussed at some length in the previous section. The importance of applying normalisations correctly has been emphasised in the literature on optimal commodity taxation by the number of cases in which they have been misunderstood. This section notes the misunderstandings that have arisen and illustrates their origins.

It has been shown that in an economy with constant returns to scale, consumer and producer prices can be normalised separately and that the standard procedure is to make one good the numeraire and set its consumer and producer prices equal. This normalisation also has the effect of setting the tax on that good to zero. The latter fact is clearly seen to be of no consequence whatsoever since the zero tax is just a result of the normalisation rule. In particular, the zero tax carries no implications about the nature of the good nor about the ability to tax that good. This follows since the good with zero tax can be chosen arbitrarily from the set of available goods.

Unfortunately, this reasoning has not been as clearly appreciated in some of the literature as it should have been. The reason for this has been the convention, as adopted in sections 3 and 4 of this chapter, of taking labour as the untaxed commodity. Since labour is often viewed as the negative of leisure, it has been inferred from this that, since leisure cannot be measured in the same way that purchases of other commodities can, the zero tax on leisure is a restriction on the permissible tax system brought about by an inability to tax leisure. In addition, the further inference is usually made that the optimal tax system aims to overcome the *missing* tax on leisure by taxing goods complementary to leisure. Particular examples of this are found in Corlett and Hague (1953) 'By taxing those goods complementary with leisure, one is to some extent taxing leisure itself' (p. 26) and Layard and Walters (1978) 'The theory of second best tells us that it we cannot tax leisure, we can do better than by taxing all other goods equiproportionately' (p. 184). Many other instances of similar statements could easily be given. This, of course, is a false interpretation. When real restrictions upon the permissible range of tax instruments are introduced the results obtained are affected. A number of such restrictions are considered in Munk (1980) where it is shown that the resulting optimal tax structure is sensitive to the precise restrictions imposed.

A further mistake that has arisen in this context can be found in Dixit (1970) and Lerner (1970). In a single-household economy, any required revenue can be raised most efficiently by a lump-sum tax on the household equal to the value of the revenue. Noticing this, it has been suggested that a set of commodity taxes which raise the price of all goods by the same proportion will have the same effect as the lump-sum tax and therefore that when all goods can be taxed, the optimal system has the same proportional tax on all goods. This conclusion is clearly in contrast to that of the Ramsey rule. The mistake in the reasoning was pointed out by Sandmo (1974) who demonstrated that such a proportional tax system would raise no revenue. This follows since households both demand goods and supply labour. A proportional tax then taxes demands but subsidises supplies and, since the value of household demand equals the value of supply, the proportional tax is just offset by the proportional subsidy. Effectively, the proportional tax on all commodities is just a rescaling of the consumer price vector which does not affect household choices.

Returning to untaxed goods, as the analysis that will now be given shows, it is correct to state that if leisure is untaxed then goods complementary with leisure should be taxed more highly but it is not correct to infer from this either that not taxing leisure is a restriction on the system or that the taxes aim to compensate for the missing tax. Taking the Ramsey rule as defined in (4.17) for a two-good and labour economy gives the necessary conditions for an optimal tax system of

$$t_1 S_{11} + t_2 S_{12} = -\theta x_1, \tag{4.79}$$

$$t_1 S_{21} + t_2 S_{22} = -\theta x_2. \tag{4.80}$$

Solving these equations, the tax rates are implicitly characterised by

$$t_1 = \left[\frac{\theta}{S}\right][S_{12}x_2 - S_{22}x_1], \tag{4.81}$$

$$t_2 = \left[\frac{\theta}{S}\right][S_{21}x_1 - S_{11}x_2], \tag{4.82}$$

where $S = S_{11}S_{22} - S_{12}S_{21}$ can be assumed to be negative by the negative semi-definiteness of the Slutsky matrix. Now define the elasticity of compensated demand by

$$\varepsilon_{ij}^c = \frac{q_j S_{ij}}{x_i}, \tag{4.83}$$

and note that by dividing (4.81) by (4.82), multiplying by $\dfrac{q_2}{q_1}$ and normalising both producer prices at unity (which can be done by selecting the units in which the commodities are measured), provides the relation

$$\frac{\dfrac{t_1}{1+t_1}}{\dfrac{t_2}{1+t_2}} = \frac{\varepsilon_{12}^c - \varepsilon_{22}^c}{\varepsilon_{21}^c - \varepsilon_{11}^c}. \tag{4.84}$$

Representing leisure by good 0, it follows from Euler's theorem and the homogeneity of degree 1 of the expenditure function in prices that

$$\sum_{j=0}^{2} q_j S_{ij} = 0, \tag{4.85}$$

and hence that after dividing by x_i

$$\varepsilon_{i0}^c + \varepsilon_{i1}^c + \varepsilon_{i2}^c = 0. \tag{4.86}$$

Therefore (4.84) can be written in the form

$$\frac{t_1}{1+t_1} = \frac{t_2}{1+t_2}\left(\frac{-(\varepsilon_{11}^c + \varepsilon_{22}^c) - \varepsilon_{10}^c}{-(\varepsilon_{11}^c + \varepsilon_{22}^c) - \varepsilon_{20}^c}\right). \tag{4.87}$$

Equation (4.87) states that if the two goods stand in the same relation to labour, so that $\varepsilon_{10}^c = \varepsilon_{20}^c$, then they should be taxed at the same rate. Otherwise the good with the lower value of ε_{j0}^c, and hence more complementary with leisure, should be taxed at the higher rate. This analysis is the basis for claims that the good complementary to the untaxed good should be taxed more.

However, it should be noted that this conclusion is simply an artefact of the homogeneity of the expenditure function rather than any fundamental result about the optimal taxes trying to compensate for the missing tax on leisure. The discussion of section 6 has already shown that the non-taxation of labour is simply a harmless normalisation and that any good could have been chosen as the untaxed commodity. In other words, good 0 could be chosen to be one of the consumption goods and good 1 labour. In that case, the direct link with leisure is then lost from (4.87). Additionally, equation (4.84) presents the tax rule in terms of own-price and cross-price elasticities of the two taxed goods without any explicit mention of the untaxed good and provides an equally acceptable point from which to seek interpretations.

This section has noted misunderstandings that have arisen in connection with the interpretation of the position of the untaxed good. Although the tax rule can be written so as to depend on the complementarity with the untaxed good, there is nothing fundamental in this observation. In addition, arguments that an optimal system would tax all goods at the same rate are unfounded since such a system would raise no revenue.

8 UNIFORM TAXES

The numerical results reported in section 5 have demonstrated that in general the structure of optimal commodity taxes will be far from uniform. However, uniform taxes are not without their supporters, see for example Hatta (1986), and it is natural to consider whether there are any circumstances in which the optimal structure should be uniform.

Conditions guaranteeing uniformity have been derived in papers by Deaton (1979, 1981) and Besley and Jewitt (1990). These papers have used a variety of representations of preferences in alternative formulations of the optimal tax problem. To present the central result in the manner closest to the analysis above, this section will present the problem in terms of *ad valorem* taxation with an indirect utility function capturing preferences.

With *ad valorem* taxation the consumer price of good i is given by $q_i = [1 + t_i]p_i$ and the optimal commodity tax problem becomes

$$\max_{\{t_1,\ldots,t_n\}} V(q_1,\ldots,q_n,w,I) \text{ subject to } R = \sum_{i=1}^{n} t_i p_i x_i. \tag{4.88}$$

For the choice of tax rate on good k the maximisation in (4.88) has the first-order condition

$$\frac{\partial V}{\partial q_k} p_k + \lambda \left[p_k x_k + \sum_{i=1}^{n} t_i p_i \frac{\partial x_i}{\partial q_k} p_k \right] = 0, \, k = 1,\ldots,n. \tag{4.89}$$

Eliminating the common factor p_k from (4.89) and using the Slutsky equation, the Ramsey rule in this case takes the form

$$\sum_{i=1}^{n} t_i p_i S_{ik} = -\theta x_k, \, k = 1,\ldots,n, \tag{4.90}$$

with $\theta = 1 - \dfrac{\alpha}{\lambda} - \sum_{i=1}^{n} t_i p_i \dfrac{\partial x_i}{\partial I}$.

Treating labour as good 0, the homogeneity of the expenditure function can be used to write

$$\sum_{i=1}^{n} q_i S_{ik} + w S_{0k} = 0, \tag{4.91}$$

where (4.91) is the generalisation of (4.85). Normalising w at 1 and using (4.92) the optimal tax rule becomes

$$S_{0k} = \theta x_k, \ k = 1, \ldots, n. \tag{4.98}$$

In this form of the Ramsey rule the tax rates are set so that the demand for each good is proportional to the rate of substitution between that good and labour. Using Shephard's lemma and the relation of the substitution terms to the expenditure function, (4.92) is equivalent to

$$C_{0k}(q_1, \ldots, q_n, w, U) = \theta C_k(q_1, \ldots, q_n, w, U), \tag{4.93}$$

with $w = 1$.

When a uniform system of taxation is optimal, so that $t_i = t$ all i, there must be some t that solves

$$C_{0k}([1 + t]p_1, \ldots, [1 + t]p_n, w, U) = \theta C_k([1 + t]p_1, \ldots, [1 + t]p_n, w, U). \tag{4.94}$$

Since the expenditure function is homogeneous of degree 1, its first derivative is homogeneous of degree 0 and its second of degree -1. Therefore (4.94) is equivalent to

$$\frac{1}{[1 + t]} C_{0k}\left(p_1, \ldots, p_n, \frac{w}{[1 + t]}, U\right) = \theta C_k\left(p_1, \ldots, p_n, \frac{w}{[1 + t]}, U\right), \tag{4.95}$$

or

$$C_{0k}(p_1, \ldots, p_n, w', U) = \theta' C_k(p_1, \ldots, p_n, w', U), \tag{4.96}$$

where $\theta' = \theta[1 + t]$ and $w' = \dfrac{w}{[1 + t]}$. For uniform taxation to be always optimal, (4.96) must hold for all producer price vectors $p_1, \ldots, p_n$ and wage rates w'. Condition (4.96) places restrictions upon the forms of cost function, and hence preferences that they represent, that will always lead to uniform taxation.

From Deaton (1979, 1981), one form of cost function that satisfies (4.96) is

$$C(p_1, \ldots, p_n, w, U) = C(c(p_1, \ldots, p_n), w, U), \tag{4.97}$$

which is called the implicitly separable cost function. More generally, Besley and Jewitt (1990) have shown that any preferences that can be defined in the form

$$f(\phi(x, x_0, U), x_0, U) = 1, \tag{4.98}$$

where x_0 is labour supply and $\phi(x, x_0, U)$ is homogeneous of degree 0 in (x, x_0) will result in uniform commodity taxes. A simple example of (4.98) is the utility function

$$U = U\left(\phi\left(\frac{x}{x_0}\right), x_0\right). \tag{4.99}$$

The important conclusion to draw from this analysis is that the conditions implying uniform taxation are restrictive and there is no reason why they should be satisfied in practice. Therefore there are no grounds for believing that the optimal tax system should be uniform.

9 PRODUCTION EFFICIENCY

Production efficiency occurs when an economy is maximising the output attainable from its given set of resources. This requires the economy to be on the boundary of its production possibility set. When such a point is attained, reallocation of inputs amongst firms cannot increase the output of one good without reducing that of another. In the special case in which each firm employs some of all of the available inputs, a necessary condition for production efficiency is that the marginal rate of substitution (MRS) between any two inputs is the same for all firms. Such a position of equality is attained, in the absence of taxation, by the profit maximisation of firms in competitive markets. Each firm sets the marginal rate of substitution equal to the ratio of factor prices and, since factor prices are the same for all firms, this induces the necessary equality in the MRSs. The same is true when there is taxation provided all firms face the same post-tax prices for inputs, that is, inputs taxes are not differentiated between firms.

In the context of commodity taxation, Diamond and Mirrlees (1971) proved the *Production Efficiency lemma*. Assuming the economy is competitive, the lemma states that the equilibrium with optimal commodity taxation should be on the frontier of the aggregate production set. This can only be achieved if private and public producer face the same shadow prices and if input taxes are not differentiated between firms. In addition, since the competitive assumption implies that any set of chosen post-tax prices can be sustained by the use of taxes on final goods alone, the latter statement also carries the implication that intermediate goods should not be taxed.

This result was seen as surprising at its time of publication because it was clearly in sharp contrast to the predictions of the Lipsey–Lancaster (1956) second-best theory that was being widely applied. Application of second-best theory, which typically suggests that one distortion should be offset by others, would imply that the distortion induced by the commodity taxes should be matched by a similar distortion in input prices. Commodity taxation is therefore a special case for which the general reasoning requires careful application.

The efficiency lemma, and the structure of the optimal commodity tax problem, can easily be explained diagrammatically for a single household two-good economy. In figure 4.2 the horizontal axis measures input use and the vertical axis output. The shaded area is the production set for the economy and the horizontal distance of the production set from the origin represents the tax revenue required in units of the input good. It is assumed that the household

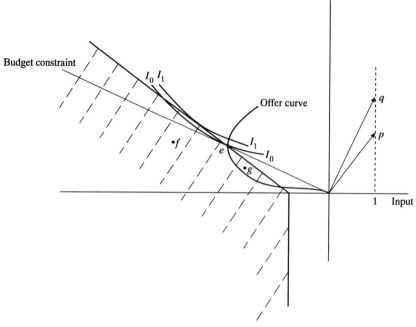

Figure 4.2   Production efficiency

supplies the input and consumes the output, so that the supply of more input from the household permits the purchase of more output. The household's budget constraint is therefore upward sloping and, in the absence of lump-sum taxes or income, must pass through the origin. Denoting the optimal set of post-tax prices by q, the budget constraint corresponding to this price vector is illustrated. Since supplying the input causes the household disutility, an increase in input supply must be compensated for by further consumption of output in order to keep utility constant. The household's indifference curves are therefore downward sloping.

The optimal tax equilibrium is given by the highest point on the household's offer curve that is in the production set; in figure 4.2 the optimum is indicated by point e. At this point the household is on indifference curve $I_0 - I_0$ and production is efficient. To ensure that firms earn zero profits when producing at the equilibrium point, producer prices, p, are determined by the normal to the production set. For both producer and consumer prices, the price of the input is normalised at 1. The difference between the two sets of prices, $t = q - p$, determines the optimal set of tax rates. It should also be noted that there are points above the indifference curve $I_0 - I_0$ which are preferred to e and which are productively feasible. These can only be reached by the use of lump-sum taxes and their existence illustrates the second-best nature of the commodity tax optimum. With the use of an optimal lump-sum tax, the household would reach indifference curve $I_1 - I_1$

To see that the optimum must be on the frontier of the production set, consider points f and g. If the equilibrium were at f, the household's welfare could be raised by reducing the use of the input whilst keeping output constant. Since this is feasible, f cannot be an optimum. From g, output could be increased without employing more input so that g cannot be an optimum. Since this reasoning can be applied to any point that is interior to the production set, the optimum must be on the boundary.

Although figure 4.2 was motivated by considering the input to be labour, a slight reinterpretation can introduce intermediate goods. Assume that there is an industry that uses one unit of labour to produce one unit of an intermediate good and that the intermediate good is then used to produce final output. Figure 4.2 then depicts the intermediate good (the input) being used to produce the output. Although the household actually has preferences over labour and final output and acts only on the markets for these goods, the direct link between units of labour and of intermediate good allows preferences and the budget constraint to be depicted *as if* they were defined directly on those variables. The production efficiency argument then follows directly as before and now implies that intermediate goods should not be taxed since this would violate the equalisation of MRSs between firms.

Moving now to a many-household competitive economy with constant returns to scale, the formal statement of the Production Efficiency Lemma can be given.

Theorem 4.1 (Diamond and Mirrlees)

Assume that social welfare is strictly increasing in the utility level of all households. If either

(i) for some i, $x_i^h \leq 0$ for all h and $x_i^{\hat{h}} < 0$ for some $\hat{h}$,

or

(ii) for some i, with $q_i > 0$, $x_i^h \geq 0$ for all h and $x_i^{\hat{h}} > 0$ for some $\hat{h}$, then if an optimum exists, the optimum has production on the frontier of the production possibility set.

Proof

Assume the optimum is interior to the production set. In case (i), increasing q_i would not reduce the welfare of any household and would strictly raise that of $\hat{h}$. Such a change is feasible since the optimum is assumed interior and the aggregate demand function is continuous. The change would raise social welfare, thus contradicting the assertion that the initial point was optimal. The same argument can be applied in case (ii) for a reduction in q_i.

When decreasing returns are permitted, Dasgupta and Stiglitz (1972) conclude that production efficiency is only desirable if the range of government instruments is sufficiently great, in effect, only if profits can be taxed at appropriate rates. Mirrlees (1972) provides further clarification of the relation of profits and production efficiency. These findings show that the constant returns to scale assumption can be relaxed. Whilst retaining the competitive assumption, one partial exemption to the Diamond–Mirrlees rule has been identified by Munk (1980) and Newbery (1986). If there are restrictions on taxes on final goods, then production efficiency is no longer necessarily desirable. In detail, Newbery demonstrates that if there are some goods whose optimal tax would be positive but the goods cannot be taxed, then input taxes should be used as partial substitutes for the missing final taxes. Similar results to those of Newbery are also given by Ebrill and Slutsky (1990), although their analysis is phrased in terms of regulated industries.

The Diamond–Mirrlees lemma therefore provides an argument for the non-taxation of intermediate goods and the non-differentiation of input taxes between firms. As noted, it has been extended from its original constant returns to scale setting. However, except for some special cases, imperfect competition invalidates the lemma and taxes on intermediate goods will raise welfare. This result will be considered in chapter 11.

10 SUMMARY

This chapter has reviewed the major contributions to the large literature on optimal commodity taxation in a competitive economy. The Ramsey rule, which represents the starting point for the modern analysis of commodity taxation, has been introduced and its standard interpretation has been given. Although efficient, the tax system this describes would be inherently inequitable. To introduce equity considerations, the economy was then extended to incorporate many households following the work of Diamond and Mirrlees. This extension clarified the effects of equity upon the optimal rates of tax and demonstrated how the equity/efficiency trade-off was resolved. The economy was then generalised further and the Diamond–Mirrlees Production Efficiency lemma was proved. Contrary to the expectations of second-best theory, this lemma showed that production efficiency is desirable in conjunction with the optimal set of commodity taxes.

The motivation behind the theory of commodity taxation is to provide practical policy recommendations. Although the analysis remains some way off fully achieving this aim, a number of interesting studies have applied these optimal tax rules to data. This line of work is still in its infancy but gradual improvements in generality have been achieved. The numerical results indicate that the optimal set of taxes may be able to achieve significant redistribution via the subsidisation of necessities.

5

INCOME TAXATION

1 INTRODUCTION

The taxation of income is a major source of revenue in most developed countries. It is also one of the most contentious. From one point of view, an income tax is seen as a direct means of effecting redistribution in order to meet objectives of equity. From another, the imposition of an income tax is viewed as a major disincentive to effort and enterprise particularly when the marginal rate of tax increases with income. The theory of income taxation shows how these competing views influence the design of the optimal tax and how the competing trade-offs are resolved.

The analysis of income taxation that is undertaken below follows from the initial contribution of Mirrlees (1971). Prior to that, there had been no formal analysis of the structure or determinants of an income tax schedule that fully captured the efficiency/equity trade-off involved in income taxation. In addition, the Mirrlees analysis also embodied the fact that the truly relevant characteristics for taxation, the unobservable ability levels of the households, can only be inferred indirectly from observed behaviour. This implies that the structure of the income tax must be compatible with the revelation of this information by households.

The chapter begins by providing a general description of the Mirrlees' economy which is the basis for the analysis. The major theoretical results that have been derived both for the general case and for the restricted constant marginal tax rate case are described. This is followed by a review of the results of a number of numerical studies. A critical analysis of the assumptions on which the simulations are based is then given and the implications of modifying these is illustrated by a brief discussion of labour supply decisions and some attempts at the direct assessment of labour supply effects. The chapter is concluded by reviewing extensions of the basic analysis, including the design of tax systems with both linear and non-linear taxes, and the issues that it omits.

2 THE MIRRLEES ECONOMY

The value of the Mirrlees' economy in the analysis of income taxation is due to the manner in which it captures the most important features of the tax design problem. These features are that the no-tax equilibrium of the economy must have an unequal distribution of income in order to introduce equity motivations for taxation. The income distribution must also be generated endogenously by the model, with households differing in the income they earn, and the income tax must affect the labour supply decisions of the households in order to introduce efficiency considerations. The economy must also be sufficiently flexible that no prior restrictions are placed on the tax functions that may be solutions. The Mirrlees' specification is the simplest that satisfies all these requirements.

To simplify and focus the analysis, it is assumed that the economy is competitive and that households in the economy differ only in the levels of skill in employment. A household's level of skill determines their hourly wage and hence income. The skill level is private information and is not known to the government. The only tax instrument of the state is an income tax. An income tax is employed both because lump-sum taxes are infeasible and because it is assumed that it is not possible for the state to observe separately hours worked and income per hour. Therefore, since only total income is observed, it has to be the basis for the tax system. The content of this restriction is best understood by considering the consequences of its relaxation. If it were relaxed, a tax could be levied that was based on income per hour; in many cases this would be a better guide to a household's potential earning power than actual income. Indeed, in the economy employed below, income per hour is precisely the ultimate target of taxation. Despite this, it does not seem unreasonable to assume that, as in practice, only total income is observed.

The income tax function is chosen to maximise social welfare subject to achieving the required level of revenue. The generality of the analysis, and the source of many of the difficulties involved in carrying it out, derives from the fact that no restrictions are placed at the outset on permissible candidates for the optimal tax function. It is intended by this that the economy determines the structure of the tax function rather than important aspects of the function being determined by a priori assumptions.

2.1 The optimisation

The optimal income tax function is chosen to maximise social welfare. This maximisation is subject to two constraints. The first constraint is that the income tax function must lead to an outcome that satisfies productive feasibility or, equivalently, meets the government's revenue requirement. The second constraint that must be satisfied is rather more complex and the way in which it is handled is of central importance for the analysis. To best understand the nature of this constraint, an alternative interpretation of the optimisation is helpful.

Rather than viewing the government as choosing an income tax function, it can be seen as assigning to each household a pre-tax income–consumption pair. The additional constraint is then that each household must find it in their own interest to *choose* the pre-tax income–consumption pair that the government intends for them rather than a pair assigned to a different household. In other words, the intended pair be must utility-maximising for the household over the set of available pairs. Due to its nature, this is termed the *self-selection* constraint. The nature of the self-selection constraint will be discussed in 2.4.

It is worthwhile noting at this point some of the difficulties involved in the analysis of the general problem. The tax function is not restricted in form so that for most tax functions the budget constraints of the households will be non-linear. In those cases for which the budget set is non-convex, there may be non-uniqueness in the solution to the individual households' maximisations and the solutions need not form a convex set. These facts prevent the behaviour of the individuals being expressible by demand functions, in contrast to the commodity tax problem of chapter 4, and therefore introduce considerable mathematical complications. It is also the reason why the self-selection constraint must be made explicit in the analysis of income taxation but not in that of commodity taxation. Mirrlees (1986) provides a thorough discussion of these issues.

2.2 Basic structure

Turning now to further details of the economy, it is assumed that there are two commodities: a consumption good and a single labour service. A household's supply of the labour service is denoted by ℓ and consumption of the good by x. The supply of labour is limited by $0 \leq \ell \leq 1$ and $x \geq 0$. When the distinction becomes necessary, the demands of different households will be distinguished by an additional index. Each household is characterised by their skill level s. The value of s gives the relative effectiveness of the labour supplied per unit of time, so a high s household is more effective in production.

If a household of ability s supplies ℓ hours of labour, they provide a quantity $s\ell$ of *effective* labour. The analysis is simplified by assuming that the marginal product of labour is constant and, for a worker of ability s, is given by s. The total productivity of a worker during the ℓ hours at work is then equal to $s\ell$. Denote the supply of effective labour of a household with ability s by $z(s) \equiv s\ell(s)$. Normalising the price of the consumption good at 1, $z(s)$ is also the household's pre-tax income in units of consumption. Denoting the *tax function* by $T(z)$ and the *consumption function* by $c(z)$, a household that earns $z(s)$ units of income can consume

$$x(s) \leq c(z(s)) = z(s) - T(z(s)) \tag{5.1}$$

units of the consumption good.

The ability parameter, s, is continuously distributed throughout the population with support S, which may be finite with $S = [S_1, S_2]$ or infinite with $S = [0, \infty]$. Typically the finite support will be used, with the infinite support

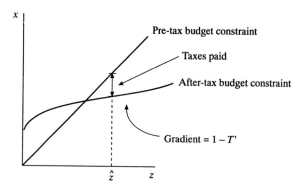

Figure 5.1   After-tax budget constraints

introduced where appropriate. The cumulative distribution of s is given by $\Gamma(s)$, so there are $\Gamma(s)$ households with ability s or less. The corresponding density function is denoted $\gamma(s)$.

All households have the same strictly concave utility function, an assumption that permits interpersonal comparability. This common utility function is denoted

$$U = U(x, \ell). \tag{5.2}$$

Each household makes the choice of labour supply and consumption demand to maximise utility subject to the budget constraint. Hence a household of ability s chooses $x(s)$, $\ell(s)$ to

$$\max U(x, \ell) \text{ subject to } x(s) \le c(s\ell(s)). \tag{5.3}$$

Define $u(s) = U(x(s), \ell(s))$ as the maximised level of utility at the optimal choices.

In the absence of income taxation, a household of ability s would face the budget constraint

$$x \le s\ell. \tag{5.4}$$

From (5.4) it can be seen that the budget constraint in (ℓ, x)-space differs with ability.

For the purposes of tax analysis, it is the budget constraint after tax, or equivalently the imposed consumption function, that is of interest. The analysis is simplified if all households face the same budget constraint and this can be achieved by setting the analysis in (z, x)-space. In this space, the pre-tax budget constraint is given by the 45° line for households of all abilities. With income taxation, the gradient of the consumption function (5.1) is equal to 1 minus the marginal rate of tax, where the marginal rate of tax, T', is defined as $\dfrac{\partial T(z)}{\partial z}$, and the vertical distance between the consumption function and the 45° line represents the total tax paid. This is illustrated in figure 5.1 for the consumer earning $\hat{z}$ units of income.

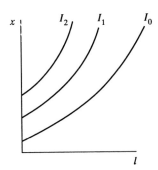

Figure 5.2   Preferences

2.3 The structure of utility

As already noted, the households have identical preferences over consumption and leisure. The utility function is continuously differentiable, strictly increasing in consumption and strictly decreasing in leisure. In addition, it satisfies

$$U_x > 0, \ U_\ell < 0, \ U_{xx} < 0,$$ (5.5)

and

$$U_\ell(x, \ell) \to -\infty \text{ as } \ell \to 1.$$ (5.6)

Condition (5.6) implies that each household will endeavour to avoid corner solutions with $\ell = 1$. It should be noted that the quantity of labour supplied is measured positively in order to conform with the literature. The indifference curves of the utility function are illustrated in figure 5.2, in which utility increases to the north west.

To allow preferences and the budget constraint to be depicted on the same diagram, the utility function can be written

$$U = U(x, \ell) = U\left(x, \frac{z}{s}\right) = u(x, z, s).$$ (5.7)

The indifference curves of $u(x, z, s)$, drawn in (z, x)-space are dependent upon the ability level of the household since it takes a high-ability household less labour time to achieve any given level of income. In fact, the indifference curves are constructed from those in (ℓ, x)-space by multiplying by the relevant value of s. This construction is shown in figure 5.3 for the single indifference curve I_0 and households of three different ability levels.

A number of the results below will require additional structure to be placed upon preferences. This involves relating the gradient of the indifference curves through a given consumption–income point for households of different abilities to the ability levels. The required assumption, termed *agent monotonicity*, was introduced by Mirrlees (1976) and named by Seade (1982).

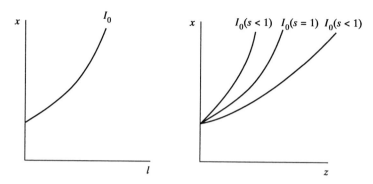

Figure 5.3   Translation of indifference curves

Agent monotonicity

The utility function (5.7) satisfies agent monotonicity if $-\dfrac{u_z}{u_x}$ is a decreasing function of s.

It should be noted that $\Phi \equiv -\dfrac{u_z}{u_x}$ is the marginal rate of substitution between consumption and pre-tax income and that agent monotonicity requires $\Phi_s \equiv \dfrac{\partial \Phi}{\partial s} < 0$. An equivalent definition of agent monotonicity is that $-\ell \dfrac{U_\ell}{U_x}$ is an increasing function of ℓ. This can be seen by noting that $-\dfrac{u_z}{u_x} = -\dfrac{U_\ell(x, z/s)}{s U_x(x, z/s)}$.

Calculating $\partial \left[-\ell \dfrac{U_\ell}{U_x} \right] \Big/ \partial \ell$ and Φ_s shows

$$\Phi_s = -\frac{1}{s^2} \frac{\partial \left[-\ell \dfrac{U_\ell}{U_x} \right]}{\partial \ell}. \tag{5.8}$$

Agent monotonicity is equivalent to the condition that, in the absence of taxation, consumption will increase as the wage rate increases. This equivalence is easily demonstrated by calculating the derivative in (5.8) and contrasting this to the rate of change of consumption with respect to the wage rate derived from the comparative statics of utility maximisation. A sufficient condition for agent monotonicity is that consumption is not inferior, i.e., it does not decrease as lump-sum income increases. This result can also be derived from the contrast between the comparative statics of utility maximisation and the derivative in (5.8).

Since the marginal rate of substitution is the gradient of the indifference curve, agent monotonicity implies that at any point in (z, x)-space the indifference curve of a household of ability s^1 passing through that point is steeper than the

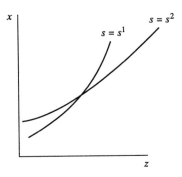

Figure 5.4   Agent monotonicity

curve of a household of ability s^2 if $s^2 > s^1$. This is illustrated in figure 5.4. The name for the condition follows from this monotonicity property that it imposes upon preferences. Agent monotonicity also implies that any two indifference curves of households of different abilities only cross once.

Theorem 5.1 shows that when the consumption function is a differentiable function of labour supply, agent monotonicity implies that gross income is an increasing function of ability. It is important to stress that no other assumption than differentiability is placed on the consumption function to derive this result.

Theorem 5.1 (Mirrlees)

When $\ell > 0$ and the sufficient conditions for utility maximisation are satisfied, $z(s)$ is an increasing function of s.

Proof

Writing the utility functions as $U(c(s\ell(s)), \ell(s))$, the first-order condition for utility maximisation, $U_\ell + U_x sc'(s\ell) = 0$, is equivalent to

$$\frac{U_\ell}{s\ell}\left[s\ell c'(s\ell) + \ell\frac{U_\ell}{U_x}\right] = 0, \tag{5.9}$$

or, since $\dfrac{U_\ell}{s\ell} < 0$

$$zc'(z) + \ell\frac{U_\ell}{U_x} = 0. \tag{5.10}$$

The second-order condition then becomes

$$\frac{\partial\left[zc'(z) + \ell\dfrac{U_\ell}{U_x}\right]}{\partial z} \leq 0. \tag{5.11}$$

The total differential of the first-order condition (5.10) with respect to s is given by

$$\frac{\partial\left[zc'(z)+\ell\dfrac{U_\ell}{U_x}\right]}{\partial z}z'(s)-\frac{\partial\left[\ell\dfrac{U_\ell}{U_x}\right]}{\partial\ell}\frac{z}{s^2}=0. \qquad (5.12)$$

Since agent monotonicity implies $-\dfrac{\partial\left[\ell\dfrac{U_\ell}{U_x}\right]}{\partial\ell}$ is negative, it follows from the second-order condition (5.11) that $z'(s)>0$.

This theorem can be reinterpreted as saying that if agent monotonicity holds and the implemented tax function has pre-tax income increasing with ability, then the second-order condition (5.11) for utility maximisation must hold. In other words, with agent monotonicity, the second-order condition and the condition that $z'(s)\geq0$ are equivalent. The importance of the condition $z'(s)\geq0$ will appear again in the discussion of self-selection.

2.4 Self-selection

In choosing the optimal tax function, it must be the case that each household will find it in their interest to choose the income–consumption pair that the government intends them to select. This self-selection constraint is now introduced formally and a convenient representation is derived.

Let $x(s)$ and $z(s)$ now represent the consumption and income levels that the government intends a household of ability s to choose. The household of ability s will choose $(x(s),z(s))$ provided that this pair generate at least as much utility as any other choice. This condition must apply to all consumption–income pairs and to all households. Written using (5.7) the self-selection constraint is as follows.

Self-selection

The self-selection constraint is satisfied if $u(x(s),z(s),s)\geq u(x(s'),z(s'),s)$ for all s,s'.

It should be noted that the utility arising from the pair $(x(s),z(s))$ is compared with that from all other possible combinations. It is this that leads to some difficulties in applying the self-selection constraint. Since the economy has a continuum of ability levels, there is an uncountable infinity of self-selection constraints for each household when expressed in the form above. Clearly, such a set of constraints cannot be easily be incorporated as a restriction on a maximisation. An important aspect of the analysis is to construct an alternative representation of the self-selection constraint that can be more easily accommodated into a maximisation problem.

In the case of linear taxation, each household pays (or receives) a fixed lump sum and the marginal rate of tax on income is constant. The imposed consumption function is linear and each household faces a convex budget set. This structure eliminates the requirement to consider the self-selection constraints since the behaviour of the household can be determined as a function of the two parameters that describe the tax function: the lump-sum payment and the marginal rate of tax. The derivation of the optimal linear income tax is therefore considerably simpler than that of the non-linear tax and resembles the analysis of commodity taxation.

When non-linear taxation is considered, the self-selection constraints must be included. This is achieved by noting that the satisfaction of the self-selection constraint is equivalent to achieving the minimum of a certain minimisation problem. If the sufficient conditions for the minimisation are satisfied by the allocation resulting from the tax function, then the self-selection constraint is satisfied.

To derive the required minimisation problem, let $u(s) = u(x(s), z(s), s)$ represent the maximised level of utility for a consumer of ability s resulting from (5.3). Now note that

$$0 = u(s) - u(x(s), z(s), s) \leq u(s') - u(x(s), z(s), s'),$$ (5.13)

so that $s' = s$ minimises $u(s') - u(x(s), z(s), s')$. Hence

$$u'(s) = u_s(x(s), z(s), s).$$ (5.14)

From the definition of $u(s)$ it follows that

$$u_x x'(s) + u_z z'(s) = 0,$$ (5.15)

is equivalent to (5.14). Condition (5.14), or equivalently (5.15), is the necessary condition (or first-order condition) for the self-selection constraint to be satisfied. Its advantage over the direct formulation of self-selection is that it provides a single condition for each value of s rather than an uncountable infinity of conditions.

The second-order condition for the self-selection constraint to be satisfied is found from the second derivative of $u(s') - u(x(s), z(s), s')$ with respect to s' to be

$$u''(s) - u_{ss}(x(s), z(s), s) \geq 0.$$ (5.16)

Again using the definition of $u(s)$

$$u''(s) = u_{sx} x'(s) + u_{sz} z'(s) + u_{ss},$$ (5.17)

which gives, by using (5.16)

$$u_{sx} x'(s) + u_{sz} z'(s) \geq 0.$$ (5.18)

Eliminating $x'(s)$ using (5.15) provides the final condition

$$\left[u_{sz} - u_{sx} \frac{u_z}{u_x} \right] z'(s) = -\frac{\Phi_s}{u_x} z'(s) \geq 0,$$ (5.19)

where Φ_s is the marginal rate of substitution introduced in the discussion of agent monotonicity. With agent monotonicity $\Phi_s < 0$, so that satisfaction of the second-order condition for self-selection is equivalent to $z'(s) \geq 0$. Any tax function that leads to an outcome satisfying (5.15) and $z'(s) \geq 0$ will therefore satisfy the self-selection constraint.

It is also worth noting a further result that can be derived directly from the conditions already stated. Since $u_x > 0$ and $u_\ell < 0$, $z'(s) \geq 0$ implies from (5.15) that any tax function satisfying the self-selection constraint must result in $x'(s) \geq 0$. The self-selection constraint therefore requires both pre-tax income and consumption to be non-decreasing with s.

3 CHARACTERISATION OF OPTIMAL TAX FUNCTION

The aim of the theoretical analysis is to provide a characterisation of the properties that the optimal tax function will have, given the specification and assumptions adopted. It will clearly not be possible to calculate the function without precisely stating the functional forms of utility, production and skill distribution. What will be achieved is the derivation of a set of restrictions that the optimal function must satisfy. This is undertaken firstly for the case where the marginal rate of tax is assumed constant. As already noted, this implies convexity of the individual budget set and allows behaviour to be expressible via demand functions which considerably simplifies the resulting analysis. The general problem is then considered. Results are derived using both the necessary conditions for the maximisation of social welfare and directly using a diagrammatic framework.

3.1 The general problem

Using the individual demand and supply functions and integrating over the population, it is possible to define total effective labour supply, Z, by

$$Z = \int_0^\infty z(s)\gamma(s)ds, \tag{5.20}$$

and aggregate demand, X, where

$$X = \int_0^\infty x(s)\gamma(s)ds. \tag{5.21}$$

The optimal tax function is then chosen to maximise social welfare, where welfare is given by the Bergson–Samuelson function

$$W = \int_{0}^{\infty} W(u(s))\gamma(s)ds, \qquad (5.22)$$

with $W'' \le 0$.

There are two constraints placed upon the maximisation of (5.22). The first is that the chosen allocation must be productively feasible. This requirement can be denoted in terms of quantities by

$$X \le F(Z), \qquad (5.23)$$

where F is the production function for the economy. This definition of productive feasibility can incorporate the government revenue requirement, expressed as a quantity of labour consumed by the government z^G, by noting that (5.23) can be written $X \le \hat{F}(Z - z^G) = F(Z)$. Alternatively, the government revenue constraint can be used in place of the production constraint to express the restriction in value terms. Denoting the level of revenue required by R, $R \equiv z^G$, the revenue constraint can be written

$$R \ge \int_{0}^{\infty} [z(s) - x(s)]\gamma(s)ds. \qquad (5.24)$$

The second constraint upon the optimisation is that it must satisfy the self-selection constraint. This has already been described in 2.4.

3.2 Linear taxation

The complexity of the general model of income taxation has led to considerable interest in the restricted case of linear taxation. With linear taxation the marginal rate of tax is constant and there is an identical lump-sum tax or subsidy for all households. The advantages of this restriction is that it ensures that the budget sets of all households are convex so that optimal choices will be unique when preferences are strictly convex. In addition, the tax system is described by just two parameters: the marginal tax rate and the lump-sum subsidy. The choice of optimal policy therefore corresponds to a standard maximisation problem. In addition, the linear tax structure corresponds to proposals for *negative income tax* schemes, in which all households below a given income level receive a subsidy from the tax system, and to the tax reform proposals of a number of countries that have reduced the number of tax rate bands.

Using the notation set out above, under a linear tax system a household with ability s supplying ℓ units of labour will pay tax of amount

$$T(s\ell) = -\tau + ts\ell, \qquad (5.25)$$

where t is the marginal rate of tax and τ is a lump-sum subsidy if positive and a tax if negative. Denoting $[1 - t]$ by ζ, the consumption function of the household is

$$x = \tau + \zeta s \ell. \tag{5.26}$$

Each household chooses consumption and labour supply to maximise utility subject to (5.26), with utility represented by (5.2). Assuming the solution to the individual maximisation is interior, the first-order conditions can be reduced to

$$-\frac{U_\ell}{U_x} = \zeta s. \tag{5.27}$$

Combined with the consumption function (5.26), (5.27) implies labour supply and consumption demand functions of the form

$$\ell = \ell(\zeta, \tau, s), x = \tau + \zeta s \ell(\zeta, \tau, s). \tag{5.28}$$

Substituted into the utility function, these determine the indirect utility function

$$U = U(\tau + \zeta s \ell(\zeta, \tau, s), \ell(\zeta, \tau, s)) = V(\zeta, \tau, s), \tag{5.29}$$

with

$$\frac{\partial V}{\partial \tau} = U_x, \frac{\partial V}{\partial \zeta} = U_x s \ell, \tag{5.30}$$

where $\dfrac{\partial V}{\partial \tau}$ is equal to the marginal utility of income.

The government's optimisation problem is to choose the parameters of the tax system to maximise social welfare subject to raising the required revenue, R. Using (5.26) and (5.29), the optimisation can be expressed as

$$\max_{\{\tau, \zeta\}} \int_0^\infty W(V(\zeta, \tau, s)) \gamma(s) ds, \tag{5.31}$$

subject to

$$\int_0^\infty [-\tau + [1 - \zeta] s \ell(\zeta, \tau, s)] \gamma(s) ds = R. \tag{5.32}$$

Using (5.30) and defining the social marginal utility of income for a household of ability s by

$$\beta(s) = W'(V(\zeta, \tau, s)) \frac{\partial V(\zeta, \tau, s)}{\partial \tau}, \tag{5.33}$$

the necessary conditions for the choice of τ and ζ respectively are

$$\int_0^\infty \beta \gamma(s) ds = \lambda \left[H - \int_0^\infty [1 - \zeta] \frac{\partial z}{\partial \tau} \gamma(s) ds \right], \tag{5.34}$$

and

$$\int_0^\infty \beta z\gamma(s)ds = \lambda \int_0^\infty \left[z - [1-\zeta]\frac{\partial z}{\partial \zeta} \right] \gamma(s)ds, \qquad (5.35)$$

where H is the population size, $H = \int_0^\infty \gamma(s)ds$.

The first use of these necessary conditions is to derive a simple expression for the optimal marginal tax rate, t, that is due to Tuomala (1985). To do this, divide (5.35) by (5.34) and denote by a bar terms of the form x/H. This gives

$$\frac{\int_0^\infty \beta z\gamma(s)ds}{\int_0^\infty \beta\gamma(s)ds} = \frac{\bar{z} - \int_0^\infty [1-\zeta]\frac{\overline{\partial z}}{\partial \zeta}\gamma(s)ds}{1 - \int_0^\infty [1-\zeta]\frac{\overline{\partial z}}{\partial \tau}\gamma(s)ds}. \qquad (5.36)$$

The term on the left-hand side of (5.36) is now denoted by $z(\beta)$ and can be interpreted as the welfare-weighted average labour supply. From totally differentiating the government revenue constraint whilst holding R constant, it can be found that

$$\frac{d\tau}{d\zeta}\bigg|_{Rconst} = \frac{-\bar{z} + \int_0^\infty [1-\zeta]\frac{\overline{\partial z}}{\partial \zeta}\gamma(s)ds}{1 - \int_0^\infty [1-\zeta]\frac{\overline{\partial z}}{\partial \tau}\gamma(s)ds}. \qquad (5.37)$$

Hence from (5.36) and (5.37)

$$z(\beta) = -\frac{d\tau}{d\zeta}\bigg|_{Rconst}. \qquad (5.38)$$

Since averaging over the population must give $\bar{z} = \bar{z}(\tau, \zeta)$, it follows from (5.38) that, holding revenue constant

$$\frac{d\bar{z}}{d\zeta}\bigg|_{Rconst} = \frac{d\bar{z}}{d\zeta} + \frac{d\bar{z}}{d\tau}\frac{d\tau}{d\zeta}\bigg|_{Rconst} = \frac{d\bar{z}}{d\zeta} - \frac{d\bar{z}}{d\tau}z(\beta). \qquad (5.39)$$

Therefore (5.36) can be written in the form

$$z(\beta) - \bar{z} = [1-\zeta]\left[\frac{d\bar{z}}{d\tau}z(\beta) - \frac{d\bar{z}}{d\zeta}\right] = -t\frac{d\bar{z}}{d\zeta}\bigg|_{Rconst}, \qquad (5.40)$$

or, recalling that $t = 1 - \zeta$,

$$t = \frac{\bar{z} - z(\beta)}{-\dfrac{d\bar{z}}{dt}\bigg|_{Rconst}}, \tag{5.41}$$

where the derivative is taken with revenue constant.

Although the tax rule in (5.41) only provides an implicit expression for t, it can be used to assess the effects of various parametric changes. If it is assumed that $\bar{z} - z(\beta)$ is positive and $\dfrac{\partial z}{\partial t}\bigg|_{Rconst}$ negative, then an increase in the disincentive effect of taxation $\left(\text{a rise in } \dfrac{\partial z}{\partial t}\bigg|_{Rconst}\right)$ would reduce the optimal tax rate. A reduction in the optimal tax would also occur, with β a decreasing function of s and z an increasing function of s, if the welfare weights were increased on the high-s households so that equity was given less weight. The effect of other variations can be addressed by similar reasoning.

From the first-order conditions it is also possible to provide general results on the sign of the tax rates. The simplest result of this form is due to Romer (1976) and Sheshinski (1972b) and is stated as theorem 5.2.

Theorem 5.2 (Sheshinski/Romer)

If (i) $\dfrac{\partial z}{\partial \tau} < 0$, *(ii)* $\dfrac{\partial z}{\partial \zeta} \geq 0$ *and* $R = 0$, *then* $t > 0$ *and* $\tau < 0$.

Proof

It is clear from (5.34) and (5.33) that $\lambda > 0$ and that $\zeta > 0$ (or else x, $\ell = 0$ for all s). Now assume that $\zeta > 1$. Then (5.34) and (i) imply that

$$\int_0^\infty [\beta - \lambda]\gamma(s)ds \leq 0. \tag{5.42}$$

Now since z is an increasing function of s in order that the second-order condition for utility maximisation is satisfied and $\beta - \lambda$ is a decreasing function

$$\int_0^\infty [\beta - \lambda]z(s)\gamma(s)ds < 0. \tag{5.43}$$

From (5.35) and (ii), however, inequality (5.43) cannot be satisfied if $\zeta \geq 1$. Hence $\zeta < 1$ which implies that the marginal tax rate $t > 0$. The negativity of τ then follows from the zero revenue condition.

The assumptions of this theorem have been weakened by Hellwig (1986) to those of agent monotonicity and non-inferiority of leisure.

The linear model has also been used to find upper bounds upon the optimal tax rate. Hellwig (1986) and Svensson and Weibull (1986) show that the optimal rate is bounded above by the optimal tax under a maxi–min social welfare function and this rate is bounded by the revenue-maximising tax rate. Svensson and Weibull (1986) also show that the upper bound given by the revenue-maximising tax rate holds under a Pareto ordering of states alone. Finally, Helpman and Sadka (1978) consider some comparative statics effects of changes in parameters. An increase in the concavity of $W(\cdot)$ is shown to raise the marginal rate of tax (as suggested after (5.41)). In contrast, the effect of a mean-preserving increase in the spread of the skill distribution cannot be unambiguously signed.

3.3 Non-linear taxation

With non-linear taxation the self-selection constraint must be taken fully into account. As shown in 2.4 this consists of (5.14) (the first-order condition) and $z'(s) \geq 0$ (the second-order condition). Most analyses of optimal income taxation, such as Mirrlees (1971) and Seade (1977), have incorporated only the first-order condition and adopt what has become known as the *first-order approach*. As shown in Mirrlees (1986) this may lead to incorrect results. In fact, Ebert (1992) presents an example in which the solution with only the first-order condition included leads to a consumption function with an interval over which it is decreasing. In contrast Brito and Oakland (1977) and Ebert (1992) impose both the first- and second-order conditions as constraints upon the maximisation and so avoid these difficulties. Given these observations, the analysis below will adopt the *second-order approach* and impose both the first-order condition and the constraint $z'(s) \geq 0$ upon the optimisation.

3.3.1 Formal optimisation

The maximisation problem has been analysed in two distinct ways. The analysis of Seade (1977) formulated the maximisation in terms of the calculus of variations and employed as choice variables the functions $x(s)$ and $\ell(s)$. In contrast, Mirrlees (1971) and Ebert (1992) employ a formulation based on Pontryagin's maximum principle. Naturally, there are slight differences between the two, but the final characterisation is the same. The optimal structure of income taxation is characterised here by applying Pontryagin's maximum principle, a good introduction to which is given in Intriligator (1971). In this framework, the level of utility, $u(s)$, pre-tax income, $z(s)$ and the tax payments of households of ability s or less, given by

$$R(s) = \int_{S_1}^{s} [z(s') - x(s')]\gamma(s')ds', \tag{5.44}$$

are taken as state variables and the derivative of gross income, $\eta(s) \equiv \dfrac{dz}{ds}$, is taken as the control variable. The level of consumption can then be found by solving $u(s) = u(x(s), z(s), s)$.

Adopting a utilitarian objective, the control variable is chosen to maximise

$$\int_{S_1}^{S_2} u(s)\gamma(s)ds, \tag{5.45}$$

subject to

$$\frac{dR}{ds} = [z(s) - x(s)]\gamma(s), \tag{5.46}$$

$$R(S_1) = R(S_2) = 0, \tag{5.47}$$

$$\frac{du}{ds} = u_s(x(s), z(s), s), \tag{5.48}$$

$$\frac{dz}{ds} = \eta(s), \tag{5.49}$$

$$\theta\left(\frac{dz}{ds}\right) = \theta(\eta(s)) \geq 0. \tag{5.50}$$

The revenue constraint is captured by (5.46) and (5.47). To simplify, it is assumed that zero revenue is to be collected and, from (5.44), this is reflected in the upper end-point condition in (5.47). The rate of change in revenue, (5.46), is derived directly from (5.44). The self-selection constraint is represented by (5.48)–(5.50). The first-order condition (5.14) is written as (5.48) and the second-order condition is included as (5.49) and (5.50). Condition (5.49) defines the rate of change of the state variable $z(s)$. The interpretation of (5.50) is that the straightforward inclusion of the second-order condition $\eta(s) \geq 0$ would lead to singularity when combined with (5.49). The second-order condition is therefore transformed to (5.50) where the differentiable function $\theta(\eta(s))$ satisfies $\theta(0) = 0$ and $\theta'(\eta) > 0$.

Introducing the adjoint variables $\lambda(s)$, $\mu(s)$, $v(s)$ and $\kappa(s)$, the Hamiltonian for the optimisation is

$$H = u(s)\gamma(s) + \lambda(s)[z(s) - x(s)]\gamma(s) + \mu(s)u_s(x(s), z(s), s) + v(s)\eta(s) + \kappa(s)\theta(s), \tag{5.51}$$

and the necessary conditions are

$$\frac{dH}{d\eta}=v+\kappa\theta'(\eta)=0,\tag{5.52}$$

$$\frac{dH}{dz}=\lambda\frac{\partial\big[[z(s)-x(s)]\gamma(s)\big]}{\partial z}+\mu\frac{\partial u_s(x(s),z(s),s)}{\partial z}=-v',\tag{5.53}$$

$$\frac{dH}{du}=\gamma(s)+\lambda\frac{\partial\big[[z(s)-x(s)]\gamma(s)\big]}{\partial u}+\mu\frac{\partial u_s(x(s),z(s),s)}{\partial u}=-\mu',\tag{5.54}$$

$$\frac{dH}{dR}=-\lambda'=0,\tag{5.55}$$

$$\kappa\frac{dz}{ds}=0,\ \kappa\geq0,\tag{5.56}$$

with transversality conditions

$$\mu(S_1)=\mu(S_2)=0,\ v(S_1)=v(S_2)=0.\tag{5.57}$$

To derive the form of these conditions that will be used below, note that from the identity $u(s)=u(x(s),z(s),s)$ it follows that

$$\frac{\partial x}{\partial z}=-\frac{u_x}{u_z}=\Phi,\tag{5.58}$$

and

$$\frac{\partial x}{\partial u}=\frac{1}{u_x}.\tag{5.59}$$

In addition

$$\frac{\partial u_s(x(s),z(s),s)}{\partial z}=u_{sx}\frac{\partial x}{\partial z}+u_z=-u_x\Phi_s,\tag{5.60}$$

and

$$\frac{\partial u_s(x(s),z(s),s)}{\partial u}=u_{sx}\frac{\partial x}{\partial u}=\frac{u_{sx}}{u_x}.\tag{5.61}$$

Now denoting $\phi(s)=\kappa(s)\theta'(\eta(s))$, (5.52)–(5.57) can be given the alternative formulation

$$-\mu u_x\Phi_s+\lambda[1-\Phi]\gamma-\phi'=0,\tag{5.62}$$

$$\mu'+\mu\frac{u_{sx}}{u_x}+\left[1-\frac{\lambda}{u_x}\right]\gamma=0,\tag{5.63}$$

$$\phi\frac{dz}{ds}=0,\ \phi\geq0,\tag{5.64}$$

$$\mu(S_1)=\mu(S_2)=0,\ \phi(S_1)=\phi(S_2)=0,\tag{5.65}$$

where the second part of (5.65) follows from (5.52).

The interpretation of these necessary conditions is best undertaken by considering separately the case in which ϕ is zero for all s and that in which it is positive for some s. In the first case, since ϕ is zero the second-order condition for the satisfaction of the self-selection constraint is not binding and pre-tax income is a strictly increasing function of ability. When this is true, the results derived from the first-order approach of Mirrlees (1971) and Seade (1977) are identical to those of the second-order approach. In particular, (5.64) and the second part of (5.65) become irrelevant, and ϕ' is eliminated from (5.62). The two remaining equations are then the standard conditions of the first-order approach describing the optimal tax function.

Now consider the case where there are some values of s for which ϕ is not zero. For such $s, z' = 0$. Hence if ϕ is positive over the interval $[s_0, s_1]$, all households with abilities falling in that interval earn the same pre-tax income. These households are therefore *bunched* at a single income level. Furthermore, because of (5.15), they must also have the same level of consumption. A point where bunching occurs can be identified by a kink in the consumption function. It is also interesting to note that although pre-tax income and consumption are identical, utility is increasing with s over the bunched households since those with higher s have to undertake less work to obtain the common income level.

3.3.2 Characterisation of the optimal tax function

The first theorem on the structure of the optimal tax function is concerned with demonstrating that if any households are unemployed at the optimum, then it will be the lowest ability households.

Theorem 5.3 (Mirrlees)

If there exists an ability level $s_0 \in S$ such that $\ell(s_0) = 0$, then $\ell(s) = 0$ for any $s < s_0$.

Proof

Assume $\ell(s_0) = 0$ and that there is some s, with $s < s_0$, such that $\ell(s) > 0$. It follows that

$$U\big(c(s\ell(s)), \ell(s)\big) < U\left(c\left(s_0 \frac{s}{s_0}\ell(s)\right), \frac{s}{s_0}\ell(s)\right), \tag{5.66}$$

since $s/s_0 < 1$ and therefore the right-hand side of (5.66) represents the utility derived with less labour supply but retaining the same level of consumption. In addition

$$U\left(c\left(s_0 \frac{s}{s_0}\ell(s)\right), \frac{s}{s_0}\ell(s)\right) < U\big(c(s_0\ell(s_0)), \ell(s_0)\big), \tag{5.67}$$

since $\ell(s_0)$ is utility maximising for the household of ability s_0. Hence if $\ell(s) > 0$, combining these inequalities gives

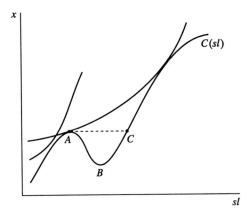

Figure 5.5   A tax rate greater than 100 per cent

$$u(s) < u(s_0).$$ (5.68)

However, if $\ell(s) = 0$, it is clear that

$$u(s) = u(s_0).$$ (5.69)

Therefore $\ell(s) > 0$ is not utility maximising and $\ell(s) = 0$ for $s \leq s_0$.

Theorem 5.3 is an interesting result since it shows, even without specifying the tax function, that the optimal tax system may generate unemployment in the sense that it results in low ability households choosing to do no work. As these households are productive whenever their ability level is non-zero, and output would increase if they did work, this carries important implications for the relation between optimal taxes and the achievement of maximum potential output.

The second result demonstrates that a marginal tax rate in excess of 100 per cent will never be optimal.

Theorem 5.4 (Mirrlees)

The consumption function $c(z)$ will be increasing in z.

Proof

Self-selection requires that $u_x x' + u_z z' = 0$ and $z' \geq 0$, therefore $x' \geq 0$. By definition, $x(s) = c(z(s))$ so that $x' = c' z'$. Hence $c' \geq 0$. Since $c(z) = z - T(z)$, the fact that $c' \geq 0$ implies that $c' = 1 - T' \geq 0 \Leftrightarrow T' \leq 1$, so the marginal tax rate is always less than or equal to 1.

To illustrate the reasoning behind theorem 5.4, consider a consumption function that has a section with gradient less than zero, that is a marginal tax rate greater than 100 per cent. Such a consumption function is shown in figure 5.5 with the decreasing section $A - B$. Because the indifference curves represent convex preferences, no household will locate between A and C, although with Leontief indifference curves there may be some households indifferent between A and C, and the consumption function with the flat section joining A and C produces an identical final allocation. Therefore downward sloping sections are redundant and there is no gain from a consumption function that has a decreasing section.

The next theorem proves that the marginal rate of tax must always be non-negative. The theorem was first proved for an additively separable utility function by Mirrlees (1971) and for a linear tax system by Sadka (1976). The generalisation of the theorem to non-linear taxes and non-separable utility was given in Seade (1982). The version of the theorem proved here relies upon strong assumptions; in particular it is assumed that there is no bunching. An extension of the theorem to take account of the possibility of bunching is contained in Ebert (1992). The theorem can also be extended to prove that the marginal tax rate must be strictly positive except for the households with the highest and lowest abilities, again see Ebert (1992).

To develop the theorem it is first necessary to note that when there is no bunching $\phi' = 0$ so that (5.62) can be written as

$$1 - \Phi = \frac{\mu u_x \Phi_s}{\lambda \gamma}. \tag{5.70}$$

Under the adopted normalisation, $1 - \Phi(s)$ is the marginal tax rate facing the household of ability s: the pre-tax price of consumption relative to income is 1 and $\Phi(s)$, being the post-tax marginal rate of substitution, is equal to post-tax relative prices. Given that λ will be proved to be positive below, the sign of the marginal rate of tax is then the opposite of that of μ. To establish that the tax is non-negative, it is therefore necessary to establish that μ is non-positive. This is the basis of the proof of the following theorem.

Theorem 5.5 (Seade)

Assuming agent monotonicity, if leisure is not an inferior good and $u_{zx} \geq 0$ then the marginal tax rate is positive.

Proof

It is first shown that non-inferiority of leisure and $u_{zx} \geq 0$ implies that u_x is a decreasing function of s. This follows since

$$\frac{du_x}{ds} = u_{xx} x' + u_{xz} z' + u_{xs}$$

$$= x' \left[u_{xx} - \frac{u_x u_{xz}}{u_z} \right] + u_{xs}, \tag{5.71}$$

where the second equality follows from the first-order condition (5.15). Non-inferiority of leisure implies $u_{xx} - \dfrac{u_x u_{xz}}{u_z} \leq 0$ and, since $u_{xs} = -\dfrac{z u_{xz}}{s}$, the assumption

that $u_{zx} \geq 0$ (and $u_{xx} < 0$) results in $\dfrac{du_x}{ds} \leq 0$.

Solving the differential equation (5.63) gives

$$\mu(s) = \int_s^{S_2} \left[1 - \frac{\lambda}{u_x} \right] \gamma(s') \exp \left[\int_s^{s'} \frac{u_{sx}}{u_x} ds'' \right] ds'. \tag{5.72}$$

Since the transversality conditions require $\mu(S_1) = \mu(S_2) = 0$ and $u_x > 0$, it follows that $\lambda > 0$. In addition, (5.55) implies that λ is a constant. Combining these observations, $\left[1 - \dfrac{\lambda}{u_x} \right]$ cannot be always positive or always negative. In fact, it must be negative for low values of s and positive for high values. This implies that $\mu(s)$ is decreasing for s less than some $\bar{s}$ and increasing for s greater than $\bar{s}$. Since $\mu(0) = 0$, $\mu(s)$ is then seen to be non-positive for all s, which completes the proof when combined with (5.70).

The theorems stated to this point have been concerned with the general structure of the tax function, rather than with particular properties. One particularly relevant property of an income tax function is progressivity. Although there are several possible definitions of progressivity, see the discussion in Lambert (1989), the one that is adopted here is to say the tax system is progressive if it has a marginal rate that increases with income. This requirement is equivalent to the condition

$$T'' \geq 0. \tag{5.73}$$

Progressivity is a feature that almost all actual income tax systems possess, an observation that illustrates the importance of investigating whether this property is always optimal.

The following theorem has obvious implications for the issue of progressivity of the tax function. It is proved both by a direct argument and by appeal to the necessary condition in (5.70).

Theorem 5.6 (Sadka/Seade)

Let the upper bound on ability, S_2, be finite. Then the marginal rate of tax must be 0 for a household of ability S_2.

Proof

Let ABC in figure 5.6 be the initial graph of $c(z) = z - T(z)$ and HBE be an indifference curve of a household with ability S_2. Since it is assumed that $T' > 0$ for ABC, it follows $c' < 1$, hence the gradient of HBE is < 1 at B. Now define a new tax T_1 as follows

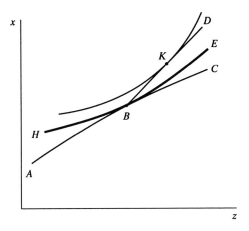

Figure 5.6   Zero rate at the top

$$T_1(z) = T(z) \text{ for } z \leq z(S_2, T),$$ (5.74)

and

$$T_1(z) = T(z(S_2, T)) \text{ all } z \geq z(S_2, T).$$ (5.75)

Under the new tax T_1, the tax payment is held constant above income level $z(S_2, T)$.

The graph of $c_1(z) = z - T_1(z)$ is then *ABD* where the section *BD* has a zero marginal rate. A household of ability S_2 will move to *K* and is evidently better off. Revenue has also not changed. Therefore this must represent an improvement in welfare and $T'(S_2) > 0$ cannot be optimal.

The alternative proof is to note that the upper bound on ability implies that $\gamma(S_2) > 0$ and the transversality condition implies $\mu(S_2) = 0$. Therefore, from (5.62),

$$1 - \Phi = \frac{\phi'}{\lambda \gamma}.$$ (5.76)

However, (5.64) and (5.65) imply ϕ' is non-positive at S_2, giving $1 - \Phi \leq 0$ at S_2. Combining this inequality with theorem 5.5, it follows that $1 - \Phi(S_2) = 0$ and the theorem is proved.

For this argument to work in the case of the infinite support, where it is natural to assume $\lim_{s \to \infty} \gamma(s) = 0$, further restrictions are necessary in order to evaluate the limiting tax rate. Details of these can be found in Seade (1977).

Theorem 5.6 is purely local in the sense that it relates only to the household of highest ability and, by continuity, to the households of similar ability. The next result of Seade's is concerned with extending the improvement further down the ability scale.

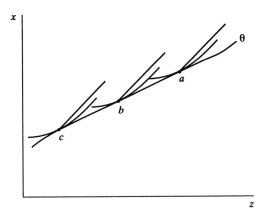

Figure 5.7   Initial schedule

Theorem 5.7 (Seade)

For a population with bounded ability, any income tax schedule with a positive marginal rate at the top of the scale can be replaced by one that leaves all households better off, inducing them to earn more income but paying the same tax.

Proof

Start with the initial schedule θ in figure 5.7 and the optimal choices, illustrated for households of three different abilities, given by the tangency points a, b and c.

It is first noted, as before, that any movement along a 45° line does not affect tax revenue since $T' = 0$ and no net payments are made out of the extra income. Further, any relocation locally up the relevant line 45° for each household will improve welfare. Hence the tax system $\hat{\theta}$ drawn in figure 5.8 improves welfare.

The tax function $\hat{\theta}$ is constructed by first selecting $\hat{a}$ for the household of highest ability and then moving the tax function around their indifference curve and attempting to cross the 45° line through b (the location of the household with second highest ability) at the highest point, then continuing downwards. This will obviously lead to a general improvement in welfare.

Such improvements can be continued until the schedule θ^* in the figure 5.9 is reached.

Point a^* obviously represents the maximum increase in utility possible without altering the level of the tax payment. The resulting schedule is then constructed by working left from a^*.

The previous two results have been concerned with the shape of the tax schedule primarily at the top end of the ability scale. The next result of this section is due to Seade (1977) and determines the tax rate facing the lowest ability household under the assumption that there is no bunching. This assumption guarantees

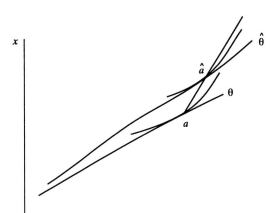

Figure 5.8   Pareto-improving schedule

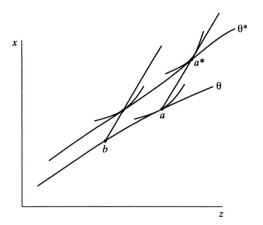

Figure 5.9   Final schedule

that the bottom of the tax function will only apply to the lowest ability household and that they will be at an interior solution rather than at a corner.

Theorem 5.8 (Seade)

If there is no bunching at the lowest income, the optimal marginal rate for the household of lowest ability is zero.

Proof

From the no-bunching condition the lowest tax rate only applies to the person of lowest ability. Applying the transversality condition (5.65) and (5.70) then gives the result.

Combining theorems 5.6 and 5.8 it is clear that, when there is no bunching at the lowest income, the tax function cannot be progressive throughout since it must begin with a zero rate and end with a zero rate. When bunching does occur at the lowest income, the outcome is different. This is summarised in theorem 5.9.

Theorem 5.9 (Ebert)

If there is bunching at the lowest income, the marginal rate of tax is strictly positive at the end of the bunching interval.

Proof

From (5.62) and (5.65) at $s = S_1$

$$\lambda[1 - \Phi(S_1)]\gamma(S_1) = \mu(S_1)u_x\Phi_s + \phi'(S_1) = 0. \tag{5.77}$$

With bunching at the lowest income, $x(s)$ and $z(s)$ are constant over some interval. Hence over this interval

$$\frac{d[1 - \Phi(s)]}{ds} = -\Phi_x x' - \Phi_z z' - \Phi_s < 0, \tag{5.78}$$

since $x' = z' = 0$. Therefore $1 - \Phi(s)$ must be positive at the end of this interval.

The same argument can be used to prove that there is no bunching at the highest income level.

Theorem 5.10 (Ebert)

There is no bunching at the highest income level.

Proof

Theorem 5.8 has already shown that the marginal tax rate on the highest income is zero. Over the interval of bunching, $1 - \Phi(s)$ must increase as s decreases and therefore becomes negative for some $s < S_2$. This contradicts theorem 5.6.

3.3.3 Summary

The major theoretical results for the analysis of the optimal non-linear tax have now been derived. These show that the optimal marginal rate of taxation must lie between 0 and 1. At the highest and lowest abilities, the tax rate must be zero. The latter finding shows that the optimal tax function cannot be progressive; a result that runs counter to observed income tax functions. It may also be optimal to force some households to choose to undertake no labour. If this is the case, it is the lowest ability households that will not work. Finally, pre-tax income and consumption must both be increasing functions of ability. To obtain further details of the structure of optimal taxes, it is necessary to consider numerical analyses.

4 NUMERICAL RESULTS

The standard analysis of optimal income taxation has been introduced above and a number of results have been derived that provide some characterisation of the shape of the tax schedule. It has been seen that the marginal rate is between 0 and 1 but as yet no idea has been developed, except for the endpoints, of how close it should be to either. Similarly, although equity considerations are expected to raise the marginal rate, this has not been demonstrated formally nor has consideration been given to how efficiency criteria, particularly the effect of taxation upon labour supply, affects the choice of tax schedule. Due to the analytical complexity of the non-linear model, these questions are best addressed via numerical analysis.

4.1 Simulations

To generate numerical results, Mirrlees (1971) assumed that the social welfare function took the form

$$W = \int_0^\infty \frac{1}{v} e^{-vU} \gamma(s)ds, \; v > 0, = \int_0^\infty U\gamma(s)ds, \; v = 0. \tag{5.79}$$

The form of (5.79) permits parametric variations of the form of the social welfare function by changes in v. Higher values of v represent greater concern for equity, with $v = 0$ representing the utilitarian case. The individual utility function was assumed to be Cobb–Douglas

$$U = \log x + \log[1 - \ell] \tag{5.80}$$

and the skill distribution log-normal

$$\gamma(s) = \frac{1}{s} \exp\left[-\frac{[\log(s+1)]^2}{2} \right], \tag{5.81}$$

with a standard deviation, σ, of 0.39. This value of the standard deviation was derived from data on the distribution of income given in Lydall (1968). There is thus an implicit assumption that the skill distribution can be inferred directly from an observed income distribution. Furthermore, this assumption implies that the skill distribution is unbounded. A selection of the numerical results of Mirrlees (1971) are given in table 5.1.

   The most important feature of the results in tables 5.1a and b are the generally low marginal rates of tax, with the maximal rate being only 34 per cent. There is also limited deviation in these rates. Relating the results to theorem 5.6, the marginal rates do become lower at high incomes but do not reach 0 because the skill distribution is unbounded. The average rate of tax is negative for low

Table 5.1. *Optimal tax schedule*

Income	Consumption	Average tax (%)	Marginal tax (%)
(a) $z^G = 0.013$, $v = 0$			
0	0.03	—	23
0.05	0.07	− 34	26
0.10	0.10	− 5	24
0.20	0.18	9	21
0.30	0.26	13	19
0.40	0.34	14	18
0.50	0.43	15	16
(b) $z^G = 0.003$, $v = 1$			
0	0.05	—	30
0.05	0.08	− 66	34
0.10	0.12	− 34	32
0.20	0.19	7	28
0.30	0.26	13	25
0.40	0.34	16	22
0.50	0.41	17	20

incomes in both tables 5.1a and b so that low-income consumers are receiving an income supplement from the government.

The set of results reported in table 5.2, also from Mirrlees (1971), show the effect of increasing the dispersion of skills. This raises the marginal tax rates but these remain fairly constant across the income range. This occurs despite the greater inequality of skills leading to a greater possible role for redistribution via the income tax. Further results on the effect of varying the dispersion of skills are given in Kanbur and Tuomala (1994). These support the finding that an increased dispersion of skills raises the marginal tax rate at each income level but show that it also has the effect of moving the maximum tax rate up the income range, so that the marginal tax rate is increasing over the majority of households.

The nature of the tax rate at the upper end of the income scale and the implications of the zero end-point result for nearby incomes has been investigated by Tuomala (1990). Tuomala's numerical results show that the marginal tax rate may be far from 0 on incomes close to the maximum. The zero end-point result is therefore only a local conclusion and does not necessarily imply that the incomes near the maximum must also be subject to low marginal tax rates.

Although the numerical simulations of Mirrlees (1971) made a number of variations in specification, these were very restricted in comparison to the potential range of formulations. In attempting to progress further, Atkinson (1972) considered the effect of changing the social welfare function to the extreme maxi–min form

Table 5.2. *Optimal tax schedule: increased dispersion of skills* ($z^G = 0.013$, $v = 1$, $\sigma = 1$)

Income	Consumption	Average tax (%)	Marginal tax (%)
0	0.10	—	50
0.10	0.15	− 50	58
0.25	0.20	20	60
0.50	0.30	40	59
1.00	0.52	48	57
1.50	0.73	51	54
2.00	0.97	51	52
3.00	1.47	51	49

$$W = \min \{U\}, \tag{5.82}$$

which places the greatest possible emphasis on equity considerations. The reasoning for doing this follows from contrasting tables 5.1a and b. From these it can be seen that increased concern for equity, v going from 0 to 1, increased the optimal marginal tax rates. The natural question would be: Could strong equity considerations lead to high marginal rates? The interest in this issue can be appreciated by recalling that the top British tax rate in the 1970s was between 70–98 per cent, dependent on the precise source of income. From this perspective the rates derived by Mirrlees were relatively low.

The effect of changing to a maxi–min social welfare function can be seen from considering table 5.3 which is based on Atkinson and Stiglitz (1980). From the table it is possible to conclude that the maxi–min criterion leads to generally higher rates. However they are again highest at low incomes and then decline. In addition, they remain relatively low.

4.2 Choice of specification

The numerical results discussed above have concentrated upon examples with the same log-normal distribution of skill and the Cobb–Douglas individual utility function. Following the analysis of Stern (1976), which is devoted to considering whether these assumptions are appropriate and the consequences of modifying them, each of these assumptions is now discussed in turn.

4.2.1 Estimation of skill distribution

The first point to consider is the determination of the skill distribution. It is natural to assume that this cannot be directly observed and must be inferred in some way from observable data. The distribution employed by Mirrlees (1971) was taken directly from an analysis of income data and therefore embodies the assumption that skill and income have the same distribution. The question that

Table 5.3. *Contrast of utilitarian and maxi–min*

Level of s	Utilitarian		Maxi–min	
	Average rate	Marginal rate	Average rate	Marginal rate
Median	6	21	10	52
Top decile	14	20	28	34
Top percentile	16	17	28	26

must be asked, considering the importance of the distribution demonstrated in table 5.2, is whether this assumption is justified.

Stern (1976) makes the point that it is generally not possible to pass from knowledge of the observed income distribution to knowledge of the underlying skill distribution unless there is full knowledge of the utility function and the tax function. This point is illustrated by the utility function $U(x,\ell) = 1 - \ell$ if $x \geq \bar{x}, = -\infty$ otherwise. If ℓ is unobserved, all that will be observed is that all consumers achieve equal incomes and have consumption level $\bar{x}$. However, consumers of high ability use little labour time to obtain this consumption level but low ability consumers require a considerable amount. From this example, it can be seen that the income distribution need not directly reflect the skill distribution. Whether the income distribution accurately reflects skills is dependent upon the other components of the economy and is not an exogenous property.

4.2.2 Labour supply

The choice of optimal income tax is concerned with maximising social welfare by reaching an efficient trade-off of equity against efficiency. The factor that is most intimately linked with the efficiency cost of taxation is the wage elasticity of labour supply or, alternatively, whether labour supply will be greatly affected by high marginal rates of taxation. This subsection briefly reviews some evidence on the effect of taxation on labour supply and then considers the implications of alternative formulations of the labour supply function.

Empirical evidence on the effect of income taxes can be found in the results of both surveys and of econometric estimates of labour supply functions. Break (1957) conducted a survey of the disincentive effect of high tax rates upon solicitors and accountants in the UK, 63 per cent of whom where subject to marginal tax rates above 50 per cent. The survey concluded that as many respondents were working harder because of the tax rates as were working less hard. A similar conclusion was obtained by Brown and Levin (1974) in a survey of the effect of income taxation on the level of overtime worked by a sample of weekly paid workers; little net effect of taxation on working hours was found.

Econometric evidence has also produced comparable results. Burtless and Hausman (1978) employ data from the Gary Negative Income Tax experiment to estimate a labour supply function and find a wage elasticity of labour supply of 0. These results, which relate primarily to the labour supply of males, suggest that there are grounds for believing the disincentive effect of income taxes for males to not be great. In contrast, the elasticity of labour supply from married females may be much higher and for this group the participation effect is also relevant. This suggests that the analysis should really treat the two groups separately. Further discussion of the relation of labour supply to taxation is given in Hausman (1985) and the evidence for the UK on female supply is surveyed in Blundell (1992).

With respect to the response of labour supply to taxation, the specification adopted for the simulations generating tables 5.1–5.3 was very restrictive due to its imposed unit elasticity of substitution between leisure and consumption. As will now be shown, alternative formulations can produce somewhat different results.

First, consider the Cobb–Douglas utility as used by Mirrlees (1971) and Atkinson (1972). The elasticity of substitution, ε, between leisure, $1-\ell$, and consumption, x, is defined as

$$\varepsilon = \frac{\dfrac{\dfrac{\partial U}{\partial x}}{\dfrac{\partial U}{\partial 1-\ell}}}{\dfrac{1-\ell}{x}} \cdot \frac{\partial\left[\dfrac{1-\ell}{x}\right]}{\partial \dfrac{\dfrac{\partial U}{\partial x}}{\dfrac{\partial U}{\partial 1-\ell}}}.$$

(5.83)

This elasticity is a unit-free measure of the rate at which consumption can be exchanged for leisure while keeping utility constant. For the Cobb–Douglas function (5.80), $\varepsilon = 1$. Hence the simulations of Atkinson (1972) and Mirrlees (1971) were based on a constant elasticity of substitution equal to 1. Given the restrictiveness of this formulation, it is natural to question its consequences and whether it is justified by data on labour supply.

Stern (1976) investigated the more general form of preferences described by the constant elasticity of substitution (CES) utility function

$$U = [\alpha[L-\ell]^{-\mu} + [1-\alpha]x^{-\mu}]^{-1/\mu},$$

(5.84)

where L is full leisure time available. L was fixed at unity in (5.80). For (5.84) the elasticity of substitution is given by

$$\varepsilon = \frac{1}{\mu+1}.$$

(5.85)

To understand the consequences that different values of ε may have, consider a consumer maximising the utility function (5.84) subject to the budget constraint

$$x = A + s\ell, \tag{5.86}$$

where s is the net wage and A is the level of lump-sum grant, which may be negative. The first-order condition for utility maximisation is

$$\left[\frac{L-\ell}{A+s\ell}\right]^{\mu+1} = \frac{\alpha}{[1-\alpha]\ell}, \tag{5.87}$$

which gives an implicit expression for ℓ. From differentiating (5.87) it can be found that

$$\frac{d\ell}{ds} = \frac{[A-\mu s\ell][L-\ell]}{s[\mu+1][A+sL]}. \tag{5.88}$$

Now from (5.85) it follows that $\mu = \dfrac{1}{\varepsilon} - 1$ so, for μ positive, it is possible that $A - \mu s\ell$, and hence $d\ell/ds$, may become negative and thus the labour supply curve bends backwards. The importance of a backward-bending labour supply function is that tax increases at high incomes will actually increase labour supply; hence the equity and efficiency factors are not directly competing. For low values of ε it is therefore to be expected that the optimal marginal rate of tax will be higher. This possibility could not arise in the specification based on the Cobb–Douglas utility function model with $\mu = 0$.

Applying the model based on (5.84) to the data of Ashenfelter and Heckman (1973) from an analysis of 3,203 American males, Stern (1976) calculated the elasticity of substitution and found that $\varepsilon = 0.408$. This value of ε is substantially less than that used by Mirrlees in the numerical simulations.

Adopting (5.84) as the individual utility function and a social welfare function of the form

$$W = \frac{1}{V} \int_0^\infty [U(x, \ell)]^v \gamma(s) ds, \tag{5.89}$$

Stern (1976) presented estimates of the optimal linear income tax. Retaining the log-normal distribution of ability with the standard deviation, the general pattern of results is summarised by the figure 5.10.

From figure 5.10 it can be seen that the Mirrlees specification $\varepsilon = 1, v = 1$ gives the lowest possible rates of taxation and that tax rates increase to 100 per cent as ε tends to 0; a proof that this always occurs is given by Stern (1976). What is important to note is that the tax rates are high for $\varepsilon = 0.0408$ and $v = -1$. Therefore high tax rates can be justified without necessarily appealing to the maxi–min criterion.

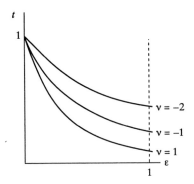

Figure 5.10   Optimal tax rate and equity

5 EXTENSIONS AND OMISSIONS

The basic Mirrlees economy described above has been extended in a number of directions and two of these are now considered. The first extension introduces a second form of labour service which allows the income tax to have indirect distributional effects via the changes in relative wages. Following this, the non-linear income tax is combined with linear taxes upon commodities and conditions are found for which commodity taxes are unnecessary. The section is completed by noting some relevant issues that are not addressed in the formal analysis.

5.1 Two forms of labour

The relevance of introducing a second form of labour service is that the economy can be designed so that the population is partitioned with those of low skill supplying a form of labour with a low wage and those of high skill supplying labour with a higher return. To obtain such a partition it is only necessary to assume that there are two distinct levels of skill: high and low. The new factor introduced by the existence of two wage levels is that the income tax can alter the relative values of these wages and, in doing so, alters the distribution of income between the two skill groups. This second route for redistribution will clearly be important in the determination of the optimal income tax.

In the first analysis of a model of this form Feldstein (1973) employed numerical techniques to investigate the effect of the relative wage variation upon the value of the optimal linear income tax. With the two forms of labour entering into a Cobb–Douglas production function, Feldstein concluded that there was little difference between the optimal tax with fixed wages and that with variable wages.

The conclusion of Feldstein was reconsidered in Allen (1982) employing an analytical, rather than a numerical, approach. The significant extension made by Allen was to use a more general form of production technology. This demonstrated that in the Cobb–Douglas case the redistribution via the income tax was reinforced by the adjustment of relative wages thus explaining the Feldstein (1973) results. However, if the elasticity of substitution between the two forms of labour is low and the labour service earning the higher wage has a negative supply elasticity, then the relative wage effect operates in the opposite direction to the income tax effect and may outweigh it. When the indirect effect does outweigh the direct effect, the optimal policy becomes a combination of lump-sum tax and a negative marginal rate of income tax.

These results indicate that the analysis of income taxation becomes rather more difficult and can generate surprising conclusions when more than one form of labour service is introduced into the model. This assumption of the standard economy may therefore be more restrictive than it at first appears.

5.2 Income and commodity taxes

The analysis of a combined tax system of linear commodity taxes and a non-linear income tax has been studied in a number of papers, most notably Atkinson and Stiglitz (1976), Mirrlees (1976) and Revesz (1986). The major results of this line of study are now briefly described.

It is assumed that there are n goods available with labour denoted as good 1 and the wage rate is w. As a normalisation rule the linear tax on good n is set at 0. With these conventions, the budget constraint facing a consumer of ability s takes the form

$$\sum_{i=2}^{n} q_i x_i = s w x_1 - T(s w x_1).\qquad(5.90)$$

To simplify the derivation, the production technology is taken to be linear so that production possibilities are constrained by the relation

$$\sum_{i=2}^{n} \int_0^\infty x_i(s)\gamma(s)ds \le \int_0^\infty s w x_1(s)\gamma(s)ds - z^G.\qquad(5.91)$$

With the linear technology, it is possible to take the producer price of each good $2,\ldots,n$ to be 1.

The optimal taxes can be found by treating $U(s)$ as the state variable and $x_i(s)$, $i=1,\ldots,n-1$ as the control variables, with $x_n(s)$ determined from the identity $U(s)=U(x_1(s),\ldots,x_n(s))$. The first-order condition for self-selection is derived from (5.14) by using the fact that $u_s = -\dfrac{U_\ell z}{s^2} = -\dfrac{U_\ell \ell}{s}$ or, in the present notation, $u_s = -\dfrac{U_{x_1} x_1}{s}$. Employing the first-order approach, the Hamiltonian for the maximisation can be written using (5.91) as

$$H=\left[U+\lambda\left[swx_1-\sum_{i=2}^{n}x_i\right]\right]\gamma(s)-\mu\frac{x_1U_{x_1}}{s}.$$ (5.92)

For the choice of $x_k(s)$, $k=2,\ldots,n-1$, using the fact that

$$\frac{\partial x_n}{\partial x_k}=-\frac{U_{x_k}}{U_{x_n}}$$ (5.93)

the necessary condition for optimality is

$$-\lambda\left[1-\frac{U_{x_k}}{U_{x_n}}\right]\gamma-\frac{\mu x_1}{s}\left[U_{x_1x_k}-U_{x_1x_n}\frac{U_{x_k}}{U_{x_n}}\right]=0, \quad k=2,\ldots,n-1.$$ (5.94)

From the necessary conditions for household utility maximisation

$$\frac{U_{x_k}}{U_{x_n}}=\frac{1+t_k}{1}.$$ (5.95)

Substituting (5.95) into (5.94), the optimality condition (5.94) can be written after some rearrangement as

$$t_k=\frac{\mu x_1 U_{x_k}}{\lambda\gamma s}\left[\frac{d\log\left[\frac{U_{x_k}}{U_{x_n}}\right]}{dx_1}\right], \quad k=2,\ldots,n-1.$$ (5.96)

The result in (5.96) reveals two facts. Firstly, if $\dfrac{d\log\left[\dfrac{U_{x_k}}{U_{x_n}}\right]}{dx_1}=0$, for all $k=2,\ldots,n-1$, which holds if the utility function is weakly separable between labour and all other commodities, then $t_k=0$ for all $k=2,..,n-1$. This is the major result of Atkinson and Stiglitz (1976). In these circumstance the commodity taxes are unnecessary and the income tax is sufficient for achieving welfare aims. This result derives from the tax system attempting to tax the innate ability of the households but, when the separability holds, there is insufficient correlation between consumption choice and ability for commodity taxation to have any effect. The second consequence of (5.96) is, holding all other variables constant, that the tax rate on a good should be positively related to the rate of change of the marginal rate of substitution between that good and labour as labour supply increases. Therefore, those goods relatively preferred by the consumers supplying most labour should be taxed more. Using a more general framework, Mirrlees (1976) strengthens this conclusion to show that the commodity tax rates should be highest on those goods for which the high ability households have the relatively strongest preference.

An alternative perspective upon the combination of income and commodity taxes has been provided by Christiansen (1984). Christiansen takes as the starting point a situation in which the income tax has been optimised but with no commodity taxes and then determines the welfare effect of introducing commodity taxes whilst holding revenue constant. The analysis provides the conclusion that goods for which demand increases if more leisure is obtained, but with no change in income, should have positive commodity taxes introduced. If no change in demand follows from the change in leisure, the tax should be zero and it should be negative if demand falls.

The results noted have determined some relations between income and commodity taxes. However, the number of alternative perspectives from which the model can be approached and the richness of the model prevent any simple and summary statement being given.

5.3 Omissions

The economy that has been studied was, by necessity, highly stylised. Although this brings undoubted analytical benefits, it does eliminate from consideration many issues that are of practical interest. Some of these are now briefly discussed.

The economy involved only a single form of labour service but with differences in the ability of households to perform this service. In reality, there are many different forms of labour in an economy which differ in the skills they require and in the working conditions they impose. The actual monetary payment for the supply of labour may only be part of the package of remuneration, and some of the return (or cost) may be entirely psychic in nature. An income tax policy designed to maximise welfare would need to take account of the entire package of characteristics that constitutes labour supply. The labour supply decision also involves more than simply the determination of the number of hours of work. As occupations differ in their characteristics, the choice between occupations is important and this choice will be affected by income taxation. For instance, an increase in taxation will be detrimental to occupations where the return is predominantly monetary. There are also intertemporal aspects to the labour supply decision such as the timing of entry to the labour force and the timing of retirement. As an income tax will introduce a distortion into such decisions, this increases the potential efficiency loss. Some of these issues are addressed in Christiansen (1988).

The preferences of the households have been taken as identical. This need not be the case and differences in preferences may arise as in chapter 4. Furthermore, the household has been viewed as supplying an homogeneous form of labour but in practice the total labour supply is often the sum of male and female components. The nature of these is often very different and empirical evidence suggests that they have markedly different responses to taxation. This observation implies that the analysis should be based upon greater detail of the structure of households. Furthermore, it also raises issues concerning the tax treatment of the individuals that constitute the household such as whether they have the option or not of being taxed as separate individuals or whether a joint household return is compulsory.

6 SUMMARY

This chapter has reviewed the formal analysis of the optimal income tax problem. The problem has been treated as one of choosing the income tax function to balance equity and efficiency considerations in an economy characterised by inequality in the distribution of income. The standard economy of Mirrlees (1971) has been described and it has been noted that this is the simplest for which the income tax problem has any real content. The major theoretical results have been derived and, although they do not provide a precise characterisation of the optimal tax schedule, they do suggest its most important properties, some of which are in conflict with the structure of observed tax schedules.

Numerical analyses have been used to investigate further the nature of the tax schedule and its dependence upon the assumed structure of the problem. Results from some of the most noteworthy of these analyses have been given above. In particular they demonstrate that the marginal rates of tax may be rather low but do increase with concern for equity. However, the conclusions are sensitive to the assumptions invoked by the model. The implications of the modification of some of these assumptions were considered.

The chapter was concluded by a consideration of two extensions. The introduction of a second form of labour service could lead to a marked change in the form of the optimal tax function if the indirect effect of taxation upon relative wages outweighed the direct effect. The optimal combination of income and commodity taxes was then considered and it was shown that weak separability of leisure would make commodity taxes redundant.

The methods of analysis can be adapted to treat other forms of non-linear taxation. It needs only a minor revision to turn the income tax into an expenditure tax with a suitable reinterpretation of the skill variable as a preference parameter. Many of the theorems derived then apply directly to this new setting. In fact, several of the studies cited, such as Mirrlees (1976) and Seade (1977) are concerned with general non-linear taxes rather than income tax *per se*.

6

POLICY REFORM

1 INTRODUCTION

The previous two chapters have considered the determination of optimal commodity and income taxes. In practice, if the derived tax rules were to be implemented it would be likely that a major upheaval of the fiscal structure would be required. To be willing to enact such a major change would require the policy maker to have considerable faith in the accuracy of the policy advice. Taking this into account, many countries have opted in favour of gradual policy reforms which involve slowly phasing in some taxes and removing others. The design of such reforms will be the subject of this chapter.

The theoretical literature on policy reform has been concerned with characterising when there exist feasible reforms that satisfy the policy maker's objectives and with determining the optimal direction of reform. For the purpose of formal analysis, reforms are always interpreted as differential changes in the vector of policy instruments. This is the limiting interpretation of the reforms being small.

This chapter will review the standard analysis that has been developed for determining the existence of worthwhile reforms in the vector of consumer prices. The inverse optimum problem, which calculates the welfare weights of households implied by a given set of policy parameters, will be related to this analysis and the concept of marginal social cost will be discussed. Several applications of these methods, including empirical investigations, will be described. In considering the practical implications of these results, it should be noted that administration costs are not considered. If such costs are significant they will reduce the potential attractiveness of a series of small reforms.

2 THE REFORM PROBLEM

The standard procedure is to take as given some initial vector of consumer prices, supporting producer prices and implied tax rates. Given these values, the equilibrium of the economy is calculated. It is clear that the values of the policy variables will determine the welfare properties of the equilibrium. Small changes in consumer prices are then considered and the question is asked: is there a feasible change that raises welfare? This is the policy reform problem. It is implicit in this description that as consumer prices change, producer prices are adjusted to maintain equilibrium.

The welfare objective has typically been either the strict Pareto principle under which an acceptable reform must raise all households' welfare or a social welfare function in which case the policy reform must raise social welfare. Both of these welfare criteria are considered below. An alternative objective, a unanimous Wicksellian criteria, is studied in Weymark (1981). Feasibility is defined in terms of the satisfaction of an aggregate production constraint or alternatively, where permissible, a government revenue constraint. When the production constraint is employed, a feasible change must result in a demand vector that is in the production set. With the revenue constraint, a given level of revenue must be collected before and after the change. Further discussion of the structure of the reform problem can be found in Feldstein (1976a).

2.1 Productive feasibility

The analysis is set within a competitive economy that has H households and n goods. The government policy variables are the n consumer prices denoted by the vector $q^T = (q_1, \ldots, q_n)$, with the superscript T denoting the transpose. All vectors are written as columns and, for vectors, the notation $x > y$ implies $x_i > y_i$ all i, $x \geq y$ implies $x_i \geq y_i$ all i and $x_i > y_i$ some i, and $x \geqq y$ implies $x_i \geq y_i$ all i. Producer prices of the n goods are written $p^T = (p_1, \ldots, p_n)$. To guarantee a separation between the production and consumption sectors, a 100 per cent profits tax is assumed as discussed in chapter 4, section 6.

Formally, the reform problem is concerned with differential changes in the policy parameters from an initial position with policy vector $q^T = (q_1, \ldots, q_n)$ to a new position with policy $q^T + dq^T = (q_1 + dq_1, \ldots, q_n + dq_n)$. The direction of change dq is restricted to be normal to q; hence $q^T dq = 0$. The set of normals to q is denoted $T(q)$ and, until indicated otherwise, all consumer price changes dq are assumed to belong to $T(q)$. Since aggregate demand is homogeneous of degree 0 in consumer prices, this is simply a normalisation and does not impose any real restriction on the set of reforms. Figure 6.1 illustrates this procedure for a two-good economy. Given initial price vector q, $T(q)$ is a line through the origin orthogonal to q. The change in policy $dq \in T(q)$ is shown to move the policy vector to $q + dq$. The homogeneity of aggregate demand implies that it is only the direction of the price vector that is relevant, not its length. It can be seen in figure 6.1 that by moving dq along $T(q)$, $q + dq$ can be made to point in any direction in the positive orthant.

The first step is to identify when a potential reform is productively feasible. For the present, feasibility will be defined by satisfaction of an aggregate production constraint. The production constraint is given in implicit form by the strictly quasi-convex and differentiable function

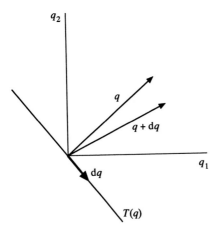

Figure 6.1   The set of policy changes

$$F(X(q)) \leq 0, \tag{6.1}$$

where

$$X(q) = \sum_{h=1}^{H} x^h(q), \tag{6.2}$$

is the aggregate demand function. The assumption of strict quasi-convexity ensures that at each point on the boundary of the production set there is a unique (up to a scalar multiple) price vector that will make that point the profit-maximising choice. Differentiability then implies, as discussed in connection with production efficiency in chapter 4, section 9, that this price vector will be proportional to the gradient vector, ∇F, of $F(\cdot)$. This assumption is relaxed in Weymark (1979b) who considers non-differentiable production constraints. Given producer prices p, the supply vector is denoted by $Y(p)$. An equilibrium is termed *tight* if $X(q) = Y(p)$ and *non-tight* if $X(q) \leq Y(p)$.

Feasibility of the policy reform requires that after the change in policy the resulting demand vector remains within the aggregate production set. It is assumed that the economy is initially on the boundary of the production set so the policy change must satisfy

$$\nabla F^T X_q dq \leq 0, \tag{6.3}$$

where

$$X_q = \begin{bmatrix} \dfrac{\partial X_1}{\partial q_1} & \cdot & \dfrac{\partial X_1}{\partial q_n} \\ & \cdot & \\ \dfrac{\partial \dot{X}_n}{\partial q_1} & \cdot & \dfrac{\partial \dot{X}_n}{\partial q_n} \end{bmatrix}, \tag{6.4}$$

is the Jacobian of the aggregate demand function. Employing the fact that producer prices are proportional to ∇F, the feasibility constraint can be written in the form

$$p^T X_q dq \leq 0. \tag{6.5}$$

Hence, as noted by Guesnerie (1977), feasible reforms are those which cause a change in aggregate demand that has a non-positive value at initial producer prices. To simplify the expressions below, the expression $-p^T X_q$ will be denoted ∇Z^T.

After a change in the consumer price vector, producer prices will also adjust in order to maintain equilibrium and it is assumed that such adjustment is in a direction that is normal to p. The following result of Guesnerie (1977) proves that, when the boundary of the production set is sufficiently smooth, the change in demand due to a differential change in the consumer price vector can be met by a supply change brought about by a differential modification of producer prices. The proof is based on the observation that when the boundary of the production set is smooth, its gradient changes continuously. In turn, the normal to the production set changes continuously around its boundary. This implies that the producer price vectors that support two nearby points, which are proportional to the normals at those points, will be similar. Figure 6.2a shows a smooth production set for which a small change in demand can be met by a differential change in the producer price vector. In figure 6.2b the production set has a kink at $y^* = (y_1^*, y_2^*)$ and to move production from $\tilde{y} = (y_1^* + \varepsilon, y_2^* - \varepsilon)$ to $\hat{y} = (y_1^* - \varepsilon, y_2^* + \varepsilon)$ requires a discrete change in producer prices.

As supply is homogeneous of degree 1 in producer prices, the Jacobian of the supply function cannot have rank n. Smoothness of the production set therefore manifests itself in the supply function having rank $n-1$. Any lower rank indicates that there are flat sections or ridges in the production set, either of which will remove the property that the normal to the production set changes continuously around the boundary of the production set. Following these preliminaries, the formal statement of the lemma can now be given.

Lemma 6.1 (Guesnerie)

If the Jacobian of the aggregate supply function has rank $n-1$ then, for any change in consumer prices such that $\nabla F^T X_q dq \leq 0$, there is at least one direction of change, dp, of producer prices such that (dq, dp) is equilibrium preserving. If $\nabla F^T X_q dq = 0$ the change dp is unique and (dq, dp) is tight equilibrium preserving.

Proof

Since aggregate supply is homogeneous of degree 0 in p, $Y_p p = 0$ and it follows from the symmetry of Y_p, where Y_p is the Jacobian of aggregate supply, that $Y_p p = 0 \Leftrightarrow p^T Y_p = 0^T$. Now define the set V by $V = \{u : p^T u = 0\}$. As $p^T Y_p u = 0$, it

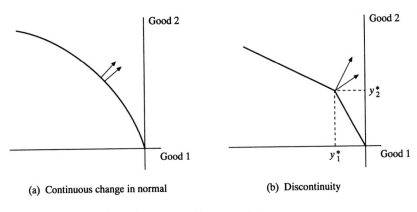

(a) Continuous change in normal   (b) Discontinuity

Figure 6.2 Smooth and non-smooth production sets

follows that $Y_p u \in V$. Hence the linear mapping, Y_p, maps from V to V. To see that the linear mapping is also one-to-one, assume that it is not, so that there exist $u^1 \in V$ and $u^2 \in V$ such that $Y_p u^1 = Y_p u^2 = u^*$. From this, $y_p[u^1 - u^2] = 0$. As the Jacobian of Y_p is of dimension $n - 1$, the set $W = \{w: Y_p w = 0\}$ is of dimension 1 and, since $Y_p p = 0$, if $w \in W$, $w = \lambda p$ for some λ. Hence $[u^1 - u^2] = \lambda p$ and $p^T[u^1 - u^2] = \lambda p^T p \neq 0$. However, as u^1 and $u^2 \in V$, $p^T u^1 = p^T u^2 = 0 \Rightarrow p^T[u^1 - u^2] = 0$. This contradiction shows the mapping must be one-to-one and onto. It then follows that on V, Y_p has an inverse Y_p^{-1}. Hence given a price change dp, $Y_p^{-1} dp = dY$, where dY is a vector of supply changes normal to dp: $dp^T dY = 0$. Thus any vector of supply changes normal to p can be obtained by a change in producer prices which is also normal to p.

Now let dq be such that $\nabla F^T X_q dq = 0$. It follows that $p^T X_q dq \equiv p^T dX = 0$. Hence $dx \in V$ and there exists $p = Y_p^{-1} dX$. Then $dY = Y_p dp = Y_p Y_p^{-1} dX = dX$, p is also unique since $dX \in V$. Therefore, if the consumer price change leads to a demand change, dX, on the boundary of the production set a producer price change can be found that matches the change in demand with an equal change, dY, in supply and is tight equilibrium preserving.

If dq satisfies $\nabla F^T X_q dq < 0$, then $p^T X_q dq \equiv p^T dX < 0$ and the argument can be repeated with $U = dX + \delta, \delta > 0$ and $p^T U = 0$ to show $dY = dU > dX$ so the change preserves equilibrium but not tight equilibrium.

The value of lemma 6.1 is that it allows the focus to be placed upon consumer prices in the knowledge that any change satisfying (6.3) can be accommodated by the adjustment of producer prices.

2.2 Improving reforms

Let $V^h(q_1, \ldots, q_n)$ denote the indirect utility function of the hth household. The level of social welfare is assumed to be determined by a Bergson–Samuelson social welfare function

$$W = W(V^1(q_1, \ldots, q_n), \ldots, V^H(q_1, \ldots, q_n)). \tag{6.6}$$

Using (6.6), the effect of the change in q upon welfare is given by

$$dW = \nabla W^T dq, \tag{6.7}$$

where

$$\nabla W^T = \left(\sum_{h=1}^{H} \frac{\partial W}{\partial V^h} \frac{\partial V^h}{\partial q_1}, \ldots, \sum_{h=1}^{H} \frac{\partial W}{\partial V^h} \frac{\partial V^h}{\partial q_n} \right). \tag{6.8}$$

The reform problem, in terms of finding a reform that raises social welfare, can now be introduced.

Welfare-improving reform (WI)

Does there exist a vector dq of reforms such that

(i) $\nabla W^T dq > 0$

and

(ii) $\nabla Z^T dq \geq 0$?

Condition (i) requires the reform to raise welfare and (ii) that it is productively feasible.

To formulate the Pareto-improving reform problem, define the vectors

$$\nabla V^{hT} = \left(\frac{\partial V^h}{\partial q_1}, \ldots, \frac{\partial V_h}{\partial q_n} \right), \quad h = 1, \ldots, H. \tag{6.9}$$

It is assumed that $\nabla V^h \neq 0$ for all h. From these vectors the matrix P is formed by using the vector ∇V^{hT} as the hth row of P. This construction leads to the following matrix

$$P = \begin{bmatrix} \nabla V^{1T} \\ \vdots \\ \nabla V^{HT} \end{bmatrix}. \tag{6.10}$$

Using P, the strict Pareto-improving reform problem can be stated formally.

Strict Pareto-improving reform (PI)

Does there exist a vector dq of reforms such that

(i) $Pdq > 0$

and

(ii) $\nabla Z^T dq \geq 0$?

Given the definition in (6.9), condition (i) is equivalent to $\nabla V^{hT} dq > 0$ for all h, so that the reform must raise the welfare of all the households. The motive for employing the strict Pareto reform, as opposed to a weak version where the reform must benefit at least one household while not harming any other, is that it leads to a simpler statement of later results.

WI and PI represent the two standard policy reform problems and it should be noted that both take the form of a system of linear inequalities. This has important implications for the analysis of reforms. It is now possible to proceed to a characterisation of when a solution exists to the problems, in terms of a non-zero vector that satisfies the relevant inequalities, and what can be concluded when such a vector does not exist.

3 CHARACTERISING POSSIBILITIES

The first approach to characterisation is to apply a *Theorem of the Alternative*. This general class of theorems states that either a set of linear inequalities has a solution or that there is a linear relationship between the component parts of the inequalities. Applied to the reform problems, this implies that either there is a solution to the reform problem or else there exists a set of weights such that the initial point is optimal with respect to the objective function determined by these weights. This section introduces the necessary Theorems of the Alternative and then discusses the interpretation of these for the two reform problems.

3.1 Solution via Theorems of the Alternative

The solution of the reform problem WI can be characterised by appeal to the Tucker Theorem of the Alternative. This, and other similar theorems, are described in detail in Mangasarian (1969).

Theorem 6.1(Tucker)

Given a matrix A and a vector B, with the number of columns of A equal to the dimension of B, exactly one of the following holds

(a) there exists a vector x such that $Ax \geq 0$, $Bx \geq 0$,
(b) there exist vectors y_1 and y_2 with $A^T y_1 + B^T y_2 = 0, y_1 > 0, y_2 \geq 0$.

Proof

See Mangasarian (1969).

For WI, the matrices A and B represent ∇W^T and ∇Z^T respectively, both are 1 by n. Condition (a) describes the case in which a feasible reform exists. Since $A \equiv \nabla W^T$, Ax is a scalar and the vector inequality $Ax \geq 0$ implies that this scalar is strictly positive. If no reform exists, so (a) cannot be satisfied, the theorem asserts the existence of a pair of vectors such that (b) is satisfied. The vectors y_1 and y_2 in (b) can be interpreted as the shadow variables in the maximisation of welfare subject to the production constraint since, if no reform exists, the initial point must be optimal. The maximisation problem that generates (b) can be clearly seen in theorem 1D9 in Takayama (1984) and the solution leads to the optimal tax rules of chapter 4. Employing (6.5) and (6.8), the optimality condition (b) can be written as

$$y_1 \sum_{h=1}^{H} \frac{\partial W}{\partial V^h} \frac{\partial V^h}{\partial q_k} - y_2 \sum_{i=1}^{n} p_i \frac{\partial X_i}{\partial q_k} = 0, \; k=1,\dots,n. \tag{6.11}$$

This is simply an alternative representation of (4.35) (p. 109) since the aggregate budget constraint $\sum_{i=1}^{n} q_i X_i = 0$ and the relation $q_i = p_i + t_i$ imply $-\sum_{i=1}^{n} p_i \frac{\partial X_i}{\partial q_k} = X_i$

$$+ \sum_{i=1}^{n} t_i \frac{\partial X_i}{\partial q_k}.$$

The solution of PI requires the use of Motzkin's Theorem of the Alternative.

Theorem 6.2 (Motzkin)
For two matrices A and B with the same number of columns, exactly one of the following holds

(a) there exists a vector x such that $Ax > 0$, $Bx \geq 0$, with $A \neq 0$,
(b) there exist vectors y_1 and y_2 with $A^T y_1 + B^T y_2 = 0, y_1 \geq 0, y_2 \geq 0$.

Proof

See Mangasarian (1969).

In terms of the reform problem PI, A represents the matrix P and is therefore H by n and B is again ∇Z^T which is 1 by n. If there is no solution then (b) applies and the H-vector y_1/y_2 defines the implicit welfare weights attached to the households if the initial state is optimal. This point is returned to in the discussion of the inverse optimum problem below. Substituting into (b) of theorem 6.2

$$\sum_{h=1}^{H} y_{1h} \frac{\partial V^h}{\partial q_k} - y_2 \sum_{i=1}^{n} p_i \frac{\partial X_i}{\partial q_k} = 0, \; k=1,\dots,n, \tag{6.12}$$

or, since $\dfrac{\partial V^h}{\partial q_k} = -\alpha^h x_k^h$ and $\alpha^h > 0$,

$$\sum_{h=1}^{H} \lambda_h x_k^h + y_2 \sum_{i=1}^{n} p_i \frac{\partial X_i}{\partial q_k} = 0, \; k=1,\dots,n, \tag{6.13}$$

where $\lambda_h = \alpha^h y_{1h} \geq 0$. This condition provides a characterisation of the Pareto optimal allocation for the chosen weights upon the households.

In summary, application of a Theorem of the Alternative to the welfare-improving and Pareto-improving reform problems demonstrates that either the initial position is an optimum or else an improving reform can be found. When a reform cannot be found, part (b) of the theorem provides a characterisation of the optimum. For the welfare-improving reform problem, the characterisation of the optimum has been discussed in chapter 4.

3.2 Geometric analysis

An alternative perspective on the existence of a solution can be provided by geometric considerations. The vector ∇Z^T defines a half space $Q(p,q)$, or simply Q, with x being in Q implying that

$$\nabla Z^T x \geq 0. \tag{6.14}$$

In terms of (6.5), the set Q, its interior Int Q and frontier Fr Q are defined by $Q = \{x: p^T X_q x \leq 0\}$, Int $Q = \{x: p^T X_q x < 0\}$ and Fr $Q = \{x: p^T X_q x = 0\}$. Therefore any vector in Q leads to a change in consumption which has a non-positive value at initial producer prices and that satisfies the production constraint.

3.2.1 Welfare-improving reform

Taking the problem WI first, the vector ∇W^T similarly defines a half space S in which all vectors, x, located in S are such that

$$\nabla W^T x \geq 0. \tag{6.15}$$

That is, all the vectors in the half space S satisfy the requirement that welfare is not decreased by a change of prices in that direction. If there is a solution to the reform problem it must be a vector that lies in the intersection of Int $S = \{x: \nabla W^T x > 0\}$ and Q. A solution will therefore exist if Int $S \cap Q$ is non-empty. In fact, only if the boundaries of S and Q are coincident can there be no solution. This discussion is summarised in theorem 6.3.

Theorem 6.3 (Guesnerie/Weymark)

If Int $S \cap Q \neq \phi$ *then the solution set to reform problem WI is non-empty. If the solution set is non-empty, a member of the solution set, dq, will lead to a tight equilibrium if $dq \in$ Fr Q and to a non-tight equilibrium if $dq \in$ Int Q.*

Proof

Directly from the preceding discussion.

In the case that the boundaries of W and S are coincident, so that there is no solution, it follows that

$$\nabla Z^T = \lambda \nabla W^T, \tag{6.16}$$

for some scalar λ. Equation (6.16) again represents the necessary condition for an optimum and is an alternative way of presenting (b) of the Tucker Theorem.

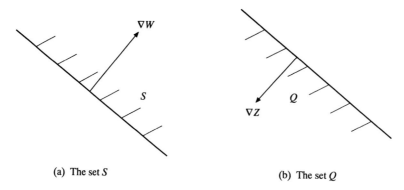

(a) The set S (b) The set Q

Figure 6.3   Welfare improvement and production feasibility

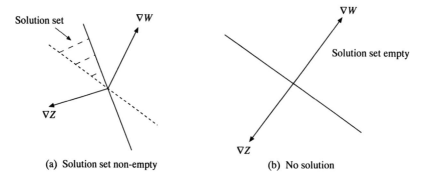

(a) Solution set non-empty   (b) No solution

Figure 6.4   Welfare-improving reform

Figure 6.3 illustrates the vectors ∇Z and ∇W and their implied half spaces for a three-good economy. With three goods, the set $T(q)$ of price changes normal to q is a plane and, to draw the diagram, this plane has been aligned with the page. The vectors ∇W and ∇Z are both shown as lying in $T(q)$. For ∇W this follows since each household is subject to the budget constraint $q^T x^h = 0$ and $\nabla W^T = -\left(\sum_{h=1}^{H} \beta^h x^h\right)$. From this $q^T \nabla W = -\left(\sum_{h=1}^{H} \beta^h q^T x^h\right) = 0$ so $\nabla W \in T(q)$. Recalling (6.5), $\nabla Z^T = -p^T X_q$ so that $q^T \nabla Z = -q^T [p^T X_q]^T = -[X_q q]^T p$. The aggregate demand function is homogeneous of degree zero in q so $X_q q = 0$ and hence $q^T \nabla Z = 0$. ∇Z is therefore in $T(q)$. Hence, in a three-good economy, ∇W and ∇Z are three-dimensional vectors that lie in the plane $T(q)$ which is coincident with the page.

Figure 6.4a depicts the existence of a welfare-improving reform. Here the interior of the intersection of S and Q is non-empty. The solution set is shown as a subset of $T(q)$. In contrast, figure 6.4b shows the arrangement of vectors that result in the solution set being empty.

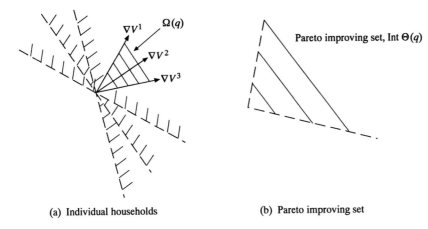

(a) Individual households

(b) Pareto improving set

Figure 6.5   Pareto-improving set

3.2.2 Pareto reform

The Pareto reform problem is analysed in two stages. In the first stage it is determined whether there exist any policy changes that will increase the welfare of all households. If such changes exist, the second stage is to check whether any are productively feasible. Only when changes exist that satisfy both stages does the Pareto reform problem have a solution.

Considering the first stage of the Pareto reform problem, each row of P determines an open half space, $P^h(q) = \{x: \nabla V^{hT} x > 0\}$, of reforms that would benefit the consumer whose preferences that row represents. As it is required that the reform must increase the utility of all households, such a reform will only exist if the intersection $\cap_{h=1}^{H} P^h(q)$ of these open half spaces is non-empty. A set of vectors ∇V^h, $h = 1, 2, 3$, that generate a non-empty Pareto-improving set is shown in figure 6.5a and the implied set of Pareto-improving reforms in figure 6.5b. Figure 6.5 is drawn by again aligning $T(q)$ with the plane of the page and utilising the fact that $\nabla V^h \in T(q)$ for all h, which follows since $\nabla V^h = -\alpha x^h$ by Roy's identity and $q^T x^h = 0$.

The intersection of the half spaces corresponding to the vectors ∇V^h will be non-empty whenever the cone generated by taking all positive linear combinations of these vectors (the rows of P) is pointed, where a set K is a cone if $k \in K$ implies $\mu k \in K$ for all $\mu \geq 0$ and a cone is pointed if $K \cap (-K) = \{0\}$. That the vectors generate a pointed cone can be viewed as capturing the fact that the preferences of the consumers are not too dissimilar. The importance of pointed cones in this context was first noted by Weymark (1979b). To illustrate these points, the vectors in figure 6.6a generate a pointed cone but those in figure 6.6b do not.

Denote by $\Omega(q)$ the cone generated by the rows of P, where $\Omega(q) = \left\{ \Omega: \Omega = \sum_{h=1}^{H} \lambda_h \nabla V^h(q), \lambda_h \geq 0 \right\}$ and define the positive polar cone to $\Omega(q)$ by

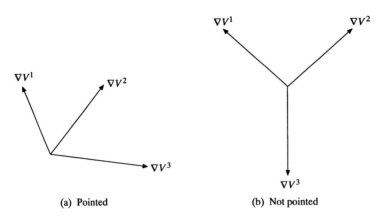

(a) Pointed   (b) Not pointed

Figure 6.6 Cones

$\Theta(q) = \{\eta: \Omega^T\eta \geq 0 \text{ for all } \Omega \in \Omega(q)\}$. If $\Omega(q)$ is pointed, $\Theta(q)$ has a non-empty interior and the interior of $\Theta(q)$, Int $\Theta(q) = \cap_{h=1}^{H} P^h(q)$, is the set of strictly Pareto-improving consumer price changes. These sets are illustrated in figure 6.5.

An alternative way of expressing this is to employ Roy's identity to note that $\nabla V^{hT}dq > 0$ is equivalent to $x^{hT}dq < 0$. The reform is then a strict Pareto improvement if it reduces the cost of the initial consumption choice for all households. Denote by $\Lambda(q)$ the cone generated by the household demand vectors, hence $\Lambda(q) = \left\{\Lambda: \Lambda = \sum_{h=1}^{H} \lambda_h x^h(q), \lambda_h \geq 0\right\}$. Let $P(q)$ be the negative polar cone of $\Lambda(q)$, $P(q) = \{\gamma: \Lambda^T\gamma \leq 0 \text{ for all } \Lambda \in \Lambda(q)\}$. $P(q)$ is the set of price changes that reduces the cost of all households' demands and the set of strict Pareto-improving reforms will be non-empty if $P(q)$ has a non-empty interior. This will be the case precisely when $\Lambda(q)$ is pointed. That $\Lambda(q)$ must be pointed for the set of reforms to be non-empty again captures the idea that the preferences, and hence demands, of the households must be similar. It should be noted that $\Omega(q) = -\Lambda(q)$, $\Theta(q) = P(q)$ and Int $P(q) = \cap_{h=1}^{H} P^h(q)$. These constructions are shown in figure 6.7.

The second stage of the Pareto-improving reform problem is undertaken by combining the Pareto-improving set with the half space Q related to the production constraint. It then follows that a feasible improving reform exists if the cone generated by the rows of P, $\Omega(q)$, is pointed, so that the Pareto-improving set is non-empty, and the intersection of Int $\Theta(q)$ with the half space Q is non-empty. This reasoning is summarised as theorem 6.4.

Theorem 6.4 (Guesnerie/Weymark)

If $\Omega(q)$ is not pointed then Int $\Theta(q) = \phi$ *and the solution set is empty. If $\Omega(q)$ is pointed then* Int $\Theta(q) \neq \phi$ *and the solution set to PI will be non-empty if* Int

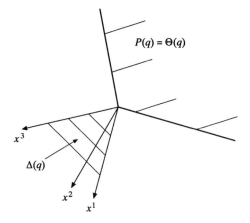

$P(q) = \Theta(q)$

x^3

$\Delta(q)$

x^2

x^1

Figure 6.7   Representation via demands

$\Theta(q) \cap Q \neq \phi$. *When the solution set is non-empty, a member of the set, dq, will lead to a tight equilibrium if dq $\in$ Fr Q and to a non-tight equilibrium if dq $\in$ Int Q.*

Proof

The theorem follows from the preceding discussion.

To determine whether the equilibrium leads to a tight or non-tight equilibrium it is sufficient to consider the location of the vector $p^T X_q$ relative to $\Lambda(q)$, the cone generated by the demand vectors. This is summarised in the following theorem.

Theorem 6.5 (Guesnerie)

Assume $p^T X_q \neq 0$ then: (a) if $p^T X_q \in -\Lambda(q)$ there exist no Pareto-improving changes; (b) if $p^T X_q \in \Lambda(q)$ there exist Pareto-improving changes but none is tight equilibrium preserving; (c) if $p^T X_q \in (\Lambda(q) \cup -\Lambda(q))^C$, where the superscript C denotes the complement, there exist Pareto-improving changes that are tight equilibrium preserving.

Proof

A formal proof can be found in Guesnerie (1977) but the theorem follows directly from the definitions and is easily demonstrated by drawing the implied diagrams, see figure 6.8.

The proof of theorem 6.5 is illustrated in figure 6.8. In (a), it can be seen that there is no improving reform. The improving reform in (b) leads to a non-tight equilibrium because any point interior to $-\Lambda$ lies inside Q. Finally, in (c) the shaded area is $(\Lambda \cup -\Lambda)^C$ and there are reforms, such as dq^*, that are tight equilibrium preserving.

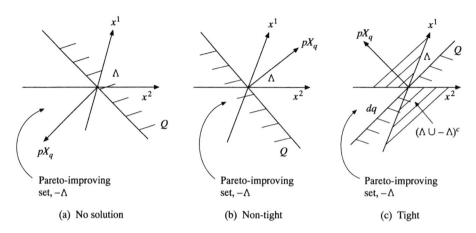

(a) No solution   (b) Non-tight   (c) Tight

Figure 6.8 Explanation of theorem 6.5

The importance of theorem 6.5 is that it demonstrates that a Pareto-improving reform may lead from an efficient point to a non-tight equilibrium with the demand vector interior to the production set. Production inefficiency may therefore be introduced as part of the reform process. This aspect of reform will be considered further in section 4.

3.3 Informational requirements

It is worth contrasting the information required to implement the Pareto-improving reform with that necessary for the welfare-improving reform and for optimal taxation. The Pareto-improving reform is based upon the gradient vectors of the households but, to determine the Pareto-improving set of reforms, it is necessary only to possess knowledge of the direction of these vectors not the length. From Roy's identity, the direction can be determined by knowledge of individual household demands; there is no requirement to observe the marginal utility of income. Such information is, in principle, directly observable. To determine whether a change satisfies productive feasibility it is sufficient to know initial producer prices and the derivatives, or elasticities, of aggregate demand. Although this information cannot be directly observed, it can be easily inferred from market data. The Pareto reform analysis can therefore be applied without the need for specifying the social welfare function. An example of such an application can be found in Ahmad and Stern (1984).

In contrast, the welfare-improving reform does require specification of the social welfare function and the individual marginal utilities so that the social welfare weights can be derived. One methodology for achieving this has been described in chapter 4, section 5 but, as noted there, that involved imposing significant restrictions upon the structure of the social marginal utilities of income. However, it is worth emphasising that it is only the direction of the welfare vector that needs to be known and not its length. The other informational requirements are as for the Pareto reform.

4 PRODUCTIVE EFFICIENCY AND MAXIMISING REFORMS

The analysis above has identified when improving reforms exist but has left two important questions unanswered. Firstly, if the solution set is non-empty, which of the reforms in the solution set should be chosen? Secondly, can any insight be obtained into when a reform will lead to an interior point of the production set?

From the definitions of the previous section, it should be noted that a reform will maintain efficiency if leads to a tight equilibrium. Producer prices are always chosen to decentralise a point on the boundary of the production set so that at a tight equilibrium, with $X(q) = Y(p)$, consumption is also on the boundary and efficiency occurs. When the equilibrium is non-tight, consumption is within the production set and the equilibrium is inefficient. That inefficient equilibria can arise due to the reform cannot therefore be ruled out and, in fact, appear to be as likely as efficient outcomes.

4.1 The possibility of inefficiency

To proceed beyond these generalities the approach of Dixit (1979) will be followed. The focus will be placed upon the welfare-improving reform problem and the optimal reform will be derived as that from the solution set that maximises the increase in welfare. It is first necessary to restrict the set from which solutions may be drawn since, in general, the solution set is a cone: if reform x raises welfare by dW, then λx, $\lambda > 0$, which is also a solution, raises welfare by λdW, hence no maximising reform exists. A procedure introduced by Dixit (1979) is to restrict consideration to vectors dq that lie on the unit sphere. This normalisation rule on the set of feasible reforms is now adopted in place of the restriction used in the previous sections. The reforms must therefore satisfy

$$\sum_{j=1}^{n} dq_j^2 = 1. \tag{6.17}$$

To reflect the fact that the reforms in question are differential, the interpretation of this normalisation is that units are such that 1 is *small*.

The optimal reform is identified as that reform on the surface of the unit sphere which maximises the increase in welfare. Writing

$$F(q_1, \ldots, q_n) \leq 0, \tag{6.18}$$

for the production constraint, where the function has been redefined to suppress the dependence upon aggregate demand, the optimal choice of reform is the solution to

$$\max_{\{dq\}} dW = \nabla W^T dq, \tag{6.19}$$

subject to the pair of constraints

$$dF = \nabla F^T dq \leq 0, \ \sum_{j=1}^{n} dq_j^2 = 1. \tag{6.20}$$

The Lagrangean for this maximisation is

$$\mathcal{L} = \nabla W^T dq - \mu \nabla F^T dq + \lambda \left[1 - \sum_{j=1}^{n} dq_j^2 \right]. \tag{6.21}$$

From (6.21), the first-order condition for the choice of the ith element of the reform vector is

$$\nabla W_i - \mu \nabla F_i - 2\lambda dq_i = 0. \tag{6.22}$$

Substituting (6.22) into the constraint on the size of the reforms provides the restriction that

$$\sum_{i=1}^{n} \left[\frac{\nabla W_i - \mu \nabla F_i}{2\lambda} \right]^2 = 1. \tag{6.23}$$

The focus of interest here is in the optimal reform, so it is assumed a non-zero solution exists to (6.19)–(6.20) and hence that $\lambda > 0$. It follows that

$$dq_i = \frac{\nabla W_i - \mu \nabla F_i}{\left[\sum_{j=1}^{n} [\nabla W_j - \mu \nabla F_j]^2 \right]^{1/2}}. \tag{6.24}$$

As the denominator of (6.24) is positive, substitution from (6.24) into the production constraint shows that productive feasibility will be satisfied if

$$\nabla F^T \nabla W - \mu \nabla F^T \nabla F \leq 0. \tag{6.25}$$

Solving (6.25) for μ, the multiplier on the production constraint, gives

$$\mu \geq \frac{\nabla F^T \nabla W}{\nabla F^T \nabla F}. \tag{6.26}$$

It is from (6.26) that production efficiency can be addressed. If $\nabla F^T \nabla W > 0$ then $\mu > 0$ and, from the complementary slackness conditions, production efficiency is preserved. Conversely, $\nabla F^T \nabla W < 0$ implies that $\mu = 0$ so that the reform will lead to a new equilibrium with productive inefficiency.

The importance of this result is the fact that for many situations, as captured by the Diamond–Mirrlees Production Efficiency lemma (theorem 4.1) and its extension by Hahn (1973), production efficiency will be desirable at the policy optimum. It would then be expected that it would also be required along the reform path. In contrast, these results show that this belief is not correct and that reform may lead to inefficiency until the optimum is reached.

The geometric interpretation of the discussion of (6.26) is that $\nabla F^T \nabla W < 0$ implies, in two dimensions, that the vectors ∇F and ∇W make an angle of more than 90°. The vector of reforms is chosen to make the narrowest feasible angle

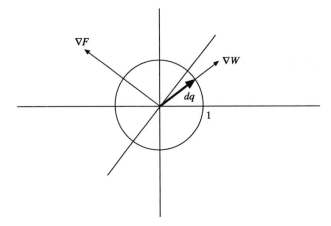

Figure 6.9   Production inefficiency after reform

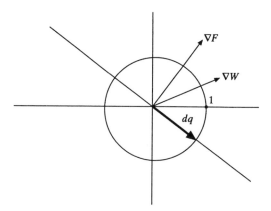

Figure 6.10   Production efficiency

with ∇W as this will maximise the increase in welfare. If $\nabla F^T \nabla W < 0$, the maximising reform lies along ∇W itself and can be defined by $dq = \delta \nabla W$, where $(\delta \nabla W)'(\delta \nabla W) = 1$. This situation is depicted in figure 6.9 for a two-good economy where the change in prices is restricted to be on the unit circle.

Production efficiency remains after the reform when $\nabla F^T \nabla W > 0$. The maximising reform is then the vector orthogonal to ∇F, thus satisfying the production constraint, that makes the smallest angle with ∇W. This represents a reform that moves the economy around the boundary of the production set. This is illustrated in figure 6.10.

To summarise the discussion, productive inefficiency may occur after the reform has taken place. Whether it occurs is dependent upon the divergence between the vector of derivatives of the welfare function and those of the production constraint. When these are similar, production efficiency is retained.

These results have been extended by Guesnerie (1977) and Fogelman, Quinzii and Guesnerie (1978) who consider policy reform as a dynamic process. At each moment in time the process is such that the reform must be Pareto improving so that individual utilities must be increasing along the reform path. In addition, the changes in demand must be capable of being matched by supply changes and consequent modification of producer prices.

The major finding of the analysis is, that to be successful, the reform process must be allowed to pass through points interior to the production set. If it is not, it may terminate at a point which is not a local Pareto optimum. Despite any inefficiencies that may occur along the path, the process will always terminate at an efficient point.

4.2 Interpretation

There are two interpretations of this result that are worth noting. The first interpretation is that the production inefficiency arises because the reform is seeking the maximum increase in welfare and there is no reason why this needs to be along the frontier. Although the initial point for the reform process and the final point are both on the frontier, the path of greatest increase in welfare is more likely to go through the production set than to follow its boundary.

The alternative interpretation rests on the observation that the initial point is not derived as the outcome of a social maximisation but is, in a sense, arbitrary. As a consequence, there is no reason to expect any relationship to hold between the gradient vectors Z and W, or between Z and the gradient vectors of individual utilities. This should be contrasted to the position at the optimum, shown in figure 6.4b, where the gradient vectors Z and W point in opposite directions. Given this arbitrary relation, it is only natural that production inefficiency may arise.

4.3 Lump-sum taxes

The analysis to this point has been concerned only with the effects of changes in the consumer price vector. It is reasonable to expect that other policy variables will be available to the government such as income taxes or methods of effecting transfer payments and the effect of these upon the reform problem needs to be considered.

Although optimal lump-sum taxes can be ruled out for the reasons discussed in chapter 2, section 4.1, a uniform lump-sum tax or subsidy cannot be dismissed so easily. As shown by Smith (1983), the incorporation of a uniform lump-sum subsidy has important implications for the reform problem. To understand the nature of these implications, it is helpful to refer back to the discussion of 4.2. Production inefficiency may arise because the gradient vectors of the indirect utility functions of the individual households are essentially arbitrary. When a lump-sum subsidy is introduced, the gradient vector of indirect utility with respect to the set of policy instruments will have a positive entry for every consumer for the effect of the lump-sum subsidy. This observation ensures a degree of similarity between the indirect utility functions of the separate households and significantly modifies the conclusions.

Consider now the consequence of introducing a lump-sum subsidy, I, to all households. From an initial point with $I=0$, a reform in I and q will lead to a Pareto improvement if

$$\nabla V^{hT} \begin{bmatrix} dI \\ dq \end{bmatrix} > 0, \text{ all } h, \tag{6.27}$$

or, using Roy's identity and eliminating the (positive) marginal utility of income, if

$$dI - x^{hT} dq > 0. \tag{6.28}$$

The change will be productively feasible if the change in demand has negative value at initial producer prices which can be expressed as

$$\sum_{h=1}^{H} p^T x_I^h dI + p^T X_q dq \leq 0, \tag{6.29}$$

where x_I^h is the derivative of household h demand with respect to lump-sum income. Since I is initially zero, the additional condition $dI \geq 0$ must also be satisfied.

Referring back to theorem 6.5, a reform will lead to inefficiency if $p^T X_q \in \Lambda(q)$. From the definition of $\Lambda(q)$, and the assumption that $p^T X_q \neq 0$, this is equivalent to the existence of $\lambda^h > 0$, all h, and $\mu > 0$ such that

$$\sum_{h=1}^{H} \lambda^h x^h - \mu p^T X_q = 0. \tag{6.30}$$

An improving reform that requires inefficiency will only exist if there exist $\lambda^h > 0$, all h, $\mu \geq 0$ and $\eta \geq 0$ such that (6.30) is satisfied and

$$\sum_{h=1}^{H} \lambda^h + \eta + \mu \sum_{h=1}^{H} p^T x_I^h = 0. \tag{6.31}$$

Since (6.30) requires $\mu > 0$, (6.31) can only be satisfied if $\sum_{h=1}^{H} p^T x_I^h < 0$. That is, to obtain production inefficiency it is necessary that the aggregate income effect must be negative. If, as is more likely, $\sum_{h=1}^{H} p^T x_I^h > 0$ then production inefficiency cannot arise. Hence, if all goods are normal, the use of a lump-sum subsidy will eliminate production inefficiency along the reform path.

The reasoning behind this argument is simple. If the government budget is balanced at the initial, efficient, point, it will be in surplus after moving to an inefficient point. The lump-sum subsidy can be used to disburse this surplus. If demand rises in response to the subsidy, which it will when goods are normal, a tight equilibrium will be achieved and efficiency restored. This represents a Pareto improvement over the inefficient position. This process will not work when $\sum_{h=1}^{H} p^T x_I^h < 0$ since the lump-sum subsidy will then reduce the value of demand further and inefficiency will increase.

A final point worth noting is that the ability to use a lump-sum subsidy ensures that the Pareto-improving set is non-empty. This follows because each vector ∇V^{hT} has a positive entry for the marginal effect of an increase in lump-sum subsidy so that the cone generated by the vectors must be pointed. With a lump-sum subsidy only the second stage of the Pareto-improving reform problem needs to be addressed.

5 THE INVERSE OPTIMUM

The motivation for the *inverse optimum* is derived from noting that when no feasible improving reform exists it follows from the Tucker's and Motzkin's theorems that the initial position is optimal given the social welfare weights. This result can have an alternative interpretation as follows. Given any initial position, it is possible to consider which set of welfare weights would make the initial point an optimum. If these weights are calculated and they do not conform with those of the policy maker, this is equivalent to saying a reform exists. The major work in this area is Ahmad and Stern (1984) who introduced the inverse optimum and applied the methodology to Indian data.

5.1 Theory

To formalise the inverse optimum, return to the welfare-improving reform problem. It is convenient to adopt as a normalisation rule that the tax on good 1 is zero and that $q_1 = p_1 = 1$; hence $dq_1 = 0$. The vector ∇W^T can then be written as

$$\nabla W^T = \left(\sum_{h=1}^{H} \frac{\partial W}{\partial V^h} \frac{\partial V^h}{\partial q_2}, \ldots, \sum_{h=1}^{H} \frac{\partial W}{\partial V^h} \frac{\partial V^h}{\partial q_n} \right) = \left(-\sum_{h=1}^{H} \beta^h x_2^h, \ldots, -\sum_{h=1}^{H} \beta^h x_n^h \right), (6.32)$$

where the second equality in (6.32) follows from (4.37). For the remainder of this section, $\beta^1, \ldots, \beta^H$ are termed the *social welfare weights* of the households. They remain, of course, a composition of social and private marginal utilities.

Employing (6.32), the first form of the inverse optimum problem can now be stated.

Inverse optimum

What must the welfare weights $(\beta^1, \ldots, \beta^H)$ be in order that the equations

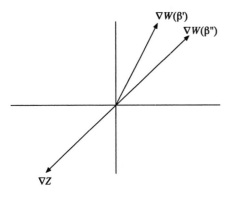

Figure 6.11   The inverse optimum

$$\nabla W^T dq > 0, \tag{6.33}$$

and

$$\nabla Z^T dq \geq 0, \tag{6.34}$$

have only the zero vector as solution?

The interpretation of this formulation is that the βs are being treated as variables and the aim is to discover the set of βs that justify the initial policy as optimal. Given these values of the social weights they can be assessed in terms of their suitable representation of social preferences. If they are obviously unacceptable, the initial policy can be seen as non-optimal.

Recalling the discussion following (6.16), the diagrammatic explanation of the inverse optimum is that β is being adjusted until the vector ∇W is such that the boundary of the half space, S, is coincident to the boundary of $Q(p,q)$. In figure 6.11, the set of weights β'' would solve the inverse optimum.

Applying the same analysis to the Pareto-improving reform, part (b) of the Motzkin theorem provides a set of non-negative weights under which no reform can be found. These can also be interpreted as the implicit social welfare weights of the households constituting the economy. Evidently, this can only be achieved if the number of goods is equal to the number of households. With too many households the βs will not be uniquely identified and with too few the equations need not have a solution. When the inverse optimum is solved it is possible that some of the β values may be negative. This indicates that a Pareto improvement may be made.

5.2 Applications

In their application of the inverse optimum analysis, Ahmad and Stern (1984) employ the same commodity groupings and Indian data set as in the work of Murty and Ray reported in chapter 4. Their first step is to take the revenue requirement as given and to solve the inverse optimum problem. As their data

Table 6.1. *Solution of inverse optimum*

Household group (Rs./month)	β
0–25	−126.37
25–32	171.36
32–40	−53.94
40–45	−438.41
45–55	241.01
55–70	33.54
70–90	−80.68
90–150	18.9
Above 150	−4.32

set has more households than goods, this is achieved by grouping the households into nine income bands to give the same number of households as goods. Table 6.1 describes the outcome of this procedure.

As can be seen from table 6.1, there is considerable variance in the welfare weights attached to the different income groups. There are also a number of negative weights which indicate that Pareto-improving reforms are possible.

Having identified the possibility of making Pareto-improving reforms, Ahmad and Stern proceed to calculate a vector of such reforms. This vector is restricted by the assumption that the tax changes must not increase or decrease the revenue raised per unit of good by more than one rupee. This normalisation rule is an alternative to (6.17). The resulting tax changes are shown in table 6.2 and the welfare effects of these in table 6.3.

The welfare change table shows clearly how welfare has increased for some groups and decreased for none. Tax changes could obviously be undertaken until the gains from reform were exhausted.

An alternative approach to the inverse optimum problem is taken by Christiansen and Jansen (1978). They approach the analysis from the perspective that the welfare weights are determined by political considerations and the form of the welfare function can be inferred from study of the political process. A vector of income changes is defined as distributively neutral if it leaves all relative welfare weights unchanged and the political process is deemed to view an equal relative increase of all incomes as neutral. Imposing an additive social welfare function

$$W = \sum_{h=1}^{H} W(M^h), \tag{6.35}$$

and defining the welfare weight of h as a function of income by

$$\beta(M^h) = \frac{\partial W(M^h)}{\partial M^h}, \tag{6.36}$$

Table 6.2. *Tax changes*

Commodity	Tax change (Rs.)
Cereals	− 0.84
Milk and milk products	+ 1.00
Edible oils	+ 1.00
Meat, fish, eggs	+ 0.47
Sugar and gur	+ 1.00
Other food	− 1.00
Clothing	− 1.00
Fuel and light	− 1.00
Other non-food	+ 0.37

Table 6.3. *Welfare changes*

Household group (Rs./month)	Welfare increase
0–25	0.005
25–32	0.03
32–40	0.02
40–45	0.04
45–55	0.09
55–70	0.09
70–90	0.05
90–150	0
Above 150	0

the political view of distributional neutrality implies that

$$\frac{\beta(M^h)}{\beta(M^{\hat{h}})}, \quad h \neq \hat{h} \tag{6.37}$$

is homogeneous of degree 1 in M^h, $M^{\hat{h}}$. From this it follows that the welfare weight function must take the form

$$\beta(M) = KM^{-v}, \tag{6.38}$$

which is identical to the form in (4.51).

This analysis is then integrated within a study of the Norwegian commodity tax system. In addition to the issues addressed in chapter 4, the design of taxes also takes into account the assumption that four of the fifteen commodity groups may have significant externality effects. When the externality effects are ignored, a value of $v = 1.706$ rationalises the choice of observed tax rates. In contrast, incorporating the externality effects provides a value of $v = 0.88$. At this value of v the social welfare function (6.35) is approximately log-linear. The difference between the two values of v show that the results of inverse optimum calculations may be highly sensitive to the correct choice of framework.

6 MARGINAL SOCIAL COST OF TAXATION

The marginal social cost has been developed as a means of assessing the potential optimality of a commodity tax system and, if the existing system is not optimal, of indicating the direction in which it should be reformed. If carefully applied, the technique is also useful for assessing other policy reforms. As above, the existence of an improving reform follows from the non-optimality of the initial position but the direction of reform is determined by assuming certain regularity conditions for the economy, where the required regularity is clarified below.

6.1 Derivation

To introduce marginal social cost the Diamond–Mirrlees economy of chapter 4 is employed. Recalling that analysis, the consumers are described by their indirect utility functions

$$U^h = V^h(q_1, \ldots, q_n, w, I^h),$$ (6.39)

and the tax revenue that must be raised is given by

$$R = \sum_{i=1}^{n} \sum_{h=1}^{H} t_i x_i^h.$$ (6.40)

Social welfare is determined by a Bergson–Samuelson social welfare function which is defined on the vector of indirect utilities

$$W = W(V^1(\cdot), \ldots, V^H(\cdot)).$$ (6.41)

Starting from an initial vector of taxes $(t_1, \ldots, t_n)$, the effect on social welfare of a change dt_k in the tax t_k on good k is given by

$$\left[\sum_{h=1}^{H} \frac{\partial W}{\partial V^h} \frac{\partial V^h}{\partial q_k} \right] dt_k.$$ (6.42)

The effect of the same change in t_k on tax revenue is

$$\left[\sum_{h=1}^{H} x_k^h + \sum_{i=1}^{n} \sum_{h=1}^{H} t_i \frac{\partial x_i^h}{\partial q_k} \right] dt_k.$$ (6.43)

Using these two terms, the marginal social cost of raising a unit of revenue by increasing the tax on good k, λ_k, is defined by (minus) their ratio

$$\lambda_k = -\frac{\displaystyle\sum_{h=1}^{H} \frac{\partial W}{\partial V^h}\frac{\partial V^h}{\partial q_k}}{\displaystyle\sum_{h=1}^{H} x_k^h + \sum_{i=1}^{n}\sum_{h=1}^{H} t_i \frac{\partial x_i^h}{\partial q_k}}.$$

(6.44)

It is clear from the first-order conditions for the optimal tax problem that at an optimum all the marginal social costs for goods $k = 1,\ldots,n$ should be equal. If they are not equal, the existing tax system is not optimal. In the case that the λs are not equal, those goods with the largest values of λ should have their taxes reduced since collecting revenue via these goods leads to a larger loss in social welfare for a unit of revenue than would taxes on low λ goods.

This procedure can be interpreted as being the first step in an iterative algorithm to find the maximum. The specific requirement that the goods with high values of λ_k should have their taxes reduced is based on the assumption that the problem has sufficient regularity so that the direct effect of t_k on λ_k dominates the cross effects caused by the adjustment of other tax rates. If this restriction is satisfied the variation in the λs indicates the correct direction of reform. Typically, the non-concavity of the tax problem prevents the application of standard theorems on the convergence of algorithms.

An interesting application of the social marginal cost is made in Newbery (1986) where the issue of taxes on intermediate goods when there is not a complete set of final goods taxes is addressed. The argument proceeds by evaluating the marginal social costs of the existing set of taxes and contrasts these with the marginal social costs of taxes on intermediate goods. If the latter costs are lower, and a condition is given by Newbery for when they will be, intermediate goods taxes should be introduced. This result also indicates the importance of a full set of commodity taxes in the proof of the Diamond–Mirrlees efficiency lemma. The marginal social cost also forms the basis of the Murty–Ray algorithm, described in chapter 4, for calculating optimal commodity taxes.

6.2 Empirical application

An empirical application of the use of the marginal social cost is given by Decoster and Schokkaert (1989). The analysis is applied to Belgian data with a twelve commodity breakdown. The welfare weights for the social welfare function are defined in the manner described in chapter 4, thus

$$\beta^h = \left(\frac{\mu^1}{\mu^h}\right)^{\varepsilon}.$$

(6.45)

The marginal social costs will evidently depend upon the chosen value of ε. A selection of the results is given in table 6.4.

Table 6.4. *Marginal social costs*

Commodity	$\varepsilon = 0$	$\varepsilon = 1.0$	$\varepsilon = 10.0$
Food	1.1192	0.8845	0.1927
Beverages	1.0254	0.8012	0.1609
Tobacco	2.4158	1.9102	0.3827
Clothing	1.1162	0.8538	0.1418
Rent	1.1469	0.8890	0.1789
Heating	1.2214	0.9688	0.2256
Durables	1.0807	0.8207	0.1310
Housing	1.0363	0.7872	0.1410
Personal care	1.1579	0.9031	0.1779
Transport	1.3067	0.9857	0.1409
Leisure	1.1792	0.9019	0.1537
Services	0.8833	0.6645	0.1300

Table 6.4 illustrates that the Belgian tax system is not optimal for any value of ε. However, for all values tobacco has the highest marginal social cost and services the lowest. The policy recommendation from this would be that the tax on tobacco should be lowered and that on services raised. Furthermore, heating also has a generally high marginal social cost. Decoster and Schokkaert also present the social marginal costs for different income groupings from which can be formed general views on the importance of various commodities to different income groupings. For instance food appears important to the low income groups with transport of no consequence. The ranking is exactly reversed for the highest income group.

7 POLITICAL CONSTRAINTS

The policy reform problem has been extended by Kanbur and Myles (1992) to include political constraints upon directions of reform. These constraints are intended to capture the fact that policy makers are invariably constrained in their choice of policy by the need, for example, to win elections, avoid riots and civil disorder and satisfy influential citizens.

The general form of a political constraint consists of a set of S functions $T_s(\xi)$: $\mathscr{R}^m \to \mathscr{R}$, $s = 1, \dots, S$ such that any policy change dq that satisfies the political constraint has the property that

$$T dq \geq 0,$$ (6.46)

where

$$T = \begin{bmatrix} \nabla T_1^T \\ \cdot \\ \nabla T_S^T \end{bmatrix}, \tag{6.47}$$

is the matrix formed from the gradient vectors of the T_s functions. One simple example arises in the case of a political elite whose welfare must not be reduced by the reform. The functions $T_s(q)$ are then the indirect utility functions of the households comprising this elite and T is formed from the gradient vectors of the indirect utility functions.

Incorporating the political constraints into the WI gives the following reform problem

Constrained welfare-improving reform (CWI)

Does there exist a vector dq of reforms such that

$$\nabla W^T dq > 0, \ \nabla Z^T dq \geq 0, \ Tdq \geq 0? \tag{6.48}$$

The structure of this problem can also be characterised by the use of a theorem of the alternative. From Mangasarian (1969)

Theorem 6.6

Either there exists a vector x with

(a) $Ax \geq 0, Bx \geq 0, Cx \geq 0,$

or there are three vectors such that

(b) $A^T y_1 + B^T y_2 + C^T y_3 = 0, y_1 > 0, y_2 \geq 0, y_3 \geq 0.$

Proof

See Mangasarian (1969).

Hence either a solution exists (case (a)) or there is some set of weights (case (b)), with the vector y_3 proportional to the Lagrange multiplier on the political constraints, for which the initial state is optimal.

The size of the solution sets to PI, WI and CWI can be contrasted. Under the normalisation rule in (6.17) that the reform vector must lie on the surface of the unit sphere, the size of a solution set can be defined as the area it covers on the surface of the sphere. Denote S^P, S^C, and S^W to be the solution sets to PI, CWI and WI respectively. The relative sizes of these solution sets are then as given in theorem 6.7.

Theorem 6.7 (Kanbur and Myles)

(a) $S^C \subseteq S^W, S^P \subseteq S^W,$

and, when the constraint is the non-reduction of the utilities of a political elite

(b) $S^P \subseteq S^C \subseteq S^W.$

Proof

To show that $S^P \subseteq S^W$ define $K_H = \left\{ x : x = \sum_{h=1}^{H} \lambda_h \nabla V^{hT}, \lambda_h \geq 0 \right\}$ which is the cone

generated by the vectors $\nabla V^h, h = 1, \ldots, H.$ As $\dfrac{\partial W}{\partial V^h} \geq 0,$ all $h, \nabla W \in K_H.$ Next, take

$H_{\nabla Z}$ and $H_{\nabla W}$ to be the half spaces defined by $H_{\nabla Z} = \{ x : \nabla Z^T x \geq 0 \}$ and $H_{\nabla W} = \{ x : \nabla W^T x \geq 0 \}.$ Using these definitions, $S^W = H_{\nabla Z} \cap \mathrm{Int} H_{\nabla W} \cap B_1$ and $S^P = H_{\nabla Z} \cap \{ K_H^+ / 0 \} \cap B_1$ where a superscript '+' indicates the positive polar of a cone and B_1 denotes the unit sphere. But, as $\nabla W \in K_H, \{ K_H^+ / 0 \} \subseteq \mathrm{Int} H_{\nabla W}.$ Hence $S^P \subseteq S^W.$

The proof that $S^C \subseteq S^W$ follows from using the rows of the matrix T to define the half space $H_{\nabla T} = \{ x : \nabla T_s^T x \geq 0 \}, s = 1, \ldots, S.$ Form this it can be seen that

$S^C = H_{\nabla Z} \cap \left[\bigcap_{s=1}^{S} H_{\nabla T} \right] \cap \mathrm{Int} H_{\nabla W} \cap B_1.$ It is then clear that $S^C \subseteq S^W.$ This proves

(a).

To prove (b), note that if the utility levels of a political elite constrain policy then T is given by the gradient vectors of the indirect utilities of the members of the elite. Index the members of the elite by $c = 1, \ldots, C$ and let

$K_C = \left\{ x : x = \sum_{c=1}^{C} \lambda_c \nabla V^{cT}, \lambda_c \geq 0 \right\}$ be the cone generated by the political con-

straints. Evidently, $K_C \subseteq K_H$ and $S^C = H_{\nabla Z} \cap K_C^+ \cap \mathrm{Int} H_{\nabla W} \cap B_1.$ Also, as $K_C \subseteq K_H$ it follows that $K_H^+ \subseteq K_C^+$ and thus $K_H^+ / 0 \subseteq K_C^+.$ From this $K_H^+ / 0 \subseteq \{ K_C^+ \cap \mathrm{Int} H_{\nabla W} \} \subseteq \mathrm{Int} H_{\nabla W}$ and $S^P \subseteq S^C \subseteq S^W.$

The result in (a) arises because ∇W is a positive linear combination of the rows of P and (b) is explained by the fact that in the case described the cone generated by T is a subset of that generated by $P.$ This theorem formalises some of the comments in Ahmad and Stern (1984).

In the presence of the political elite, the optimal tax problem is

$$\max_{\{q_2, \ldots, q_n\}} W = W\big(V^1(q_1, q_2 \ldots, q_n), \ldots, V^H(q_1, q_2 \ldots, q_n) \big), \tag{6.49}$$

subject to the political constraint

$$V^c(q_1, q_2 \ldots, q_n) \geq \bar{V}^c, \text{ all } c \in C, \tag{6.50}$$

where C is the set of elite households, and the production constraint

$$F\big(X(q_1, q_2, \ldots, q_n) \big) \leq 0. \tag{6.51}$$

Solving (6.49)–(6.51), the optimal policy is characterised by

$$\sum_{h=1}^{H} \frac{\partial W}{\partial V^h} \frac{\partial V^h}{\partial q_i} + \sum_{c=1}^{C} \mu^c \frac{\partial V^c}{\partial q_i} - \lambda \nabla F^T \frac{\partial X}{\partial q_i} = 0, \ i = 1, \ldots, n, \qquad (6.52)$$

and

$$\lambda F = 0, \ \lambda \geq 0, \ \mu^c(V^c - \bar{V}^c) = 0, \ \mu^c \geq 0, \ c = 1, \ldots, C. \qquad (6.53)$$

From (6.52) and (6.53), it can be seen that the effect of the constraint is to raise the effective welfare weight on the constraining households from $\dfrac{\partial W}{\partial V^c}$ to $\dfrac{\partial W}{\partial V^c} + \mu^c$, with the complementary slackness conditions, (6.53), guaranteeing that μ^c is non-negative. From this it can be seen that the implicit effect of the constraint is to shift the optimal policy in favour of the constrained household by effectively giving greater concern for social welfare to them.

This result does have important implications for the analysis of the inverse optimum problem. Working back from the solution to (6.52) would generate the effective weights $\dfrac{\partial W}{\partial V^c} + \mu^c$ which, whenever a constraint is effective, will differ from the true weights $\dfrac{\partial W}{\partial V^c}$. Therefore whenever political constraints are binding, it is not possible to recover the welfare function from observed policy. The inverse optimum can only recover the combined values of the welfare weights and the additional multipliers.

8 CONCLUSIONS

This chapter has reviewed the economic analysis of policy reform and has introduced some of the important analytical tools and results. The importance of the Theorems of the Alternative has been stressed since these theorems show that either an improving reform is possible or that the initial point is optimal. An alternative insight into the existence of reforms was provided by a geometric approach that relied on the properties of convex cones.

One of the most important conclusions to emerge from the analysis was that temporary inefficiency may arise during a process of reform. This finding should be contrasted to the efficiency lemma of chapter 4 which showed the desirability of production efficiency at the optimum. It should also be stressed that, although the theory was developed in the context of price reform in a Diamond–Mirrlees economy, the method of considering the effects of differential policy reform can be usefully applied beyond this particular framework.

7

RISK

1 INTRODUCTION

Risk is a factor that is evident throughout economic activity. Firms must choose between investment plans for which neither the cost nor the return can be known with certainty, households purchase goods whose value in use is determined by the state of nature and the government receives uncertain revenues and allocates funds to projects with unknown outcomes. Although the Arrow–Debreu economy is capable of incorporating risks of these kinds, so that they can be viewed as having already been covered by previous analysis, the special features involved with risk justify a separate chapter devoted to the subject.

The interpretation of the Arrow–Debreu economy in the presence of risk is discussed first and the Pareto optimality of equilibrium is reconsidered with particular focus placed upon the number of markets necessary to sustain optimality. This analysis is at the level of generality of previous chapters. The reasons why there may be too few markets to sustain optimality and whether this may justify government intervention are also considered. Individual attitudes to risk, in terms of measures of risk aversion, are then contrasted to social attitudes. Alternative perspectives on social attitudes, including the Arrow–Lind theorem supporting risk neutrality of government, are contrasted. A more general framework is then presented which shows how social attitudes to risk can be derived from the social insurance effects of projects and the weighting of households in the social welfare function.

A more specific interpretation of risk in terms of assets with random returns is then adopted and household maximisation is analysed in further detail. Reactions to taxation are determined under various assumptions about the loss-offset provisions of the tax system, the return on the safe asset and the number of risky assets available. Two alternative perspectives on the nature of risk and the interaction with taxation are then described. The first is the standard utility maximisation analysis of labour supply but is extended to include uncertainty about the wage. This is followed by a consideration of choice between occupations where one occupation has a known return and the other an uncertain payoff.

Several different approaches to the design of income taxation with risk are described. The first set of analyses consider risks which are purely individual: some households may do well and others badly. The unifying feature of these is shown to be the welfare gains that can be achieved by the use of a distorting income tax due to the social insurance that the tax can provide. The social insurance effect is such that it is preferable to raise revenue from a set of *ex ante* identical households using the optimal income tax rather than a uniform lump-sum tax. These results are contrasted to those that apply under purely aggregate risk where the entire population either gains or loses. In the latter case, taxation cannot provide social insurance.

Before proceeding, two points are worth noting. In common with most recent literature, no distinction is made here between risk and uncertainty; the two terms are employed interchangeably. Secondly, the analysis of tax evasion is reserved for later analysis in chapter 12. Although tax evasion is an example of choice with risk, it is somewhat special because of its illegality. In addition, the substantial literature on tax evasion merits separate consideration.

2 GENERAL EQUILIBRIUM WITH RISK

Risk can be incorporated into the Arrow–Debreu economy with very few formal modifications; effectively all that needs to be done is to increase the number of goods and prices in an appropriate manner. The results of the previous analysis then follow as in chapter 2. The classic presentations are given in Arrow (1963) and Debreu (1959). Radner (1982) provides an extensive survey of the relevant literature.

The major focus here will be placed on the simplest case in which all contracts are formed in period 0 and the uncertainty is about the state of the world that will occur in the only other period, period 1, in which contracts are fulfilled and consumption takes place. In this setting it is not necessary to distinguish commodities by their time of availability. The extension to many time periods (though retaining a single period in which contracts are formed) will be briefly discussed; none of the essential conclusions is modified.

2.1 Risk in the Arrow–Debreu economy

To formalise the notion of risk, a set of alternative *states of the world* is introduced. The set of states is intended to be an exhaustive list of all potential states that differ in an economically relevant way. The relation of these states to risk is that any realisation of random events will lead to one of the states, s, where the states are indexed $s = 1, \ldots, S$, and that there are sufficient states to cover all possible different realisations.

Each good in the economy is differentiated by its place and state of availability. Contracts are made prior to the realisation of the state and will correspondingly specify the place of delivery and the state in which delivery will be made. Since goods will only be delivered if the relevant state occurs, the term *contingent commodities* is often used since delivery is contingent upon the specified state occurring.

The production set of each firm is extended, in a manner compatible with the extended list of commodities, to include all feasible input–output combinations of contingent commodities. A production plan is then a list of inputs and outputs of all goods in all states. Denoting the price vector of the n goods in state s by $p_s = (p_{1s}, \ldots, p_{ns})$, the extended list of prices becomes $p = (p_1, \ldots, p_s)$. Firm j chooses a production plan $y^j = (y^j_{11}, \ldots, y^j_{n1}, \ldots, y^j_{nS})$ to maximise profits $\pi^j = py^j$. With a known price vector this provides a clearly defined level of profits. The structure of this profit maximisation problem is formally identical to that introduced in chapter 2 and, given the strict convexity of the production set, the outcome will be continuous supply and profit functions. It should be noted that these are supplies of contingent commodities which will only be delivered if the relevant state occurs.

The preferences of each household h are assumed to be representable by a von Neumann–Morgernstern (1953) utility function

$$U^h = \sum_{s=1}^{S} \rho_s^h U_s^h(x_s^h), \tag{7.1}$$

where $x_s^h = (x_{1s}^h, \ldots, x_{ns}^h)$ is the vector of consumption of the n goods in state s and $(\rho_1^h, \ldots, \rho_s^h)$ are the probabilities that household h assigns to the possibility of states 1 to S occurring. The structure of (7.1) allows each of the within-period utility functions to be state dependent.

If the endowment vector of h in state s is ω_s^h, their budget constraint is

$$\sum_{s=1}^{S} p_s x_s^h \leq \sum_{s=1}^{S} p_s \omega_s^h + \sum_{j=1}^{m} \theta_j^h \pi^j. \tag{7.2}$$

Once the price vector is known, the budget constraint in (7.2) is clearly determined. The household will then choose their demand for each contingent commodity to maximise utility subject to (7.2) and subject to the demand being in the consumption set of the household; the consumption set being defined in terms of contingent commodities. As in chapter 2, if (i) the utility function is continuous and strictly quasi-concave, (ii) the consumption set is closed, convex and has a lower bound and (iii) the endowment is interior to the consumption set, this maximisation will generate continuous demand functions for all goods. It should be noted that in this context quasi-concavity of the utility function implies risk aversion; see Arrow (1963) and Debreu (1959).

An equilibrium for the economy is a price vector such that demand is equal to supply for all contingent commodities. Whichever state arises, it is then the case that the demand for commodities in that state is equal to the supply. Since the economy is only a reinterpretation of that without uncertainty, the method of establishing the existence of equilibrium remains the same. In particular, the same set of assumptions applied to the extended definitions of the production and consumption sets remain sufficient for the existence of equilibrium.

2.2 Efficiency

In considering the efficiency of the equilibrium that will result from trade, it is necessary to distinguish between *ex ante* and *ex post* efficiency. An equilibrium is *ex ante* efficient if no redistribution of contingent consumption levels can be found that is Pareto improving in terms of expected utilities. Conversely, *ex post* efficiency would be achieved if no reallocation could take place of actual consumption levels in the state that occurred that would be Pareto-improving in terms of realised utilities.

The formal equivalence between the economy with certainty and that with uncertainty implies immediately that the equilibrium will be Pareto efficient in the *ex ante* sense; the proof of the First Theorem of Welfare Economics is directly applicable. Now let $\tilde{M}_s^h \equiv p_s x_s^h$ be the equilibrium value of the contingent commodities demanded by h in state s. Then, relative to the vector of income levels $(\tilde{M}_s^1, \ldots, \tilde{M}_s^H)$, the equilibrium allocation in any state s is also Pareto efficient in the *ex post* sense: once the state has been realised no reallocation of consumption exists that is Pareto improving. This result is explained by viewing households being endowed in state s with incomes $(\tilde{M}^1, \ldots, \tilde{M}^H)$ and then equilibrium being reached given these incomes. The outcome must be Pareto efficient.

A further observation merits attention. If no trade were to take place until the state were realised, the income of household h in state s, $\hat{M}_s^h$, would be given by the value of the state-contingent endowment, $\hat{M}_s^h \equiv \hat{p}_s \omega_s^h$, where $\hat{p}_s$ is the equilibrium price vector that would be realised once state s had occurred. It is also correct to observe that the equilibrium then reached in state s would be Pareto efficient in an *ex post* sense. However, there is no reason to expect that the income vector $(\tilde{M}_s^1, \ldots, \tilde{M}_s^H)$ is a simple rescaling of $(\hat{M}_s^1, \ldots, \hat{M}_s^H)$ nor that the equilibria reached with the two income distributions are identical. Both are Pareto efficient but they will generally be based upon different income distributions. The difference between the two income distributions arises because the trade in contingent commodities allows households to reallocate their purchasing power between states on the basis of their attitudes to risk and assessment of the probabilities of the states occurring. Further discussion of this issue can be found in Dreze (1970–1).

The equivalence between the economy with uncertainty and that with certainty also justifies the direct application of the Second Theorem of Welfare

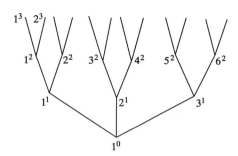

Figure 7.1   Time and uncertainty

Economics. When the required convexity and continuity assumptions are satisfied, any allocation that is Pareto efficient in an *ex ante* sense can be decentralised as a competitive equilibrium with appropriate lump-sum transfers. If there are no restrictions upon policy instruments, the government can therefore achieve a socially optimal outcome by lump-sum redistribution and operation of competitive markets. It should be noted that the lump-sum transfers will be in terms of contingent commodities and will generally be state dependent.

2.3 Including time

The introduction of time in addition to uncertainty can be achieved following the procedure due to Debreu (1959). Assume that there are T time periods, indexed $t = 1, \ldots, T$, during which consumption can take place and a further period, labelled 0, in which all trades are enacted. Period 0 occurs prior to periods during which consumption can take place. At time T there is a set of possible states of the world that may occur; these are indexed $s^T = 1^T, \ldots, S^T$. It is assumed that there is a unique series of states from period 0 through to T by which state s^T can be realised. Therefore, given a realisation of s^T, the previous states of the economy are determined. These assumptions are illustrated in figure 7.1. The states of the economy at each time period can be represented by the vertices of a tree. If $T = 3$, it can be seen that the realisation of state 1^3 implies that states 1^2, 1^1 must also have occurred.

A commodity can now be defined by its place of availability and by the vertex of the tree at which it is available. Specifying the vertex uniquely identifies the time and state in which the commodity is available. Since no delivery will take place unless the relevant vertex occurs, these commodities again represent contingent claims for delivery. Profit and utility maximisation can be defined in terms of these contingent commodities and continuous supply and demand functions derived.

It should be appreciated that this formulation of time and uncertainty does not alter any of the essential structures of the economy. The previous reasoning therefore continues to apply: under the standard assumptions an equilibrium will exist, a competitive equilibrium will be Pareto-efficient and any Pareto efficient equilibrium can be decentralised. In an economy with this structure, both time and uncertainty can be incorporated without the efficiency of the competitive equilibrium being destroyed.

2.4 Complete markets

When assessing the relevance of these results there are several issues that have to be considered. In addition to the points raised in chapter 2 concerning the strict applicability of the economy and the use of lump-sum taxation, it is now also important to consider the number and arrangement of markets in the economy. The economies described above have possessed a *complete* set of markets, that is, when markets open at the start of the economy trades can be organised for every good in any state and, in the extended economy, for any time. In short, the economy is assumed to possess markets for all state-contingent commodities. This requirement is naturally far too demanding for any actual economy to satisfy; it is not even likely that the products that will be available in the future will be known today. In reality there are well-organised futures markets in a small number of financial, industrial and agricultural products but certainly not for the majority of products. Furthermore, even when there are futures markets there is no necessary implication that state-contingent contracts can be written and enforced. Hart (1975a) demonstrates that if markets are incomplete the outcome of competitive trade will not be Pareto efficient and may even fail to be efficient relative to the set of markets that are open. In effect, when markets are incomplete the economy can become trapped in an equilibrium which is Pareto dominated. It is consequently unlikely that assumptions of this economy can be satisfied and hence its welfare properties cannot be appealed to as descriptive of reality.

There is, however, an alternative form of the economy, due to Arrow (1963), that is rather more tenable. This alternative interpretation reduces the number of futures markets that have to be operational and brings the economy closer to what is observed in practice. To formalise this idea it is simplest to return to the economy with uncertainty but a single period of consumption. Assume that there exists a set Σ of securities, with S members, such that security $s \in \Sigma$ pays one unit of numeraire commodity if state s occurs and nothing otherwise. Security s has price q_s. Economic activity is then organised in two stages. Firstly, households allocate their incomes to the purchase of securities. Hence securities will be purchased by household h to satisfy the budget constraint

$$M^h = \sum_{\sigma=1}^{S} q_\sigma z_\sigma^h, \tag{7.3}$$

where M^h is the income of h and z_σ^h is the quantity of security σ purchased by h. Naturally, this procedure will determine the income of consumer h in state σ to be z_σ^h. The second stage of the economy occurs after the state has been realised and involves the households using their income from security purchases to buy the commodities that are available in that state.

The central feature of this reinterpretation is that it leads to precisely the same equilibrium as the economy with a full set of futures markets. To see this, assume that in the original economy household h chose to purchase the vector $(x_{1s}^h, \ldots, x_{ns}^h)$ in state s. Given the equilibrium price vector, this choice will cost the household an amount given by

$$\sum_{i=1}^{n} p_{is} x_{is}^h. \tag{7.4}$$

If securities are purchased so that

$$z_\sigma^h = \sum_{i=1}^{n} p_{is} x_{is}^h, \text{ all } s = 1, \ldots, S, \sigma = s, \tag{7.5}$$

the household can guarantee the necessary income to purchase the optimal consumption plan. They will, of course, also choose this level of income since it was defined by the optimality of the consumption vector. The final step is to note that, since the total income to be allocated to securities is defined by the value of the contingent endowments and the profits of firms, this remains the same in both interpretations of the economy. The prices of the securities are then determined on their market so that precisely the correct levels of income are transferred forward. In summary, if for each state there exists a unique security that has a unit return in that state and zero return in all others, the equilibrium of the economy will be the same as that with a full set of futures markets. It therefore has the same welfare properties and the Two Theorems can be proved to hold.

Two further points are worth making about this economy. Firstly, the use of securities has economised upon the number of markets that are required to achieve optimality. The initial economy employed nS markets whereas the alternative possessed S security markets and n goods markets since the goods market was only opened after the state was realised. There is therefore greater likelihood that the optimum will be attained in the latter case. Secondly, although the economy was introduced in terms of the S elementary securities that had returns in only a single state, it will also function when securities have returns in several states provided the returns are such that the securities can be combined so that any vector of returns across the states can be achieved; see the discussion in Duffie and Sonnenschein (1989). This property of the securities is generally termed *spanning* in the literature. The applicability of this economy is therefore broader than the initial description may have suggested.

2.5 Comments

The discussion above has demonstrated that the Arrow–Debreu economy may be extended to accommodate uncertainty and that, when extended, it retains the welfare properties of the economy with certainty. However, the extension required either an expansion of the number of markets or the introduction of security markets. The first interpretation probably has little to commend it other than formal elegance since economies with complete sets of markets are not observed in practice. The second is rather more applicable and does suggest how economies actually attempt to cope with the existence of uncertainty but, although securities certainly exist, it is not clear that they actually satisfy the spanning property. Furthermore, the structure of the economy also places very strong informational requirements upon the participants. In order to determine the optimal purchase of securities, it is necessary for the household to know the prices that will rule in each possible state that may be realised; this is implicit in the statement of (7.5). It must also be the case that all the agents agree upon the prices that will be ruling in each state. This position is clearly untenable.

Although the interpretation of general equilibrium with risk shows that there is no formal difference between the economy with certainty and that with uncertainty, the structure of the latter makes it apparent that even less emphasis should be placed upon its welfare properties than was placed upon those of the certainty economy. As before, the economy provides a benchmark case against which other, more restricted, economies should be placed. As already noted, the existence of a market failure is not a sufficient condition for supporting government intervention since the government may also be restricted by some of the features of the economy that prevent the market being efficient. In every case it must be verified that the government can actually achieve a better outcome than the market.

3 PRIVATE AND SOCIAL ATTITUDES TO RISK

It is typically assumed that households prefer a certain outcome to a risky outcome with the same expected payoff. That such risk aversion exists is supported by the observation that the purchase of insurance policies is commonplace. The holding of shares with limited liability and of money, which pays no interest, can be similarly explained by the desire to avoid risk. Given that society is the sum of its members, does it follow from this that the government, as the representative of society, should also act in a risk-averse manner? The answer to this question has important implications for policy choice since a risk-averse government would undertake fewer risky projects than a risk-neutral one and would structure policies to avoid uncertainty in revenues and expenditures.

This section will first recall some aspects of the theory of household attitudes to risk and of the measurement of risk aversion. This is followed by a summary of alternative views on social attitudes to risk including the Arrow–Lind theorem that asserts the risk neutrality of the government. The section is completed by an analysis of the valuation of projects in a contingent-commodity framework with, possibly, incomplete markets.

3.1 Private attitudes

Consider household h which derives utility level $U^h = U^h(M)$, $U^{h\prime}(\cdot) > 0$, from certain income M. Assuming that the preferences of the household satisfy the assumptions of von Neumann–Morgernstern expected utility theory, so that the utility function is unique up to affine transformations, the expected utility of receiving income level $\tilde{M}$ with probability ρ and $\hat{M}$ with probability $1 - \rho$ is given by

$$\mathscr{E}[U^h] = \rho U^h(\tilde{M}) + [1 - \rho]U^h(\hat{M}), \tag{7.6}$$

where $\mathscr{E}[\cdot]$ is the expectations operator. If $\rho\tilde{M} + [1 - \rho]\hat{M} = M$ then household h is *risk averse* if and only if

$$U^h(M) > \rho U^h(\tilde{M}) + [1 - \rho]U^h(\hat{M}). \tag{7.7}$$

The interpretation of (7.7) is that a risk-averse household would not take on an actuarially fair bet. If the inequality was reversed the household would be a *risk lover*. Equality in (7.7) would imply *risk neutrality*.

For (7.7) to hold for all actuarially fair bets the marginal utility of income for h must be decreasing, that is $U^{h\prime\prime} < 0$. Equivalently, the utility function $U^h(M)$ must be strictly concave. A measure of the degree of risk aversion of a household must therefore involve the second derivative of utility. By itself, this cannot act as a measure since it is not invariant of the particular transformation of utility chosen. Two measures that are invariant to such transformations are given by the Arrow–Pratt (Arrow 1965, Pratt 1964) measures of *absolute* and *relative* risk aversion defined respectively by

$$\textit{Absolute risk aversion, } R_A(M) = \frac{-U^{h\prime\prime}}{U^{h\prime}},$$

and

$$\textit{Relative risk aversion, } R_R(M) = \frac{-M U^{h\prime\prime}}{U^{h\prime}}.$$

It is often hypothesised (for instance in Arrow 1965) that $R_A(M)$ is a decreasing function of M and that $R_R(M)$ is an increasing function. The first of these hypotheses implies that the willingness to take small bets of fixed size increases with income, an observation that is not implausible. The second implies that as the level of wealth and the size of bets increase in the same proportion, the willingness to accept the bet should fall. This observation is not as immediately appealing as the first.

Now consider a risk-averse household assessing whether to undertake a risky investment project, for example the purchase of securities. The concavity of the utility function that follows from the assumption of risk aversion, implies that the expected return to the household of the investment is less than the expected value of the returns. This is simply a more general restatement of (7.7). An alternative view is that the household discounts the returns for the risk involved at a higher rate than is justified by the probabilities of the outcomes alone. In any case, a risk-averse household will not undertake a project that has an expected value of zero.

An alternative perspective can be obtained by using the concept of a risk premium. Consider a household facing a random income M and choose the fixed income level M_0 such that

$$U(M_0) = \mathscr{E}[U(M)]. \tag{7.8}$$

Now set $M_0 = \bar{M} - \kappa$ where $\bar{M} = \mathscr{E}[M]$. From (7.8) this implies that

$$\mathscr{E}[U(M)] = U(M_0) = U(\bar{M} - \kappa). \tag{7.9}$$

The value κ is termed the *risk premium* and it can be interpreted as the amount the household would be willing to pay to avoid the risk associated with the random income M. It should be clear that as risk aversion increases, so will the value of the risk premium that the household will pay. In fact, denoting the variance of the random variable M by σ^2, Pratt (1964) shows that the risk premium and risk aversion are related by $\kappa = \frac{1}{2}\sigma^2 R_A(M_0) +$ higher-order terms.

3.2 Social attitudes

The implication of household risk aversion for the social treatment of risk has received considerable discussion and several alternative positions have been proposed. These are based upon differing views on the role of the government, its relation to the agents that compose the society over which it governs and its relative ability at dissipating risk.

A first view, propounded most forcefully by Hirshleifer (1964, 1966) and Sandmo (1972) is that the government should really not be given any privileged role with respect to risk bearing. In a perfect capital market, the decisions and attitudes to risk of the agents that constitute those markets are reflected in the equilibrium levels of discounting that are applied to risky projects since the market functions to allocate risks efficiently. As the market captures the views of agents, it is then argued that the government can do no better than to adopt the market rate of discounting when making its own project appraisal decisions. A further development of this argument would be to suggest that if the government did use a discount rate lower than the market rate, it would adopt projects that were socially undesirable and which displaced private-sector projects with higher returns.

An alternative view, stated for example in Samuelson (1964) and Vickrey (1964), is that the government is in an advantageous position with respect to accepting risk relative to private-sector agents. This advantage arises due to the size of the public sector and the number and variety of projects that it undertakes. If the returns from its various projects are not perfectly positively correlated, it is possible for the government to pool the risks arising from the projects and therefore lessen the overall uncertainty of its returns. The argument is then completed by noting that an ability to pool risks allows a lower discount factor to be applied to any single risky project than would be done if the project were undertaken separately in the private sector.

There are several arguments that can be raised against this view. Firstly, projects should be evaluated individually by the public sector and not as a package as implied by the risk-pooling argument. Packaging projects may result in some being adopted which are socially undesirable. Secondly, if the government is able to reduce risk by pooling, it should confer the advantages of doing so on the private sector rather then simply exploit them in the choice of public-sector project. One method of doing so is by direct subsidy of the private sector in order to allow previously marginal projects to be adopted.

Rather than focus on the risk pooling ability of government, Arrow and Lind (1970) argue in favour of a lower discount factor for the public sector on the grounds of the ability of the public sector to spread risk. A simple version of this argument would go as follows. Although each taxpayer is risk averse, the total cost of a project will be divided between taxpayers with each carrying only a small amount of the cost and therefore only a fraction of the risk. Provided that the number of taxpayers is sufficiently great, that the project is not large relative to the economy as a whole and that the (random) cost to any taxpayer of the project is not correlated with any existing uncertainty in their income stream, then as the number of taxpayers increases the risk premium of each taxpayer and the total risk premium to society tends to zero. Given this, the public sector should act as if it were risk neutral.

To prove this theorem, consider an economy with H identical households who have identically distributed random incomes, M, and concave, bounded, strictly increasing and differentiable utility functions $U(M)$ which satisfy the axioms of expected utility theory. The government carries all costs of investment in a project and receives all returns. The payoff, less costs, is denoted by Π. Its budget is to be balanced in the absence of the project so positive returns from the project are given equally to the taxpayers (by reducing taxes) and costs are carried by the taxpayers (by raising taxes).

The first step is to write the payoff to the project in the form $\Pi = \bar{\Pi} + X$ where $\bar{\Pi} = \mathscr{E}[\Pi]$ and $\mathscr{E}[X] = 0$. Now consider an individual household and let s, $0 \le s \le 1$, be their share of the returns of the project. This household would pay a risk premium $\kappa(s)$ to avoid the risk where $\kappa(s)$ is defined by $\mathscr{E}[U(M + s\bar{\Pi} + sX)] = U(M + s\bar{\Pi} - \kappa(s))$. The value of $\kappa(s)$ is the cost to the household of bearing the risk. With these definitions, theorem 7.1 can now be proved.

Theorem 7.1 (Arrow and Lind)

Assume that cov $(M, \Pi) = 0$ *and that* $s = \dfrac{1}{H}$. *The total cost of risk bearing,*

$H\kappa(s) = H\kappa \left(\dfrac{1}{H}\right) \equiv Hk(H)$, *then tends to zero as H tends to infinity.*

Proof

Differentiating expected utility with respect to s gives

$$\frac{\partial}{\partial s} \mathscr{E}[U(M + s\bar{\Pi} + sX)] = \mathscr{E}[U'(M + s\bar{\Pi} + sX)[\bar{\Pi} + X]]. \tag{7.10}$$

Setting $s = 0$ and employing the fact that cov $(M, \Pi) = 0$, which implies cov $(M, X) = 0$, it follows that

$$\mathscr{E}[U'(M)[\bar{\Pi} + X]] = \bar{\Pi}\mathscr{E}[U'(M)] \tag{7.11}$$

From the equality in (7.11), using the definition of a derivative shows that

$$\lim_{s \to 0} \frac{\mathscr{E}[U(M + s\bar{\Pi} + sX) - U(M)]}{s} = \bar{\Pi}\mathscr{E}[U'(M)], \tag{7.12}$$

or, equivalently under the assumption that $s = \dfrac{1}{H}$

$$\lim_{H \to \infty} H\mathscr{E}\left[U\left(M + \frac{\bar{\Pi} + X}{H}\right) - U(M)\right]$$

$$= \lim_{H \to \infty} H\mathscr{E}\left[U\left(M + \frac{\bar{\Pi}}{H} - k(H)\right) - U(M)\right] = \bar{\Pi}\mathscr{E}[U'(M)], \tag{7.13}$$

where the second equality follows from the definition of the risk premium.

Noting that $\lim_{H \to \infty} \dfrac{\bar{\Pi}}{H} - k(H) = 0$, the definition of a derivative can be used to write

$$\lim_{H \to \infty} \frac{\mathscr{E}\left[U\left(M + \dfrac{\bar{\Pi}}{H} - k(H)\right) - U(M)\right]}{\dfrac{\bar{\Pi}}{H} - k(H)} = \mathscr{E}[U'(M)]. \tag{7.14}$$

Using (7.14) to divide through (7.13) gives

$$\lim_{H \to \infty} [\bar{\Pi} - Hk(H)] = \bar{\Pi}, \tag{7.15}$$

or

$$\lim_{H \to \infty} Hk(H) = 0. \tag{7.16}$$

The limit in (7.16) proves the theorem.

Although a formally attractive theorem, this result is not entirely persuasive. The most obvious shortcoming is the assumed independence between private and public risk. These risks may well be highly correlated, for instance in a recession both public- and private-sector incomes will fall. More importantly, the theorem overlooks existing private-sector institutions for risk sharing. Foremost amongst these are insurance and joint-stock companies and the theorem does not prove that the public sector can spread risk any more effectively than these institutions. Furthermore, if there is an element of self-selection in the adoption of private-sector risk, it may be the case that risk in the private sector is borne by those who are risk lovers and that the private sector is, in aggregate, less than risk neutral.

To provide further insight into these issues, consider the following analysis due to Grinols (1985) which is based on the state-preference economy of section 2 augmented by the existence of a stock market. The economy is assumed here to last for two periods. There is no uncertainty in the first period, labelled 0, but any one of S possible states, $s = 1, \ldots, S$, may arise in the second period. Trades must be completed in the first period. It is possible to trade shareholdings in firms and to enact futures trades for some, or all, goods. A shareholding in a firm entitles the owner to a share in the production of the firm proportional to the shareholding and this is the only means by which households can obtain consumption in period 1. To motivate a social role for government risk taking, the analysis will focus on the case where there are incomplete futures markets.

A consumption plan for household h, $h = 1, \ldots, H$, is written $x^h = (x_0^h, x_1^h, \ldots, x_S^h)$ of which $e^h = (e_0^h, e_1^h, \ldots, e_S^h)$ is derived from the public sector and $x^h - e^h$ is from the private sector; the consumption set is X^h. Household h owns an initial endowment ω_0^h of the input; no endowments are held of the state-contingent commodities. The production plan for firm $j, y^j = (y_0^j, y_1^j, \ldots, y_S^j)$, is chosen from the production set Y^j. The production set is defined so that $y_0^j \leq 0$ is the input and $y_s^j \geq 0$ is the output if state s occurs. Government production is denoted $e = (e_0, e_1, \ldots, e_S)$ with $e_0 \leq 0$, $e_s \geq 0$, and is chosen from the production set Y^g.

The important feature of the economy is that inefficient risk bearing may arise due to forward markets being incomplete. If the forward market does not exist for good i, there will be no price quoted in period 0 for delivery of good i in period 1. In order to determine its optimal production plan a firm must decide upon a value for the missing prices. This is assumed to be done by weighting the valuations of the firm's shareholders of good i by the level of final shareholding. This approach, and possible alternatives, are discussed in Diamond (1967), Dreze (1974) and Grossman and Hart (1979). Formally, denote the price vector that firm j perceives to be ruling by $p^j = (p_0^j, \ldots, p_S^j)$ and normalise so that $p_0^j = 1$, all j. The vector of marginal rates of substitution for consumer h is written

$$q^h = \left(\frac{U_0^h}{U_0^h}, \ldots, \frac{U_S^h}{U_0^h} \right) = (1, q_1^h, \ldots, q_S^h).$$ Letting $\bar{\theta}_j^h$ be the shareholding of h in firm j

before trade in shares and θ_j^h be the shareholding after trade, the perceived prices for firm j are given by

$$p^j = \sum_{h=1}^{H} \theta_j^h q^h. \tag{7.17}$$

It should be noted that the economy with complete markets is a special case of (7.17). With complete markets, trade results in the marginal rates of substitution being equalised across households and, since the shareholdings must sum to 1, (7.17) then states the usual relation that price is equal to the (common) marginal rate of substitution.

With the share price for firm j represented by r^j, an equilibrium of the economy is defined as follows.

Equilibrium

An equilibrium is an array $[\{\hat{p}^j\},\{\hat{r}^j\},\{\hat{y}^j\},\{\hat{x}_0^h\},\{\hat{\theta}_j^h\}]$ such that:

For all $j=1,\ldots,m$, $\hat{y}^j$ maximises $\hat{p}^j y^j$ for $y^j \in Y^j$;
For all $h=1,\ldots,H,(\hat{x}_0^h,\hat{\theta}_1^h,\ldots,\hat{\theta}_m^h)$ maximises $U^h(x_0^h,x_1^h,\ldots,x_S^h)$ subject to

(i) $x^h \in X^h$,

(ii) $x_0^h + \sum_{j=1}^{m} \theta_j^h r^j \leq \omega_0^h + \sum_{j=1}^{m} \bar{\theta}_j^h [\, r^j + y_0^j\,] + e_0^h,$

(iii) $x_s^h - e_s^h - \sum_{j=1}^{m} \theta_j^h y_s^j \leq 0,\ s=1,\ldots,S.$

Conditions (ii) and (iii) capture the first- and second-period budget constraints. In (ii) the initial ownership of a share in a firm implies that the household must provide a share of the input to the firm proportional to the shareholding.

It is now possible to consider the evaluation of public-sector projects. The comparison will be made between the valuation that a typical private firm, say j, would place on a project and that which the government would adopt. To remove one reason for these to differ, it is assumed the returns to the public-sector project are distributed in precisely the same proportions as the returns to the private firm. Therefore, the proportion of the public-sector project that is distributed to h, Θ^h, satisfies $\Theta^h = \theta_j^h$. To value public projects, the government employs a social welfare function that is a weighted sum of the household valuations

$$W(x) = \sum_{h=1}^{H} a^h \sum_{s=0}^{S} q_s^h x_s^h, \tag{7.18}$$

where $a^h \geq 0$, all h, and $\sum_{h=1}^{H} a^h = H$. A project is interpreted as a differential change in consumption $dx = (dx_0^1,\ldots,dx_S^H)$. Such a project is valued by the social welfare function at

$$W(dx) = \sum_{h=1}^{H} a^h \sum_{s=0}^{S} q_s^h dx_s^h = \sum_{h=1}^{H} a^h \Theta^h \sum_{s=0}^{S} q_s^h dx_s^h. \tag{7.19}$$

Conversely, a change in production dx_s is valued by firm j at

$$F^j(dx) = \sum_{h=1}^{H} \sum_{s=0}^{S} \theta_s^h q_s^h dx_s. \tag{7.20}$$

Employing the restriction that $\Theta^h = \theta_j^h$, the valuation in (7.19) and that in (7.20) are related by

$$W(dx) = F^j(dx) + \sum_{h=1}^{H} [a^h - 1] \Theta^h \sum_{s=0}^{S} q_s^h dx_s. \tag{7.21}$$

It is immediately apparent from (7.21) that if all households were weighted equally in the social welfare function, so that $a^h = 1$, private and social valuations would be equal. If (7.18) is viewed as a linear approximation of a standard Bergson–Samuelson social welfare function, then there is no reason why the weights should be equal. Consequently, there is no reason to expect equality of private and social valuations.

To further investigate the difference in valuations when households are not weighted equally requires a further distinction to be drawn. A public project is said to be *contained within the private sector* if the vector of returns dx can be achieved by a portfolio of holdings in the existing private-sector firms. If this is the case, then existing trading arrangements ensure that the valuations of households and firms are equalised for such a project. Conversely, a public project is *outside the private sector* if its returns cannot be duplicated by the purchase of shareholdings in firms. A project outside the private sector has the property that it extends the set of securities that are available and permits further risk spreading.

For a project contained within the private sector it follows that $\sum_{s=0}^{S} q_s^h dx_s^h$
$= F^j(dx)$, all $h = 1, \ldots, H$ and $j = 1, \ldots, m$. Using this relation in (7.21) then gives

$$W(dx) = F^j(dx) \left[1 + \sum_{h=1}^{H} [a^h - 1] \left[\Theta^h - \frac{1}{H} \right] \right] = F^j(dx)[1 + \text{cov}(a^h, \Theta^h)]. \tag{7.22}$$

The interpretation of (7.22) is that a project contained within the private sector should be valued more highly by the public sector than by the private sector when its returns accrue disproportionately to those households that have a high weighting in the social welfare function. If the returns accrue to those with a low weighting, the public sector should value the project less than the private sector. The major implication of (7.22) is therefore the demonstration that there is no *a priori* reason for the public sector to employ a discount rate that is uniformly higher or lower than that of the private sector. As regards the choice of project, if $[1 + \text{cov}(a^h, \Theta^h)] > 0$, any project that satisfies $F^j(dx) > 0$, and hence would be undertaken by the private sector, also satisfies $W(dx) > 0$ so that it would also be undertaken by the public sector. This result also emphasises the role played by the assumption of the Arrow–Lind theorem that private and public risks are uncorrelated. The argument of Hirshleifer (1966) that the government should employ the same discount rate as private firms follows from assumption of complete futures markets which implies that all projects are within the private sector. Similarly, Sandmo (1972) although assuming incomplete futures markets, reaches the identical conclusion by considering only projects within the private sector.

As already noted, a project that is outside the private sector introduces a set of payoffs that cannot be duplicated by shareholdings in firms. If such a project is undertaken, households affected by the project will need to adjust their portfolios of assets to achieve optimal risk taking. If the portfolio adjustment raises utility, then the project can be viewed as providing *social insurance* and this will raise the welfare valuation of that project. It is also possible that the portfolio adjustment may reduce utility in which case the welfare valuation of the project will be reduced.

To formalise these observations, the project $dx \equiv (dx_0, dx_\sigma)$, $dx_\sigma \in \mathcal{R}^s$, is written in the form $dx = d\tilde{x} + d\hat{x}$, where $d\tilde{x}$ is that part of the project that can be obtained by combining existing private-sector returns and $d\hat{x}$ is the uninsurable part. Expressed alternatively, $d\tilde{x} \equiv (dx_0, d\tilde{x}_\sigma)$ can be written as a linear combination of basis vectors of the form (dx_0, y_σ^j) where y_σ^j are the future returns of firm j and is therefore the projection of dx on to the space spanned by the future returns of the firms. The uninsurable part of the project, representing an addition to the existing set of risky assets, takes the form $d\tilde{x} \equiv (0, d\hat{x}_\sigma)$ and is orthogonal to the space of existing risks.

Substituting into (7.21) determines the relation between social and private valuations as

$$W(dx) = F^j(dx) + F^j(d\tilde{x}) \sum_{h=1}^{H} [a^h - 1]\Theta^h + \sum_{h=1}^{H} [a^h - 1]\Theta^h \sum_{s=0}^{S} q_s^h d\tilde{x}_s$$

$$= F^j(d\hat{x})[1 + \text{cov}(a^h, \Theta^h)] + F^j(d\tilde{x}) + \sum_{h=1}^{H} [a^h - 1]\Theta^h \sum_{s=0}^{S} q_s^h d\tilde{x}_s. \quad (7.23)$$

The evaluation of the project can therefore be divided into three components. The first is the evaluation of the part of the project that lies within the private sector and can be interpreted in the manner following (7.22). The second and third components are the firm's and the households' evaluations of the component of the project that is uninsurable. Since this part of the project is not traded, these need not be equal. These can be positive or negative; hence the social evaluation may be above or below the private valuation. There is therefore no *a priori* reason for believing the social valuation to be above or below the private valuation. In the Arrow–Lind case for which the public project is entirely uncorrelated with private returns, $d\tilde{x}$ would be zero and as the number of households increased without limit the final term would tend to zero. This leaves the government evaluation equal to the valuation of the risk-neutral firms.

3.3 Summary

This section has considered alternative perspectives on the relation between private and social attitudes to risk. There is, of course, some merit in each of these proposals and it was shown how each could be generated as a special case of a general state-preference economy. As a final approach to this issue, Glazer (1989) has considered social attitudes to risk from a political perspective and has argued that strategic voting behaviour may lead to projects being adopted by the public sector that could only be rationalised by a discount rate below that of the private sector. This emphasises that the political outcome may remain distinct from that which is economically efficient.

4 HOUSEHOLD CHOICE AND TAXATION

Although the contingent commodity framework used in the previous sections has the appeal of generality, this is also its shortcoming as a vehicle for developing simple insights into the interaction between taxation and risk taking. A literature has therefore developed that focuses upon household portfolio choice when there are only two assets available: one safe, one risky. If it is further assumed that there are only two potential future states of the world, the household decision problem can be represented diagrammatically. This approach, and its extensions, will be the subject matter of this section.

Consider a household with a given initial wealth, Ω, to divide between the two available assets. One of the assets, termed the *safe* asset, yields a known return r. The other, the *risky* asset, has a random return ξ which is distributed with density $\gamma(\xi)$ and variance σ^2. $\gamma(\xi)$ has support on $(-1, \infty)$. The household is concerned only with their final level of wealth, Y, and seeks to maximise $\mathscr{E}[U(Y)]$ by choosing the amount, a, of their initial wealth invested in the risky asset. The household is assumed to be risk averse; hence $U''(Y) < 0$. The effects of two taxes will be analysed: a wealth tax, denoted t_w, and an income tax, t_m.

In order to specify the payoff to the household from a given portfolio, it is first necessary to clarify the provisions in the tax system for offsetting losses (negative returns) against taxable income. If all losses can be offset, the tax system is said to have *full loss offset*. The other extreme is termed *no loss offset*. Between the extremes lie systems with *partial loss offset*. The relevance of loss offset provisions is in their effect upon the expected post-tax return from the risky asset and the distribution of tax revenues. With full loss offsets, an income tax reduces both the potential gains from holding the risky asset and the potential losses. Conversely, with no loss offset only the gains are reduced. These distinct effects upon the structure of post-tax returns show why the effects of taxation will be dependent upon loss offset provisions. In addition, in all but the no loss offset case, the government will incur some risk in the form of potentially reduced tax revenues whenever the household holds some of the risky asset. The extent of loss offset then determines the degree to which the government shares the household's risk.

Although full loss offset may seem at first sight a practically uninteresting case, it should be noted that the investment behaviour under consideration may only be a part of the broader economic activity of the household. When the household earns income in addition to that derived from investment, then any loss on investments can be set against other income in the determination of taxable income. If all sources of income are taxed at the same rate, the tax system would then appear as if it had full loss offset provisions.

Having clarified these distinctions, the analysis will first consider the effect of a wealth tax and then turn to the income tax. The formal results will be developed for the general case described above but will be diagrammatically illustrated for the special two-state case in which the risky asset either yields a high return or a low return. The majority of the results are due to Mossin (1968) and Stiglitz (1969a).

4.1 Wealth taxation

The wealth tax is levied upon the final wealth of the consumer that is determined after the realisation of the return on the random asset. Provided that the final wealth of the household is positive, the loss offset provisions are not relevant for the determination of the effect of the tax.

When the realised return on the random asset is ξ, the final wealth of the household with wealth tax $t_w < 1$ is

$$Y = \big[[\Omega - a][1+r] + a[1+\xi]\big][1 - t_w]. \tag{7.24}$$

It then follows that the expected utility of the household can be calculated as

$$\mathscr{E}[U(Y)] = \int_{-1}^{\infty} U\big([[\Omega - a][1+r] + a[1+\xi]][1 - t_w]\big)\gamma(\xi)d\xi. \tag{7.25}$$

Differentiating with respect to a and assuming that $\mathscr{E}[\xi] > r$, which is necessary and sufficient for an interior solution with $a > 0$ (see Arrow (1970)), the optimal portfolio satisfies

$$[1 - t_w]\mathscr{E}[U'(Y)[\xi - r]] = 0, \tag{7.26}$$

and

$$\mathscr{E}[U''(Y)[\xi - r]^2] = 0. \tag{7.27}$$

From (7.25) and (7.26) it can be seen that the effect of the wealth tax is equivalent to a reduction in initial wealth Y. An increase in the rate of tax will decrease the proportion invested in the risky asset if the wealth elasticity of demand for the risky asset, $\dfrac{\partial a}{\partial \Omega}\dfrac{\Omega}{a}$, is greater than 1, will leave it unchanged if

$\dfrac{\partial a}{\partial \Omega}\dfrac{\Omega}{a}=1$ and increase it if $\dfrac{\partial a}{\partial \Omega}\dfrac{\Omega}{a}<1$. The effect of the taxation in this case is straightforward.

To illustrate this result, assume that the risky asset provides a high return ξ_1 with probability ρ_1 in state 1 and a low return ξ_2 with probability ρ_2 in state 2; $\xi_1 > r > \xi_2$. Investing all wealth in the risky asset will lead to final wealth of $\Omega[1 + \xi_1][1 - t_w]$ in state 1 and $\Omega[1 + \xi_2][1 - t_w]$ in state 2. Alternatively, if all income is invested in the safe asset, final wealth will be $\Omega[1 + r][1 - t_w]$ in both states. The expected utility of the household is given by

$$\mathscr{E}[U(Y)] = \rho_1 U\big(\big[[\Omega - a][1 + r] + a[1 + \xi_1]\big][1 - t_w]\big) \\ + \rho_2 U\big(\big[[\Omega - a][1 + r] + a[1 + \xi_2]\big][1 - t_w]\big). \tag{7.28}$$

The indifference curves of (7.28) and the budget opportunities facing the household are illustrated in figure 7.2.

In figure 7.2 the budget constraint is given by AB and the chosen portfolio is at O. The proportion of wealth placed in the risky asset is AO/AB. The effect of an increase in the wealth tax or, equivalently, of a reduction in wealth is to move points A and B towards the origin with the new budget line being parallel to the old. Repeated for a series of changes in wealth, this will trace out the wealth-portfolio locus of optimal portfolios. This is shown in figure 7.3.

If the wealth-portfolio locus is a ray through the origin, as in figure 7.3, the proportion of wealth invested in the risky asset is constant as wealth or the rate of wealth taxation change. This occurs when the wealth elasticity of demand for the risky asset is equal to 1. When the wealth elasticity is greater than 1 the wealth-portfolio locus will bend downwards away from the ray and the proportion invested in the risky asset will fall as the rate of tax increases. Conversely, a wealth elasticity less than 1 will lead to a wealth-portfolio locus that rises more quickly than the ray and a consequent increase in the proportion invested in the risky asset as the wealth tax increases.

4.2 Income tax

As already noted, it is necessary in the case of an income tax to specify the loss offset provisions in the tax code. The analytically simpler case of full loss offset will be treated first and then partial loss offset will be considered.

4.2.1 Full loss offset

To initially simplify the analysis, it will first be assumed that $r = 0$ so the safe asset has a zero return. Under this assumption, when the realised return on the random asset is ξ, the final wealth of the household with income tax $t_m < 1$ is

$$Y = \Omega - a + a[1 + \xi[1 - t_m]] = \Omega + a\xi[1 - t_m], \tag{7.29}$$

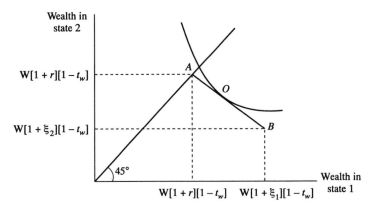

Figure 7.2   Portfolio choice

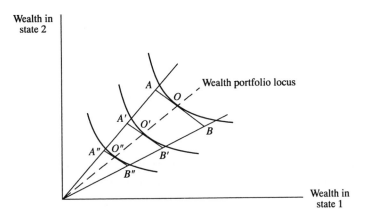

Figure 7.3   Wealth-portfolio locus

so that the expected utility of the household becomes

$$\mathcal{E}[U(Y)] = \int_{-1}^{\infty} U(\Omega + a\xi[1-t_m])\gamma(\xi)d\xi. \tag{7.30}$$

Assuming that solution to the decision problem is interior, the optimal portfolio satisfies

$$[1-t_m]\mathcal{E}[U'(Y)\xi] = 0. \tag{7.31}$$

The effect of a change in the tax rate upon the portfolio is found by differentiating (7.31) with respect to t_m. This gives

$$\mathcal{E}\left[U''(Y)\left[\frac{\partial a}{\partial t_m}\xi[1-t_m]-a\xi\right]\xi[1-t_m]-U'(Y)\xi\right] = 0. \tag{7.32}$$

Employing the first-order condition (7.31) implies that equation (7.32) can be reduced to $\mathscr{E}\left[U''(Y)\left[\dfrac{\partial a}{\partial t_m}\xi[1-t_m]-a\xi \right]\xi[1-t_m] \right]=0$ or

$$\frac{\partial a}{\partial t_m}=\frac{a}{1-t_m}. \tag{7.33}$$

From (7.33) it can be seen that the holding of the risky asset is increased as the rate of income tax increases. With full loss offset, an income tax encourages the household to increase the holding of risky assets.

The surprising aspect of the result in (7.33) is that the response of the household to the change in taxation is independent of the structure of preferences. It should be noted, however, that this is strongly dependent upon the assumption that the safe asset has zero return. The reasoning lying behind (7.33) is that the change in a described there is such that it keeps the mean final wealth of the household, $\mathscr{E}[Y]=\Omega+a\mathscr{E}[\xi][1-t_m]$, the variance of final wealth, $\mathrm{var}\,[Y]=a^2\sigma^2[1-t_m]^2$, and all higher moments of the final wealth distribution constant. Since the riskiness of the portfolio does not increase for the household, social risk taking must have increased due to the government holding part of an increased level of risky assets.

In terms of the two-state economy, the result is illustrated in figure 7.4. The assumption of zero return on the safe asset implies that point A is not affected by taxation. Point B moves inward to B'. Provided that the change in the tax rate is not so great as to push the household to a corner solution, the original choice of returns, O, is still available but this now implies a greater holding of the risky asset. The attainment of O requires the increase in investment in the risky asset given by (7.33).

When the return to the risky asset is non-zero the result is less clear. The level of expected utility is given by

$$\mathscr{E}[U(Y)]=\int_{-1}^{\infty} U(\Omega[1+r[1-t_m]]+a[\xi-r][1-t_m])\gamma(\xi)d\xi. \tag{7.34}$$

Maximising (7.34) by the choice of a and differentiating the resulting first-order condition with respect to t_m gives

$$\frac{da}{dt_m}=\frac{\mathscr{E}\left[U''(Y)[\xi-r]\right]}{\mathscr{E}\left[U''(Y)[\xi-r]^2\right]}\frac{\Omega r}{1-t_m}+\frac{a}{1-t_m}. \tag{7.35}$$

The first term of (7.35) can be viewed as a wealth, or income, effect on asset demand whilst the second term is in the nature of a substitution effect. Since these two conflict, no unequivocal conclusion can be given on the effect of the income tax on portfolio composition.

Further insight can be gained by observing that the concavity of the utility function implies $\mathscr{E}\left[U''(Y)[\xi-r]^2\right]<0$. To evaluate the term $\mathscr{E}\left[U''(Y)[\xi-r]\right]$ note that the wealth elasticity of demand for the risky asset is equal to

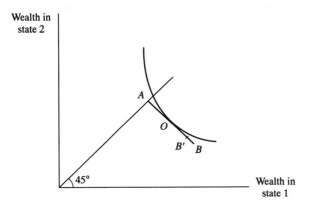

Figure 7.4   Income tax with zero return on safe asset

$$\frac{da}{d\Omega}\frac{\Omega}{a} = -\frac{1 + r[1 - t_m]}{1 - t_m}\frac{\mathcal{E}\big[U''(Y)[\xi - r]\big]}{\mathcal{E}\big[U''(Y)[\xi - r]^2\big]}\frac{\Omega}{a}.\tag{7.36}$$

Therefore the sign of $\mathcal{E}\big[U''(Y)[\xi - r]\big]$ is opposite to that of the wealth elasticity of demand. Relating this to (7.35), if the wealth elasticity of demand for the risky asset is negative, this further increases the level of demand for the risky asset caused by the tax increase. When the elasticity is positive, the increase in demand is reduced below $\dfrac{a}{1 - t_m}$. Substituting from (7.36) into (7.35) determines the effect of the tax as

$$\frac{da}{dt_m} = -\frac{\Omega r}{1 + r[1 - t_m]}\frac{da}{d\Omega} + \frac{a}{1 - t_m}.\tag{7.37}$$

Returning to the two-state case, the effect of the income tax is illustrated in figure 7.5. The effect of the income tax is to shift the budget constraint from AB to $A'B'$ and the optimal choice from O to O'. As drawn, the proportion of wealth invested in the risky asset remains constant (the move down the dashed line from O to O'). An altered portfolio composition would be shown by a move above or below the dashed line.

4.2.2 Imperfect loss offsets

When loss offset provisions are imperfect, taxation has an asymmetric effect upon the post-tax returns to the household. The government takes a share of positive returns but carries no responsibility, or at most a limited responsibility, for any losses. It should therefore be expected that this will reduce the demand for the risky asset relative to a system with full loss-offset. Due to the existence of competing income and substitution effects, the validity of such a claim depends upon the basis for comparison adopted (for instance, at constant revenue or at constant tax rate) and the method of specifying an imperfect loss offset.

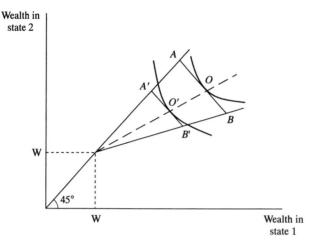

Figure 7.5   Effect of an income tax

An analysis of imperfect loss offsets can be found in both Mossin (1968) and Stiglitz (1969a) but the approach taken here is based on the more general analysis of Eeckhoudt and Hansen (1982). Let the income tax on positive returns be fixed at t_m and denote the tax on negative returns by t_n with $0 \le t_n \le t_m$. If $t_n = t_m$ the tax system has perfect loss offset and if $t_n = 0$ there are no offset provisions. A move away from full loss offset can be interpreted as a reduction in t_n.

The return to the household investing amount a in the risky asset is negative if $[\Omega - a]r + a\xi < 0$. Hence for $\xi < -\dfrac{[\Omega - a]r}{a}$ the tax rate t_n is applicable. For other values of ξ returns are taxed at t_m. The expected utility of the household is therefore

$$\mathcal{E}[U(Y)] = \int_{-1}^{-\frac{[\Omega-a]r}{a}} U\big(\Omega[1 + r[1 - t_n]] + a[1 - t_n][\xi - r]\big)\gamma(\xi)d\xi$$

$$+ \int_{-\frac{[\Omega-a]r}{a}}^{\infty} U\big(\Omega[1 + r[1 - t_m]] + a[1 - t_m][\xi - r]\big)\gamma(\xi)d\xi. \qquad (7.38)$$

The first-order condition for the choice of a to maximise (7.38) follows as

$$\frac{\partial \mathcal{E}[U(Y)]}{\partial a} = \int_{-1}^{-\frac{[\Omega-a]r}{a}} U'\big(\Omega[1 + r[1 - t_n]] + a[1 - t_n][\xi - r]\big)[1 - t_n][\xi - r]\gamma(\xi)d\xi$$

$$+ \int_{-\frac{[\Omega-a]r}{a}}^{\infty} U'\big(\Omega[1 + r[1 - t_m]] + a[1 - t_m][\xi - r]\big)[1 - t_m][\xi - r]\gamma(\xi)d\xi.$$

$$(7.39)$$

The negativity of the second-order condition implies that sgn. $\left\{\dfrac{\partial a}{\partial t_n}\right\} = $ sgn. $\left\{\dfrac{\partial^2 \mathcal{E}[U(Y)]}{\partial a \partial t_n}\right\}$. Calculating the latter derivative gives

$$\frac{\partial^2 \mathscr{E}[U(Y)]}{\partial a \partial t_n} = \int_{-1}^{-\frac{[\Omega - a]r}{a}} \left[U'[\xi - r] + U''[1 - t_n][\xi - r][[\Omega - a]r + a\xi] \right] \gamma(\xi) d\xi.$$

(7.40)

Since the integration is conducted over values of ξ for which $[\xi - r] < 0$ and $[\Omega - a]r + a\xi < 0$, the concavity of the utility function implies that $\dfrac{\partial^2 \mathscr{E}[U(Y)]}{\partial a \partial t_n}$ > 0. An increase the loss offset provisions (t_n increasing) therefore increases the household's investment in the risky asset. Phrased alternatively, the household's purchases of the risky asset will fall as the loss offset provisions are reduced.

A similar analysis is conducted by Diamond and Stiglitz (1974) but with the tax rate adjusted as loss offset is changed in order to keep utility constant. The same general result is also shown to hold in that case. With respect to the effect of changes in the tax rate on positive returns, Mossin (1968) shows that the result is indeterminate due to the conflict between income and substitution effects even when the return on the safe asset is zero. Since these results are straightforward to generate, they are not reproduced here.

4.3 Generalisations

The results given above are based on a specification that is restrictive in a number of directions. The analysis has been entirely partial equilibrium and the use to which tax revenues were put was not considered. It was assumed that there was a safe asset; such an asset need not exist. The restriction to two assets is unjustifiable. Some of the consequences of relaxing these restrictions will now be considered.

With respect to the use of tax revenue, it can always be assumed that this is used to purchase a public good and that all households' preferences are separable between final wealth and levels of the public good. Similar reasoning was used in chapters 4 and 5. It is possible to consider the implications of tax revenue being distributed between households but, since no particular mechanism for redistribution suggests itself as most appropriate and the results are mechanism dependent, few general insights can be gained from this. The partial equilibrium nature of the results will be relaxed somewhat in section 6 when the design of the tax system will be addressed.

Although it may appear innocuous, the assumption that there exists a safe asset is rather a strong one. An obvious candidate for this role is holding cash which earns a known nominal return of zero. However, if there is inflation the real return will be less than the nominal return and, if there is uncertainty about future levels of inflation, the real return will be uncertain. The same comments apply to any asset whose nominal return is fixed but whose real return may vary. Fortunately, the analysis is not critically dependent upon the existence of a safe asset and can be reworked to include two risky assets.

Introducing further risky assets leads to a number of complications. Firstly, the extent of risk taking cannot be as easily measured as in the one safe one risky economy where the degree of risk taking is given by the proportion of income invested in the risky asset. Secondly, basic comparative statics results on the relation of the investment in the risky asset to wealth (with decreasing absolute risk aversion and increasing relative risk aversion the amount invested increases with wealth whilst the proportion falls, see Arrow (1965)) no longer apply except in rather special cases, some of which are noted in Cass and Stiglitz (1972). As shown by Hart (1975b) with more than one risky asset (plus one safe one) it is generally possible to construct the returns to the risky assets in such a way that converse comparative statics results can be derived.

Despite these difficulties, Sandmo (1977) demonstrates that some results still apply. Consider a household faced with the choice between n risky assets and a safe asset that pays return r. Let the return on risky asset k, $k = 1, \ldots, n$, be given by ξ_k and the amount that asset purchased be denoted a_k so that final wealth is

$$Y = \Omega\big[1 + r[1 - t_m]\big] + \sum_{k=1}^{n} a_k\, [\xi_k - r][1 - t_m]. \tag{7.41}$$

The effect of changes in the tax rate upon the demand for asset k is then given by

$$\frac{\partial a_k}{\partial t_m} = -\frac{\Omega r}{1 + r[1 - t_m]}\frac{\partial a_k}{\partial \Omega} + \frac{a_k}{1 - t_m}, \quad k = 1, \ldots, n. \tag{7.42}$$

This result has precisely the form of (7.37).

5   LABOUR SUPPLY AND OCCUPATIONAL CHOICE

The choice of portfolio is not the only uncertain decision that a typical household will have to take. It may not be unusual for labour supply decisions to be taken before the actual level of the wage is realised. This can occur in some forms of self-employment (such as farming) where production takes place prior to the return being realised and, even if the nominal wage is known, future price variation can make the real wage random. An alternative source of uncertainty can arise in the choice of occupation; in particular between entering paid employment with (possibly) known return and some form of entrepreneurship that has a random return. In both these examples, the tax system interacts with the uncertainty in determining household choice.

5.1   Labour supply

The analysis of labour supply under certainty is restricted in the number of clear predictions that it provides about the effects of taxation due to the inherent conflict between income and substitution effects. It does, however, provide two clear conclusions. Firstly, if taxation is raised on exogenous non-labour income then labour supply is increased provided that leisure is non-inferior. Secondly, income-compensated increases in taxation upon earned income reduce labour supply.

To see the implications of the introduction of uncertainty for these conclusions, consider augmenting the standard analysis of labour supply by assuming, as in Eaton and Rosen (1980), that the household does not know the wage that they will receive but instead holds a probability distribution over possible wages. Denoting labour supply by x_0 and consumption by x_1, the taxpayer chooses labour supply to maximise expected utility, $\mathscr{E}[U(x_0, x_1)]$, given the constraint that

$$x_1 = wx_0[1 - t]] + I, \tag{7.43}$$

where t is the tax rate and I is lump-sum income. Assuming an interior solution, the necessary condition for maximisation is

$$\mathscr{E}[U_0 + U_1[1 - t]w] = 0. \tag{7.44}$$

From (7.44), the effect of an increase in lump-sum income can be found to be

$$\frac{dx_0}{dI} = -\frac{\mathscr{E}[U_{01} + U_{11}[1 - t]w]}{S}, \tag{7.45}$$

where $S < 0$ is the second-order condition for maximisation. If the utility function is separable, so that $U_{01} = 0$, concavity with respect to consumption implies that $U_{11} < 0$ and hence $\dfrac{dx_0}{dI} < 0$. An increase in lump-sum income, which is received with certainty, therefore reduces labour supply. This result is in agreement with that which would be derived with a certain wage.

Now consider the effect of an increase in the tax rate that is compensated for by an increase in lump-sum income. The effect of this upon labour supply is given by

$$\frac{dx_0}{dt}\bigg|_{comp.} = \frac{dx_0}{dt} + \bar{w}x_0\frac{dx_0}{dI}, \tag{7.46}$$

in which $\bar{w}x_0 dt$, with $\bar{w}$ the expected wage, is the compensation required for the tax change dt. Calculating (7.46) gives

$$\frac{dx_0}{dt}\bigg|_{comp.} = \frac{\mathscr{E}[U_1 w + [U_{11}[1 - t] + U_{01}]wx_0[w - \bar{w}]]}{S}. \tag{7.47}$$

With certainty $w = \bar{w}$ so that the tax increase would unambiguously reduce labour supply. In contrast, the effect of uncertainty is to make the sign of $\mathscr{E}[[U_{11}[1 - t] + U_{01}]wx_0[w - \bar{w}]]$ ambiguous and it is possible for a compensated increase in the tax rate to raise labour supply.

Uncertainty can therefore have the effect of reversing the direction of labour supply responses to changes in taxation and the results of the certainty analysis are not directly applicable. The results developed above will be employed in the analysis of tax design in section 6.

5.2 Occupational choice

The analysis of occupational choice involves a different decision framework from that of the choice of labour supply. As emphasised by Kanbur (1980), occupation is not really a variable that can be continuously adjusted and it is more reasonable to think of a discrete choice being taken between entering alternative occupations which differ in the certainty of their returns. The discreteness of the choice prevents the household obtaining insurance against risk by combining a portfolio of employment in several occupations. Analyses of the interaction between taxation and occupational choice are given in Kihlstrom and Laffont (1983) and in Kanbur (1980). The presentation given below is based on the latter.

Consider an economy in which each of the set of identical households has a choice between either supplying 1 unit of labour and receiving the competitive wage w with certainty or becoming an entrepreneur and accepting uncertainty in earnings. Those households who choose to become entrepreneurs choose the quantity of labour they employ in order to maximise

$$\mathscr{E}\left[U(R(y,\xi)-wy)\right], \tag{7.48}$$

where $U(\cdot)$ is the von Neumann–Morgernstern concave utility of income function common to all households, y is the quantity of labour employed and $R(y,\xi)$ is the revenue from entrepreneurial activity when value ξ of the random variable is realised. It is the dependence of revenue on ξ and the randomness of ξ that is the source of uncertainty in the return from entrepreneurship. It is assumed that each household holds a common belief about the distribution of ξ. The maximisation of (7.48) leads to a labour demand from each entrepreneur of $y=y(w)$. If the proportion of the population becoming entrepreneurs is denoted by ρ, an equilibrium for the economy, in the absence of taxation is given by a wage rate, $\hat{w}$, and a proportion $\hat{\rho}$ such that

(i) $\hat{\rho}y(\hat{w})=1-\hat{\rho}$,

and

(ii) $\mathscr{E}\left[U(R(y(\hat{w}),\xi)-\hat{w}y(\hat{w}))\right]=U(\hat{w})$.

Condition (i) is the full employment condition that balances the labour demand from entrepreneurs with the labour supply of those choosing the risk-free occupation. The second condition equates the expected return from the occupations so that there is no incentive at equilibrium to change occupation.

One course of action open to a government faced with this economy is the differential treatment of income from the risky and the safe activity. If such differentiation is feasible, it is natural to investigate which of the two forms of income should carry the lowest rate of tax. To formalise this, let income from entrepreneurship be taxed at rate t and that from the risk-free labour supply be subsidised at rate s. Post-tax incomes in the two occupations are then given by

$$M_n^e = [1-t] \left[R(y(\hat{w}), \xi) - \hat{w}y(\hat{w}) \right] = [1-t] M^e, \tag{7.49}$$

and

$$M_n^s = [1+s]\hat{w} = [1+s]M^s, \tag{7.50}$$

in entrepreneurship and safe labour supply respectively. The analysis now determines the direction that a balanced budget reform of the tax system should take beginning in an initial position with $t=s=0$. Assuming a utilitarian social welfare function, the level of per-capita welfare is

$$W = \rho \mathscr{E} \left[U([1-t][R(y(\hat{w}), \xi) - \hat{w}y(\hat{w})]) \right] + [1-\rho] U([1+s]\hat{w}) = U([1+s]\hat{w}), \tag{7.51}$$

since, in equilibrium, $\mathscr{E} \left[U([1-t][R(y(\hat{w}), \xi) - \hat{w}y(\hat{w})]) \right] = U([1+s]\hat{w})$. In order that the budget remains balanced, the tax and subsidy must satisfy the budget constraint

$$\rho t \mathscr{E} [R(y, \xi) - wy] - [1-\rho]sw = 0. \tag{7.52}$$

Hence

$$ds = \left[\frac{\mathscr{E}[M^e]}{wy} + t \frac{\partial \frac{\mathscr{E}[M^e]}{wy}}{\partial t} \right] dt = \left[\frac{\mathscr{E}[M^e]}{wy} \right] dt, \tag{7.53}$$

where the second equality follows from evaluating at the initial point with $t=0$. From (7.51) the effect of a balanced budget reform upon social welfare is

$$\frac{dW}{dt} = U' \left[[1+s] \frac{dw}{dt} + w \frac{ds}{dt} \right]. \tag{7.54}$$

Differentiating the equilibrium condition guaranteeing equivalence of utilities and evaluating at $t=s=0$ provides the relation

$$\frac{dw}{dt} \left[y\mathscr{E}[U'] + U' \right] + \mathscr{E}[M^e U'] + wU' \frac{ds}{dt} = 0. \tag{7.55}$$

Combining (7.53), (7.54) and (7.55) and evaluating at $t=s=0$ provides the final expression

$$\frac{dW}{dt} = U' \left[\frac{\mathscr{E}[M^e]\mathscr{E}[U'] - \mathscr{E}[M^e U']}{y\mathscr{E}[U'] + U'} \right]. \tag{7.56}$$

The concavity of the utility function implies that marginal utility and income are negatively correlated; hence $\mathscr{E}[M^e]\mathscr{E}[U'] > \mathscr{E}[M^e U']$. Using this inequality shows that (7.56) is positive. From this it can be concluded that starting from the initial position with zero taxes the government can raise welfare by taxing the risky occupation whilst subsidising the safe occupation. Furthermore, as shown by Kanbur (1980), with non-increasing absolute risk aversion and non-decreasing relative risk aversion such a tax reform will reduce the proportion of the population that chooses the risky occupation. The analysis provides a clear prediction that, given the use of differentiated income taxes as available policy tools, the government should attempt to reduce entry into the risky occupation.

A similar analysis can be conducted to characterise the structure of a linear income tax that is common to earnings from both occupations. Denoting the parameters of the income tax by τ and t, post-tax income is given by

$$M_n^i = [1 - t]M^i - \tau, i = e, s. \tag{7.57}$$

Since the marginal rate of tax is t and the average rate $\dfrac{\tau}{M^i} + t$, the tax is *progressive* if $\tau < 0$ and *regressive* if $\tau > 0$. The direction of reform from an initial position with no taxation can be found, as above, by differentiating the equilibrium conditions and the revenue constraint and evaluating at $\tau = 0, t = 1$. Noting that welfare is a monotonically increasing function of the post tax wage, M_n^s, the direction of reform can be found by noting that

$$\left. \frac{dM_n^s}{dt} \right|_{t=0} = \frac{\mathscr{E}[RU'] - \mathscr{E}[R]\mathscr{E}[U']}{y\mathscr{E}[U'] + U'} < 0, \tag{7.58}$$

where the negative sign follows from observing that R and U' are negatively correlated. Social welfare is therefore raised by the introduction of a progressive linear income tax with $\tau < 0$ and $t > 0$. This form of tax reduces the risk carried by entrepreneurs since it raises their income in the worst state relative to that in the best state.

This analysis of occupational choice is applied to the taxation of profit in Peck (1989) and is extended to include heterogeneous households in the analysis of optimal linear income taxation in Boadway *et al.* (1991).

6 OPTIMAL TAXATION

In designing optimal taxation in the presence of uncertainty, it is necessary to face several issues that did not arise in the analysis under certainty. There is first the appropriate definition of a government budget constraint and whether this should be satisfied in an expected sense, which was implicitly what was imposed in the previous section, or whether a separate budget constraint should be enforced in each state of the world. The choice of policy instruments is also broader since taxes may potentially be differentiated across states in addition to being differentiated across goods. When risks in the economy are purely private and uncorrelated across individuals, there is also a role for taxation in providing social insurance in addition to raising revenue and effecting redistribution.

Given this list of extensions beyond the analysis of certainty, it is clear that the results given below cannot deal comprehensively with all of these. In fact, the existing literature has made only initial investigations into each of them and none is yet treated in an exhaustive fashion. The discussion is divided between an analysis of tax design with private risk and that with aggregate risk.

6.1 Private risk

The majority of the literature on optimal income taxation under uncertainty has focused upon the social insurance role played by taxation. This has been achieved either by considering identical households who make a single-period labour supply decision in the face of uncertainty about the wage they will receive or by considering households with two-period lives, who may all be identical, but face uncertainty about the second period of their lives. In both cases income taxation, by providing the households with partial insurance against wage variations, can increase welfare through a channel that does not exist without uncertainty.

To develop the first result, the labour supply analysis described in (7.43) to (7.47) is employed and the optimal linear income tax is characterised for a population of identical households. With a linear income tax, the budget constraint of a typical household becomes

$$x_1 = [1-t]wx_0 - \tau + I, \tag{7.59}$$

and the government budget constraint, which is required to hold in an expected sense, expressed in per-capita terms is

$$R = t\mathscr{E}[wx_0] - \tau. \tag{7.60}$$

Assuming that the population is sufficiently large and employing the fact that the identical households all choose the same level of labour supply, over the entire population (7.60) is equivalent to

$$R = t\mathscr{E}[w]x_0 - \tau = t\bar{w}x_0 - \tau, \tag{7.61}$$

where $\bar{w}$ is the expected wage.

The optimal tax structure can be found by solving

$$\max_{\{t\}} = \mathscr{E}[U(x_0, x_1)] = \mathscr{E}[U(x_0, [1-t]wx_0 + I + t\bar{w}x_0 - R)], \tag{7.62}$$

where $x_0 = x_0(t, \tau) = x_0(t, t\bar{w}x_0 - R)$. The first-order necessary condition for (7.62) follows from differentiation as

$$\mathscr{E}\left[[U_0 + U_1[[1-t]w + t\bar{w}]] \left[\frac{\partial x_0}{\partial t} + wx_0 \frac{\partial x_0}{\partial I} \right] + U_1[\bar{w}x_0 - wx_0] \right] = 0. \tag{7.63}$$

From (7.63), the optimal tax is characterised in the following proposition.

Theorem 7.2 (Eaton and Rosen)

The optimal value of $t \in (0, 1)$.

Proof

From (7.44) $\mathscr{E}[U_0 + U_1[1 - t]w] = 0$. In addition, (7.46) shows that $\left[\dfrac{\partial x_0}{\partial t} + wx_0 \dfrac{\partial x_0}{\partial I}\right]$ is formed as an expectation on the distribution of w. Using these, (7.63) reduces to

$$\mathscr{E}\left[[U_1 t\bar{w}]\left[\frac{\partial x_0}{\partial t} + wx_0 \frac{\partial x_0}{\partial I}\right] + U_1[\bar{w}x_0 - wx_0]\right] = 0. \tag{7.64}$$

Evaluating at $t = 0$ gives

$$\mathscr{E}[U_1[\bar{w}x_0 - wx_0]] = -x_0 \operatorname{cov}(U_1, w) > 0, \tag{7.65}$$

since $\dfrac{dU_1}{dw} = U_{11}x_0 < 0$. Therefore $t = 0$ is not optimal. When $t \geq 1, x_0 = 0$ and the first-order condition reduces to

$$\bar{w}\mathscr{E}\left[[U_1]\left[\frac{\partial x_0}{\partial t} + wx_0 \frac{\partial x_0}{\partial I}\right]\right] < 0, \tag{7.66}$$

where the inequality follows from noting that (7.47) implies $\dfrac{\partial x_0}{\partial t} + wx_0 \dfrac{\partial x_0}{\partial I}$ is negative when $x_0 = 0$. Finally, any value of $t < 0$ can be shown by a revealed preference argument to be dominated by $t = 0$ since a negative value of t increases the variability of income.

The important aspects of theorem 7.2 become clear when it is contrasted with the case of certainty. Under certainty, the optimal way to raise revenue from a set of identical households is to employ a lump-sum tax which will raise the required revenue without introducing any distortions. This can be seen in the derivations above by noting that certainty implies $\bar{w} = w$ and that $t = 0$ then solves the first-order condition. Viewed this way, the proposition states that lump-sum taxes are not the most efficient way to collect revenue in the presence of uncertainty. This seemingly surprising result can be explained by repeating the observation that income taxation provides partial insurance against the risk due to the uncertain wage. That the optimal rate of tax is non-zero is then simply a reflection of the fact that the gain from insurance initially outweighs the loss of welfare arising from the inefficiency caused by the distorting nature of the tax.

An alternative perspective on the social insurance role of income taxation has been provided by Varian (1980), who considers households that face a two-period decision problem. In the first period the household works for a known wage and divides income between consumption and saving. Uncertainty is introduced by assuming that the level of consumption in the second period is equal to savings plus a random component with zero mean. The interpretation of this framework is that initially identical households differ in the *luck* they have in choosing the correct form of deposit for their savings. For instance, if different portfolios of stocks were chosen by different households, the final value of these would be expected to differ.

Formalising this discussion, each of the identical households receives a fixed income of w which is divided between savings, x, and consumption, $w - x$. Consumption in the second period in the absence of taxation is $x + \varepsilon$, where ε is a random variable with zero mean that is independently and identically distributed across the population. It is assumed that the government cannot observe x and ε separately but can only monitor their sum $x + \varepsilon$. A tax system can then be seen to take the form of the imposition of a budget constraint such that second period consumption is given by $c(x + \varepsilon)$.

Under the assumption of identical households, the optimal tax system is chosen to solve the following maximisation programme

$$\max_{\{c(\cdot)\}} U(w - x) + \mathscr{E}\left[U\big(c(x + \varepsilon)\big)\right], \tag{7.67}$$

subject to

$$\mathscr{E}\left[c(x + \varepsilon)\right] = x, \tag{7.68}$$

$$U'(w - x) - \mathscr{E}\left[U'\big(c(x + \varepsilon)\big)\right]c'(x + \varepsilon) = 0. \tag{7.69}$$

The constraint (7.68) restricts the tax system to break even in expected terms and (7.69) is the first-order condition for optimal savings choice by each of the households.

In the case of a linear consumption function with gradient γ and intercept Γ, (7.68) can be solved to write $\Gamma = [1 - \gamma]x$ and (7.69) used to write $x = x(\gamma)$. Together these allow the objective function, (7.67), to be written entirely in terms of γ as

$$\max_{\{\gamma\}} U(w - x(\gamma)) + \mathscr{E}\left[U\big(\gamma[x(\gamma) + \varepsilon] + [1 - \gamma]x(\gamma)\big)\right]. \tag{7.70}$$

Setting the derivative of (7.70) equal to zero and employing (7.69) the gradient of the consumption function can be characterised implicitly by

$$\gamma = \frac{U'(w - x(\gamma))x'(\gamma)}{U'(w - x(\gamma))x'(\gamma) - \mathscr{E}\left[U'(x(\gamma) + \gamma\varepsilon)\varepsilon\right]}. \tag{7.71}$$

Since an increase in ε reduces $U'(x(\gamma) + \gamma\varepsilon)$, $\mathscr{E}\left[U'(x(\gamma) + \gamma\varepsilon)\varepsilon\right] < 0$. From (7.71) it is then clear that γ lies between 0 and 1. The reason for this finding is once again the social insurance role of the income tax. The numerical calculations presented in Varian (1980) also show that as the degree of risk aversion rises so does the level of the marginal rate of tax, an observation which reinforces the insurance interpretation of the tax system.

In the case of a general non-linear consumption function, Varian establishes that the marginal rate of tax must be less than 1, as in the standard income tax analysis, but that the marginal rate of tax may be non-zero on the household with the highest value of $x + \varepsilon$. The latter result follows from the absence of the disincentive effect in this framework; high second-period income is due to luck rather than effort.

Diamond, Helms and Mirrlees (1980) also consider an economy where individuals have a two-period horizon but introduce uncertainty by allowing the possibility that a given individual will be unable to work in the second period of their life (for instance through ill health). Since the government cannot distinguish between those who are unable to work in the second period and those who choose not to work, there is an additional moral hazard problem in the creation of social insurance to cover the risk in the second period. Numerical simulations for economies based on Cobb–Douglas preferences show that linear taxation, although having some effect, is of limited value in providing social insurance.

The analyses of optimal income taxation described above have focused on the role of income taxation in providing social insurance in economies with uncertainty. The same conclusion arises from each despite the somewhat different formulations of the source of uncertainty: the social insurance value of income taxation outweighs its disincentive effects. Therefore, even when no revenue is to be raised, social welfare can be increased by the introduction of an optimal linear income tax. Even when revenue is to be raised, the linear income tax is preferred to a uniform lump-sum tax for a population of identical households.

6.2 Aggregate risk

In the presence of aggregate risk taxation cannot have a social insurance role. This being the case, the focus is now shifted to the design of a tax system that is efficient in its collection of revenue. To make the situation precise, the single-household economy of Christiansen (1993) is considered in which the household allocates an exogenous income between a safe and a risky asset. The incomes accruing from the two assets are tax at differentiated rates and the aim of the analysis is to characterise the form of the tax structure. Tax revenue is used to provide a public good. The aggregate risk is captured in the variable return to the risky asset. In this framework, taxation affects the division of risk between private and public consumption.

Denoting the exogenous wealth of the household by Ω and investment in the risky asset by a, the consumption level of the household in state s is given by

$$x_s = \Omega + [1 - t_r]r[\Omega - a] + [1 - t_\xi]\xi_s a, \tag{7.72}$$

where ξ_s is the return to the risky asset in state s and t_r, t_ξ are the tax rates on the income from the safe and risky asset respectively. The tax rates are chosen subject to the constraint that expected government revenue is equal to expenditure, $\bar{g}$, or

$$\mathcal{E}\left[t_r r[\Omega - a] + t_\xi \xi a\right] = \bar{g}. \tag{7.73}$$

The form of the government budget constraint is not inconsequential with uncertainty. Expressing it in terms of expected revenue permits variations in the level of revenue, and hence expenditure, across states of nature. This formulation therefore leaves an element of risk in public consumption. An alternative would be to fix the level of expenditure, and required revenue, in each state. This would remove the uncertainty about the level of public consumption. Except when utility is linear in public consumption or when there is a large number of taxpayers with uncorrelated risks so that expected and actual tax revenue are equal, the specification of the budget constraint will affect the optimal tax system. Further discussion of this issue can be found in Christiansen (1993).

Assuming that the household derives utility from private consumption and government spending and that the utility function is linear in g, social welfare is given by

$$W = \mathcal{E}\left[U(\Omega + [1 - t_r]r[\Omega - a] + [1 - t_\xi]\xi a)\right] + \mathcal{E}[g]. \tag{7.74}$$

The optimal tax rates are found by maximising (7.74) subject to (7.73).

To characterise the tax rates, first note from (7.73) that if expected revenue is to remain constant, t_r and t_ξ are related by

$$\frac{dt_r}{dt_\xi} = -\frac{a\mathcal{E}[\xi] + \left[t_\xi \mathcal{E}[\xi] - t_r r\right]\dfrac{\partial a}{\partial t_\xi}}{r[\Omega - a]}. \tag{7.75}$$

Differentiating (7.74) with respect to t_ξ whilst varying t_r so as to keep revenue constant gives

$$\frac{dW}{dt_\xi} \equiv -\mathcal{E}\left[U_x\left[\frac{dt_r}{dt_\xi}r[\Omega - a] - \xi a\right]\right] = 0. \tag{7.76}$$

Substituting (7.75) and the first-order condition for household portfolio choice

$$\mathcal{E}[U_x \xi] = -\frac{\mathcal{E}[U_x][1 - t_r]r}{[1 - t_\xi]}, \tag{7.77}$$

into (7.76) and rearranging, the optimal tax rates satisfy

$$\frac{t_\xi \mathcal{E}[\xi] - t_r r}{[1 - t_\xi]\mathcal{E}[\xi] - [1 - t_r]r} = \frac{1}{\hat{a}}, \tag{7.78}$$

where $\hat{a} = \dfrac{[1 - t_\xi]}{a}\dfrac{\partial a}{\partial t_\xi}$ is the elasticity of demand for the risk asset with respect to $[1 - t_\xi]$. The characterisation of optimal taxes in (7.78) is in the form of an inverse elasticities rule in which the inverse of the elasticity is inversely related to the ratio of the net tax on the risky asset and the net return on the risky asset.

7 CONCLUSIONS

In a competitive economy with complete markets, the presence of uncertainty does not destroy the Pareto optimality of the equilibrium and suitably interpreted versions of the Two Theorems still apply. Indeed, efficiency is still achieved even if for each state there is only a single asset that has a positive return in that state. Despite these results there may still be a role for the public sector in an economy with complete markets if the public sector is able to bear risk more efficiently than the private sector. Whether the public sector should discount for risk at a lower rate than the private sector has been the subject of some dispute and alternative perspectives on this issue were presented in section 3. In brief, the treatment of risk by the public sector is dependent upon the form of the risk that is involved, in the terminology used above whether it is inside or outside the private sector.

The effects of income and wealth taxation upon portfolio choice were considered and can be viewed as an example of how taxation affects risk taking. They also illustrated the manner in which the use of taxation turns the government into a partner in a household's risk-taking activities. This also emphasised the distinction between private and social risk taking, with social risk entering through the variability of government revenue. Similar effects were also noted in the treatment of taxation and labour supply with an uncertain wage and in the study of occupational choice.

The design of optimal taxes involves issues that do not arise in an economy with certainty, in particular the specification of the government budget constraint and the range of policy tools. Furthermore, in addition to the revenue-raising and redistributional roles of taxation, there is now the possibility that taxation can also provide social insurance by transferring from those who are benefiting from high random returns to those who are suffering low returns. This effect is sufficiently strong that a distortionary income tax can raise welfare in an economy of individuals who are identical except for random components in their wealth. More interestingly, the optimal linear income tax is preferable to a uniform lump-sum tax.

8

CORPORATE TAXATION

1 INTRODUCTION

The corporation is treated as a separate entity for tax purposes in all developed countries. It has been subject to numerous tax instruments with a variety of different motivations. The transfers between the corporation and its stockholders result in the behaviour of the corporation also being influenced by the structure of the personal tax system, most notably through the favourable tax treatment of capital gains. The intention of this chapter is to describe the relevant tax instruments and to determine their effects. This will give an insight into the many issues that arise in the analysis of corporate taxation.

This chapter is distinguished from those that precede it by its focus upon the effects of taxation rather than upon optimisation exercises. There are several reasons for this. Input taxes have often been employed in many countries and the effects of such taxes are important because of this, but it has already been shown that they would not form part of an optimal tax system for a competitive economy. Therefore there is no need for a further study of optimisation. In simple settings where shareholders exercise direct control, the corporation cannot be identified as an entity distinct from its owners. A coherent tax structure would then involve a comprehensive income tax on owners, covering all sources of earnings, with no need for separate taxation of the corporation. Although the effects of corporation taxation are still of interest in such a framework since they suggest issues that may arise in more complex settings, optimisation is again of limited interest. When the setting becomes more complex, and the existence of managers leads to a separation between ownership and control, the task of clarifying the effects of taxation is difficult enough, without considering optimisation.

The next section will discuss the various taxes to which the corporation has been subject and will consider the rationale for treating the corporation as a distinct taxable entity. The incidence of a range of taxes will then be considered in a two-sector general equilibrium economy. This form of economy was popular in the 1970s following the work of Harberger (1962) and stills remains instructive. The incidence results will be derived in the simplest setting but a number of extensions will also be described. As a tool for studying taxation of the corporation, the two-sector economy is restricted by its static nature and its lack of integration with the personal tax system. These features prevent the study of dividends and bonds and the consequences of preferential tax treatment of some sources of income. Adopting an intertemporal framework, section 4 will consider the effect of taxation upon the policy of the corporation under both certainty and uncertainty.

2   TAXATION OF THE FIRM

As has already been noted, the corporation (and the firm generally) has been subject to a range of taxes. This section will describe a number of these but with particular focus placed upon the corporate profits tax. This mirrors the emphasis upon this tax in the literature. A brief description will also be given of how the corporate tax system interacts with the personal tax system.

2.1   Input and output taxes

The most prevalent form of input tax has been that levied upon the employment of labour. In the US, the Social Security tax provides a notable example and the economics of this are discussed further in chapter 14. National Insurance payments play a similar role in the UK. Both the Social Security tax and National Insurance raise the cost of labour for the employer relative to the price of capital and other inputs. Another example of a tax on labour is the Selective Employment Tax which was levied in the UK between 1966 and 1973. The rate of Selective Employment Tax was sector-specific: it taxed employment in service industries and subsidised it in manufacturing. For further discussion of the effects of this tax see Reddaway (1970).

Factor subsidies have also been used to promote additional investment. Such subsidies have the effect of lowering the cost of additional units of capital relative to labour. These subsidies are often provided in the form of depreciation allowances but cash subsidies to some forms of investment in defined geographical areas were available under the 1972 Industry Act in the UK. The corporate profits tax has often been interpreted as a tax on capital in the corporate sector. This interpretation is explained further in 2.2.

Viewing the provision of finance as an input to the corporation, there has also been differential treatment of payment to providers of finance. Interest payments to bondholders may be tax deductible for the firm, in contrast to dividends which are taxed. Provision of finance by equity holders may lead to capital gains which are taxed under the personal tax system at a different rate from interest received from bondholdings or from dividends. How these various provisions affect the choice of financial policy for the firm is investigated in section 4.

The Value Added Tax (VAT) levied by the European Union is essentially a tax on the output of the firm. The tax is based on the value added in production. Alternative taxes on output include production and turnover taxes. In contrast to the VAT, these are based on the gross output of the firm rather than its net output.

2.2 Profit tax

A tax on corporate profits is levied in all developed countries and is significant in the level of revenue it raises. Its economic effects have also been extensively analysed and this will be the focus of much of the analysis below. The discussion here will simply set the scene and point up some of the issues that are addressed below.

With full allowance for capital expenditure, the firm will optimise, by choice of capital and labour, the level of after-tax profits given by

$$\pi = [1 - \tau_c][pF(K, L) - wL - rK], \tag{8.1}$$

where τ_c is the rate of profit taxation, p is the product price, r the rental rate on capital, L the labour employed and K the level of capital. It is clear from (8.1) that, provided the tax rate is not greater than 100 per cent, the firm's optimal choice of inputs will be unaffected by the imposition of the tax. In this circumstance, the profit tax will not cause any substitution effects in the pattern of input use by the firm. This should not be taken as a claim that the tax is completely without distortion. Since the firm's net of tax profit is reduced by the tax, its return to its owners will fall and this may cause substitution in the asset holdings of households and changes, for example, in their labour supply.

The results are modified if payments to capital cannot be deducted before tax. In this case the firm seeks to maximise

$$\pi = [1 - \tau_c][pF(K, L) - wL] - rK, \tag{8.2}$$

or equivalently

$$\pi = [1 - \tau_c][pF(K, L) - wL - r\zeta K], \tag{8.3}$$

where $\zeta = \dfrac{1}{1 - \tau_c}$. If the tax rate is positive, the corporation tax raises the price of capital relative to that of labour. Denoting total tax payments by Γ, assuming constant returns to scale it follows that

$$pF(K, L) = wL + rK + \Gamma, \tag{8.4}$$

which is the identity that total income must equal total disbursements. Substituting from (8.4) into (8.2) and using the zero profit identity gives

$$\pi = [1 - \tau_c][rK + \Gamma] - rK = 0,\tag{8.5}$$

or

$$\Gamma = \tau_c rK.\tag{8.6}$$

Given (8.6) it can be seen that with constant returns to scale and with the non-deductibility of capital costs, the corporate profits tax can be seen equally as a tax on the value of capital use. Indeed, this is the interpretation that has been adopted in much of the incidence literature that is discussed in section 3.

2.3 Personal taxes

The discussion of corporation tax given above provides a starting point for a more detailed analysis but, because of the form of most tax codes, the corporation tax cannot be considered in isolation from other aspects of the tax system. To briefly illustrate this consider a firm about to finance an extra unit of investment. This investment can be paid for either from retained earnings, from additional borrowing or from the issue of new equity. The fact that interest on borrowing may be tax deductible leads to an obvious incentive to borrow rather than issue equity. Also, the equity holders of the firm may experience capital gains and these will be taxed but at a lower rate than dividends. The response of the firm to corporation tax cannot then be seen in isolation from the capital gains tax. Furthermore, dividends may be taxed twice: once as profit to the firm and then as income for a shareholder. The decision of the firm in issuing dividends must then be considered with the corporation tax. Finally, the static nature of the analysis does not permit the discussion of investment. The corporation tax, by affecting financial policy, will affect the cost of investment and this needs to be addressed. Each of these points is considered in turn in the remaining sections of the chapter.

2.4 Why tax the corporation?

Having made these points about the structure and effects of taxes, there remains a further issue that must be addressed. This is the reason why the corporation is taxed at all. If the corporation is seen merely as earning income and transmitting this to its ultimate owners, then there is no reason why the corporation should be taxed. Instead, the tax liability should be placed upon its owners alone. Kay and King (1990) provide a forceful exposition of this viewpoint. This arguments reflects the view that the corporation does not have a personality or existence of its own other than that given to it in law.

The alternative perspective is that incorporation carries legal and economic privileges and that the corporation tax is a tax upon the gains enjoyed from the benefit of these privileges. Foremost among these privileges is the limited liability that the shareholders in the corporation enjoy in the event of bankruptcy. Another possible view, and one reflected in US Tax Reform Act of 1986 which shifted the tax burden from the personal sector to the corporate sector, is that corporations can afford to pay taxes and should therefore carry their share of the burden. There is also the argument, already explored above, that corporation tax is taxing rent so is a distortion-free way of raising revenue. As already noted, there are limits to how far this argument can be pushed since it relies at the very least on the tax being levied on true economic profit.

Ultimately, the effect of a tax depends upon how it affects the individuals in the economy and the correctness, or otherwise, of taxing the corporation depends upon the final incidence of the tax. If the tax can achieve objectives that other taxes cannot, and so raise social welfare, then there is a justification for its existence. In a sense, many of the arguments noted above simply direct attention away from the main justification for introducing any form of taxation, which is to achieve specified aims. As is always the case in Second-Best theory, although a policy instrument may have no role in the First-Best, its use may still be justified in other circumstances.

3 TAX INCIDENCE

One aspect that has already been stressed in earlier chapters is that the *economic incidence* of a tax is rarely the same as the *legal incidence*. Legal incidence relates to who has to formally pay the tax to the tax collection agency whereas economic incidence is identified by the agents who suffer reduced welfare due to the imposition of the tax. Since there are general equilibrium repercussions to any tax change, the identification of economic incidence is not always a straightforward exercise.

In terms of the corporation tax, Harberger (1962) was the first to present a comprehensive analysis of incidence. The framework employed was that of a two-sector economy with two factors of production: capital and labour. One of the sectors of the economy was treated as incorporated and capital in that sector bore the legal incidence of the corporation tax. This framework permitted identification of the real effects of the corporation tax in terms of an *output effect*, capturing the change in the relative outputs of the two goods, and an *input substitution effect*, representing the adjustment of inputs within sectors. In addition, Harberger also calculated the change in relative factor rewards in order to determine the economic incidence of the tax in terms of whether the tax burden fell on capital or labour.

In the period since its publication, the Harberger analysis has been subject to many extensions and modifications, many of which are detailed in the surveys of Mieszkowski (1969) and McLure (1975). The analysis of this section will describe the *Harberger economy* and show how this can be employed to derive results on the incidence of the corporation tax and a range of other tax instruments. Some of the extensions will then be described. The analytical technique used to solve the incidence question follows closely the original development of Harberger (1962) and its description in Shoven and Whalley (1972).

3.1 Tax incidence in the Harberger economy

The Harberger economy is competitive with two goods, denoted 1 and 2, and two factors of production, capital and labour. The factors of production are in fixed supply. The initial equilibrium for the economy is defined in the absence of taxation and the effect of introducing infinitesimal taxes is then considered. This point must be stressed since it has not always been clarified in some of the literature. The extension of the analysis to finite taxes is described in 3.2.1.

To simplify the analysis by eliminating income effects, it is assumed that the government spends the tax revenue it receives in the same way that consumers would have done in the absence of taxes. In conjunction with the fact that taxes are infinitesimal, this implies that income does not need to be considered as a determinant of demand. The demand for good 1 is further assumed to depend only upon the ratio of consumers prices or

$$X_1 = X_1 \left(\frac{q_1}{q_2} \right). \tag{8.7}$$

Since demand is determined by the price ratio, the underlying utility function must be homothetic; see Rapanos (1991). Denoting the compensated elasticity of demand by ε, total differentiation of (8.7) gives

$$\frac{dX_1}{X_1} = \varepsilon \, \frac{d\left(\dfrac{q_1}{q_2} \right)}{\dfrac{q_1}{q_2}}. \tag{8.8}$$

The elasticity appearing in (8.8) is compensated since the marginal propensities to consume of households and government are assumed equal so that the income effect in government demand exactly offsets that in consumer demand. This leaves only the substitution effect. Units of measurement of the commodities are chosen so that the initial consumer prices are equal to unity. Equation (8.8) can then be approximated by

$$\frac{dX_1}{X_1} = \varepsilon [dq_1 - dq_2]. \tag{8.9}$$

Production in sector i is determined by the differentiable and homogeneous of degree 1 production function

$$X_i = F^i(K_i, L_i). \tag{8.10}$$

Total differentiation of the production relation (8.10) gives

$$dX_i = \frac{\partial F^i}{\partial K_i} dK_i + \frac{\partial F^i}{\partial L_i} dL_i, \tag{8.11}$$

which can be divided by X_i to read

$$\frac{dX_i}{X_i} = f_K^i \frac{dK_i}{K_i} + f_L^i \frac{dL_i}{L_i}, \tag{8.12}$$

where

$$f_K^i = \frac{\frac{\partial F^i}{\partial K_i} K_i}{X_i}, \tag{8.13}$$

is the relative share of capital in output (or the partial elasticity of output with respect to capital) and f_L^i is defined similarly.

Let $\hat{r}_i$ be the price paid by users of capital in sector i and $\hat{w}_i$ be the price paid for labour. The definition of the elasticity of substitution, s_i, between inputs then implies

$$\frac{d\left(\frac{K_i}{L_i}\right)}{\frac{K_i}{L_i}} = s_i \frac{d\left(\frac{\hat{r}_i}{\hat{w}_i}\right)}{\frac{\hat{r}_i}{\hat{w}_i}}. \tag{8.14}$$

The set of input taxes that are to be considered include sector-specific taxes and general taxes on capital and labour. Incorporating these taxes into factor prices and taking an approximation linearises (8.14) to

$$\frac{dK_i}{K_i} - \frac{dL_i}{L_i} = s_i[dr + dT_{K_i} + dT_K - dw - dT_{L_i} - dT_L], \tag{8.15}$$

where r is the price received by owners of capital, T_{K_i} the sector-specific tax on capital and T_K the general tax on capital. The notation is interpreted similarly for the taxes T_{L_i} and T_L on labour. Units of measurement are also chosen for inputs so that initial prices are unity. Given this, the tax rates can be interpreted as being either *ad valorem* or specific since, for example, the differential of $r[1 + T_{K_i}]$ equals $dr + dT_{K_i}$ when $r = 1$ and $T_{K_i} = 0$ which is equal to the derivative of $r + T_{K_i}$.

The assumptions of competitive behaviour and homogeneity of the production functions imply that factor payments are equal to revenue in both sectors. Hence

$$p_i X_i = \hat{w}_i L_i + \hat{r}_i K_i, \tag{8.16}$$

which when totally differentiated gives

$$p_i dX_i + X_i dp_i = \hat{w}_i dL_i + L_i d\hat{w}_i + \hat{r}_i dK_i + K_i d\hat{r}_i. \tag{8.17}$$

Profit-maximising input choice equates the marginal revenue product of the input to its price so

$$\frac{\partial F^i}{\partial K_i} = \frac{\hat{r}_i}{p_i},$$ (8.18)

and

$$\frac{\partial F^i}{\partial L_i} = \frac{\hat{w}_i}{p_i}.$$ (8.19)

Substituting (8.18) and (8.19) into (8.11) gives

$$dX_i = \frac{\hat{w}_i}{p_i} dL_i + \frac{\hat{r}_i}{p_i} dK_i.$$ (8.20)

Given (8.20), (8.17) reduces to

$$dp_i = \frac{L_i}{X_i} d\hat{w}_i + \frac{K_i}{X_i} d\hat{r}_i.$$ (8.21)

As initial input prices are unity, (8.13) and (8.18) imply that at the initial equilibrium $f^i_K = \dfrac{K_i}{X_i}$ and (8.20) that $f^i_L = \dfrac{L_i}{X_i}$. Hence (8.21) becomes

$$dp_i = f^i_L d\hat{w}_i + f^i_K d\hat{r}_i.$$ (8.22)

Incorporating taxes (8.22) can be written

$$dq_i = f^i_L [dw + dT_{L_i} + dT_L] + f^i_K [dr + dT_{K_i} + dT_K] + dT_{c_i} + dT_c,$$ (8.23)

where T_{c_i} is the sector-specific consumption tax and T_c the general consumption tax.

This completes the initial derivations. The solution for the effect of the introduction of the taxes into the economy is given by equations (8.9), (8.12), (8.15) and (8.23). These equations will shortly be solved but first a preliminary result is given that shows how various sets of taxes are *equivalent* in the sense that they have the same effect upon the equilibrium. This result is due to Mieszkowski (1967) and is stated as theorem 8.1

Theorem 8.1

When levied at the same rate the following equivalencies hold:

(i) T_{K_i} *and* T_{L_i} *to* T_{c_i}, $i = 1, 2$;
(ii) T_K *and* T_L *to* T_c;

and

(iii) T_{c_1} *and* T_{c_2} *to* T_c.

Proof

To prove (i) it is first noted that taxes only appear in (8.15) and (8.23). When introduced at the same rate, $dT_{K_i} = dT_{L_i}$ and the taxes cancel from (8.15). From Euler's theorem $f_L^i + f_K^i = 1$ so that from (8.23) the increases in dT_{K_i} and dT_{L_i} are equivalent to an equal increase in dT_{c_i}. This establishes that the effect of raising dT_{K_i} and dT_{L_i} is identical to that of raising dT_{c_i}.

The same argument applies to show the equivalence of T_K and T_L to T_c, where it must be noted that the change in rates affects both sectors. Finally (iii) is proved by noting that the tax changes involved only affect (8.23).

The explanation lying behind (i) of theorem 8.1 is that the pair of tax changes T_{K_i} and T_{L_i} together raise the price of factors equally for sector i, so that no substitution between factors occurs. The consequent increase in costs has the same effect upon the equilibrium as a consumption tax T_{c_i}. In the case of (ii), the pair of taxes raises the price of inputs equally in both sectors and so is equivalent to a general consumption tax. The same general reasoning applies to the pair of consumption taxes in (iii).

The equivalence demonstrated in theorem 8.1 shows that only a restricted set of taxes need be considered. To maintain the focus upon corporation taxation, the taxes upon labour will now be set at zero. In addition, the general consumption tax will not be considered. In the present context with no saving and fixed labour supply, the general consumption tax is equivalent to an income tax. A change in its value leads only to an income effect and not a substitution effect so that it is of limited interest as a source of inefficiency. Due to the equivalence result, it is also assumed that $dT_{c_2} = 0$. To understand the reason for the final restriction, it is best to return to the original motivation for the analysis. Harberger (1962) was concerned with distortion that would arise through the taxation of capital in the corporate sector while capital in the non-corporate sector remained untaxed. Under this interpretation, only one of the two sectors should bear a corporation tax. Correspondingly, it is assumed that sector 1 can be treated as incorporated but sector 2 cannot. Hence the capital tax in sector 2, dT_{K_2}, is set at zero. Finally, the wage rate is chosen as numeraire so that $dw = 0$ throughout.

Adopting these restrictions and substituting (8.23) for $i = 1, 2$ into (8.9) provides

$$\frac{dX_1}{X_1} = \varepsilon\left[f_K^1[dr + dT_{K_1} + dT_K] + dT_{c_1} - f_K^2 dr \right]. \tag{8.24}$$

Equating (8.24) to (8.12) and rearranging

$$\varepsilon[f_K^2 - f_K^1]dr + f_K^1 \frac{dK_1}{K_1} + f_L^1 \frac{dL_1}{L_1} = \varepsilon\left[f_K^1[dT_{K_1} + dT_K] + dT_{c_1} \right]. \tag{8.25}$$

Since the supply of factors is fixed, it follows that $dK_2 = -dK_1$ and $dL_2 = -dL_1$. Employing these facts, (8.15) for $i = 2$ can be transformed to

$$s_2 dr + \frac{K_1}{K_2}\frac{dK_1}{K_1} - \frac{L_1}{L_2}\frac{dL_1}{L_1} = 0, \tag{8.26}$$

and for $i = 1$ rearrangement of (8.15) gives

$$-s_1 dr + \frac{dk_1}{K_1} - \frac{dL_1}{L_1} = s_1 dT_{K_1} + s_1 dT_K. \tag{8.27}$$

Taken together, (8.25), (8.26) and (8.27) provide a three-equation system determining the dependence of the endogenous variables dr, dK_1, and dL_1 upon the tax changes dT_{K_1}, dT_K and dT_{c_1}.

Taking the sector-specific capital tax first, it follows from the solution of the system that

$$\frac{dr}{dT_{K_1}} = \left[\varepsilon f_K^1 \left[\frac{K_1}{K_2} - \frac{L_1}{L_2} \right] + s_1 \left[f_K^1 \frac{L_1}{L_2} + f_L^1 \frac{K_1}{K_2} \right] \right] A, \tag{8.28}$$

where

$$A = \left[\varepsilon [f_K^2 - f_K^1] \left[\frac{K_1}{K_2} - \frac{L_1}{L_2} \right] - s_2 - s_1 \left[f_K^1 \frac{L_1}{L_2} + f_L^1 \frac{K_1}{K_2} \right] \right]^{-1}. \tag{8.29}$$

To interpret (8.28) it is first necessary to establish that A is positive. To see this, note that ε, s_1 and s_2 are negative. Now if sector 2 is relatively capital intensive then $f_K^2 > f_K^1$ and $\frac{K_1}{K_2} < \frac{L_1}{L_2}$. The converse inequalities apply if sector 1 is the most capital intensive. In either case the product of the two terms is negative thus ensuring A is positive. The next point to note is that since it has been assumed that $dw = 0$, a negative value of dr implies that the imposition of the tax reduces the return to capital relative to that of labour whilst a positive value indicates an increase in the relative return of capital. The input substitution and output effects of the tax can clearly be seen in (8.28). The output effect is determined by the elasticity of demand whilst the input substitution effect is dependent upon the value of the elasticity of substitution.

Given these preliminaries, the next theorem follows from (8.28).

Theorem 8.2 (Harberger)

(i) $\dfrac{dr}{dT_{K_1}}$ *can only be positive if sector 1 is more capital intensive than sector 2.*

(ii) *If* $|s_1| > |\varepsilon|$ *then* $\dfrac{dr}{dT_{K_1}} < 0$.

(iii) *As* $|s_2|$ *increases without limit,* $\dfrac{dr}{dT_{K_1}}$ *tends to zero.*

(iv) *Assume* $\dfrac{K_1}{L_1}=\dfrac{K_2}{L_2}$. *Then if* $|s_1|=|s_2|$, *it follows that* $\dfrac{dr}{dT_{K_1}}=\dfrac{-K_1}{K_1+K_2}$ *and capital*

bears the full burden of the tax. If $|s_1|>|s_2|$, $\dfrac{dr}{dT_{K_1}}>\dfrac{-K_1}{K_1+K_2}$ and if $|s_1|<|s_2|$,

$\dfrac{dr}{dT_{K_1}}<\dfrac{-K_1}{K_1+K_2}$.

(v) *If* $|s_1|=|s_2|=0$, *then the incidence of the tax depends only on factor proportions.*

Proof

(i) In (8.28), only the term $\varepsilon f_K^1\left[\dfrac{K_1}{K_2}-\dfrac{L_1}{L_2}\right]$ can be positive. Hence for $\dfrac{dr}{dT_{K_1}}>0$ it

is necessary that $\dfrac{K_1}{K_2}-\dfrac{L_1}{L_2}<0$, which is the condition that sector 1 is more

labour intensive.

(ii) If $|s_1|>|\varepsilon|$ then $s_1 f_K^1\dfrac{L_1}{L_2}-\varepsilon f_K^1\dfrac{L_1}{L_2}<0$ so $\dfrac{dr}{dT_{K_1}}<0$.

(iii) This follows from observing that s_2 only appears in the denominator of

(8.28) so , all else equal, an increase in s_2 reduces the absolute value of $\dfrac{dr}{dT_{K_1}}$.

(iv) The expressions are obvious after substitution. Their interpretation follows from noting that the total tax burden is $K_1 dT_{K_1}$ so if the price of capital net of

tax falls by $dr=\dfrac{K_1 dT_{K_1}}{K_1+K_2}$, then capital has borne the entire tax.

(v) From substitution.

It is the calculations of (iv) of theorem 8.2 that describe the means of calculating

the economic incidence of the tax. Since a value of $dr=\dfrac{K_1 dT_{K_1}}{K_1+K_2}$ implies that

capital bears the entire burden of the tax, incidence can be determined by

contrasting this with the value of $\dfrac{dr}{dT_{K_1}}$ given by (8.28). If the value in (8.28) is

higher then labour is also carrying some of the burden of the tax. What (iv) achieves is to provide the answer to the incidence question under a specific set of assumptions. Following the same line of enquiry, Harberger substituted into (8.28) employing values from empirical studies in the US and reached the conclusion that capital generally bears the entire tax burden. The value of this conclusion is naturally restricted by the assumptions made about the economy in which it is derived. Much of the work following Harberger was concerned with testing the result under alternative assumptions. Some of this work will be described in the section 3.2.

Returning to the analysis of the present economy, it can easily be calculated that the introduction of the capital tax in sector 1 reduces employment of capital in that sector. The effect upon labour use in sector 1 is given by

$$\frac{dL_1}{dT_{K_1}} = L_1 \left[s_1 s_2 f_K^1 - \varepsilon f_K^1 \left[s_2 + s_1 \frac{K_1}{K_2} \right] - s_1 \varepsilon [f_K^2 - f_K^1] \frac{K_1}{K_2} \right] A. \tag{8.30}$$

In general, the change in labour use cannot be signed because of the conflicting input substitution and output effects but (8.30) permits the effect of various sets of restrictions on the elasticity of demand and elasticity of substitution to be tested. As an example, when the elasticity of demand is zero, labour demand in sector 1 increases as labour is substituted for capital. The effect of the sector-specific output tax upon the return to capital is

$$\frac{dr}{dT_{C_1}} = \varepsilon \left[\frac{K_1}{K_2} - \frac{L_1}{L_2} \right] A, \tag{8.31}$$

so that whenever the elasticity of demand is non-zero the change in the price of capital depends entirely upon the relative capital intensity of sector 1.

These results are intended to be indicative of what can be achieved in the context of the two-sector Harberger economy. Although only a limited number of taxes have been considered here, the same methods can determine the incidence effect of a broad range of tax instruments. However, the assumptions of the economy are rather restrictive and more is to be gained by relaxing these than by extending the set of taxes.

3.2 Extensions

Since the publication of Harberger (1962), many extensions of the analysis have been completed. Included among these are studies that have simply addressed the same issues but under alternative assumptions and others that have applied the analysis, often under very similar assumptions, to different issues. A survey of the latter, which will not be covered here, can be found in McLure (1975). In addition, Jones (1965, 1971) and McLure (1974) have developed alternative analytical techniques for studying the Harberger economy. The extensions that are now discussed are those that modify the structure of the Harberger economy in order to relax the restrictiveness of its assumptions.

3.2.1 Income effects

The discussion of the demand function (8.7) described how income effects were eliminated by the assumptions that infinitesimal taxes were introduced from an initial position with no taxation and that the government spent the tax revenue in the same way as consumers. This assumption has been relaxed in two ways. Mieszkowski (1967) considers demand to be derived from two distinct groups of consumers whilst Ballentine and Eris (1975) retain the Harberger specification but incorporate income effects for non-infinitesimal tax changes.

The consumers in Mieszkowski (1967) are comprised of workers, who earn income from the supply of labour, and capitalists, who receive the return from capital. In such a framework, a number of anomalies may arise when compared to the standard Harberger analysis. For instance, when these two groups have very divergent spending propensities and the elasticities of substitution in production are small, a tax on capital in the capital intensive sector may increase demand for that sector's commodity and increase the price of capital relative to labour. Since the same general principles are involved, this analysis also suggests the possibilities that would arise if the government did not spend its revenue in the same way as consumers.

Ballentine and Eris (1975) write the underlying demand function as

$$X_1 = X_1(q_1, q_2, rK + L + rt_{K_1}K_1),$$ (8.32)

where $rK + L$ is the income of consumers and $rt_{K_1}K_1$ the revenue of the government from the tax on capital in sector 1. The dependence of demand on total income implies the assumption that government and consumer spending patterns are identical. Taking the total derivative of (8.32) gives

$$\frac{dX_1}{X_1} = \varepsilon \left[\frac{dq_1}{q_1} - \frac{dq_2}{q_2} \right] + \frac{m}{X_1} \left[[K + t_{K_1}K_1]dr + rK_1 dt_{K_1} + rt_{K_1} dK_1 - X_1 dq_1 - X_2 dq_2 \right],$$ (8.33)

where m is the marginal propensity to consume good 1. Solving the system with (8.9) replaced by (8.33) gives the result

$$\frac{dr}{r} \frac{1 + t_{K_1}}{dt_{K_1}} = \frac{\varepsilon \Theta_{K_1} A + s_1 B - m q_1 C \Theta_{K_1} s_1 \dfrac{L_1}{L_2}}{\varepsilon [\Theta_{K_2} - \Theta_{K_1}] A - s_1 B - s_2 + m q_1 C \Theta_{K_1} \left[s_1 \dfrac{L_1}{L_2} + s_2 \right]},$$ (8.34)

where $\Theta_{K_i} = \dfrac{r[1 + t_{K_i}]K_i}{q_i X_i}$, $A = \dfrac{K_1}{K_2} - \dfrac{L_1}{L_2}$, $B = \Theta_{L_i} \dfrac{K_1}{K_2} + \Theta_{K_i} \dfrac{L_1}{L_2}$, $\Theta_{L_1} = \dfrac{wL_1}{q_1 X_1}$ and $C = \dfrac{t_{K_1}}{1 + t_{K_1}}$.

The value of (8.34) is that it permits the incorporation of finite taxes into the analysis. For zero initial taxes, it reduces to (8.28). It follows from (8.34) that when sector 1 is capital intensive, capital will bear more of the burden of any finite tax than labour (i.e., $dr < 0$). This extends (i) of theorem 8.2 to finite initial taxes. Similarly (iii) and (v) of theorem 8.2 extend to finite taxes but (ii) and (iv) do not. In addition, (8.34) shows that if $s_1 = s_2 = -1$ and the elasticity of substitution in consumption, σ, also equals -1, then the fall in payment to capital due to the tax exactly equals government revenue. To see this note that the homotheticity of demand implies

$$mq_1 = \frac{q_1 X_1}{q_1 X_1 + q_2 X_2},$$ (8.35)

and

$$\varepsilon = \frac{q_2 X_2}{[q_1 X_1 + q_2 X_2]\sigma}. \tag{8.36}$$

With these restrictions, (8.34) reduces to

$$\frac{dr}{r}\frac{1+t_{K_1}}{dt_{K_1}} = -\frac{K_1}{K}, \tag{8.37}$$

so

$$\frac{dr}{dt_{K_1}}K = \frac{dr}{r}\frac{1+t_{K_1}}{dt_{K_1}}\frac{r}{1+t_{K_1}} = -\frac{rK_1}{1+t_{K_1}}. \tag{8.38}$$

The effect of the tax change upon government revenue, $R = rt_{K_1}K_1$, is

$$\frac{dR}{dt_{K_1}} = rK_1 + t_{K_1}K_1\frac{dr}{dt_{K_1}} + t_{K_1}r\frac{dK_1}{dt_{K_1}}$$

$$= rK_1 + \frac{dr}{r}\frac{1+t_{K_1}}{dt_{K_1}}\frac{rt_{K_1}K_1}{1+t_{K_1}}\left[1 - \frac{s_2}{A} - \frac{L_1 s_1}{L_2 A}\right] - \frac{rt_{K_1}K_1}{1+t_{K_1}}\frac{L_1 s_1}{L_2 A}. \tag{8.39}$$

Substituting into (8.39) using (8.37) and the restriction that $s_1 = s_2 = -1$ gives

$$\frac{dR}{dt_{K_1}} = -\frac{rK_1}{1+t_{K_1}}, \tag{8.40}$$

thus demonstrating that the fall in income to capital is equal to government revenue.

3.2.2 Imperfect competition

Monopoly was first introduced into the analysis by Harberger in the original 1962 article. This was achieved by including a mark-up, representing the presence of some monopoly element, in the pricing equation for sector 1. Doing this for $i = 1$, (8.23) becomes

$$dq_i = \left[f_L^i [dw + dT_{L_i} + dT_L] + f_K^i [dr + dT_{K_i} + dT_K] + dT_{c_i} + dT_c \right][1+\mu], \tag{8.41}$$

where μ is the monopoly mark-up. Although this is a straightforward method of incorporating imperfect competition, it is not entirely persuasive since it omits the optimisation of firms in the determination of the mark-up. In addition, it also changes the nature of the sector-specific tax on capital. It was argued in section 2 that this could be viewed as a corporation tax in a competitive economy with constant returns to scale. The introduction of a mark-up in the pricing equation now implies the existence of pure profits which, in turn, prevent this interpretation of the sector-specific capital tax.

   With the monopoly mark-up included, the effect of the capital tax upon the return to capital is given by

$$\frac{dr}{dT_{K_1}} = \left[\varepsilon f_K^1 [1 + \mu] \left[\frac{K_1}{K_2} - \frac{L_1}{L_2} \right] + s_1 \left[f_K^1 \frac{L_1}{L_2} + f_L^1 \frac{K_1}{K_2} \right] \right] \hat{A},$$

(8.42)

where

$$\hat{A} = \left[\varepsilon \left[f_K^2 - f_K^1 [1 + \mu] \right] \left[\frac{K_1}{K_2} - \frac{L_1}{L_2} \right] - s_2 - s_1 \left[f_K^1 \frac{L_1}{L_2} + f_L^1 \frac{K_1}{K_2} \right] \right]^{-1}.$$

(8.43)

Comparison of (8.42)–(8.43) with (8.28)–(8.29) shows that the inclusion of the monopoly mark-up does not affect in any fundamental way the content of theorem 8.2.

An alternative formulation of imperfect competition is given in Atkinson and Stiglitz (1980) but this is based on a particular specification of monopolistic competition with a precise functional form for utility. Although instructive, it is not able to address the full range of issues associated with imperfect competition. A more general presentation of monopolistic competition is given in Anderson and Ballentine (1976). They conclude that the existence of imperfect competition does not much alter the incidence of taxation, concurring with the findings of Harberger (1962), and that, compared to the competitive case, imperfect competition amplifies the welfare loss caused by the introduction of a distortionary taxation.

In contrast to these static analyses, Davidson and Martin (1985) study a dynamic economy in which collusion can arise in the repeated game played by the imperfectly competitive firms. The output level in the collusive equilibrium is partly determined by the need to make deviation from the collusive level an unprofitable strategy. Deviation is rewarded by increased profits in the period in which it takes place followed by reduced profits in all future periods as the firms switch to punishment strategies. Full details of this form of equilibrium can be found in Friedman (1977). Whether deviation is profitable then depends on the rate at which future profits are discounted. In fact, as the discount rate rises so must the collusive output level. The relation of this to the incidence of capital taxation is due to the fact that the firms will use the net return to capital, r, as the discount rate. The corporation tax then affects r in the manner already analysed above and this effect then leads, via changes in the collusive output level, to changes in other factor and product prices. Consequently, even though capital may be in fixed supply, a general tax on capital which applies to all sectors is shifted rather than absorbed by capital because of the effect of the discount rate on the collusive equilibrium output level.

3.2.2 Intermediate goods

The main effect of the introduction of intermediate goods into the Harberger economy is to increase the possibilities for substitution between inputs. Unless the technology is Leontief with fixed input coefficients, these substitution possibilities modify the conclusions on tax incidence. In a series of papers, Bhatia (1981, 1982a, 1982b, 1986) has addressed these issues.

In an economy where there is a single intermediate good which is not used for final consumption, Bhatia (1981) shows that (i), (iii) and (v) of theorem 8.2 still apply to the extended economy but (ii) cannot be proved in the presence of intermediate goods. In addition to this, it is also proved that when factor proportions in the final goods industries are the same, an increase in the sector-specific capital tax will be a burden to capital relatively more than to labour so long as capital and labour, and capital and the intermediate good, are not complementary to each other in the taxed sector. Bhatia (1982b) considers the contrast between a corporation tax and a VAT. It is shown that neither of these tax instruments affects relative prices if input coefficients are fixed and the elasticity of demand is zero. When input coefficients are variable, only a VAT applied at an equal rate to all industries is neutral.

4 TAXATION AND FINANCE

An important issue in the study of corporate taxation is the question of how the tax system affects the financing of a firm and the investment plans of the firm. To finance investment, a firm has three sources of funds. The firm can issue new equity, it can issue bonds or it can employ retained earnings. The issue of new equity makes the firm liable for future dividend payments, but does not commit the firm to any specific level of payment, whereas bonds involve a fixed commitment to pay interest and, eventually, to redeem the bonds. A profit-maximising firm will naturally wish to choose the mix of these three instruments that finance the investment at minimum cost. Furthermore, the extent of future investment will in turn be determined by the cost of finance, usually referred to as the *cost of capital*. The focus is therefore upon how the tax system influences the means of finance and the cost of capital.

Most of the issues involved can be treated adequately under the assumption of certainty with all agents in the economy fully informed of the future prospects of the firm. However, the assumption of certainty does imply some restrictions. With certainty, there can be no possibility of any firm becoming bankrupt since such a firm would simply not operate. In contrast, in an economy with uncertainty there may be some states of nature in which a firm is unable to meet its obligations, essentially the contractual payments to bondholders, and therefore has to go into bankruptcy. The consequences of this will be discussed further below. A second issue that arises in the presence of uncertainty is that of the objective of the firm. In an economy with certainty, there will be unanimous agreement of the shareholders that the firm should maximise its profits. This need not be the case with uncertainty if there are incomplete markets. Generally, the problem facing the firm is that of aggregating the diverse preferences of its shareholders into a single objective. One possible resolution of this problem has already been noted in section 3 of chapter 7. The issues that arise with uncertainty have not been fully resolved and this limits what can be said about the effects of taxation.

The following section will discuss the essential aspects of the tax system that will be analysed. The differential tax treatment of different forms of transfer from the corporate to the private sector imply that the analysis must involve an integrated treatment of both corporate and personal taxation. The effects of taxation are then derived under the assumption of certainty with an emphasis upon the financial decisions of the firm. Uncertainty will then be introduced and the Modigliani–Miller theorem proved. Some further aspects of taxation will then be discussed.

4.1 Systems of corporate and personal taxation

The tax system that is now described is commonly termed the *classical system* and is in use in the US and many other countries. This is to be distinguished for the *imputation system* used in the UK and the *two-rate system*; these are described later.

The motivation behind the classical system is that the corporate tax is a tax on the benefits that follow from incorporation. As such, the tax liability of the corporation is treated as entirely distinct from that of the shareholders of the company. Consequently, profits are taxed at the rate set for corporation tax, dividends are taxed at the personal income tax rate applicable to the shareholders who receive them, as is interest received by the bondholders of the firm, and a separate rate applies to capital gains which is levied on realisation of those gains. Interest paid by the firm is tax deductible. Many of the consequences of this tax system with respect to corporate finance follow from the distortions introduced by the differential tax treatment of dividends and interest payments. In what follows, the rate of corporation tax will be denoted τ_c, dividends are taxed at the personal rate τ_p and capital gains at the rate τ_g. To reflect the reality of tax codes, it is assumed that $\tau_g < \tau_p$.

One of the perceived difficulties of the classical system is the double taxation of dividends: they are taxed once as corporate profit and then again as personal income. The imputation system represents an attempt to avoid this double taxation by integrating the corporate and personal tax systems. It does this by giving each shareholder a credit for the tax paid by the company on the profit out of which dividends are paid. In essence, any profits distributed as dividends are deemed to have already been subject to personal tax at what is known as the *rate of imputation*. The shareholder receiving the dividend is then only liable for the difference between the rate of imputation and their personal tax rate. In the UK the rate of imputation is equal to the standard rate of tax. A further alternative system that has been employed in the UK and in West Germany and Japan is the *two-rate system*. Under this system different tax rates apply to distributed and undistributed profits with the latter being taxed at a higher rate. This is designed to partly offset the double taxation of dividends inherent in the classical system. King (1977) provides further discussion of alternative systems of corporation tax.

4.2 Finance and investment with certainty

The study of the effect of taxation upon the corporation has gradually developed from the initial static analysis of Stiglitz (1973, 1976) and King (1975) through to fully intertemporal presentations such as Auerbach (1979) and Bradford (1981). Results derived in a static setting can be instructive but are unable to capture many aspects of the problem. For example, one of the notable features of the personal tax system is the favourable treatment of capital gains relative to other sources of income but, since capital gains are essentially intertemporal in nature, this aspect cannot be captured in a static framework. The same can be said of the more general fact that the value of the firm is determined by the flow of funds it provides to the household sector. The approach taken here will be to focus entirely upon the intertemporal analysis originally developed in Auerbach (1979) and extended in Auerbach and King (1983).

To motivate the approach taken to the analysis of corporation taxation, it is worth first looking at the investment decision in a simple two-period economy. Consider a firm that is entirely owned by a single household. Assume that the firm can undertake an investment project which requires the input of one unit of the economy's single commodity. Under what conditions should the firm make the investment? If the household faces a price ratio of $\frac{p_1}{p_2} = 1 + r$ for consumption in the present period (good 1) against consumption in the future period (good 2) and can lend or borrow as it likes at interest rate r, then the firm should undertake the investment project if the return in units of consumption in period 2 is greater than $1 + r$. If this inequality is satisfied then the firm is able to provide, via the investment project, units of good 2 more cheaply than the consumer can purchase them on the market. Effectively, undertaking the investment expands the budget set of the firm's owner. Furthermore, since the household will be maximising utility subject to the intertemporal budget constraint, the rate of interest will also be equal to the household's personal rate of time preference.

In this context, the interest rate is termed the *cost of capital* and plays a key role in determining the choice of investment projects. The conclusion of the example illustrates a general truth about the investment decision: the firm should undertake any investment that gives a rate of return of at least the rate of interest. In addition, the firm should continue making investments until the marginal investment just achieves the rate of interest. These observations underline the role played by the cost of capital and are now applied to the analysis of corporate and personal taxation. Further discussion of the cost of capital from this perspective can be found in Auerbach (1983) who also considers the effect of imperfections in capital markets.

4.2.1 No personal taxes

The problem of firm financial policy and investment strategy in the presence of a corporation tax is first approached in the absence of personal taxes. The analysis assumes that the firm can finance future investment through either issuing new equity, by issuing bonds or through the use of retained earnings. The timing of transactions is as follows. At the beginning of each period the firm distributes dividends to the shareholders of the previous period, it pays interest on its debt and repays the principal (the bonds issued by the firm are assumed to have a term of one period) and sells new shares ex-dividend. Interest payments are tax deductible for the firm. The actions of the firm in period t are chosen so as to maximise the wealth of those who hold shares in the firm at the beginning of period t. The construction that follows determines the level of wealth and its dependency upon the structure of the tax system.

At the beginning of period t the firm chooses an investment policy, a debt policy and an equity policy. Together these determine its dividend policy. An investment policy is characterised by the set of cash flows that arise as a result of the investment rather than by looking directly at the investment itself. Such an investment policy is denoted by a vector $z = (z_t, z_{t+1}, z_{t+2}, \ldots)$ where z_t is the firm's cash flow at the beginning of period t net of corporation tax. Since bonds have a term of one period, a bond policy, $B = (B_t, B_{t+1}, B_{t+2}, \ldots)$, describes both the number of bonds that will be issued in each period and the total stock of debt of the firm in that period. An equity policy is denoted $V^n = (V_t^n, V_{t+1}^n, V_{t+2}^n, \ldots)$ with each V_t^n being the value of new equity sold at the start of t. It follows that these policies imply the dividend policy through the identity

$$D_t = z_{t+1} + B_{t+1} + V_{t+1}^n - [1 + i_t[1 - \tau_c]]B_t, \tag{8.44}$$

where D_t is the value of dividends paid at the beginning of period $t+1$ to the shareholders of period t and i_t is the interest rate paid to bondholders.

After the payments of dividends in period t, the value of the firm's equity is denoted V_t^o. Following the sale of new equity the value of the total stock of equity is

$$V_t = V_t^o + V_t^n. \tag{8.45}$$

In period $s \geq t$, some of the dividends paid will go to equity issued before the beginning of t whilst the remainder will be received by holders of equity issued from t onwards. The proportion of equity in period s that is in existence before the beginning of t is

$$\mu_t^s = [1 - \eta_t][1 - \eta_{t+1}] \ldots [1 - \eta_s], \tag{8.46}$$

with $\eta_t = V_t^n / V_t$. In an efficient market, the value of the firm will equal the discounted value of future dividends. Hence, letting ρ_t be the discount rate applied by equity holders, the value of the equity at the beginning of t is

$$V_t^o = \sum_{s=t}^{\infty} \left[\prod_{u=t}^{s} [1 + \rho_u]^{-1} \right] \mu_t^S D_t. \tag{8.47}$$

Now noting that

$$V_t^o = \frac{1 - \eta_t}{1 + \rho_t} [D_t + V_{t+1}^o], \tag{8.48}$$

and

$$\frac{1 + \rho_t}{1 - \eta_t} V_t^o = [1 + \rho_t] V_t, \tag{8.49}$$

it follows that

$$\rho_t V_t = D_t + V_{t+1}^o - V_t. \tag{8.50}$$

The firm aims to maximise the wealth of existing shareholders and this wealth is given by

$$W_t^o = V_t^o + D_{t-1}, \tag{8.51}$$

which after substituting from (8.44) and (8.45) is equal to

$$W_t^o = V_t + z_t + B_t - \left[1 + i_{t-1}[1 - \tau_c] \right] B_{t-1}. \tag{8.52}$$

As the last term of (8.52) is pre-determined at t, maximising W_t^o is equivalent to maximising

$$\hat{W}_t^o = V_t + z_t + B_t. \tag{8.53}$$

The firm therefore acts to maximise the sum of security market value (equity plus bonds) plus current cash flow. From (8.50)

$$V_t = \frac{1}{1 + \rho_t} [V_{t+1} + A_t], \tag{8.54}$$

where $A_t = D_t - V_{t+1}^n$, which on solving for V_t gives

$$V_t = \sum_{s=t}^{\infty} \left[\prod_{u=t}^{s} [1 + \rho_u]^{-1} \right] A_s. \tag{8.55}$$

The result in (8.55) shows that the value of the firm is independent of the level of dividends and new equity issues. From the definition of A_t it can be seen that a one unit increase in dividends financed by a unit increase in the value of new equity has no effect on the value of the firm, nor has an equal reduction in both. In particular, the firm has no reason to sell new equity in order to pay increased dividends.

Rearranging (8.54) and adding to both sides gives

$$V_t[1 + \rho_t] + B_t + i_t B_t[1 - \tau_c] = V_{t+1} + D_t + B_{t+1} - B_{t+1} + B_t + i_t B_t[1 - \tau_c]. \tag{8.56}$$

Using the definition of the dividend in (8.44) to replace D_t, (8.56) becomes

$$V_t[1+\rho_t]+B_t+i_tB_t[1-\tau_c]=V_{t+1}+B_{t+1}+z_{t+1}, \tag{8.57}$$

or

$$B_t+V_t=\frac{V_{t+1}+B_{t+1}+z_{t+1}}{1+b_ti_t[1-\tau_c]+[1-b_t]\rho_t}, \tag{8.58}$$

where $b_t=\dfrac{B_t}{V_t+B_t}$ is the leverage of the firm. Combining (8.58) with (8.53) relates the level of shareholder wealth in two consecutive periods by

$$\hat{W}_t^o=z_t+[1+r_t]^{-1}\hat{W}_{t+1}^o, \tag{8.59}$$

with $r_t=b_ti_t[1-\tau_c]+[1-b_t]\rho_t$. The interpretation of r_t is that this is now the cost of capital for the firm since it is the weighted average rate of return that has to be paid for finance. The weights are determined by the present financial structure of the firms in terms of its leverage. When the firm can exercise choice over its financial structure it will aim to minimise r_t; more will be said about this shortly. Solving (8.59) under the assumption that there is convergence

$$\hat{W}_t^o=z_t+\sum_{s=t+1}^{\infty}\left[\prod_{u=t}^{s-1}[1+r_u]^{-1}\right]z_s. \tag{8.60}$$

From (8.60) it can be seen that the wealth of shareholders is equal to the present value of future after-tax cash flows discounted using the cost of capital derived above and it is this that the firm's policy should be chosen to maximise.

In considering the choice between bond financed investment and investment via the sale of new equity, it should be noted that both these policies keep the stream of cash flows constant. Their only effect is felt through the change in the cost of capital and the firm should choose b_t to minimise r_t. Assuming that the firm takes ρ_t and i_t as parametric, when the rates of return on bonds and equity differ there is no general presumption about the nature of the choice and the outcome is dependent upon the corporation tax rate. However, in the central case in which the rates of return are equal, bond financing is always preferred. This reasoning is summarised as theorem 8.3

Theorem 8.3

(i) If $i_t[1-\tau_c]>\rho_t$ then it is optimal to choose $b_t=0$ so finance is by equity alone.
(ii) If $i_t[1-\tau_c]=\rho_t$ then the firm is indifferent about the value of b_t.
(iii) If $i_t[1-\tau_c]<\rho_t$ then it is optimal to choose $b_t=1$ so finance is by bonds alone.

In particular, if $i_t=\rho_t$ then bond financing is preferred if $\tau_c>0$ and the firm is indifferent about its financial policy if $\tau_c=0$.

Proof

All these results follow from differentiating the definition of r_t. Doing this gives

$$\frac{\partial r_t}{\partial b_t} = i_t[1 - \tau_c] - \rho_t. \tag{8.61}$$

When this is non-zero a corner solutions follows. If it is zero, indifference arises.

The results in theorem 8.3 encompass several of the most well-known findings in the study of corporation taxation and its effects upon financing. The conclusion that the firm is indifferent about its financial policy in the absence of taxation is the Modigliani–Miller theorem applied to the case of certainty. It will be shown in section 4.3 how this can be extended to the case of uncertainty. The superiority of bond financing over equity financing when the discount rates are equal is usually attributed to Stiglitz (1973). As the theorem shows, this preference for bond financing is entirely due to the preferential treatment of bonds under the corporation tax.

4.2.2 Integration with personal taxes

The analysis developed above can be easily modified to incorporate the provisions of the personal tax system provided that it is assumed that capital gains are taxed on accrual in each period. This is counter to the usual practice under which capital gains are taxed upon realisation but is a necessary assumption since analysing taxation upon realisation would require a comprehensive study of household choice over time in order to link taxation with timing of asset sales. Undertaking this would remove the transparency of the analysis. What the analysis will capture are the consequences of the basic fact that capital gains are typically taxed at a lower rate than other sources of income.

When dividend income and capital gains are taxed, the net dividend received by the shareholders is

$$\Delta_t = [1 - \tau_p]D_t - \tau_g[V^o_{t+1} - V_t], \tag{8.62}$$

and (8.47), giving the value of the firm in period t, becomes

$$V^o_t = \sum_{s=t}^{\infty} \left[\prod_{u=t}^{s} [1 + \rho_u]^{-1} \right] \mu^s_t \Delta_t. \tag{8.63}$$

Following the same method of derivation as in (8.48) and (8.49)

$$\rho_t V_t = \Delta_t + V^o_{t+1} - V_t. \tag{8.64}$$

The wealth of shareholders is still given by (8.51) but after substitution can be written as

$$W^o_t = [1 - \tau_g]V_t + [1 - \tau_p][B_t - [1 + i_{t-1}[1 - \tau_c]]B_{t-1} + z_t] - [\tau_p - \tau_g]V^n_t + \tau_g V_{t-1}. \tag{8.65}$$

Since terms with subscripts $t - 1$ are pre-determined at time t, maximisation of W^o_t is equivalent to maximising

$$\hat{W}_t^o = [1 - \tau_g] V_t + [1 - \tau_p][B_t + z_t] - [\tau_p - \tau_g] V_t^n. \tag{8.66}$$

Substituting for Δ_t and V_{t+1}^o in (8.64) and simplifying gives

$$\left[\frac{1 + \rho_t - \tau_g}{1 - \tau_g} \right] V_t = \left[\frac{1 - \tau_p}{1 - \tau_g} \right] D_t - V_{t+1}^n + V_{t+1}. \tag{8.67}$$

Employing the definition of A_t and solving gives the value of the firm as

$$V_t = \sum_{s=t}^{\infty} \left[\sum_{u=t}^{s} \left[\frac{1 + \rho_u - \tau_g}{1 - \tau_g} \right]^{-1} \right] \left[\left[\frac{1 - \tau_p}{1 - \tau_g} \right] A_t - \left[\frac{\tau_p - \tau_g}{1 - \tau_g} \right] V_{t+1}^n \right]. \tag{8.68}$$

The value given in (8.68) implies the following theorem which can be found in Pye (1972) and King (1974).

Theorem 8.4

Given an investment policy, z, and a bond policy, B, if $\tau_p > \tau_g$ a decrease in V_s^n for any $s > t$ increases V_t.

Proof

Since $A_t = D_t - V_{t+1}^n = z_{t+1} + B_{t+1} - [1 + i_t[1 - \tau_c]]B_t$, any change in V_s^n only has a direct effect upon V_t. Given $\tau_p - \tau_g > 0$, a decrease in V_s^n for any $s > t$ will increase V_t.

The significant implication of theorem 8.4 is that the increases in value for the firm achieved by reducing new equity issues need not be exhausted when $V_s^n = 0$. In fact, provided dividends remain positive, the firm would wish to repurchase its own equity (i.e., choose V_s^n to be negative) rather than increase dividends. This result arises entirely from the preferential tax treatment given to capital gains relative to dividends and emphasises how directly the structure of the personal tax system can affect the financial behaviour of the firm. In practice, firms are restricted in their freedom to repurchase shares. To do so in the UK requires a court order whilst in the US the Internal Revenue Code prohibits firms from repurchasing shares in lieu of distribution dividends.

As a consequence of theorem 8.4 it becomes reasonable to assume that the firm will not issue new equity. Hence V_t^n will now be taken as zero for all t. Following the derivation in (8.56) to (8.60), the wealth of the shareholders is given by

$$\hat{W}_t^o = [1 - \tau_p] \left[z_t + \sum_{s=t+1}^{\infty} \left[\prod_{u=t}^{s-1} [1 + r_u]^{-1} \right] z_s \right], \tag{8.69}$$

where the cost of capital is

$$r_t = \frac{b_t i_t [1 - \tau_c][1 - \tau_p] + [1 - b_t]\rho_t}{[1 - \tau_g] - [\tau_p - \tau_g]b_t}. \tag{8.70}$$

The financial policy of the firm can be inferred from (8.70) through the firm attempting to minimise the cost of capital. To do this, note that after tax a bondholder receives $[1-\tau_p]i_t$ from each bond held. If households are to hold both debt and equity simultaneously then their post-tax returns must be equal so it follows that $[1-\tau_p]i_t = \rho_t$ where ρ_t is the return on equity defined in (8.64). This observation provides the basis for theorem 8.5.

Theorem 8.5

The firm will employ only equity financing if $[1-\tau_c][1-\tau_g] > [1-\tau_p]$ and will employ only debt financing if $[1-\tau_c][1-\tau_g] < [1-\tau_p]$.

Proof

Differentiating (8.70) with respect to b_t gives

$$\frac{dr_t}{db_t} = \frac{[1-\tau_p]\left[i_t[1-\tau_c][1-\tau_g] - \rho_t\right]}{\left[[1-\tau_g] - [\tau_p - \tau_g]b_t\right]^2}, \tag{8.71}$$

so the firm will choose only debt if $i_t[1-\tau_c][1-\tau_g] < \rho_t$ and only equity if the inequality is reversed.

Now suppose that $[1-\tau_p]i_t = \rho_t$ so both debt and equity are held. If $[1-\tau_c][1-\tau_g] > [1-\tau_p]$ then it follows that $i_t[1-\tau_c][1-\tau_g] > \rho_t$ and the firm would switch to an equity-only policy. Conversely, if $[1-\tau_c][1-\tau_g] < [1-\tau_p]$ then $i_t[1-\tau_c][1-\tau_g] < \rho_t$ and the firm will issue only debt.

The significant content of theorem 8.5 is its demonstration that the financial policy of the firm is determined solely by the structure of the corporate and personal tax systems. As in theorem 8.3, higher values of the corporate tax work in the direction of favouring debt finance as do increases in capital gains tax. Conversely, an increase in the personal tax rate favours equity finance. It is also important to notice that the theorem predicts that a firm will never use both equity and debt financing except in the special case that $i_t[1-\tau_c][1-\tau_g] = \rho_t$.

4.2.3 Conclusions

The analysis of the firm under certainty has made a number of strong predictions concerning the effect of the tax system upon the financing of the firm. Without taxation, the certainty version of the Modigliani–Miller theorem shows that the firm is indifferent about its choice of financial policy. The introduction of taxation directly alters this conclusion, with the corporation tax always working in the direction of favouring bond finance. The results also emphasise how directly financial policy is affected by the personal tax system.

4.3 Uncertainty

The analysis above has been restricted by the assumption that all actions by the firm lead to known future outcomes. Although a valuable assumption for generating insights into financial policy, it is a poor reflection of reality especially where long-term investments are considered. Uncertainty is now introduced but it must be noted at the outset that the resulting analysis cannot be as comprehensive as that conducted under certainty. Much of the reason for this follows from the need to include the differing risk characteristics of equity and bonds in the portfolio choice problem of consumers. If the firm does not become bankrupt, bonds always pay a known return whereas the return to equity, in both dividend and capital gain, will be dependent upon the state of nature. In addition, if a firm becomes bankrupt the equity of that firm will be worthless whereas bondholders will receive a share in the remaining value of the firm.

The Modigliani–Miller theorem has already entered the earlier discussion and this section begins with a formal demonstration of the theorem for the case of uncertainty. This will provide a sufficient set of assumptions under which the value of the firm is independent of the choice of financial policy. Following this, the effects of introducing taxation upon financial policy are discussed.

4.3.1 The Modigliani–Miller theorem

The Modigliani–Miller theorem extends the observation in theorem 8.3, that in the absence of taxes the value of the firm is independent of its financial policy, to an economy with uncertainty. It was first published in Modigliani and Miller (1958) and extended by Stiglitz (1969b). The limitation of both of these derivations is that they were basically static and did not capture the intertemporal aspects of the firm's decision. The theorem was extended to a multi-period setting in Stiglitz (1974) and it is upon this that the following is based.

Consider an economy with m firms and H households. All firms use one input to produce an output of the same commodity. A plan for the firm is a choice of investment levels for each period t and, implicit in what follows, a production technique contingent on the state of nature that arises at t. The investment level of firm j at time t in state of nature $s(t)$ is denoted by $I_j(t, s(t))$ and the level of gross profit by $\pi_j(t, s(t))$. These are taken as given. The firm can use two financial instruments: bonds and equity. Both of these are sold on perfect markets. A bond represents a promise to pay one unit of output in period t. The price of a bond with maturity at time τ in period t in state s is $p(t, s(t), \tau)$. It is assumed that there is no bankruptcy so it must be the case that $p(t, s, t) = 1$, all s, t.

Now suppressing the state of nature, investment can be written

$$I_j(t) = \sum_{\tau=t+1}^{\infty} \left[p(t, \tau)[B_j(t, \tau) - B_j(t-1, \tau)] \right] + q_j(t)[v_j(t) - v_j(t-1)] + \Psi_j(t),$$

$$(8.72)$$

where $B_j(t, \tau)$ denotes the number of bonds at the end of period t with maturity at τ, $q_j(t)$ the price of a share in the jth firm at t, $v_j(t)$ the number of shares outstanding at the end of period t and $\Psi_j(t)$ retained earnings. Hence the level of investment must be equal to the change in value of outstanding bonds plus the value of the change in the number of shares plus retained earnings. Define

$$V_j^e(t) = q_j(t)v_j(t) \tag{8.73}$$

to be the value of equity outstanding at the end of period t and

$$V_j^o(t) = q_j(t)v_j(t-1) \tag{8.74}$$

to be the value outstanding at the beginning of the period. From these definitions it follows that $V_j^e(t) - V_j^o(t)$ is the value of the change in the number of shares and $V_j^o(t-1) - V_j^e(t)$ is the capital gain or loss between periods. Since there are no taxes, the gross profits of the firm must be either held as retained earnings or distributed as dividends or used to redeem bonds. Thus

$$\pi_j(t) = B_j(t-1, t) + D_j(t) + \psi_j(t), \tag{8.75}$$

where $D_j(t)$ denotes dividend payments in period t.

The value of the jth firm at the beginning of period t before the bonds maturing in that period are redeemed is given by the present value of the outstanding bonds plus the value of equity

$$W_j^o(t) = V_j^o(t) + \sum_{\tau=t}^{\infty} p(t, \tau)B_j(t-1, \tau), \tag{8.76}$$

and the value at the end of period t is

$$W_j^e(t) = V_j^e(t) + \sum_{\tau=t+1}^{\infty} p(t, \tau)B_j(t, \tau). \tag{8.77}$$

Hence

$$D_j(t) = \pi_j(t) - I_j(t) + W_j^e(t) - W_j^o(t). \tag{8.78}$$

Turning now to the household side of the economy, let $w^{ho}(t)$ be the wealth of h at beginning of t, $w^{he}(t)$, be wealth at end of t, $v_j^{he}(t)$ be ownership of h in j at the end of t and $B^h(t, \tau)$ be their ownership of bonds with maturity τ. The assumption that there is no bankruptcy makes all firms' bonds identical so they must have the same pricing structure. The wealth of h is therefore given by

$$w^{he}(t) = \sum_{j=1}^{m} v_j^{he}(t) + \sum_{\tau=t+1}^{\infty} p(t, \tau)B^h(t, \tau), \tag{8.79}$$

or

$$w^{he}(t) = \sum_{j=1}^{m} \theta_j^h(t)W_j^e(t) + \sum_{\tau=t+1}^{\infty} p(t, \tau)\left[B^h(t, \tau) - \sum_j \theta_j^h(t)B_j(t, \tau) \right], \tag{8.80}$$

where $\theta_j^h(t) = \dfrac{v_j^{he}(t)}{v_j^e(t)}$ is the share of h in the equity of firm j at the end of t. Similarly

$$w^{ho}(t+1) = \sum_j \theta_j^h(t) W_j^o(t+1) + \sum_{\tau=t+1}^{\infty} p(t+1,\tau) \left[B^h(t,\tau) - \sum_j \theta_j^h(t) B_j(t,\tau) \right].$$

(8.81)

During period t household h receives dividends of $\sum_{j=1}^{m} \theta_j^h D_j$ and consumes $x^h(t)$ so the wealth levels at the beginning and end of t are related by

$$w^{he}(t) = w^{ho}(t) - x^h(t) + \sum_{j=1}^{m} \theta_j^h(t-1) D_j(t),$$

(8.82)

and the level of consumption is determined by

$$x^h(t) = \sum_{j=1}^{m} \theta_j^h(t-1) \left[\pi_j(t) - I_j(t) + W_j^e(t) - \sum_{\tau=t}^{\infty} p(t,\tau) B_j(t-1,\tau) \right]$$

$$+ \sum_{\tau=t}^{\infty} p(t,\tau) B^h(t-1,\tau) - w^{he}(t), \text{ all } h, t.$$

(8.83)

The description of the economy is completed by noting that equilibrium requires the value of ownership claims on firm j to equal the value of equity or

$$\sum_{h=1}^{H} V_j^{he}(t) = \sum_{h=1}^{H} \theta_j^h(t) V^{je}(t) = V^{je}(t), \text{ all } j, t,$$

(8.84)

and for the supply of bonds to equal the demand

$$\sum_{j=1}^{m} B_j(t,\tau) = \sum_{h=1}^{H} B^h(t,\tau), \text{ all } t, \tau.$$

(8.85)

The following theorem can then be proved.

Theorem 8.6 (Modigliani–Miller/Stiglitz)

Assume that there exists an equilibrium for the economy. Then there is another equilibrium in which any firm (or group of firms) has changed its financial policy but in which the value of the firm and of all its bonds are unchanged. In addition, the portfolio changes of investors are given by

$$\Delta B^h(t,\tau) = \sum_{j=1}^{m} \theta_j^h(t) \Delta B_j(t,\tau), \text{ all } t, \tau, j,$$

(8.86)

and

$$\Delta \theta_j^h(t) = 0, \text{ all } h, j, t.$$

(8.87)

Proof

Assume that $w^{he}(t)$, $p(t,\tau)$ and $W_j^e(t)$ remain unchanged after the change in financial policy. Under this assumption, it is clear from (8.81) that the changes in portfolio described in (8.86) and (8.87) are feasible. From (8.83), if these changes are undertaken then $x^j(t+1)+w^{he}(t+1)$ remains constant. Hence if $x^j(t+1)$ is unchanged, so is $w^{he}(t+1)$. In addition, for periods before the change in financial policy, wealth levels will be unchanged. Consequently, any consumption stream that was feasible before the change in financial policy remains feasible after the change. Furthermore, the original consumption stream must still be optimal since the opportunity set has not changed.

It remains to show that the markets for equity and bonds remain in equilibrium. From (8.87) it is clear that the equity market must be unaffected. For the bond market, it follows from (8.86) that

$$\sum_{j=1}^{m}\sum_{h=1}^{H}\theta_j^h(t)\Delta B_j(t,\tau)=\sum_{j=1}^{m}\Delta B_j(t,\tau). \tag{8.88}$$

Since all markets are unaffected, this justifies the original assumption that wealth, prices and values remained unchanged.

The basis of theorem 8.6 is that any change in financial policy by firms can be neutralised by adjustment of household portfolio composition. In this way, the equilibrium before the change can be maintained. The theorem does, however, rely on some strong assumptions. Firstly, it requires that households are unrestricted in their borrowing and lending and face the same rates on loans as the firms. Secondly, it was assumed that there was no bankruptcy. The effect of this assumption is to make all bonds maturing at some given date perfect substitutes regardless of the firm that issued them. This assumption is clearly an inappropriate one. The role of the bankruptcy assumption is discussed further in Hellwig (1981) who shows that the theorem can be extended to include potential bankruptcy provided that, when only securities issued by firms can act as collateral on loans, short selling of securities is permitted. However when moral hazard is incorporated as a feature of loan contracts, even this theorem does not apply.

4.3.2 Uncertainty and financial policy

In an economy with a full set of Arrow–Debreu contingent commodities, the profit level of the firm is certain, as described in chapter 7, despite the underlying uncertainty. This follows from the contingent production plan having a certain value at the known prices for contingent commodities. Since an increase in profits of a firm expands the budget set of all its shareholders, they will be in unanimous agreement that the firm should maximise profit. The implication of these observations are that with a full set of markets the results on the interaction of taxation and financial policy are the same under uncertainty as for certainty. Additional content to the problem can therefore only be given in an economy with incomplete markets.

With incomplete markets, there may no longer be unanimity between the shareholders about the objective of the firm. King (1977) presents an example where households receive the same utility from consumption but differ in the probabilities they assign to the occurrence of alternative states. As a consequence, their von Neumann–Morgernstern expected utility functions differ. Because of these differences, there may be a conflict of interest between shareholders since the expected utility of a policy is a product of the returns earned by the firm in the various states and the probabilities assigned to those states. In addition to the lack of unanimity, the shareholders may prefer the firm not to choose the policy that maximises the value of the firm. The explanation for this is that shareholders are also concerned with the prices of the goods they consume. If the actions of the firm affect both wealth and relative prices, then wealth maximisation need not be optimal. This aspect is investigated in Taggart (1980) who shows how the incompleteness of market prevents the equalisation of shareholders marginal rates of substitution between current and future consumption. This was also the reasoning behind the valuation adopted in the analysis of incomplete markets in (7.17).

The requirement of including incomplete markets and analysing the firm's decision problems when there is potentially no unanimity between shareholders makes further progress difficult to obtain. One contribution that is worth noting in this context is that of Auerbach and King (1983). Although this is restricted by being developed within a framework in which households are concerned only with the mean and variance of returns, so limiting the generality of preferences, it does develop a number of important conclusions. It is shown that two forms of equilibrium can arise. The first form of equilibrium arises when there is a firm whose returns are spanned by the returns of the other firms. When this occurs, value maximisation is optimal by firms but households will be specialised in their purchases. Because of taxes, some households will prefer to purchase only equity whilst others will purchase only debt. The value of each firm will be independent of its financial policy. In the alternative equilibrium value maximisation is not optimal and households will hold both debt and equity. However, for either of the equilibria to exist, constraints upon the activities of households must be imposed. There must be a limit upon the extent of borrowing that can be undertaken and no household's aggregate portfolio can be short sold. The force of these restrictions is to prevent infinite trades to take advantage of tax arbitrage.

5 CONCLUSIONS

This chapter has considered the effect of corporate taxation upon both the productive activities of the firm and its choice of financial policy. These represent the two channels through which the corporation interacts with the other agents in the economy. The structure of the chapter involved a process of moving from the analysis of the productive decisions of the corporation in the Harberger economy to the combination of financial and investment decisions in an uncertain environment. The analysis of financial policy emphasised the importance of both the corporate tax system and the personal tax system for the determination of financial policy. The effect of taxation in determining financial policy is emphasised most emphatically when contrasted with the conclusion of the Modigliani–Miller theorem which asserts the irrelevance to the firm's value of the choice between equity and debt.

Part III

RELAXING THE ASSUMPTIONS

9

PUBLIC GOODS

1 INTRODUCTION

When a public good is provided, it can be consumed collectively by all households. Such collective consumption violates the assumption of the private nature of the goods in the Arrow–Debreu competitive economy. The existence of public goods then leads to a failure of the competitive equilibrium to be efficient. This implies a potential role for the state in public good provision to overcome the failure of the market.

The formal analysis of public goods began with Samuelson (1954) who derived the rule characterising efficient levels of provision and, after defining some necessary terms, this will also be the starting point of this chapter. Efficient provision will be considered for pure public goods and for public goods subject to congestion. The theme of efficiency is continued into the study of Lindahl equilibria with personalised prices. Following this, the analysis of private provision demonstrates the nature of the outcome when prices are uniform and illustrates why a competitive market fails to attain efficiency.

If government provision is to be justified, it must be shown that the government can improve upon the market outcome. Section 6 shows what can be achieved when policy instruments are restricted to commodity taxation and uniform lump-sum taxes. In seeking the attainment of an efficient outcome, the government is faced with informational constraints of which the lack of knowledge of household preferences is the most significant. Section 7 on mechanism design shows why households may choose to misrepresent their preferences and how mechanisms can be designed to overcome this. Finally, the chapter is completed by a review of experimental evidence on private provision and preference revelation, and the use of market data to elicit valuations.

2 DEFINITIONS

A public good can be distinguished from a private good by the fact that it can provide benefits to a number of users simultaneously whereas a private good can, at any time, only benefit a single user. If the public good can accommodate any number of users then it is said to be *pure*. It is *impure* when congestion can occur. This section defines a public good, clarifies the distinction between pure and impure and develops its economic implications.

2.1 Pure public goods

The pure public good has been the subject of most of the economic analysis of public goods. In some ways, the pure public good is an abstraction that is adopted to provide a benchmark case against which other results can be assessed. Before proceeding, it should be noted that public goods can take the form of inputs into production in addition to their more commonly presented role as objects of consumption. A simple translation of the comments below can be made in order to allow them to describe the public good as an input.

A pure public good has the following two properties.

Non-excludability

If the public good is supplied, no household can be excluded from consuming it except, possibly, at infinite cost.

Non-rivalry

Consumption of the public good by one household does not reduce the quantity available for consumption by any other.

The implication of non-excludability is that consumption cannot be controlled efficiently by a price system since no household can be prevented from consuming the public good if it is provided. It is evident that a good satisfying this condition does not fit into the framework of the competitive economy used to derive the Two Theorems of Welfare Economics in chapter 2. In the form given, those theorems are inapplicable to an economy with public goods.

From the property of non-rivalry it can be deduced that all households can, if they so desire, simultaneously consume a level of the public good equal to its total supply. If it is possible for households not to consume the public good, then some may consume less. In the latter case, the public good may satisfy *free disposal*, so that consumption can be reduced at no cost, or else disposal can be costly. Further discussion of the modelling of free disposal is given in Milleron (1972) and of costly disposal in Oakland (1987). When all households must consume, or want to consume, to the maximum, the welfare level of each household is dependent on the total public good supply.

In reality, it is difficult to find any good that satisfies both the conditions of non-excludability and non-rivalry precisely. For example, the transmission of a television signal will satisfy non-rivalry but exclusion is possible at finite cost. Similar comments apply, for example, to defence spending which will eventually be rivalrous and from which exclusion is possible.

2.2 Impure public goods and congestion

In practice, public goods tend to eventually suffer from congestion when usage is sufficiently great. Obvious examples include parks and roads. Congestion results in a reduction in the return the public good gives to each user as the use of a given supply by households increases. Such public goods are termed impure. The utility derived by each household from an impure public good is an increasing function of the level of supply and a decreasing function of its use. There are a number of ways of representing the effect of congestion upon preferences and some of these will be described when optimal provision is characterised.

To obtain further insight into these definitions it may be helpful to think of a continuum of types of good running from purely private goods, for which there is complete rivalry and exclusion at zero cost, to pure public goods. Figure 9.1 illustrates the possible division of the consumption of one unit of a good between two households for the two extremes and for an impure public good. With a pure public good it is possible for both to consume a maximum of one unit. In contrast, the private good must be divided between the households. The consumption possibilities for an impure public good lie between these limits.

3 OPTIMAL PROVISION

The characterisation of the efficient provision of a pure public good was first published in Samuelson (1954) and was followed by a diagrammatic explanation in Samuelson (1955). For this reason, the rule for efficient provision is typically called the *Samuelson rule*. The following analysis will derive the Samuelson rule for a pure public good, with and without free disposal, and for public inputs and public goods with congestion.

3.1 Pure public good

To provide a reasonably simple derivation of the efficiency rule it will be assumed that there is available a single public good and, initially, that disposal is not possible. The latter assumption implies that all households must consume a

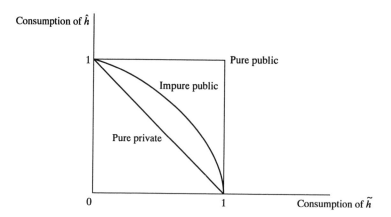

Figure 9.1   Consumption possibilities for one unit of good

quantity of the public good equal to its supply. The extension to many public goods is entirely straightforward.

The economy consists of H households, indexed $h = 1, \ldots, H$. Each household has a utility function

$$U^h = U^h(x^h, G), \tag{9.1}$$

where x^h is the consumption of household h of the vector of private goods and G is the supply of the public good. The fact that total supply, G, appears in all households' utility functions indicates that the public good is pure.

It is assumed that the combinations of x^h, $h = 1, \ldots, H$, and G that the economy can produce are constrained by production possibilities. The implicit representation of the production set is written

$$F(X, G) \leq 0, \tag{9.2}$$

where

$$X = \sum_{h=1}^{H} x^h. \tag{9.3}$$

To characterise the set of first-best, or Pareto efficient, allocations the government chooses x^h, $h = 1, \ldots, H$, and G to maximise the utility level of the first household, constrained by the requirement that households 2 to H obtain given utility levels and by the requirement that the allocation is productively feasible. Varying the given utility levels for households 2 to H traces out the set of Pareto-efficient allocations. The Lagrangean for this maximisation problem can be written

$$\mathscr{L} = U^1(x^1, G) + \sum_{h=2}^{H} \mu^h [U^h(x^h, G) - \bar{U}^h] - \lambda F(X, G), \tag{9.4}$$

where $\bar{U}^h$ is the utility level that must be achieved by $h=2,\ldots,H$. Assuming that the specified utility levels can be reached simultaneously, the necessary condition describing the choice of a component x_i^h from x^h is

$$\frac{\partial \mathcal{L}}{\partial x_i^h} \equiv \mu^h \frac{\partial U^h}{\partial x_i^h} - \lambda \frac{\partial F}{\partial X_i} = 0, \ h = 1, \ldots, H, \tag{9.5}$$

with $\mu^h = 1$ for $h = 1$. At an optimum (9.5) holds for all $i = 1, \ldots, n$. For the choice of the level of public good, optimising with respect to G gives

$$\frac{\partial \mathcal{L}}{\partial G} \equiv \sum_{h=1}^{H} \mu^h \frac{\partial U^h}{\partial G} - \lambda \frac{\partial F}{\partial G} = 0. \tag{9.6}$$

Solving (9.5) for μ^h, substituting into (9.6) and rearranging gives

$$\sum_{h=1}^{H} \frac{\dfrac{\partial U^h}{\partial G}}{\dfrac{\partial U^h}{\partial x_i^h}} = \frac{\dfrac{\partial F}{\partial G}}{\dfrac{\partial F}{\partial X_i}}, \ i = 1, \ldots, n. \tag{9.7}$$

To interpret (9.7) note that each term in the summation on the left-hand side is

$$\frac{\dfrac{U^h}{\partial G}}{\dfrac{\partial U^h}{\partial x_i^h}}, \tag{9.8}$$

which is the marginal rate of substitution between the public good and the ith private good for the hth household. The right-hand side of (9.7) is the marginal rate of transformation between the public good and private good i. Equation (9.7) can thus be written as

$$\sum_{h=1}^{H} MRS_{Gi}^h = MRT_{Gi}. \tag{9.9}$$

Equation (9.9) is the Samuelson rule which states that Pareto-efficient provision of the public good occurs when the marginal rate of transformation between the public good and each private good is equated to the sum, over all households, of the marginal rates of substitution.

The result in (9.9) should be contrasted to the corresponding rule for efficient provision of two private goods i and j

$$MRS_{ji}^h = MRT_{ji}, \text{ all } i, j \text{ and } h. \tag{9.10}$$

The difference between (9.9) and (9.10) occurs due to the fact that an extra unit of public good increases the utility of all households so that the social benefit of this extra unit is found by summing the marginal benefit, measured by the *MRS*, to individual households. At an optimum, this is equated to the marginal cost given by the marginal rate of transformation. In contrast, an extra unit of private good only increases the welfare of its single recipient and an optimum occurs when marginal benefits are equalised across households and to marginal cost.

Two points must be noted in the interpretation of this result. Firstly, although non-excludability has been adopted as a defining characteristic of a pure public good, it played no role in the derivation of the Samuelson rule. In fact, the optimal level of provision is not dependent on the degree of excludability. Instead, excludability is only relevant for determining feasible provision mechanisms. Secondly, although the Samuelson rule is deceptively simple in form, care should be taken before believing that it can be easily implemented. In order to derive the rule it was assumed that the government had complete control over the allocation of resources. Equivalently the government could employ lump-sum taxation to redistribute income and to finance the provision of the public good, with decentralisation of the provision of private goods. It has already been argued in chapter 2 that optimal lump-sum taxes can rarely be employed in practice and the same observation negates the implementation of the Samuelson rule. This conclusion has motivated the investigation of alternative forms of finance and the contrast of the resulting allocations to the first-best Samuelson rule.

3.2 Free disposal

If free disposal of the public good is possible it is no longer necessary that each household need consume the total quantity provided. If it is assumed that all households wish to consume some of the public good, the utility level of household h can be written $U^h = U^h(x^h, g^h)$, where g^h is the consumption of the public good by h, and the constraint $g^h \leq G$, all h, added to the maximisation in (9.4). The resulting Lagrangean is

$$\mathscr{L} = U^1(x^1, g^1) + \sum_{h=2}^{H} \mu^h [U^h(x^h, g^h) - \bar{U}^h] - \lambda [F(X, G)] + \sum_{h=1}^{H} \rho^h [G - g^h]. \quad (9.11)$$

The version of the Samuelson rule that applies in this case is given by

$$\sum_{h=1}^{H} \frac{\dfrac{\partial U^h}{\partial g^h}}{\dfrac{\partial U^h}{\partial x_i^h}} = \frac{\dfrac{\partial F}{\partial G}}{\dfrac{\partial F}{\partial X_i}}, \quad (9.12)$$

with the condition $\dfrac{\partial U^h}{\partial g^h} = 0$ if $g^h < G$. The interpretation of (9.12) is that the marginal benefit of increasing provision of the public good is set equal to the marginal cost but allowing for the possibility that some households may be satiated with the public good and receive no benefit from additional provision.

This derivation can be extended to permit some households to consume a zero quantity of the public good by introducing the constraint $g^h \geq 0$ into the maximisation. It is also straightforward to remove the free disposal assumption and replace it with costly disposal. Oakland (1987) provides a derivation of the relevant version of the Samuelson rule in these cases.

3.3 With congestion

For many public goods congestion is a very real phenomenon. Naturally, congestion reduces the benefit that all households receive from their use of the public good and therefore modifies the rule for efficient provision.

In the presence of congestion, the welfare of a household is typically written as dependent upon the total supply of the public good and the usage of the public good by all households. One approach to this (Oakland 1972) is to write

$$U^h = U^h(x^h, g^1, \ldots, g^H, G), \tag{9.13}$$

with $\dfrac{\partial U^h}{\partial G} > 0$, $\dfrac{\partial U^h}{\partial g^h} \geq 0$ and for $j \neq h$, $\dfrac{\partial U^h}{\partial g^j} < 0$. It is the sign of the latter term that captures the congestion effect. If disposal of the public good is not possible then $g^h = G$ all h and (9.13) collapses to

$$U^h = U^h(x^h, G, H). \tag{9.14}$$

A specialisation of (9.14) will be employed in chapter 12. Alternative specifications which employ a household production approach have been suggested by Sandmo (1973) and Muzondo (1978), who consider production processes using private and public goods, and Ebrill and Slutsky (1982) who focus on the combination of public goods with scarce time.

If (9.13) is employed and the Lagrangean formed as in (9.11), the resulting necessary conditions for the maximisation can be combined to give

$$\sum_{j=1}^{H} \frac{\dfrac{\partial U^j}{\partial g^h}}{\dfrac{\partial U^j}{\partial x_i^j}} = \frac{\rho^h}{\lambda} \frac{\partial F}{\partial X_i}, \quad i = 1, \ldots, n, \ h = 1, \ldots, H, \tag{9.15}$$

and

$$\sum_{h=1}^{H} \frac{\dfrac{\partial U^h}{\partial G}}{\dfrac{\partial U^h}{\partial x_i^h}} + \sum_{h=1}^{H} \sum_{j=1}^{H} \frac{\dfrac{\partial U^j}{\partial g^h}}{\dfrac{\partial U^j}{\partial x_i^j}} = \frac{\dfrac{\partial F}{\partial G}}{\dfrac{\partial F}{\partial X_i}}, \quad i = 1, \ldots, n. \tag{9.16}$$

If, at the optimum, $g^h < G$ for all h, then from the complementary slackness conditions $\rho^h = 0$ and (9.15) states that each household's use of the public good should be expanded until the private return is exactly balanced by the sum of negative externalities that this inflicts on other households. Additionally, the second term in (9.16) will be identically zero and (9.16) will describe the standard Samuelson rule.

If some, or all, households are not satiated at the optimum, so that $g^h = G$ for some households, then the second term in (9.16) is positive and the left-hand side of the equation provides a measure of benefit in excess of that used in the standard Samuelson rule. This excess arises due to an increase in provision of the public good affecting utility both directly and through the reduction in congestion that is brought about.

3.4 Public input

The characterisation of efficiency conditions for economies with pure public inputs began with Kaizuka (1965). The subsequent literature, which has also analysed congestible public inputs, is discussed in Feehan (1989).

To derive the efficiency conditions for the supply of a pure public input, consider an economy with m firms each using labour and the public good to produce a single form of output. Denoting the labour use of firm j by ℓ^j, the firm's production function is given by

$$y_j = f^j(\ell^j, G). \tag{9.17}$$

The public good is produced by using labour alone according to the production function $G = \phi(\ell^G)$. This is assumed to have an inverse $\ell^G = \Theta(G), \Theta(G) \equiv \phi^{-1}(G)$. The equilibrium conditions, that supply must equal demand for goods and labour, are given by

$$\sum_{h=1}^{H} x^h = \sum_{j=1}^{m} y^j = \sum_{j=1}^{m} f^j(\ell^j, G), \tag{9.18}$$

and

$$\sum_{h=1}^{H} \ell^h = \sum_{j=1}^{m} \ell^j + \Theta(G). \tag{9.19}$$

For this economy, an optimum allocation is found from the Lagrangean

$$\mathcal{L} = U^1(x^1, \ell^1) + \sum_{h=1}^{H} \mu^h[U^h(x^h, \ell^h) - \bar{U}^h] + \lambda \left[\sum_{h=1}^{H} x^h - \sum_{j=1}^{m} f^j(\ell^j, G) \right]$$

$$+ \rho \left[\sum_{h=1}^{H} \ell^h - \sum_{j=1}^{m} \ell^j - \Theta(G) \right]. \tag{9.20}$$

Carrying out the maximisation in (9.20) provides the efficiency criteria

$$\frac{\dfrac{\partial U^h}{\partial \ell^h}}{\dfrac{\partial U^h}{\partial x^h}} = -\frac{\partial f^j}{\partial \ell^j} \quad h=,\ldots,H \text{ and } j=1,\ldots,m. \tag{9.21}$$

and

$$\sum_{j=1}^{m} \frac{\partial f^j}{\partial G} = \frac{\partial f^j}{\partial \ell^j} \, \Theta', j=1,\ldots,m. \tag{9.22}$$

The first condition, (9.21), ensures that the marginal rate of substitution between labour and consumption is equated between households and this value is set equal to (minus) the firms' common marginal product of labour. This is a standard efficiency condition. Condition (9.22) is the form of the Samuelson rule for the public input and requires the sum of marginal products of the public inputs for the firms to equal the private good foregone in producing marginally more public good.

This completes the analysis of rules for efficient provision and from this point the focus will be placed upon pure public goods. The Samuelson rule may characterise the set of Pareto-efficient outcomes but, as noted, it cannot in general be implemented. This motivates the study of feasible allocation mechanisms and the comparison of their outcomes to those that satisfy the Samuelson rule.

4 PERSONALISED PRICES AND THE LINDAHL EQUILIBRIUM

Now that the rule for Pareto-efficient provision has been derived the natural question is whether there is any form of economy in which competitive behaviour will lead to an efficient outcome. The equilibrium in the standard model of chapter 2 will not be Pareto efficient in the presence of public goods. This arises from the fact that consumers differ in the valuation they place upon a given supply of the public good. Insisting that they all pay an identical price for the supply cannot therefore be efficient.

Following this reasoning, it would appear likely that Pareto efficiency would result if each consumer could pay an individual or *personalised price* for the good. In this way, each will be paying a price that reflects their valuation. Allowing such personalised prices represents an extension of the Arrow–Debreu economy which assumed that each commodity had a single price. The equilibrium with personalised prices is often called a *Lindahl equilibrium* after its introduction by Lindahl (1919).

Two variants of the Lindahl equilibrium will be described in this section. The first is for a simple economy with two households in which the price of the public good is given by the share of the cost of the public good each household must cover. Following this, it is shown how efficiency can be sustained in a competitive economy with truly personalised prices. The section is completed by analysing the relationship of the Lindahl equilibrium, and its extensions, to the core.

4.1 Simple model

The first formal analysis of the Lindahl equilibrium can be traced to Johansen (1963) who provided an analytical interpretation of Lindahl's (1919) equilibrium concept. With a single public good, the central aspect of this formulation is that each household bases their consumption decision upon the share, τ^h, of the cost of provision of the public good that they must pay. Assuming that the demand of household h for the public good increases without limit as $\tau^h \to 0$, an equilibrium can be defined as a set of cost shares, $\{\tau^1, \ldots, \tau^H\}$, that sum to 1 and are such that they lead all households to demand the same quantity of the public good. The importance of this equilibrium is that it satisfies the Samuelson rule and is therefore Pareto efficient despite the existence of the public good. If there are many public goods, a cost share can be introduced for each public good and optimality again achieved.

To illustrate these ideas in the simplest setting, consider an economy with two households who have an endowment of ω^h units, $h = 1, 2$, of the numeraire which they supply inelastically to the market. Each household therefore has a fixed income of ω^h. There is a single private good produced with constant returns to scale using the numeraire alone and the units of measurement of this good are chosen so that a unit of output requires one unit of numeraire input. The price of the private good is therefore also equal to 1. Production of the public good is subject to constant returns to scale and each unit requires p_G units of labour. The marginal rate of transformation in production between the public good and the private good is therefore constant at p_G.

Assume that each household has a utility function such that

$$U^h = U^h(x^h, G), \quad h = 1, 2, \tag{9.23}$$

where x^h is the quantity consumed of the single private good and G is the quantity of the public good. Utility is non-decreasing in x^h and G. Now let G^h denote the quantity of the public good that household h would like to see provided when faced with the budget constraint

$$x^h + \tau^h p_G G^h = \omega^h. \tag{9.24}$$

In (9.24) $p_G G^h$ is the total cost of providing the good and τ^h the fraction of this paid by h. From (9.23) and (9.24) household h chooses G^h to maximise

$$U^h = U^h(\omega^h - \tau^h p_G G^h, G^h). \tag{9.25}$$

The necessary condition for this maximisation is

$$\frac{U_G^h}{U_x^h} = p_G \tau^h. \tag{9.26}$$

Solving (9.26) for G^h generates the Lindahl reaction function

$$G^h = L^h(\tau^h; \omega^h), \tag{9.27}$$

which describes the household's demand for the public good as a function of the cost share it faces and its initial endowment. If the second-order condition for maximising (9.25) is satisfied and the utility function is strictly concave, then $L^h(\cdot)$ is a decreasing function of τ^h.

A *Lindahl equilibrium* is a pair of cost shares $\{\hat{\tau}^1, \hat{\tau}^2\}$ such that

(i) $\hat{\tau}^1 + \hat{\tau}^2 = 1$,

and

(ii) $L^h(\hat{\tau}^h; w^h) = G^* \geq 0$, $h = 1, 2$.

The first condition guarantees that sufficient revenue will be obtained to finance the equilibrium public good provision and the second condition that the households will both be satisfied with the supply. It follows from the fact that utility is non-decreasing in G that the cost shares will be non-negative.

The nature of the Lindahl equilibrium is illustrated in figure 9.2. The Lindahl reaction functions are formed as the loci of the vertical points on the indifference curves of the utility function in (9.25) and the equilibrium is given by the intersection of the functions. At this point, the indifference curves for the two households are tangential and the equilibrium is therefore Pareto efficient. To demonstrate the latter point, note that (9.26) must hold for both households at the equilibrium. Summing for the two households then gives

$$\sum_{h=1}^{2} \frac{U_G^h}{U_x^h} = \sum_{h=1}^{2} MRS_{Gx}^h = \sum_{h=1}^{2} \tau^h p_G = p_G = MRT_{Gx}. \tag{9.28}$$

Since (9.28) is the Samuelson rule for this economy, it demonstrates that the Lindahl equilibrium is Pareto efficient. This establishes a form of the First Theorem of Welfare Economics for the Lindahl equilibrium. The relation of the Lindahl equilibrium to the Second Theorem will be investigated formally below. For the present, it is sufficient to note that by redistributing the initial endowment it is possible to generate a new Lindahl equilibrium which represents another point in the set of Pareto-efficient outcomes.

4.2 A general treatment

The analysis of the Lindahl equilibrium in terms of cost shares clearly indicates how the reasoning can be generalised. In the budget constraint (9.25) the price of a unit of public good for household h is given by $p_G \tau^h$. Whenever the cost shares differ, the households face different prices for the public good. It is the existence

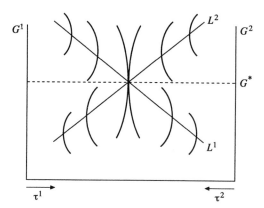

Figure 9.2   The Lindahl equilibrium

of these personalised prices that leads to the attainment of efficiency. The asymmetry between private and public goods should also be noted: with private goods all households face the same prices but demand different quantities; with public goods the households face different prices but, at the equilibrium, demand the same quantity.

The presentation of the Lindahl equilibrium via cost shares and reaction functions has the benefit of simplicity but, as careful study of the previous section shows, it does not make it obvious how general theorems on the existence of equilibrium or the welfare properties of the equilibrium can be obtained. To develop these it is preferable to exploit the fact that the use of personalised prices allows the Lindahl equilibrium to be expressed as the equilibrium of a suitably defined competitive economy. Since standard existence and welfare theorems apply to the competitive economy, they naturally apply to the Lindahl equilibrium. This approach to the Lindahl equilibrium was developed by Foley (1970), Milleron (1972) and Roberts (1973, 1974).

To formalise this idea consider an economy in which there are s non-disposable public goods available with these public goods used only for final consumption. The aggregate production set of the economy is denoted Y and, with n private goods available, $Y \subset \mathcal{R}^{n+s}$. It is assumed that Y is a closed, convex cone that contains the origin and thus that the technology satisfies constant returns to scale. A production plan is written in the form $(g; y)$ where the first s elements represent public goods and the final n private goods. It is assumed that no public good is required as an input: if $(g; y) \in Y$ then $(\hat{g}; y) \in Y$ where $\hat{g}_i = g_i$ if $g_i > 0$ and $\hat{g}_i = 0$ if $g_i < 0$. Each household, h, from the set of H households possesses a consumption set $X^h \subset \mathcal{R}^{n+s}$ with a consumption choice for the household denoted $(g^h; y^h)$. Household h has continuous preferences over X^h represented by the utility function $U^h(g^h; y^h)$, where $U^h(\cdot)$ is strictly monotonic and quasi-concave. The endowment of h is denoted by $\omega^h = (0; \omega^h)$. There are no endowments of public goods.

A state of this economy is an array $\{g, x^1, \ldots, x^H\}$ of public and private good vectors. A *feasible* state is now defined.

Feasibility

(i) $(g; x^h) \in X^h$ for all $h = 1, \ldots, H$,

(ii) $\left(g; \sum_{h=1}^{H} [x^h - w^h] \right) \in Y.$

Condition (i) ensures the consumption allocation is in the consumption set for each household and (ii) that it is productively feasible.

The relevance of personalised prices has already been discussed and they are now employed to define the Lindahl equilibrium. Let p_G^h be the price vector for public goods faced by h and p be the common vector of private goods prices. The formal definition of a Lindahl equilibrium can now be given.

Lindahl equilibrium

A Lindahl equilibrium with respect to the endowment $\{\omega^1, \ldots, \omega^H\}$ is a feasible allocation $\{\hat{g}, \hat{x}^1, \ldots, \hat{x}^H\}$ and a price system $\{\hat{p}_G^1, \ldots, \hat{p}_G^H, \hat{p}\} \geq 0$ such that

(i) $\left[\sum_{h=1}^{H} \hat{p}_G^h; \hat{p} \right] \cdot \left[\hat{g}; \sum_{h=1}^{H} [\hat{x}^h - \omega^h] \right] \geq \left[\sum_{h=1}^{H} \hat{p}_G^h; \hat{p} \right] \cdot [g; y]$ for all $(g; y) \in Y,$

(ii) $\hat{p}_g^h \hat{g} + \hat{p}\hat{x}^h \leq \hat{p}\omega^h,$

(iii) $U^h(\hat{g}; \hat{x}^h) \geq U^h(g; x^h)$ for all $(g; x^h) \in X^h$ such that $\hat{p}_G^h g + \hat{p}x^h \leq \hat{p}\omega^h.$

This definition is a direct extension of that in 4.1.

The first issue concerning this economy is the existence, or otherwise, of an equilibrium. Although this is not of direct relevance here, it is worth making some comments. To develop an existence proof, both Foley (1970) and Milleron (1972) construct a quasi-economy in which the commodity space is expanded to allow each public good for each household to be treated as a separate good. Consumption sets, preferences and the production set are redefined to be compatible with this. Equilibrium is then proved to exist, under assumptions closely related to those in section 9 of chapter 2, for the quasi-economy and this equilibrium is shown to be an equilibrium for the original economy. The alternative approach adopted by Roberts (1973) is to work directly with the Lindahl economy and to construct a mapping from the price space for private goods and the quantity space for public goods into the same two spaces. A fixed point of this mapping is shown to exist and to be the equilibrium for the economy. Further discussion of these proofs can be found in Roberts (1974) and an extension to non-convex production sets in Bonnisseau (1991). From these results, it can be concluded that under relatively weak conditions a Lindahl equilibrium exists and it is justifiable to proceed to an analysis of its welfare properties.

   Given the existence of a Lindahl equilibrium and the obvious parallel of this to the competitive equilibrium, it follows that a version of the First Theorem must hold. The proof of this exactly mirrors that for the standard competitive economy: assume the equilibrium is not Pareto efficient and that there exists a preferred allocation; the preferred allocation can then be shown not to be feasible.

Theorem 9.1 The First Theorem for Lindahl Economies (Foley)

The Lindahl equilibrium is Pareto efficient.

Proof

See Foley (1970).

Since the Samuelson rule describes the set of Pareto-efficient allocations, it follows that the Lindahl equilibrium also satisfies the Samuelson rule.

To prove the equivalent of the Second Theorem, which is that any Pareto optimum can be decentralised as a Lindahl equilibrium, requires the application of a separation theorem as in the proof of theorem 2.4. The proof proceeds by constructing two convex sets which have no interior points in common and can therefore be separated. The normal to the separating hyperplane is then taken as a set of equilibrium prices which are such that the Pareto-efficient output is profit maximising and each consumption plan is cost minimising over choices yielding at least as much utility.

The proof given is based on Foley (1970) and requires the following additional assumption: given the feasible allocation $\{g, x^1, \ldots, x^H\}$ there exists, for all h, $\{g, \tilde{x}^h\}$ such that $\tilde{x}^h < x^h$ and $\tilde{x}^h \in X^h$. When the price vector is positive this assumption states that, given any consumption plan, there is always an alternative plan with lower value. Using this assumption, the Second Theorem for Lindahl economies can now be proved.

Theorem 9.2 The Second Theorem for Lindahl Economies (Foley)

If a feasible allocation $\{\hat{g}, \hat{x}^1, \ldots, \hat{x}^H\}$ is Pareto efficient, there exists a price vector $p = (p_G^1, \ldots, p_G^H, p) \geq 0$ such that

(a) $\left[\sum\limits_{h=1}^{H} p_G^h ; p \right] \cdot \left[\hat{g}; \sum\limits_{h=1}^{H} [\hat{x}^h - \omega^h] \right] \geq \left[\sum\limits_{h=1}^{H} p_G^h ; p \right] \cdot [g; y] \text{ for all } (g; y) \in Y,$

(b) $\text{if } U^h(g; x^h) > U^h(\hat{g}; \hat{x}^h) \text{ then } p_G^h g + p x^h > p_G^h \hat{g} + p \hat{x}^h.$

Proof

Define the set $F = \{(g^1, \ldots, g^H; y): g^1 = \ldots = g^H = g \text{ and } (g; y) \in Y\}$. Since Y is a convex cone, F is also a convex cone. It is also non-empty since $0 \in F$. Next, define the

$\text{set } D = \left\{ (g^1, \ldots, g^H; y): y = \sum\limits_{h=1}^{H} y^h \text{ with } U^h(g^h; y^h + \omega^h) > U^h(\hat{g}^h; \hat{x}^h) \right\}. \ D \text{ is convex}$

and non-empty due to the quasi-concavity and monotonicity of utility.

As $\{\hat{g}, \hat{x}^1, \ldots, \hat{x}^H\}$ is Pareto efficient, D and F have no points in common. Therefore there exists a separating hyperplane with normal $(p_G^1, \ldots, p_G^H, p) \neq 0$ and a scalar r such that

(i) for all $(g^1, \ldots, g^H; y) \in F$, $\sum_{h=1}^{H} p_G^h g^h + py \leq r$

and

(ii) for all $(g^1, \ldots, g^H; y) \in \bar{D}, \bar{D}$ the closure of D, $\sum_{h=1}^{H} p_G^h g^h + py \geq r$.

Since the allocation $\{\hat{g}, \hat{x}^1, \ldots, \hat{x}^H\}$ is Pareto efficient, monotonicity of preferences implies $(\hat{g}, \ldots, \hat{g}; \hat{y}) \in \bar{D}$ and the feasibility of the allocation implies that $(\hat{g}, \ldots, \hat{g}; \hat{y}) \in F$. Hence $\sum_{h=1}^{H} p_G^h \hat{g} + p\hat{y} = r \geq \sum_{h=1}^{H} p_G^h g + py$ for all $(g; y) \in Y$. This proves (a).

Since F is a convex cone containing zero, $r \geq 0$ However, if $r > 0$ then it could be increased without limit by expanding any plan that gave positive profit. Hence $r = 0$. Since preferences are monotonic, $p \geq 0$ or (ii) would be violated by increasing the consumption on any good with a negative price. Similarly, $p = 0$, $p_G^h \geq 0$ cannot arise since public goods with positive prices could then be produced using costless inputs (public goods are not needed as inputs) and profit would be positive. Hence $p \geq 0$.

Suppose $U^k(g^k; x^k) > U^h(\hat{g}^k; \hat{x}^k)$. Then $\left(g^1, \ldots, g^H; \sum_{h=1}^{H} [x^h - \omega^h]\right)$ where $x^h = \hat{x}^h$, $g^h = \hat{g}^h$, all $h \neq k$, is in $\bar{D}$ so $\sum_{h=1}^{H} p_G^h g^h + p \sum_{h=1}^{H} [x^h - \omega^h] \geq \sum_{h=1}^{H} p_G^h \hat{g} + p \sum_{h=1}^{H} [\hat{x}^h - \omega^h]$. But, as only the terms relating to k in the inequality differ, this reduces to $p_G^k g^k + px^k \geq p_G^k \hat{g} + p\hat{x}^k$. Suppose this was an equality. Then the assumption that for any feasible allocation there is a point in the consumption set of k with lower value implies that along the line joining the point of lower value to $(g^k; x^k)$ there is, by continuity, a point of lower value than $(g^k; x^k)$ and preferred to $(\hat{g}; \hat{x}^k)$. This would imply the existence of a point in $\bar{D}$ contradicting (ii). Therefore the inequality is strict and (b) is established.

Theorems 9.1 and 9.2 demonstrate how the Lindahl equilibrium replicates the properties of the competitive equilibrium for economies with public goods. Implicit in the Second Theorem is the fact that the distribution of resources is chosen so that the Pareto efficient allocation satisfies the budget constraint of each household. To achieve this objective, starting from an arbitrary initial allocation, requires the use of lump-sum transfers or taxation. This makes the Second Theorem for Lindahl economies subject to the criticisms discussed in connection with theorem 3.2.

4.3 Core equivalence

One of the observations supporting the use of the competitive equilibrium notion is, that for economies with large numbers of consumers, the set of core allocations shrinks to the set of competitive equilibrium. This was stated below as theorem 2.2. In this way, identical equilibrium allocations are isolated using two very different concepts of equilibrium. If it were also true that the core of an economy with public goods shrank to the set of Lindahl equilibria as the number of consumers increased, this would provide similar support for the use of the Lindahl equilibrium concept.

Unfortunately, this is not the case. It is true that the Lindahl equilibrium is in the core, and this will be proved below, but Muench (1972) presents an example for which the set of core allocations is larger than the set of Lindahl equilibria despite the economy possessing a continuum of consumers. The relevance of the continuum is that Aumann (1964) demonstrated that the core and competitive equilibrium are equivalent in this case. Therefore, although the Lindahl equilibrium has many of the properties of the competitive equilibrium, it does not satisfy the same core equivalence so that its relation to the core cannot be appealed to in support of the equilibrium concept. The failure of core equivalence can be traced to the fact that when a coalition, say S, attempts to improve upon a given allocation it must be able to provide, from its own resources, quantities of the public goods. Since there are returns to coalition size in the provision of public goods, it is difficult for coalitions to improve upon existing allocations.

The result that the Lindahl equilibrium is in the core is given in the following theorem.

Theorem 9.3 (Foley)

If $\{\hat{g}, \hat{x}^1, \ldots, \hat{x}^H; \hat{p}_G^1, \ldots, \hat{p}_G^H, \hat{p}\}$ is a Lindahl equilibrium for the endowment vector $\{\omega^1, \ldots, \omega^H\}$, it is in the core with respect to $\{\omega^1, \ldots, \omega^H\}$.

Proof

Suppose the coalition S can improve upon the allocation $\{\hat{g}, \hat{x}^1, \ldots, \hat{x}^H\}$ with the allocation $\{g; x^1, \ldots, x^H\}$. Since the new allocation is preferred by all members of S, it follows from the definition of a Lindahl equilibrium that

$$\sum_{i \in S} \hat{p}_G^i g + \hat{p} \sum_{i \in S} x^i > \sum_{i \in S} \hat{p}_G^i \hat{g} + \hat{p} \sum_{i \in S} \hat{x}^i = \hat{p} \sum_{i \in S} \omega^i.$$

Since $\hat{p}_G^i \geq 0$ for all i, $\sum_{i=1}^{H} \hat{p}_G^i \geq \sum_{i \in S} \hat{p}_G^i$ so that $\hat{g} \geq 0$ implies $\sum_{h=1}^{H} \hat{p}_G^h g + \hat{p} \sum_{i \in S} [x^i - \omega^i] > 0.$

The latter condition contradicts profit maximisation in the Lindahl equilibrium and proves the theorem.

4.4 Cost–share equilibria

At the heart of the Lindahl equilibrium is the concept of personalised pricing. In the economy described in 4.2 the cost that household h faces for the public good provision, $p_G^h g$, is a linear function of the quantity of provision. In a natural generalisation of this framework Mas-Colell (1980b), Mas-Colell and Silvestre (1989) and Weber and Wiesmeth (1991) have investigated the implications of permitting monotonic cost functions $\phi^h(G)$ which are not necessarily linear for economies with a single public good.

The main result of this literature is the equivalence theorem of Weber and Wiesmeth which proves that the set of cost–share equilibria is identical to the set of core allocations. The additional flexibility offered by the non-linear cost–shares is therefore sufficient to provide the equivalence that is absent in the linear Lindahl equilibrium. However, since it is already difficult to envisage linear personalised pricing being applied in practice, non-linear personalised pricing would seem devoid of practical interest.

4.5 Comments

The Lindahl equilibrium demonstrates how efficiency can be attained in an economy with public goods by the use of personalised prices. The personalised prices succeed in equating the individual valuations of the supply of public goods to the cost of production in a way that uniform pricing cannot. These are important observations that support the relevance of the Lindahl equilibrium concept.

Unfortunately, the Lindahl equilibrium is not without fault. It is central to the equilibrium that each household should face a price system that is designed to capture that household's evaluation of the public good supply. When it participates in the public goods market each household is the only purchaser at its particular price ratio and is not in the position it would be in a competitive market of being one purchaser among many. In a competitive equilibrium there is no incentive for the household to act in any other way than just to purchase its most preferred consumption plan. In contrast, the fact that the household is in a stronger position in the Lindahl equilibrium raises the very clear possibility that it can gain by false revelation of preferences in an attempt to adjust equilibrium prices to its advantage. Such strategic behaviour on the part of households undermines the foundation of the Lindahl equilibrium. If it does occur, the Lindahl equilibrium with strategic behaviour no longer possesses the efficiency properties set out above. The consequences of strategic behaviour, and responses to it, will be discussed further in section 7.

5 PRIVATE PROVISION OF PUBLIC GOOD

The characterisation of optimal provision in section 3 was concerned with an economy in which the government provided the public good and was unrestricted in its policy instruments. This first-best outcome is now contrasted to the equilibrium of an economy in which the public good is funded entirely by the voluntary contributions of individual households. Economies with government provision alone and those with only private provision should be seen as the two extreme cases since in practice, as charitable donations indicate, public goods are usually provided by a combination of both methods. The focus of the analysis will be upon the welfare properties of the private provision equilibrium and the level of public good supply relative to efficient levels. In addition, the effect of the number of households on supply and changes in the income distribution will also be considered.

In order to analyse private provision, it is necessary to make an assumption about how each household expects their contribution to the provision of public goods to affect the contributions of others. The assumption that was made in the initial literature on private provision (for example Bergstrom, Blume and Varian (1986), Chamberlin (1974, 1976), Cornes and Sandler (1985), McGuire (1974) and Young (1982)) was the standard Nash assumption: in planning their contribution, each household takes the contribution of the others as given. This is not the only permissible assumption and alternatives have been investigated; some of these will be discussed briefly in 5.6.

5.1 Equilibrium

The equilibrium with private provision will be derived in the economy used to introduce the Lindahl equilibrium. The economy therefore has H households who each have an endowment of ω^h units of the numeraire which they supply inelastically. The income of each household is fixed at ω^h. The single private good is produced with constant returns to scale using the numeraire alone and a unit of output requires one unit of numeraire input. The price of the private good is equal to one. Production of the public good is subject to constant returns to scale and each unit requires p_G units of labour. The price of the public good is constant at p_G.

Each household has a utility function

$$U^h = U^h(x^h, G), \quad h = 1, \ldots, H, \tag{9.29}$$

where x^h is the quantity of private good consumed, $G = \sum_{h=1}^{H} g^h$ and g^h is the contribution of h. The contribution towards the public good by all households other than h, $\bar{G}_h$, is defined by

$$\bar{G}_h = G - g^h. \tag{9.30}$$

Using the budget constraint $x^h + p_G \tau^h G^h = \omega^h$, utility can be written in terms of $\bar{G}_h$ and g^h as follows

$$U^h(x^h, G) = U^h(\omega^h - p_G g^h, g^h + \bar{G}_h) = V^h(g^h, \bar{G}_h, p_G). \tag{9.31}$$

Household h chooses g^h to maximise (9.31) given $\bar{G}_h$ and subject to $g^h \in \left[0, \dfrac{\omega^h}{p_G} \right]$.

Indifference curves of $V^h(\cdot)$ can be drawn in $(g^h, \bar{G}_h)$ space. Increasing $\bar{G}_h$ will always lead to a higher attainable level of V for given g^h, g^h is limited by the budget constraint and preferred sets are convex.

Since the household takes the provision of others as given when maximising, the optimal choice of g^h for a given value of $\bar{G}_h$ occurs at the tangency of the indifference curve and the horizontal line at $\bar{G}_h^*$. This is shown in figure 9.3 and the solid locus, the Nash reaction function, traces out the optimal choices of g^h as $\bar{G}_h$ varies. The gradient of the reaction function, when the chosen value of g^h is interior, can be derived by noting that for all g^h on the reaction function

$$g^h = \operatorname{argmax} \ U^h(\omega^h - p_G g^h, g^h + \bar{G}_h). \tag{9.32}$$

Differentiating this, g^h solves

$$- U_x^h p_G + U_G^h = 0. \tag{9.33}$$

Now considering variations in g^h and $\bar{G}_h$ that satisfy the first-order condition (9.33),

$$\frac{dg^h}{d\bar{G}_h} = \frac{U_{xG}^h p_G - U_{GG}^h}{U_{xx}^h p_G^2 - 2U_{xG}^h p_G + U_{GG}^h}, \tag{9.34}$$

which is always negative when $U_{xG}^h > 0$.

Alternatively, taking incomes as fixed, (9.33) can be solved to express g^h as a function of $\bar{G}_h$. The reaction function can then be written as

$$g^h = \rho^h(\bar{G}_h), \ \rho^h(\bar{G}_h) \in \left[0, \frac{\omega^h}{p_G} \right]. \tag{9.35}$$

This function traces out the optimal response of the household to the supply $\bar{G}_h$ of the other households.

The equilibrium of the private provision economy occurs at a set of choices for the households such that all the reaction functions are simultaneously satisfied.

Private provision equilibrium

A private provision equilibrium is an array of contributions $\{\hat{g}^h\}, \hat{g}^h \in \left[0, \frac{\omega^h}{p_G} \right]$,

such that $\hat{g}^h = \rho^h(\bar{G}_h)$ for all $h = 1, \ldots, H$, with $\bar{G}_h = \sum_{\substack{j=1, \\ j \neq h}}^{H} \hat{g}^j$.

If $\hat{g}^h > 0$ household h is termed a *contributor* and is a *non-contributor* if $\hat{g}^h = 0$. The set of contributors is denoted C.

The proof that such an equilibrium exists employs the standard argument for demonstrating the existence of a Nash equilibrium. Assuming that preferences are strictly convex, the composite function $R(g^1, \ldots, g^H) \equiv (\rho^1, \ldots, \rho^H)$ defines a

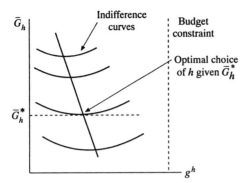

Figure 9.3   Indirect preferences over private provision

continuous function from the compact, convex set $\times_{H=1}^{H}\left[0, \dfrac{\omega^{h}}{p_{G}}\right]$ to itself. From Brouwer's theorem $R(g^{1}, \ldots, g^{H})$ has at least one fixed point and a fixed point of $R(g^{1}, \ldots, g^{H})$ is clearly a private provision equilibrium.

It has also been shown that under weak conditions the private provision equilibrium is unique. Given $\bar{G}_{h}$, (9.32) determines the contribution of h as a function of income, $g^{h} = f^{h}(\omega^{h})$. Bergstrom, Blume and Varian (1986, 1992) show that the restriction $0 < \dfrac{\partial f^{h}(\omega^{h})}{\partial \omega^{h}} < 1$ is sufficient to prove uniqueness. This restriction is simply the requirement that both private and public goods are normal.

For a two-household economy the private provision equilibrium can be presented diagrammatically. The households solve the following maximisations

Household 1: $\max_{\{g^{1}\}} U^{1}(\omega^{1} - p_{G}g^{1}, g^{1} + g^{2})$, with g^{2} fixed.
Household 2: $\max_{\{g^{2}\}} U^{2}(\omega^{2} - p_{G}g^{2}, g^{1} + g^{2})$, with g^{1} fixed.

The solution to these maximisations are given by the reaction functions $g^{1} = \rho^{1}(g^{2})$ and $g^{2} = \rho^{2}(g^{1})$. The equilibrium is then a pair $\hat{g}^{1}, \hat{g}^{2}$ such that

$$\hat{g}^{1} = \rho^{1}(\hat{g}^{2}), \hat{g}^{2} = \rho^{2}(\hat{g}^{1}). \tag{9.36}$$

This equilibrium is illustrated in figure 9.4 in which the reaction functions are simultaneously satisfied at their intersection.

5.2 Pareto improvements

It is a property of Nash equilibria that they are not, in general, Pareto efficient and, although no agent can improve their welfare when acting independently, a simultaneous change in actions can benefit all agents. This observation applies to the private provision equilibrium in which a simultaneous increase in contributions will raise all households' welfare.

To demonstrate this it is first observed, as is always the case, that the set of

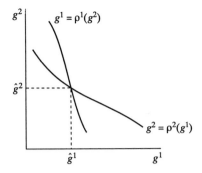

Figure 9.4   Private provision equilibrium

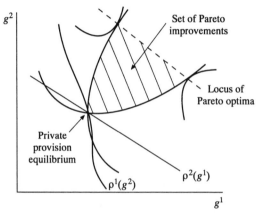

Figure 9.5   Non-optimality of private provision

Pareto-efficient allocations are the points of tangency of the households' indifference curves. In contrast, it follows from the construction of the reaction function in figure 9.3 and the structure of equilibrium in figure 9.4 that for the two-household economy the private provision equilibrium occurs at a point where two households' indifference curves are at right angles. The set of Pareto-efficient allocations and the private provision equilibrium are shown in figure 9.5. Since the private provision equilibrium is not Pareto efficient, there exist Pareto improvements and these are given by the shaded area.

It is also apparent in figure 9.5 how an increase in both the households' contributions can lead to a Pareto improvement. Therefore, local improvements in welfare can be achieved by an increase in the provision of public goods. Compared to Pareto-preferred allocations, the private provision equilibrium leads to an undersupply of public goods.

5.3 Quantity of provision

The result described above, that the private provision equilibrium is Pareto-dominated by allocations with a higher level of public good, has often been

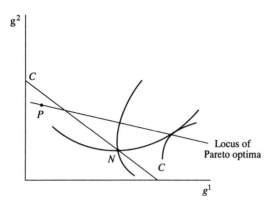

Figure 9.6   The possibility of oversupply

interpreted as demonstrating that private provision leads to undersupply relative to the socially optimal level. However, a global optimum of a Paretian social welfare function may lie anywhere on the locus of Pareto-efficient allocations and not necessarily on that part of the locus that Pareto dominates the private provision equilibrium.

Buchanan and Kafoglis (1963) demonstrated that it was possible for counter examples to be constructed in which the quantity of a public good is decreased as the economy moves towards the optimum from the private provision equilibrium. The possibility of such anomalies arising is illustrated in figure 9.6. The private provision equilibrium occurs at point N and the set of Pareto-efficient allocations are given by the locus of tangencies of the indifference curves.

The line CC represents an aggregate level of public good supply equal to that in the private provision equilibrium. For the optimum to have less of the public good simply requires the locus of Pareto optima to cut the line CC and for social welfare to be maximised at some point below CC. If the optimal point is P a reduction in the total supply of the public good is required in the move from the private provision equilibrium to the optimum. It should also be noted that if the locus does cross CC, a social welfare function can always be found that places the optimum below CC.

As shown by Diamond and Mirrlees (1973), such anomalies can only be ruled out by placing restrictions upon the second derivatives of the households' utility functions. There are no fundamental reasons why restrictions upon second derivatives should be satisfied and hence anomalous cases may well occur even in the two-household model. Therefore, although local results can be established without too much difficulty, it is not straightforward to provide global comparisons.

5.4 The number of households

It has already been established that the private provision equilibrium is not Pareto efficient. A further issue that has been addressed (Chamberlin 1974, 1976;

McGuire 1974) is how the deviation from efficiency depends upon the number of households that may potentially contribute. The natural expectation would be that an increase in the number of households would lead to greater divergence as each household expected all others to contribute. However, as is often the case, the actual result differs somewhat from this expectation. In addition, the limiting properties of equilibrium, as the number of households increases without limit, will be analysed following the approach of Andreoni (1988a).

To consider the consequence of variations in the number of households, assume that all the households are identical in terms of both preferences and endowments. Assuming both goods are normal, the uniqueness result then justifies the study of symmetric equilibria. For an economy with H households, it follows that at the symmetric equilibrium

$$g = \frac{\bar{G}}{H-1}, \tag{9.37}$$

where g is the households' common contribution. In terms of $(g - \bar{G})$ space, an allocation satisfying (9.37) must lie somewhere on a ray through the origin with gradient $H-1$ and, for each level of H, the equilibrium is given by the intersection of the appropriate ray with the reaction function. The welfare optima, if all households are treated equally, are the locus of tangencies between the rays and the indifference curves. This is shown in figure 9.7.

Whether the quantity of public good at the private provision equilibrium increases as H increases is dependent upon the gradient of the reaction function. If $\rho'(\bar{G}) < 1$, then provision, given by Hg, is an increasing function of H. When $\rho'(\bar{G}) = 1$, provision is independent of H and it is a decreasing function of H if $\rho'(\bar{G}) > 1$. These conditions can be related to the structure of preferences via (9.34). For instance, with the utility function

$$U(x, G) = x + K(G), \tag{9.38}$$

the reaction curve has a gradient of -1 since $U^h_{xx} = U^h_{xG} = 0$ and the total level of provision is independent of the number of households.

The effect of increasing the number of households upon the divergence between the private provision equilibrium and the equal-treatment welfare optima is not so easily determined. It can be seen in figure 9.7 that this is dependent upon the curvature of the indifference curves between the two equilibria and, as shown by Cornes and Sandler (1984a), both income and substitution effects are involved. What can be said is that examples can be constructed, such as the case shown in figure 9.7, in which the divergence decreases as H increases. The opposite result can also be shown to be possible.

The natural extension of the above analysis is to consider the equilibrium level of provision as the number of households tends to infinity. An idea of what will occur with identical households can be seen by considering the consequence of the ray in figure 9.7 becoming vertical: provision will tend to the level at which the reaction function crosses the vertical axis and the provision of each household will tend to zero. This result is due to Chamberlin (1974). Now

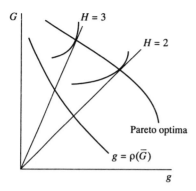

Figure 9.7 Equilibria and optima for various *H*

consider an economy where all households have the same preferences but differ in their endowments. The following theorem is due to Andreoni (1988a).

Theorem 9.4 (Andreoni)

For an economy of H households with identical preferences and endowments distributed according to a continuous density function $\gamma(\omega)$ with support $(0,\Omega)$, then as H increases to infinity:

(i) the proportion of the population contributing decreases to zero;
(ii) only the households with the highest endowment contribute;
(iii) total contributions increase to a finite value;
(iv) the average contribution decreases to zero.

Proof

The maximisation of household h can be written $\max_{\{x^h,G\}} U^h(x^h,G)$ subject to the constraints $x^h + G = \omega^h + \bar{G}_h$ and $G \geq \bar{G}_h$. This yields the demand function $G = \max\{\zeta(\omega^h + \bar{G}_h), \bar{G}_h\}$. It is assumed that private and public goods are normal so $0 < \zeta' < 1$. If $G > \bar{G}_h$, the demand function can be inverted to give $g^h = \omega^h - \phi(G)$ where $\phi(g) = \zeta^{-1}(G) - G$ and $0 < \phi'(G) < \infty$. Define by ω^* the level of endowment above which the household becomes a contributor and note that $\omega^* = \phi(G)$. Then

$$g^h = \omega^h - \omega^* \text{ if } \omega^h > \omega^*,$$
$$0 \qquad \text{ if } \omega^h \leq \omega^*.$$

Hence $G = \displaystyle\sum_{h=1}^{H} g^h = \sum_{\omega^h > \omega^*} [\omega^h - \omega^*] = \phi^{-1}(\omega^*).$

Now consider the function $M_H(s) \equiv \dfrac{\phi^{-1}(s)}{H} = \dfrac{1}{H}\displaystyle\sum_{\omega > s}(\omega^h - s)$ which, for given

endowments for the H households, has solution $s = \omega_H^*$. Now add to the vector of endowments by making random draws from the density $\gamma(\omega)$. By the law of large numbers, $M_H(s)$ tends to $M(s)=\int_s^\Omega[\omega-s]\gamma(\omega)d\omega$ as H tends to infinity.

Denote the solution to this equation ω^{**}, then $\lim_{H\to\infty}\omega_H^*=\omega^{**}$. Since ω_H^* is bounded and ϕ^{-1} is finite, $\lim_{H\to\infty}M_H=\lim_{H\to\infty}\dfrac{\phi^{-1}(\omega_H^*)}{H}=0$. It then follows

that $M(\omega^{**})=\int_{\omega^{**}}^\Omega[\omega-\omega^{**}]\gamma(\omega)d\omega=0$. From this, $\omega^{**}=\Omega$ and $\lim_{H\to\infty}\omega_H^*$

$=\Omega$.

From this result, (i), (ii) and (iv) follow immediately. (iii) follows from noting that $G=\phi^{-1}(\Omega)$.

This theorem has been generalised by Andreoni (1988) to economies with heterogeneous preferences. In that case, the same conclusions hold with the addition that the set of contributors will converge to a set of individuals of a single type.

5.5 Invariance results

The private provision equilibrium is characterised by some surprising invariance properties. Changes in the endowment distribution that satisfy certain conditions will not affect the total level of provision. An increase in exogeneous public good supply, for instance through the government providing some public good in addition to the private sector, will not affect total supply in the limit. Public provision therefore crowds out private provision on a one-for-one basis. These results are now demonstrated.

In most economic situations a change in the endowment, or income, distribution will affect the equilibrium except when households have identical affine Engel curves. For the private provision equilibrium, Warr (1983) proved the much stronger result that, provided all households contribute, the total level of public good is independent of the endowment distribution. This result was extended by Bergstrom, Blume and Varian (1986) to allow for the possibility of non-contributors. This result is given in the following theorem.

Theorem 9.5 (Bergstrom, Blume and Varian)

The total provision of the public good is unaffected by any income redistribution that leaves the set of contributors, C, unchanged.

Proof

It was shown in the proof of the previous theorem that $G=\sum_{h\in C}g^h=\sum_{h\in C}[\omega^h-\omega^*]$ and that ω^* is independent of the income distribution. From this equality it follows trivially that any redistribution of income that does not change the set of contributors will leave G unchanged.

To consider the effect of an exogeneous increase in public good supply, let the exogeneous increase be denoted by $d\Gamma$. The response of household h to this change is given by

$$dg^h = \gamma' [d\bar{G}_h + d\Gamma] - d\bar{G}_h - d\Gamma, \tag{9.39}$$

where $d\bar{G}_h$ is the total response of households other than h. Rearranging and summing across all households gives

$$dG = - \frac{\sum_{h=1}^{H} \dfrac{1-\gamma'}{\gamma'}}{1 + \sum_{h=1}^{H} \dfrac{1-\gamma'}{\gamma'}} d\Gamma, \tag{9.40}$$

from which the total change in supply can be calculated as

$$dG + d\Gamma = \frac{1}{1 + \sum_{h=1}^{H} \dfrac{1-\gamma'}{\gamma'}} d\Gamma \geq 0. \tag{9.41}$$

Assuming normality, so that γ' is strictly less than 1, there exists β such that $H\beta \leq \sum_{h=1}^{H} \dfrac{1-\gamma'}{\gamma'}$. Substituting into (9.40) this implies

$$dG + d\Gamma \leq \frac{1}{1 + H\beta} d\Gamma. \tag{9.42}$$

From (9.42) the invariance result of Andreoni (1988a) follows as a consequence of noting that the total change in supply tends to zero as H tends to infinity. For large populations, an exogeneous increase in public good supply is exactly met by a reduction in private provision. Expressed differently, any government provision will crowd out an exactly equal amount of private provision.

5.6 Alternative formulations

The properties of the private provision equilibrium that have been derived have been taken as indicative of the failure of the equilibrium concept to accurately capture reality. The conclusion that only the richest household in a large population will contribute is not an accurate representation of, for example, charitable contributions in the United States. Nor does the average level of contribution appear to be close to zero. Crowding out has been estimated to be of the order of a 5 to 28 cent reduction for each dollar of government spending (Abrams and Schmitz 1984), not the one-for-one predicted by the analysis. At the private provision equilibrium an increase in contribution by one household will lead to a reduction by all others. This feature has also been criticised as an inaccurate representation of reality. These observations have led a number of authors to investigate alternative maximisation procedures for the households and different preference structures with the view to generating equilibria whose properties are more in accord with empirical observations.

The simplest modification to the private provision equilibrium is to consider conjectural variations that differ from the Nash conjecture. In the maximisation in (9.32) each household takes the contributions of others as given when making their decision. The alternative to this is to assume that the household views the choices of others as being dependent upon their decision and takes this variation into account when maximising. Including this variation, the first-order condition (9.33) would become

$$-U_x^h p_G + U_G^h \left[1 + \sum_{j=1, j \neq h}^{H} \frac{\partial g^j}{\partial g^h} \right] = 0, \tag{9.43}$$

where the terms $\dfrac{\partial g^j}{\partial g^h}$ are the conjectural variations. Cornes and Sandler (1984b) investigate the effects of alternative values for the conjectural variation and show that if they are positive the equilibrium will have greater total public good supply than the Nash equilibrium. Despite this modification, Dasgupta and Itaya (1992) demonstrate that the invariance to the distribution of endowment still holds for any constant conjectures.

Consistent conjectures are those which agree with the actual responses of the households involved, that is $\dfrac{\partial g^j}{\partial g^h}$ must be equal to the change in contribution that j would make if h were to change theirs. Sugden (1985) argues that the only consistent conjectures are for all the terms $\dfrac{\partial g^j}{\partial g^h}$ to be negative. If this is the case, equilibrium provision of the public good will be zero under reasonable assumptions.

Moving to non-Nash conjectures can therefore alter the equilibrium level of the public good but does not necessarily eliminate the invariance properties. Overall, this approach must be judged as somewhat arbitrary. There are sensible game-theoretic motives for focusing upon the Nash equilibrium and these are not matched by any other set of conjectures. If the Nash equilibrium of the private provision economy does not agree with observations, it would seem that the objectives of the households and the social rules they observe should be reconsidered, not the conjectures they hold when maximising.

One approach to modified preferences has been taken by Andreoni (1989, 1990) who considers the case of impure altruism given by the utility function $U^h = U^h(x^h, G, g^h)$. Here the contribution of h provides both a public and a private return. This representation of utility leads to equilibria that are not invariant and produce predictions closer to observed behaviour. There remains the problem of why a pure public good should provide the private benefit.

A final modification that has been considered is to remove the individualism by modifying the rules of social behaviour. Sugden (1984) considers the principle of reciprocity by which each household considers the contributions of others and contrasts them to what contribution they feel they should make. If the contributions of others match, or exceed, what is expected then household h is assumed to feel under an obligation to make a similar contribution. Formalising this notion, Sugden (1984) proves that the outcome will be Pareto efficient if all households agree upon the expected contributions. In all other cases Pareto improvements can be made by increasing supply. Bordignon (1990) has provided a formalisation of Kantian behaviour that leads to similar conclusions.

5.7 Summary

In the absence of government intervention, public good provision will be left to the private contributions of households. The basic model of private provision is built upon the assumption of Nash behaviour and it has been shown that this leads to an inefficient outcome. In addition, the equilibrium level of provision is invariant to changes in the income distribution and exogenous changes in public good supply. These properties, and the limiting behaviour of the equilibrium, are at variance with empirical observations. Alternative conjectures have been analysed but these are entirely arbitrary and do not provide a better explanation of reality. Altering the structure of preferences and the social rules do provide improved predictions but no alternative has yet received convincing arguments in its favour.

6 FINANCE BY TAXATION

The rules for efficient provision derived in section 3 require for their implementation that there are no restrictions upon the tax instruments that can be employed by the government or, equivalently, that the government has complete control over resource allocation. When optimal lump-sum taxes are not an available policy instrument the rule for provision, and the resulting level of provision, must take account of the method of finance. In particular, the gain in welfare enjoyed due to the provision of the public good has to be offset against any distortions caused by the method of finance. This section considers the implications of methods of financing in an economy with a set of identical consumers, which effectively behaves as a single-consumer economy with no distributional aspects, and in a Diamond–Mirrlees economy with many consumers.

6.1 Identical consumers

In an economy with many identical consumers, if a lump-sum tax can be employed at all it must be feasible to choose the optimal lump-sum tax. To provide content to the analysis it is therefore assumed that the only tax instruments available to the government to finance the public good are commodity taxes. This will be relaxed when differentiated consumers are considered and restricted lump-sum taxes become meaningful. The aim of the analysis is to determine how the distortions caused by the commodities taxes affect the Samuelson rule and the level of provision. This is undertaken by following the work of Atkinson and Stern (1974).

Each of the identical consumers maximises their utility $U(x,G)$ subject to the budget constraint $qx=0$ where q is the vector of post-tax prices and x the vector of net demands. There is one change from the standard commodity tax model: revenue must now equal expenditure, G, on the public good

$$H \sum_{i=1}^{H} t_i x_i = G. \tag{9.44}$$

Market clearing implies that the revenue constraint and the production constraint may be used interchangeably as argued in chapter 2 above. The production constraint is used and is written in the form $F(X,G)=F(Hx,G)=0$. It is assumed that

$$F_1 = \frac{\partial F}{\partial X_1} = 1, \tag{9.45}$$

and good 1 is taken to be the numeraire with $q_1 = p_1 = 1$. Pre-tax prices are chosen so that $F_k = p_k$.

For the choice of optimal tax rates, t, and the quantity of public good, the appropriate Lagrangean is

$$\mathcal{L} = HV(q,G) - \lambda F(X(q,G),G). \tag{9.46}$$

From this, the first-order condition for the choice of G is

$$\frac{\partial \mathcal{L}}{\partial G} \equiv H \frac{\partial V}{\partial G} - \lambda \left[\sum_{i=1}^{n} F_i \frac{\partial X_i}{\partial G} + F_G \right] = 0, \tag{9.47}$$

which, using the definition of pre-tax prices, can be written

$$H \frac{\frac{\partial V}{\partial G}}{\alpha q_k} = \frac{p_k}{q_k} \frac{\lambda}{\alpha} \frac{F_G}{F_K} + \frac{\lambda}{\alpha q_k} \sum_{i=1}^{n} p_i \frac{\partial X_i}{\partial G}, \tag{9.48}$$

where α is the marginal utility of income for each consumer. From each consumer's first-order condition for the utility maximising choice of good k, $\frac{\partial U}{\partial x_k} = \alpha q_k$. Therefore the term

$$H \frac{\dfrac{\partial V}{\partial G}}{\alpha q_k} = H \frac{\dfrac{\partial U}{\partial G}}{\dfrac{\partial U}{\partial x_k}}, \tag{9.49}$$

is the sum of marginal rates of substitution between the public good and private good k.

Evaluating the first-order condition (9.48) for $k = 1$, so that $q_1 = 1$, it can be rearranged to give

$$\frac{F_G}{F_1} = \frac{\alpha}{\lambda} H \frac{\dfrac{\partial U}{\partial G}}{\dfrac{\partial U}{\partial x_1}} - \sum_{i=1}^{n} [q_i - t_i] \frac{\partial X_i}{\partial G}, \tag{9.50}$$

but since the consumers' budget constraints imply $\sum_{i=1}^{n} q^i \dfrac{\partial X_i}{\partial G} = 0$, (9.50) can be written

$$MRT_{G,1} = \frac{\alpha}{\lambda} \sum_{h=1}^{H} MRS_{G,1}^h + \frac{\partial \sum_{i=1}^{n} t_i X_i}{\partial G}. \tag{9.51}$$

The expression in (9.51) represents the Samuelson rule for optimal provision with distorting commodity taxation. It differs from the first-best rule (9.9) in two ways: the sum of marginal rates of substitution is multiplied by the term α/λ which may not be equal to one and there is an additional term on the right-hand side. This additional term measures the effect of public good provision upon tax revenue due to substitutability or complementarity in demand between the public good and the private goods.

The revenue effect implies that if provision of the public good increases tax revenue, which will be the case for example if it is a complement to highly taxed goods, this reduces the cost, measured by the MRT, of providing the public good. This factor tends to increase provision above the level determined by the Samuelson rule. The converse holds if provision reduces tax revenue.

To isolate the first effect assume that $\dfrac{\partial \sum_{i=1}^{n} t_i X_i}{\partial G} = 0$ so that the public good is

revenue neutral. In this case the departure from the first-best is determined by $\dfrac{\alpha}{\lambda}$

alone. To proceed further, consider the choice of tax rate for good k. From the Lagrangean

$$H \frac{\partial V}{\partial q_k} = \lambda \sum_{i=1}^{n} F_i \frac{\partial X_i}{\partial q_k} = \lambda \frac{\partial \sum_{i=1}^{n} p_i X_i}{\partial t_k}. \tag{9.52}$$

Using Roy's identity and the fact that

$$\frac{\partial \sum_{i=1}^{n} p_i X_i}{\partial t_k} + \frac{\partial \sum_{i=1}^{n} t_i X_i}{\partial t_k} = \frac{\partial \sum_{i=1}^{n} q_i X_i}{\partial t_k} = 0, \tag{9.53}$$

(9.52) can be written

$$\frac{\alpha}{\lambda} = \frac{\dfrac{\partial \sum_{i=1}^{n} t_i X_i}{\partial t_k}}{X_k}. \tag{9.54}$$

Finally, using the Slutsky equation,

$$\frac{\alpha}{\lambda} = 1 - \sum_{i=1}^{n} t_i \frac{\partial X_i}{\partial I} + \sum_{i=1}^{n} t_i \frac{S_{ik}}{X_k}. \tag{9.55}$$

From (9.55) it can be seen that the divergence of α/λ from 1 can be separated into two components: (i) a revenue effect given by $\sum_{i=1}^{n} t_i \frac{\partial X_i}{\partial I}$, and (ii) a distortionary effect $\sum_{i=1}^{n} t_i \frac{S_{ik}}{X_k}$. From the negative semi-definiteness of the Slutsky matrix it follows that

$$\sum_{i=1}^{n} t_i \frac{S_{ik}}{X_k} \leq 0. \tag{9.56}$$

The negativity in (9.56) has the effect of tending to reduce α below λ. This would imply that the true benefit of the public good is less than the ΣMRS In contrast, the second effect $\sum_{i=1}^{n} t_i \frac{\partial X^i}{\partial I}$ cannot be unambiguously signed. If it were positive then α would be less than λ. This would be the case if all taxed goods were normal, but this may not be the case.

In summary, when the public good has to be financed by distortionary taxation there is a divergence of MRT from ΣMRS. This divergence can be broken down into the effect of provision on tax revenue and two further components: one of which always reduces the benefit measure so that the benefit becomes something less than ΣMRS, the other is also likely to reduce it though this cannot be guaranteed. An alternative perspective upon this issue can be found in Christiansen (1981) who derives sufficient conditions for the standard cost–benefit calculation of comparing the MRT to the ΣMRS to be valid even when there are distributional objectives. Adopting the Mirrlees' formulation of labour supply described in chapter 5 but with a public good and a second private good incorporated in utility, Christiansen shows that weak separability of utility between work effort and all other goods combined with the optimal taxation of

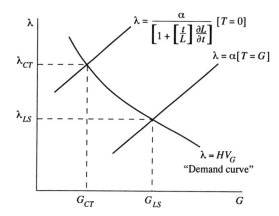

Figure 9.8   Comparison of lump-sum and commodity tax finance

income is sufficient to eliminate the distributional factors and leave only the basic cost–benefit calculation. Outside of these special cases, the additional effects described above must be included in the optimality calculation.

The analysis above has been addressed to finding the appropriate benefit measure in the presence of distortion and has not directly answered the question of whether more or less public good should be provided when its provision is financed by distortionary taxation. Unfortunately no complete answer can be given to this.

Consider an economy where finance is possible either through a lump-sum tax T or a tax t is levied upon the single factor of production L. The Lagrangean is

$$\mathscr{L} = HV(t, T, G) + \lambda[HT + tHL - G], \tag{9.57}$$

with first-order necessary conditions

$$V_t + \lambda\left[L + t\frac{\partial L}{\partial t}\right] = 0, \tag{9.58}$$

$$HV_G - \lambda = 0, \tag{9.59}$$

$$HT + HtL - G = 0. \tag{9.60}$$

T is treated as a parameter that can vary from 0 to G.

To provide an answer on the level of provision it would be necessary to demonstrate that (9.58) for $T=0$ and $T=G$ could be drawn as, for example, in figure 9.8. In the case shown provision is lower when distortionary taxes are employed. However, to actually show that $G_{CT} < G_{LS}$, where subscripts refer to 'commodity taxes' or 'lump sum', it is necessary to contrast λ_{CT} and λ_{LS}. The analysis has only been able to determine α/λ which is not sufficient for this purpose. The question of output levels therefore remains unanswered.

In terms of examples, Atkinson and Stern (1974) show that for the utility function

$$U(X, L, G) = a \log X + [1-a] \log[1-L] + f(G), \tag{9.61}$$

the level of provision of public good is lower with commodity taxation than for the first-best. Wilson (1991a) has extended this conclusion to the function

$$U(X, L, G) = U(\omega(X, 1 - L), G), \tag{9.62}$$

where $\omega(X, 1 - L)$ is of the CES form and G is assumed to be a normal good. No example has been published that has higher provision with commodity taxation than at the first-best. This lends a degree of support for the conclusion that the first-best level will exceed the second-best.

6.2 Differentiated households

Allowing the households to differ in their income and preferences provides motivation for considering restricted forms of lump-sum taxation. Even though an optimal set of lump-sum taxes may not be feasible, it may well remain possible to levy a uniform lump-sum tax. At the margin, such taxes have the property of providing a non-distortionary source of finance.

Now consider an economy with an arbitrary, but non-zero, set of commodity tax rates and implied consumer prices which are taken as fixed. Since the private sector of the economy is distorted by the existence of the commodity taxes, the non-distortionary uniform lump-sum tax provides a means by which resources can be moved from the distorted sector into provision of the public good. It does not then seem unreasonable that if the private sector is sufficiently distorted, more resources would be moved to the public sector than at the first-best optimum. This will result in the second-best provision of the public good being above the first-best.

This reasoning has been formalised by Wilson (1991b) who derives a condition that determines the relative levels of public good provision and provides examples to confirm that second-best provision may be greater than first-best.

6.3 Summary

The results have shown how distortionary financing affects the form of the Samuelson rule. Although there is a presumption that when finance is entirely by commodity taxation the second-best level of provision will fall below the first-best, this has not been formally established and the form of (9.51) suggests that it cannot be. In contrast, when some financing can be undertaken by lump-sum taxation their non-distortionary nature provides a reason for second-best provision to rise above first-best and examples have been constructed to confirm this.

7 MECHANISM DESIGN

That a household will choose the action that leads to the maximisation of their welfare is one of the basic assumptions of economic theory. If applied

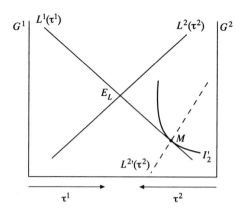

Figure 9.9 Manipulating the Lindahl equilibrium

consistently, this assumption implies that a household will behave dishonestly if it is in their interests to do so. This simple observation has surprisingly important implications for the theory of public goods.

The analysis of the Lindahl equilibrium assumed that households were honest in revealing their reactions to the announcement of cost shares. However, there will be a gain to households who attempt to cheat, or *manipulate*, the allocation mechanism. By announcing preferences that do not coincide with their true preferences, it is possible for a household to modify the outcome in their favour provided that others do not do likewise. To see this, consider a two-household economy in which household 1 act honestly and household 2 know the preferences of 1. In figure 9.9, honesty on the part of household 2 would lead to the equilibrium E_L. However, by claiming their preferences to be given by the Lindahl reaction function $L^{2\prime}(\tau^2)$, rather than the true function $L^2(\tau^2)$, the equilibrium can be driven to point M which represents the maximisation of 2's utility given the Lindahl reaction function $L^1(\tau^1)$ of 1.

Due to this problem, attention has focused upon the design of allocation mechanisms that overcome attempted manipulation. As will be shown, the design of some of these mechanisms leads households to reveal their true preferences. From this property is derived the description of these mechanisms as *preference revelation mechanisms*.

The general form of allocation mechanism can be described as a game in which each household has a strategy set and chooses a strategy from this set in order to maximise their payoff. The aim of the analysis is to determine when a game can be constructed such that the equilibrium strategies lead to the allocation that the policy maker wishes to see implemented. The game will be one of incomplete information since it is natural to assume that each household has knowledge only of their own payoff function. For such games a number of equilibrium concepts may be employed. Of these, most attention in the early literature was upon the dominant strategy equilibrium, where each household have a dominant strategy regardless of the choices of others, and the Nash equilibrium in which the chosen strategy must be optimal given that other households play their equilibrium strategy. In the setting of incomplete information the dominant strategy equilibrium has the appealing property that, since a dominant strategy is the best response to any choice by opponents, households do not need to form any expectations about how others will play the game. Consequently, the difficulties caused by the incomplete information are overcome. More recent work has also considered Bayesian equilibria in which the information problem is explicitly modelled.

7.1 Definitions

The set of potential public projects from which the choice is to be made is denoted by $\mathcal{G}$, where $\mathcal{G}$ is a compact set, and a typical element of $\mathcal{G}$ is denoted G. There are H households who have preferences over the public projects and over monetary transfers, t_h, where the monetary transfers arise as part of the game that is played by the households. For the present, each household is assumed to have additively separable preferences given by

$$U^h(G, t_h) = v^h(G) + t_h. \tag{9.63}$$

The representation of preferences in (9.63) is interpreted as being net of the costs of the project imputed to household h. It is then possible to term $v^h(G)$ the valuation of project G by household h.

The strategy space of household h is given by S^h and $S = \prod_{h=1}^{H} S^h$. A strategy choice for household h is denoted by $s^h \in S^h$ with a set of strategy choices for the households denoted $s = (s^1, \ldots, s^H)$. A *game form*, Γ, consists of a strategy space and a payoff function, $\gamma^h(s)$, for each household. If the outcome of the game is determined by a decision function $d: S \to \mathcal{G}$, which determines the project chosen given the announced strategies, and a transfer rule $t: S \to \mathcal{R}^H$, $t(s) = t_1(s), \ldots, t_H(s))$, determining the transfer to each household, it is termed a *mechanism*. A mechanism is therefore composed of a set of strategy spaces, $\{S^h\}$, and a function $f: S \to \mathcal{G} \times \mathcal{R}^H$, $f \equiv [d(s), t_1(s), \ldots, t_H(s)]$ where the accepted project is $d(s)$ and $t_h(s)$ is the transfer received by household h. Once determined, the decision $d(s)$ and the transfers $t_h(s)$ are enacted by the government or *centre*.

A *revelation mechanism* is a mechanism for which the strategy space of each household is the set of possible valuation functions and a strategy is the announcement of a valuation function. The set of possible valuation functions for h is denoted V^h. In the case that the strategy space is the set of possible valuations, let the reported valuation of h be given by $w^h(\cdot)$. A *direct revelation mechanism* is then defined as a revelation mechanism such that $d(w)$

$$= d(w^1(\cdot), \ldots, w^H(\cdot)) \in \left\{ G^* : G^* \in \mathcal{G} \text{ and } \sum_{h=1}^{H} w^h(G^*) = \max \sum_{h=1}^{H} w^h(G), G \in \mathcal{G} \right\} \text{ or,}$$

equivalently, $d(w) \in \text{argmax}_{G \in \mathcal{G}} \sum_{h=1}^{H} w_h(G)$. A direct revelation mechanism therefore has the property that the chosen project maximises the sum of reported valuations and is therefore optimal given those valuations. To ensure that the maximum exists, it is assumed the each $v^h(G)$ is upper semi-continuous. The reported valuations must then also be restricted to be upper semi-continuous.

7.2 Dominant strategies

If a dominant strategy exists for each participant of a game, a strong argument can be made that the participants will play those strategies. In addition, the existence of dominant strategies removes any need to consider how the participants form expectations about the strategy choice of their opponents and difficulties introduced by the existence of incomplete information are overcome. If the preference revelation problem can be solved by a mechanism involving dominant strategies, there are persuasive reasons for recommending its use. These observations provide the motivation for the study of dominant strategy mechanisms.

A direct revelation mechanism with decision function $d(w)$ and associated transfers $\{t_h(w)\}$ is termed *strongly individually incentive compatible* (s.i.i.c.) if truth telling is a dominant strategy. Announcement of the truth will be a dominant strategy for all agents if and only if

$$v^h \in \mathrm{argmax}_{w^h \in V^h} v^h\big(d(w^h, w^{-h})\big) + t_h(w^h, w^{-h}), \forall\, w^{-h}, h = 1, \ldots, H, \tag{9.64}$$

where $w^{-h} = (w^1, \ldots, w^{h-1}, w^{h+1}, \ldots, w^H)$, so that the true valuation maximises the payoff. To demonstrate the existence of a mechanism that satisfies (9.64), first note that from the definition of a direct revelation mechanism it follows that $d(w)$ has the property that

$$v^h \in \mathrm{argmax}_{w^h \in V^h} v^h\big(d(w^h, w^{-h})\big) + \sum_{\substack{j=1, \\ j \neq h}}^{H} w^j\big(d(w^h, w^{-h})\big), h = 1, \ldots, H. \tag{9.65}$$

Hence truthful revelation by h maximises the sum of the payoff to h and the payoffs, in terms of announced valuations, to the other households. Now write the transfers in the form

$$t_h(w) = \sum_{\substack{j=1 \\ j \neq h}}^{H} w^j\big(d(w)\big) + r^h(w), h = 1, \ldots, H, \tag{9.66}$$

which can always be done by suitable choice of the functions $r^h(w)$. Using (9.66), the dominant strategy condition (9.64) can be written

$$v^h \in \mathrm{argmax}_{w^h \in V^h} v^h\big(d(w^h, w^{-h})\big) + \sum_{\substack{j=1, \\ j \neq j}}^{H} w^j\big(d(w^h, w^{-h})\big) + r^h(w^h, w^{-h}),$$

$$h = 1, \ldots, H. \tag{9.67}$$

Contrasting (9.67) and (9.65) it can be seen that social and individual objectives will coincide whenever $r^h(w^h, w^{-h})$ is independent of w^h. Following its introduction in Groves (1973), a *Groves scheme* is defined by a set of transfers such that

$$t_h(w) = \sum_{\substack{j=1 \\ j \neq h}}^{H} w^j(d(w)) + r^h(w^{-h}), \quad h = 1, \ldots, H, \tag{9.68}$$

and a *Groves mechanism* is a direct revelation mechanism with the transfer rule given by (9.68). The reasoning above can then be summarised in the following theorem which was originally proved in Groves and Loeb (1975).

Theorem 9.6 (Groves and Loeb)

A Groves mechanism is strongly individually incentive compatible.

Proof

Directly from comparing (9.65) and (9.67) after substitution of (9.68).

The interpretation of the Groves mechanism is that the transfers are designed so that the only effect the strategy choice of a household can have upon the size of the transfer is via the effect that the decision on the public project, based upon that strategy, has upon other households' welfare. There is no direct effect on the transfer. This mechanism can be viewed as internalising the external consequences of the strategy choice of each household, since the external consequences are given by the welfare effects on other households of the public decision. In a *Clarke mechanism*, which was introduced by Clarke (1971), the functions $r^h(w^{-h})$ are given by

$$r_h(w^{-h}) = -\sum_{\substack{j=1 \\ j \neq h}}^{H} w^j(d_h(w^{-h})), \quad h = 1, \ldots, H, \tag{9.69}$$

where $d_h(w^{-h})$ is the maximiser of $\sum_{\substack{j=1 \\ j \neq h}}^{h} w^j(G)$. In this case the transfer is exactly the change in welfare of other households due to the influence of household h on the public project decision. This is a special case of the Groves mechanism.

Having demonstrated the existence of an s.i.i.c. mechanism it is natural to consider whether there are any alternative mechanisms that will also serve the same purpose. The following analysis will show that there are not: the Groves mechanism is the only s.i.i.c. direct revelation mechanism. To demonstrate this result, which is due to Green and Laffont (1977), it is first necessary to provide the following definition.

Direct revelation mechanism

A direct revelation mechanism satisfies

(i) the *transfer independence property* if $t_h(w)$ is independent of G^*, i.e., if for $w^{-h}, w^h, w^{h'}$ such that $G^*(w^{-h}, w^h) = G^*(w^{-h}, w^{h'})$ then $t_h(w^{-h}, w^h) = t_h(w^{-h}, w^{h'})$;

(ii) the *compensation property* if $t_h(w^{-h}, w^h) - t_h(w^{-h}, w^{h'}) = \sum\limits_{\substack{j=1, \\ j \neq h}}^{H} w^j(G^*)$

$- \sum\limits_{\substack{j=1, \\ j \neq h}}^{H} w^j(G^{*\prime})$, where G^* *maximises* the sum of announced valuations given

w^h and $G^{*\prime}$ is the maximising project given announcement $w^{h'}$.

It is immediately clear from this definition that the transfer independence and compensation properties uniquely characterise the Groves mechanism. A direct revelation mechanism is therefore a Groves mechanism if and only if it satisfies transfer independence and compensation.

The proof that the Groves mechanism is the only s.i.i.c. direct revelation mechanism can now be undertaken by demonstrating that if transfer independence and compensation are not satisfied by a direct revelation mechanism, it cannot be s.i.i.c. Therefore it follows from the equivalence of these conditions to the Groves mechanism that the Groves mechanism is the unique s.i.i.c. direct revelation mechanism. The relevant theorem is as follows.

Theorem 9.7 (Green and Laffont)

An s.i.i.c. direct revelation mechanism must satisfy the transfer independence and compensation properties.

Proof

First assume that there exists an s.i.i.c. direct revelation mechanism for which transfer independence is not satisfied. Then there are $w^{-h}, w^h, w^{h'}$ with the same optimal G^* but with $t_h(w^{-h}, w^h) > t_h(w^{-h}, w^{h'})$. Now let $v^h = w^{h'}$ and note that $t_h(w^{-h}, w^h) + v^h(G^*) > t_h(w^{-h}, v^h) + v^h(G^*)$. The choice of v^h is then not a dominant strategy. An s.i.i.c. direct revelation mechanism must therefore satisfy transfer independence.

Now assume that the mechanism does not satisfy the compensation property. There then exist $w^{-h}, w^h, w^{h'}$ such that G^* maximises $\sum\limits_{\substack{j=1, \\ j \neq h}}^{H} w^j + w^h$ over $\mathscr{G}$, $G^{*\prime}$

maximises $\sum\limits_{\substack{j=1, \\ j \neq h}}^{H} w^j + w^{h'}$ over $\mathscr{G}$ and $t_h(w^{-h}, w^h) - t_h(w^{-h}, w^{h'}) = \sum\limits_{\substack{j=1, \\ j \neq h}}^{H} w^j(G^*) =$

$$\sum_{\substack{j=1,\\j\neq h}}^{H} w^j(G^{*\prime})+\varepsilon \text{ for some } \varepsilon>0.$$

Let $\tilde{w}^{h\prime}$ be defined by $\tilde{w}^{h\prime}(G^*)= -\sum_{\substack{j=1,\\j\neq h}}^{H} w^j(G^*),\ \tilde{w}^{h\prime}(G^{*\prime})= -\sum_{\substack{j=1,\\j\neq h}}^{H} w^j(G^{*\prime})+\frac{\varepsilon}{2}$

and $\tilde{w}^{h\prime}(G)= -c$ for $G\neq G^*$ or $G^{*\prime}$ with $c>\max_{G\in\mathcal{G}} \sum_{\substack{j=1,\\j\neq h}}^{H} w^j(G)$. Since $\tilde{w}^{h\prime}$ is upper

semi-continuous, it is a permissible valuation announcement.

Now note that $G^{*\prime}=\text{argmax}_{G\in\mathcal{G}} \sum_{\substack{j=1,\\j\neq h}}^{H} w^j(G)+\tilde{w}^{h\prime}(G)$, since it has been shown

that the mechanism must satisfy transfer independence, $t_h(w^{-h},w^{h\prime}) = t_h(w^{-h},\tilde{w}^{h\prime})$. Hence

$$t_h(w^{-h},w^h)-t_h(w^{-h},w^{h\prime})=t_h(w^{-h},w^h)-t_h(w^{-h},\tilde{w}^{h\prime})$$

$$= \sum_{\substack{j=1,\\j\neq h}}^{H} w^j(G^*)-\sum_{\substack{j=1,\\j\neq h}}^{H} w^j(G^{*\prime})+\varepsilon$$

$$= \tilde{w}^{h\prime}(G^*)+\tilde{w}^{h\prime}(G^{*\prime})+\frac{\varepsilon}{2}.$$

Rearranging gives $t_h(w^{-h},w^h)+\tilde{w}^{h\prime}(G^*)>t_h(w^{-h},\tilde{w}^{h\prime})+\tilde{w}^{h\prime}(G^{*\prime})$. Letting $v^h \equiv \tilde{w}^{h\prime}$ then contradicts the assumption that the mechanism was s.i.i.c since truth is not the dominant strategy. A s.i.i.c. direct revelation mechanism must therefore satisfy the compensation property.

In the form given, theorem 9.7 only restricts the valuation functions to be in the class of semi-continuous functions. However, restricting the set from which valuation functions may be drawn does not extend the set of direct revelation mechanisms. As proved by Holmstrom (1979), provided the domain of valuation functions is smoothly connected (that is, there exists a differentiable deformation of one valuation function in the domain into any other), the Groves scheme will be unique.

These results permit the study of s.i.i.c. direct revelation mechanisms to be undertaken by studying only the properties of the Groves mechanisms. Although it has been shown that a Groves mechanism can implement the correct choice of project, it should not be presumed that it will necessarily lead to a fully efficient equilibrium. To be efficient the mechanism must also have the property that the sum of transfers must be identically zero, in which case the mechanism is termed *balanced*. If it is negative some resources are being taken from the households and not used to produce welfare elsewhere. It may be felt that these resources could be redistributed to the households but if this were done incentives would be introduced for the households to choose their announced valuation taking into consideration the effect it would have upon the redistribution. The s.i.i.c. aspect of the mechanism would then fail. Conversely, if the sum of transfers is positive, some resources are being transferred from the centre to the households and the centre is bearing the cost of implementing the mechanism.

To investigate the possibilities, assume that the valuation functions are differentiable and can be given a one-dimensional parametrisation. Let household h be described by the preference parameter $\theta^h \in \Theta^h$ where Θ^h is an open interval of $\mathcal{R}$ and assume the valuation function $v^h(G, \theta^h)$ is smooth. Finally, assume that for any array of household preferences $\theta = (\theta^1, \ldots, \theta^H)$, there exists a differentiable function $G^*(\theta) > 0$ such that $G^*(\theta) = \operatorname{argmax}_{G>0} \sum_{h=1}^{H} v^h(G, \theta^h)$. The following theorem describes the conditions necessary for the existence of a balanced mechanism.

Theorem 9.8 (Green and Laffont)

There exists a balanced mechanism if and only if

$$\sum_{h=1}^{H} \frac{\partial^{H-1}}{\partial\theta^1, \ldots, \partial\theta^{h-1}, \partial\theta^{h+1}, \ldots, \partial\theta^H} \left[\frac{\partial v^h}{\partial G} \frac{\partial G^*}{\partial\theta^h} \right] \equiv 0.$$

Proof

In the case described the transfer functions will depend only on the parameter vector θ. Denoting the true preference parameter of h by $\tilde{\theta}^h$, truth will be the dominant strategy if $\tilde{\theta}^h = \operatorname{argmax}_{\theta^h \in \Theta^h} v^h(G^*(\theta), \tilde{\theta}^h) + t_h(\theta)$ for all θ^{-h}. This will only apply if $\frac{\partial v^h}{\partial G} \frac{\partial G^*}{\partial\theta^h} + \frac{\partial t_h}{\partial\theta^h} \equiv 0$ when evaluated at $\tilde{\theta}^h$ for all θ^{-h}. Integrating with respect to θ^h then gives $t^h(\theta^h, \theta^{-h}) = \int -\frac{\partial v^h}{\partial\theta^h} \frac{\partial G^*}{\partial\theta^h} d\theta + r_h(\theta^{-h})$, where $r_h(\theta^{-h})$ is arbitrary.

The mechanism is therefore balanced if $\sum_{h=1}^{H} \left[-\int \frac{\partial v^h}{\partial\theta^h} \frac{\partial G^*}{\partial\theta^h} d\theta + r_h(\theta^{-h}) \right] \equiv 0$.

Differentiating this condition for a balanced mechanism with respect to $\theta^1, \ldots, \theta^H$ gives $\sum_{h=1}^{H} \frac{\partial^{H-1}}{\partial\theta^1, \ldots, \partial\theta^{h-1}, \partial\theta^{h+1}, \ldots, \partial\theta^H} \left[\frac{\partial v^h}{\partial G} \frac{\partial G^*}{\partial\theta^h} \right] \equiv 0$ which establishes necessity. Sufficiency is proved by integrating the stated condition successively to obtain the condition for a balanced mechanism.

Since the condition required for the Groves mechanism to be balanced even in the simple environment of parametrised preferences is restrictive, this theorem demonstrates that it will not be possible to always find a balanced mechanism. This result is established formally by Green and Laffont (1979) who prove that there exists no Groves mechanism that is balanced for all possible valuations. It is therefore unlikely that a Groves mechanism will achieve full efficiency. The lack of efficiency is, of course, the price that has to be paid for the revelation of information.

These negative conclusions are somewhat diminished as the size of the population of households increases. As shown by Green and Laffont (1979) and Rob (1982), the likelihood that any household receives a negative transfer (i.e., pays a tax) tends to zero as the population increases without bound and the expected total transfer also tends to zero. These results imply that the limiting outcome is approximately efficient.

A important assumption that has been employed up to this point has been the additive separability of preferences described in (9.63). Given the restrictiveness of this assumption, it would be hoped that this was simply a convenient assumption that could be dropped when necessary. Unfortunately this is not the case. Bergstrom and Cornes (1983) have shown that the Groves mechanism will still function successfully if preferences are given by

$$U^h(x^h, G) = A(G)x^h + B^h(G), \quad h = 1, \dots, H, \tag{9.70}$$

where $A(G)$, which is assumed to be known, is common to all individuals and x^h is the quantity of private good consumed by h. This, however, is only a minor extension.

The possibility of proving a general result on the existence of an s.i.i.c. is ruled out by the Gibbard–Satterthwaite theorem. To describe the content of this theorem, consider a set Ξ of social states and a set of economic agents. Each of the H economic agents has a preference order, P^h, defined over Ξ. Let Π be the set of possible preference orders. A *social choice function* (SCF) is defined as a function from $\times_{h=1}^H \Pi$ into Ξ which assigns to any $P \in \times_{h=1}^H \Pi$ a social state $\xi \in \Xi$. An SCF, W, is *manipulable* at the preference profile P if there exists $P^{h\prime}$ such that $W(P^1, \dots, P^{h\prime}, \dots, P^H)$ is preferred by h, with preference P^h, to $W(P^1, \dots, P^h, \dots, P^H)$. Manipulability means that h can alter the social decision to one they prefer by announcing a set of preferences, $P^{h\prime}$, which differ from their true preferences. The SCF is s.i.i.c. if there is no set of preferences, P, at which it is manipulable. Now let the range of the SCF, W, be $\Xi' \subseteq \Xi$. The SCF is *dictatorial* when for any $\xi \in \Xi'$, $\xi \neq W(P)$, $W(P)$ is preferred by h to ξ. Agent h is then said to be the dictator.

Given these preliminaries, the Gibbard–Satterthwaite theorem can now be stated.

Theorem 9.9 (Gibbard–Satterthwaite)

If Ξ' has at least three alternatives, an SCF with range Ξ' satisfying s.i.i.c. and having an unrestricted domain (so no restrictions on preferences are permitted) is dictatorial.

Proof

See Laffont (1987).

The implication of the Gibbard–Satterthwaite theorem is that the search for a mechanism that will efficiently implement social decisions in all circumstances is a futile one. As has been shown, the Groves mechanism illustrates that implementation can occur in some restricted circumstances but there is little hope for proceeding very far beyond this. This negative conclusion provides the motivation for studying equilibrium concepts that are weaker than dominant strategies.

7.3 Nash equilibrium

The simplest alternative equilibrium concept is that of Nash equilibrium, so that each household's strategy has to be optimal only against the optimal choices of other households. This weakening of the equilibrium concept does open up new possibilities and the work of Groves and Ledyard (1977) demonstrates that Nash equilibrium can lead to optimality. However, there remain difficulties with the interpretation of the Nash equilibrium concept in the context of games with incomplete information. These will be discussed further below after the results that can be obtained are described.

Consider a set Ξ of social states and an SCF, W, $W: \times_{h=1}^{H} \Pi \to \Xi$. The game form Γ *implements* W if, for every $P \in \times_{h=1}^{H} \Pi$, the set of equilibrium strategies for Γ, denoted $E_\Gamma(P)$, is non-empty and $\Gamma(E_\Gamma(P)) \subseteq W(P)$. A set of strategy choices $(s^{1*}, \ldots, s^{H*})$ are a *Nash equilibrium* for the game form Γ if and only if for all h

$$\gamma^h(s^{h*}, s^{-h*}) > \gamma^h(s^h, s^{-h*}), \forall s^h \in S^h. \tag{9.71}$$

The first result of this section, due to Dasgupta *et al.* (1979), concerns the relationship between truthful implementation in Nash equilibrium and in dominant strategies.

Theorem 9.10 (Dasgupta, Hammond and Maskin)

The social choice function W can be truthfully implemented in Nash strategies if and only if it can be truthfully implemented in dominant strategies.

Proof

If W can be implemented in dominant strategies, it can be implemented in Nash since a dominant strategy equilibrium is a Nash equilibrium. Now assume that the game form Γ truthfully implements W in Nash strategies. For all $P \in \times_{h=1}^{H} \Pi$, truthful revelation is then a Nash equilibrium. This implies that for all h, for all $P \in \times_{h=1}^{H} \Pi$, and for all $P^{h\prime} \in \Pi, \gamma^h(P^h, P^{-h}) > \gamma^h(P^{h\prime}, P^{-h})$. Truth is therefore the dominant strategy.

The implication of this theorem is that there is nothing to be gained by considering Nash equilibria in direct mechanisms since the same result could be obtained by considering only dominant strategies. If the Nash equilibrium is to be of value in extending the set of circumstances in which implementation can take place it will be necessary to consider mechanisms in which individuals do not announce their true preferences at the equilibrium.

The major contribution of Groves and Ledyard (1977) was to provide a mechanism that was balanced and which led to a Pareto optimal allocation. Assume that there are available K public goods and denote the price vector (to the public sector) of these public goods by p_G. The Groves–Ledyard mechanism then restricts the strategy space of each household to be $\mathscr{R}^K$. This can be given the interpretation that each household announces the incremental adjustment they would like to be made to the sum of public goods supplies requested by other households. With this restricted strategy space, the mechanism clearly does not elicit the valuation functions from the households. For a set of strategy choices $(s^1, \ldots, s^H)$ the decision function is given by $d(s) \equiv \sum_{h=1}^{H} s^h$ and the transfer functions by

$$t_h(s) \equiv -\left[\alpha^h p_G \sum_{j=1}^{H} s^j + \frac{\beta}{2} \left[\frac{H-1}{H} [s^h - \mu(s^{-h})]^2 - \sigma(s^{-h})^2 \right] \right], \quad h = 1, \ldots, H,$$

$$(9.72)$$

where $\sum_{j=1}^{H} \alpha^h = 1, \beta > 0, \mu(s^{-h}) \equiv \dfrac{1}{H-1} \sum_{\substack{j=1, \\ j \neq h}}^{H} s^j$ and $\sigma(s^{-h})^2 \equiv \dfrac{1}{H-2} \sum_{\substack{j=1, \\ j \neq h}}^{H} [s^j - \mu(s^{-h})]^2$.

Under this transfer rule the transfer from household h increases as their request deviates further from the average of other requests and is reduced as the squared standard error of the others' requests increases.

Although the Groves–Ledyard mechanism is balanced and achieves Pareto optimality, difficulties still remain. In the context of the private ownership economy with government in which they embedded the mechanism, there is no reason to believe that the mechanism is individually rational. That is, after participating in the mechanism a household may be left with a utility level lower than that given by their initial endowment. In these circumstances the rational act for the household would be not to engage in trade but to simply consume their endowment. Imposing individual rationality, Hurwicz (1979a, 1979b) demonstrates, under mild continuity and convexity restrictions, that the set of Lindahl allocations is a subset of the Nash equilibria and all interior Nash equilibria are Lindahl allocations.

These results would seem to suggest that implementation in Nash strategies provides an attractive means of overcoming the failings of the dominant strategy mechanisms. Unfortunately, Nash mechanisms are not without their failings. The major difficulty is the level of knowledge implied by the equilibrium concept. Interpreted literally, it requires each household to know the preferences of the others and to be able to solve the game for the set of equilibrium strategies. Such common knowledge amongst the households is in sharp contrast to the lack of knowledge of the centre. Although it has been argued that there may be situations when this is appropriate (see Moore and Repullo 1988), the public goods problem is almost certainly not amongst them. Alternatively, the Nash equilibrium could be seen as being achieved as the outcome of some iterative process but, again, this falls outside the scenario envisaged.

7.4 Bayesian equilibria

Bayesian equilibria, in which each household holds a probability distribution over the distribution of preferences in the population and maximise expected utility subject to this, have also been considered most notably by d'Aspremont and Gérard-Varet (1979) and Laffont and Maskin (1982). Although Bayesian equilibria can generate fully efficient outcomes, in common with Nash equilibria they suffer from informational difficulties. In order that a household can calculate an equilibrium strategy the probability distributions held by the households must be common knowledge. In addition, Bayesian mechanisms suffer from multiplicity of equilibria. These points alone are sufficient to cast serious doubt upon the relevance of Bayesian equilibria.

7.5 Conclusions

This review of mechanism design has included some positive results and some negative ones. It has been shown possible to achieve efficient, though not always fully efficient, outcomes when preferences are separable using dominant strategies. Unfortunately, the Gibbard–Satterthwaite theorem shows that this result cannot be extended to apply to all possible forms of preferences. Efficiency is attainable using Nash equilibrium but the informational requirements of the equilibrium concept appear unsustainable in the public goods context. The same is also true of Bayesian equilibrium. The mechanism design problem is therefore far from fully solved.

8 EXPERIMENTAL EVIDENCE AND MARKET DATA

The previous section has considered the design of mechanisms to elicit households' valuations of public goods. The presumption that such a mechanism is required is based on the view that households act always to maximise welfare even when this involves dishonesty. Whether this view is justified has been tested in numerous experiments and the results of a number of these are described in section 8.1. Although households may have an incentive to not reveal their true preferences in markets involving public goods, this does not apply in markets for private goods. This suggests the possibility that behaviour in markets for private goods may reveal information about preferences for public goods.

8.1 Experimental evidence

The analysis of private provision demonstrated that the equilibrium will not be Pareto efficient and that, compared to Pareto-improving allocations, too little of the public good will be supplied. A simple explanation of this result can be given in terms of each household relying on others to contribute and hence deciding to contribute little themselves. In a sense, each household is free-riding on others' contributions and, since all attempt to free-ride, the total contribution fails to reach an efficient level. The similar, but distinct, concept of misrevelation of preferences was analysed in the previous section. If asked to reveal their valuation of a public good, each household will typically have strategic motives for revealing a false valuation in order to manipulate the allocation mechanism in their favour.

The experimental literature on public goods has attempted to test the predictions of these theories and to evaluate methods of overcoming misrevelation. Unfortunately, some of the literature has not been sufficiently careful in the distinction between free-riding and misrevelation with the result that some papers discuss examples of misrevelation and then conduct an experiment that tests the free-riding hypothesis. With this in mind, the results of a number of these experiments are now discussed.

Marwell and Ames (1981) report the findings of a series of experiments. The basic structure of the experiments, which was maintained in many later experiments, was to give participants a number of tokens that could be invested in either an *individual exchange* or a *group exchange*. The individual exchange had a set repayment per token that was independent of the total investment by the individual and of the total investment by the group. This should be interpreted as the purchase of a private good. In contrast, the return from the group exchange was dependent upon the investment into the group exchange of the other participants and an investment in the group exchange by any participant led to a payment to all participants. The group exchange therefore has the properties of a pure public good. The rates of return were made known to the participants and the total return from investment was paid to the participant. It was therefore in the interests of each participant to maximise their payoff. The structure of payoffs were such that the private provision equilibrium would result in no investments in the public good although the efficient outcome would involve only investment in the public good. Each participant made a single investment decision.

Although the structure of payoffs, the distribution of tokens and the nature of the public good (divisible or lumpy) changed between experiments, the results were remarkably consistent. In the first eleven experiments, the average investment in the public good lay between 28 per cent and 87 per cent of tokens with most observations falling in the 40–50 per cent range. In the twelfth experiment, with a group of first-year graduates in economics, the investment in the public good fell to 20 per cent. These results clearly do not support the predictions of the private provision model.

Isaac, Walker and Thomas (1984) modified the experiment by repeating the investment decision over ten rounds with the view that this should allow time for the participants to learn about free-riding and develop the optimal strategy. The results from this experiment are not as clear as in Marwell and Ames (1981) and a wider range of investments occurs. Free-riding is not completely supported but some instances are reported in which it does occur. However, this finding should be treated with caution since having ten rounds of the game introduces aspects of repeated game theory. While it remains true that the only credible equilibrium of the repeated game is the private provision equilibrium of the corresponding single-period game, it is possible that in the experiments some participants may have been attempting to establish cooperative equilibria by playing in a fashion that invited cooperation. Additionally, those not trained in game theory may have been unable to derive the optimal strategy even though they could solve the single-period game. Similar comments apply to Kim and Walker (1984) who also employ a repeated game framework. In their experiments free-riding was found to occur but some odd responses involving occasional large investments in the public good also arose.

The repeated game framework was also applied by Isaac, McCue and Plott (1985) who conducted nine experiments with undergraduate economists. It was found that the contributions to the public good fell short of the Lindahl level but remained above the zero level that would occur in the private provision equilibrium. It is interesting to note that in experiments in which the Lindahl level was announced after five or six rounds, the contributions then increased. Allowing communication also raised contributions but less noticeably. Overall, the experiments show some evidence of free-riding but do not conform exactly to the predictions of the private provision equilibrium. Isaac and Walker (1988) use the same format to examine the effect of group size upon free-riding. The results show that increasing group size leads to increased divergence from the efficient outcome when accompanied by a decrease in marginal return from the public good but the results do not support a pure numbers-in-group effect. This finding is compatible with the theoretical finding that the effect of group size on the divergence from optimality was in general indeterminate.

The results above indicate that there is little evidence of free-riding in single-period, or one-shot, games but in the repeated games the contributions fall towards the private provision level as the game is repeated. Andreoni (1988b) suggests two reasons for these findings and attempts to choose between them. The first possibility is that the decay could be due to learning as the participants are initially unable to solve the game and only learn the optimal strategy by repeated play. Alternatively, the pattern of contributions observed may be a strategic choice where some cooperation in the early stages is part of that strategy. To distinguish between the two explanations, one set of participants in the experiment were placed in different groups after each round of investment.

Since the groups were randomly chosen, this prevented any benefit existing from playing a long-term strategy. Alongside these varying groups were three groups which remained fixed throughout the ten rounds of the experiment. If the strategic explanation is correct, the fixed groups should have higher contribution levels in the early stages of the game. In addition to the groups playing a fixed number of ten rounds, an identical number of participants, again split into fixed and varying groups, were subject to ten rounds of the game and then told the game was to be restarted for another ten rounds. If learning is the correct explanation, restarting should not affect the level of contributions.

The results do not confirm either hypothesis. Contributions by the members of fixed groups were always less than those made by members of the variable groups and in both cases remained above the level that would be achieved in the private provision equilibrium After the restart the level of contributions was temporarily higher for the variable groups. For the fixed groups there was a lasting increase in contribution after the restart.

Taken together, these experiments do not provide great support for the equilibrium based on the private provision economy with Nash behaviour. In the single-period games free-riding is unambiguously rejected. Although it appears after several rounds in repeated games, the explanation for the strategies involved is not entirely apparent. Neither a strategic nor a learning hypothesis is confirmed. What seems to be occurring is that the participants are initially guided more by a sense of fairness than by Nash behaviour. When this fairness is not rewarded, the tendency is then to move towards the Nash equilibrium. The failure of experimentation to support free-riding lends some encouragement to the views of Johansen (1977), that although such behaviour may be individually optimal, it is not actually observed in practice.

In a series of papers Bohm (1971, 1972, 1984) has suggested a procedure for dealing with misrevelation, has provided experimental results and has described the outcome of the procedure in practice. To provide a practical method for determining the valuation of a public good, Bohm suggests running two preference revelation mechanisms simultaneously. The first mechanism should be designed to lead to an underreporting of the true valuation of the project and the second to an overreporting. The direction of misrevelation can easily be controlled by the link between reported valuation and the charge levied for use of the public good. For instance, if the charge is credibly announced to be zero then overreporting will always take place if provision of the public good is dependent upon reported valuations being greater than its cost. If those whose valuations are sought are randomly allocated between the first and second mechanism then upper and lower bounds are obtained on the valuation of the public good with the true valuation lying somewhere in the interval. The decision to provide the public good is then taken if all points in the interval are greater than the cost and it is not provided if all points are less than the cost. A level of cost lying in the interval indicates potential indifference between provision and non-provision of the public good at the given level of cost.

Bohm (1972) conducted an experimental implementation of this procedure on 200 people from Stockholm who had to evaluate the benefit of seeing a previously unshown TV programme. The participants were divided into four groups which faced the following payment mechanisms: (i) pay stated valuation, (ii) pay a fraction of stated valuation such that costs are covered from all payments, (iii) pay a low flat fee and (iv) no payment. Although the first two provide an incentive to underreport and the latter two to overreport, the experiment found that there was no significant difference in the stated valuations, suggesting that misrevelation may not be as important as suggested by the theory. In the practical application, Bohm (1984) describes how the choice of whether to collect statistics on housing is determined by obtaining the local government valuations of these. Two alternative contracts were offered, the first had payment as a proportion of valuation with the proportion chosen to cover costs and the second had a fixed payment for any valuation over a given figure. A valuation below this figure resulted in exclusion from the use of the statistics. The results indicated that valuations were on average lower (SEK 827) for those offered the first contract than for those offered the second (SEK 889) with the valuation interval being small. This work suggests that the misrevelation problem is not as great as the theory predicts and that simple procedures may well exist that overcome the actual degree of misrevelation.

In assessing these results, it must be borne in mind that the experimental procedures are always subject to the criticism that the participants do not treat them in the way they would act in real situations. The rewards involved are usually small and the experiment is always somewhat artificial. Furthermore, the participants may not be a representative sample of the population.

8.2 Market data

When acting in a competitive market, households have no incentive to reveal false information about their preferences. At the parametric price they face, their only decision is the quantity to buy and if they do not buy the quantity that is optimal for them the only effect is to reduce their welfare. This simple observation can sometimes provide the basis for constructing valuation schedules for public goods.

To focus the following discussion, consider the case of housing. Viewed in a characteristics framework (see Lancaster 1966 or Gorman and Myles 1987), a house is treated as a collection of attributes and the value to a purchaser of a house is determined by their assessment of the set of attributes. Equally, the cost of supplying a house is also dependent upon the attributes supplied. As shown by Rosen (1974), willingness-to-pay and willingness-to-supply schedules determine the equilibrium price as a function of characteristics. Now consider that part of the attraction of any house is the environmental quality of its locality, for example whether there is a nearby park. There is obviously no market for environmental quality as such, but if the prices of a variety of houses are observed that differ in their environmental quality then a valuation of this can be derived by observing the prices at which they trade. The difference in price of two houses that are identical in all respects except for environmental quality captures the value of the environmental difference.

These observations lead into the theory of hedonic analysis of price which is the statistical formalisation of the method just described. Examples of the application of hedonics can be found in Griliches (1971), Ball (1973) and Brookshire *et al.* (1982). It must be noted that the method does have shortcomings, particularly in that many public goods may have no private goods market associated with them.

9 CONCLUSIONS

This chapter has reviewed the standard analysis of the efficient level of provision of a public good leading to the Samuelson rule and its generalisations. These efficiency rules generate allocations that can only be achieved if the government is unrestricted in its policy tools or, as the Lindahl equilibrium demonstrated, personalised pricing can be employed. If a uniform price must be charged, it was shown that private provision would not generate a Pareto-efficient outcome and that it would be Pareto improving for each household to increase their contribution towards provision of the public good. Such results provide a natural role for the government to participate in financing and provision and the consequences of financing public goods by distortionary taxation were analysed.

One aspect of public goods that prevents the government making efficient decisions is the government's lack of knowledge of households' preferences and willingness to pay for public goods. Mechanisms were shown to exist that could overcome the incentives for households to misreveal their preferences but for the most relevant equilibrium concept, that of dominant strategies, these were restricted in the forms of preferences to which they applied. Despite these rather negative theoretical conclusions, experimental evidence indicates that household behaviour when confronted with decision problems involving public goods does not conform with the theoretical prediction and that the private provision equilibrium may not be as inefficient as theory suggests. Furthermore, misrevelation has not been confirmed as the inevitable outcome.

10

EXTERNALITIES

1 INTRODUCTION

An externality represents a connection between economic agents which lies outside the price system of the economy. As the level of externality generated is not controlled directly by price, the standard efficiency theorems on market equilibrium cannot be applied. The market failure that can result raises a potential role for correction through policy intervention.

Externalities and their control are a subject of increasing practical importance. The greenhouse effect is one of the most significant examples of the consequences of an externality but there are any number of others, from purely local environmental issues to similarly global ones. Although these may not appear at first sight to be economic problems, many of the policy responses to their existence have been based on the economic theory of externalities. The purpose of this chapter is to demonstrate the consequences of the existence of externalities and to the review policy responses that have been suggested. In particular, it will be shown how the unregulated economy generally fails to reach an efficient outcome and to what degree this can be corrected using standard tax instruments.

The chapter begins with a discussion of alternative definitions of an externality which differ in whether they focus on effects or consequences. Adopting an effect-based definition, it is then shown how the market generally fails to achieve efficiency. This lack of efficiency is contrasted to the claim of the Coase theorem that efficiency will be eliminated by trade. An emphasis is placed on the role of missing markets and inefficiency in bargaining with incomplete information. The design of the optimal set of corrective, or Pigouvian, taxes is then addressed under alternative assumptions about the feasible degree of differentiation among different households and firms. The chapter is completed by contrasting the use of taxes with direct control through tradable licences and the value of internalisation.

2 EXTERNALITIES

Although the nature of an externality as an effect inflicted by one agent upon another may seem very clear at an intuitive level, once a formalisation is attempted a number of issues arise that need to be resolved. Of most importance is the question of whether the existence of an externality should be judged by its effects or by its consequences. Since both approaches have some merit, but can lead to different classifications, there is no universally agreed definition of an externality. This section discusses two alternative definitions and describes the representation of externalities adopted in the following analysis.

2.1 Definitions

In the literature there have been a number of alternative definitions of an externality and several attempts at providing classifications of various types of externality; a survey is presented in Baumol and Oates (1988). There are two major categories of definition, the first of which defines an externality by its effects and the second by the reason for its existence and its consequences.

The first definition of an externality is the most commonly adopted and is based on the effects of externalities.

Externality (1)

An externality is present whenever some economic agent's welfare (utility or profit) includes real variables whose values are chosen by others without particular attention to the effect upon the welfare of the other agents they affect.

This is a very broad definition but does have the advantage of allowing an externality to be recognised from its effects. The definition also implicitly distinguishes between two broad categories of externality. A *production externality* is said to exist when the effect of the externality is upon a profit relationship and a *consumption externality* is present whenever a utility level is affected. Clearly, an externality can be both a consumption and a production externality simultaneously. For a household, an externality can affect either the consumption set or the utility function. In either case, final welfare will be affected. Similarly, for a firm, an externality may determine the structure of the production set or it may enter the profit function directly.

The difficulty with this definition is its dependence upon the institutional context in which it is placed. The following example of Heller and Starret (1976) illustrates this point. In a barter economy with two households, the utility of each household is dependent upon the quantity that the other household is willing to give up in exchange. From the definition above, this must clearly count as an externality although such a classification seems inappropriate. If the institutional setting is altered by the introduction of competitive markets then the externality is removed. Furthermore, it is precisely the non-existence of functioning markets for external effects that leads them to be classified as externalities. Based on this reasoning, Heller and Starret (1976) provide an alternative definition of externalities that relates to the existence, or otherwise, of markets and the consequences of the externality.

Externality (2)

An externality is present whenever there is an insufficient incentive for a potential market to be created for some good and the non-existence of this market leads to a non-Pareto-optimal equilibrium.

Although the conditions of the second definition are stronger than those of the first so that, for a given institutional framework, the externalities it identifies will be a subset of those identified by the first, in most cases the two definitions will delineate precisely the same set of effects as externalities. Moreover, since the focus below will be placed upon externalities in a competitive economy, the effects of varying the market institution upon the set of externalities will be of limited interest. On this basis, the first definition is adopted as the determinant of what constitutes an externality. The second definition is still important, however, due to it directing attention to the question of why some markets exist and some do not.

2.2 Representation

Having defined an externality, it is possible to move on to the formal representation. Denote, as in chapter 2, the array of consumption vectors $x = \{x^1, \ldots, x^H\}$ and the array of production vectors $y = \{y^1, \ldots, y^m\}$. It is assumed that consumption externalities enter the utility functions of the households and that production externalities enter the production sets of the firms. At the most general level, this assumption implies that the utility functions take the form

$$U^h = U^h(x, y), \quad h = 1, \ldots, H, \tag{10.1}$$

and the production set is described by

$$Y^j = Y^j(x, y), \quad j = 1, \ldots, m. \tag{10.2}$$

In this formulation the utility functions and the production sets are dependent upon the entire arrays of consumption and production vectors. The expressions in (10.1) and (10.2) represent the general form of the externality problem and in some of the discussion below a number of further restrictions will be employed. In particular, the case where the total externality effect is due to the sum of contributions will be used on a number of occasions.

It is immediately apparent from (10.1) and (10.2) that the actions of the agents in the economy will no longer be independent or determined solely by prices.

The linkages via the externality result in the optimal choice of each agent being dependent upon the actions of others. Viewed in this light, it becomes apparent why the efficient functioning of the competitive economy will generally not be observed in an economy with externalities.

Before proceeding to analyse potential inefficiency of the market outcome, it is worth noting that an economy based on the utility and production functions defined in (10.1) and (10.2) may still possess a competitive equilibrium even though this equilibrium may not be Pareto optimal. Provided demand and supplies remain continuous functions of their arguments, the proof of the existence of equilibrium can proceed along the lines sketched in chapter 2. Further details can be found in Arrow and Hahn (1971) and McKenzie (1955). There are two additional difficulties that arise in the proof of equilibrium in an economy subject to externalities which concern the boundedness of the economy and the convexity of production sets. Boundedness is a technical point that is not of great importance here, a detailed discussion can be found in Osana (1973). The possible non-convexity of production sets is of rather more importance and will be considered in section 4.3.2.

3 MARKET INEFFICIENCY

It has been implicit throughout the discussion above that the presence of externalities will result in the competitive equilibrium failing to be Pareto optimal. The immediate implication of this fact is that incorrect quantities of goods, and hence externalities, will be produced. It is also clear that a non-Pareto-optimal outcome will never maximise welfare. This provides scope for economic policy to raise welfare. The purpose of this section is to demonstrate how inefficiency can arise in a competitive economy. Cases where externalities do not lead to inefficiency will also be described. The results are developed in the context of a simple two-consumer model since this is sufficient for the purpose and also makes the relevant points as clear as possible.

3.1 Equilibrium and inefficiency

Consider a two-household economy where the households have utility functions

$$U^1 = U^1(x_1^1, x_2^1, x_1^2), \tag{10.3}$$

and

$$U^2 = U^2(x_1^2, x_2^2, x_1^1). \tag{10.4}$$

The externality effect in (10.3) and (10.4) is generated by consumption of good 1 by the other household. The externality will be *positive* if U^h is increasing in x_1^j, $h \neq j$, and *negative* if decreasing.

To complete the description of the economy, it is assumed that the supply of good 2 comes from an endowment to the households whereas good 1 is produced from good 2 by a competitive industry that uses one unit of good 2 to produce one unit of good 1. Normalising the price of good 1 at one, the structure of production ensures that the equilibrium price of good 2 must also be one. Given this, all that needs to be determined for this economy is the division of the initial endowment into quantities of the two goods.

In specifying demand it is necessary to make an assumption concerning the treatment of the externality effect by the households in their maximisation decisions. The standard assumption is that both households take the level of externality as given when they maximise. Although this may seem inappropriate for a two-household economy, two points should be stressed. Firstly, this analysis is illustrative and, in the more relevant case of many households, the effect of each on external effects would be negligible and the assumption is rather more tenable. Secondly, it is also possible that the households may be aware of the externality but not of its cause. They therefore take the quantity as given when maximising.

Incorporating this assumption into the maximisation decision of the households, the competitive equilibrium of the economy is described by the equations

$$\frac{\frac{\partial U^h}{\partial x_1^h}}{\frac{\partial U^h}{\partial x_2^h}} = 1, \ h = 1,2, \tag{10.5}$$

$$x_1^h + x_2^h = \omega_2^h, \ h = 1,2, \tag{10.6}$$

and

$$x_1^1 + x_1^2 + x_2^1 + x_2^2 = \omega_2^1 + \omega_2^2. \tag{10.7}$$

It is equations (10.5) that are of primary importance at this point. For household h these state that the ratio of private benefits from each good, determined by the marginal utilities, is equated to the ratio of private costs. The external effect does not appear directly in the determination of the equilibrium.

To characterise the set of Pareto-optimal allocations, the technique employed is to maximise the utility of household 1 subject to holding household 2 at a fixed level of utility and subject to the production possibilities. Varying the fixed level of household 2's utility will then trace out the set of Pareto optimal allocations. The resulting equations will then be contrasted to (10.5). In detail, the Pareto optima are the solution to

$$\max_{\{x_i^h\}} U^1(x_1^1, x_2^1, x_1^2) \text{ subject to } U^2(x_1^2, x_2^2, x_1^1) \geq \bar{U}^2,$$
$$\text{and } \omega_2^1 + \omega_2^2 - x_1^1 - x_1^2 - x_2^1 - x_2^2 \geq 0. \tag{10.8}$$

Denoting the Lagrange multiplier on the first constraint by μ, the solution is characterised by the conditions

$$\frac{\dfrac{\partial U^1}{\partial x_1^1}}{\dfrac{\partial U^1}{\partial x_2^1}} + \mu \frac{\dfrac{\partial U^2}{\partial x_1^1}}{\dfrac{\partial U^1}{\partial x_2^1}} = 1, \tag{10.9}$$

and

$$\frac{\dfrac{\partial U^2}{\partial x_1^2}}{\dfrac{\partial U^2}{\partial x_2^2}} + \mu^{-1} \frac{\dfrac{\partial U^1}{\partial x_1^2}}{\dfrac{\partial U^2}{\partial x_2^2}} = 1. \tag{10.10}$$

In (10.9) and (10.10) the externality effect can be seen to affect the optimal allocation between the two goods via the derivatives of utility with respect to the externality. If a positive externality, these will raise the value of the left-hand terms. They will decrease them if a negative externality. The value of μ can be interpreted as the relative social welfare weight given to the second household and it will change as $\bar{U}^2$ changes. For example, if the optimum had been derived by maximising a utilitarian social welfare function, then μ would be identically 1. It can then be seen that at the optimum with a positive externality the marginal rate of substitution of both households is above its value in the market outcome. The converse is true with a negative externality. Since the marginal rates of substitution can be interpreted as valuations, it can be seen that the externality leads to a divergence between the private valuations of consumption given by (10.5) and the corresponding social valuations in (10.9) and (10.10). This observation has the implication that the market outcome is not Pareto optimal. It is also tempting to conclude that if the externality is positive then more of good 1 will be consumed at the optimum than under the market outcome. However this is not always the case, a point that is discussed in section 5.

There is one further point worth noting. When a richer production structure is added to the model, the question of whether it is always optimal for firms to produce on the frontier of their production sets arises. The answer to this is given by Murakami and Negishi (1964) who provide an example that has an optimum with inefficiency. However, if it is optimal for at least one firm to be inefficient then the outputs of that firm must cause a negative externality on other, efficient, firms and the inputs must cause a positive externality. This is a fairly restrictive condition so that productive inefficiency is probably not of great consequence.

3.2 Pareto-irrelevant externalities

Although it conveys the message that externalities generally lead to a failure of the competitive economy to achieve Pareto optimality, the simplicity of the preceding analysis is somewhat misleading. As shown by Osana (1972), Rader

(1972) and Parks (1991) there are certain classes of preferences for which the competitive equilibrium is Pareto optimal.

To see how this may arise, assume that the preferences of household h can be represented by a utility function of the form

$$U^h = x_1^h x_2^h [x_1^j x_2^j]^{\rho^h}, \tag{10.11}$$

where the term $[x_1^j x_2^j]^{\rho^h}$, captures the externality effect on h arising from the consumption of j. With these preferences, the competitive equilibrium is then characterised by

$$\frac{x_1^h}{x_2^h} = 1, \, h = 1,2. \tag{10.12}$$

The necessary conditions determining a Pareto optimum can be written

$$x_k^1 [x_1^2 x_2^2]^{\rho^1} + \mu \rho^2 x_1^2 x_2^2 [x_1^1 x_2^1]^{\rho^2 - 1} x_k^1 = \lambda, \, k = 1,2, \tag{10.13}$$

and

$$x_1^1 x_1^2 \rho^1 [x_1^2 x_2^2]^{\rho^1 - 1} x_k^2 + \mu x_k^2 [x_1^1 x_2^1]^{\rho^2} = \lambda, \, k = 1,2. \tag{10.14}$$

Dividing the equation for $k = 1$ in (10.13) by that for $k = 2$ gives (10.12). Repeating this for (10.14) also gives (10.12). The existence of the externality therefore does not affect the efficiency of the competitive equilibrium.

Parks (1991) shows that the Pareto irrelevant externalities arise when the preferences of the households have the general form

$$U^h = U^h(f^1(x^1), f^2(x^2), \ldots, f^H(x^H)). \tag{10.15}$$

In (10.15) the functions $f^h(x^h)$ can be interpreted as the private utility that h derives from their consumption x^h. The total utility of each household is then given as a Bergson–Samuelson function of the vector of private utilities. Although for each household this Bergson–Samuelson function must be defined on the true private utilities, it can differ between households as it would in the example of (10.11) if $\rho^1 \neq \rho^2$. It is straightforward to show that the competitive equilibrium derived from the private maximisation of $f^h(x^h)$ is described by the same necessary conditions as a Pareto optimum obtained from the maximisation of (10.15).

The form of (10.15) clearly demonstrates that it is interdependent utilities that give rise to Pareto-irrelevant externalities. The result arises because the externality effects exactly offset each other when the optimal allocation is determined. Other forms of externality, such as Meade's (1952) *atmosphere externality* which is a function of the sum of consumption of one of the goods, cannot satisfy this condition and will be Pareto relevant.

4 THE COASE THEOREM

The Coase theorem is central to understanding the policy implications of externalities. It does this through indicating those situations in which market activities will eliminate the effects of externalities and suggests new perspectives on why market solutions to externalities may fail and appropriate policy responses. This section states the Coase theorem and then explores its interpretations and implications.

4.1 The theorem

As Coase (1960) never formally stated the theorem but merely described it via examples, a number of alternative interpretations of the theorem have resulted. In very general terms, the theorem asserts that if allowed to function freely the market will achieve an efficient allocation of resources. A generally agreed version of the Coase theorem is as follows.

The Coase theorem

In a competitive economy with complete information and zero transaction costs, the allocation of resources will be efficient and invariant with respect to the legal rules of entitlement.

Stated in this form, the theorem makes two distinct claims. Following Regan (1972), these are termed the *efficiency* thesis and the *invariance* thesis. In a given situation it is possible for one of these to be valid whilst the other is false. No attempt will be made to prove the theorem in the conventional sense. As the discussion will make clear, it is close to being tautological in some circumstances and false in others.

The legal rules of entitlement, or *property rights*, are of central importance to the Coase theorem. These rules determine the rights of the agents in the economy, for example the right to unpolluted air or the right to enjoy silence, and determine the direction in which compensation payments will be made if the right is violated. If valid, the implication of the Coase theorem is that there is no need for policy intervention with regard to externalities except to ensure that property rights are clearly defined. When they are, private agreements over compensation will generate a Pareto-optimal outcome. This conclusion naturally runs counter to the standard assessment of the consequences of externalities and explains why the Coase theorem has been of considerable interest.

A natural expectation would be that the assignment of rights will determine the equilibrium level of an externality, for example that the level of pollution under a polluter-pays system will be less than that under a pollutee-pays one. The invariance thesis of the Coase theorem states that this is incorrect and that the equilibrium level of externality is independent of the assignment of property rights. To show how this may work, consider the example of a factory that is polluting the atmosphere of a neighbouring house. When the firm has the right to pollute the householder can only reduce the pollution by paying the firm a sufficient amount of compensation to make it worthwhile to stop production or to find an alternative means of production. Let the amount of compensation the firm requires be C. Then the cost to the householder of the pollution, Γ, will either be greater than C, in which case they will be willing to compensate the firm and the externality will cease, or it will be less than C and the externality will be left to continue. Now consider the outcome under the polluter pays principle. The cost to the firm of stopping the externality now becomes C and the compensation required by the household is Γ. If C is greater than Γ the firm will be willing to compensate the household and continue producing the externality, if it is less than Γ it stops the externality. Considering the two cases, it can be seen the outcome is determined only by Γ relative to C and not by the assignment of property rights which is essentially the content of the Coase theorem.

That the invariance thesis of the Coase theorem is usually false is easily seen from the example. The change in property rights between the two cases will cause differences in the final distribution of income due to the direction of compensation payments. The invariance thesis can only be correct if there are no income effects. Since income effects will generally exist, the invariance thesis is false. Attention is now paid only to the efficiency thesis.

4.2 Markets for externalities

In the study of externalities considerable emphasis has been placed on the value of markets for externalities. This arises because, if the externalities were actually traded, the market outcome would be Pareto optimal. The failure of the competitive equilibrium to achieve optimality can then be seen as arising from the necessary markets being missing from the economy. The idea that externalities could be overcome by the introduction of markets for external effects was first introduced by Arrow (1969) and employed by Meyer (1971). Starret (1972) provided the formal development of the idea and the proofs of the central results; the analysis now described is based closely on Starret (1972).

To demonstrate the role of markets, consider an economy with three firms, labelled $j = 1, 2, 3$, and two goods. An externality is introduced by assuming that the production set for each firm depends upon the production plans of the other firms. The production set, Y^1, of firm 1 is therefore defined on a six-dimensional space with a typical element $(y_1^1, y_2^1, y_1^2, y_2^2, y_1^3, y_2^3)$. Clearly, firm 1 only has direct choice upon the first two elements of this set. The same comments apply to the production sets of firms 2 and 3, where these firms have direct control over the second and third pairs of entries respectively.

Now let y^j be the output vector of firm j. The economy's production set is

$$Y=\left\{y:y=\sum_{j=1}^{3} y^j, y^j \in Y^j, j=1,...,3\right\}.$$ (10.16)

Provided there is no point interior to the production set which is Pareto optimal, the efficient production plan will be a point, $\bar{y}$, on the boundary of Y and, if Y is convex, this will imply a price vector q under which $\bar{y}$ maximises qy over all y in Y. Under this interpretation the price system q captures the true social rates of transformation between the goods. The optimality question can now be phrased formally as determining whether there exists any arrangement of trade in this economy such that the equilibrium is Pareto optimal, so demonstrating the First Theorem of Welfare Economics, and whether there exists a price system which will lead, by profit maximisation of the individual firms, to the production plan $\bar{y}$ and hence demonstrating that the Second Theorem of Welfare Economics applies.

Before proceeding, it may be worth recalling how the Two Theorems of Welfare Economics were demonstrated in chapter 2. For the First Theorem, it is sufficient for it to hold that all agents are maximising subject to parametric prices with no external effects. The proof of the Second Theorem required that the firms' production sets were independent and that the price vector which ensured the optimal allocation was profit maximising for the economy as a whole also had the property that it was profit maximising for individual firms to choose the quantities that lead to the optimal output. These observations indicate that for the Theorems to apply the important point is to define the production sets so that they are independent between firms.

The required independence can be obtained by delineating goods both by the firm that produces them and by the firm upon which they have an externality effect. Thus define good y_i^{kj} to be the net output of good i by firm j as observed by firm k. The production set of firm k is now defined on the variables $(y_1^{k1}, y_2^{k1}, y_1^{k2}, y_2^{k2}, y_1^{k3}, y_2^{k3})$, $k=1, 2, 3$. A count of the commodities shows that this leads to there being eighteen different goods. In addition, the production sets of the firms are formally independent since the goods over which any firm exercises choice do not appear in the production set of any other firm. To complete the argument, a set of prices are introduced that correspond to the number of goods in the artificial markets. The price vector faced by firm k is therefore written $(p_1^{k1},...,p_n^{km})$. Since none of the agents now faces an external effect, it follows that if agents act competitively and an equilibrium exists for the economy including the markets for external effects, then the equilibrium must be Pareto optimal. It is also possible to appreciate that there are now sufficient prices to allow the control of firms' decisions that is necessary for decentralisation. In particular, it is possible to choose the prices such that the identity $y_i^{kj} = y_i^{k'j}$, all k, j, k', i is satisfied.

Starret (1972) proves the following result which extends the Second Theorem to the economy with markets for externalities.

Theorem 10.1

The price vector $(p_1^{11}, \ldots, p_n^{mm})$ can be chosen such that the profit-maximising production plans of the firms have the property that they sum to the optimal aggregate output $\bar{y}$ and the prices satisfy $\sum\limits_{k=1}^{m} p_i^{kj} = q_i$.

Proof

See Starret (1972).

Theorem 10.1 shows that the prices can be chosen so that individual profit maximisation generates the chosen level of output and that the prices on the artificial markets are equal to the true social costs. In other words, the equality states that the total cost of a unit of good i for firm j, including all the externality effects it has upon other firms, sums to the social cost. In this way, the externality effects are brought into the price system. The motivation for this result is that each good can be seen as a bundle of commodities traded on the artificial markets and the price of the bundle is the sum of the prices of its components. An alternative way of viewing it is to note that the direct price of a unit of good i for firm j is p_i^{jj}. Taking q_i to be the consumer price of good, it follows from the identity

$$q_i = p_i^{jj} + \sum_{k=1, k \neq j}^{m} p_i^{kj}, \tag{10.17}$$

that the sum $\sum\limits_{k=1, k \neq j}^{m} p_i^{kj}$ can be seen as total tax payments per unit of good i by firm j to cover the externality effects. Equation (10.17) therefore captures the basic duality between prices on artificial markets and corrective taxes. To summarise, if artificial markets are created for the externalities, so that they are treated as distinct goods according to the firm that produces them and the firm that they affect, then a price system defined over these constructed commodities can support the optimal allocation. In addition, this price system can also be interpreted as defining a set of optimal taxes to counter the externalities.

This analysis can be given two alternative interpretations. Firstly, it can be taken as prescriptive of what should be done to overcome inefficiency due to the existence of externalities in the sense that if there is an externality problem then this can be overcome by the introduction of markets for external effects. Secondly, it can be treated as a proof of the efficiency thesis of the Coase theorem as it shows that if externalities can be traded on competitive markets then the equilibrium must be efficient. In this context, the Coase theorem becomes almost tautological. If the markets exist then, as in the second definition of an externality, there must actually be no externalities. As regards policy prescriptions, since trading artificial commodities is equivalent to trading property rights, the analysis can also be interpreted as showing that policy should be directed to facilitating the exchange of property rights.

4.3 Non-existence of markets

The discussion of the previous section has shown that if the economy has sufficient markets and if these markets function competitively, then the equilibrium will be Pareto optimal even in the presence of externalities. From the construction, it is clear that this argument presumes that each externality will have its own market. The question that is now addressed is, given their obvious desirability, why a complete set of such markets are not observed in practice.

4.3.1 Property rights

The first difficulty in proposing the results above as a solution to the problem of externalities lies with the assignment of property rights in the market. When considering trade for commodities defined in the usual sense it is clear who is the purchaser and who is the supplier and, therefore, the direction in which payment should be transferred. However, when externalities are interpreted as commodities, this is no longer the case.

If property rights are not clearly specified, it may not be obvious who should be seen as the recipient of payment. For example, consider the case of air pollution. It may be that it is acknowledged that the polluter should pay with the implicit recognition of the right to clean air. On the other hand, tradition may have established a right to pollute, with clean air something that should have to be paid for. When neither tradition is generally accepted, the direction in which payment should go remains unclear. As a consequence, without clearly specified property rights, the markets may not function since none of the parties involved would be willing to accept the responsibility for payment and costly litigation would diminish the gain from the existence of the market. These observations suggest that the clarification of property rights should constitute that first step in the construction of a policy towards externalities.

4.3.2 Non-convexities

It has been implicit in the discussion up to this point that the standard assumptions on convexity, particularly of production sets, will still be applicable to the economy despite the existence of externalities. Without convexity, maximising choices may not be continuous functions of underlying variables and no equilibrium may exist. When there is no equilibrium, policy proposals based on its assumed existence, with or without the artificial markets, will be of little value. Furthermore, even if an equilibrium exists it may not be decentralisable. Although convexity is not too contentious without externalities, this is not

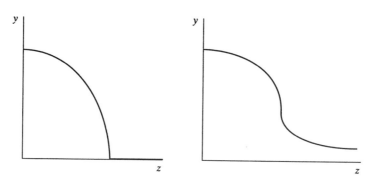

Figure 10.1   Non-convexity

the case with externalities. As noted by Starret (1972) there are strong reasons for doubting its applicability.

As an example of the first reason for the possible failure of the convexity assumption, consider the case of a negative production externality. For a firm that is affected, if this has the effect of driving its output to zero regardless of the level of other inputs then the production set will not be convex. Two ways in which this may occur are illustrated in figure 10.1 where the output, y, of the firm is drawn as a function of the level, z, of some externality for a given level of inputs.

In the left-hand diagram, output becomes identically zero after some level of the externality is reached. The right-hand diagram does not have the zero output level but shows output driven asymptotically to zero. In both these case the production set of the firm is not convex.

In such cases the economy based on artificial markets will fail to have an equilibrium. Suppose the firm were to receive a positive price for accepting externalities. The optimal behaviour for the firm would then be to produce zero output and offer to accept an arbitrarily large quantity of externalities. Since its output is already zero the externalities can do it no further harm, so that this plan will lead to an unbounded level of profits. If the price for accepting externalities were zero, the same firm would not accept any. The demand for externalities is therefore discontinuous and an equilibrium need not exist. If the externality were positive, the firm would choose a production plan involving an arbitrarily large negative quantity of the externality which again leads to unbounded profit.

The second reason for non-convexity is due to Meade (1952). It is often assumed that once all inputs are properly accounted for, all firms will have constant returns to scale since they can always replicate their behaviour. That is, if a fixed set of inputs (i.e., a factory and staff) produce output y, doubling all those inputs must produce $2y$ since they can be split into two identical subunits (e.g., two factories and staff) producing an amount y each. Now consider a firm subject to a negative externality and assume that it has constant returns to all inputs including the externality. From this view, there are constant returns from the perspective of society. Now consider the firm doubling all its inputs but with the externality held at a constant level. Since the externality is a negative one, it becomes diluted by the increase in other inputs and output must more than double. The firm therefore faces private increasing returns to scale. With such increasing returns, the firm's profit-maximising decision may not have a well-defined finite solution and market equilibrium may again fail to exist.

Further analysis of these issues is given in Otani and Sicilian (1977). Their theorem demonstrates that convexity is inconsistent with a set of reasonable assumptions describing the consequences of external effects. This simply formalises the arguments above. However they also note that by not permitting firms to demand negative quantities of inputs or supply a negative quantity of output the problem does not occur with positive externalities. Therefore non-convexity appears more of an issue for negative externalities.

These comments have been of a fairly negative nature since non-convexities are the source of severe difficulties for conclusions based on competitive behaviour. Although they may not be of critical importance in practice, they do act as a warning that decentralised solutions may not be appropriate for dealing with externalities.

4.3.3 Transaction costs

If the exchange of commodities would lead to mutually beneficial gains for two parties, the commodities will be exchanged unless the cost of doing so outweighs the benefits. Such *transactions costs* may arise from the need for the parties to travel to a point of exchange or from the legal costs involved in formalising the transactions. They may also arise due to the search required to find a trading partner. Whenever they arise, transactions cost represent a hindrance to trade and, if sufficiently great, will lead to no trade at all taking place. The latter results in the economy having a missing market.

The existence of transaction costs is often seen as the most significant reason for the non-existence of markets in externalities. To see how they can arise, consider the problem of pollution caused by car emissions. If the economy above is applied literally, then any driver of a car must purchase pollution rights from all of the agents that are affected by the car emissions each time, and every time, that the car is used. Obviously, this would take an absurd amount of organisation and, since considerable time and resources would be used in the process, would certainly not correspond to the frictionless market envisaged in the Arrow–Debreu economy. In many cases it seems likely that the welfare loss due to waste of resources in organising the market would outweigh any gains from having the market.

Despite these negative conclusions, the transactions cost perspective upon the Coase theorem still has policy value. The prescription arising from it is that the cost of transferring legal entitlements between agents should be reduced as far as possible to permit trade.

4.3.4 Missing markets and side payments

If markets for external effects are missing, it may be possible for direct transfers, or side payments, between agents to overcome this and achieve efficiency. One way to formalise this idea has been considered by Bigelow (1993). Assume that two agents are initially faced with playing a bimatrix non-constant sum one-shot game. Denote the payoff of this game to 1, if agent 1 chooses strategy i and agent 2 strategy j, by $\Gamma^1(i,j)$ and the payoff to 2 by $\Gamma^2(i,j)$. Without side payments, there is no reason why the Nash equilibrium of the game should be efficient. Side payments can be introduced by allowing agent h, $h = 1$, 2, to offer agent k an outcome contingent payment of $\Lambda^k(i,j)$ if strategies i, j are chosen for the original game. Incorporating these side payments, the payoff for 1 if i,j is chosen is $\Gamma^1(i,j) + \Lambda^1(i,j) - \Lambda^2(i,j)$ and for 2 is $\Gamma^2(i,j) + \Lambda^2(i,j) - \Lambda^1(i,j)$. An equilibrium for the game with side payments is then a set of side payments which are chosen optimally given that the resulting strategies form a Nash equilibrium for the game where the payoffs include side payments.

A missing market is then represented by an original matrix game in which the payoff of one agent is not affected by the action of the other. Bigelow (1993) then proves that the existence of side payments is sufficient to ensure that an efficient equilibrium is achieved. In contrast when two markets are missing, so any form of payoff may arise in the original matrix game, an equilibrium may not exist in the game with side payments and when it does, it need not be efficient. Although they are rather stylised, these results do show the limitations of side payments in achieving efficiency when there are missing markets.

4.4 Bargaining

When external effects are traded, there will generally only be one agent on each side of the market. This *thinness* of the market undermines the assumption of competitive behaviour that can support the efficiency hypothesis. In such circumstances, the Coase theorem has been interpreted as implying that bargaining between the two agents will take place over compensation for external effects and that this bargaining will lead to an efficient outcome. Such a claim requires substantiation.

Bargaining can be interpreted as taking the form of either a *cooperative* game between agents or as a *non-cooperative* game. When it is viewed as cooperative, the tradition since Nash (1950) has been to adopt a set of axioms which the bargain must satisfy and to derive the outcomes that satisfy these axioms. The requirement of Pareto optimality is always adopted as one of the axioms so that the bargained agreement is necessarily efficient. If all bargains over compensation payments were placed in front of an external arbitrator, then the Nash bargaining solution would have some force as descriptive of what such an arbitrator should try and achieve. However, this is not what is envisaged in the Coase theorem which focuses on the actions of markets free of any regulation.

Although appealing as a method for achieving an outcome agreeable to both parties, the fact that Nash bargaining solution is efficient does not demonstrate the correctness of the Coase theorem.

The literature on bargaining in a non-cooperative context is best divided between games with complete information and those with incomplete information, since this distinction is of crucial importance for the outcome. One of the central results of non-cooperative bargaining with complete information is due to Rubinstein (1982) who considers the division of a single object between two players. The players take it in turns to announce a division of the object and in each period an offer and an acceptance or rejection are made. Both players discount the future so are impatient to arrive at an agreed division. Rubinstein shows that the game has a unique subgame perfect equilibrium with agreement reached in the first period. The outcome is Pareto optimal.

The important point is the complete information assumed to prevail in this representation of bargaining. The importance of information for the nature of outcomes has been already been emphasised on several occasions and its consequences are equally important for bargaining. In the simple bargaining problem of Rubinstein (1982) the information that must be known is the preferences of the two agents, captured by their rates of time discount. When these discount rates are private information the attractive properties of the complete information bargain are lost and, as shown by Rubinstein (1985), there may be many potential equilibria with the equilibria being dependent upon the precise specification of the structure of bargaining.

In the context of externalities it seems reasonable to assume that information will be incomplete since there is no reason why the agents involved in bargaining an agreement over compensation for an external effect should be aware of the other's valuation of the externality. The formalisation of this situation given by Myerson and Satterthwaite (1983) considers the sale of an object (which would be the property right) from one agent to another. Each agent knows their own valuation at the time of bargaining but is uncertain about that of the other agent. The characterisation of bargaining is then undertaken by determining the form of *Bayesian incentive-compatible* and *individually rational direct* mechanisms for reaching agreement (see the definitions in chapter 9, section 8). Application of the *revelation principle*, which asserts that for any Bayesian equilibrium there is an equivalent mechanism that involves truthful revelation, justifies the restriction to incentive compatible direct mechanisms.

Agent 1 initially owns the object and agent 2 wishes to purchase. The valuation of the object by 1 is denoted v^1 and that of 2 by v^2. Household j, $j = 1, 2$, believes v^i, $i \neq j$, to be distributed with density function $f_i(v^i)$ which has strictly positive support on $[a_i, b_i]$ and cumulative distribution $F_i(v^i)$. The outcome is determined by a function $p(v^1, v^2)$ which represents the probability that the object is transferred and a function $q(v^1, v^2)$ that is the payment that must be made. Given a pair of such functions, the expected payment as viewed by 1 is given by

$$\bar{q}_1(v^1) = \int_{a_2}^{b_2} q(v^1, w^2) f_2(w^2) dw^2, \tag{10.18}$$

and the cost expected by 2 is

$$\bar{q}_2(v^2) = \int_{a_1}^{b_1} q(w^1, v^2) f_1(w^1) dw^1. \tag{10.19}$$

Similarly, the probability of transfer expected by 1 is

$$\bar{p}_1(v^1) = \int_{a_2}^{b_2} p(v^1, w^2) f_2(w^2) dw^2, \tag{10.20}$$

and by 2

$$\bar{p}_2(v^2) = \int_{a_1}^{b_1} p(w^1, v^2) f_1(w^1) dw^1. \tag{10.21}$$

Employing (10.18) and (10.20), the expected payoff of 1 can be written

$$U^1(v^1) = \bar{q}_1(v^1) - v^1 \bar{p}_1(v^1), \tag{10.22}$$

and that of 2

$$U^2(v^2) = v^2 \bar{p}_2(v^2) - \bar{q}_2(v^2). \tag{10.23}$$

The characterisation of the mechanism begins by noting that incentive compatibility implies for agent 1 that

$$U^1(v^1) = \bar{q}_1(v^1) - v^1 \bar{p}_1(v^1) \geq \bar{q}_1(w^1) - v^1 \bar{p}_1(w^1), \tag{10.24}$$

and

$$U^1(w^1) = \bar{q}_1(w^1) - w^1 \bar{p}_1(w^1) \geq \bar{q}_1(v^1) - w^1 \bar{p}_1(v^1), \tag{10.25}$$

for any v^1 and w^1. Taken together, (10.24) and (10.25) give

$$[w^1 - v^1] \bar{p}_1(v^1) \geq U^1(v^1) - U^1(w^1) \geq [w^1 - v^1] \bar{p}_1(w^1). \tag{10.26}$$

Choosing $w^1 > v^1$ shows that $\bar{p}_1(v^1) \geq \bar{p}_1(w^1)$ so that the probability is decreasing in valuation. Differentiating (10.26) with respect to v^1 and letting $w^1 \to v^1$ shows that $U_1'(v^1) = -\bar{p}_1(v^1)$. Integrating gives

$$U^1(v^1) = U^1(b_1) + \int_{v^1}^{b_1} \bar{p}_1(w^1) dw^1. \tag{10.27}$$

Repeating the argument for agent 2 shows that $\bar{p}_2(\cdot)$ is increasing and

$$U^2(v^2) = U^2(a_2) + \int_{a_2}^{v^2} \bar{p}_2(w^2) dw^2. \tag{10.28}$$

The central result of Myerson and Satterthwaite (1983) can now be stated.

Theorem 10.2 (Myerson and Satterthwaite)

If the intervals $[a_i, b_i]$, $i = 1, 2$, have an intersection with non-empty interior (so there is a positive probability of gains from trade) and neither is a subset of the other then there is no efficient mechanism that satisfies incentive compatibility.

Proof

Substituting for $U^1(v^1)$ and $U^2(v^2)$ in (10.27) and (10.28) using (10.22) and (10.23) and summing the resulting equations gives

$$\bar{q}_1(v^1) - \bar{q}_2(v^2) = v^1 \bar{p}_1(v^1) - v^2 \bar{p}_2(v^2) + U^1(b_1) + U^2(a_2) + \int_{v^1}^{b_1} \bar{p}_1(w^1) dw^1$$

$$+ \int_{a_2}^{v^2} \bar{p}_2(w^2) dw^2. \tag{10.29}$$

As there is no outside agency involved, the expected income of 1 is equal to the expected payment of 2 or $\mathscr{E}[\bar{q}_1(v^1)] = \mathscr{E}[\bar{q}_2(v^2)]$. The expectation of the right-hand side of (10.29) is therefore zero. Taking the expectation and integrating by parts gives

$$U^1(b_1) + U^2(a_2) = - \int_{a_1}^{b_1} \left[v^1 + \frac{F_1(v^1)}{f_1(v^1)} \right] \bar{p}_1(v^1) f_1(v^1) dv^1$$

$$+ \int_{a_2}^{b_2} \left[v^2 - \frac{1 - F_2(v^2)}{f_2(v^2)} \right] \bar{p}_2(v^2) f_2(v^2) dv^2. \tag{10.30}$$

Replacing $\bar{p}_1(v^1)$ and $\bar{p}_2(v^2)$ using (10.18) and (10.20) and noting that individual rationality requires $U^1(b_1) \geq 0$, $U^2(a_2) \geq 0$, (10.30) implies

$$0 \leq \int_{a_2}^{b_2} \int_{a_1}^{b_1} \left[\left[v^2 - \frac{1 - F_2(v^2)}{f_2(v^2)} \right] - \left[v^1 + \frac{F_1(v^1)}{f_1(v^1)} \right] \right] p(v^1, v^2) f_1(v^1) f_2(v^2) dv^1 dv^2. \tag{10.31}$$

Condition (10.31) must be satisfied by any incentive compatible and individually rational mechanism.

An efficient outcome requires $p(v^1, v^2) = 1$ if $v^1 < v^2$ and $p(v^1, v^2) = 0$ if $v^1 > v^2$. Under such a mechanism, $\bar{p}_1(v_1) = 1 - F_2(v_1)$ and $\bar{p}_2(v_2) = F_1(v_2)$. Substituting these restrictions into the right-hand side of (10.31) gives

$$\int_{a_2}^{b_2} \int_{a_1}^{\min\{v^2, b_1\}} [v^2 f_2(v^2) + F_2(v^2) - 1] f_1(v^1) dv^1 dv^2$$

$$- \int_{a_2}^{b_2} \int_{a_1}^{\min\{v^2, b_1\}} [v^1 f_1(v^1) + F_1(v^1)] f_2(v^2) dv^1 dv^2$$

$$= \int_{a_2}^{b_2} [v^2 f_2(v^2) + F_2(v^2) - 1] F_1(v^2) dv^2 - \int_{a_2}^{b_2} \min\{v^2 F_1(v^2), b_1\} f_2(v^2) dv^2$$

$$= -\int_{a_2}^{b_2} [1 - F_2(v^2)] F_1(v^2) dv^2 + \int_{b_1}^{b_2} [v^2 - b_1] f_2(v^2) dv^2$$

$$= -\int_{a_2}^{b_2} [1 - F_2(v^2)] F_1(v^2) dv^2 - \int_{b_1}^{b_2} [F_2(v^2) - 1] dv^2$$

$$= -\int_{a_2}^{b_1} [1 - F_2(w)] F_1(w) dw < 0. \tag{10.32}$$

Contrasting (10.32) and (10.31) shows that an efficient outcome contradicts individual rationality.

Theorem 10.2 shows how asymmetric information leads to inefficiency in the outcome of bargaining. The incentive for each agent to attempt to exploit their private information prevents all the gains from trade being exhausted. Rob (1989) and Mailath and Postlewaite (1990) extend this inefficiency result to economies in which the externality caused by one agent affects many agents. As the number of agents increases the effect of each upon the externality becomes negligible. The degree of inefficiency can therefore increase as the number of agents increases.

The efficiency thesis of the Coase theorem relies on agreements being reached on the compensation required for external effects. The results above suggest that when information is incomplete, bargaining between agents will not lead to an efficient outcome.

4.5 Conclusions

In summary, the Coase theorem suggests that externalities can be overcome by decentralised trading between affected parties. In practice it is difficult to imagine that its conditions are actually satisfied so that it cannot be given too much weight as a foundation for the formulation of policy. The arguments above provide some fairly powerful reasons why the full set of markets required for optimality may not exist. Furthermore they also show why bargaining between affected parties is also unlikely to achieve efficiency.

5 WELFARE-IMPROVING CHANGES

A natural expectation would be that if the production of a good generated a negative externality, then too much of that good would be produced at the competitive equilibrium and welfare could be raised by reducing output. The same point would apply to consumption externalities. If this reasoning was always correct, it would provide a simple rule of thumb for policy to follow. This section investigates the truth of this statement for a model with a single externality. The claim is shown to be true for marginal changes but, as will be discussed, must be treated with care when non-marginal changes are involved.

5.1 Local results

Consider an economy that has a single externality that is generated by the firms in the economy at a level that is related to their output of good 1. The quantity of externality generated by firm j, z^j, is determined by

$$z^j = z^j(y_1^j).$$
(10.33)

The total quantity of externality then amounts to

$$z = \sum_{j=1}^{m} z^j = \sum_{j=1}^{m} z^j(y_1^j).$$
(10.34)

It is assumed that the externality affects both the consumers, via their utility functions, and the firms, via their production sets. The utility of household h is therefore denoted

$$U^h = U^h(x_1^h, \ldots, x_n^h, z).$$
(10.35)

From (10.35) it can be seen that utility is a function only of the total quantity of the externality and is not related to its distribution across firms. The production set of each firm is written in implicit form as

$$\{y_1^j, \ldots, y_n^j \mid f^j(y_1^j, \ldots, y_n^j, z) \leq 0\}, j = 1, \ldots, m.$$
(10.36)

The analytical procedure is now to start at a competitive equilibrium and to calculate the effect of a differential increase in the output of good 1 by all firms, with an offsetting change in the consumption and production of all other goods. This effect is then converted into a social valuation via a utilitarian aggregation procedure. If the social valuation of the increase has a negative value, then welfare will be raised by reducing the output of good 1 by all firms.

The competitive equilibrium allocation must satisfy both the definition, (10.34), of the level of the externality and it must be productively feasible for the firms, that is (10.36) must be met for all j. In addition, an equilibrium allocation has to meet the market clearance condition

$$\sum_{h=1}^{H} x_i^h \le \omega_i + \sum_{j=1}^{m} y_i^j, \ i=1,\ldots,n, \tag{10.37}$$

where ω_i is the total endowment of good i.

It is now assumed that the constraints (10.34), (10.36) and (10.37) are met with equality so that the effect of the increase in the output of good 1 can be calculated by total differentiation. Carrying out the differentiation gives

$$dz = \sum_{j=1}^{m} \frac{dz^j}{\partial y_1^j} \, dy_1^j, \tag{10.38}$$

$$\sum_{h=1}^{H} dx_i^h = \sum_{j=1}^{m} dy_i^j, \ i=1,\ldots,n, \tag{10.39}$$

and

$$df^j = \sum_{i=1}^{n} f_i^j dy_i^j + f_z^j dz = 0, \ j=1,\ldots,m. \tag{10.40}$$

Equation (10.40) can be rearranged to give the equivalent form

$$\sum_{i=1}^{n} f_i^j dy_i^j = -f_z^j dz, \ j=1,\ldots,m. \tag{10.41}$$

To derive an expression for the social value of this change in the production plan, it is first noted that utility maximisation of household h leads to the equalities

$$U_i^h = \lambda p_i, \ U_n^h = \lambda p_n, \tag{10.42}$$

where λ is the Lagrange multiplier on the household's budget constraint. If p_n is normalised at 1, then

$$\frac{U_i^h}{U_n^h} = p_i, \tag{10.43}$$

is a measure of the value of good i to household h relative to the other goods. To generate a measure of change in social welfare, the effect of rearrangement in production is defined as

$$dW = \sum_{i=1}^{n} \sum_{h=1}^{H} \left[\frac{U_i^h}{U_n^h} \right] dx_i^h + \sum_{h=1}^{H} \left[\frac{U_z^h}{U_n^h} \right] dz. \tag{10.44}$$

If dW is positive, the modification of production is assumed to be of positive value for society.

The aim now is to express dW in terms of the output of good 1 so that it can be ascertained whether a reduction in the externality producing good will raise welfare. The first step is to note from the resource balance equation that any change in consumption must be met with an equal change in production. Hence

$$\sum_{h=1}^{H} dx_i^h = \sum_{j=1}^{m} dy_i^j, \ i=1,\dots,n. \tag{10.45}$$

In addition, the fact that the initial point is assumed to be a competitive equilibrium implies that the firms must be equating the marginal rate of transformation between any two goods to the ratio of their prices. In particular, taking all other goods relative to good n gives

$$MRT_{i,n}^{j} = \frac{f_i^j}{f_n^j} = p_i, \ i=1,\dots,n, \text{ all } j. \tag{10.46}$$

Using (10.45) and (10.46), dW can be written

$$dW = \sum_{i=1}^{n} \sum_{j=1}^{m} \left[\frac{f_i^j}{f_n^j} \right] dy_i^j + \sum_{h=1}^{H} \left[\frac{U_z^h}{U_n^h} \right] dz. \tag{10.47}$$

From (10.41) the terms in f_i^j can be eliminated to provide

$$dW = \left[-\sum_{j=1}^{m} \left[\frac{f_z^j}{f_n^j} \right] + \sum_{h=1}^{H} \left[\frac{U_z^h}{U_n^h} \right] \right] dz. \tag{10.48}$$

Finally, using the externality generation process defined in (10.38) gives

$$dW = \left[-\sum_{j=1}^{m} \left[\frac{f_z^j}{f_n^j} \right] + \sum_{h=1}^{H} \left[\frac{U_z^h}{U_n^h} \right] \right] \sum_{j=1}^{m} z_1^j dy_1^j. \tag{10.49}$$

The expression in (10.49) captures the welfare effect of a feasible change in the production of good 1 by all firms. To interpret this condition, note that

$$f_z^j > 0, f_n^j > 0, \ z_1^j > 0, \text{ all } j, \text{ and } U_z^h < 0, \ U_n^h > 0, \text{ all } h. \tag{10.50}$$

Therefore, if dy_1^j is positive for all firms, dW is negative. Hence a reduction in the output of good 1 by all firms, that is $dy_1^j < 0$ all j, would raise welfare.

In conclusion, a reduction in the output of an externality-producing good from its level determined at the competitive equilibrium will raise welfare. This is the intuitively plausible result that agrees with the presumption that it should always be the intention of policy to reduce the level of a negative externality. By reversing the signs of f_z^j, all j, and U_z^h, all h, it is also clear that (10.49) implies that the quantity of a good producing a positive externality should be increased from its competitive equilibrium level. The methodology employed to derive this result is clearly analogous to the more general policy reform analysis of chapter 6. The methods of that chapter could be employed to extend the model to several externalities and corresponding changes in several outputs.

5.2 Global results

In addition to the usual caveats that must be applied to any result, such as the appropriateness of the model within which it was derived, the claim of the previous section is restricted by a further consideration. Since the formal analysis considered only the consequence of a differential change in the output of good 1, the result is purely *local* in that it refers to the correct course of action only in the locality of the competitive equilibrium. It must therefore not be read as suggesting that the output of good 1 should be reduced regardless of the starting point or that the optimal level of the output of good 1 is less than that at the competitive equilibrium. Both the latter statements are examples of *global* results and could only be supported by stronger arguments.

A global result would relate the production and consumption arrays $\{x^c\}$, $\{y^c\}$ at the competitive equilibrium to the optimal arrays $\{x^o\}$, $\{y^o\}$. In fact, as shown in Baumol and Oates (1988), a comparison between these arrays can only be made under stronger assumptions than have so far been adopted. In particular, even with a single externality, convexity of the production sets becomes essential.

Buchanan and Kafoglis (1963) demonstrate that it also possible for counter examples to be constructed in which, for example, the quantity of a positive externality is decreased as the economy moves towards the optimum. Consider a two-consumer, two-good, economy with a single positive consumption externality. For each consumer, the externality arises from the other's consumption of good 2. Under these assumptions the utility functions are of the form

$$U^1 = U^1(x_1^1, x_1^2, x_2^1), \ U^2 = U^2(x_1^1, x_1^2, x_2^2). \tag{10.51}$$

As each consumer maximises their utility taking the other consumer's contribution to the externality as fixed, the equilibrium occurs at a point at which the indifference curves cross at right angles. This is precisely the same argument as for the private provision of public goods in chapter 9. Therefore, as shown in chapter 9, section 5.3, it is possible for there to be too much consumption of goods causing positive externalities at the market outcome relative to the social optimum and too little of goods causing negative externalities.

The conclusion of this section is that although local results can be established without too much difficulty it is not straightforward to provide global comparisons. However, since many policy recommendations are only concerned with marginal changes, this is not of too great a consequence for the formulation of practical policies.

6 CORRECTIVE TAXATION

In response to the non-optimality of the market equilibrium in the presence of externalities, a natural policy to adopt is the imposition of a set of taxes to correct for the distortions. Such taxes, often termed *Pigouvian taxes* following the work of Pigou (1920), will be the subject of this section. Before proceeding to characterise optimal taxes, it is first necessary to clarify several important issues regarding the extent to which the taxes may be differentiated.

Taxation has already been implicit in much of the discussion of artificial markets and was made explicit in (10.17). The content of the first subsection will be to derive a set of taxes of the form of those described in (10.17) for a model of consumption externalities. The perspective chosen emphasises the fact that the rates of tax need to be differentiated between commodities and between consumers. This is a far stronger requirement than that normally imposed upon models of commodity taxation and, arguably, is not administratively feasible. When the requirement that the taxes must be uniform across consumers is imposed, the first-best allocation cannot, in general, be sustained except for some special cases. This leads to the choice of taxes that will generate the optimal second-best outcome. Uniform taxes are considered in the second subsection.

6.1 Non-uniform taxation

It has already been argued in the analysis of artificial markets that the first-best can be sustained by a system of personalised prices and that the components of these prices can be given the interpretation of taxes as in (10.17). The analysis involved asserting the existence of such prices by exploiting the convexity of the model but did not discuss the means by which such prices could be calculated. To remedy this, optimal taxes are now reconsidered for a model of consumption externalities.

Let the utility of household h be given by

$$U^h = U^h(x_1^{h1}, x_1^{h2}, \ldots, x_1^{hH}, x_2^{h1}, \ldots, x_n^{hH}), \tag{10.52}$$

where the externality effects have been included as artificial commodities with $x_i^{h\tilde{h}}$ denoting the consumption of good i by $\tilde{h}$ as viewed by h. The aggregate quantity, X_i, of good i is defined by

$$X_i = \sum_{h=1}^{H} x_i^{hh}, \tag{10.53}$$

and the production feasibility constraint is expressed as

$$F(X_1, \ldots, X_n) \leq 0. \tag{10.54}$$

Following Meyer (1971), the optimal taxes can be characterised by calculating a Pareto optimum for the economy set out above. Such an optimum appears as the solution to the maximisation problem

$$\max_{\{x_1^{11}, \ldots, x_n^{HH}, X_1, \ldots, X_n\}} \sum_{h=1}^{H} \beta^h U^h(x_1^{h1}, x_1^{h2}, \ldots, x_1^{hH}, x_2^{h1}, \ldots, x_n^{hH}), \tag{10.55}$$

subject to

$$X_i \geq \sum_{h=1}^{H} x_i^{hh}, \; 0 \geq F(X_1 \ldots, X_n), x_i^{hh} = x_i^{\tilde{h}h}, \; i=1,\ldots,n, h, \tilde{h}=1,\ldots,H, h \neq \tilde{h}.$$

$$(10.56)$$

The final set of constraints capture the consistency condition that the consumption of h as viewed by $\tilde{h}$ must equal the actual consumption of h. Let λ_i, $i=1,\ldots,n$ denote the Lagrange multipliers on the first n constraints, λ_0 be the multiplier on the production feasibility constraint and $\xi_i^{\tilde{h}h}$, $i=1,\ldots,n$, $h=1,\ldots,H$ be the multipliers on the remaining $H(H-1)n$ constraints.

For the choice of good x_i^{hh}, the first-order condition is

$$\beta^h \frac{\partial U^h}{\partial x_i^{hh}} - \lambda_i - \sum_{\tilde{h}=1, \tilde{h} \neq h}^{H} \xi_i^{\tilde{h}h} = 0,$$

$$(10.57)$$

and for good $x_i^{\tilde{h}h}$,

$$\beta^{\tilde{h}} \frac{\partial U^{\tilde{h}}}{\partial x_i^{\tilde{h}h}} + \xi_i^{\tilde{h}h} = 0.$$

$$(10.58)$$

It can be seen in (10.58) that the multipliers $\xi_i^{\tilde{h}h}$ are proportional to the externality effect. In addition, dividing two of the first-order conditions (10.57) for goods i and j for a consumer, h, gives

$$\frac{\dfrac{\partial U^h}{\partial x_i^{hh}}}{\dfrac{\partial U^h}{\partial x_j^{hh}}} = \frac{\lambda_i + \displaystyle\sum_{\tilde{h}=1, \tilde{h} \neq h}^{H} \xi_i^{\tilde{h}h}}{\lambda_j + \displaystyle\sum_{\tilde{h}=1, \tilde{h} \neq h}^{H} \xi_i^{\tilde{h}h}},$$

$$(10.59)$$

which would be the first-order condition for the choice of the consumer if they faced prices given by $\lambda_i + \sum_{\tilde{h}=1, \tilde{h} \neq h}^{H} \xi_i^{\tilde{h}h}$ for good i, a fact first noted by Davis and Whinston (1962). Therefore the multipliers $\xi_i^{\tilde{h}h}$ can be treated as the per-unit tax rate on consumer h for each unit of good $x_i^{\tilde{h}h}$ they generate. The total tax paid on a unit of consumption, that is for each unit of good x_i^{hh}, is then the sum of these individual taxes. This is the same interpretation as given after (10.17). Note that from (10.58), if the externality is negative, the individual tax component will be positive.

From the above it can be concluded that for the Pareto optimum to be achieved the taxes must have the potential to be differentiated among consumers so that each consumer effectively faces a personalised price for each good. As will be noted below, there are some cases where the effects are symmetric across consumers so that they actually face the same optimal prices but these are the exception rather than the rule. These results have precisely the same interpretation as the demonstration in chapter 9 that the Lindahl equilibrium with personalised prices can decentralise the optimum level of public good provision.

Indeed, public goods can be treated entirely as a special case of the more general externality framework.

The remaining first-order conditions take the form

$$\lambda_i - \frac{\partial F}{\partial X_i} = 0. \tag{10.60}$$

These equations imply that the marginal rates of transformation between each pair of goods is equated to the ratio of the λs. Since the λs can be interpreted as pre-tax prices this has the implication that there is production efficiency and hence the optimal tax system distorts only the consumption side of the economy in response to a consumption externality.

This discussion has demonstrated that a set of taxes can be derived that will support a Pareto optimum in the presence of externalities. However, these taxes will in general need to be differentiated both across goods and across consumers. If the model was extended to include production externalities, the taxes would also need to be differentiated across firms. Theorem 2.5 investigated some of the consequences of attempting to implement a tax system with this degree of differentiation and showed that such attempts were most likely to fail. Since they are based on private information of a similar nature, this general conclusion also applies to the differentiated Pigouvian taxes that support the first best. Consequently, although a first-best outcome can be achieved if the necessary information were available, the implied tax scheme is unlikely to be implementable.

6.2 Uniform taxation

Uniform taxation refers to the situation in which the taxes can be differentiated across goods but not across consumers. As already noted, such taxes will not in general be sufficient to sustain the first-best outcome. This subsection begins, however, with a discussion of circumstances in which uniform taxes will sustain the first best. Following this, the determinants of the level of taxes are considered and the important distinction between direct and indirect tax instruments is introduced.

6.2.1 Attainment of first best

Considering the problem set out in (10.55) and (10.56), uniform taxation will be the solution to this problem when, for a given good i, all the multipliers $\xi_i^{\tilde{h}h}$ have the same value for all h and $\tilde{h}$. The first case in which this will occur is the relatively uninteresting one of identical consumers with each given the same weight in social welfare. Under these conditions the derivatives of utility in (10.58) will be the same for all h and the claim then follows.

Rather more interesting is the example of Meade's (1952) additive atmosphere externality. The level, γ, of such an externality is determined by the relation

$$\gamma = \gamma \left(\sum_{h=1}^{H} x_i^h \right), \gamma' \ge 0. \tag{10.61}$$

From (10.61) the level of the externality is determined as an increasing function of the sum of individual consumption of good i. What is important about the form of this externality generating process is that the marginal contribution of each individual to the total is identical. As will now be shown, for this form of externality uniform taxation generates the first best.

To simplify the notation, assume a two-consumer, two-good economy; neither of these restrictions is of any consequence. With the atmospheric externality the utility functions are written

$$U^h = U^h(x_1^h, x_2^h, \gamma), \ h = 1, 2, \tag{10.62}$$

and, assuming that the externality is generated by the consumption of good 1, γ is determined by

$$\gamma = \gamma(x_1^1 + x_1^2). \tag{10.63}$$

The optimum is then characterised as arising from the solution to

$$\max_{\{x_1^1, \dots, x_2^2, X_1, X_2, \gamma\}} \sum_{h=1}^{2} \beta^h U^h, \tag{10.64}$$

subject to

$$X_i \ge \sum_{h=1}^{2} x_i^h, \ 0 \ge F(X_1, X_2), \gamma = \gamma(x_1^1 + x_1^2). \tag{10.65}$$

This problem generates the first-order conditions

$$\beta^h \frac{\partial U^h}{\partial x_1^h} - \lambda_1 + \xi_1 \frac{\partial \gamma}{\partial x_1^h} = 0, \ h = 1, 2, \tag{10.66}$$

$$\beta^h \frac{\partial U^h}{\partial x_2^h} - \lambda_2 = 0, \ h = 1, 2, \tag{10.67}$$

$$\lambda_i - \lambda_0 \frac{\partial F}{\partial X_i} = 0, \ i = 1, 2, \tag{10.68}$$

and

$$\beta^1 \frac{\partial U^h}{\partial \gamma} + \beta^2 \frac{\partial U^2}{\partial \gamma} + \xi_1 = 0. \tag{10.69}$$

As $\dfrac{\partial \gamma}{\partial x_1^1} = \dfrac{\partial \gamma}{\partial x_1^2}$, (10.66) and (10.69) have the implication that the consumers should face the same shadow prices for the two goods or, equivalently, that the tax rate on good 1 should not be differentiated across the consumers. Therefore uniform taxes can sustain the first best in the presence of the atmosphere externality. Alternative derivations of this result, for external economies of scale in production, can be found in Aoki (1971) and Chipman (1970). A more detailed characterisation of optimal taxes with the atmospheric externality can be found in Sandmo (1975).

6.2.2 Direct and indirect taxes

When uniform taxation cannot generate the first best, the range of tax instruments that are available is of great importance. To aid the discussion, it is first necessary to distinguish between *direct taxes*, which are levied on the activity that causes the externality, and *indirect taxes* that are levied on some activity that is related, via demand or supply functions, to the externality generating activity. For example, if the use of a car causes air pollution then a tax on motoring would be a direct tax and a tax on petrol an indirect tax. Although only direct taxes have been sufficient in the example considered above, it is clear that when direct taxes are restricted to be uniform the extra instrument of an indirect tax may raise welfare further, a point made clearly by Green and Sheshinski (1976).

The analysis that is now developed will consist of two parts. The first will consider only direct taxes and will aim to characterise the factors that determine their level. This will be followed by the introduction of indirect taxes and the factors that determine the optimal mix of direct and indirect taxes will then be of primary importance.

To provide clear conclusions, the first step will be to restrict the individual utility functions to be linear in all commodities except that causing the externality. Aggregating the non-externality commodities into a single commodity and labelling this good 2, the utility functions are assumed to take the form

$$U^h = U^h(x_1^1, \ldots, x_1^H) + x_2^h. \tag{10.70}$$

In addition, the utility functions are assumed to have the concavity and separability properties as below

$$\frac{\partial^2 U^h}{\partial x_1^h \partial x_1^h} < 0, \; \frac{\partial^2 U^h}{\partial x_1^h \partial x_1^{\tilde{h}}} = 0, \; h \neq \tilde{h}. \tag{10.71}$$

The zero cross derivative implies that there are no connections between the effect on utility of different households' contributions to the externality.

For consumer h with income M^h, solving the utility maximisation problem

$$\max_{\{x_1^h, x_2^h\}} \; U^h(x_1^1, \ldots, x_1^H) + x_2^h \text{ s.t. } [p_1 + t_1]x_1^h + x_2^h = M^h, \tag{10.72}$$

where the price of good 2 is normalised at 1, generates the demand function

$$x_1^h = x_1^h(p_1 + t_1). \tag{10.73}$$

Now assuming, as in Diamond (1973a), that any tax revenue is returned to the consumers via lump-sum taxes, the social welfare function can be written in the form

$$W = \sum_{h=1}^{H} U^h\left(x_1^1(p_1+t_1),\ldots,x_1^H(p_1+t_1)\right) - p_1 \sum_{h=1}^{H} x_1^h(p_1+t_1) + \sum_{h=1}^{H} M^h. \quad (10.74)$$

Differentiating (10.74) with respect to t_1, setting the expression equal to zero for a maximum, and using the first-order condition from (10.72), the optimal tax can be written implicitly as

$$t_1 = \frac{-\sum_{h=1}^{H} \sum_{\tilde{h}=1,\tilde{h}\neq h}^{H} \dfrac{\partial U^{\tilde{h}}}{\partial x_1^h} \dfrac{\partial x_1^h}{\partial t_1}}{\sum_{h=1}^{H} \dfrac{\partial x_1^h}{\partial t_1}}. \quad (10.75)$$

From (10.75) it can be seen that the optimal tax is given by the sum of externality effects weighted by the demand derivatives.

The simple characterisation in (10.75) was derived on the basis of a number of strong assumptions. In particular, the separability between the effects of different households' contributions to the externality is almost indefensible. When this is removed, however, the possibility is opened for rather more surprising results to emerge. For example, Diamond (1973a) is able to construct a two-consumer example which has $t_1 = 0$ as the optimal solution despite the presence of a negative externality. This line of reasoning is developed further by Green and Sheshinski (1976) who introduce a third good that enters into the non-linear part of the utility function. With this formulation they permit indirect taxation of the third commodity and demonstrate that an optimum may involve a zero direct tax but a non-zero indirect tax.

These results are placed into a common framework by Balcer (1980) whose analysis is now described. The previous model is extended by assuming a utility function of the form

$$U^h(x_1^h, x_3^h) + \bar{U}^h(x_1^1, \ldots, x_1^{h-1}, x_1^{h+1}, \ldots, x_1^H) + x_2^h. \quad (10.76)$$

In (10.76), the externality effect remains separable from the direct level of consumption of good 1 but it is distinguished from (10.72) by the inclusion of good 3 in the first component of the utility function. The focus of the analysis is on the effect of the substitutability/complementarity relation between good 1 and 3 and the structure of the optimal taxes.

Retaining the assumption that all tax revenues are returned to the consumers via lump-sum transfers, the welfare function can be written

$$W = \sum_{h=1}^{H} U^h(x_1^h, x_3^h) + \sum_{h=1}^{H} \bar{U}^h(x_1^1, \ldots, x_1^{h-1}, x_1^{h+1}, \ldots, x_1^H) - p_1 \sum_{h=1}^{H} x_1^h$$

$$- p_3 \sum_{h=1}^{H} x_3^h + \sum_{h=1}^{H} M^h. \quad (10.77)$$

By differentiating the welfare function with respect to these tax rates and defining

$$\Theta_i^N \equiv \sum_{h=1}^{H} \frac{\partial x_N^h}{\partial t_i}, \quad \tilde{U}_h \equiv \sum_{\bar{h}=1,\bar{h}\neq h}^{H} \frac{\partial \bar{U}^{\bar{h}}}{\partial x_1^{\bar{h}}}, \quad \tilde{U}\Theta_i^N \equiv \sum_{\bar{h}=1}^{H} \bar{U}_h \frac{\partial x_N^h}{\partial t_i}, \quad N=1,3, \; i=1,3, \quad (10.78)$$

the optimal taxes can be implicitly expressed as

$$t_1 = \frac{-\tilde{U}\Theta_1^1}{\Theta_1^1}\left[\frac{\Theta_2^2 - \Theta_1^2[\tilde{U}\Theta_2^1/\tilde{U}\Theta_1^1]}{\Theta_2^2 - \Theta_1^2\Theta_2^1/\Theta_1^1}\right], \qquad (10.79)$$

and

$$t_2 = \frac{\tilde{U}\Theta_1^1}{\Theta_1^1}\left[\frac{\Theta_2^1 - \Theta_1^1[\tilde{U}\Theta_2^1/\tilde{U}\Theta_1^1]}{\Theta_2^2 - \Theta_1^2\Theta_2^1/\Theta_1^1}\right]. \qquad (10.80)$$

The first result that can be derived form these expressions is that if

$$\frac{\tilde{U}\Theta_2^1}{\Theta_2^1} = \frac{\tilde{U}\Theta_1^1}{\Theta_1^1}, \qquad (10.81)$$

then $t_2=0$ and t_1 is given by (10.75). This will occur if the either the externality is of the atmospheric kind so that $\tilde{U}_h$ is the same for all h or if the consumers are identical. As has been noted above, these are the situations for which a uniform tax can sustain the first-best so the present conclusion is simply an application of that result.

In other situations the values of the tax rates are determined by two factors: the degree of aggregate complementarity ($\Theta_1^2<0$) or substitutability ($\Theta_1^2>0$) and how those individuals that cause a greater amount of externality at the margin view the good. When the larger offenders view the goods as complements and the goods are aggregate complements then $t_2<0$ and t_1 is less than the value determined by the Diamond formula. Moving to aggregate substitutability makes t_1 greater than the Diamond value whilst the signs are all reversed when larger offenders view the goods as substitutes.

6.3 Summary

These results conclude the analysis of the determination of tax rates. Although the economies have been restricted in comparison to some of those in previous sections, they have illustrated some of the most important determinants of the tax rates. In particular, it has been shown that uniform taxation cannot sustain the first-best except in restricted circumstances and that optimality will often require the use of taxes on related goods. However, even when taxes on related goods are included the first-best will generally not be achievable. Indirect taxes can also be motivated in situations where direct taxes cannot be employed, such as when emissions cannot be monitored directly but the level of production that generates them can be. Finally, the effect of the related goods depends on their substitutability or complementarity to the externality producing good and upon how the larger contributors to the externality view the goods.

7 TRADABLE LICENSES

The motivation underlying the use of corrective pricing is that the unregulated market will produce incorrect quantities of externalities but, by altering the relative cost of generating an externality, taxation can lead to the optimal quantity of an externality. When phrased in this way, it may then actually appear simpler to limit directly the quantity of externalities rather than to attempt to influence them via the price system. An obvious way to do this, first suggested by Dales (1968), is to introduce licences that permit the generation of an externality and to allow agents to produce externalities only to the extent of the licences they hold. Allowing the licences to be traded should lead to them being held by the agents who value them most highly resulting in efficient generation of externalities. Set against these observations has to be the fact that the markets on which permits are traded may be thin so that the competitive outcome will not be achieved.

Administratively, the use of licences has much to recommend it. The calculation of tax rates requires considerable information to correctly forecast their relationship to externalities generated. In addition, changes in other prices will affect the optimal tax rates and in a dynamic setting the taxes will need continuous adjustment. These problems are avoided entirely by licences. In a spatial economy, the control of the spatial distribution of externalities will only be achieved through taxation if the tax rates are spatially differentiated which raises the information necessary for their design. In contrast, licences can restrict the right to emit externalities to a given area and control the spatial allocation directly. Despite these points, when the properties of licences and taxes are considered in detail, the choice between the two is not as clear-cut as these administrative advantages may suggest.

7.1 Certain costs and benefits

The basis of the argument in favour of licences, which is given in more detail in Parish (1972), is that a market in pollution quotas would see them purchased by those who value them most highly and that such purchasers would give the best return to society for the given level of pollution. The quantity of licences would determine the level of an externality that would be generated, which it is presumed would be set at the optimal level, whilst the bidding for them would see this quantity allocated efficiently between alternative sources. The tradable licence system therefore attains an efficient outcome.

When all costs and benefits are known with certainty by both the government and individual agents, tradable permits and taxation are equivalent in their effects to a redistribution of income. This result is demonstrated for a very rich spatial economy in Montgomery (1972), for an exchange economy in Bergstrom (1976) and for a competitive market with entry and exit by Pezzey (1992). The distribution of income resulting from licences is dependent upon the method of distribution of licences. If each externality generating agent is sold a quantity of licences equal to their optimal quantity at the market clearing price then no further trading will take place and the distribution of income will be identical to that with taxation. Alternatively, the licences may be distributed free, possibly in proportion to agents' existing level of generation of externality, which will lead to a redistribution of income from the government to the externality generators relative to the tax solution. Other than these income differences, the choice between the two systems under certainty will primarily depend on administrative convenience.

7.2 Prices versus quantities

When costs and benefits are uncertain, the equivalence argument does not apply. To see how this can arise, assume that the level of externality generation can be reduced at some cost but that this cost is uncertain. If a quantity constraint is chosen based on expected costs, this will lead to the level of externalities being too high relative to the optimum when a low value of cost is realised. Conversely, if a tax, or charge, is introduced this will result in excessive reduction when the cost of reduction is revealed to be low. The consequences of this observation were first formalised by Weitzman (1974) who derived a condition determining which of quantity control or pricing would be preferable.

Consider the regulation of a single agent producing an externality and let ρ denote a reduction in the level of the externality from some initial baseline. The emission of this externality can be controlled either by announcing a Pigouvian tax of t per unit of externality or by directly announcing the reduction that must be achieved. Although the assumption of a single agent prevents any trading in the licences, the argument can be extended to many agents with the licences traded between then. The cost of reducing the externality is given by $C(\rho,\theta)$ where θ is a random variable whose distribution is known to the regulator but whose realisation is not observed at the time the policy must be announced. The benefits are represented by $B(\rho,\eta)$ where η is also random with the distribution known but the realisation not observed until after the policy is announced. It is assumed that $\mathscr{E}[\theta]=\mathscr{E}[\eta]=0$ and $\mathscr{E}[\theta\eta]=0$.

When the regulation policy takes the form of an announcement of the reduction in externality that must be achieved, the optimal reduction, $\hat{\rho}$, is defined by

$$\hat{\rho}=\operatorname{argmax}_{\{\rho\}} \mathscr{E}[B(\rho,\eta)-C(\rho,\theta)], \qquad (10.82)$$

so that it satisfies

$$\mathscr{E}[B_1(\hat{\rho},\eta)]=\mathscr{E}[C_1(\hat{\rho},\theta)]. \qquad (10.83)$$

When a charge per unit of externality is employed, a maximising agent will reduce the externality up to the point where the charge is equal to the marginal cost of reductions *after* the realisation of the random variable θ. This gives the equality

$$t = C_1(\rho, \theta). \tag{10.84}$$

When $C_{11} \neq 0$, (10.84) can be solved to write

$$\rho = h(t, \theta). \tag{10.85}$$

The optimal value of t, denoted $\tilde{t}$, is then defined by

$$\tilde{t} = \text{argmax}_{\{t\}} \, \mathscr{E}\big[B(h(t, \theta), \eta) - C(h(t, \theta), \theta)\big], \tag{10.86}$$

so that

$$\mathscr{E}\big[B_1(h(\tilde{t}, \theta), \eta)h_1(\tilde{t}, \theta)\big] = \mathscr{E}\big[C_1(h(\tilde{t}, \theta), \theta)h_1(\tilde{t}, \theta)\big]. \tag{10.87}$$

Using (10.84) in (10.87) gives

$$\tilde{t} = \frac{\mathscr{E}\big[B_1(h(\tilde{t}, \theta), \eta)h_1(\tilde{t}, \theta)\big]}{\mathscr{E}[h_1(\tilde{t}, \theta)]}, \tag{10.88}$$

and a level of externality reduction $\tilde{\rho} = h(\tilde{t}, \theta)$. This level of externality reduction is known only after θ is realised.

To permit a comparison of the two methods of regulation, the costs and benefits are approximated around $\hat{\rho}$ by the quadratic expansions

$$C(\rho, \theta) = C^1 + [C^2 + \theta][\rho - \hat{\rho}] + \frac{C^{3^2}}{2}[\rho - \hat{\rho}]^2, \tag{10.89}$$

and

$$B(\rho, \eta) = B^1 + [B^2 + \eta][\rho - \hat{\rho}] + \frac{B^{3^2}}{2}[\rho - \hat{\rho}]^2. \tag{10.90}$$

From (10.89), differentiation gives $C_1(\rho, \theta) = [C^2 + \theta] + C^3[\rho - \hat{\rho}]$ and from (10.90) $B_1(\rho, \eta) = [B^2 + \eta] + B^3[\rho - \hat{\rho}]$. The equality in (10.83) then implies that $C^2 = B^2$. Solving (10.84) using (10.89) gives the reaction of the agent as

$$\rho = h(t, \theta) = \hat{\rho} + \frac{t - C^2 - \theta}{C^3}, \tag{10.91}$$

hence

$$h_1(t, \theta) = \frac{1}{C^3}. \tag{10.92}$$

Substituting (10.92) into (10.88), cancelling the terms in C^3 and taking the expectation of $B_1(\rho, \eta)$ gives

$$\tilde{t} = B^2 - \frac{B^3}{C^3} C^2 + \frac{B^3}{C^3} t. \tag{10.93}$$

From the equality of B^2 and C^2, it follows that $\tilde{i} = C^2$. Using this result in (10.91) yields

$$\tilde{\rho} = \hat{\rho} - \frac{\theta}{C^3}. \tag{10.94}$$

To determine which of fee and quantity regulation is superior, define the additional gain from using taxation relative to quantity control by

$$\Gamma = \mathcal{E}\left[[B(\tilde{\rho}, \eta) - C(\tilde{\rho}, \theta)] - [B(\hat{\rho}, \eta) - C(\hat{\rho}, \theta)]\right]. \tag{10.95}$$

Substituting into (10.94) using the derived terms

$$\Gamma = \frac{\sigma^2[B^3 + C^3]}{2C^{3^2}}, \tag{10.96}$$

where $\sigma^2 = \mathcal{E}[\theta^2]$. The result in (10.96) is easily interpreted. From the approximations in (10.89) and (10.90) it can be seen that a natural assumption would be $B^3 < 0 < C^3$. Therefore taxation will be preferable if the gradient of the marginal benefit function is less (in absolute value) than that of marginal cost. When the opposite holds, quantity restrictions are preferred.

This analysis has been extended to a number of other regulatory schemes by Laffont (1977), Ireland (1977), Yohe (1978), Dasgupta, Hammond and Maskin (1980) and Chen (1990) (not all of which are directly applicable to the control of externalities). However, all these analyses are restricted by the employment of quadratic approximations. Therefore, beyond the observation that charges and quantities are not equivalent under uncertainty, no general principles have been derived from this line of analysis.

7.3 Non-linear pricing

The differing effects of fees and licences suggests that, rather than relying on either one alone, it would be best to combine the instruments. Roberts and Spence (1976) prove that such a combined system reduces expected social costs below the level achievable by either fees or licences alone. This, though, does not exhaust the possibilities.

Spence (1977) observes that control by licences can be interpreted as a non-linear pricing system in which the price of the right to emit an externality is zero (or the cost of the licence) until the quantity permitted by the licence is reached. For any quantity above this level, the price becomes infinite. In contrast, fees represent a linear price system for the externalities. It follows from these observations that if the set of permissible pricing systems is extended to the set of continuous functions, both fees and licences, or any combination of the two, will be dominated by a suitably chosen non-linear pricing system from this set. In such a system, the price for emitting externalities is dependent upon the quantity emitted. These results show that the choice between price and quantity is therefore irrelevant and all that really matters is the selection of the optimal non-linear pricing system. Although the optimal non-linear price system can be characterised using methods similar to those of chapter 5, its value is limited by the considerable administrative difficulties involved with the implementation of such a system.

8 INTERNALISATION

A further method of externality control, as first discussed by Davis and Whinston (1962), is to encourage the internalisation of the externality so that private and social costs become the same. The essence of the internalisation is that if firm A causes a negative externality only upon firm B, then the firm formed by merging both A and B will take account of the externality when choosing its optimal behaviour. Hence, no inefficiency will arise. Such arguments have also been proposed as providing part of the rationale concerning the existence of the firm.

Internalisation though is not without its difficulties. To highlight the first of these, consider an industry in which the productive activity of each firm in the industry causes an externality for the other firms in the industry. In this situation the internalisation argument would suggest that the firms become a single monopolist. If this were to occur, welfare loss would then arise due to the monopolistic behaviour and this may actually be greater than the initial loss due to the externality. Although this is obviously an extreme example, the internalisation argument always implies the construction of larger economic agents and a consequent increase in market power. The welfare loss due to market power then has to be offset against the gain from eliminating the effect of the externality.

The second difficulty is that the economic agents involved may simply not wish to be amalgamated into a single unit. This objection is particularly true when applied to consumption externalities since if a household generates an externality for their neighbour it is not clear that they would wish to form a single household unit, particularly if the externality is a negative one.

In summary, internalisation will eliminate the consequences of an externality in a very direct manner by ensuring that private and social costs are equated. However it is unlikely to be a practical solution when many distinct economic agents contribute separately to the total externality and it has the disadvantage of leading to increased market power.

9 CONCLUSIONS

Externalities are a prevalent feature of economic life and their existence can lead to inefficiency in an unregulated competitive economy. Although the Coase theorem suggests that such inefficiencies will be eliminated by private trading in competitive markets, a number of objections can be raised to this conclusion. Amongst these are the lack of well-defined property rights, the thinness of markets and the incomplete information of market participants. Each of these impediments to efficient trading undermines the practical value of the Coase theorem.

The obvious policy response to the externality problem is the introduction of a system of corrective Pigouvian taxes with the tax rates being proportional to the marginal damage inflicted by externality generation. When sufficient differentiation of these taxes is possible between different agents, the first best outcome can be sustained but such a system is not practical due to its informational requirements. Restricting the taxes to be uniform across agents allows the first-best to be achieved in some special cases but, generally, leads to a second-best outcome. An alternative system of control is to employ marketable licences. These have administrative advantages over taxes and lead to an identical outcome in conditions of certainty. With uncertainty, licences and taxes have different effects and combining the two can lead to a superior outcome.

11

IMPERFECT COMPETITION

1 INTRODUCTION

In the previous chapters, the assumption of competitive behaviour has been maintained throughout. It is often best to view this as a useful restriction for developing initial ideas and eliminating unnecessary complication. As a representation of reality it is clearly flawed, an observation easily supported by casual empiricism. This chapter relaxes the competitive assumption and reviews some of the major results that have been derived within the framework of imperfect competition.

The first point to note is that there are numerous forms of imperfect competition which vary with respect to the nature of products, the strategic variables of the firms, the objectives of the firms and the possibility of entry. Products may be homogeneous or differentiated and the strategic variables of the firms can either be prices or quantities with, possibly, additional instruments such as investment or advertising. The firms' objectives may be individual profit maximisation or, alternatively, joint profit maximisation. Entry may be impossible, so that an industry is composed of a fixed number of firms, it may be unhindered or incumbent firms may be following a policy of entry deterrence. To avoid some of this complexity, this chapter will focus primarily upon economies with quantity setting oligopoly and homogeneous products although at some points conjectures are introduced to permit flexibility. This form of oligopoly has the advantage of being equivalent to monopoly when the industry has a single firm and, under most circumstances, to competition as the number of firms increases without limit. This makes the economy both straightforward and flexible.

A second point of some relevance is that tax incidence is more complex with imperfect competition. Under the competitive assumption any taxes are simply passed forward by the firms since price is always set at marginal cost. In contrast, prices on imperfectly competitive markets are set at a level above marginal cost and an increase in cost due to taxation need not be reflected in an identical increase in price. To determine the actual change it is necessary to work through the comparative statics of the industry in question. In addition to the price effects, imperfectly competitive firms may also earn non-zero profits and the effect of taxation on these must also be determined.

The initial sections of this chapter focus on issues related to the construction and analysis of a general equilibrium economy with imperfect competition. After introducing the economy that forms the basis of the chapter, it is shown why the equilibrium is not Pareto optimal and measures of the welfare loss due to imperfect competition are described. This is followed by an analysis of commodity tax incidence and optimal tax rules. The chapter is completed by a reconsideration of the necessity for production efficiency.

2 IMPERFECT COMPETITION AND GENERAL EQULIBRIUM

The first formal general equilibrium economy with imperfect competition can be attributed to Negishi (1961). Also of significance are Arrow and Hahn (1971), Gabszewicz and Vial (1972), Roberts and Sonnenschein (1977), Cornwall (1977) and the survey by Hart (1985). Unlike the Arrow–Debreu formulation of the competitive economy there is not a single, generally accepted framework but a number of alternative specifications. The economies are differentiated by the assumptions made about the form of demand function known by the firms and on the relation of demand to profit.

2.1 Objective and subjective demand

The first distinction to note is that between economies that employ *objective* demands and those using *subjective* demands. This distinction arises from the information that the firms comprising an imperfectly competitive industry must possess in order to know their profit function. In a competitive economy, a firm need only observe the set of market prices to determine its profit-maximising strategy. In contrast an imperfectly competitive firm requires the knowledge of the demand function for its product. Naturally this is a far greater informational requirement than just the knowledge of prices and, when literally interpreted, implies that the firms need to be able to solve the economy to generate the excess demands.

Faced with this informational problem, Negishi (1961) assumed that the firms actually knew only a linear approximation to their true demand functions, with the restriction that the linear approximation was equal to the true demand at equilibrium prices. The latter condition ensures that the firms generate the profit levels that they were expecting. Such demands have been labelled subjective since they exist only as beliefs held by firms. This approach has been extended by

Gary-Bobo (1989) to consider firms that perceive knowledge of a kth order Taylor expansion of their true demand. When $k \geq 1$ the equilibria coincide with the equilibrium arising from the true demands.

In an economy with objective demand, such as Gabszewicz and Vial (1972), it is assumed that the firms actually know their demand functions. Despite the informational burden this imposes, it does overcome the problems of the subjective approach in that it does not require specification of how the firms form the subjective demands or of how they may seek to revise them. In the analysis of this chapter only the objective approach is followed. This can be supported on the grounds of simplicity and the fact that since subjective demands are typically chosen equal to objective demands at equilibrium, the equilibrium of the economy should not be affected by the choice.

The assumptions concerning the distribution of profits and their effect upon demand is another area in which alternative economies differ. If returned to consumers as dividends, whenever income effects are non-zero a firm's profits must appear as an argument of its demand function. This causes some difficulties for the specification of the firm's maximisation problem since the quantity to be maximised (profit) appears as an argument in the objective function. When this occurs, standard results on maximisation are not applicable.

There have been three responses to this. The first is to assume the structure of the economy is such that there are no income effects. This approach is exemplified by the work of Hart (1982) in which the economy is divided into separate sectors and the firms distribute profit generated in one sector to consumers who purchase in a different sector. In this way, although aggregate demand depends on profit, the demand for each firm is independent of its own profit level. However, assumptions such as this have the disadvantage of being highly artificial. The second response is more direct and simply involves assuming that all profits are taxed at a rate of 100 per cent so that profit income accrues to the government alone. This assumption has the disadvantage of eliminating the motive for the choice of profit-maximising strategy for the firms. The final approach is to meet the problem directly and to extend the analysis to suit. This has the drawback of leading to greater complication in the results. The approach taken below will be to adopt a combination of the latter two possibilities, with the choice made to suit the purpose.

To complete this discussion of the choice of structure, it should be noted that intermediate goods are almost never included in general equilibrium economies with imperfect competition. This exclusion is due to the difficulty of formulating the derived demand for such goods when a number of firms have market power. For a discussion of this point, see Hart (1985). Although they are similarly excluded from most of the discussion below, they do occur at two points: in the discussion of the extent of welfare loss due to imperfect competition and in the treatment of production efficiency.

2.2 Price normalisations

Prior to setting out the details of the economy, it is necessary to describe the method of price normalisation that is to be employed. For competitive general equilibrium economies, the permissible price normalisations are well known and have been described in chapter 2: the price vector may be transformed in any way provided the ratios of prices remain unaffected. The same claim cannot be made for economies with imperfect competition and the general class of permissible normalisation rules is more restricted than for the competitive economy.

Since the work of Gabszewicz and Vial (1972) it has been recognised that normalisation rules that would not affect a competitive equilibrium will have real effects upon equilibrium with imperfect competition as the following example demonstrates. Consider an economy with one single-product monopolist producing at zero cost and whose profit-maximising output is finite. Now imagine a representation of this economy which, for analytical simplicity, uses a normalisation rule that selects the monopolist's good as the numeraire. The monopolist's profit-maximising output in the representation of the economy then becomes unbounded and so the normalisation rule has altered the real equilibrium. Since this normalisation rule is known not to affect competitive equilibria, this example demonstrates that the class of normalisation rules that do not affect equilibrium is smaller for imperfect competition than for the competitive model. The actual rules employed by Gabszewicz and Vial are essentially arbitrary and were no doubt used for computational convenience. The same general comment applies to Dierker and Grodal (1986). In contrast, both Negishi (1961) and Cornwall (1977) restrict prices to the unit simplex in order to exploit the resulting compactness properties of this set. Cornwall notes that this choice will affect the equilibrium except in the special case of the Negishi model with linear subjective demand. Roberts (1980d) employs leisure as the numeraire and notes that the equilibrium is generally not numeraire free. It is not clear whether the market for the numeraire is competitive or not. Neither Guesnerie and Laffont (1978) nor Roberts and Sonnenschein (1977) use or discuss a price normalisation. Finally, each economy in the survey paper of Hart (1985) employs a different method of price normalisation.

As the variety of price normalisations noted above illustrates, there is no common approach but there is general agreement that some price normalisations will affect the real equilibrium. In Cripps and Myles (1989), it is shown that the equilibrium is invariant to any normalisation rule that is defined as a function of competitive goods prices but is independent of the prices of goods traded on imperfectly competitive markets. For the economies described below, a simple version of this rule is adopted: labour is assumed to be traded on a competitive market and the wage rate is taken as numeraire.

2.3 The economy

The general equilibrium economy with imperfect competition that will form the basis for the analysis of commodity taxation and production efficiency is now introduced. The economy is based upon that used for the analysis of commodity taxation by Myles (1989a). It will be assumed that there is a fixed number of firms in each industry but the economy can easily be extended to allow for entry.

Consider an economy with $n+1$ goods, indexed $i=0,1,\ldots,n$, where good 0 is chosen to be labour. It is assumed that the labour market is competitive and that consumers' endowments are of labour alone. The n goods are partitioned into two subsets. The first subset consists of goods $i=1,\ldots,K$ and these are assumed to be produced by competitive industries, each employing a constant returns to scale technology that has labour as the only input. The assumptions of constant returns and a single input imply that for each good there is a constant c^i that describes the labour input per unit of output. With a wage rate p_0, the competitive assumption implies marginal cost pricing so that

$$p_i = c^i p_0, \ i=1,\ldots,K. \tag{11.1}$$

Since profits are zero under constant returns to scale, equation (11.1) is a complete description of the competitive sector.

The remaining $n-K$ goods are produced by imperfectly competitive industries. In the industry producing good i, there are m_i firms, indexed $j=1,\ldots,m_i$. The demand function for good i is denoted by

$$X_i = X_i(p_0,\ldots,p_n,\pi), \tag{11.2}$$

where the aggregate level of profit, π, is equal to the sum of profits of all firms

$$\pi = \sum_{i=K+1}^{n} \sum_{j=1}^{m_i} \pi_i^j. \tag{11.3}$$

The demand function in (11.2) is taken to be the true demand for the economy so it is one of objective demand. Assuming that (11.2) is strictly monotonic in p_i, it can be solved to give the inverse demand function for good i

$$p_i = \phi_i(p_0,\ldots,p_{i-1},X_i,p_{i+1},\ldots,p_n,\pi). \tag{11.4}$$

To analyse the firms' decisions, it is assumed that quantities are the strategic variable. Hence each firm in industry i chooses its output level to maximise profits. Denoting a typical firm by j, the firm chooses x_i^j to maximise

$$\pi_i^j = \phi_i(p_0,\ldots,p_{i-1},X_i,p_{i+1},\ldots,p_n,\pi)x_i^j - C_i^j(x_i^j), \tag{11.5}$$

where $C_i^j(x_i^j)$ is the cost function of the firm. The Cournot assumption is adopted so that when choosing x_i^j firm j takes as fixed the outputs, $x_i^{j'},j'$ $=1,\ldots,m_i,j'\neq j$, of all other firms in its industry. In addition, the Cournot assumption is extended to the other arguments of (11.4) so the firm also takes as given the prices on all other markets and the profit levels of all firms other than itself.

Totally differentiating (11.5) under these assumptions gives

$$d\pi_i^j \left[1 - x_i^j \frac{\partial \phi_i}{\partial \pi} \right] = dx_i^j \left[p_i + x_i^j \frac{\partial \phi_i}{\partial X_i} - \frac{\partial C_i^j}{\partial x_i^j} \right]. \tag{11.6}$$

Assuming that the income effect in demand is sufficiently weak that the left-hand side satisfies

$$\left[1 - x_i^j \frac{\partial \phi_i}{\partial \pi} \right] > 0, \tag{11.7}$$

then the first-order condition that the firms decision must satisfy is given by

$$p_i + x_i^j \frac{\partial \phi_i}{\partial X_i} - \frac{\partial C_i^j}{\partial x_i^j} = 0. \tag{11.8}$$

In addition to satisfying this condition, at an equilibrium any choice for the firm must also have the property that it is consistent with the assumptions made on the profit levels and outputs of other firms. That is, the chosen level of output must also satisfy the profit identity

$$\pi_i^j - \phi_i(p_0, \ldots, p_{i-1}, X_i, p_{i+1}, \ldots, p_n, \pi)x_i^j - C_i^j(x_i^j) = 0. \tag{11.9}$$

Simultaneously solving (11.8) and (11.9) for the m_i firms comprising industry i, the output and profit of firm j can be expressed in terms of the prices charged on other markets and the profits levels of firms in other industries. This gives the following two equations:

$$\pi_i^j = \gamma_i^j \left(p_0, \ldots, p_{i-1}, p_{i+1}, \ldots, p_n, \sum_{\substack{i' = K+1 \\ i' \neq i}}^{n} \sum_{j'=1}^{m_{i'}} \pi_{i'}^{j'} \right), \tag{11.10}$$

$$x_i^j = \sigma_i^j \left(p_0, \ldots, p_{i-1}, p_{i+1}, \ldots, p_n, \sum_{\substack{i' = K+1 \\ i' \neq i}}^{n} \sum_{j'=1}^{m_{i'}} \pi_{i'}^{j'} \right). \tag{11.11}$$

Equation (11.11) can now be used to replace aggregate output, X_i, in (11.4) by the sum of individual firms' outputs and (11.10) to substitute for the profits levels of firms in industry i. This determines an equilibrium price on market i as

$$p_i = \Phi_i \left(p_0, \ldots, p_{i-1}, p_{i+1}, \ldots, p_n, \sum_{\substack{i' = K+1 \\ i' \neq i}}^{n} \sum_{j'=1}^{m_{i'}} \pi_{i'}^{j'} \right). \tag{11.12}$$

Using equations (11.10) and (11.12), a general equilibrium can now be defined formally.

Imperfectly Competitive Equilibrium

An imperfectly competitive equilibrium is an array $[\{p_i\},\{\pi_i^j\}]$ such that

(i) $p_i = c^i p_0$, $i = 1, \ldots, K$,

(ii) $p_i = \Phi_i \left(p_0, \ldots, p_{i-1}, p_{i+1}, \ldots, p_n, \sum_{\substack{i'=K+1 \\ i' \neq i}}^{n} \sum_{j'=1}^{m_{i'}} \pi_{i'}^{j'} \right)$, $i = K+1, \ldots, n$

and

(iii) $\pi_i^j = \gamma_i^j \left(p_0, \ldots, p_{i-1}, p_{i+1}, \ldots, p_n, \sum_{\substack{i'=K+1 \\ i' \neq i}}^{n} \sum_{j'=1}^{m_{i'}} \pi_{i'}^{j'} \right)$, $i = K+1, \ldots, n$, $j = 1, \ldots, m_i$.

This definition of the equilibrium incorporates both the profit maximisation of the firms and the existence of positive levels of profit. It should be noted that the economy takes as given the demand functions of the households, rather than using their preference relation, and restricts demand to depend only upon total profits. It is therefore being implicitly assumed in the above statement that there is some array of shareholdings that determine the allocation of profits to households and that the households are maximising utility given their income levels and consumption sets. Since the emphasis here is upon the consequences of the non-competitive behaviour of the firms, it does not seem necessary to provide the details of the consumption sector since these remain as for the competitive economy.

It is considerably more problematic to prove the existence of an equilibrium for the imperfectly competitive economy than for the competitive case. The first difficulty arises from the maximisation defined in (11.5). If this is to have a unique solution that is continuous in the variables parametric to the individual firm, then the profit function of the firm must be strictly concave as a function of its own output. Unfortunately, strict concavity is a strong requirement since it imposes severe restrictions upon the demand function facing the firm. As shown by Roberts and Sonnenschein (1977) it is possible to construct economies in which the concavity fails. Moving from the single firm to the economy, the equilibrium requires that the output and profit functions given in the definition should all be satisfied simultaneously. Although similar in nature to simultaneously solving the excess demand functions for a competitive economy, there is less structure in the imperfectly competitive economy and stronger assumptions are necessary to ensure the existence of a solution. Despite these difficulties, given that it is assumed an equilibrium exists, the characterisation of equilibrium above is straightforward and can be employed in further analysis.

3 IMPERFECT COMPETITION AND WELFARE

Imperfect competition is one of the standard examples of market failure which lead to the non-achievement of Pareto optimality. It is on this basis that economic policy is usually suggested as necessary in the presence of imperfect competition in order to reduce inefficiency.

3.1 Failure of Pareto optimality

To demonstrate that imperfect competition does not generate a Pareto optimum, it is necessary to provide a suitable characterisation of Pareto optimality. There are several ways in which this can be done. Firstly, by consideration of the competitive equilibrium it can be appreciated that competitive firms price at marginal cost and that this is one of the conditions for Pareto optimality. Contrasting this to the pricing policy implicit in (11.8), it can be seen that whenever $\dfrac{\partial \phi_i}{\partial X_i}$ is non-zero, price will not be equal to marginal cost in the imperfectly competitive industry. Further investigation of the relation of prices to costs, or the mark-up over costs, with imperfect competition can be found in Cowling and Waterson (1976).

A second method of comparison is to return to the economy summarised in (9.1) and (9.2) but without the inclusion of the public good. Repeating the analysis given there, the conclusion that follows is that at a Pareto optimum the ratio of shadow prices for any pair of goods, given by the λs, should be equal to the ratio of rates of transformation. In addition, at a competitive equilibrium the ratio of shadow prices is equal to the ratio of market prices

$$\frac{p_i}{p_k} = \frac{\lambda_i}{\lambda_k} = \frac{\dfrac{\partial F}{\partial X_i}}{\dfrac{\partial F}{\partial X_k}}. \tag{11.13}$$

For the economy with imperfect competition, assuming that there is a single firm in each imperfectly competitive industry in order to simplify the construction, the production possibilities are constrained by the relation that the sum of labour demand from the competitive and imperfectly competitive sectors satisfies

$$\sum_{i=1}^{K} a_i X_i + \sum_{i=K+1}^{n} \frac{C_i(x_i)}{p_0} - \omega_0 \leq 0, \tag{11.14}$$

where $C_i(x_i)$ is the cost function of the single firm in industry i and ω_0 is the initial endowment of labour. For two goods i and k produced by imperfectly competitive firms, it follows from (11.14) that

$$\frac{\dfrac{\partial F}{\partial X_i}}{\dfrac{\partial F}{\partial X_k}} = \frac{\dfrac{\partial C_i}{\partial x_i}}{\dfrac{\partial C_k}{\partial x_k}}. \tag{11.15}$$

Hence using (11.8),

$$\frac{p_i + x_i \dfrac{\partial \phi_i}{\partial X_i}}{p_k + x_k \dfrac{\partial \phi_k}{\partial X_k}} = \frac{\dfrac{\partial F}{\partial X_i}}{\dfrac{\partial F}{\partial X_k}}. \tag{11.16}$$

Equation (11.16) captures the notion of market failure due to the lack of price-taking behaviour. The prices should be proportional to the marginal rates of transformation which capture the social cost of producing each good. However, the fact that the imperfectly competitive firms take the effect of their actions upon prices into account eliminates the direct proportionality.

3.2 Measures of welfare loss

It has been shown that the imperfectly competitive equilibrium is not Pareto optimal. Following from this, the equilibrium cannot maximise the value of any social welfare function that satisfies the Pareto criterion defined in chapter 2. This observation then makes it natural to consider what the degree of welfare loss may actually be, either for a real economy or for simulated examples. The assessment of monopoly welfare loss has been a subject of some dispute in which calculations have provided a range of estimates from the effectively insignificant to considerable percentages of potential welfare.

Contributions to the literature on monopoly welfare loss can be characterised according to three criteria: the welfare measure used, whether data or simulations are employed and whether the underlying model is of general or partial equilibrium. The choice between welfare measures can effectively be reduced either to calculating welfare loss triangles (in terms of National Income in Harberger (1954) and Gross Corporate Product in Cowling and Mueller (1978)) or to specifying an explicit welfare function and using this to evaluate welfare loss, a methodology whose case has been argued most forcefully by Bergson (1973). The earlier contributions were primarily concerned with the use of data to calculate losses for actual economies (Harberger for the USA, Cowling and Mueller for the UK and USA) but more recent work has concentrated on the use of simulations to calculate potential losses (Bergson 1973, Kay 1983). Dickson and Yu (1989) employ a mix of both data and simulation. With respect to the form of model, the vast majority of contributions have adopted a partial equilibrium framework. There are some exceptions to this, most notably Ireland (1978), Kay (1983) and Myles (1994).

The initial study of monopoly welfare loss is usually attributed to Harberger (1954) who considered the effect of monopolisation in United States manufacturing industry for the period 1924–28. From the data it is concluded that welfare loss is equal to 0.08 per cent of national income. Clearly if this figure is accurate, then monopoly welfare loss was insignificant in the United States. In contrast to Harberger, Cowling and Mueller (1978) include the cost of advertising in the measure of welfare loss on the interpretation that advertising is undertaken with the intention of maintaining a monopoly position. This naturally raises their estimates. Their analysis of welfare loss in the United States is based on data for 734 firms between 1963 and 1966 and concludes that welfare loss is between 4 per cent and 13 per cent of Gross Corporate Product. For the United Kingdom, Cowling and Mueller conclude that the top 103 firms in 1968 to 1969, accounting for a third of GNP, generated a welfare loss of between 3.9 per cent and 7.2 per cent of Gross Corporate Product. This contrasts with the loss of 0.2 per cent to 3 per cent using the Harberger measure for the same data set. These two sets of figures clearly provide conflicting evidence, as do the numerous other contributions that are surveyed in Sawyer (1981). The actual extent of welfare loss therefore remains an open question.

Turning now to measures of welfare loss in simulation models, these have generated far higher figures than analyses of data. Using a constant elasticity of substitution utility function, Bergson (1973) produces a range of estimates from 0.06 per cent of national income to 39.03 per cent The drawback to these figures is that they are calculated on the basis of hypothesised price–cost mark-ups rather than having the mark-up determined as the equilibrium of a specified economy. Kay (1983) employs a model with one consumption good that is produced by a monopolist using a single form of labour service. With the utility function

$$U = \frac{x_1^{1-\varepsilon}}{\varepsilon} - x_0, \tag{11.17}$$

a range of estimates were calculated ranging from 3 per cent of GNP when $\varepsilon = 0.1$ to 134 per cent when $\varepsilon = 0.9$. In addition, the loss was above 10 per cent for all values of $\varepsilon > 0.3$.

The analyses described above have considered monopoly power to be present only in the markets for final goods and have implicitly taken intermediate goods markets to be competitive. When the outputs of imperfectly competitive industries are used both as intermediate inputs and for final consumption, welfare loss can only be increased by the additional distortion of input prices. In a general equilibrium economy with intermediate goods, Myles (1994) finds welfare loss figures ranging from 11 per cent of the attainable utility level to 79 per cent.

It can be appreciated from this discussion that there have been a broad range of estimates of monopoly welfare loss. The figures generated by simulation studies are generally greater than those arising from data and indicate that, theoretically, monopoly may be very damaging in terms of reduced welfare.

4 COMMODITY TAXATION

The use of commodity taxation when there is imperfect competition has the additional motivation, beyond those of raising revenue and redistributing welfare present in the analysis of commodity taxation in chapter 4, of attempting to reduce the welfare loss due to non-competitive behaviour. There is consequently a counter-distortionary role for commodity taxation even in a single consumer model with a zero revenue requirement.

Compared to the competitive model there are several factors that complicate tax analysis when imperfect competition is introduced. Firstly, the analysis of tax incidence is more complex in the imperfectly competitive case. With competition, commodity taxes are simply passed forward by the firms since they always price at marginal cost. In contrast, prices on imperfectly competitive markets are set at a level above marginal cost and an increase in cost due to taxation need not be passed directly to consumers. The actual change in price can only be determined by working through the comparative statics of the industry in question. The analysis of taxation therefore begins with a consideration of tax incidence. Secondly, in addition to the price effects, imperfectly competitive firms may also earn non-zero profits and the effect of taxation upon these must also be determined. As with the incidence of taxes upon prices, the profit effects have to be calculated from the comparative statics of each industry.

With imperfect competition it is also necessary to note that *ad valorem* and specific taxation do not have identical effects. That is, for a given level of post-tax price, the two methods of taxation may lead to different levels of revenue. To reduce the level of complexity below, the major part of the analysis of this chapter will the conducted in terms of specific taxes. The interaction of specific and *ad valorem* taxes is considered in section 5.

After a review of tax incidence, two economies will be analysed. The first economy has a single consumer and three goods. This is employed to investigate the factors that determine the levels of taxation when the taxes are used solely to counter the distortions due to non-competitive behaviour. The second economy characterises optimal taxes using the imperfectly competitive economy introduced in section 2.3 and provides a non-competitive variant of the Diamond–Mirrlees optimal commodity tax rule.

4.1 Tax incidence

Tax incidence is concerned with the effect of taxation upon prices and profit levels. Although tax incidence was of considerable importance in the determination of the optimal tax rules of chapter 4, the structure of the competitive economy that was used to derive the Ramsey rule simplifies tax incidence to such an extent that a formal discussion of incidence was not required. In addition, in the more general economy of section 6 of chapter 4, the separation of producer and consumer sectors again obviates the need for an analysis of tax incidence. With imperfect competition, an analysis of tax incidence is essential.

To emphasise the points made above, it is worth looking again at the effects of commodity taxation in the competitive model. Retaining the assumption that labour is the only input implies, with the wage rate as the untaxed numeraire, that there is a set of fixed producer prices $p_0, \ldots, p_K$ in the competitive sector. It then follows immediately that

$$q_i = p_i + t_i, \ i = 1, \ldots, K, \tag{11.18}$$

and from this that

$$\frac{\partial q_i}{\partial t_i} = 1, \tag{11.19}$$

and

$$\frac{\partial q_i}{\partial t_k} = 0, \ i \neq k. \tag{11.20}$$

Equation (11.19) states that the commodity tax is forward shifted at the rate of 100 per cent, that is, the entire tax is shifted by the firm on to the consumer. Equation (11.20) illustrates that there is no interaction between the price of a good produced by a competitive industry and the tax on any other good. It is these results that give the competitive tax rules their precise structure.

To illustrate the important features of tax incidence with imperfect competition a simple, but flexible, example will now be considered. Consider a single industry and assume that this industry is composed of m_i firms, each with the same cost function and beliefs about the other firms' reactions. These assumptions ensure that there will be a symmetric equilibrium, with all firms producing the same output level. The inverse demand function facing the industry is denoted

$$q_i = \phi_i \left(\sum_{j=1}^{m_i} x_i^j, q_k \right), \tag{11.21}$$

where x_i^j is the output of firm j and q_k is some representative other price. The second price is introduced in order to allow consideration of the consequences of its variation. Note that the prices are represented by qs to denote that they are post-tax consumer prices. Each of the m_i firms aims to maximise

$$\pi_i^j = x_i^j \phi_i \left(x_i^j + \sum_{\substack{j'=1 \\ j' \neq j}}^{m_i} x_i^{j'}, q_k \right) - t_i x_i^j - C(x_i^j), \tag{11.22}$$

where $C(x_i^j)$ is the cost function that is the same for all firms in industry i and t_i is the specific tax levied on the output of the ith industry.

The flexibility in the example is introduced by assuming that each firm holds a *conjecture* about how the other firms will respond to changes in its output level. By suitable choice of the conjecture, it is possible for the model to generate all outcomes from competitive pricing to monopoly pricing. The conjecture, λ, can be defined formally as

$$\lambda = \frac{\partial \left(x_i^j + \sum_{\substack{j'=1 \\ j' \neq j}}^{m_i} x_i^{j'} \right)}{\partial x_i^j}. \tag{11.23}$$

As will be made clear after inspection of the first-order condition (11.24) below, if $\lambda = m_i$ monopoly pricing arises, $\lambda = 1$ represents Cournot behaviour and $\lambda = 0$ generates the Bertrand equilibrium with competitive marginal cost pricing. Employing the definition of the conjecture, the first-order condition for profit maximisation for firm j is

$$\frac{\partial \pi_i^j}{\partial x_i^j} \equiv q_i - t_i + x_i^j \lambda \frac{\partial \phi_i}{\partial X_i} - \frac{\partial C}{\partial x_i^j} = 0. \tag{11.24}$$

The first question concerning tax incidence is the calculation of the effect of changing t_i upon the equilibrium values of π_i^j, $j = 1, \ldots, m_i$, and q_i. These effects are derived by first noting that the symmetry assumption implies that $x_i^j = x_i$, all j and hence that

$$q_i = \phi_i \left(\sum_{j=1}^{m_i} x_i^j, q_k \right) = \phi_i(m_i x_i, q_k). \tag{11.25}$$

Totally differentiating the first-order condition (11.24) by varying all outputs and the tax rate gives

$$dx_i \left[m_i \frac{\partial \phi_i}{\partial X_i} + \lambda \frac{\partial \phi_i}{\partial X_i} + x_i m_i \lambda \frac{\partial^2 \phi_i}{\partial X_i^2} - \frac{\partial^2 C}{\partial x_i^2} \right] = dt_i. \tag{11.26}$$

From the inverse demand function

$$dq_i = m_i \frac{\partial \phi_i}{\partial X_i} dx_i. \tag{11.27}$$

Using (11.27) to eliminate dx_i from (11.26) determines the effect of the tax change upon the equilibrium price as

$$\frac{dq_i}{dt_i} = \frac{m_i \frac{\partial \phi_i}{\partial X_i}}{[m_i + \lambda] \frac{\partial \phi_i}{\partial X_i} + x_i m_i \lambda \frac{\partial^2 \phi_i}{\partial X_1^2}}. \tag{11.28}$$

where it has been assumed for simplicity that marginal cost is constant. The expression $\dfrac{dq_i}{dt_i}$ is termed the degree of *forward shifting* of the tax and, except when the equilibrium is in the sense of Bertrand with $\lambda = 0$, it can be seen from (11.28) that $\dfrac{dq_i}{dt_i}$ is not necessarily equal to 1.

It is standard practice to distinguish between *overshifting*, in which case the price rises by more than the increase in tax, and *undershifting*, for when it rises by less. This distinction will be seen to be important in the determination of relative tax rates. To proceed further, it is assumed that the equilibrium is stable in the sense of Seade (1980), for which a sufficient restriction is that the denominator of (11.28) is negative. Using the stability restriction, it follows from (11.28) that overshifting, which is equivalent to $\dfrac{dq_i}{dt_i} > 1$, occurs for non-zero λ when

$$m_i \frac{\partial \phi_i}{\partial X_i} < [m_i + \lambda] \frac{\partial \phi_i}{\partial X_i} + x_i m_i \lambda \frac{\partial^2 \phi_i}{\partial X_i^2}. \tag{11.29}$$

Since both the left- and right-hand sides of (11.29) are negative, it can be rearranged to give the equivalent condition for overshifting

$$\frac{\partial \phi_i}{\partial X_i} > - x_i m_i \frac{\partial^2 \phi_i}{\partial X_i^2}. \tag{11.30}$$

Condition (11.30) above can be viewed in two ways. Firstly, it represents a restriction on the convexity of the inverse demand function since, if overshifting is to occur, it is necessary that $\dfrac{\partial^2 \phi_i}{\partial X_i^2}$ is positive. Secondly, it can be phrased in terms of Seade's (1985) E by defining

$$E \equiv \frac{- X_i \dfrac{\partial^2 \phi_i}{\partial X_i^2}}{\dfrac{\partial \phi_i}{\partial X_i}}, \tag{11.31}$$

where E measures the elasticity of the slope of the inverse demand function. In terms of E, condition (11.30) states that overshifting occurs when $E > 1$, that taxes are shifted at a rate of 100 per cent when $E = 1$ and undershifted when $E < 1$.

Turning now to profits, the profit level of firm j can be written as a function of the tax rate

$$\pi_i^j(t_i) = x_i(t_i)[q_i(t_i) - t_i] - C(x_i(t_i)). \tag{11.32}$$

Differentiating profits with respect to t_i gives

$$\frac{d\pi_i^j}{dt_i} = x_i \left[\frac{\partial q_i}{\partial t_i} - 1 \right] + \frac{\partial x_i}{\partial t_i} \left[q_i - t_i - \frac{\partial C_i}{\partial x_i} \right]. \tag{11.33}$$

Now using (11.24), (11.26) and (11.28) provides the expression

$$\frac{d\pi_i^j}{dt_i} = \frac{-\left[2x_i \frac{\partial \phi_i}{\partial X_i} + x_i^2 m_i \lambda \frac{\partial^2 \phi_i}{\partial X_i^2}\right]}{[m_i + \lambda] \frac{\partial \phi_i}{\partial X_i} + x_i m_i \lambda \frac{\partial^2 \phi_i}{\partial X_i^2}}. \tag{11.34}$$

The result in (11.34) provides the interesting conclusion that the firm's profit level may actually increase as the tax rate increases, a result first shown by Seade (1986). The sufficient condition for this to occur can be found from (11.34) to be $E > 2$. This possibility arises due to the tax change moving the oligopolistic equilibrium closer to the monopoly outcome. Further results along these lines can be found in de Meza (1982), Dierickx, Matutes and Neven (1988), Myles (1987) and Stern (1987).

The tax incidence analysis above comprises what have been termed the *direct* effects of taxation, where direct refers to the fact that they relate to the effect of the tax levied on the industry under consideration. In addition to the direct effects there may also arise *indirect* or *induced* changes in prices and profits in imperfectly competitive industry i due to changes in the tax rates on industries other than i. From (11.20) and the fact that profits are zero for the competitive industries, these induced effects do not arise in the competitive model.

To evaluate the induced effects upon price, (11.24) can be differentiated with respect to q_k to give

$$\frac{dq_i}{dq_k} = \frac{\lambda \left[\frac{\partial \phi_i}{\partial q_k}\left[\frac{\partial \phi_i}{\partial X_i} + x_i m_i \frac{\partial^2 \phi_i}{\partial X_i^2}\right] - x_i m_i \frac{\partial \phi_i}{\partial X_i} \frac{\partial^2 \phi_i}{\partial X_i \partial q_k}\right]}{[m_i + \lambda]\frac{\partial \phi_i}{\partial X_i} + x_i m_i \lambda \frac{\partial^2 \phi_i}{\partial X_i^2}}. \tag{11.35}$$

Provided the inverse demand for good i is not independent of q_k, the induced price effect is almost always non-zero. Inspection of (11.35) shows that the change in q_i may be of either sign. That is, the induced effect may increase or decrease the price of good i.

To illustrate the importance of this factor assume that good k is produced by a competitive industry so that the inverse demand function can be written as

$$q_i = \phi_i \left(\sum_{j=1}^{m_i} x_i^j, p_k + t_k\right). \tag{11.36}$$

Hence $\dfrac{dq_i}{dq_k}$ calculated above is equal to $\dfrac{dq_i}{dt_k}$ so, in optimising over t_k, these induced effects must be taken into account. Similar reasoning also holds when industry k is imperfectly competitive but the additional, non-linear, relation of q_k to t_k must be included. To complete this analysis, it should also be noted that there will be an induced effect of changes in q_k upon the profit levels in industry i.

To summarise this section, it has been noted that with imperfect competition taxes may be undershifted or overshifted. Overshifting implies that the final price rises by more than any increase in tax, undershifting the converse. The rate of shifting is determined by the degree of concavity or convexity of the demand function facing the industry and the cost functions of the firms that compose that industry. Concavity of demand leads to undershifting and sufficient convexity to overshifting. When marginal cost is constant, the relevant factor is Seade's E, the elasticity of the gradient of the demand function. The dependence of the market price upon the demand function introduces a further factor. If a price of another good alters, due perhaps to a tax levied on it, then this will affect the demand function and hence the market price of the imperfectly competitive industry in question. These induced price changes are considered in detail in Myles (1987, 1989a). To the above effects must also be added the effects of taxation upon the profit levels of the firms which are not always as straightforward as may be expected.

4.2 Optimal taxes

It is now possible to move beyond the study of tax incidence to a consideration of the factors that determine optimal rates of commodity taxation in imperfectly competitive economies. The analysis will first focus on tax reform in a two-good and labour economy in order to highlight the importance of the tax incidence results. This will then be extended to a construction of optimal tax rules in the general equilibrium economy detailed at the start of this chapter.

4.2.1 An illustration

To begin the analysis of tax design, consider the following simple economy taken from Myles (1987) in which the tax analysis consists of characterising the welfare-improving tax reform starting from an initial position with no commodity taxation. The economy has a single consumer and a zero revenue requirement so the taxes are used merely to correct for the distortion introduced by the imperfect competition. There are two consumption goods, each produced using labour alone. Good 1 is produced with constant returns to scale by a competitive industry. It has post-tax price $q_1 = p_1 + t_1$. The second good is produced by an imperfectly competitive industry that faces inverse demand

$$q_2 = \phi_2 \left(\sum_{j=1}^{m_2} x_2^j, q_1 \right). \tag{11.37}$$

It is assumed that the preferences of society can be represented by an indirect utility function

$$V = V(p_0, q_1, q_2), \tag{11.38}$$

where p_0 is the price of labour. Profits are assumed to be taxed at a rate of 100 per cent and the revenue used to purchase labour.

Rather than repeat the tax incidence analysis, the direct and induced effects of taxation are understood to have been constructed as above. They are then denoted

$$h_1 \equiv \frac{dq_2}{dt_1},$$

(11.39)

and

$$h_2 \equiv \frac{dq_2}{dt_2}.$$

(11.40)

The expression of these effects at a general level has the advantage that it is unnecessary to specify the particular model of imperfect competition in order to derive results. A specific formulation is only needed when the results require evaluation.

The tax reform problem now involves finding a pair of tax changes dt_1, dt_2 that raise welfare whilst collecting zero revenue. If the initial position is taken to be one with zero commodity taxes, the problem can be phrased succinctly as finding dt_1, dt_2 from an initial position with $t_1 = t_2 = 0$ such that $dV > 0$, $dR = 0$, where tax revenue, R, is defined by

$$R = t_1 X_1 + t_2 X_2.$$

(11.41)

This framework ensures that one of the taxes will be negative, the other positive and the aim is to provide a simple characterisation of the determination of the relative rates. It should be noted that if both industries were competitive the solution would be $dt_1 = dt_2 = 0$ so that non-zero tax rates emerge due to the distortion caused by the imperfect competition.

From differentiating the indirect utility function, it follows that the effect of the tax change upon welfare is

$$dV = \frac{\partial V}{\partial q_1} \frac{\partial q_1}{\partial t_1} dt_1 + \frac{\partial V}{\partial q_2} \frac{\partial q_2}{\partial t_1} dt_1 + \frac{\partial V}{\partial q_2} \frac{\partial q_2}{\partial t_2} dt_2.$$

(11.42)

Since $q_1 = p_1 + t_1$, (11.19) implies $\dfrac{\partial q_1}{\partial t_1} = 1$. Using this fact and the definition of the tax incidence terms h_1 and h_2

$$dV = \left[\frac{\partial V}{\partial q_1} + \frac{\partial V}{\partial q_2} h_1 \right] dt_1 + \left[\frac{\partial V}{\partial q_2} h_2 \right] dt_2.$$

(11.43)

From the revenue constraint

$$dR = 0 = X_1 dt_1 + X_2 dt_2,$$

(11.44)

where the fact that $t_1 = t_2 = 0$ initially has been used. Solving (11.44) for dt_1

$$dt_1 = -\frac{X_2}{X_1} dt_2.$$

(11.45)

Substituting (11.45) into the welfare expression determines the welfare change as dependent upon dt_2 alone

$$dV = \left[\frac{\partial V}{\partial q_2} h_2 - \frac{X_2}{X_1} \frac{\partial V}{\partial q_1} - \frac{X_2}{X_1} \frac{\partial V}{\partial q_2} h_1 \right] dt_2. \tag{11.46}$$

Finally, using Roy's identity

$$dV = \left[-\alpha X_2 h_2 + \alpha X_2 + \frac{X_2}{X_1} \alpha X_2 h_1 \right] dt_2. \tag{11.47}$$

It then follows if

$$X_1 [1 - h_2] + X_2 h_1 < 0, \tag{11.48}$$

then $dt_2 < 0$. From (11.48), the output of the imperfectly competitive industry should be subsidised and the competitive industry taxed when h_2 is large, so that overshifting is occurring, and h_1 is negative. These are, of course, sufficient conditions. In general, the greater the degree of tax shifting the more likely is subsidisation. The explanation for this result is that if firms overshift taxes, they will also do the same for any subsidy. Hence a negative dt_2 will be reflected by an even greater reduction in price. If h_1 is also negative, the tax on the competitive industry secures a further reduction in the price of good 2.

The conclusion of this analysis is that the rate of tax shifting is important in the determination of relative rates of taxation. Although the economy is simplified by abstracting away from profit effects, it does demonstrate that with imperfect competition commodity taxation can be motivated on efficiency grounds alone.

4.2.2 Optimal taxes

The insights of the example are now employed to provide a characterisation of optimal commodity taxes when there is also a positive revenue requirement. This analysis is therefore a development of the commodity tax theory of chapter 4 to incorporate imperfect competition. The economy to be used is based on Myles (1989a) and involves introducing commodity taxes into the general equilibrium economy described at the start of this chapter. To simplify notation, only a single-consumer tax rule will be constructed. The extension to many consumers is straightforward.

Treating labour as an untaxed numeraire with a wage rate p_0, the post-tax price of good i from the competitive sector when the commodity tax is set at t_i is given by

$$q_i = c^i p_0 + t_i, \ i = 1, \ldots, K. \tag{11.49}$$

Profits remain zero for all firms in the competitive sector.

Introducing taxes into the definition of profit for the imperfectly competitive firms, each firm in industry i chooses its output level to maximise

$$\pi_i^j = [\phi_i(q_0, \ldots, q_{i-1}, X_i, q_{i+1}, \ldots, q_n, \pi) - t_i]x_i^j - C_i^j(x_i^j), \tag{11.50}$$

where inverse demand, $\phi_i(\cdot)$, is now dependent on post-tax prices. Simultaneously solving the first-order condition that results from maximising (11.50) and the profit identities for the m_i firms comprising industry i, the output and profit of firm j in industry i can be expressed by the following two equations:

$$\pi_i^j = \gamma_i^j \left(q_0, \ldots, q_{i-1}, t_i, q_{i+1}, \ldots, q_n, \sum_{\substack{i'=K \\ i' \neq i}}^{n} \sum_{j'=1}^{m_{i'}} \pi_{i'}^{j'} \right), \tag{11.51}$$

$$x_i^j = \sigma_i^j \left(q_0, \ldots, q_{i-1}, t_i, q_{i+1}, \ldots, q_n, \sum_{\substack{i'=K \\ i' \neq i}}^{n} \sum_{j'=1}^{m_{i'}} \pi_{i'}^{j'} \right). \tag{11.52}$$

It should be noted that the arguments of (11.51) and (11.52) are the prices and profits of other industries and the tax rate on industry i. Aggregating output and using the inverse demand function determines an equilibrium price on market i

$$q_i = f^i \left(q_0, \ldots, q_{i-1}, t_i, q_{i+1}, \ldots, q_n, \sum_{\substack{i'=K \\ i' \neq i}}^{n} \sum_{j'=1}^{m_{i'}} \pi_{i'}^{j'} \right). \tag{11.53}$$

The derivatives of f^i and γ_i^j are precisely the tax incidence terms calculated in the previous section for which it was assumed that all other variables are constant.

The general equilibrium of the economy with taxation is then the simultaneous solution to

$$q_i = c^i p_0 + t_i, \ i = 1, \ldots, K, \tag{11.54}$$

$$q_i = f^i \left(q_0, \ldots, q_{i-1}, t_i, q_{i+1}, \ldots, q_n, \sum_{\substack{i'=K \\ i' \neq i}}^{n} \sum_{j'=1}^{m_{i'}} \pi_{i'}^{j'} \right), \ i = K+1, \ldots, n \tag{11.55}$$

and

$$\pi_i^j = \gamma_i^j \left(q_0, \ldots, q_{i-1}, t_i, q_{i+1}, \ldots, q_n, \sum_{\substack{i'=K \\ i' \neq i}}^{n} \sum_{j'=1}^{m_{i'}} \pi_{i'}^{j'} \right), \ i = K+1, \ldots, n, j = 1, \ldots, m_i. \tag{11.56}$$

Solving equations (11.55) and (11.56) simultaneously for all imperfectly competitive goods' prices and firms' profits determines the equilibrium level of prices and profits in the imperfectly competitive industries as functions of the tax rates and the competitive prices

$$q_{K+1} = \Phi^{K+1}(q_0, \ldots, q_K, t_{K+1}, \ldots, t_n),$$
$$\vdots$$
$$q_n = \Phi^n(q_0, \ldots, q_K, t_{K+1}, \ldots, t_n),$$
$$\pi_{K+1}^1 = \Omega^{1, K+1}(q_0, \ldots, q_K, t_{K+1}, \ldots, t_n), \tag{11.57}$$
$$\vdots$$
$$\pi_n^{m_n} = \Omega^{m_n, n}(q_0, \ldots, q_K, t_{K+1}, \ldots, t_n).$$

These equations can be used to determine the effects of changes in the government control variables.

Before proceeding to a derivation of the optimal tax rules, it is helpful to understand the relation between equations (11.57) and (11.51)–(11.53). To do this it is necessary to realise that the derivatives of (11.57) capture the effect of the tax changes taking into account the general equilibrium adjustment of all other prices and profits whilst those of (11.51)–(11.53) capture only the partial equilibrium effects holding other prices and profits constant.

The choice of optimal commodity taxes are the solution to the maximisation

$$\max_{\{t_1,\dots,t_n\}} \mathcal{L} = V(q_0,\dots,q_n,\pi) + \lambda \left[\sum_{i=1}^{n} t_i X_i - R \right],\qquad(11.58)$$

subject to

$$q_i = p_i + t_i,\ i = 1,\dots,K,\qquad(11.59)$$

$$q_i = \Phi^i(q_0,\dots,q_K,t_{K+1},\dots,t_n),\ i = K+1,\dots,n,\qquad(11.60)$$

and

$$\pi_i^j = \Omega^{j,i}(q_0,\dots,q_K,t_{K+1},\dots,t_n),\ i = K+1,\dots,n,\ j = 1,\dots,m_i.\qquad(11.61)$$

From this system, differentiation with respect to the tax rate of a typical good, k, from the competitive sector provides the first-order condition

$$\frac{\partial V}{\partial q_k} + \sum_{s=K+1}^{n} \frac{\partial V}{\partial q_s}\Phi_k^s + \frac{\partial V}{\partial \pi}\sum_{s=K+1}^{n}\sum_{j=1}^{m_s}\Omega_k^{j,s} +$$

$$\lambda\left[X_k + \sum_{i=1}^{n} t_i\frac{\partial X_i}{\partial q_k} + \sum_{i=1}^{n}\sum_{s=K+1}^{n} t_i\frac{\partial X_i}{\partial q_s}\Phi_k^s + \sum_{i=1}^{n}\sum_{s=K+1}^{n}\sum_{j=1}^{m_s} t_i\frac{\partial X_i}{\partial \pi}\Omega_k^{j,s} \right] = 0.\quad(11.62)$$

In (11.62) the subscripts on Φ^s and $\Omega^{j,s}$ denote the argument with respect to which the function is differentiated.

This first-order condition is distinguished from its equivalent for the competitive model, (4.7), by the inclusion of the effects of the induced price and profit changes, given respectively by the terms Φ_k^s, and $\Omega_k^{j,s}$. Using Roy's identity and the Slutsky equation, (11.62) can be written

$$\sum_{i=1}^{n} t_i S_{ki} = -\theta X_k + \left[\frac{1}{\lambda}\right]\Gamma^k,\ k = 1,\dots,K,\qquad(11.63)$$

where

$$\theta = 1 - \frac{\alpha}{\lambda} - \sum_{i=1}^{n} t_i\frac{\partial X_i}{\partial \pi},\qquad(11.64)$$

and

$$\Gamma^k = \alpha \sum_{s=K+1}^{n} X_s\Phi_k^s - \alpha \sum_{s=K+1}^{n}\sum_{j=1}^{m_s}\Omega_k^{j,s} + \lambda \sum_{i=1}^{n}\sum_{s=K+1}^{n} t_i\frac{\partial X_i}{\partial q_s}\Phi_k^s +$$

$$\lambda \sum_{i=1}^{n} \sum_{s=K+1}^{n} \sum_{j=1}^{m_s} t_i \frac{\partial X_i}{\partial \pi} \Omega_k^{j,s}. \tag{11.65}$$

If the term $\left[\frac{1}{\lambda}\right] \Gamma^k$ were not included, (11.65) would be identical to the standard Ramsey rule so this additional term can be interpreted as the modification required to incorporate imperfect competition. As can be seen from its definition, Γ^k is determined by the induced price and profit effects which would not be present in a competitive model. Retaining the standard interpretation of the Ramsey rule given in chapter 4, an analysis of the constituents of Γ^k shows that the reduction in compensated demand for good k is smaller when a tax on this good increases the prices of imperfectly competitive goods ($\Phi_k^s > 0$), reduces profits ($\Omega_k^{j,s} < 0$) and the induced tax changes lower tax revenue.

Repeating the derivation for a typical good k from the imperfectly competitive sector gives the first-order condition for the choice of tax rate t_k

$$\frac{\partial V}{\partial q_k} \Phi_k^k + \sum_{\substack{s=K+1 \\ s \neq k}}^{n} \frac{\partial V}{\partial q_s} \Phi_k^s + \frac{\partial V}{\partial \pi} \sum_{s=K+1}^{n} \sum_{j=1}^{m_s} \Omega_k^{j,s}$$

$$+ \lambda \left[X_k + \sum_{i=1}^{n} \sum_{s=K+1}^{n} t_i \frac{\partial X_i}{\partial q_s} \Phi_k^s + \sum_{i=1}^{n} \sum_{s=K+1}^{n} \sum_{j=1}^{m_s} t_i \frac{\partial X_i}{\partial \pi} \Omega_k^{j,s} \right] = 0. \tag{11.66}$$

After employing Roy's identity and the Slutsky equation, (11.66) becomes

$$\sum_{i=1}^{n} t_i S_{ki} = -\theta^k X_k + \left[\frac{1}{\lambda}\right] \Gamma^k, \quad k = K+1, \dots, n, \tag{11.67}$$

where

$$\theta^k = \frac{1}{\Phi_k^k} - \frac{\alpha}{\lambda} - \sum_{i=1}^{n} t_i \frac{\partial X_i}{\partial \pi}, \tag{11.68}$$

and

$$\Gamma^k = \frac{1}{\Phi_k^k} \left[\alpha \sum_{\substack{s=K+1 \\ s \neq k}}^{n} X_s \Phi_k^s - \alpha \sum_{s=K+1}^{n} \sum_{j=1}^{m_s} \Omega_k^{j,s} + \lambda \sum_{\substack{i=1 \\ i \neq k}}^{n} \sum_{s=K+1}^{n} t_i \frac{\partial X_i}{\partial q_s} \Phi_k^s \right.$$

$$\left. + \lambda \sum_{i=1}^{n} \sum_{s=K+1}^{n} \sum_{j=1}^{m_s} t_i \frac{\partial X_i}{\partial \pi} \Omega_k^{j,s} \right]. \tag{11.69}$$

In (11.67) the term $\left[\frac{1}{\lambda}\right] \Gamma^k$ again represents a correction to the competitive Ramsey rule for the existence of the induced price and profit effects. The interaction of its constituent parts with the reduction in compensated demand can be broken down precisely as for (11.65). The distinction between (11.65) and (11.69) is that for the latter θ^k is dependent upon the good k under consideration due to the appearance of the tax-shifting term in (11.69). Since θ^k is inversely related to Φ_k^k, the greater the degree of overshifting the smaller will be the reduction in compensated demand. This result is the natural generalisation of that derived for the two-good example.

To summarise this discussion, for a good produced by a competitive industry the standard Ramsey tax rule is adjusted by the incorporation of an additional term that captures the induced effects of the tax on that good. For goods from imperfectly competitive industries, the tax rule incorporated the correction term for the induced effects and the reduction in compensated demand was inversely related to the degree of tax shifting. The tax incidence results in (11.28), (11.34) and (11.35) capture the fact that the direct and induced effects are dependent upon industrial conduct via the value of the conjecture, λ. Consequently the tax rules (11.63) and (11.67) show that industrial conduct is as important as tastes in determining relative rates of taxation.

5 *AD VALOREM* AND SPECIFIC TAXES

In the competitive model there is no distinction between the effects of specific taxes, which are an addition to the unit costs of production, and *ad valorem* taxes, which represent a proportional reduction in the received price. That is, for a given increase in consumer price, the two forms of taxation will raise an identical level of revenue. Although discussions of commodity taxation are generally phrased in terms of specific taxes, as was chapter 4, a similar analysis can be conducted for *ad valorem* taxes and, as shown by Hatta (1986), the form of the optimal tax rules are not affected by the choice. When imperfect competition is under consideration, the equivalence between the two forms of taxation no longer applies. This distinction has been emphasised by Kay and Keen (1983) and Delipalla and Keen (1992). Myles (1995a) shows the potential gains that can be obtained by combining the two forms of taxation. The purpose of this section is to review these results.

5.1 Tax incidence

Returning to the economy used to derive the tax incidence results above and denoting the specific and *ad valorem* taxes levied on industry i by t_i^s and t_i^v respectively, the profit of firm j is

$$\pi_i^j = x_i^j q_i [1 - t_i^v] - t_i^s x_i^j - C(x_i^j).$$ (11.70)

The first-order condition for profit maximisation at a symmetric equilibrium is then

$$[1 - t_i^v]\left[q_i + \gamma \frac{\partial \phi_i}{\partial X_i} X_i \right] - t_i^s = \frac{\partial C}{\partial x_i^j},$$ (11.71)

where $\gamma = \lambda/m_i$. Now defining A by

$$A = -\frac{\dfrac{\partial^2 C}{\partial x_i^{j^2}}}{\lambda[1-t_i^v]\dfrac{\partial \phi_i}{\partial X_i}},$$

(11.72)

the procedure used in (11.26) to (11.28) can be repeated to give the effects of the taxes upon price as

$$\frac{dq_i}{dt_i^s} = \frac{1}{[1-t_i^v][1+\gamma[1+A-E]]},$$

(11.73)

where E is as defined in (11.31), and

$$\frac{dq_i}{dt_i^v} = \Theta \frac{dq_i}{dt_i^s}, \quad \Theta = \frac{\dfrac{\partial C}{\partial x_i^j}+t_i^s}{1-t_i^v}.$$

(11.74)

With respect to aggregate profits, the effects of the taxes are

$$\frac{d\pi}{dt_i^s} = -\frac{\gamma X_i[2+A-E]}{[1+\gamma[1+A-E]]},$$

(11.75)

and

$$\frac{d\pi}{dt_i^v} = q_i \frac{d\pi}{dt_i^s} - \frac{\gamma q_i X_i[1-\gamma]}{\varepsilon_q^d[1+\gamma[1+A-E]]},$$

(11.76)

with ε_q^d the price elasticity of demand.

These equations indicate that the incidence effects of specific and *ad valorem* taxes are not identical. It can therefore be expected that they have different welfare implications. The first step to understanding the welfare effects is to consider starting from a position with both taxes zero and then varying the taxes whilst holding revenue at zero. Such a reform satisfies the equation

$$0 = q_i dt_i^v + dt_i^s.$$

(11.77)

The effect of the reform on the price level is determined by

$$dq_i = \frac{dq_i}{dt_i^v} dt_i^v + \frac{dq_i}{dt_i^s} dt_i^s.$$

(11.78)

Using (11.77), this reduces to

$$dq_i = [\Theta - q_i]\frac{\partial q_i}{\partial t_i^s} dt_i^v.$$

(11.79)

Since (11.71) implies $\Theta < q_i$ and $\dfrac{\partial q_i}{\partial t_i^s} > 0$, it can be seen from (11.79) that the consumer price will be lower if the reform is chosen to satisfy $dt_i^v > 0$. Therefore a positive *ad valorem* tax and a negative specific tax can generate budget-neutral reductions in consumer price.

Strengthening this finding, Delipalla and Keen (1992) prove that if the specific tax is restricted to be non-negative, then the solution of the problem

$$\max_{\{t_i^s, t_i^v\}} V(q_i) + \pi \text{ subject to } [t_i^v q_i + t_i^s] X_i = R \tag{11.80}$$

will have zero as the optimal value of t_i^s. The reason for this result is described in Venables (1986): raising the *ad valorem* tax reduces the perceived effect of changes in output upon prices and leads, in the limit, to the competitive state in which a change in output has no effect on price. Therefore, the *ad valorem* tax is lessening the consequences of imperfect competition.

5.2 Optimal combinations

Relaxing the restriction that the specific tax be non-negative, the optimal combination of *ad valorem* and specific taxation can eliminate the welfare loss due to imperfect competition. In particular, the use of the pair of tax instruments can lead to the set of prices that maximise welfare given the budget constraint. Such prices are often termed *Ramsey prices* and, as already discussed in chapter 4, they arise as the solution to the problem of choosing optimal public-sector prices subject to a budget constraint and as the optimal prices in the analysis of commodity taxation. Bös (1986) clearly elucidates the major principles of Ramsey pricing in the public sector context and provides a number of alternative characterisations of the relevant optimality conditions.

To show that Ramsey prices can be generated despite the imperfect competition, consider an economy that has one consumer, a government and an industry that produces the single consumption good using labour as the only input. The government levies taxes and uses the revenue to purchase labour. The labour required by the firms and government is supplied by the consumer through a competitive market with the wage rate as numeraire. All profit income is paid as a dividend to the consumer. The single industry is oligopolistic with m firms indexed by $j = 1, \ldots, m$. The inverse demand function facing the industry is given by $p = p(X)$, with first derivative $p_X < 0$. Each firm has the cost function $C = C(x_j)$ where $F \equiv C(0) \geq 0$ and $C_x > 0$. The common conjecture of the firms on the value of $\dfrac{dX}{dx_i}$ is denoted by λ, with $0 < \lambda \leq m$. If government receives all profits or if production is under state control, the Ramsey price, p^*, is the solution to

$$\max_{\{p\}} V(p, I) \text{ subject to } R + \sum_{j=1}^{m} C(x_j) = pX(p), \ I = 0, \tag{11.81}$$

so that it maximises welfare given the budget constraint and the restriction that lump-sum income be zero. In the single-sector economy, the solution to (11.81) will also satisfy the budget constraint

$$p^*X(p^*) = R + mC(m^{-1}X(p^*)), \tag{11.82}$$

where the assumption of symmetry between firms has been imposed. The Ramsey price p^* is optimal given that the existing number of firms is maintained; changes in the number of firms are not considered.

The first-order condition for profit maximisation of a typical oligopolistic firm is

$$[1 - t^v]p - C_x - t^s + [1 - t^v]\gamma p_X X = 0, \tag{11.83}$$

where $\gamma = \lambda/m$. Since the symmetry implies that $x_j = x = X/m$, all $j = 1, \ldots, m$, (11.83) can be solved to express the equilibrium level of output as a function of the tax rates. This solution is denoted

$$X = \xi(t_v, t_s). \tag{11.84}$$

Substituting (11.84) into the inverse demand function then determines the equilibrium price conditional on the taxes. Hence

$$p = p(\xi(t_v, t_s)) = \rho(t_v, t_s). \tag{11.85}$$

Finally, using (11.83) and the profit identity determines the equilibrium profit level as

$$\pi_j = \pi = \varsigma(t^v, t^s), \text{ all } j = 1, \ldots, m. \tag{11.86}$$

Employing (11.84)–(11.86), a combination of *ad valorem* and specific taxation can generate Ramsey pricing if it is possible to find a pair $\{t^{v*}, t^{s*}\}$ such that the following three conditions are satisfied simultaneously

(i) $\rho(t^{v*}, t^{s*}) = p^*$,
(ii) $\varsigma(t^{v*}, t^{s*}) = 0$,
(iii) $[t^{v*}\rho(t^{v*}, t^{s*}) + t^{s*}]\xi(t^{v*}, t^{s*}) = R$. $\qquad$ (11.87)

If (11.87(i)) and (11.87(iii)) are satisfied, then $\pi_i = [[1 - t^v]p - t^s]\dfrac{X}{m} - C$

$$= \left[\rho - \frac{R}{\xi}\right]\frac{\xi}{m} - C \text{ using (11.87(iii))}, \quad = \left[\rho - \frac{R}{\xi}\right]\frac{1}{m}[\rho\xi - R - mC] = 0 \text{ using}$$

(11.87(i)) and (11.81). Therefore the satisfaction of (11.87(i)) and (11.87(iii)) implies (11.87(ii)) and the optimal tax scheme need solve only two of the three equations. In the analysis below, the focus is placed upon (11.87(i)) and (11.87(iii)).

To give the problem content, it is assumed that the revenue requirement is sufficiently small that it can be achieved by use of either of the tax instruments alone. This ensures that the use of both instruments occurs through choice. Defining $\psi_1 = \{t^s, t^v : \rho(t^s, t^v) = p^*\}$ and $\psi_2 = \{t^s, t^v : [t^v \rho(t^s, t^v) + t^s]\xi(t^s, t^v) = R\}$, the first lemma relates the relative positions of these curves to the profit levels of the firms.

Lemma 11.1

If, for a given value of t^v, denoted $\hat{t}^v$, $\bar{t}^s$ and $\tilde{t}^s$ are defined by $(\bar{t}^s, \hat{t}^v) \in \psi_1$, $(\tilde{t}^s, \hat{t}^v) \in \psi_2$, and for all pairs $\{t^s, t^v\}$ that solve (11.87(i)), $\dfrac{t^v C_x + t^s}{1 - t^v} < -[1 - \gamma] p_X X$, then $\bar{t}^s < \tilde{t}^s$ if $\varsigma(\tilde{t}^s, \hat{t}^v) > 0$, and $\bar{t}^s > \tilde{t}^s$ if $\varsigma(\tilde{t}^s, \hat{t}^v) < 0$.

Proof

Using (11.81), define $G(t^s; \hat{t}^v) \equiv p(\xi(t^s, \hat{t}^v)) \xi(t^s, \hat{t}^v) - R - mC(m^{-1}\xi(t^s, \hat{t}^v))$. The derivative of $G(t^s; \hat{t}^v)$ is given by $\dfrac{\partial G}{\partial t^s} = [p - C_x + Xp_X] \dfrac{\partial \xi}{\partial t^s}$. Given that $\dfrac{\partial \xi}{\partial t^s} < 0$, $\dfrac{\partial G}{\partial t^s}$ is positive if $[p - C_x + Xp_X] < 0$. From (11.82) $p - C_x + Xp_X = \dfrac{t^s + t^v C_x}{1 - t^v} + [1 - \gamma] p_X X$ which is negative by assumption.

Since $\dfrac{\partial G}{\partial t^s} > 0$ it is clear that if $G(t^s; \hat{t}^v)$ evaluated at $(\tilde{t}^s, \hat{t}^v)$ is positive then the solution to $G(\bar{t}^s, \hat{t}^v) = 0$ is reached by reducing t^s and hence $\bar{t}^s < \tilde{t}^s$. The converse holds if $G(t^s; \hat{t}^v)$ is negative at $(\tilde{t}^s, \hat{t}^v)$. Now note that if $[\hat{t}^v p + \tilde{t}^s]X = R$, then $G = pX - R - mC = pX - mC - X[t^v p + t^s] = [[1 - t^v]p - t^s]X - mC = m\pi$. Therefore $G(\tilde{t}^s; \hat{t}^v) > 0$ if $m\pi = m\varsigma(\tilde{t}^s, \hat{t}^v) > 0$ and $G(\tilde{t}^s, \hat{t}^v) < 0$ if $m\pi = m\varsigma(\tilde{t}^s, \hat{t}^v) < 0$.

The assumption that $\dfrac{t^v C_x + t^s}{1 - t^v} < -[1 - \gamma] p_X X$ is clearly very weak. The right-hand side is always positive but, since only values of t^v satisfying $t^v \leq 1$ need be considered and $t^s < -C_x$ for most points in ψ_1, the left-hand side is generally negative.

The next result determines the change in profit on the ψ_1 curve as t^v increases.

Lemma 11.2

Profit is monotonically decreasing along the ψ_1 curve as t^v increases.

Proof

The lemma is directly proved by total differentiation along ψ_1. See Myles (1995a).

The implication of lemma 11.1 is that the ψ_1 curve lies outside the ψ_2 curve whenever the firms earn positive profits on the ψ_2 curve. Hence if there are points on the ψ_2 curve such that the firms earn negative profits then the continuity implies that the two curves must cross at some point prior to this. From this observation follows theorem 11.1.

Theorem 11.1

If there exist t_n^s, t_n^v such that $t_n^v < 1$, $[t_n^v \rho (t_n^s, t_n^v)] \xi (t_n^s, t_n^v) = R$ and $\varsigma (t_n^s, t_n^v) < 0$, then there exists a unique pair (t^{s*}, t^{v*}) with $t^{v*} < 1$ that generates Ramsey pricing.

Proof

The statements in the proposition imply, by lemma 11.1, that ψ_1 must lie to the right of ψ_2 at t_n^s, t_n^v. Therefore, since assumption 1 implies $\pi \geq 0$ when evaluated at $\hat{t}^s$, where $\hat{t}^s$ is defined by $(\hat{t}^s, 0) \in \psi_2$, there must be some point at which ψ_1 and ψ_2 cross and at this point $t^v < 1$. The crossing point therefore determines the taxes that generate Ramsey pricing. The crossing point is also unique since if the curves intersected more than once lemma 11.2 would be violated.

Theorem 11.1 has demonstrated that Ramsey pricing can be generated when the firms become unprofitable at some combinations of taxes that satisfy the revenue requirement. This provides the first possible form of optimal tax policy. The economic reasoning lying behind this result is that the use of an *ad valorem* tax reduces the perceived market power of the imperfectly competitive firms by lowering marginal revenue whilst the specific tax can be targeted as a subsidy towards covering fixed costs.

For the case of constant marginal cost, the positivity of F is a necessary condition that profit become negative at some point on the ψ_2 curve. This can be seen by solving (11.87(i)) to (11.87(iii)). Doing this shows that the levels of t^v and t^s are characterised implicitly by

$$[1 - t^v] = -\frac{Fm}{\gamma p_X X^2}, \quad t^s = -m \left[\frac{C(m^{-1}X)}{X} + \frac{F}{\gamma p_X X^2} \right], \tag{11.88}$$

where X and p_X are evaluated at the Ramsey price and quantity. From (11.88), t^v can only be less than 1 when F is positive.

The optimal policy when there is no pair of tax rates on the ψ_2 curve that lead to negative profits can be found by applying the following lemma.

Lemma 11.3

Tax revenue is monotonically increasing along the ψ_1 curve as t^v increases.

Proof   see Myles (1995a)

Theorem 11.2

If there does not exist t_n^s, t_n^v such that $t_n^v < 1$, $[t_n^v \rho (t_n^s, t_n^v) + t_n^s] \xi (t_n^s, t_n^v) = R$ and $\varsigma (t_n^s, t_n^v) < 0$, then the optimal policy to let $t^v \to 1$ with t^s determined by the ψ_2 curve. If, $\lim \pi = 0$ as $t^v \to 1$ along ψ_2 then Ramsey pricing is generated in the limit.

Proof

Lemma 11.1 shows tax revenue is less on ψ_1 than ψ_2 for given t^v. From lemma 11.3, the two curves must then converge as t^v increases. Hence the optimal policy is always to let t^v tend to 1 to move as close to ψ_1 as possible since this takes the price closer to the Ramsey price. The second part of the proposition follows from Lemma 11.1.

It is therefore possible for the combination of specific and *ad valorem* taxation to support Ramsey pricing in imperfectly competitive economies and such an optimal tax system has the effect of eliminating the welfare loss due to monopoly power. The use of both tax instruments is able to achieve rather more than the use of a single instrument.

6 PRODUCTION EFFICIENCY AND THE TAXATION OF LABOUR

The important Diamond–Mirrlees production efficiency lemma was discussed in chapter 4. Since this implied that all producers should face the same shadow prices, there was no need for taxes upon intermediate goods in an optimal tax structure. The result was based on several assumptions, amongst them being those of competition and of constant returns to scale. Although the latter can be relaxed without harming the essence of the conclusion, the former cannot. The purpose of this section is investigate why production efficiency fails when there is imperfect competition and to consider the consequences for the taxation of intermediate goods. It was also assumed in chapter 4 that labour could act as an untaxed numeraire. Although valid in a competitive economy, the non-taxation of labour is an additional restriction with imperfect competition. The consequences of relaxing this are also explored.

6.1 Production efficiency

If taxes upon intermediate goods are introduced these will affect the vector of input prices faced by producers. With competition, a change in input costs is reflected in final prices only to the extent to which it affects marginal cost. In contrast, this simple relationship is lost when imperfect competition is introduced. A change in input costs operates through the cost function and then through the optimisation of the firm. As with commodity taxation, a change in production costs may be overshifted or undershifted in final price. By manipulating input prices through taxation, tax design can exploit these shifting effects, and the profit effects, in order to gain welfare increases.

These issues have been analysed by Myles (1989b) and Konishi (1990). Myles (1989b) considers economies with fixed numbers of firms whereas Konishi (1990) analyses free-entry Cournot oligopoly in which a number of competitive industries produced goods that were used as inputs by the oligopoly and as final consumption goods. Both focus only upon the efficiency aspects of taxation and find that, in general, welfare can be raised by the taxation of intermediate goods. The relative rates of tax between different industries are dependent upon returns to scale. Konishi shows that taxation should encourage the use of intermediate goods that are demanded elastically and reduce the use of those with inelastic demand. This has been termed the *production side Ramsey rule*.

To demonstrate the nature of these results, consider an economy in which a competitive industry's entire output is sold as an intermediate good to a monopolist whose output constitutes the economy's final good. Attention is focused upon efficiency arguments by assuming the existence of a single consumer who consumes the final goods, receives the monopoly's profits and supplies labour. Each firm in the competitive industry is assumed to have a fixed coefficient production function and units are normalised so that each unit of output requires one unit of labour. Writing p_0 for the wage rate, the post-tax price of the competitive industry's good, which is labelled 1, is

$$q_1 = p_0 + \varsigma_1, \tag{11.89}$$

where ς_1 is the tax levied upon the intermediate good. Directly from (11.89)

$$\frac{\partial q_1}{\partial \varsigma_1} = 1. \tag{11.90}$$

The monopoly produces with costs given by

$$C(q_1, p_0, X_2) + X_2 t_2, \tag{11.91}$$

where X_2 is the firm's output level and t_2 the level of commodity tax. The monopolist chooses its price, q_2, to maximise profit, π, where

$$\pi = [q_2 - t_2] X_2 (q_2, p_0, \pi) - C(q_1, p_0, X_2), \tag{11.92}$$

$X_2(\cdot)$ being the demand function. The presence of π on both sides of (11.92) captures the income effects that occur in a general equilibrium model. Assuming the condition in (11.7) is satisfied, the profit-maximising choice is characterised by

$$X_2 + \left[q_2 - t_2 - \frac{\partial C}{\partial X_2} \right] \frac{\partial X_2}{\partial q_2} = 0, \tag{11.93}$$

and the second-order condition is

$$2 \frac{\partial X_2}{\partial q_2} + \left[q_2 - t_2 - \frac{\partial C}{\partial X_2} \right] \frac{\partial^2 X_2}{\partial q_2^2} - \left[\frac{\partial X_2}{\partial q_2} \right]^2 \frac{\partial^2 C}{\partial X_2^2} < 0. \tag{11.94}$$

In addition, the equilibrium must also satisfy the profit identity (11.92).

Treating (11.92) and (11.93) as a two-equation system, they can be differentiated and solved to give the tax incidence terms

$$\frac{\partial \pi}{\partial \varsigma_1} = -\frac{\dfrac{\partial C}{\partial q_1}}{1 - \dfrac{\partial X_2}{\partial \pi}\left[q_2 - t_2 - \dfrac{\partial C}{\partial X_2}\right]}, \tag{11.95}$$

$$\frac{\partial \pi}{\partial t_2} = -\frac{X_2}{1 - \dfrac{\partial X_2}{\partial \pi}\left[q_2 - t_2 - \dfrac{\partial C}{\partial X_2}\right]}, \tag{11.96}$$

$$\frac{\partial q_2}{\partial \varsigma_1} = -\frac{\dfrac{\partial X_2}{\partial q_2}\dfrac{\partial^2 C}{\partial q_1 \partial X_2}}{2\dfrac{\partial X_2}{\partial q_2} + \left[q_2 - t_2 - \dfrac{\partial C}{\partial X_2}\right]\dfrac{\partial^2 X_2}{\partial q_2^2} - \left[\dfrac{\partial X_2}{\partial q_2}\right]^2 \dfrac{\partial^2 C}{\partial X_2^2}}$$
$$+ \frac{\dfrac{\partial C}{\partial q_1}\left[\dfrac{\partial X_2}{\partial \pi} + \dfrac{\partial^2 X_2}{\partial \pi \partial q_2}\left[q_2 - t_2 - \dfrac{\partial C}{\partial X_2}\right] - \dfrac{\partial X_2}{\partial \pi}\dfrac{\partial X_2}{\partial q_2}\dfrac{\partial^2 C}{\partial X_2^2}\right]}{\left[1 - \dfrac{\partial X_2}{\partial \pi}\left[q_2 - t_2 - \dfrac{\partial C}{\partial X_2}\right]\right]\left[2\dfrac{\partial X_2}{\partial q_2} + \left[q_2 - t_2 - \dfrac{\partial C}{\partial X_2}\right]\dfrac{\partial^2 X_2}{\partial q_2^2} - \left[\dfrac{\partial X_2}{\partial q_2}\right]^2 \dfrac{\partial^2 C}{\partial X_2^2}\right]}, \tag{11.97}$$

and

$$\frac{\partial q_2}{\partial t_2} = -\frac{\dfrac{\partial X_2}{\partial q_2}}{2\dfrac{\partial X_2}{\partial q_2} + \left[q_2 - t_2 - \dfrac{\partial C}{\partial X_2}\right]\dfrac{\partial^2 X_2}{\partial q_2^2} - \left[\dfrac{\partial X_2}{\partial q_2}\right]^2 \dfrac{\partial^2 C}{\partial X_2^2}}$$
$$+ \frac{X_2\left[\dfrac{\partial X_2}{\partial \pi} + \dfrac{\partial^2 X_2}{\partial \pi \partial q_2}\left[q_2 - t_2 - \dfrac{\partial C}{\partial X_2}\right] - \dfrac{\partial X_2}{\partial \pi}\dfrac{\partial X_2}{\partial q_2}\dfrac{\partial^2 C}{\partial X_2^2}\right]}{\left[1 - \dfrac{\partial X_2}{\partial \pi}\left[q_2 - t_2 - \dfrac{\partial C}{\partial X_2}\right]\right]\left[2\dfrac{\partial X_2}{\partial q_2} + \left[q_2 - t_2 - \dfrac{\partial C}{\partial X_2}\right]\dfrac{\partial^2 X_2}{\partial q_2^2} - \left[\dfrac{\partial X_2}{\partial q_2}\right]^2 \dfrac{\partial^2 C}{\partial X_2^2}\right]}. \tag{11.98}$$

The first term of (11.98) is the direct effect of the change in tax upon price and, as shown above, it may be greater than 1. Assuming $\dfrac{\partial^2 X_2}{\partial \pi \partial q_2} > 0$, the second term will certainly be negative if marginal cost decreases with output. This negativity captures the fact that the tax lowers profits, which then leads to a reduction in demand. The same interpretation applies to (11.97).

To demonstrate that the intermediate good should be taxed, it is worth first considering the tax reform problem of finding the direction of change in taxation, from an initial position with both taxes zero, that raises welfare whilst maintaining a balanced budget. Formally stated, starting from an initial position with $\varsigma_1 = t_2 = 0$, the sign of $d\varsigma_1$, dt_2 such that $dV > 0$ and $dR = 0$ will be determined where $V = V(p_0, q_2, \pi)$ is the single consumer's indirect utility function, which acts as the measure of social welfare, and $R = \varsigma_1 X_1 + t_2 X_2$.

To characterise the solution, first differentiate the utility function and the revenue constraint to give

$$dV = \left[\frac{\partial V}{\partial q_2} \frac{\partial q_2}{\partial \varsigma_1} + \frac{\partial V}{\partial \pi} \frac{\partial \pi}{\partial \varsigma_1} \right] d\varsigma_1 + \left[\frac{\partial V}{\partial q_2} \frac{\partial q_2}{\partial t_2} + \frac{\partial V}{\partial \pi} \frac{\partial \pi}{\partial t_2} \right] dt_2, \tag{11.99}$$

and

$$dR = X_1 d\varsigma_1 + X_2 dt_2 = 0. \tag{11.100}$$

From Shephard's lemma, $X_1 = \dfrac{\partial C}{\partial q_1}$ so (11.100) gives

$$dt_2 = - \frac{\dfrac{\partial C}{\partial q_1}}{X_2} d\varsigma_1. \tag{11.101}$$

Substituting (11.101) and (11.95)–(11.98) into (11.99)

$$dV = \frac{\partial V}{\partial q_2} \frac{\dfrac{\partial X_2}{\partial q_2} \dfrac{\partial^2 C}{\partial X_2 \partial q_1} - \dfrac{\dfrac{\partial C}{\partial q_1} \dfrac{\partial X_2}{\partial q_2}}{X_2}}{2 \dfrac{\partial X_2}{\partial q_2} + \left[q_2 - t_2 - \dfrac{\partial C}{\partial X_2} \right] \dfrac{\partial^2 X_2}{\partial q_2^2} - \left[\dfrac{\partial X_2}{\partial q_2} \right]^2 \dfrac{\partial^2 C}{\partial X_2^2}} d\varsigma_1. \tag{11.102}$$

Using (11.102), the direction of reform can be summarised in theorem 11.3.

Theorem 11.3

$d\varsigma_1 \neq 0$ if $X_2 \dfrac{\partial^2 C}{\partial X_2 \partial q_1} - \dfrac{\partial C}{\partial q_1} \neq 0$. In particular, $d\varsigma_1 > 0$ if $X_2 \dfrac{\partial^2 C}{\partial X_2 \partial q_1} - \dfrac{\partial C}{\partial q_1} < 0$ and $d\varsigma_1 < 0$ if $X_2 \dfrac{\partial^2 C}{\partial X_2 \partial q_1} - \dfrac{\partial C}{\partial q_1} > 0$.

Proof

Since $\dfrac{\partial V}{\partial q_2}$, $\dfrac{\partial X_2}{\partial q_2}$ and the denominator of the second term in (11.102) are negative, the result follows from inspection.

Assuming that $\mathrm{sgn.} \left\{ X_2 \dfrac{\partial^2 C}{\partial X_2 \partial q_1} - \dfrac{\partial C}{\partial q_1} \right\} = \mathrm{sgn.} \left\{ X_2 \dfrac{\partial^2 C}{\partial X_2 \partial p_0} - \dfrac{\partial C}{\partial p_0} \right\}$, so the production function is well behaved, theorem 11.3 can be stated in terms of returns to scale.

Theorem 11.4

If the monopolist produces with constant returns to scale, $d\varsigma_1 = 0$. Increasing returns imply $d\varsigma_1 > 0$ and decreasing returns that $\varsigma_1 < 0$.

Proof

If the monopolist produces with constant returns to scale, $C(q_2, p_0, X_2) = c(q_2, p_0)X_2$. From this, $X_2 \dfrac{\partial^2 C}{\partial X_2 \partial q_1} - \dfrac{\partial C}{\partial q_1} = 0$ and hence $d\varsigma_1 = 0$. The rest follows from noting that increasing returns imply $X_2 \dfrac{\partial^2 C}{\partial X_2 \partial q_1} - \dfrac{\partial C}{\partial q_1} < 0$ and decreasing returns that $X_2 \dfrac{\partial^2 C}{\partial X_2 \partial q_1} - \dfrac{\partial C}{\partial q_1} > 0.$

Theorem 11.3 demonstrates clearly that with imperfect competition there will typically be a case for the taxation of intermediate goods providing the monopolist does not produce with constant returns to scale. The basis for these taxes are the different rates at which the intermediate tax and the final tax affect the consumer price. In terms of theorem 11.4, when the monopolist has decreasing returns the input should be subsidised in an attempt to induce a larger level of output by cost reductions. Although the precise structure of these statements is due to the simple model used, the same features would also be of importance in any larger model.

As discussed in chapter 4, the analysis of perfect competition with decreasing returns has demonstrated that production efficiency is desirable when profits are correctly taxed. This can be investigated for imperfect competition by introducing a profits tax into the analysis above. Writing η (< 1) for the rate of profit taxation, the demand function now becomes

$$X_2 = X_2(q_2, p_0, [1 - \eta]\pi). \tag{11.103}$$

Including the revenue from the profits tax, the new revenue constraint is

$$\eta\pi + \varsigma_1 X_1 + t_2 X_2 = 0, \tag{11.104}$$

and, for a given value of η, the differential of this is

$$\left[\eta \frac{\partial \pi}{\partial t_2} + X_2\right] dt_2 + \left[\eta \frac{\partial \pi}{\partial \varsigma_1} + X_1\right] d\varsigma_1 = 0. \tag{11.105}$$

Repeating the tax incidence analysis, differentiating the utility function and substituting from (11.105) again generates (11.102). Consequently, the characterisation of policy given in theorem 11.3 is still valid independently of the value of the profit tax. This is in contrast to the Dasgupta and Stiglitz (1972) result for competitive economies.

These results demonstrate clearly that non-taxation of intermediate goods is not theoretically justified in economies with imperfect competition. Although they do not match the generality of the competitive economy of Diamond and Mirrlees, they are sufficiently rich in possibilities to highlight the major factors. Furthermore, the conclusion that intermediate goods should be taxed is merely strengthened by increasing the complexity of the economies.

6.2 Taxation of labour

Turning now to the taxation of labour, it should first be noted that in analyses of commodity taxation labour is treated as an untaxed numeraire in economies with constant returns and as taxed at a uniform rate when there are decreasing returns. The arguments of Munk (1980) justify these choices of normalisation in competitive economies and their optimality is assured via the Production Efficiency lemma. With imperfect competition, however, treating labour as an untaxed numeraire places an additional restriction upon the tax system.

The taxation of labour in the presence of imperfect competition is addressed in Myles (1995b). As in the case of the taxation of intermediate goods, it is the non-linear relation of final price to labour cost that is the key factor. Providing the response of final price to the wage rate differs across industries, then it will be justifiable on welfare grounds to use a labour tax that is differentiated across industries. By subsidising labour in industries where price is very responsive to labour cost and taxing those were it is not, a welfare-improving reduction in the price level can be achieved. The rate of response of price to tax is again determined by demand conditions, summarised by Seade's E, and returns to scale in the production process. The determinants of relative tax rates are the returns to scale of each industry and industrial conduct within the industry. Optimal taxes relate the reduction in supply from each industry due to the tax system to the returns to scale of the industry, the effect of the tax upon price and the interaction of the industry with the economy.

7 OTHER FORMS OF REGULATION

The focus of this chapter has been upon the effects of commodity taxation in imperfect economies and the optimisation of such taxes. In practice, a number of forms of regulation have been employed to reduce the welfare loss arising from the existence of imperfect competition. The most important distinction between these is whether the firm is taken into public ownership or remains in the private sector. The forms of regulation used in these cases may differ but the aim remains the same: to encourage the firm to act in a socially efficient manner.

When faced with imperfect competition, the most obvious policy response would be the encouragement of competition. This could be done by removing any barriers to entry and by providing initial inducements for competitors to become active. The limits to the operation of this policy are confronted when *natural monopoly* arises. The essence of natural monopoly is that the production technology has the property that output can always be produced more cheaply by one firm than it can by two or more. This property, termed subadditivity by Baumol *et al.* (1977), is a necessary condition for natural monopoly to arise. Stated formally, a subadditive cost function satisfies

$$C(y) < \sum_{j=1}^{k} C(y_k), y = \sum_{j=1}^{k} y_k, k \geq 2. \tag{11.106}$$

With natural monopoly, the market will not sustain more than one firm nor can it be socially optimal to have more than one firm, otherwise costs will not be minimised. It is therefore necessary to devise some policy other than introducing competition.

The two policy options that have been most widely employed are public ownership and private ownership with a regulatory body controlling behaviour. The most significant difference between these is that under public control the government is as informed as the firm about demand and cost conditions. It can therefore determine the behaviour of the firm using the best available information. Although this information may not be complete, so policy can only maximise the objective function in an expected sense, the best that is possible will be achieved. In contrast, when the firm is in private ownership, the government, via the regulatory body, may well be far less informed about information pertinent to the operating conditions of the firm than the firm itself. Information about cost structures and market conditions are likely to remain private and the firm may have strategic reasons for not revealing this accurately.

When the firm is run under public ownership, the level of price should be chosen to maximise social welfare subject to the budget constraint placed upon the firm. The firm may be required to break even or to generate income above its cost. Alternatively, it may be allowed to run a deficit which is financed from other tax revenues. In any case, as already noted in chapter 4, the structure of the decision problem for the government mirrors that in determining optimal commodity taxes and will generate the Ramsey price for the firm.

Assume all other markets in the economy are competitive. The Ramsey price for public firm subject to a break-even constraint will then be equal to marginal cost if this satisfies the constraint. If losses arise at marginal cost, then the Ramsey price will be equal to average cost. The literature on public-sector pricing has extended this reasoning to situations in which marginal cost and demand vary over time such as in the supply of electricity. Doing this leads into the theory of peak-load pricing (see Brown and Sibley (1986) and Dreze (1964)). When other markets are not competitive, the Ramsey prices will reflect the distortions elsewhere (see Bös (1986)). The principles involved are the same in all cases.

As an alternative to public ownership, a firm may remain under private ownership but be made subject to the control of a regulatory body. This introduces possible asymmetries in information between the firm and the regulator. Faced with limited information, one approach considered in the theoretical literature is for the regulator to design an incentive mechanism that achieves a desirable outcome. An example of such a regulatory scheme is the two-part tariff studied in Baron (1989) and Lockwood (1995) in which the payment for the commodity involves a fixed fee to permit consumption followed by a price per unit for consumption, with these values being set by the regulator. Alternatively, the regulator may impose a constraint on some observable measure of the firm's activities. Adopting the framework characteristic of regulation in the US, Averch and Johnson (1962) study the optimisation of the firm under the constraint that it must not exceed a given rate of return upon the capital employed. Even more simple are the regulatory schemes in the UK which involve restricting prices to rise at a slower rate than an index of the general price level.

8 CONCLUSIONS

This chapter has shown how imperfect competition leads to a failure to attain Pareto optimality. As with all such failures, this opens a potential role for government intervention to promote efficiency. Estimates of the welfare loss due to imperfect competition have been constructed from both observed data and from numerical simulations. These vary widely from the almost insignificant to considerable proportions of attained welfare. On balance, it is likely, however, that imperfect competition is of significance.

There are numerous ways in which imperfect competition can be represented. The subjective and objective demand approaches were discussed and a number of unresolved issues were highlighted. An economy incorporating quantity-setting oligopoly using objective demand, and conjectural variations when interesting, was then adopted and it was shown how this could be employed to determine the structure of optimal commodity taxation. The tax rules derived were direct generalisations of those for the competitive economy and their implementation would require information additional to the competitive rules.

In contrast to the competitive case, specific and *ad valorem* taxation are not equivalent with imperfect competition. In a choice between the instruments, *ad valorem* taxation is more effective since it has the effect of reducing perceived monopoly power. Combining the instruments can lead to further gains and, if correctly chosen, the welfare loss due to the monopoly power can be eliminated entirely Finally, imperfect competition was also shown to invalidate the general argument for production efficiency, so that taxes on intermediate goods could be justified.

12

TAX EVASION

1 INTRODUCTION

An implicit assumption that supported the analysis of taxation in the previous chapters was that firms and consumers honestly report their taxable activities. Although acceptable for providing simplified insights into the underlying issues, this assumption is patently unacceptable when confronted with reality. The purpose of this chapter can therefore be seen as the introduction of practical constraints upon the free choice of tax policy. Tax evasion, the intentional failure to declare taxable economic activity, is pervasive in many economies as the evidence given in the following section makes clear and is therefore a subject of practical as well as theoretical interest.

After reviewing evidence on the extent of tax evasion, the chapter considers the tax evasion decision of consumers. This decision is represented as a choice under uncertainty and naturally employs the techniques of chapter 7. Within this framework, the optimal degree of auditing and of punishment is considered. This is then extended to include decisions over labour supply, since the choice of occupation can determine opportunities for evasion, and the role of public goods and social norms. The analysis predicts the relationship between the level of evasion, tax rates and punishments. The results of experiments that investigate these are discussed. A more developed analysis of the optimal choice of audit is then given. The analysis of tax evasion is then completed by consideration of evasion by firms.

2 THE EXTENT OF TAX EVASION

The importance of developing a theoretical understanding of tax evasion can only be assessed by estimating the actual extent of evasion. If such evasion constitutes a significant activity within the economy, then a theory of evasion is of potential use in designing structures that minimise evasion at least cost and ensuring that policies are optimal given that evasion occurs.

Due to its very nature, the measurement of tax evasion and unreported economic activity is fraught with difficulty and uncertainty. Tax evasion should be distinguished from tax avoidance, which is the reorganisation of economic activity, possibly at some cost, to lower tax payment. Tax avoidance is legal, tax evasion is not. This illegality makes surveys prone to error if the fear of prosecution remains and, by definition, tax evasion is not measured in official statistics. The estimates reported below therefore rely on a number of methods of inference which naturally leaves them open to error. They should be regarded primarily as rough approximations. In addition to measurement errors, there is also the issue of what should be included. Illegal activities, such as the supply of drugs or smuggling generally, would not be included in measured GDP even if they were known. It is open to debate as to whether they should be included in measures of the hidden economy.

One of the earliest published studies of tax evasion is the analysis by Rey (1965) of the Italian General Sales Tax. This tax is levied on all exchanges of goods and services, with some exceptions, and in 1961 raised revenue equal to approximately 4 per cent of GNP. The tax had several methods of collection and of the largest of these, which raised two thirds of revenue, Rey estimated that evasion was equal to 52.46 per cent of actual yield. This is clearly a significant degree of evasion.

In a article that proved the starting point for many studies, Gutmann (1977) attempted to measure the extent of unobserved economic activity, or the *hidden economy*, in the USA. Based on the observation that transactions in the hidden economy are invariably financed by cash rather than cheque or credit, Gutmann used the growth of currency in circulation relative to demand deposits as an indirect measure of unobserved activity. This procedure resulted in an estimate of $176 bn. for illegal GNP in 1976 which was approximately 10 per cent of legal, measured activity. This figure is in accordance with that reported by the Internal Revenue Service in 1979 which estimated unreported income in 1976 to be between $75 bn. and $100 bn. or 7 per cent to 9 per cent of reported income.

Feige (1979) attempted to measure the same activity as Gutmann but employing a different methodology. The method of Feige was to work from the observation that total economic activity, including both measured and unmeasured sectors, is equal to the price level times transactions. An estimate of the unmeasured sector is then provided by the ratio of the value of measured income to that of transactions. The major difficulty with this approach is determining the number of transactions that actually occur. Feige achieved this by using data on the life-span in months of bank notes in circulation relative to the number of times it is expected each note can be used. This analysis provides an estimate of the unmeasured sector in 1976 of $369 bn., which is 22 per cent of GNP, and $704 bn., 33 per cent, in 1978. Given the size of these estimates, Feige concludes that official statistics must be very misleading.

Applying the same methodology to the UK, Feige (1981) calculates that the unobserved sector produced a GNP of £28 bn. in 1979 which was equal to 15 per cent of measured GNP. This estimate must be set against the reported comments of an ex-Chairman of the Inland Revenue that undeclared income could amount to 7.5 per cent of GNP. An alternative approach to measurement of the UK unobserved sector has been taken by Pissarides and Weber (1989) who employ data from the 1982 Family Expenditure Survey. By assuming that income and expenditure are reported accurately by employees whose employer filed their income report, an estimate of the expenditure function for these households then gives the true relation between income and expenditure. Observing the expenditure of other households then permits an estimate to be made of their income and, consequently, their tax evasion. The final estimate is that the unobserved economy is 5.5 per cent of GDP. Finally, Feige and McGee (1983) report an estimate of 10 per cent for unobserved activity in Sweden and Smith (1981) presents a useful summary table of results.

Even when the possible degrees of error are taken into account, the impression that these estimates give is that undeclared economic activity, and hence tax evasion, is a significant part of total economic activity in many western economies. Although the methods employed are imperfect, they cannot be dismissed entirely. Such an observation clearly justifies further study of the causes and consequences of tax evasion.

To close this section, it is worth noting that implicit in many discussions is the assumption that tax evasion reduces tax revenue. However, as shown by Peacock and Shaw (1982), if unreported activity has a multiplier effect and would take place at a lower level if it were subject to taxation, then estimates of revenue loss will be overstated, even to the extent that evasion may lead to no revenue loss at all. This effect is enhanced by the possibility that evasion may encourage participation in taxed activities. As the analysis of Peacock and Shaw is based on a simple Keynesian model, this is a point that could bear further investigation.

3 EVASION AS A DECISION WITH RISK

The decision to evade taxation fits naturally into the framework of choice under risk. Since not all tax evaders are caught by the tax authorities, risk arises since an individual who evades tax stands a chance of succeeding with the evasion, and hence having increased wealth, or a chance of being caught and punished. As an initial approximation, the individual can be viewed as choosing the extent of tax to evade, subject to the probability of being caught and punished, to maximise expected utility. The earliest formal analyses of this decision were given by Allingham and Sandmo (1972), Srinivasan (1973) and Yitzhaki (1974). These differ only in the structure of the punishments and that Srinivasan imposes risk neutrality by assuming the individual's objection is the maximisation of expected income. The derivation given below will be based primarily upon Yitzhaki. A diagrammatic presentation can be found in Cowell (1985a).

The taxpayer receives an exogeneous income M which is known to the taxpayer but not to the tax collector. The analysis is simplified by assuming that declared income, X, is taxed at a constant rate t. If the taxpayer is caught evading, which occurs with probability p, a fine $F > 1$ is placed upon evaded tax. The taxpayer's aim is to choose X so as to maximise a von Neumann–Morgernstern utility function. This decision problem can be written as

$$\max_{\{X\}} \mathcal{E}[U(X)] = [1-p]U(M-tX) + pU(M-tX-Ft[M-X]), \tag{12.1}$$

where $\mathcal{E}$ is the expectation operator and $Ft[M-X]$ is the total fine paid when caught evading. Defining $Y = M - tX$ and $Z = M - tX - Ft[M-X]$, the first- and second-order conditions for maximising (12.1) are

$$p[F-1]U'(Z) - [1-p]U'(Y) = 0, \tag{12.2}$$

and

$$S \equiv t\big[[1-p]U''(Y) + [F-1]^2 pU''(Z)\big] \leq 0. \tag{12.3}$$

It is assumed that $U' > 0$ and $U'' < 0$.

For tax evasion to take place, the solution to (12.2) must have $X < M$. When (12.3) holds for all X, this will occur when the derivative $\dfrac{\partial \mathcal{E}[U]}{\partial X}$ is negative when evaluated at $X = M$ implying that X must be reduced to arrive at the optimum. Calculating the derivative at $X = M$, tax evasion will occur whenever $pF < 1$. It is assumed from this point that this condition is satisfied.

The aim of the analysis is to determine how the level of tax evasion is affected by changes in the model's variables. There are four such variables that are of interest: the income level M, the tax rate t, the probability of detection p and the fine rate F. The computation of these effects is a straightforward exercise in comparative statics using (12.2) and (12.3). Totally differentiating (12.2) with respect to X and p and rearranging gives

$$\frac{dX}{dp} = -\frac{[F-1]U'(Z) + U'(Y)}{S} > 0, \tag{12.4}$$

so that an increase in the probability of detection raises the level of income declared and reduces evasion. This is a clearly expected result since an increase in the likelihood of detection lowers the payoff from evading and makes evasion a less attractive proposition. Repeating the procedure for a change in the fine rate upon evaded tax provides the expression

$$\frac{dX}{dF} = -\frac{pU'(Z) - p[F-1]U''(Z)t[M-X]}{S} > 0. \tag{12.5}$$

As expected, an increase in the fine leads to a reduction in the level of tax evasion.

There is therefore no ambiguity about the effects of the two punishment variables upon the level of evasion.

The next variable to consider is the tax rate upon declared income. Differentiating (12.2) with respect to X and t gives

$$[S]dX + [[1-p]U''(Y)X - p[F-1]U''(Z)X - p[F-1]U''(Z)[M-X]]dt = 0. \qquad (12.6)$$

The first-order condition (12.2) implies that $p[F-1]U'(Z) = [1-p]U'(Y)$ and this can be used to write the second-bracketed term in (12.6) as

$$[1-p]U''(Y)X - p[F-1]U''(Z)X - p[F-1]U''(Z)[M-X] =$$

$$[1-p]U'(Y)\left[\frac{[1-p]U''(Y)X}{[1-p]U'(Y)} - \frac{p[F-1]U''(Z)X}{p[F-1]U'(Z)} - \frac{p[F-1]U''(Z)[M-X]}{p[F-1]U'(Z)}\right]. \qquad (12.7)$$

Using the Arrow–Pratt measure of absolute risk aversion $R_A(I) = \dfrac{-U''(I)}{U'(I)}$ to simplify (12.7), the effect of the tax rate upon tax evasion is given by

$$\frac{dX}{dt} = -\frac{[1-p]U'(Y)[X[R_A(Z) - R_A(Y)] + F[M-X]R_A(Z)]}{S}. \qquad (12.8)$$

Since R_A is positive, for an increase in the tax rate to increase the level of income declared it is sufficient that $R_A(Z) - R_A(Y) > 0$. Thus if absolute risk aversion decreases as income increases, higher tax rates will lead to greater income declarations and a reduction in evasion. This result has provoked considerable discussion since it runs counter to the intuitive expectation that an increase in tax rates should provide a greater incentive to evade. Such a relationship is supported by the observation that estimates of the unofficial economy suggest that it has grown in periods when the average tax burden has increased.

Differentiating (12.2) with respect to X and M and repeating the substitution used in (12.7) determines the effect of an increase in income upon evasion as

$$\frac{dX}{dM} = \frac{FtR_A(Z) - [R_A(Z) - R_A(Y)]}{FtR_A(Z) - t[R_A(Z) - R_A(Y)]}. \qquad (12.9)$$

The condition $R_A(Z) - R_A(Y) > 0$ then implies, since $t < 1$, that $\dfrac{dX}{dM} < 1$ and hence declared income rises less fast than actual income implying that tax evasion rises with income.

In assessing the latter two results it should be stressed that the restriction that absolute risk aversion decreases with income cannot be regarded as universally acceptable so there remains some degree of uncertainty as to the validity of the presumption that higher tax rates and higher income lead to greater tax evasion. In addition, these results are also sensitive to the precise form of the punishment for evasion. If the fine is determined as in Allingham and Sandmo (1972) by

$f[M-X], f > t$, rather than $Ft[M-X]$, then the effect neither of the tax rate or of income can be unambiguously signed even with decreasing absolute risk aversion.

Before proceeding to a discussion of the choice problem of the tax authorities, it is worth noting two directions in which the analysis has been extended. Cross and Shaw (1982) have conducted a joint determination of evasion and avoidance activities, where avoidance refers to legal but costly means of altering activity in order to reduce total tax payments. They highlight the possible complementarities between the two activities so that an increase in the level of one of the activities leads to a reduction in the cost of the other. For instance, if tax can be avoided by claiming expenses, there is little additional cost involved in inflating an expenses claim and therefore evading taxation. A second direction taken has been to embed the evasion decision within a more general choice problem by introducing additional assets with risky returns. This then makes tax evasion only one of a portfolio of activities that have risky returns. As shown by Landskroner, Paroush and Swary (1990) even in this generalised setting the comparative statics results remain much as given above with decreasing absolute risk aversion still being the critical factor. A further extension of the analysis, the choice of labour supply, will be discussed in more detail in section 5.

4 OPTIMAL AUDITING AND PUNISHMENT

In developing the comparative statics properties of the tax evasion decision, it has been assumed that the probability of detection, or of *auditing*, and the fine levied when detected are constant. This is correct from the viewpoint of the tax evader but from the perspective of the tax collector they are variables which can be chosen to attain specified objectives. The present section will consider the choice of these variables within the simplest framework; an alternative perspective is given in section 9.

From (12.4) and (12.5) it can be seen that both an increase in the probability of detection and of the fine will reduce evasion. Therefore, as noted by Allingham and Sandmo (1972), the two instruments are substitutes with respect to reducing evasion since a reduction in one can be compensated for by an increase in the other. For this to be strictly true it must also be the case that increases in the instruments also raise additional revenue, a property that is now demonstrated to be satisfied.

Following Kolm (1973), if it is assumed that the taxpayer of the previous section is a representative of a large population of identical taxpayers, then the average tax revenue from a taxpayer is equal to the expected revenue from each. The level of average revenue is then given by

$$R = tX + pFt[M-X].$$
(12.10)

Differentiating with respect to p determines the effect of an increase in the probability of detection upon revenue as

$$\frac{\partial R}{\partial p} = Ft[M - X] + t[1 - pF]\frac{\partial X}{\partial p} > 0, \tag{12.11}$$

where the positivity follows from (12.4) and the interior-solution assumption $pF < 1$. Repeating for the fine rate gives

$$\frac{\partial R}{\partial F} = pt[W - X] + t[1 - pF]\frac{\partial X}{\partial F} > 0, \tag{12.12}$$

which is positive by (12.5). These results confirm that the two instruments are indeed substitutes.

It is now possible to consider the determination of the optimal values of p and F. A natural assumption is that detection is costly in the sense that resources are used in the auditing procedure. Thus increases in p require additional expenditure. In contrast, there are no differences in the cost of alternative levels of F and, effectively, increases in F are costless to produce. Given this, it is clear what the optimal, revenue-maximising combination of p and F should be: p should be set to zero and F increased without limit. This structure provides maximum deterrence at zero cost. In the words of Kolm (1973), the optimal policy should be to hang tax evaders with probability zero. This result is also supported by the analysis of Christiansen (1980) which shows, with a slightly different specification, that when the detection probability and the fine are adjusted to keep the expected gain from tax evasion constant, tax evasion will be reduced by an increase in the fine so that the fine is the more efficient deterrent. Further development of this result, introducing non-proportional taxes, can be found in Koskela (1983).

There are several comments that can be made in respect of this result. Firstly, it has been assumed that the aim of the tax collector was to choose the probability and the fine in order to maximise tax revenue. This runs in contrast to the position of previous chapters in which social welfare is maximised subject to a revenue constraint. If this latter viewpoint is accepted in the present context and the set of choice variables extended to also include the tax rate, then an interior solution may exist. This will be considered when public goods are introduced in section 6. Secondly, the level of the fine may not be under the direct control of the tax collector but may be determined by the courts relative to punishments for other crimes. In this case, the only choice variable is the probability of detection and if detection is costly an interior solution is again likely to exist. Finally, if a majority of the population are evading taxation, there is little public support for strong enforcement since each consumer may perceive the threat of punishment to outweigh any gains that may accrue from additional tax revenue.

This section has considered the determination of the optimal values of detection probability and fine within a tax-revenue maximisation context and in this particular case the optimum involved zero detection and maximal punishment. This result should be contrasted to those of later sections in which the structure is somewhat modified.

5 TAX EVASION AND LABOUR SUPPLY

The labour supply decision with evasion has two important components. Firstly, there is the question of how the possibility for evasion and non-declaration of income affects the labour supply decision in terms of the comparative statics of labour supply. Secondly, there is also the issue of occupational choice. If some forms of employment have greater possibilities for evasion than others, then each household must reach a decision on the quantity of each form of employment to be undertaken. The tax system and the punishments for evasion will clearly have an influence upon this decision.

5.1 Labour supply

Allowing labour supply to be variable introduces an additional degree of flexibility. However, this is not without cost. As shown by Pencavel (1979) virtually none of the comparative statics effects of parameter changes can be unambiguously signed when labour supply is variable. The only exception to this is that an increase in lump-sum income reduces declared income when the marginal rate of tax is non-decreasing. This failure to provide definite results arises from the conflict between income and substitution effects. If the substitution effects alone are considered, then it is possible to derive specific results.

If hours of labour supply are denoted by x_1 and utility is additively separable with the form

$$U = R(x_1) + S(wx_1),$$ (12.13)

where wx_1 is the income level achieved, then Andersen (1977) shows that

$$\left.\frac{\partial x_1}{\partial t}\right|_{Uconst.} < 0, \quad \left.\frac{\partial[wx_1 - X]}{\partial t}\right|_{Uconst.} > 0,$$ (12.14)

where $wx_1 - X$ is the level of evaded income. Therefore an increase in the tax rate, holding utility constant, reduces labour supply but increases the level of evaded income. If evaded income is taxed at a penalty rate f when discovered, then the effects of increases in f are

$$\left.\frac{\partial x_1}{\partial f}\right|_{Uconst.} < 0, \quad \left.\frac{\partial[wx_1 - X]}{\partial f}\right|_{Uconst.} > 0,$$ (12.15)

so that an increase in the penalty rate, with utility constant, reduces labour supply and evaded income. Finally, if relative risk aversion increases with income and is greater than 1, then an increase in the probability of detection reduces evaded income.

These results do indicate that some conclusions can be derived when the labour supply decision is introduced. However, these are almost entirely restricted to substitution effects for a separable utility function. Once such restrictions are invoked, it is not surprising that the conclusions do not differ greatly from those with exogeneous income.

5.2 Allocation of hours

It has been assumed above that tax evasion takes the form of a simple failure to declare some of the income earned. In practice tax evasion is also linked to occupational choice, with some occupations providing greater opportunities for evasion than others. Furthermore, within an occupation it may also possible to divide labour time between an official market, the income from which must be declared, and an unofficial market from which the income earned is not declared. It is upon this latter aspect that the focus will now be placed.

Two wages are now defined: w^r, the wage in the registered or official market and w^u, the unofficial market wage. Since the recipient of the wages does not pay tax when working on the unofficial market, it is assumed that $w^u < w^r$. This has the implication that the gain from evading tax is split between the supplier and employer of unofficial labour. Compatible with these wage rates are the hours of labour x_1^u, x_1^r. The income level when evasion is not detected is given by

$$w^u x_1^u + w^r x_1^r [1-t], \tag{12.16}$$

and when detected

$$w^u x_1^u [1-f] + w^r x_1^r [1-t]. \tag{12.17}$$

The consumer chooses x_1^u, x_1^r to maximise expected utility subject to the constraints (12.16) and (12.17).

The aim is to determine how the allocation of labour between the two markets is affected by changes in the tax and punishment parameters. However, it has already been noted that, in general, few of these effects are actually signed. In order to derive concrete results, it is necessary to place restrictions upon the utility function. As shown by Cowell (1981), with a utility function of the form

$$U = U(M, 1 - x_1^u - x_1^r), \tag{12.18}$$

where M is total income and the time endowment is normalised at 1, the important restriction is that

$$\frac{\partial \left[\dfrac{U_1}{U_2} \right]}{\partial M} = 0, \tag{12.19}$$

where $U_1 \equiv \dfrac{\partial U}{\partial M}$, $U_2 \equiv \dfrac{\partial U}{\partial L}$, with L, the leisure consumed, defined by $L = 1 - x_1^u - x_1^r$. The important consequence of this restriction is that it determines the total labour supply, $x_1^u + x_1^r$, as a function of the post-tax wage on the official market and any lump-sum income.

To produce easily interpretable results, a precise functional form that satisfies (12.19) is now employed. Following Isachsen and Strom (1980), the utility function is defined by

$$U = \log M + \log L. \tag{12.20}$$

The maximisation facing the consumer can then be written

$$\max_{\{x_1^u, x_1^r\}} [1-p]\left[\log(w^r x_1^r [1-t] + w^u x_1^u) + \log(L)\right] \\ + p\left[\log(w^r x_1^r [1-t] + w^u x_1^u [1-f]) + \log(L)\right]. \tag{12.21}$$

To guarantee an interior maximum, the assumption

$$w^u[1-p] > w^r[1-t], \tag{12.22}$$

is adopted. Solving the first-order conditions for a maximum of (12.21) it can be found that

$$\frac{x_1^r}{x_1^u} = \frac{w^u\left[[1-p][1-f]w^r[1-t] + pw^r[1-t] - [1-f]w^u\right]}{w^r[1-t]\left[[1-p]w^u + p[1-f]w^u - w^r[1-t]\right]}. \tag{12.23}$$

Differentiating (12.23) and using (12.22) shows that

$$\frac{\partial\left[\frac{x_1^r}{x_1^u}\right]}{\partial f} > 0, \quad \frac{\partial\left[\frac{x_1^r}{x_1^u}\right]}{\partial p} > 0, \tag{12.24}$$

so that an increase in either the fine rate on undeclared income or the probability of detection reduces the proportion of time spent in the unofficial labour market. In addition

$$\frac{\partial\left[\frac{x_1^r}{x_1^u}\right]}{\partial t} < 0, \tag{12.25}$$

so an increase in the tax rate reduces the proportion of time spent in the official labour market and increases tax evasion. It should be noted that this result is in contrast to that for the exogeneous income model.

It is the last of these results that is probably the most important since it supports the general presumption that the growth in unofficial economic activity is due to increases in taxation. However, it should be recalled that it was derived on the basis of a particular form of utility function and does not constitute a general finding.

This section has studied two particular assumptions about the method of reporting income and the flexibility of labour supply. The first involved the household having complete freedom in choice of hours and reporting whatever level of income they felt to be optimal. In the second, labour supply was still variable but evasion was only possible on unofficial income. These are not the only possible sets of assumptions, for instance it is likely that hours of work are fixed in the official market and that changes in supply can only be made in the unofficial market. Cowell (1985b) presents a summary of results to be obtained from the different sets of assumptions; the results differ only in minor details.

6   PUBLIC GOODS

When the objective of the policy maker is revenue maximisation, it was shown above that the optimal choice of detection probability and fine was to have infinite punishment with zero probability of detection. The reason for the optimality of this extreme strategy was that the objective function did not take account of the welfare of the taxpayers nor the use to which the revenue would be put. Once these are incorporated, the choice problem has more content.

The simplest means by which to close the system is to assume that tax revenue is used to supply a public good from which all households derive welfare. This provides the motivation for the existence of taxation. In addition to this, it is also necessary to include a cost function for the detection probability, reflecting the fact that catching tax evaders requires the input of resources. Combining these features with a suitable welfare function then provides a well-specified maximisation problem.

The specification of the welfare function raises some interesting issues in this context. Since the government, whose preferences are captured by the social welfare function, would prefer all taxpayers to act honestly and does not hesitate to punish those who do not, should it take account of the welfare of evaders when formulating policy? Since tax evasion is only a minor crime it may seem that tax evaders should not be excluded from consideration by society. However, this cannot be claimed to constitute a general proposition about all crimes since there probably reaches a point where a crime is so heinous that its perpetrator does not merit attention in the formulation of society's preferences. Although there is no clear set of guidelines to answer this question, the tradition in the literature, for instance Kolm (1973) and Sandmo (1981), has been to adopt a utilitarian framework in which the utilities of evaders are included in social welfare. This is probably for analytical simplicity rather than for philosophical reasons.

6.1   The valuation of public funds

Following Kolm (1973), let there be a population of n identical consumers, where n is intended to be a large number. If p is the true probability of being detected when evading tax and all the population evade tax, then np consumers are caught evading and $[1-p]n$ are not. With a cost function $C(p)$, $C(0) \geq 0$, $C' > 0$, representing the cost of achieving the probability p of detection and tax revenue $R = tX + pf[m - X]$, where f is the fine rate, the level of public good supply is given by

$$G = R - C = tX + pf[M - X] - C(p).\tag{12.26}$$

The expected welfare of a typical consumer is then defined by a utility function that is additively separable in private consumption and public good consumption

$$\mathscr{E}[U] = [1 - p]U(Y) + pU(Z) + V(G),\tag{12.27}$$

where $Y = M - tX$ and $Z = M - tX - f[M - X]$. The level of G is certain for the individual consumer due to the assumption that n is large. Given that G is parametric for the individual, the analysis of (12.1) is appropriate here and the action of each consumer is to choose the optimal value of X. Due to the separability assumption, the optimal X depends only upon p, t and f, hence

$$X = X(t,p,f),\tag{12.28}$$

with partial derivatives denoted X_t, X_p and X_f.

Invoking the large number assumption again, social welfare is given by

$$W = n[[1 - p]U(Y) + pU(Z) + V(G)],\tag{12.29}$$

since exactly np of the population are caught evading. Defining the per-capita variables $g = G/n$, $r = R/n$ and $c(p) = C(p)/n$, maximising (12.29) is equivalent to maximising

$$\bar{W} = [1 - p]U(Y) + pU(Z) + V\left(\frac{nG}{n}\right) = [1 - p]U(Y) + pU(Z) + v(g),\tag{12.30}$$

with

$$g = r - c(p) = tX + pf[M - X] - c(p).\tag{12.31}$$

Differentiating (12.30) with respect to the choice variables t, p and f and noting that the optimality of X implies that $[1 - p]U'(Y)t + pU'(Z)[f - t] = 0$, the first-order conditions are

$$\frac{d\bar{W}}{dt} = X[v' - \mathscr{E}[U']] + v'[t - pf]X_t = 0,\tag{12.32}$$

$$\frac{d\bar{W}}{df} = p[M - X][v' - U'(Z)] + v'[t - pf]X_f = 0,\tag{12.33}$$

and

$$\frac{d\bar{W}}{dp} = U'(Z) - U'(Y) + v'p[M - X] - v'c' + v'[t - pf]X_p = 0,\tag{12.34}$$

where

$$\mathscr{E}[U'] = [1 - p]U'(Y) + pU'(Z).\tag{12.35}$$

It has already been demonstrated in (12.4) and (12.5) that X_p and X_f are both positive. In addition, if it is assumed that $X_t < 0$, then the first-order conditions imply that the marginal utilities can be ranked as $U'(Y)<\mathscr{E}[U']<v'<U'(Z)$. The central inequality is reversed if $X_t>0$. In particular it follows that

$$\frac{v'}{\mathscr{E}[U']}=\frac{1}{1-\left[1-\dfrac{pf}{t}\right]\dfrac{t}{X}\dfrac{\partial X}{\partial t}},\tag{12.36}$$

so that the ratio of the marginal utility of public income to the consumer, v', to the marginal utility of private income, $\mathscr{E}[U']$, is affected by the effect of changes in the tax rate upon the declared level income. Since this valuation of public funds would be employed in any cost–benefit calculations, it can be seen that tax evasion should be taken into account when determining all public decisions.

The main conclusion to be drawn from endogenising the use of revenue and formulating the objective function in terms of social welfare is that it is possible to generate an interior solution for the detection probability and the level of the fine for evasion. As such, these variables are subject to the same basic considerations as other instruments of public policy.

6.2 Congestible public goods

The second effect that public goods may have is to modify the response of the household to changes in tax rates. It has been noted that the standard prediction is that an increase in the tax rate will lower evasion; a result that runs counter to expectations. If households feel that public goods are overprovided then an increase in the tax rate will lead to even greater overprovision. As the greater provision exacerbates the initial feeling of overprovision, the households may well alter the extent of their tax evasion; in particular circumstances, decreasing absolute risk aversion will lead to increased evasion. This aspect could not arise in the previous model where the additive separability of the utility function ensured that the evasion decision was independent of the level of public goods provided. This intuitive argument has been formalised by Cowell and Gordon (1988).

Define the level of evaded income by $E\equiv M-X$ so that the gain from evasion is tE if evasion in undetected and $-tEf$ if detected. The household can then be viewed as choosing a quantity tE of a random asset which has return $r=1$ with probability $1-p$ and return $r=-f$ with probability p. Hence consumption can be defined as the random quantity

$$x=[1-t]M+rtE.\tag{12.37}$$

The revenue raised from taxation is

$$R=n[tM+\bar{r}tE]-nc(p),\tag{12.38}$$

where the large population has been used to replace the random variable r by its mean $\bar{r}=1-p-pf$. In contrast to section 6.1 the quantity of public good available to each individual is also dependent upon the size of the population; an assumption that is intended to capture congestion effects. In detail

$$G = \frac{R}{\psi(n)}, \quad \lim_{n \to \infty} \frac{1}{\psi(n)} = 0, \quad \lim_{n \to \infty} \frac{n}{\psi(n)} = \frac{1}{\bar{\psi}} > 0.$$ (12.39)

If the $n-1$ other households each evade an amount $\bar{E}$, then the evasion E of the nth household determines the level of public good as

$$G = \frac{n[tM - c(p)] - [n-1]\bar{r}tE}{\psi(n)} - \frac{rtE}{\psi(n)} = \bar{G}(n,t) - \frac{rtE}{\psi(n)}.$$ (12.40)

In determining their consumption, it is assumed that the household takes $\bar{G}(n,t)$ as fixed. This is the Nash assumption as employed in the analysis of the private provision of public goods in chapter 9. It is important to note that in writing (12.40) it is assumed that the household takes account of how their choice of evasion affects the level of public good provision. Effectively, the population is sufficiently large that the mean can be substituted into (12.38) but not so large that the effect of each household is negligible. Without this assumption, the essential link between evasion and provision is lost. The best interpretation to give this is that a small number economy is considered and the limit assumption is imposed in (12.42) and (12.47) to provide a simplification.

By choosing their level of evasion, E, each household seeks to maximise the von Neumann–Morgernstern utility function

$$U = \mathscr{E}[U(x,G)],$$ (12.41)

with G defined by (12.40). The first-order condition for this maximisation is

$$\mathscr{E}\left[U_x r - \frac{U_G}{\psi(n)} r \right] = 0.$$ (12.42)

Imposing the limit assumption in (12.39), the first-order condition reduces to

$$\mathscr{E}[U_x r] = 0.$$ (12.43)

As noted, the aim of the analysis is to determine the effect of changes in the tax rate, t, upon the level of tax evasion. To do this, the first-order condition (12.43) is differentiated with respect to t and tE to give

$$\frac{d[tE]}{dt} = \frac{\mathscr{E}[U_{xx}r]M - \mathscr{E}[U_{xG}r]\frac{\partial G}{\partial t}}{\mathscr{E}[U_{xx}r^2]}.$$ (12.44)

At the symmetric Nash equilibrium, the level of the public good is given by

$$G = \frac{n[tM-c(p)] - n\bar{r}tE}{\psi(n)}.$$ (12.45)

Hence differentiating

$$\frac{\partial G}{\partial t} = \frac{nM}{\psi} - \frac{n\bar{r}}{\psi}\frac{\partial tE}{\partial t}.$$ (12.46)

Substituting (12.46) into (12.44) provides the final characterisation

$$\frac{d[tE]}{dt} = \frac{\mathcal{E}[U_{xx}r]M - \mathcal{E}[U_{xG}r]\dfrac{M}{\bar\psi}}{\mathcal{E}[U_{xx}r^2] - \mathcal{E}[U_{xG}r]\dfrac{\bar r}{\bar\psi}},$$
(12.47)

where the limit assumption has again be used on the terms $\dfrac{n}{\psi}$.

To determine the sign of (12.47), it is first noted that stability of the Nash equilibrium implies that the denominator is negative. Therefore the sign is the opposite of the numerator. In general, the sign of the numerator cannot be restricted so the model can therefore generate a positive relationship between evaded tax and the tax rate, in contrast to the model without public goods. In order to be more precise, consider the special case where $\dfrac{U_G}{U_x}$ is independent of x.

This assumption implies that

$$U_x U_{xG} - U_{xx} U_G = 0,$$
(12.48)

and hence $\mathcal{E}[U_{xG}r] = \mathcal{E}[U_{xx}r]m$, where $m = \dfrac{U_G}{U_x}$. Using this restriction, (12.47) can be written

$$\frac{d[tE]}{dt} = \frac{\mathcal{E}[U_{xG}r]M\left[1 - \dfrac{m}{\bar\psi}\right]}{\mathcal{E}[U_{xx}r^2] - \mathcal{E}[U_{xG}r]\dfrac{m\bar r}{\bar\psi}}.$$
(12.49)

To complete the analysis, note that the effect on utility of an increase in t is given by

$$\frac{d\mathcal{E}[U]}{dt} = M\left[\frac{\mathcal{E}[U_G]}{\bar\psi} - \mathcal{E}[U_x]\right] = M\left[\frac{m}{\bar\psi} - 1\right].$$
(12.50)

If this expression is positive, it suggests public goods are underprovided since the consumer would welcome an expansion of the public sector. Returning to (12.49), since the denominator is negative, tax evasion will increase whenever $\left[1 - \dfrac{m}{\bar\psi}\right]$ is positive. Therefore an increase in tax rate will increase evasion when public goods are overprovided.

The introduction of public goods represents one way of closing the system so that tax revenue raised has some beneficial effect. It has been demonstrated how such closure can lead to an interior solution for the punishment variables and thus places these within the standard framework of public economics. In addition, it was also demonstrated that tax evasion alters the cost of raising public funds and that this should be taken into account in any cost–benefit calculations. Finally, the introduction of public goods may lead to the degree of tax evasion increasing as the tax rate increases, a result more in conformity with a priori expectations.

7 EMPIRICAL EVIDENCE

The theoretical analysis of tax evasion has predicted the effect that changes in various parameters will have upon the level of tax evasion. In some cases, such as the effect of the probability of detection and the fine, these are unambiguous. In others, particularly the effect of changes in the tax rate, the effects depend upon the precise specification of the tax system and upon assumptions concerning attitudes towards risk. Given these uncertainties, it is valuable to investigate empirical evidence in order to see how the ambiguities are resolved in practice. Furthermore, analysis of empirical evidence also allows the investigation of the relevance of other parameters, such as source of income, and other hypotheses on tax evasion, for example the importance of social norms.

There have been three basic approaches taken in studying tax evasion. The first has been to collect survey or interview data and from these to infer the extent of evasion and some qualitative aspects of its relationship to various parameters. Secondly, econometric analysis has been applied to both survey data and to standard economic statistics. Such analysis provides a more quantitative determination of the relationships. Finally, tax evasion experiments have been conducted which provide an opportunity of designing the environment to permit the investigation of particular hypotheses.

An early example of the use of interview data can be found in the study of Norwegian taxpayers by Mork (1975). The methodology was to interview individuals in order to ascertain their actual income levels. This information was then contrasted to that given on the tax returns of the same individuals and indicated a steady decline of declared income as a proportion of reported income as income rose. This result is in agreement with that of the comparative statics analysis.

Combining econometrics and survey methods, Spicer and Lundstedt (1976) sought to investigate the importance of attitudes and social norms in the evasion decision; the data were taken from a 1974 survey in the United States. Econometric analysis revealed that the propensity to evade taxation was reduced by an increased probability of detection and an increase in age. Surprisingly, an increase in income reduced the propensity to evade. With respect to the attitude and social variables, an increase both in the perceived inequity of taxation and of the number of other tax evaders known to individual made evasion more likely. The extent of tax evasion was also increased by the attitude and social variables but was also increased by the experience of the taxpayer with previous tax audits. This study clearly demonstrated the importance of social variables in addition to the economic variables.

Clotfelter (1983) estimated tax evasion equations using data from the Internal Revenue Services Taxpayer Compliance Measurement Program survey of 1969. These indicated that tax evasion did, in fact, increase as marginal tax rates increased and was decreased when wages were a significant proportion of income. This result was supported by Crane and Nourzad (1986) employing the difference between income and expenditure figures in National Accounts from the United States for the period 1947–81. Although their major focus was the fact that inflation raised evasion, the results also showed that increased marginal tax rates also raised evasion. In contrast to this, the study of Geeroms and Wilmots (1985) of Belgian data found precisely the converse conclusion with tax increases leading to less evasion. Therefore these econometric studies do not resolve the ambiguity about the relation between marginal tax rates and tax evasion.

Turning now to experimental studies, Friedland, Maital and Rutenberg (1978) employed a tax evasion *game* in which participants were given a monthly income and a set of tax and punishment parameters. Given these, they were requested to make tax declarations. The major findings of this study were that evasion increased with the tax rate and, that keeping the net gain from evasion constant, evasion fell as the fine was increased and the detection probability reduced. This result is in agreement with the theoretical analysis of Christiansen (1980). Further results showed that women evaded more often than men but evaded lower amounts and that purchasers of lottery tickets, presumed to be less risk averse, were no more likely to evade than non-purchasers but evaded greater amounts when they did evade. A similar experiment was conducted by Becker, Büchner and Sleeking (1987) but with the inclusion of endogenous transfers of tax revenue back to the taxpayers and with income being earned by the participants. With respect to the propensity to evade, a high transfer had a negative effect as did the probability of detection and, surprisingly, the perceived level of tax. Income level had a positive effect and hence raised the propensity to evade. Only the audit probability had a significant effect on the level of evasion.

Finally, Baldry (1986) contrasted the findings of two sets of experiments. The first was framed as a tax evasion decision and this determined that some participants never evaded tax and that the decision to evade was influenced by the tax schedule. This experiment was then repeated as a simple gamble with the same payoffs. The finding was then that all participants betted and each made the maximum bet. From these contrasting findings, it can be concluded that there is more to tax evasion than gambling and that the moral and social dimensions are of importance.

The important lessons to be drawn from these results are that the theoretical predictions are generally supported, with the exception of the effect of the tax rate which remains uncertain, and that tax evasion is rather more than a simple gamble; there are attitudinal and social aspects to the evasion decision. This latter observation naturally carries implications for further theoretical analysis of the evasion decision. In particular, the fact that some taxpayers never evade requires explanation.

8 HONESTY AND SOCIAL NORMS

The feature that distinguishes tax evasion from a simple gamble is that taxpayers submitting incorrect returns feel varying degrees of anxiety and regret. To some, being caught would represent a traumatic experience which would do immense damage to their self-image. To others, it would be only a slight inconvenience. The innate belief in honesty of some taxpayers is not captured by the representation of tax evasion as a gamble nor are the non-monetary costs of detection and punishment captured by preferences defined on income alone. The first intention of this section is to incorporate these features into the analysis and to study their consequences.

The empirical results show a positive connection between the number of tax evaders known to a taxpayer and the level of that taxpayer's own evasion. This observation suggests that the evasion decision is not made in isolation by each taxpayer but is made with reference to the norms and behaviour of the general society of the taxpayer. Given the empirical significance of such norms, the second part of this section focuses on their implications.

To introduce the concept of a preference for honesty into the utility function, the simplest approach is to adopt a function of the form

$$U = U(x) - \chi E, \tag{12.51}$$

where χ is the measure of the taxpayers honesty and, with E the extent of evasion, χE is the utility cost of deviating from complete honesty. It is assumed that taxpayers are characterised by their value of χ but are identical in all other respects.

Combining (12.51) with the budget constraint (12.37), individual maximisation leads to the first-order condition for choice of E

$$\mathscr{E}[U'(x)rt] - \chi = 0. \tag{12.52}$$

E will only be positive when the marginal utility of evasion is greater than zero at a zero level of evasion. Formally, evasion will occur when $V_0 - \chi > 0$, where $V_0 = [1 - p - pf]tU'(M[1-t])$. Hence those taxpayers characterised by values of χ that satisfy $V_0 - \chi > 0$ will evade and those with higher values of χ will not. The population is therefore separated into two parts with *honest* taxpayers not evading whilst *dishonest* will evade. The term honest does not have its standard meaning in this context since all taxpayers with finite χ will evade if the expected gain is sufficiently great.

The comparative statics with respect to the punishment and income parameters are not too different from those of the model described by (12.1). The major difference is that the aggregate effect is composed of the changes in the level of evasion by existing evaders and the marginal changes as either more or fewer taxpayers evade. Since these effects work in the same direction, there is no change in the predicted effects on aggregate or individual evasion.

The effect of an increase in the tax rate is given in the following theorem from Gordon (1989).

Theorem 12.1 (Gordon)

With decreasing absolute risk aversion, there exists some $\chi^* < V_0$ such that $\dfrac{\partial E}{\partial t} < 0$

if $\chi < \chi^*$ and $\dfrac{\partial E}{\partial t} > 0$ if $V_0 > \chi > \chi^*$.

Proof

By differentiation of (12.52), the effect of the tax change can be found to be

$$\frac{\partial E}{\partial t} = \frac{\mathscr{E}\left[U''(x)rt[M - rE]\right] - \dfrac{\chi}{t}}{\mathscr{E}\left[U''(x)rt[M - rE]\right]}.\tag{12.53}$$

For $\chi = 0$, (12.53) reduces to (12.8) which has already been shown to be negative. In the limit as χ tends to V_0 (12.53) is clearly positive since E is tending to 0 from a positive value. As the decreasing absolute risk aversion implies the numerator is monotonic in χ, the sign of $\dfrac{\partial E}{\partial t}$ must change once as stated in the theorem.

This analysis predicts that there will be some evaders who increase the extent of their evasion as the tax rate increases. In addition to this effect, an increase in t also raises V_0 so that previously honest taxpayers will begin to evade. It is therefore possible, though not unambiguous, that the introduction of the utility cost of evasion can generate a positive relation between the tax rate and the extent of evasion.

Social norms have been incorporated into the evasion decision in two distinct ways. Gordon (1989) introduces the social norm as an additional element of the utility cost to evasion. The additional utility cost is assumed to be an increasing function of the proportion of taxpayers who do not evade. This formulation is intended to capture the fact that more utility will be lost, in terms of *reputation*, the more out of step the taxpayer is with the remainder of society. The consequence of this modification is to reinforce the separation of the population into evaders and non-evaders. This approach has been developed further by Myles and Naylor (1995a) who show that reputation effects can lead to multiple equilibria and epidemics of evasion.

An alternative approach has been taken by Bordignon (1993) who explicitly imposes a social norm upon behaviour. The social norm is based on the concept of Kantian morality and, effectively, has each individual assessing their *fair* contribution in tax payments towards the provision of public goods. This calculation then provides an upper bound on the extent of tax evasion. To calculate the actual degree of tax evasion each taxpayer then performs the expected utility maximisation calculation, as in (12.1), and evades whichever is the smaller out of this quantity and the previously determined upper bound. This formulation is also able to provide a positive relation between the tax rate and evaded tax for some range of taxes and to divide the population into those who evade tax and those who do not.

The introduction of psychic costs and of social norms is capable of explaining some of the empirically observed features of tax evasion which are not explained by the standard expected utility maximisation hypothesis. It does this modifying the form of preferences but the basic nature of the approach is unchanged. The obvious difficulty with these changes is that there is little to suggest precisely how social norms and utility costs of dishonesty should be formalised.

9 OPTIMAL AUDITING WITH AN INDEPENDENT REVENUE SERVICE

In the analysis of the optimal fine and detection probability conducted in section 4, it was assumed that both instruments were under the control of the authority that also determined the rate of tax. In practice it is more likely that there is a distinction between the agencies that determine each of these variables. Taxes are set by the exchequer, detection rates by a revenue service, and punishments by the courts in relation to those for other offences. If this view is adopted, it is more appropriate to analyse the determination of the optimal rate of detection in isolation taking as given the rate of tax and the fines that will be levied. Having identified the revenue service as an agency in its own right, it follows that its objective can be identified as the maximisation of revenue collected less the cost of enforcing its verification policy.

As noted by Reinganum and Wilde (1985), tax evasion is distinguished from many other forms of crime in that the tax evader is required to make a report of their income to the revenue service and it is on the basis of this report that the revenue service makes the decision whether to investigate or not. Consequently the reports can be viewed as a signal from the taxpayer about their true income and the revenue service can attempt to extract information from this signal. Formalising this, given their observed income, which is private information, each taxpayer files an income report and the revenue service decides to audit, or not, on the basis of this report. The reported income is chosen to maximise the welfare of the taxpayer and the audit probabilities are chosen to maximise the net revenue of the revenue service.

To complete the description, the distinction must also be drawn between an equilibrium with *pre-commitment* and that without. With pre-commitment the revenue service is bound by a pre-announced audit policy which it cannot alter in the light of taxpayers responses even if the audit policy is then non-optimal. The assumption of pre-commitment reduces the model to a principal–agent problem in which the revenue service (the principal) designs the contract for the taxpayer (the agent). Without pre-commitment the audit policy must remain optimal given the choices of the taxpayers. There is hence a degree of simultaneity in the choices and the Nash equilibrium concept becomes appropriate.

Taking the no-commitment model first, Reinganum and Wilde (1986) consider a verification policy as a function $\rho = p(X)$, where X is the taxpayers reported income. Given a report of income X, the function $p(X)$ determines the probability ρ with which evasion will be detected. Given a true income level of M the taxpayer chooses X to maximise

$$\mathscr{E}[U(X)] = p(X)[M[1-t] - tf[M-X]] + [1 - p(X)][M - tX]. \qquad (12.54)$$

The specification in (12.54) embodies the assumption of risk neutrality so the consumer is attempting to maximise expected income. Given $p(X)$, the maximisation in (12.54) determines a report as a function of true income. This function is denoted $r(M)$, hence the report is given by $X = r(M)$.

When it receives an income report the revenue service must form an expectation of the true income level of the person filing that report. Let these beliefs be captured by a function $\tau(X)$, that is if income X is reported the revenue service believes the taxpayer to be of true income $\tau(X)$. Defining the cost of achieving a probability ρ of detection as $c(\rho)$, the expected revenue from a taxpayer making report X is given by

$$R(X, \rho; \tau) = \rho[t\tau(X) + ft[\tau(X) - X]] + [1 - \rho]tX - c(\rho). \qquad (12.55)$$

Given its beliefs, the revenue service chooses ρ to maximise $R(X, \rho; \tau)$.

The equilibrium that is to be defined is assumed to be a separating equilibrium in which each income type files a different report. This implies that the report function $r(M)$ is monotonic in M; in particular it is natural to assume that $r(M)$ is monotonically increasing in M. A separating equilibrium can then be defined.

Separating equilibrium

A set of functions $\{\bar{\tau}(X), \bar{p}(X), \bar{r}(M)\}$ is a separating equilibrium if $\bar{r}(M)$ is monotonically increasing and

(i) given $\bar{\tau}(X), \bar{p}(X)$ maximises $R(X, \rho: \tau)$;
(ii) given $\bar{p}(X), \bar{r}(M)$ maximises $\mathscr{E}[U(X)]$;

and

(iii) $\bar{\tau}(\bar{r}(M)) = M$.

Condition (iii) is the consistency condition for the beliefs of the revenue service and simply asserts that they cannot be consistently wrong in their assessment of the income levels from the reports that they are given.

For each value of X the optimal audit probability can be found by differentiating (12.55). This provides the necessary condition

$$t[1+f][\tau(X)-X]-c'(p)=0. \tag{12.56}$$

Assuming that c'' is positive, this is also a sufficient condition for the choice of audit probability. From (12.54), the taxpayer's optimal report must satisfy

$$p(r(M))tf-p'(r(M))t[1+f][M-r(M)]-t[1-p(r(M))]=0. \tag{12.57}$$

The second-order condition is

$$2p'(r(M))t[1+f]-p''(r(M))t[1+f][M-r(M)]\leq0. \tag{12.58}$$

The consistency condition $\bar{\tau}(\bar{r}(M))=M$ can be given the alternative formulation $\bar{\tau}(\bar{r}(M))=\bar{r}^{-1}(X)$, where $\bar{r}^{-1}(X)$ is the inverse of the function $\bar{r}(M)$. Using this identity (12.56)–(12.58) can rewritten

$$t[1+f][r^{-1}(X)-X]-c'(p(X))=0, \tag{12.59}$$

$$p(X)tf-p'(X)t[1+f][r^{-1}(X)-X]-t[1-p(X)]=0, \tag{12.60}$$

and

$$2p'(X)t[1+f]-p''(X)t[1+f][r^{-1}(X)-X]\leq0. \tag{12.61}$$

The advantage of these transformed equations is that they are now in terms of X and can be used to characterise the reporting and auditing strategies.

Since (12.59) and (12.60) must hold for all X they can be differentiated to give

$$t[1+f][r^{-1'}(X)-1]-c''(p(X))p'(X)=0, \tag{12.62}$$

$$p'(X)t[1+f][2-r^{-1'}(X)]-p''(X)t[1+f][r^{-1'}(X)-X]=0. \tag{12.63}$$

The form of the optimal audit function is then given in the following theorem.

Theorem 12.2 (Reinganum/Wilde)

$p'(X)<0$ and $r^{-1'}(X)\in(0,1)$.

Proof

For (12.62) to hold either $p'>0$ and $r^{-1'}>1$ or $p'<0$ and $r^{-1'}<1$. Similarly, for (12.63) to hold either $p'>0$ and $r^{-1'}<0$ or $p'<0$ and $r^{-1'}>0$. These requirements can only be consistent when $p'<0$ and $0<r^{-1'}<1$. This proves the theorem.

Theorem 12.2 has the implication that the equilibrium effort at verification diminishes the higher is the level of reported income. In addition the identity $r^{-1'}=1/r'$ and the result $0<r^{-1'}<1$ imply that $r'(M)>1$ and hence that tax evasion declines with income since $M-r(M)$ is decreasing in M. The second of these two conclusions may seem surprising but if evasion increased with income the revenue service would have an incentive to raise the audit probability on high incomes.

This analysis has been extended to a social custom model of tax evasion in Myles and Naylor (1995b). The existence of the social custom results in the equilibrium being characterised by some taxpayers evading whilst others pay their taxes honestly. This leads to there being pooling of honest and dishonest taxpayers at some income report levels. The optimal audit schedule is still decreasing over the reports by evaders, with the probability of audit reaching zero at the highest income report of a tax evader. An increase in the fine rate raises the audit probability (where positive), in direct contrast to the analysis of section 4 where the two instruments are substitutes.

Turning now to the analysis with pre-commitment, somewhat different results are obtained. Allowing pre-commitment permits the adoption of strategies by the revenue service which involve a zero probability of auditing some income levels. In fact, as shown by Scotchmer (1987), the optimal policy takes the form of a cut-off rule in which income reports above a certain level are not audited at all. Since this leads all taxpayers with an income above the cut-off level to file a report at the cut-off, this can only be an equilibrium when pre-commitment is allowed because if there were no commitment the revenue service would gain by reneging on the zero audit probability and catching all the evaders at the cut-off point. This optimal strategy is clearly an exaggeration of the decreasing audit probability shown to be optimal without commitment.

The consequence of the cut-off rule is that the official tax which is proportional at rate t becomes regressive since actual tax payment is constant on incomes above the cut-off point and the effective tax function is regressive. This observation illustrates the general point that with tax evasion the properties of the effective tax function may well be very different from those of the official tax function. This is a point pursued further by Cremer, Marchand and Pestieau (1990) who also note the difficulties in determining optimal taxes due to the non-convexity of the social welfare function.

10 TAX EVASION BY FIRMS

The analysis of the previous sections has been concerned with the tax evasion decisions of households. To complement this, and to provide the results needed for considering optimal taxation with evasion, it is also necessary to consider tax evasion by firms. Firms can evade taxation either by misreporting sales or profit or by making false declarations about input use. It is possible that all three methods may be required simultaneously to disguise evasion if the information gathering process of the revenue service is sufficiently thorough. The analysis given below is simplified, however, by considering only the underreporting of sales. Tax evasion will be analysed in both competitive and imperfectly competitive markets.

10.1 Competitive firms

The tax evasion decision for competitive firms has been analysed by Virmani (1989), Yamada (1990) and Cremer and Gahvari (1993), with each employing a slightly different structure; the analysis given here follows Cremer and Gahvari. Consider a competitive industry producing with a constant marginal cost c whose output is subject to a specific tax t. Each firm in the industry can choose to reveal only a fraction ϕ of its sales to the revenue service. However, to conceal output requires the use of resources by the firms. The resource cost of concealing each unit of output is determined by a convex function $G(1 - \phi)$ of the proportion of sales concealed. The probability that evasion is detected is given by ρ. The penalty rate on evaded tax is given by $\tau - 1$.

Denoting the market price of output as q, a typical firm in the industry maximises expected profit given by

$$\pi^e = [q - c - [1 - \phi]G(1 - \phi) - [1 - \rho]\phi t - \rho[t + [\tau - 1][1 - \phi]t]]y, \qquad (12.64)$$

where y is its output. Given that y is positive, ϕ is chosen to maximise

$$q - c - [1 - \phi]G(1 - \phi) - [1 - \rho]\phi t - \rho[t + [\tau - 1][1 - \phi]t]. \qquad (12.65)$$

Defining $g(1 - \phi) \equiv [1 - \phi]G(1 - \phi)$, the necessary condition for choice of ϕ is

$$g'(1 - \phi) = [1 - \rho\tau]t. \qquad (12.66)$$

The second-order condition is naturally satisfied by the assumption that $G(1 - \phi)$ is a convex function. Equation (12.66) therefore characterises the optimal ϕ. Defining the expected tax rate, t^e, by

$$t^e = [\phi + [1 - \phi]\rho\tau]t, \qquad (12.67)$$

the competitive assumption implies that market price must be equal to expected marginal cost or

$$q = c + g + t^e, \qquad (12.68)$$

where g and t^e are evaluated at the optimal value of ϕ.

These equations allow the comparative statics effects of changes in the underlying parameters to be calculated. Taking changes in the tax rate first, differentiation of (12.66) gives

$$\frac{d\phi}{dt} = -\frac{[1 - \rho\tau]}{g''} < 0, \qquad (12.69)$$

so that reported sales decrease as the tax rate increases. The effect upon the expected tax rate follows from (12.67) as

$$\frac{dt^e}{dt} = [\phi + [1 - \phi]\rho\tau] - \frac{[1 - \rho\tau]^2 t}{g''}. \qquad (12.70)$$

This effect may be positive or negative since an increase in t directly raises the expected tax but causes an indirect decrease as evasion rises. Finally, using (12.69) and (12.70), the effect upon price is

$$\frac{dq}{dt} = [\phi + [1 - \phi]\rho\tau], \ 0 < \frac{dq}{dt} < 1. \tag{12.71}$$

The post-tax price rises but by less than the amount of the tax since some of the tax increase is absorbed in increased evasion.

The effect of changes in the probability of detection are also derived from (12.66) to (12.68). The results are given by

$$\frac{d\phi}{d\rho} = \frac{t\tau}{g''} > 0, \tag{12.72}$$

$$\frac{dt^e}{d\rho} = [1 - \phi]t\tau + \frac{[1 - \rho\tau]t^2\tau}{g''} > 0, \tag{12.73}$$

and

$$\frac{dq}{d\rho} = [1 - \phi]t\tau > 0. \tag{12.74}$$

Hence an increased probability of evasion raises the proportion of sales declared, the expected tax and the market price. It can be seen from the last result that an increase in the probability has an ambiguous effect upon welfare since it raises the price level to the detriment of consumers.

These results are generally without surprises but they indicate that tax evasion can be incorporated into the analysis of the competitive firm. They will also be employed in the characterisation of optimal taxes below. Before considering imperfect competition, it should be noted that Virmani (1989) studies firms with U-shaped average costs and establishes the result that with tax evasion production will not take place at minimum average cost. This raises a channel through which tax evasion can lead to production inefficiency.

10.2 Imperfect competition

Tax evasion by monopolistic firms has been studied by Marrelli (1984) and evasion by oligopolisitc firms by Marrelli and Martina (1988). Both authors assumed that the firms were risk averse. Since this is not standard practice the analysis below will assume risk neutrality. The case of monopoly will be reviewed here; the extension to oligopoly is straightforward.

The structure remains as that for the competitive firm but with the addition that the price is chosen by a profit-maximising monopolist. Denoting the demand function by $X(q)$, the price and level of evasion are chosen to maximise

$$\pi^e = X(q)[q - c - g(1 - \phi) - [1 - \rho]\phi t - \rho[t + [\tau - 1][1 - \phi]t]]. \tag{12.75}$$

For the choice of ϕ, the first-order condition is

$$X(q)[g'(1-\phi)-[1-\rho\tau]t]=0. \tag{12.76}$$

Assuming that $X(q)$ is positive, this is simply the condition given in (12.66) again. In addition, since $X(q)$ can be cancelled from (12.76), q does not appear in the condition determining ϕ. Hence the evasion decision is independent of the pricing decision. The converse is not true since the evasion decision determines the expected level of costs, inclusive of tax, and therefore the level of price. To see this formally, note that the first-order condition for the choice of q is given by

$$X'(q)[q-c-g(1-\phi)-[1-\rho]\phi t-\rho[t+[\tau-1][1-\phi]t]]+X(q)=0, \tag{12.77}$$

where (12.77) is evaluated at the optimal ϕ.

The qualitative nature of the comparative statics are sufficiently similar to those of the competitive model not to require close study. However, it is worth noting that tax overshifting will occur when

$$E>2-[\phi+[1-\phi]\rho\tau]. \tag{12.78}$$

Contrasting this to (11.31), tax evasion reduces the possibility of overshifting whenever $\rho\tau<1$ and increases it if $\rho\tau>1$. Therefore, the higher the rate of punishment, the more likely is overshifting of taxation.

11 OPTIMAL TAXATION WITH EVASION

The existence of tax evasion clearly has implications for the determination of optimal taxes. It has been noted above that optimal auditing policies will not generally result in complete elimination of evasion. Therefore the design of taxes should take this into explicit account. With respect to commodity taxation, the evasion of firms implies that the relationship between tax and price will be modified by the existence of evasion. For income taxation, tax evasion has the effect of altering the elasticity of labour supply due to the possibility of working in the shadow economy. These factors are now incorporated into the relevant optimal tax problems.

11.1 Commodity taxation

Consider a single-consumer competitive economy with n industries as described in section 4 of chapter 4. Normalising the wage rate to unity, industry i will have a constant marginal cost of c_i. Given a tax t_k on good k, the result in (12.68) shows that the post-tax price will be

$$q_k=c_k+g_k+t_k^e, \tag{12.79}$$

where $t_k^e=[\phi_k+[1-\phi_k]\rho_k\tau]t_k$ is the expected tax payment per unit of output of a firm in industry k and the tax evasion cost, g_k, the evasion choice, ϕ_k, and the detection rate, ρ_k, are all industry specific. Employing the argument that each industry is composed of a large number of firms permits the claim that actual and expected tax revenue are equal so that

$$R = \sum_{i=1}^{n} t_i^e X_i. \tag{12.80}$$

In the optimal tax problem, the choice variables of the government are the set of tax rates $(t_1, \ldots, t_n)$ and the detection probabilities $(\rho_1, \ldots, \rho_n)$. The problem can be written

$$\max_{\{t_1, \ldots, t_n, \rho_1, \ldots, \rho_n\}} V(q_1, \ldots, q_n) \text{ subject to } \sum_{i=1}^{n} t_i^e X_i - C(\rho_1, \ldots, \rho_n) = R, \tag{12.81}$$

where $C(\rho_1, \ldots, \rho_n)$ is the cost of implementing the chosen set of detection probabilities. This problem has the associated Lagrangean

$$\mathcal{L} = V(q_1, \ldots, q_n) + \lambda \left[\sum_{i=1}^{n} t_i^e X_i - C(\rho_1, \ldots, \rho_n) - R \right]. \tag{12.82}$$

Differentiating with respect to t_k gives the first-order condition

$$\left[A_k - \frac{\alpha}{\lambda} \right] X_k + \sum_{i=1}^{n} t_i^e \frac{\partial X_i}{\partial q_k} = 0, \tag{12.83}$$

where

$$A_k \equiv \frac{\dfrac{\partial t_k^e}{\partial t_k}}{\dfrac{\partial q_k}{\partial t_k}}. \tag{12.84}$$

For the optimal choice of audit probability, the first-order condition is

$$\left[B_k - \frac{\alpha}{\lambda} \right] X_k + \sum_{i=1}^{n} t_i^e \frac{\partial X_i}{\partial q_k} = \frac{C_k}{[1 - \phi_k] t_k \tau}, \tag{12.85}$$

where the right-hand side follows from (12.74) and

$$B_k \equiv \frac{\dfrac{\partial t_k^e}{\partial \rho_k}}{\dfrac{\partial q_k}{\partial \rho_k}}. \tag{12.86}$$

The fundamental result of Cremer and Gahvari (1993) is now found by subtracting (12.85) from (12.83). Replacing $[1 - \phi_k] t_k \tau$ by $\dfrac{\partial q_k}{\partial \rho_k}$ and then solving provides the conditions

$$\frac{\dfrac{\partial q_k}{\partial t_k}}{\dfrac{\partial q_k}{\partial \rho_k}} = \frac{\dfrac{\partial t_k^e}{\partial t_k}}{\dfrac{\partial t_k^e}{\partial \rho_k} - \dfrac{C_k}{X_k}}, \quad k = 1, \ldots, n. \tag{12.87}$$

The interpretation of these equations are that the taxes and detection probabilities should be adjusted until the rate of substitution between tax and probability, holding the price of good k constant, and hence welfare constant, given by the term on the left equals the rate of substitution holding tax revenue constant, which is the right-hand term. This equality of rates of substitution provides the obvious balance between the effects of the alternative instruments.

To provide a direct contrast between the tax rule in (12.83) and its counterpart with no evasion given by (5.16), the Slutsky equation can be used to write (12.83) as

$$\sum_{i=1}^{n} t_i^e S_{ki} = \left[\sum_{i=1}^{n} t_i^e \frac{\partial X_i}{\partial I} + \frac{\alpha}{\lambda} - A_k \right] X_k. \tag{12.88}$$

This differs from the standard Ramsey rule in two ways. Firstly, it is in terms of the expected rather than the actual taxes. Secondly, the term A_k enters and hence the right-hand side is raised or lowered depending on whether A_k is less than or greater than zero. A_k measures the rate at which the expected tax rate increases relative to price as the nominal tax is raised. It is therefore preferable to tax those goods where A_k is relatively high. This is reflected in (12.88) where a high value of A_k leads to a greater reduction in compensated demand.

11.2 Income taxation

Sandmo (1981) considers the determination of an optimal linear income tax in the presence of tax evasion. Taxpayers are divided into two groups. The first group consists of taxpayers who have a choice of allocating some, or all, of their labour to an unobserved sector and hence avoiding income tax. The second group of taxpayers do not have this option open to them and must pay tax upon all their earned income. An optimal income tax is then derived by maximising a utilitarian social welfare function. This resulting tax rule provides an implicit characterisation of the optimal marginal tax and can be partitioned into two parts: the first being the standard formula for the optimal marginal tax and the second being a correction term for the existence of tax evasion. If a higher tax rate leads to substitution towards labour in the unobserved sector then this makes the correction term positive and implies a tendency for the marginal rate of tax to be increased. This result is in marked contrast to the view that tax evasion should be offset by lower marginal rates of tax.

12 SUMMARY

Tax evasion is an important and significant phenomenon that affects both developed and developing economies. Although there is residual uncertainty surrounding the accuracy of measurements, even the most conservative estimates suggest the hidden economy in the UK and US to be at least 10 per cent of the measured economy. The substantial size of the hidden economy, and the tax evasion that accompanies it, requires understanding so that the effects of policies that interact with it can be correctly forecast.

The predictions of the standard Allingham–Sandmo representation of tax evasion as a choice with risk were derived and contrasted with empirical and experimental evidence. This showed that although it is valuable as a starting point for a theory of evasion, the Allingham–Sandmo representation ignores some key aspects of the evasion decision, most notably the effects of morals and the social interactions between taxpayers. In addition, tax evasion also impinges upon the broader issues of labour supply and the allocation of hours between markets and occupations. It was shown how each of these issues could be incorporated into the evasion decision.

Part IV

INTRODUCING REAL TIME

13

OVERLAPPING GENERATIONS ECONOMIES

1 INTRODUCTION

The overlapping generations economy, so called because of its assumed demographic structure, was introduced by Samuelson (1958). It has since proved useful in many areas of economics including macroeconomic growth theory, public economics and monetary economics. One of the economy's major points of interest is the welfare properties of its equilibrium. Even when the standard competitive assumptions are imposed, the equilibrium of the overlapping generations economy may not be Pareto optimal. This is in marked contrast to the Arrow–Debreu competitive economy.

Despite its value in many areas, as demonstrated by the previous chapters, there are several shortcomings of the Arrow–Debreu economy when applied to intertemporal issues. The first is that it is essentially static and, although it can be interpreted as intertemporal, this is not completely satisfactory as noted in chapter 2. It would seem to be stretching the interpretation too far to accept trading in a single period for all goods into the indefinite future. Trades in the economy are carried out by barter and there is simply no role for money. This is a consequence of the assumptions that agents are assumed to know universally the terms of trade between commodities and that any sequence of transactions can be completed without cost or hindrance. The equilibrium of the economy is also Pareto optimal, so there can be no inefficiency in investment or in the choice of production techniques. Finally, the economy implicitly assumes the lives of each agent to be at least as long as the length of the economy itself. In many ways, the economy is simply too rich: it can cover all possibilities but can never describe anything in detail.

These observations provide the motivation for the study of overlapping generations economies. By structuring the evolution of the population and introducing time in a very real sense, the overlapping generations economy is able to address many issues of interest in public economics. The potential failure of its competitive equilibrium to be Pareto optimal provides an efficiency-based justification for assessing the benefits of government intervention. In addition to possessing inefficient equilibria, overlapping generations economies can also generate cyclical equilibria without any requirement for exogenous shocks. Furthermore it is possible for fiat money to be valuable and for a continuum of equilibria to exist. All these features will be discussed below.

This chapter sets out the structure of both the pure exchange overlapping generations economies and an aggregate economy with production due to Diamond (1965). A version of the economy proposed by Samuelson is introduced first, and the failure of efficiency demonstrated. The economy is then generalised and placed in an Arrow–Debreu format in order to make the comparison with the finite economy as sharp as possible. This generalised economy is employed to characterise efficient equilibria. Money, dynamics and indeterminacy are then considered. For the aggregate production economy, the focus is placed on characterising its steady state and the welfare properties of the steady state equilibrium.

2 OVERLAPPING GENERATIONS EXCHANGE ECONOMIES

The features of the overlapping generations economy that have been noted above are most clearly identified in economies without production and it is these that have been most extensively analysed. For exchange economies it is straightforward to reinterpret an overlapping generations economy as a special case of the Arrow–Debreu economy described in chapter 2 in which the lifetime of each household is finite but, over the lifetime of the economy, there are an infinite number of households and goods. It is this double infinity that gives an overlapping generations economy its unique structure.

Following a general description of a typical overlapping generations economy, this section will demonstrate the failure of Pareto optimality in the simple economy first described by Samuelson (1958). Although instructive in itself, this style of presentation of the economy does not make clear the link between overlapping generations economies and the Arrow–Debreu economy. A more general economy is therefore introduced which is cast in a form that emphasises the parallels between it and the Arrow–Debreu economy. This general form of an overlapping generations economy is then employed to demonstrate the most important features of the equilibria of such economies.

An overlapping generations economy is explicitly intertemporal. Time is divided into discrete periods with the basic interval of time being equal to the length of time that elapses between the birth of one generation and that of the following generation. There is no final period for the economy. The population of households alive at any point in time in a typical overlapping generations economy consists of a set of finitely lived consumers. At each date is born a cohort of young consumers and, if the rate of growth is positive, each cohort is

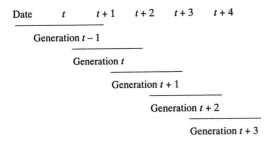

Date	t	$t+1$	$t+2$	$t+3$	$t+4$

Generation $t-1$

Generation t

Generation $t+1$

Generation $t+2$

Generation $t+3$

Figure 13.1   Structure of generations

larger than the previous. In this and the following chapters, the term household is reserved for a sequence of consumers linked by family ties. The lifespan of each consumer is assumed to be two periods; it will be shown below that this is not a significant restriction. The structure of the population is illustrated in figure 13.1 where the solid lines represent the lifespan of the generations. Each generation is identified with the period in which its members are born. The figure shows the motivation for the name applied to these economies.

An equilibrium for the economy is a sequence of prices that equate demand to supply in each time period. In this section it is assumed that there is no production and no storage of commodities. Since the absence of storage possibilities prevents any of the endowment of one period being carried over to the next period, the supply in each period is equal to the fixed endowment. The existence of the infinite population makes the definition of a Pareto optimum non-trivial; alternative concepts will be defined later.

2.1 The Samuelson economy

The *Samuelson economy* is defined as one in which all consumers are identical, except for their date of birth, and in which there is a single good available. Each consumer receives their endowment of this good entirely in the first period of their life. Since there is no storage, the only means by which a consumer can enjoy consumption in the second period of their life is by organising a series of trades in which they deliver some quantity of the good in the first period of their life and receive a delivery in the second period. It is the possibility, or otherwise, of organising such trades that will determine the efficiency of the competitive equilibrium.

The consumption in period s of a consumer born in period t is denoted x_t^s so that their utility level is given as $U = U(x_t^t, x_t^{t+1})$. Such a consumer will be referred to as belonging to generation t. It is assumed that the utility function satisfies $\lim_{x_t^t \to 0} \dfrac{\partial U}{\partial x_t^t} = \lim_{x_t^{t+1} \to 0} \dfrac{\partial U}{\partial x_t^{t+1}} = \infty$ so that the consumer strictly desires consumption in both periods of their life. The consumer's endowment, which for a consumer of generation t is received entirely in period t, comprises ω_t^t units of the good. If prices p_t and p_{t+1} hold in periods t and $t+1$, the budget constraint of the consumer is

$$p_t x_t^t + p_{t+1} x_t^{t+1} = p_t \omega_t^t. \tag{13.1}$$

Defining $1 + r_{t+1} = \dfrac{p_t}{p_{t+1}}$, the budget constraint can be written in the alternative form

$$[1 + r_{t+1}][\omega_t^t - x_t^t] - x_t^{t+1} = 0, \tag{13.2}$$

which can be interpreted as saying that any savings out of the endowment earn interest at rate r_{t+1}.

Generation t is defined as the set of consumers who are born in period t. The population grows at rate n, so that if generation t is of size H_t then $H_{t+1} = [1 + n]H_t$. An allocation is feasible for the economy if consumption by the two generations alive at each point in time is no greater than the total endowment. At time t the consumption levels of the generations must satisfy

$$x_{t-1}^t H_{t-1} + H_t x_t^t = H_t \omega_t^t, \tag{13.3}$$

where equal treatment of the identical households in each generation has been assumed. Using the assumed growth path of the population, (13.3) can be written as

$$[1 + n][\omega_t^t - x_t^t] - x_{t-1}^t = 0. \tag{13.4}$$

From (13.4) a steady state equilibrium for the economy, in which the endowment and the consumption levels are independent of t, is restricted to satisfy

$$[1 + n][\omega^1 - x^1] - x^2 = 0, \tag{13.5}$$

where x^1 and x^2 denote the steady state consumption levels in the first and second period of life and ω^1 is the constant first-period endowment. From these equalities can be proved the following theorem due to Samuelson (1958) and Gale (1973).

Theorem 13.1 (Gale, Samuelson)

There are at most two possible steady state equilibria. Either (i) $r_{t+1} = n$, all t or (ii) $x^1 = \omega^1$, all t.

Proof

In the steady state (13.2) reduces to $[1 + r][\omega^1 - x^1] - x^2 = 0$. Contrasting with (13.5) proves the theorem.

It is interesting to note that there is actually no economic behaviour behind theorem 13.1 and that it is simply a consequence of the accounting constraints.

The economic implications follow from studying the welfare properties of the two steady state equilibria.

Consider case (i) first. Assume that the steady state consumption levels x^1, x^2 chosen by the consumers when $r_{t+1}=n$, all t yield less utility than an alternative pair of stationary consumption levels $\bar{x}^1$, $\bar{x}^2$. Revealed preference implies that since x^1, x^2 were chosen, $\bar{x}^1$, $\bar{x}^2$ must be more costly so that, from the budget constraint (13.2),

$$[1+n][\omega^1 - \bar{x}^1] - \bar{x}^2 < 0. \tag{13.6}$$

However, (13.6) implies that the pair $\bar{x}^1$, $\bar{x}^2$ cannot satisfy (13.5) and hence must be infeasible. It follows that $r_{t+1}=n$ and the associated choices x^1, x^2 represent a Pareto-optimal outcome for the economy. The optimality of this equilibrium has led to it being termed the *Golden rule* path for the economy. Conversely, the equilibrium in case (ii) with $x^1=\omega^1$ is clearly not Pareto optimal. Given the assumptions made about the form of the utility function, each consumer would be willing to trade consumption in the first period of their life for consumption in the second period at any finite price.

Since there are two steady state equilibria with one strictly dominating the other, it is now necessary to identify which will arise as an equilibrium of a competitive economy. To sustain a market equilibrium with $r_{t+1}=n$ it is necessary that consumers are able to trade some of their endowment for consumption in the second period of their life since $r_{t+1}=n$ implies that the price of second period consumption in terms of first period consumption is finite. Such a trade would require the household to form a contract which involved transferring consumption in period t to a second party and receiving, from the same second party, consumption in $t+1$. Unfortunately, the only economic agents alive in both period t and $t+1$ are all members of the same generation and they are all trying to enact the same trade. This absence of trading partners therefore prevents the equilibrium $r_{t+1}=n$ being sustained as a competitive outcome. In contrast, the autarkic outcome $x^1=\omega^1$ can be sustained as a competitive equilibrium since, by default, it involves no trade. Implicitly, this equilibrium requires the price of consumption in the second period of life relative to that in the first period being infinite or, equivalently, $r_{t+1}=-1$.

The Samuelson economy therefore leads to an outcome in which there exists a single steady state equilibrium that can be supported by competitive behaviour and this equilibrium is not Pareto optimal. The existence of a competitive equilibrium that is not Pareto optimal, in contradiction to the First Theorem of Welfare Economics, is just one of a number of surprising features that overlapping generations economies possess. Although the Samuelson economy forces this equilibrium by preventing any possibility of all consumers simultaneously transferring consumption from the first to the second period of their lives, the same possibility will be shown to hold in more general economies below. In addition, only the steady state equilibria have so far been described. More attention will be paid to non-steady state equilibria below.

2.2 Overlapping generations as Arrow–Debreu economies

It would not be unreasonable to suspect that the source of the failure of Pareto optimality lay in the fact that the Samuelson economy in particular, and overlapping generations economies in general, were of an entirely different nature from the competitive Arrow–Debreu economy described in chapter 2. Such differences could possibly stem from trades being enacted sequentially in the overlapping generations in contrast to the completion of trades prior to economic activity in the Arrow–Debreu economy. Alternatively, the restriction that consumers conduct trades only during their own lifespan may be felt to account for the failure of optimality, so that if consumers could trade in any period the inefficiency would perhaps be removed. Two final possibilities may be that the endowment pattern was responsible for the inefficiency or that the assumption of identical consumers was responsible.

It will now be shown that none of these claims is justified. This will be achieved by setting out the structure of a general form of overlapping generations economy in an Arrow–Debreu format as in Balasko and Shell (1980). Several features will be made more precise including specifying the time periods over which the economy operates. Once this is done, it will be seen that the overlapping generations economy is simply a special case of the Arrow–Debreu economy in which there are an infinite number of consumers and goods. Hence, although the structure of the Samuelson economy was certainly responsible for producing such stark findings, none of the assumptions was strictly necessary for producing the inefficiency result.

2.2.1 The economy

In each time period $t = 1, 2, 3, \ldots$ of the economy there is a finite number n of goods, none of which can be stored. The consumers are indexed by their date of birth. Each consumer lives for two periods so those born in period t are alive during periods t and $t+1$. At the start of the economy in period 1 there is a generation, labelled generation 0, whose lives finish at the end of period 1. To provide some simplification, each generation consists of a single consumer.

The consumption of commodity i by the consumer born in t during period s is denoted by $x_t^{s,i}$. The lifespans of the consumers are reflected in their preferences by assuming that the consumers only derive utility from consuming during the periods they are alive. The utility of the consumer born at t is thus given by $U_t = U_t(x_t)$, $t = 0, 1, \ldots$ with $x_0 = x_0^1 = (x_0^{1,1}, \ldots, x_0^{1,n})$ for $t = 0$ and $x_t = (x_t^t, x_t^{t+1})$ $= (x_t^{t,1}, \ldots, x_t^{t,n}, x_t^{t+1,1}, \ldots, x_t^{t+1,n})$ for $t = 1, 2, \ldots$. The utility function is assumed to be strictly quasi-concave, differentiable and all its first-order partial derivatives are strictly positive. The indifference curves are also assumed not to cross any of the coordinate axes. Each consumer receives an endowment in each period they are alive. These endowments are denoted $\omega_0 = \omega_0^1 = (\omega_0^{1,1}, \ldots, \omega_0^{1,n})$ for $t = 0$ and

$\omega_t = (\omega_t^t, \omega_t^{t+1}) = (\omega_t^{t,1}, \ldots, \omega_t^{t+1,n})$ for $t = 1, 2, \ldots$ The notation x_0 is used to refer to both the vector x_0^1 and the sequence $(x_0^1, 0, 0, \ldots)$. Similarly, x_t represents (x_t^t, x_t^{t+1}) and $(0, \ldots, 0, x_t^t, x_t^{t+1}, 0, 0, \ldots)$. The same convention also applies to the endowments and to the demands defined below.

The price of good i in period t is represented by $p^{t,i}$ so that $p^t = (p^{t,1}, \ldots, p^{t,n})$ and $p = (p^1, p^2, \ldots)$. The price normalisation $p^{1,1} = 1$ is employed. Using these definitions of the prices, the demands of the consumer comprising generation 0 solve

$$\max_{\{x_0^1\}} U_0(x_0^1) \text{ subject to } p^1 x_0^1 \leq p^1 \omega_0^1 = M_0, \tag{13.7}$$

while those of generation $t = 1, 2, \ldots$ solve

$$\max_{\{x_t^t, x_t^{t+1}\}} U_t(x_t^t, x_t^{t+1}) \text{ subject to } p^t x_t^t + p^{t+1} x_t^{t+1} \leq p^t \omega_t^t + p^{t+1} \omega_t^{t+1} = M_t. \tag{13.8}$$

These maximisations result in demand functions $x_0 = x_0(p^1, M_0)$ and $x_t = x_t(p^t, p^{t+1}, M_t)$ or, alternatively, $x_0 = x_0(p, M_0)$ and $x_t = x_t(p, M_t)$. These demand functions can be treated equally as mapping into either a vector or a sequence. For instance, for $t = 0$ the demand maps either to x_0^1 or into a sequence $x_0^1, x_0^2, \ldots$ with a positive entry for x_0^1 alone. Given these demand functions, a competitive equilibrium for the overlapping generations economy can be defined.

Competitive equilibrium

A competitive equilibrium is a sequence $p^1, p^2, \ldots$ of strictly positive prices such that $\sum_t x_t(p, M_t) = \sum_t \omega_t$.

The proof of the existence of an equilibrium is sketched in the next section.

2.2.2 Existence of equilibrium

The proof of the existence of an equilibrium is of interest not only in its own right but also because of the insight it gives into the non-uniqueness of equilibrium. A formal proof of existence will not be given here but instead a fairly detailed description of the steps involved is provided.

The first step in the proof is to truncate the economy at period t and to consider the existence of a solution to the equations

$$x_0^1(\cdot) + x_1^1(\cdot) = \omega_0^1 + \omega_1^1, \tag{13.9}$$

$$x_1^2(\cdot) + x_2^2(\cdot) = \omega_1^2 + \omega_2^2, \tag{13.10}$$

$$\ldots$$

$$x_{t-1}^t(\cdot) + x_t^t(\cdot) = \omega_{t-1}^t + \omega_t^t, \tag{13.11}$$

It should be clear that the solutions of (13.9) to (13.11), which is termed the *truncated economy* E_t, will determine a set of prices $\hat{P}$ with typical member

$\hat{p}^1, \hat{p}^2, \ldots, \hat{p}^{t+1}$. The equations must have a solution since adding the additional equation $x_t^{t+1}(\cdot) = \omega_t^{t+1}$ to (13.9)–(13.11) gives a set of equilibrium conditions for a $t+1$ period Arrow–Debreu economy. As this extended set of equations must have a solution, the reduced set certainly does. Thus any sequence of prices $p = p^1, p^2, \ldots$ can be treated as an equilibrium for the t-period truncated economy provided it agrees with some $\hat{p}^1, \hat{p}^2, \ldots, \hat{p}^{t+1}$ from $\hat{P}$ in its first $t+1$ elements. Alternatively, the truncated economy determines the first $t+1$ elements of a price sequence with the remaining elements being indeterminate.

The next step is to provide upper and lower limits for possible equilibrium prices. Assume that the endowment of each consumer is strictly positive. In equilibrium each consumer must reach a level of utility at least equal to that of their endowment and their maximum consumption level is limited by the total endowment of the economy. The set of possible equilibrium consumptions for a consumer is therefore given by the intersection of the set above the indifference curve through the endowment and below the total endowment. Since the indifference curves of each consumer's utility function do not cross the coordinate axes, this set is compact and the set of possible gradients of the indifference curves through points in this set is also compact. Measuring the gradient relative to that of good 1, the desirability assumption implies that the gradients are bounded above zero but are also finite. Hence for each time period t there is an lower bound α^t and an upper bound β^t on the gradient of the indifference curves and hence on the possible equilibrium prices.

The above reasoning shows that the equilibrium prices for the t-period truncated economy E_t belong to a compact set which is a subset of the possible equilibrium prices for E_{t-1}. As t tends to infinity, a sequence of non-empty compact sets is generated with each being a subset of the previous set. Such an infinite sequence of sets has a non-empty intersection. An element of the infinite intersection is an equilibrium price system for the economy. This proves the existence of an equilibrium.

2.2.3 Welfare properties

It has already been shown that the equilibrium of an overlapping generations economy need not be Pareto optimal, even though it is characterised by competitive behaviour and an absence of externalities or any other standard source of market failure. The purpose of the present section is to formalise definitions of Pareto optimality that are appropriate for infinite economies and to characterise Pareto-optimal equilibria via the structure of the supporting price sequences.

Pareto optimality is usually tested by considering whether there exists any reallocation of resources that can raise the welfare of one consumer without reducing that of any other. In a finite economy this is a sufficient description. However, in an infinite economy it is necessary to consider the number of consumers that can be involved in any reallocation of resources. Searching for improving allocations where only a finite number of consumers can have their allocation altered will clearly provide different results from allowing allocations to be altered for an infinite number of consumers. Accordingly, the distinction is made between *weak Pareto optimality* and *Pareto optimality* as follows.

Pareto optimality

The allocation $\{x_0, x_1, x_2, \ldots\}$ is Pareto optimal if there is no allocation $\{x'_0, x'_1, x'_2, \ldots\}$ with $\sum_t x_t = \sum_t x'_t$, $U_t(x'_t) \geq U_t(x_t)$, all t and $U_{t'}(x'_{t'}) > U_{t'}(x_{t'})$ for some t'.

Weak Pareto optimality

The allocation $\{x_0, x_1, x_2, \ldots\}$ is weakly Pareto optimal if there is no allocation $\{x'_0, x'_1, x'_2, \ldots\}$ with $\sum_t x_t = \sum_t x'_t$, $x_t = x'_t$ for all but a finite number of t, $U_t(x'_t) \geq U_t(x_t)$ all t and $U_{t'}(x'_{t'}) > U_{t'}(x_{t'})$ for some t'.

To understand the distinction between these forms of optimality, consider the following example from Shell (1971). Each consumer has a linear utility function, so that utility is the sum of consumption levels in the two periods, and each consumer is endowed with one unit of the single available good in each period of life. The competitive equilibrium in this case must have consumption equal to the endowment. Now consider a series of transfers in which the consumer who is born in period 1 transfers their first period endowment to the consumer who was born in period 0 and, in each successive period, the consumer born in that period transfers their endowment to the consumer born in the previous period. Compared to the competitive outcome, all consumers born from period 1 onwards still attain a utility level of 2 but the consumer born in period 0 has their utility raised from 1 to 2. The transfer has therefore achieved a Pareto improvement and the competitive equilibrium was not Pareto optimal. In making this Pareto improvement, the allocation of an infinite number of consumers has been changed. More importantly, it can easily be seen that a Pareto improvement could not be made if only a finite number of consumers were involved in the reallocation. The competitive equilibrium is therefore weakly Pareto optimal but not Pareto optimal.

The conclusions of this example will now be shown to be generally applicable. That is, competitive equilibria will be shown to be weakly Pareto optimal but not necessarily Pareto optimal. The first of these statements is proved in the following theorem.

Theorem 13.2 (Balasko and Shell)

Every competitive equilibrium is weakly Pareto optimal and every weakly Pareto-optimal allocation is a competitive equilibrium allocation for a suitable assignment of endowments.

Proof

Given an allocation $x=\{x_0,x_1,x_2,...\}$, the price sequence $p=(p^1,p^2,p^3,...)$ is said to support the allocation x if and only if for all $t=0,1,2,...x_t$ maximises $U_t(\cdot)$ subject to $px_t\leq M_t$ for some sequence of incomes M_t.

It is easy to see that every competitive equilibrium allocation x, with its associated equilibrium price sequence p, is supported by p when the income sequence is given by $\{M_t\}=\{p\omega_t\}$. Conversely, if an allocation x is supported by a price sequence p, there exists a sequence of endowments $\{\omega_t\}$ such that x is a competitive equilibrium and the equilibrium prices are given by p. To see this, note that if p supports x then, from utility maximisation, $x_t=x_t(p,px_t)$ for $t=0$, $1,2,...$. If the endowment sequence is chosen so that $\omega_t=x_t$ the claim follows. Given these observations connecting competitive equilibria and supporting price sequences, the proof is completed by showing that an allocation is weakly Pareto optimal if and only if there exists a price sequence which supports it.

To show that any allocation supported by a price sequence is weakly Pareto optimal, let x be supported by p and assume that x is not weakly Pareto optimal. Therefore, since weak Pareto optimality is concerned with allocations that differ in only a finite number of components, the assumption that x is not weakly Pareto optimal implies that there exists x' with $x_t'=x_t$ for $t\geq t'$, $\sum_t x_t=\sum_t x_t'$ and $U_t(x_t')\geq U_t(x_t)$ with at least one strict inequality for $t<t'$. From revealed preference $px_t'\geq px_t$ with strict inequality for at least one $t<t'$. Hence $\sum_{t=0}^{t'-1} px_t'>\sum_{t=0}^{t'-1} px_t$, contradicting $\sum_t x_t=\sum_t x_t'$ and $x_t'=x_t$ for $t\geq t'$.

Finally, it is necessary to show that an allocation x is weakly Pareto optimal only if there exists a price sequence that supports it. It is obvious that an allocation is weakly Pareto optimal if and only if the first t elements of the allocation sequence are Pareto optimal for any truncated economy E_t, $t=0,1,2,...$. The allocation x_0 is uniquely supported in E_0 by $p^1=\theta\nabla U_0(x_0)$ with θ chosen so that $p^{1,1}=1$. The argument is now completed by induction by showing that, given unique supporting prices $p^1,p^2,...,p^t$ for $x_0,...,x_{t-1}$, in E_{t-1} there exists a unique p^{t+1} such that $p^1,p^2,...,p^{t+1}$ supports $x_0,...,x_t$ in E_t. Assume that p'^t,p'^{t+1} support x_t so that $p'^t,p'^{t+1}=\phi\nabla U_t(x_t)$ for some $\phi>0$. Now since $x_0,...,x_t$ is Pareto optimal in E_t, $p'^t=\gamma\nabla U_t(\cdot,x_t^{t+1})$ with x_t^{t+1} fixed and $p'^t=\varphi\nabla U_{t-1}(x_{t-1}^{t-1},\cdot)$ with x_{t-1}^{t-1} fixed. But, by the assumption that $p^1,p^2,...,p^t$ supports $x_0,...,x_{t-1}$, $p^t=\kappa\nabla U_{t-1}(x_{t-1}^{t-1},\cdot)$. Hence $p'^t=\frac{\varphi}{\kappa}p^t$. Now define $p^{t+1}=\frac{\kappa}{\varphi}p'^{t+1}$. $p^1,p^2,...,p^{t+1}$ clearly supports $x_0,...,x_t$ in E_t and the proof is completed.

The characterisation of Pareto-optimal allocations is somewhat more complex than that of weakly Pareto optimal. To provide necessary and sufficient conditions requires considerable work. As a consequence, the theorem that is proved below describes only sufficient conditions. An informal description of the necessary and sufficient conditions is also given. To permit proof of the theorem, a description of Pareto-improving sequences of feasible transfers is required. Let x be a given feasible allocation. The sequence $h=(h_0, h_1, \ldots)$ is a *feasible sequence of commodity transfers* if $x+h$ is a feasible allocation and $\sum_t h_t = 0$. Since commodities can only be transferred between consumers who are alive at the same time, it follows that $h_0 = h_0^1 = -h_1^1$ and, for $t \neq 0$, $h_t = (h_t^t, h_t^{t+1})$ $= (-h_{t-1}^t, -h_{t+1}^{t+1})$. A sequence of transfers is *Pareto improving* on the allocation x if $U_t(x_t + h_t) \geq U_t(x_t)$ for all t and with strict inequality for at least one t. The following theorem gives sufficient conditions for an allocation to be Pareto optimal.

Theorem 13.3 (Balasko and Shell)

A weakly Pareto-optimal allocation x supported by prices p is Pareto optimal if the sequence $(x_0, x_1, \ldots)$ is bounded from above and $\liminf_{t \to \infty} \|p^t\| = 0$.

Proof

The first step in the proof is to show that if an element of a sequence of Pareto-improving transfers, from an initial weakly Pareto-optimal position, is positive at $t = t_0$, it is positive for all $t \geq t_0$. To show this, assume the converse. Hence there exists $t_1 > t_0$ such that $h_{t_1} = 0$. Now, since $\sum_t h_t = 0$, the structure of

transfers implies that $\displaystyle\sum_{t=t_0}^{t_1} h_t = 0$ and $\displaystyle\sum_{t>t_1} h_t = 0$. Therefore the sequence h_t $= (0, \ldots, 0, h_{t_0}, \ldots, h_{t_1}, 0, \ldots, 0)$ would be feasible and $U_t(x_t + h_t) \geq U_t(x_t)$ for all $0, 1, \ldots$.   Due   to   strict   quasi-concavity   of   utility,   the   sequence $(0, \ldots, 0, \lambda h_{t_0}, \ldots, \lambda h_{t_1}, 0, \ldots, 0), 0 < \lambda < 1$, would be Pareto improving. This sequence has only a finite number of non-zero elements; a contradiction to the supposition that the initial state was weakly Pareto optimal which establishes the claim.

The second step is to show that the transfers involved in a Pareto improvement can be ranked in terms of their values. In particular, it is now shown that

$$p^{t+1} h_{t+1}^{t+1} \leq p^t h_t^t \leq \ldots \leq p^1 h_1^1 = -p^1 h_1^1 = -p^1 h_0^1 \leq 0,$$

with strict inequality for $t \geq t_0$, t_0 as defined above. To prove this, first note that for generation 0, $U_0(x_0 + h_0) \geq U_0(x_0)$ which, by revealed preference, implies that $p^1[x_0^1 + h_0^1] \geq p^1 x_0^1$ or $p^1 h_0^1 \geq 0$. For generation 1, $p^1 h_1^1 + p^2 h_1^2 \geq 0$ so that $p^2 h_1^2 \geq p^1 h_1^1$. From the structure of transfers, $h_1^1 = -h_0^1$ and $h_1^2 = -h_2^2$ hence $p^2 h_2^2 \leq p^1 h_1^1 = -p^1 h_0^1 \leq 0$. This construction can be continued for all t with strict inequality holding for $t \geq t_0$.

The proof is completed by noting that $(x_0, x_1, \ldots)$ is bounded from above and that $\liminf_{t\to\infty} \|p'\| = 0$. Assume that there exists a Pareto-improving sequence of transfers. For such a set of transfers, it follows that for $t \geq t_0, p'h'_t$ $< p^{t_0+1}h^{t_0+1}_{t_0+1} < p^{t_0}h^{t_0}_{t_0} = 0$. The assumed boundedness of $(x_0, x_1, \ldots)$ implies that h'_t is also bounded and the assumption that $\liminf_{t\to\infty} \|p'\| = 0$ implies that $\liminf_{t\to\infty} \|p'h'_t\| = 0$. This contradicts the preceding inequality and establishes that under the conditions of the theorem the allocation x is Pareto optimal.

It should be noted how this result provides a characterisation of Pareto optimality in terms of the price sequence that supports an allocation rather than in terms of the allocation itself. The restriction that the sequence of allocations is bounded above prevents the economy enjoying unlimited growth.

The result described in theorem 13.3 is not the most general that is available. Since $\liminf_{t\to\infty} \|p'\| = 0$ is a sufficient condition for Pareto optimality, it leaves open the possibility that there may be important cases in which this is not satisfied but which are Pareto optimal. After placing further regularity assumptions upon the curvature and gradient of indifference curves and bounding feasible allocation sequences above and below, Balasko and Shell (1980) prove the following.

Theorem 13.4 (Balasko and Shell)

A weakly Pareto optimal allocation x *is Pareto optimal if and only if*
$$\sum_t \frac{1}{\|p'\|} = +\infty, \text{ where } p \text{ is the price sequence that supports } x.$$

Proof

See Balasko and Shell (1980).

It should be noted that $\liminf_{t\to\infty} \|p'\| = 0$ implies $\sum_t \dfrac{1}{\|p'\|} = +\infty$ but not the converse. For instance, in the Samuelson economy with no population growth, so that $n = 0$, if trades could be organised the Pareto-optimal equilibrium would be supported by the price sequence $p = (1,1,\ldots)$ which satisfies $\sum_t \dfrac{1}{\|p'\|} = +\infty$ but not $\liminf_{t\to\infty} \|p'\| = 0$. This characterisation of Pareto optimality will be employed further in the discussion of dynamics for overlapping generations economies.

2.2.4 General demographic structure

The demographic structure of two-period lifetimes may seem unduly restrictive and potentially responsible for some of the more surprising conclusions. However, this is not the case and, as shown by Balasko, Cass and Shell (1980), it is possible to transform economies with more general demographic structures into two-period economies by suitable relabelling. The restriction to two-period lives therefore involves no loss of generality.

The basis for this procedure is to distinguish between real calendar time and (artificial) time used for labelling lifespans. Let calendar time be labelled $s = 0, 1, 2, \ldots$ At $s = 0$, out of the set of consumers alive at that time, the consumer with the greatest future longevity is identified. It is then assumed that $s = 0$ represents the end of the first half of their life. The second half of their life ends at their date of death, say s_1. Economic time is then constructed so that $t = 1$ is associated with s_1. The same process is repeated at s_1: the consumer with the greatest longevity is identified and viewed as being at the end of their first period of life. Their date of death, s_2, is then associated with $t = 2$.

Proceeding in this way, the economic periods are constructed so the consumers live at most two periods. It is possible that some may be born, for instance, at a date $s > 0$ and die at $s < s_1$. Such consumers are regarded as having single-period lifespans. The construction is completed by treating all commodities available between $s = 0$ and $s = s_1$ as being traded at $t = 1$. This is repeated for $t = 2, \ldots$. Preferences are then defined over vectors of goods at t and $t + 1$.

2.3 Money, dynamics and indeterminacy

As noted in the introduction, overlapping generations economies differ from finite economies in more ways than simply that their competitive equilibria may be inefficient. Three of these further differences are now briefly discussed.

2.3.1 Money

In a standard competitive economy that exists over a finite number of periods, fiat money whose only use is as a store of value would be worthless. This conclusion can be established by a simple backward induction argument. Money is clearly worthless in the final period since it has no further use as a store of value. Seeing that it is worthless in the last period, no consumer would wish to purchase money in the second to last period so that it is also worthless in that period. This argument can be continued backward until the beginning of the economy. Money is therefore worthless unless it is arbitrarily assumed that it must be used as a means of exchange.

This backward induction argument cannot be applied to the infinite overlapping generations economy and the possibility then arises that fiat money may have value. This can be shown most clearly by returning to the Samuelson economy. The inefficiency in that economy arose because consumers have no opportunity for turning their first-period endowment into second-period consumption. Money provides such a possibility. As first shown by Samuelson (1958), the introduction of money can permit the attainment of Pareto optimality provided that all generations believe money to be valuable and are willing to accept money in exchange for goods.

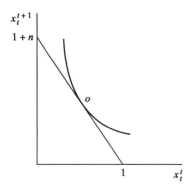

Figure 13.2   Efficient allocation

This argument can be illustrated simply as follows. Assume that each consumer is endowed with one unit of the single consumption good when young and none when old and that if generation t has H_t identical members then $H_{t+1} = [1+n]H_t$. In each period the feasible allocations are given by

$$H_t x_t^t + H_{t-1} x_{t-1}^t = H_t,$$ (13.12)

or, in per-capita terms,

$$x_t^t + \frac{x_{t-1}^t}{[1+n]} = 1.$$ (13.13)

From (13.13) the structure of the population ensures that the feasible allocation to any individual must be constrained by

$$x_t^t + \frac{x_t^{t+1}}{[1+n]} = 1.$$ (13.14)

This constraint is shown in figure 13.2. As already argued, the only competitive equilibrium for this economy is the autarkic outcome with consumption allocation $(x_t^t, x_t^{t+1}) = (1,0)$ whereas the efficient outcome is shown as the tangency between indifference curve and constraint (13.14) at point o.

Introducing money increases the set of potential trades consumers may make. Suppose at time 0 a quantity of M units of money is divided equally between those already alive (the generation who will be old in period 1) and that they and all following generations believe this money to have value. In period t a consumer then solves the maximisation

$$\max_{\{x_t^t, x_t^{t+1}\}} U(x_t^t, x_t^{t+1}) \text{ subject to } p_t = M_t^d + p_t x_t^t, p_{t+1} x_t^{t+1} = M_t^d,$$ (13.15)

where M_t^d is money demand. This maximisation implies a demand function for real balances of the form $\dfrac{M_t^d}{p_t} = M\left(\dfrac{p_t}{p_{t+1}}\right)$ so that equilibrium on the money market in period t requires

$$H_t M \left(\frac{p_t}{p_{t+1}}\right) p_t = M. \tag{13.16}$$

Equating this to money demand in period $t+1$, which must equal the same stock, provides the equilibrium condition

$$M \left(\frac{p_t}{p_{t+1}}\right) \frac{p_t}{p_{t+1}} = [1+n] M \left(\frac{p_{t+1}}{p_{t+2}}\right). \tag{13.17}$$

At a steady state solution with $\dfrac{p_t}{p_{t+1}} = \dfrac{p_{t+1}}{p_{t+2}} \equiv 1+\rho$, this equation is solved when $1+\rho = 1+n$. Combining the budget constraints in (13.15) and employing the solution to (13.17) shows that at the steady state with $1+\rho = 1+n$, each consumer faces the budget constraint

$$x_t^t + \frac{x_t^{t+1}}{[1+\rho]} = x_t^t + \frac{x_t^{t+1}}{[1+n]} = 1. \tag{13.18}$$

The constraint in (13.18) is identical to (13.14). Faced with this budget constraint, each consumer will choose the efficient consumption point o. This observation demonstrates how the introduction of money that is valued allows the decentralisation of the Pareto-efficient outcome by extending the range of allocations that can be sustained through competitive behaviour. It should be noted that the discussion has been restricted to the steady state.

The fact that money can have value in an overlapping generations economy is another surprising aspect of these economies. Equally surprising are the potential efficiency gains from the introduction of a commodity with no actual consumption value. Although money will not receive further analysis in the chapters that follow, these observations provide an insight into the results that can emerge. Further properties of monetary equilibria are discussed in Balasko and Shell (1981) and Hahn (1982).

2.3.2 Dynamics

The analysis to this point has characterised the steady state solutions of the Samuelson economy and investigated the existence and welfare properties of equilibria for the generalised economy. The intention now is to consider the possible dynamics of non-steady state solutions. The dynamics of overlapping generations economies were first investigated by Gale (1973), who provided an example of an economy with two-period cycles, and then in detail by Grandmont (1985). The work of Grandmont revealed the potential complexity of the dynamics that can arise.

The structure of dynamics can most easily be seen by considering a slightly modified version of the Samuelson economy. It is now assumed that there is a single consumer in each generation and that an endowment is received in both periods of life. In addition, the preferences of all consumers are identical and can be represented by a utility function that is separable between consumption in the first and second periods of life.

The budget constraint for each consumer is given by

$$[1+r_{t+1}][\omega_t^t - x_t^t] + \omega_t^{t+1} - x_t^{t+1} = 0, \tag{13.19}$$

so that maximisation of the utility function $U(x_t^t, x_t^{t+1}) = U^1(x_t^t) + U^2(x_t^{t+1})$ results in the necessary condition

$$U^{1\prime}(x_t^t) - [1+r_{t+1}]U^{2\prime}(x_t^{t+1}) = 0. \tag{13.20}$$

Eliminating $[1+r_{t+1}]$ by using the budget constraint (13.19) reduces (13.20) to

$$[\omega_t^t - x_t^t]U^{1\prime}(x_t^t) + [\omega_t^{t+1} - x_t^{t+1}]U^{2\prime}(x_t^{t+1}) = 0. \tag{13.21}$$

The aggregate feasibility condition for the economy requires that total consumption does not exceed the total endowment or

$$\omega_t^t - x_t^t + \omega_{t-1}^t - x_{t-1}^t = 0. \tag{13.22}$$

Taken together, (13.21) and (13.22) fully describe the dynamic evolution of the economy from any feasible initial starting value of x_0^1. Given x_0^1, (13.22) determines x_1^1 and then, using the value of x_1^1, (13.21) determines x_1^2. Returning to (13.22), x_2^2 can then be found. Repeating this process, whilst taking account of non-negativity constraints, provides the entire sequence of consumption levels for the economy. Although some of the consumption patterns that will arise in this dynamic process appear not to be feasible trades given what has been said above, two modifications can overcome this objection. As noted by Gale (1973), a fictitious central clearing house could be introduced that can organise trades that would not otherwise be possible. Alternatively, money could be introduced with only minor modification to the analysis.

The above argument provides a simple constructive approach to the dynamics but it provides limited insight into the dynamic processes that may emerge; for example it neither confirms nor refutes the possible existence of periodic cycles. To proceed further in this direction, (13.22) can be used to substitute for x_t^t in (13.21) giving

$$[x_{t-1}^t - \omega_{t-1}^t]U^{1\prime}(\omega_t^t + \omega_{t-1}^t - x_{t-1}^t) + [\omega_t^{t+1} - x_t^{t+1}]U^{2\prime}(x_t^{t+1}) = 0. \tag{13.23}$$

The structure of (13.23) is (implicitly) that of a non-linear first-order difference equation relating x_t^{t+1} to x_{t-1}^t. Hence given the consumption in the second period of life for members of generation $t-1$, (13.23) determines the second-period consumption of generation t. First-period consumption levels can then be read from (13.22). If it is further assumed that all generations receive an identical pattern of endowments, so that $\omega_t^t = \omega_1$, $\omega_t^{t+1} = \omega_2$, all t, (13.23) reduces to

$$[x_{t-1}^t - \omega_2]U^{1\prime}(\omega_1 + \omega_2 - x_{t-1}^t) + [\omega_2 - x_t^{t+1}]U^{2\prime}(x_t^{t+1}) = 0. \tag{13.24}$$

The relevance of this assumption is that if $x_s^{s+1} = x_t^{t+1}$ then $x_s^s = x_t^t$ so that if the consumer of generation s has the same second-period consumption as that of t, they also have identical first-period consumption. The structure of the economy then ensures that generations s and t face identical nominal variables and choose identical real variables. If such equivalence occurs every k generations, the economy can be said to possess a cycle of period k.

The next step is to show that such cycles can actually occur. Gale (1973) demonstrated that if the utility function has the form $U(x_t^t, x_t^{t+1}) = 10x_t^t - 4x_t^{t^2} + 4x_t^{t+1} - x_t^{t+1^2}$ and the endowment $(\omega_t^t, \omega_t^{t+1}) = (0,2)$ then there exists a cycle of period 2 with consumption levels $x_t^t = \dfrac{5 - \sqrt{5}}{6} = x_{t+2}^{t+2}, x_{t+1}^{t+1} = \dfrac{5 + \sqrt{5}}{6} = x_{t+3}^{t+3}.$ One of the interesting features of such a cycle is that it is driven entirely by equilibrium behaviour under certainty and is not the consequence of random shocks hitting the economy or of false expectations.

Now return to (13.24). Theorem 13.1 shows that (13.24) has two steady state solutions, that is there are two values of x_{t-1}^t such that $x_{t-1}^t = x_t^{t+1}$. Hence, if the locus of pairs of (x_{t-1}^t, x_t^{t+1}) that solve (13.24) are drawn in (x_{t-1}^t, x_t^{t+1}) space, the locus must cross the 45° line twice. The gradient of the locus can be calculated as

$$\frac{dx_t^{t+1}}{dx_{t-1}^t} = \frac{U^{1\prime}[1 - A_1[\omega_2 - x_{t-1}^t]]}{U^{2\prime}[1 - A_2[x_t^{t+1} - \omega_1]]}, \tag{13.25}$$

where $A_i = -\dfrac{U^{i\prime\prime}}{U^{i\prime}}$ is the coefficient of absolute risk aversion in period i of life. At the autarkic steady state with consumption equal to the endowment the gradient is equal to $\dfrac{U^{1\prime}}{U^{2\prime}} > 0.$ The locus therefore cuts the 45° line from below at the autarkic steady state and hence must cut it from above at the Pareto-efficient steady state.

If the second-period endowment is sufficiently low that the efficient steady state level of second-period consumption is greater than the endowment, then the locus of solutions to (13.24) will appear as in figure 13.3. Point a denotes the autarkic equilibrium and b the efficient steady state. In particular, if the second-period endowment is 0 then the autarkic steady state will be the origin.

Starting with a value of x_0^1 on the horizontal axis, x_1^2 can be found on the vertical axis by reading off the graph of the curve. Translating this value through the 45° line back on to the horizontal axis then allows x_2^3 to be plotted on the vertical. In this way, the dynamics of consumption in the second-period of life for each generation of consumers can be traced on the diagram. There is a significant mathematical literature on systems that have the form shown in figure 13.3 and only a sketch of the most important will be given here. Further details of the mathematics can be found in Collet and Eckmann (1980) and simple surveys are given in Baumol and Benhabib (1989) and Boldrin and Woodford (1990).

The possible forms of dynamic behaviour that the system may display can be placed into four general categories. These are:

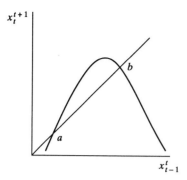

Figure 13.3   Dynamic solution

1 Convergence
The system may converge to a steady state.
2 Convergence to a cycle
After an initial period the system settles down to a cycle in which the same points are visited after specific intervals. An example of an economy with a cycle of period 2 has already been described.
3 Non-cyclical
Here the system never returns to the same point twice. The system may simply be erratic or it may be drawn to a *strange attractor* in which case it becomes arbitrarily close to some cycle.
4 Chaotic
In the case of chaos the system never returns to the same point and has *sensitive dependence on initial conditions*. That is, two solution paths that start at two initial points an ε apart will, after a finite time, be a significant distant apart. This has the implication that such a system cannot be investigated by numerical simulation since rounding errors will be sufficient to invalidate the analysis.

To delineate conditions under which each of these would arise requires considerable further formalisation which is not worth undertaking here. However, two further points are worth noting. Firstly, if for some starting point the system has a cycle of period 3, then starting points can be found that will give a cycle of any desired order. This is an implication of *Sarkovskii's theorem*: if a system has a cycle of period 3, it has cycles of all orders. Grandmont (1985) actually provides conditions under which such a cycle exists in an overlapping generations economy. Secondly, it is difficult to determine if an observed chaotic times series is generated by a deterministic system or is actually random.

There are two important conclusions that follow from this discussion. The first is economies may be constructed whose dynamics reproduce the properties of observed economic time series. Observed series generate cyclical behaviour of fairly stable periodicity. Such cycles can be generated by few economies other than the overlapping generations economy, except for exceptional sets of parameter values. This gives the overlapping generations economy an important role in the analysis of business cycles. Secondly, the fact that the economy can generate endogenous cycles provides a natural motivation for a counter-cyclical policy. The policy implications of these dynamics have been investigated in detail by Grandmont (1985).

In the context of policy reactions to cycles it may seem surprising to note that the cycles, with the exception of the autarkic 1-cycle, are actually Pareto optimal. The argument behind this conclusion is the observation that if the economy is cyclical equilibrium prices must also be cyclical. During the time span of the economy the same prices must therefore be repeated an infinite number of times. This implies $\sum_t \dfrac{1}{\|p^t\|} = +\infty$, hence the cycle must be Pareto optimal.

2.3.3 Indeterminacy

A theorem of Debreu (1970) shows that almost all competitive economies of the form described in chapter 2 have a finite number of isolated equilibria so that each equilibrium is locally unique. That a similar conclusion does not apply to overlapping generations economies has been shown by Gale (1973), Geanakoplos and Polemarchakis (1984) and Kehoe and Levine (1985). For overlapping generations economies robust examples can be constructed that have a continuum of equilibria so that both finiteness and local uniqueness do not apply. Such indeterminacy imposes considerable problems for analysis. Comparative statics exercises are not possible and the concept of perfect foresight along such indeterminate paths is implausible. The introduction of money compounds the problem by introducing a further dimension to the indeterminacy.

The problem of indeterminacy is inherent in all applications of overlapping generations economies. It is sidestepped in the chapters that follow, as well as in much of the literature, by focusing only upon steady states. As has already been shown, there are just two steady states for the Samuelson economy and in the aggregate production economy discussed next it is possible for there to be a unique steady state.

2.4 Summary

This section has described the overlapping generations economy and has illustrated a number of the important properties that such economies possess. In contrast to standard competitive economies, the equilibria of an overlapping generations economy need not be Pareto optimal, though all are weakly Pareto optimal, and there may be an uncountable infinity of equilibria. Furthermore, fiat money can play a socially useful role in leading to the attainment of a Pareto optimum and, consequently, may be valued.

These features of overlapping generations economies undermine many of the presumptions developed from analysis of standard competitive economies. Due to this, it has proved an important tool in the study of public economics. The version of the overlapping generations economy that will be employed in the following chapters is less general than that described in this section but the results here provide the foundation of the analysis.

3 AN AGGREGATE PRODUCTION ECONOMY

The overlapping generations economies described above involved no production but only exchange of commodities. Each generation of consumers received their endowment and then traded. In contrast, the overlapping generations economy described in Diamond (1965) introduced a production process that involved both capital and labour. This extension permits the analysis of many interesting topics, including the assessment of the efficiency of choice of capital–labour ratio.

In the *Diamond economy* each consumer again lives for just two periods. They work only during the first period of their life and inelastically supply one unit of labour. This unit of labour is their entire endowment. In their second period of life they are retired and supply no labour. Income earned by a consumer during the first period of their life is divided between consumption and savings. Second-period consumption is equal to savings plus accumulated interest. With the exception of their date of birth, all consumers are identical. At each date is born a cohort of consumers and the population grows at a constant rate.

The economy has a single consumption good which is produced using capital and labour. Available capital consists of a stock of the single good and is generated by the savings of the previous period. Capital does not depreciate during the production process. The production function exhibits constant returns to scale. The level of production is chosen so as to maximise profits. Finally, all markets are competitive. The existence of capital as a store of value allows consumers to carry purchasing power from one period to the next.

3.1 Consumers

All consumers have identical preferences which, for the consumer born in period t, are represented by the utility function

$$U = U(x_t^t, x_t^{t+1}),$$
(13.26)

where x_t^t is the consumption level of the single good when the consumer is young and x_t^{t+1} consumption when old. There is no disutility from labour supply.

To construct the budget constraint of a typical consumer, note that labour income must be divided between consumption and savings and that each consumer supplies one unit of labour. With the price of the consumption good in period t denoted p_t, consumption and savings, s_t, must satisfy

$$W_t = p_t x_t^{t+1} + p_t s_t.$$
(13.27)

where W_t is the wage received for the single unit of labour. The value of second-period consumption must be equal to the value of savings, hence

$$p_{t+1}x_t^{t+1}=p_t s_t. \tag{13.28}$$

Combining (13.27) and (13.28) and defining the interest rate by $r_{t+1}=\dfrac{p_t-p_{t+1}}{p_{t+1}}$, the budget constraint becomes

$$\frac{W_t}{p_t}\equiv w_t=x_t^t+\frac{x_t^{t+1}}{[1+r_{t+1}]}, \tag{13.29}$$

where w_t is the real wage. Employing the definition of the interest rate also gives $x_t^{t+1}=[1+r_{t+1}]s_t$. Note that the relevant interest rate is r_{t+1} since interest is notionally paid in period $t+1$.

From (13.26) and (13.29) the utility-maximising consumption plan satisfies the first-order condition

$$\frac{U_1(x_t^t,x_t^{t+1})}{U_2(x_t^t,x_t^{t+1})}=[1+r_{t+1}]. \tag{13.30}$$

Equation (13.30) relates the intertemporal marginal rate of substitution to the rate of transformation and is a simple extension of the standard condition for optimal choice. The simultaneous solution of (13.30) and (13.29) provides demand functions of the form

$$x_t^{t+i}=x_t^{t+i}(w_t,r_{t+1}),\ i=0,\ 1. \tag{13.31}$$

3.2 Production

The productive sector of the economy is described by an aggregate production function

$$Y_t=F(K_t,L_t), \tag{13.32}$$

where K_t is the capital stock in period t and L_t aggregate labour supply. Since each young consumer inelastically supplies one unit of labour, $L_t=H_t$. The production function can either be interpreted literally as representing the technology of a single firm or as the aggregate production function of a set of identical firms. A formal demonstration of such an aggregation argument is given in Sargent (1979). As capital does not depreciate, consumption and saving must satisfy

$$F(K_t,L_t)+K_t=H_t x_t^t+H_{t-1}x_{t-1}^t+H_t s_t. \tag{13.33}$$

The production function therefore gives net output not including the non-depreciating capital.

It is assumed that $F(K_t,L_t)$ satisfies constant returns to scale and is therefore homogeneous of degree 1 so that $F(vK_t,vL_t)=vF(K_t,L_t)$ for all positive v. As the size of the population is growing at rate n, what matters as a measure of the output of the economy is not total output but output per head. The homogeneity of production permits the analysis to be phrased in these terms. To see this, set $v = \dfrac{L_t}{L_t}$ in (13.33) and use the homogeneity to extract the numerator of v. This gives

$$Y_t = L_t F\left(\frac{1}{L_t} K_t, \frac{1}{L_t} L_t\right) = L_t F\left(\frac{K_t}{L_t}, 1\right) = L_t f\left(\frac{K_t}{L_t}\right). \tag{13.34}$$

Now define

$$y_t = \frac{Y_t}{L_t}, \; k_t = \frac{K_t}{L_t}. \tag{13.35}$$

Then output per unit of labour is determined by a function that has the capital–labour ratio as its sole argument

$$y_t = f(k_t). \tag{13.36}$$

As the labour market is competitive, profit maximisation in the choice of labour by firms implies that the marginal product of labour must be equated to the real wage. The marginal product of labour is derived by noting that

$$Y_t = L_t f\left(\frac{K_t}{L_t}\right), \tag{13.37}$$

so that

$$\frac{\partial y_t}{\partial L_t} = f\left(\frac{K_t}{L_t}\right) - L_t f'\left(\frac{K_t}{L_t}\right) \frac{K_t}{L_t^2} = f(k_t) - k_t f'(k_t). \tag{13.38}$$

The optimum choice of labour therefore satisfies

$$w_t = f(k_t) - k_t f'(k_t). \tag{13.39}$$

Similarly, the optimum choice of capital equates the rate of interest to the marginal product

$$r_t = f'(k_t). \tag{13.40}$$

3.3 Equilibrium

At the equilibrium it is necessary that consumers maximise utility, firms maximise profit and all markets clear. For capital market equilibrium, the relevant condition is that capital used must be equal to the level of savings, since capital is the only store of wealth. To derive the capital market equilibrium condition, first note that the population of young consumers is of size H_t in period t, so the equality of total savings with capital available in period $t+1$ implies that

$$H_t[w_t - x_t^t] = K_{t+1}. \tag{13.41}$$

Dividing through (13.41) by H_t, recalling that $H_{t+1} = H_t[1+n]$ and $H_t = L_t$, gives

$$w_t - x_t^t = k_{t+1}[1+n]. \tag{13.42}$$

When equation (13.42) is satisfied, there is equilibrium in the capital market.

Collecting equations, the equilibrium evolution through time of the economy is determined as the simultaneous solution to

$$\frac{U_1(x_t^t, x_t^{t+1})}{U_2(x_t^t, x_t^{t+1})} = [1 + r_{t+1}], \tag{13.43}$$

$$w_t = x_t^t + \frac{x_t^{t+1}}{[1+r_{t+1}]}, \tag{13.44}$$

$$w_t = f(k_t) - k_t f'(k_t), \tag{13.45}$$

$$r_t = f'(k_t), \tag{13.46}$$

$$w_t - x_t^t = k_{t+1}[1+n]. \tag{13.47}$$

These equilibrium equations can be used to provide a simple description of the evolution of the capital stock through time which can then be used to generate the time paths of the other endogenous variables. To do this recall that the simultaneous solution of (13.43) and (13.44) provides demand functions of the form

$$x_t^{t+i} = x_t^{t+i}(w_t, r_{t+1}), \ i = 0, \ 1. \tag{13.48}$$

From the determination of w_t described in (13.45), and from stepping (13.46) one period forward, it follows from substitution into the demand function that

$$x_t^t = x_t^t(f(k_t) - k_t f'(k_t), f'(k_{t+1})). \tag{13.49}$$

Now substituting (13.49) into the capital market equilibrium equation (13.47) gives the final expression

$$f(k_t) - k_t f'(k_t) - x_t^t(f(k_t) - k_t f'(k_t), f'(k_{t+1})) = [1+n]k_{t+1}. \tag{13.50}$$

Equation (13.50) has as its only arguments the capital–labour ratio in periods t and $t+1$ and it represents the basis for studying the dynamic equilibrium of the economy. Assuming that (13.50) can be solved for k_{t+1} in terms of k_t, the relation can be written

$$k_{t+1} = v(k_t). \tag{13.51}$$

The intertemporal evolution of the capital–labour ratio is summarised in (13.51) in the sense that it determines k_{t+1} for given k_t. As with (13.23), (13.51) is a non-linear first-order difference equation and the potential dynamics that were discussed in connection with that equation are again relevant here.

To analyse (13.51) first assume that, for all k_t

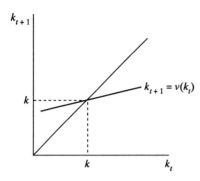

Figure 13.4   Stable convergence to steady state

$$\left|\frac{\partial k_{t+1}}{\partial k_t}\right| < 1, \tag{13.52}$$

which, after implicitly differentiating (13.50), will hold if

$$\left|\frac{\left[\dfrac{\partial x_t^t}{\partial w_t} - 1\right] k_t f''}{1 + n + \dfrac{\partial x_t^t}{\partial r_{t+1}} f''}\right| < 1. \tag{13.53}$$

In this case, if the system given by (13.50) has a stationary solution with $k_t = k_{t+1} = k$, all t, it will be globally stable. That is, if there is a fixed point such that

$$f(k) - kf'(k) - x_t^t(f(k) - kf'(k), f'(k)) = k[1 + n], \tag{13.54}$$

then the system will always converge to k regardless of the initial level of the capital stock. A stable system of this form is illustrated figure 13.4.

The system in figure 13.4 also has the property that the $v(k_t)$ function is monotonically increasing. This may be a reasonable restriction and it certainly rules out many forms of badly behaved solutions. Sufficient conditions for the function $v(k_t)$ to be increasing in k_t are that

a) $\dfrac{\partial x_t^t}{\partial w_t} > 0, \dfrac{\partial x_t^{t+1}}{\partial w_t} > 0,$

and

b) $\dfrac{\partial x_t^t}{\partial r_{t+1}} < 0.$

Condition (a) is the requirement that both goods are normal. The importance of (a) is that it implies $\dfrac{\partial x_t^t}{\partial w_t} < 1$. Together conditions (a) and (b) guarantee that the numerator and denominator of (13.53) are positive. Of course further restrictions are needed to ensure that the derivative is less than 1.

Alternatively assume that for some values of k_t

$$\left| \frac{\partial k_{t+1}}{\partial k_t} \right| > 1,$$ (13.55)

and that $v(k_t)$ is first increasing and then decreasing with a unique maximum which can occur if second period consumption is inferior. This provides the hump-shaped relationship of figure 13.3 and permits the possibility of the complex dynamics discussed following that figure. The Diamond economy can therefore potentially generate convergent, cyclical, non-cyclical and chaotic behaviour in the capital–labour ratio and hence in output per head.

3.4 Steady state solution

Although the dynamic solution is of much potential interest, the focus of most analyses of overlapping generations economies in public economics has been placed upon steady state equilibria. A *steady state* is the situation in which the economy repeats itself period after period in the sense that the capital–labour ratio, the output–labour ratio and the interest rate are constant over time. The steady state is typically interpreted as constituting the long-run equilibrium for the economy. The typical policy analysis characterises the steady state and performs comparative statics exercises as the policy variables are modified. Such exercises will be the subject matter of chapters 14 and 15. The present concern is the characterisation of the steady state and the analysis of its welfare properties.

Since all nominal variables and per-capita variables are constant in the steady state, the time subscripts are now dropped. Denoting the steady state value of the capital–labour ratio by k and the interest rate by r, the budget constraint can be written

$$x^1 + \frac{x^2}{1+r} = w,$$ (13.56)

where x^1 and x^2 are first- and second-period consumption levels. Using the facts that $w = f(k) - kf'(k)$ and $r = f'(k)$, the budget constraint can be written

$$x^1 + \frac{x^2}{1+f'(k)} = f(k) - kf'(k).$$ (13.57)

From capital market equilibrium

$$w - x^1 = [1+n]k,$$ (13.58)

or

$$f(k) - kf'(k) - x^1 = [1+n]k.$$ (13.59)

The points to be made about the properties of the steady state can be derived from using (13.59) to eliminate x^1 from (13.57). Differentiating the equation obtained gives

$$\frac{dk}{dx^2} = \frac{1}{[1+n][1+f'+kf'']} > 0. \tag{13.60}$$

It is therefore possible to solve for k as a function of x^2. This solution is denoted $k = k(x^2)$. The next step is to substitute the solution for k into (13.59) to give

$$f(k(x^2)) - k(x^2)f'(k(x^2)) - x^1 = [1+n]k(x^2). \tag{13.61}$$

The solutions to equation (13.61) generates a locus of pairs (x^1, x^2) termed the *consumption possibility frontier* and, using $k = k(x^2)$, an implied value of k. Each point on this frontier is potentially a steady state with the actual steady state that arises as the competitive equilibrium being determined by consumer preferences. There are basic economic reasons for expecting the locus to describe a non-monotonic relationship between x^1 and x^2. For low values of x^2 the capital–labour ratio is also low so that total production, and hence x^1, must also be small. As x^2 increases the capital–labour ratio grows and permits x^1 to rise. Eventually, the capital–labour ratio will become too large and x^1 will again fall. As an example, for the Cobb–Douglas production function

$$f(k) = k^\alpha, \ 0 < \alpha < 1, \tag{13.62}$$

the locus has the shape shown in figure 13.5.

The importance of this construction is the following interpretation. The long-run steady state will generate some value of k as the equilibrium of the economy. This value of k implies a pair (x^1, x^2) on the consumption possibility locus. The question then arises as to whether the k determined in this manner, or equivalently the consumption pair (x^1, x^2), has any efficiency properties. That is, are some values of k preferable to others and, if so, will the economy have an optimal value of k as its equilibrium? The answers to these questions are considered next.

3.5 Golden rules

It is possible to define the optimal value of k in a number of ways. The simplest is to view the optimum as the level of the capital–labour ratio that maximises per-capita consumption in the steady state. The relation that this level of capital satisfies is termed the *Golden rule* and the resulting capital–labour ratio is the Golden rule level. The analysis of the Golden rule is undertaken in 3.5.1. Alternatively, optimality can be defined in terms of the maximisation of a social welfare function. When the social welfare function is chosen as a discounted sum of utilities, the *modified Golden rule* is obtained. This is derived in 3.5.2. Such rules are important throughout the theory of economic growth.

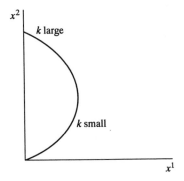

Figure 13.5   Consumption possibility locus

3.5.1 The Golden rule

This section considers the maximisation of consumption per period or, equivalently, consumption per capita, a procedure that leads to the Golden rule level of the capital–labour ratio. The following section will relate the Golden rule to Pareto optimality and dynamic efficiency.

The objective of the central planner is

$$\max x_t^l H_t + x_{t-1}^l H_{t-1},$$

(13.63)

which, since $H_{t-1} = \dfrac{H_t}{[1+n]}$, can be expressed in per-capita terms as

$$\max x_t^l + \frac{x_{t-1}^t}{[1+n]}.$$

(13.64)

Since the maximisation will be restricted to the choice between steady states, (13.64) reduces to

$$\max x^1 + \frac{x^2}{[1+n]}.$$

(13.65)

The constraint facing the central planner is that consumption in any period must be equal to total output less additions to the capital stock. Hence

$$x_t^l H_t + x_{t-1}^l H_{t-1} = H_t f(k_t) - H_t [k_{t+1}[1+n] - k_t].$$

(13.66)

At a steady state equilibrium (13.66) reduces to

$$x^1 + \frac{x^2}{[1+n]} = f(k) - nk.$$

(13.67)

The optimisation in (13.65) is therefore equivalent to $\max_{\{k\}} f(k) - nk$. From this maximisation the first-order condition

$$f'(k) - n = 0$$

(13.68)

is obtained. Hence the optimal k, k^*, should be chosen such that

$$f'(k^*) = n. \tag{13.69}$$

The capital–labour ratio k^* is termed the Golden rule capital–labour ratio and it is the optimal ratio in the sense that it maximises consumption per head.

Returning to the competitive economy, since $f' = r$, if the competitive economy reaches a steady state equilibrium with $r = n$, this equilibrium will satisfy the Golden rule. Since no other equilibrium will, this identifies $r = n$ as the Golden rule rate of interest. To understand the structure of the Golden rule competitive equilibrium, (13.57) and (13.59) can be used to show that the gradient of the consumption possibility locus is given by

$$\frac{dx^1}{dx^2} = - \frac{kf' + 1 + n}{[1+n][1+f'+kf'']}. \tag{13.70}$$

When $f' = n$, (13.70) reduces to $\dfrac{dx^1}{dx^2} = -\dfrac{1}{[1+n]}$. When facing a rate of interest $r = n$ consumer maximisation implies that $\dfrac{U_1(x^1, x^2)}{U^2(x^1, x^2)} = [1+n]$. Therefore at the Golden Rule the consumers' budget constraints, maximal indifference curves and the consumption possibility locus have identical gradients. This is illustrated in figure 13.6.

3.5.2 The modified Golden rule

The modified Golden rule is derived by choosing the growth path of the economy to maximise a social welfare function defined as the discounted sum of future utilities. This social welfare function is denoted by

$$\sum_{t=0}^{\infty} \gamma^t U(x_t^t, x_t^{t+1}). \tag{13.71}$$

Although the size of population in each generation does not enter explicitly into (13.71), it can be incorporated via the definition of the discount factor γ.

The objective of the social planner is to maximise (13.71) subject to the production constraint upon the economy which is summarised in (13.66). Dividing through by H_t, (13.66) becomes

$$k_t + f(k_t) = [1+n]k_{t+1} + x_t^t + \frac{x_{t-1}^t}{1+n}. \tag{13.72}$$

Substituting into (13.71) for x_{s-1}^{s-1} and x_s^s using (13.72), social welfare can be written

$$\sum_{t=0}^{\infty} \gamma^t U(x_t^t, x_t^{t+1}) = \sum_{t=0}^{s-2} \gamma^t U(x_t^t, x_t^{t+1})$$

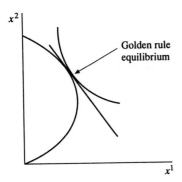

Figure 13.6   Golden rule competitive equilibrium

$$+\gamma^{s-1}U\left(k_{s-1}+f(k_{s-1})-[1+n]k_{s}-\frac{x_{s-2}^{s-1}}{1+n}, x_{s-1}^{s}\right)$$

$$+\gamma^{s}U\left(k_{s}+f(k_{s})-[1+n]k_{s+1}-\frac{x_{s-1}^{s}}{1+n}, x_{s}^{s+1}\right)+\sum_{t=s+1}^{\infty}\gamma^{t}U(x_{t}^{t}, x_{t}^{t+1}). \quad (13.73)$$

From (13.73) the optimal choice of x_{s-1}^{s} and k_{s} is determined by

$$\gamma^{s-1}\frac{\partial U(x_{s-1}^{s-1}, x_{s-1}^{s})}{\partial x_{s-1}^{s}}-\frac{\gamma^{s}}{[1+n]}\frac{\partial U(x_{s}^{s}, x_{s}^{s+1})}{dx_{s}^{s}}=0. \qquad (13.74)$$

and

$$-\gamma^{s-1}\frac{\partial U(x_{s-1}^{s-1}, x_{s-1}^{s})}{\partial x_{s-1}^{s-1}}[1+n]+\gamma^{s}\frac{\partial U(x_{s}^{s}, x_{s}^{s+1})}{dx_{s}^{s}}[1+f']=0. \qquad (13.75)$$

Along the optimal growth path, (13.74) and (13.75) must hold for all values of s.
Moving to the steady state, (13.74) and (13.75) become

$$U_{2}-\frac{\gamma}{[1+n]}U_{1}=0, \qquad (13.76)$$

and

$$1+n=\gamma[1+f']. \qquad (13.77)$$

Equation (13.77) is the modified Golden rule which relates the optimal
capital–labour ratio to the rate of population growth and the discount factor.
Since social welfare defined by (13.71) is only properly defined if $\gamma<1$, the
modified Golden rule results in a lower capital–labour ratio than the standard
Golden rule. This is due to the impatience implied by the discounting leading to
higher consumption in the present and less accumulation. The interpretation of
(13.76) is that the steady state must involve optimal intertemporal allocation of
consumption for each consumer when faced with an implied interest rate
satisfying $1+r=\dfrac{\gamma}{[1+n]}$.

3.6 Pareto optimality

Having now characterised the Golden rule capital–labour ratio and the corresponding rate of interest, it is possible to relate this to the question of Pareto optimality. To do this, first note that if $k > k*$ then $r < n$. The converse is true if $k < k*$. This is a simple consequence of the concavity of the production function. These two cases will now be discussed in turn, beginning with $k > k*$.

A capital–labour ratio above $k*$ represents an economy that has overaccumulated along the growth path. In such an economy it would be feasible for the consumers alive in any period with $k > k*$ to consume some of the existing capital stock so as to reduce the stock to the level $k*$. Such consumption would have two consequences. It would raise the welfare of the existing generations because it increases their present consumption at no cost. Secondly, it would raise the welfare of all following generations because it would place the economy on the Golden rule path and would consequently maximise their consumption. Thus, such consumption of the excess of the capital stock above the Golden rule level would lead to a Pareto improvement. Therefore, any steady state with $k > k*$ and $r < n$ is not Pareto optimal. Such states are called *dynamically inefficient*.

When $k \leq k*$ no such Pareto improvements can be found. Any act of investment that raises the welfare of the following generations must be undertaken at a cost to the existing generations in foregone consumption. Therefore all such states, including the Golden rule and modified Golden rule states, are Pareto optimal and are termed *dynamically efficient*.

The importance of this discussion is that when $r < n$ the equilibrium is not Pareto optimal despite the economy satisfying all the standard competitive assumptions. To illustrate that the failure of Pareto optimality does not require an unusual structure to be placed on the economy, consider the following example from Diamond (1965). The utility function of the single consumer in each generation is given by

$$U(x_t^t, x_t^{t+1}) = \beta \log x_t^t + (1 - \beta) \log x_t^{t+1}, \tag{13.78}$$

and the production function is $y = Ak^\alpha$. The steady state interest then can be calculated to be

$$r = \frac{\alpha[1 + n]}{[1 - \beta][1 - \alpha]}. \tag{13.79}$$

This will only be equal to the Golden rule rate when

$$n = \frac{\alpha}{[1 - \beta][1 - \alpha] - \alpha}. \tag{13.80}$$

If preferences and production do not satisfy this condition, and there is no reason why they should, the economy will not grow on the Golden rule growth path. This example illustrates that a Golden rule economy will be the exception rather than the norm.

4 CONCLUSIONS

Overlapping generations economies have a number of interesting features that are not shared with standard Arrow–Debreu economies. The competitive equilibria can be inefficient, complex endogenous dynamics can be generated, fiat money may be valuable as a store of value and its existence can raise the level of welfare and indeterminacy in equilibria may exist. In the context of public economics, it is the first of these that is arguably the most important since it provides a role for corrective policies in the absence of any additional market failure.

More importantly, the structure of the economy permits the analysis of the effects of policies that are essentially intertemporal in nature. This will be utilised in the analysis of social security in chapter 14 and debt and taxation in chapter 15. In both cases, the nature of inefficiency in overlapping generations economies and the structure of Golden rules will be central in explaining the results of policy analysis.

14

SOCIAL SECURITY

1 INTRODUCTION

The provision of social security to provide cover against disability and the inability to work due to old age is a feature of all developed economies. Such programmes are large, both in terms of the proportion of population receiving benefits and in terms of the total payments as a proportion of national income. The programmes are not without their difficulties. Thompson (1983) describes the adjustments made to the US programme following overly optimistic forecasts of real earnings growth. The expected increase in the ratio of retired to employed due to greater life expectancy will also place the system under pressure. There is also evidence, see Kotlikoff (1989), that social security programmes are required due to the inadequate savings and insurance purchases of the elderly which would not support them through retirement. These observations show that the analysis of social security and its economic impact is a subject of practical importance.

The first issue in the analysis of social security is its effect upon the equilibrium of the economy and, particularly, upon the level of the capital stock. If a social security programme has the form of a forced saving programme, so that consumers are provided with greater second-period earnings than they would naturally choose, then the programme may raise the capital stock. This outcome will be beneficial in an undercapitalised economy. Conversely, if the programme simply transfers earnings from those who are working to those who are retired, savings and hence the level of capital may fall. It can be judged from the difference in outcomes of these simple scenarios that the consequence of the existence of social security is closely dependent upon the programme's structure. In addition to its effects on savings, the interaction between social security and the retirement decision may also be significant.

A second major issue that arises is the effect of demographic change upon the social security programme. Present trends are for the proportion of retired consumers to increase and for the retired to live longer. At a practical level, this raises the question of whether the working population can continue to fund social security. A related, but more theoretical, issue is the question of whether there exists an optimal rate of population growth. This issue arises from the observation that if the rate of population growth increases, there are more workers to support each retired consumer but the level of capital per worker is reduced. This trade-off suggests there may be an optimal growth rate.

The introduction of a social security programme results in a transfer of resources towards the generation that benefits on the introduction of the programme and away from later generations. This raises the question of how such a programme receives the support that is required for it to be introduced at all. The mechanism by which the level of benefits in the programme are selected also needs to be addressed. Furthermore, the reasons why the private sector cannot provide insurance cover on terms at least as attractive as those offered by social security must also be addressed.

This chapter begins by setting out the important distinction between fully funded and pay-as-you-go social security. The economic effects of these two polar forms of programme are markedly different. An optimal social security programme is then characterised under the strong assumptions of certainty and fixed labour supply. A number of extensions of the basic result are considered including an analysis of optimal population growth. Determination of the level of social security by majority voting and various justifications for social security are then considered including altruism, myopia and aggregate uncertainty. The final section analyses the effect of introducing individual uncertainty about the length of life.

2 FULLY FUNDED AND PAY-AS-YOU-GO

The financing of social security can have important implications for the economic effects of the programme and for its sustainability in the face of demographic change. The purpose of this section is to define alternative structures of financing and to broadly sketch their differing effects.

To make the definitions as precise as possible, assume that the economy is one with overlapping generations and that each consumer lives for just two periods. Each consumer supplies labour during their first period of life and is retired in the second period. Finally, there is one capital good available, purchases of which provide a repository for savings.

In a *fully funded* system each consumer when young make contributions towards social security via a social security tax and the contributions are used to purchase capital by the social security programme. Total capital in the economy is then given by the sum of private capital and the publicly owned capital of the social security programme. Total pension benefits received by a consumer when retired are then equal to their contribution to the programme plus interest received. Such a programme satisfies the equalities pensions = social security tax plus interest = capital plus return.

A fully funded social security system effectively forces each consumer to save an amount at least equal to the tax they pay. Consumers may, of course, choose to save more. If, in the absence of social security, all consumers chose to save an amount in excess of the tax levied by the programme then, holding all else constant, a fully funded system will simply replace private saving by an equivalent amount of public saving. If these conditions are met, a fully funded system will have no effect upon the equilibrium outcome. In more general settings with a variety of investment opportunities, the possibility must be considered that the rate of return on private savings may differ from that on public savings. When it does, a fully funded system may affect the equilibrium.

In contrast to the fully funded system, a *pay-as-you-go* social security programme does not own any capital. Instead, a pay-as-you-go system relies on the contributions of the young of each generation to provide the pensions of the old of the previous generation. Such a programme therefore satisfies the equality

total benefits received by generation $t-1$ = contributions of generation t.

The system presently in operation in the US is of this form since the capital it owns would only fund approximately two months of benefit payments (see Thompson 1983).

A pay-as-you-go system leads to an intergenerational reallocation of resources whereas a fully funded system can at most cause an intertemporal reallocation for each generation. From this observation it can be seen immediately that the two systems will have rather different welfare implications, some of which will be investigated in the following sections.

Systems that fall between these two extremes will be termed *non-fully funded*. Such systems own some of the capital stock but the payments made in a period may be greater than or less than the revenue, composed of tax payments and interest, received in that period. The difference between the two will comprise investment, or disinvestment, in capital.

3 AN OPTIMAL PROGRAMME

The analysis of this section presents Samuelson's (1975a) characterisation of an optimal social security programme. The assumptions under which this will be undertaken are strong. In particular, it is assumed that labour supply is completely inelastic and that the date of retirement cannot be varied. The relaxation of these restrictions, and others, in later sections will place the results of this section in context.

Given that the competitive equilibrium may be non-optimal in an overlapping generations economy, there is potentially a role for a social security to enhance efficiency. In fact, in the discussion of Pareto optimality in chapter 13, a simple form of social security programme was shown to be Pareto improving over the competitive outcome. That example involved each young consumer transferring a unit of the good to the old consumer of the previous generation. This series of transfers, which is essentially a pay-as-you-go social security programme, raised the welfare of the generation that were old when the programme was introduced and left that of all later generations unaffected. This argument is further formalised in Aaron (1966).

To proceed beyond this result, consider a Diamond economy in which there exists a social security programme. The programme taxes each worker an amount τ and pays each retired person a pension β. The programme also owns a quantity K_t^s of capital. Equivalently, it can be said to own k_t^s, $k_t^s = K_t^s/L_t$, of capital per unit of labour. A social security programme will be *optimal* if the combination of τ, β and k_t^s is feasible for the programme and leads the economy to the Golden rule.

A *feasible social security* programme must satisfy the budget identity

$$\beta L_{t-1} = \tau L_t + r_t k_t^s L_t - [k_{t+1}^s L_{t+1} - k_t^s L_t], \tag{14.1}$$

which states that pension payments must be equal to tax revenue plus return on capital holdings less investment in capital. Since the population grows at rate n, in a steady state the identities $L_{t-1} = \dfrac{L_t}{1+n}$, $L_{t+1} = [1+n]L_t$ and $k_{t+1}^s = k_t^s \equiv k^s$, and can be used in (14.1) to generate the steady state budget identity

$$\frac{\beta}{[1+n]} = \tau + [1+r]k^s - [1+n]k^s. \tag{14.2}$$

Employing the equilibrium conditions $r = f'(k)$, where k denotes the total capital stock, the budget constraint of a consumer under the programme can be written

$$x^1 + \frac{x^2}{[1+r]} = f(k) - rk - \tau + \frac{\beta}{[1+r]}. \tag{14.3}$$

Note that the pension, β, which is received in the second period, is discounted since $x^1 + s = w - \tau$ and $[1+r]s + \beta = x^2$; hence $s = \dfrac{x^2 - \beta}{1+r}$. The budget identity of the programme can be used to eliminate β in the individual's budget constraint to give

$$x^1 + \frac{x^2}{[1+r]} = f(k) - rk - \tau + \frac{[1+n]}{1+r}\left[\tau + [r-n]k^s\right]. \tag{14.4}$$

Equilibrium in the capital market requires that private savings be equal to total capital less capital owned by the social security programme. This condition can be expressed as

$$w - x^1 - \tau = [1+n][k - k^s]. \tag{14.5}$$

Substitution for x^1 from the individual budget constraint (14.4) gives

$$\frac{x^2}{[1+r]} - \frac{[1+n]}{[1+r]} \left[\tau + [r - n]k^s \right] = [1+n][k - k^s]. \tag{14.6}$$

The equilibrium of the economy is then the simultaneous solution to

$$x^1 + \frac{x^2}{[1+r]} = f(k) - rk - \tau + \frac{[1+n]}{[1+r]} \left[\tau + [r - n]k^s \right], \tag{14.7}$$

$$f'(k) = r, \tag{14.8}$$

$$\frac{U_1}{U_2} = [1+r], \tag{14.9}$$

and

$$\frac{x^2}{[1+r]} - \frac{[1+n]}{[1+r]} \left[\tau + [r - n]k^s \right] = [1+n][k - k^s]. \tag{14.10}$$

These equations represent the private budget constraint, the choice of production technique, individual choice and the capital market equilibrium respectively.

The aim now is to investigate the effect that the social security policy can have upon the equilibrium. In particular, is it possible to design a policy that will generate the Golden rule? To see why this may be possible it should be noted that the failure of the competitive equilibrium without intervention to be efficient results from the savings behaviour of individuals which may lead to over- or underaccumulation of capital. With the correct choice of social security programme the government can effectively force-save for individuals. This alters the steady state level of the capital stock and hence the growth path of output.

Equations (14.7) to (14.10) determine the endogenous variables k, x^1, x^2, w and r conditionally upon the exogenous variables τ and k^s describing the social security programme. The solution of (14.7) to (14.10) provides the following system

$$k = k(\tau, k^s), \ x^1 = x^1(\tau, k^s), \ x^2 = x^2(\tau, k^s), \ r = r(\tau, k^s), \ w = w(\tau, k^s). \tag{14.11}$$

For a social security programme to achieve the Golden rule, there must exist a pair $\{\tau, k^s\}$ that satisfies the equality

$$r(\tau, k^s) = n. \tag{14.12}$$

To see the values that should be chosen, set $r = n$ in the capital market equilibrium condition (14.10) and employ the functional relationships (14.11) to give

$$\frac{x^2(\tau, k^s)}{[1+n]} = \tau + [1+n][k(\tau, k^s) - k^s]. \tag{14.13}$$

From (14.13) can be determined the set of pairs of $\{\tau, k^s\}$ that will give the Golden rule rate of growth. Since this is one equation in two variables, there will in general be a continuum of solutions rather than a single unique solution. If there exists a solution for τ when $k^s = 0$, then the optimum can be sustained by a pay-as-you-go system.

The structure of this social security programme is that the young in each generation give up some consumption, in the form of tax payments, to the old on the understanding that they will receive a similar a gift when old. There is consequently an element of trust involved in the transactions that support the social security policy. This should be contrasted to the failure of Pareto optimality in the Samuelson economy due to the lack of intergenerational trades.

To show that the optimal programme will not be fully funded, note that a fully funded programme must satisfy the identity

$$\beta L_{t-1} = \tau L_{t-1}[1+r] = k^s L_t[1+r]. \tag{14.14}$$

The substitution of (14.14) into the equilibrium conditions (14.7)–(14.10) shows that they reduce to the original market equilibrium conditions described in (13.43)–(13.47). The fully funded system therefore replaces private capital by public capital and does not affect the consumption choices of individual consumers. It can therefore have no real effect on the equilibrium and, if the initial steady state were not at the Golden rule, a fully funded social security programme cannot restore efficiency.

This analysis has demonstrated how a correctly designed social security programme can generate the Golden rule equilibrium, provided that it is not of the fully funded kind. A fully funded system simply replaces private savings by public savings and does not affect the growth path. In contrast a non-fully funded system can affect the aggregate levels of savings and hence the steady state capital–labour ratio. The results have been concerned only with the comparison between steady states. Burbidge (1983a) discusses the stability of the steady states and presents some simulations of the adjustment paths that are followed. The optimality result can also be extended, as in Gigliotti (1984), to show that a social security programme can be designed such that the implied steady state maximises the discounted sum of future utilities and achieves the modified Golden rule.

4 SOME EXTENSIONS

The optimality result of the previous section was derived under strong assumptions. Foremost amongst these was the inelastic supply of labour. One obvious consequence of the provision of a pension is to encourage retirement and through this mechanism to reduce labour supply. An induced increase in retirement raises the proportion of retired to working consumers and reduces the welfare gains obtained from the implementation of social security. The provision of a pension will also affect the savings decision. There will be an incentive to reduce saving since a pension is simply a substitute for private saving. Conversely, earlier retirement suggests the need to raise savings to cover the longer retirement period. The resolution of these effects will have important implications for the level of the capital stock. Variable labour supply, and other extensions to the basic analysis, are now considered.

4.1 Labour supply and retirement

The interaction between social security provision and the retirement decision has been analysed from both partial equilibrium and general equilibrium perspectives. Although the important results of the former will be noted, it is the latter that is of primary interest here.

Under the assumptions of perfect capital markets, actuarial fairness and known lifespan, Kotlikoff (1979) shows that the provision of social security will not affect the retirement decision. This is simply a result of pensions being equivalent to private savings in that the provision of pensions does not alter the opportunity set of a consumer. An increase in pension simply replaces private savings on a one-for-one basis. Relaxing each assumption in turn, Crawford and Lilien (1981) show that the effect on the date of retirement is in general ambiguous but a progressive system tends to advance retirement for low-income workers. Diamond and Mirrlees (1986) focus on the problems raised by the government's inability to distinguish between those unable to work and those who choose not to work. When consumers are forced to retire due to an inability to work, but with no prior warning of this, it is shown that the optimal social security programme will have benefits rising with the age of retirement.

Although suggestive, these analyses do not address the interaction between the retirement decision and the equilibrium of the economy. There are clearly important connections between these since early retirement reduces labour supply while reduced savings lower the equilibrium capital stock. A simple extension of the Samuelson analysis by Hu (1979) that incorporates endogenous retirement is now discussed.

The production side of the economy and the structure of the population remains as in section 3. What distinguishes the present economy is that although all consumers must supply one unit of labour in the first period of their life, they can choose what proportion of the second period of life they spend working. To provide a motive for retirement, utility is increasing in the length of the period of retirement.

Expressed formally, the utility function is assumed to take the form

$$U^t = U(x_t^t, x_t^{t+1}, \alpha_t),\tag{14.15}$$

where α_t, $0 \leq \alpha_t \leq 1$ is the proportion of the second period of life that is spent in retirement. Again denoting the tax paid toward the social security programme whilst working by τ and the pension by β, the consumer's budget constraint is

$$x_t^1 + \frac{x_t^{t+1}}{1+r_{t+1}} = w_t - \tau + \frac{[1-\alpha_t][w_{t+1}-\tau]}{1+r_{t+1}} + \frac{\alpha_t\beta}{1+r_{t+1}}, \qquad (14.16)$$

or, in the steady state

$$x^1 + \rho x^2 = w - \tau + \rho[1-\alpha][w-\tau] + \rho\alpha\beta. \qquad (14.17)$$

Maximising utility leads to the necessary conditions

$$\frac{\partial U}{\partial x^2} = \rho \frac{\partial U}{\partial x^1}, \qquad (14.18)$$

and

$$\frac{\partial U}{\partial \alpha} = \rho[w - \tau - \beta] \frac{\partial U}{\partial x^1}. \qquad (14.19)$$

From (14.18) and (14.19) can be derived consumption demands and a retirement decision that are dependent upon w, ρ, τ and β. It is assumed that the optimal α satisfies $0 < \alpha < 1$. If the upper bound were attained the model would be identical to that already analysed.

The total population at time t is denoted by P_t. With growth rate n, the proportion of the total population that is in the second period of life, θ, is given by

$$\theta = \frac{H_{t-1}}{H_t + H_{t-1}} = \frac{H_{t-1}}{[1+n]H_{t-1} + H_{t-1}} = \frac{1}{2+n}. \qquad (14.20)$$

The social security programme is assumed to operate on the pay-as-you-go basis. Noting that benefits are only paid once a consumer has retired, the programme satisfies the budget identity

$$P_t\theta\alpha\beta = L_t\tau = P_t l\tau, \qquad (14.21)$$

where L is total labour supply and l is average labour supply given by $[1-\theta+\theta[1-\alpha]] = [1-\theta\alpha]$ since proportion $1-\theta$ of the population work full-time and proportion θ work for fraction $[1-\alpha]$ of the time. Equation (14.21) reduces to

$$\alpha\theta\beta = [1-\alpha\theta]\tau. \qquad (14.22)$$

The decision problem of firms is unaffected by the existence of the social security programme. In the steady state capital and labour demands satisfy $r = f'(k)$ and $w = f(k) - kf'(k)$, where the capital-labour ratio $k = K/L$. These equations can be solved to express the interest rate as a function of the wage rate or $w = \phi(r)$. This relationship is termed the *factor price frontier* and is the locus of pairs of w, r that are consistent with equilibrium for firms. Since $dr = f''dk$ and

$$dw = -kf''dk, \frac{dw}{dr} = -k.$$

The optimal social security programme can be derived by maximising (14.15) with respect to the level of the pension, β, taking into account the dependence of the choice variables on β and the budget constraint of the programme. Differentiating (14.15) and using (14.18) and (14.19) gives

$$\frac{dU}{d\beta} = \frac{\partial U}{\partial x^1} \left[\frac{dx^1}{d\beta} + \rho \frac{dx^2}{d\beta} + \rho[w - \tau - \beta] \frac{d\alpha}{d\beta} \right], \tag{14.23}$$

where the total derivatives $\dfrac{dx^i}{d\beta}, i = 1, 2$ and $\dfrac{d\alpha}{d\beta}$ take account of the induced change in τ via (14.22). The derivative of the budget constraint (14.17) can then be substituted into (14.23) to give

$$\frac{dU}{d\beta} = \frac{\partial U}{\partial x^1} \left[[1 + \rho - \alpha\rho] \frac{d[w - \tau]}{d\beta} + [w - \tau - x^2 - \alpha[w - \tau - \beta]] \frac{d\rho}{d\beta} + \alpha\rho \right]. \tag{14.24}$$

Using the second-period budget constraint $w - \tau + [1 + r]s = x^2 + \alpha[w - \tau - \beta]$, where s is first-period saving, (14.24) becomes

$$\frac{dU}{d\beta} = \frac{\partial U}{\partial x^1} \left[[1 + \rho - \alpha\rho] \frac{d[w - \tau]}{d\beta} - [1 + r]s \frac{d\rho}{d\beta} + \alpha\rho \right]. \tag{14.25}$$

By definition, $\dfrac{d\rho}{dr} = -\rho^2$ and, from the factor price frontier $\dfrac{dr}{dw} = -\dfrac{1}{k}$. Since the level of capital is given by $K = P\theta s$ and total labour supply $L = Pl = P[1 - \alpha\theta]$, $k = \dfrac{\theta s}{[1 - \alpha\theta]}$. Substituting these definitions into (14.24), using $\dfrac{d\rho}{d\beta} = \dfrac{d\rho}{dr}\dfrac{dr}{dw}\dfrac{dw}{d\beta}$ and collecting terms

$$\frac{dU}{d\beta} = \frac{\partial U}{\partial x^1} \left[\left[1 + \rho - \frac{\rho}{\theta} \right] \frac{dw}{d\beta} - [1 + \rho - \alpha\rho] \frac{d\tau}{d\beta} + \alpha\rho \right]. \tag{14.26}$$

Finally, since $\theta = \dfrac{1}{2 + n}$ and $\rho = \dfrac{1}{1 + r}$, $\left[1 + \rho - \dfrac{\rho}{\theta} \right] = [r - n]\rho$, the optimal pension solves

$$\frac{dU}{d\beta} = \frac{\partial U}{\partial x^1} \left[[r - n]\rho \frac{dw}{d\beta} - [1 + \rho - \alpha\rho] \frac{d\tau}{d\beta} + \alpha\rho \right]. \tag{14.27}$$

The contrast between this result and the conclusion drawn from the economy in which no labour can be supplied in the second period of life can be seen by setting $\alpha = 1$ in (14.27). From (14.22), when $\alpha = 1$, $\dfrac{d\tau}{d\beta} = \dfrac{\theta}{1 - \theta}$. Substituting into (14.27) then gives

$$\frac{dU}{d\beta}\bigg|_{\alpha=1} = \frac{\partial U}{\partial x^1}\left[[r-n]\rho\frac{dw}{d\beta} - \left[\frac{\theta}{1-\theta}\right]\left[\frac{r-n}{1+n}\right]\right] = 0. \tag{14.28}$$

Since $\frac{\partial U}{\partial x^1} > 0$, the solution to (14.28) must have $r = n$ so that the programme achieves the Golden rule.

When $0 < \alpha < 1$, it then follows that $r = n$ will not be achieved at the solution to (14.27). Assuming that $\frac{d\tau}{d\beta} > 0$, if $\frac{dw}{d\beta} < 0$ then the programme will lead to a rate of interest less than the growth rate of population. The converse holds if $\frac{dw}{d\beta} > 0$.

The conclusion to be drawn from this analysis is that the decentralisation of the Golden rule by the use of a social security programme will not be desirable when the retirement decision is endogenous. This is because the tax used to pay for pensions introduces a distortion into the choice problem of each consumer. Although the programme can aid the dynamic efficiency of the economy by affecting the level of the capital stock, this has to be set against the inefficiency caused by the tax. Continuous-time versions of this analysis are presented in Hu (1978) and Sheshinski (1978).

In addition to affecting the retirement decision, social security will also have an impact upon the labour supply decision itself. This impact will be particularly pronounced when a household framework is adopted and the distinction is made between the male and female labour supply. Since female labour supply is typically more elastic than male supply, it will be female labour supply that is proportionately more affected by the social security programme. Simulation evidence on the strength of these effects is presented by Craig and Batina (1991). They consider an economy in which each generation is composed of an equal number of males and females. Pairs of males and females then form households and jointly choose their labour supplies to maximise a household utility function. Except for the fact that they now supply two forms of labour, male and female, these households are equivalent to the consumers of the economies above. It is assumed that the two forms of labour are close, but not perfect, substitutes in a CES production function. Since they are not perfect substitutes, the equilibrium wage rates may differ.

The social security programme considered by Craig and Batina contains provisions other than a simple retirement benefit. The retirement benefit is determined by the value of earnings prior to retirement and may be different between males and females. Furthermore, each female has the option of choosing either a pension based on their own earnings history or one based on their spouse's earnings. The social security programme is financed by a tax on labour earnings, a lump-sum tax and an additional tax upon labour earnings when, in the second period of life, these rise above a cut-off level. Incorporating these provisions, the budget constraint of a household whose members are born in period t is given by

Table 14.1. *Effect of social security*

	w/w'	L_t	L_{t+1}	L'_t	L'_{t+1}	$x_t/'x_{t+1}^t$
Without programme	1.790	0.478	0.232	0.434	0.084	0.561
With programme	1.804	0.503	0.095	0.462	0	0.470

$$x_t' + \frac{x_t^{t+1}}{1+r_{t+1}} = [1-t]\left[w_t L_t + w_t' L_t' + \frac{w_{t+1}L_{t+1} + w_{t+1}'L_{t+1}'}{1+r_{t+1}}\right] - T$$

$$+ \left[\frac{\beta[w_t L_t + w_{t+1}L_{t+1}] + \beta'[1-\delta][w_t'L_t' + w_{t+1}'L_{t+1}'] + B}{1+r_{t+1}}\right]$$

$$+ \left[\frac{\sigma\delta[w_t L_t + w_{t+1}L_{t+1}]}{1+r_{t+1}}\right] - \left[\frac{\tau[w_{t+1}L_{t+1} + w_{t+1}'L_{t+1}' - a]}{1+r_{t+1}}\right]. \quad (14.29)$$

In (14.29) the primes denote variables relating to the female, β is the benefit rate on own earnings, $\delta=0$ if the wife chooses a pension based on her earnings and $\delta=1$ if she chooses that based on that of her spouse. σ is the benefit rate on spouse's earnings. B is the lump-sum benefit, T the lump-sum tax, t the tax rate on earnings and τ the tax on second-period earnings above the level a.

For a programme with $t=0.15$, $\beta=\beta'=0.2$, $\sigma=0.1$ and $\tau=0.5$, the results obtained are summarised in table 14.1. The primary effects of the programme are to shift labour supply towards the beginning of the life-cycle for both males and females and to increase the level of household consumption in the second period of life relative to that in the first period. Lifetime labour supply of both males and females falls. The programme also causes a slight shift in relative wages in favour of males.

These results demonstrate how the introduction of a social security programme affects the allocation of labour and consumption over the lifecycle. In particular, it acts as a disincentive to supply labour in the later stages of life. The reduction of total labour supply that is caused will also have consequences for the level of output that is produced and the capital–labour ratio.

4.2 Effect on savings and capital

With a pay-as-you-go social security programme in operation, any effect that the existence of the programme has upon private savings is reflected directly in the level of the capital stock since, by definition, the programme owns no capital. Social security has two conflicting effects upon the level of private saving. The first effect is the substitution of social security for private savings which naturally reduces the level of saving. Offsetting this effect is the likelihood that social security will bring forward retirement. If this does occur, private saving should rise in order to cover the increased length of retirement. At this level of generality, the net effect is indeterminate.

In contrast to the earlier evidence of Cagan (1965) and Katona (1964) which showed that consumers covered by private pensions did not save less than those not covered, Feldstein (1974) estimated that the existence of the US social security programme reduced private savings by 30–50 per cent. This evidence was based on the estimation of a consumption function that included social security wealth as one of the explanatory variables. The central estimate suggested that, during the 1960s, the capital stock was 38 per cent lower with the social security programme than it would have been without. Although widely cited, these results have not always been replicated in later studies. Danziger, Haveman and Plotnick (1981) suggest that the true figure should be somewhere in the range of 0–20 per cent whilst Aaron (1982) concludes that there is simply a lack of agreement amongst the studies. As an example of conflicting findings, work by Lee and Chao (1988) estimates labour force participation and personal savings, simultaneously taking into account private pensions. Although social security wealth is found to encourage retirement, the payment of contributions to social security has an insignificant effect on private savings.

Whether it is possible for a theoretical economy to exhibit a similar responsiveness to the introduction of social security as that suggested by Feldstein has been investigated by Kotlikoff (1979) in an analysis involving a continuous-time formulation of endogenous retirement. Consider an economy of identical individuals which has a population growth rate of n and endogenous labour-augmenting technical progress at rate g. The latter assumption implies that the wage rate is also growing at rate g. At each point in time, the fraction of the existing population that have lived out their lifespan of D years will be replaced by new consumers. Each consumer chooses their consumption stream and date of retirement to maximise discounted utility.

Denoting instantaneous utility by $U(x(t))$, discounted utility is given by

$$U = \int_0^D U(x_t(t))e^{-\rho t}dt, \tag{14.30}$$

where ρ is the rate of time preference. Utility (14.30) is maximised subject to the budget constraint

$$\int_0^D x_t(t)e^{-rt}dt = \int_0^R W[1-\tau]e^{-[r-g]t}dt + \int_R^D \beta e^{-[r-g]t}dt. \tag{14.31}$$

In writing (14.31), it is assumed that both the wage, W, and the pension, β, are growing at rate g. The pay-as-you-go identity for the social security programme is given by

$$\beta = \frac{\tau W[1-\theta]}{\theta}, \tag{14.32}$$

with $\dfrac{[1-\theta]}{\theta}$, the ratio of those working to those retired, given by

$$\frac{1-\theta}{\theta} = \frac{\displaystyle\int_0^R e^{-nt}dt}{\displaystyle\int_D^R e^{-nt}dt}. \tag{14.33}$$

At each point in time, additions to the capital stock are equal to the savings of those working plus the savings of those who are retired. For a working consumer born at date t, their savings are

$$\frac{dK_t(t)}{dt} = W[1-\tau]e^{gt} - x_t(t) + rK_t(t), \tag{14.34}$$

whilst for a retired consumer

$$\frac{dK_t(t)}{dt} = \beta e^{gt} - x_t(t) + rK_t(t). \tag{14.35}$$

Solving (14.34) provides the capital owned by a consumer born in t and solving (14.35) determines the capital of a retired consumer. Total capital can then be found by integrating over the population. The total savings provided by consumers can then be equated with the capital demanded by firms and equilibrium computed.

Adopting an instantaneous utility function of the form $U = \dfrac{x_t(t)^{1-\alpha}}{1-\alpha}$ and a Cobb–Douglas production function, the simulation results of Kotlikoff for the effect of the introduction of a social security programme with a value of τ of 0.1 are summarised in table 14.2. Inspection of table 14.2 demonstrates that a social security programme can have effects with the order of magnitude identified by Feldstein. The reductions in the capital stock range from 10 per cent to 21 per cent which, although somewhat less than 38 per cent, are still significant. Even in very simple economies it is therefore possible for the introduction of pay-as-you-go social security to substantially reduce the capital stock and with it the output of the economy.

4.3 Ricardian equivalence

Ricardian equivalence originally referred to the proposition that the method of financing government expenditure, whether through taxes or borrowing, was irrelevant. To illustrate this, consider the following example. To reduce the level of taxation by D in period t, the government sells quantity D of bonds. To repay the bonds the following period, the government must levy additional taxes in

Table 14.2. *Effect on capital stock*

Net rate of interest	Age of retirement	Rate of time preference	Reduction in capital stock
	42	0.0160	−0.213
0.05	45	0.0120	−0.190
	50	0.0058	−0.104
	42	0.0232	−0.212
0.06	45	0.0196	−0.189
	50	0.0148	−0.102

Note: Parameters: $\alpha = 1$, $D = 55$, $r = 0.05$, $\tau = 0.01$, $r = n + g$, $n = g$

$t + 1$ of $[1 + r]D$. Since the discounted value of this increase in taxation is exactly equal to the value of the original tax cut, the net wealth of the economy is unchanged when viewed from period t. The bond-financed plan is therefore equivalent to keeping the initial level of taxation unchanged, illustrating the principle of Ricardian equivalence.

Ricardian equivalence will be discussed in detail in chapter 15 but a further point needs to be made here in order to relate the argument to the analysis of social security. Returning to the example above, it would seem that if some of the households alive at time t were no longer alive at $t + 1$ then the equivalence would fail since they would benefit from the reduced tax payment but would avoid the increased tax. To make this point stronger, assume the bonds mature N periods after issue. The argument of the example would still apply if the population remained unchanged over the N period but it now seems less reasonable to expect this.

There is, as first noted by Barro (1974), a mechanism that will maintain equivalence even if the population changes between issue and redemption of bonds. Suppose that each consumer has a single identified descendant and that they care about their own level of consumption and about the utility level of their descendant. Such intergenerational altruism then links finitely lived consumers into a household whose lifespan is as long as that of the economy. The altruism will manifest itself in consumers choosing to leave bequests to their descendants and it is via the bequest motive that Ricardian equivalence arises. To see this point, assume that the bonds are purchased by generation t but the tax liability is borne by generation $t + 1$. If generation t raises its bequest to $t + 1$ by exactly the amount necessary for $t + 1$ to meet their increased tax liability then the consumption plans of both generations will remain unaffected by the switch from tax-finance to bonds thus maintaining the equivalence result. Although there are, of course, limitations to this result which are described in chapter 15, it does have implications for the analysis of social security.

One implication of Ricardian equivalence has, in fact already been described. The discussion of a fully funded social security programme in section 2 noted that such a programme would leave the equilibrium of the economy unaffected. The fully funded system requires that the pensions received by each generation are equal to the taxes that they paid. In this case an increase in tax when young is accompanied by the receipt of a pension when old which is equal in value to the tax plus interest. This is simply the opposite of the initial example of equivalence and a slight modification of that argument shows why it has no net effect. The households reduce their private savings by the amount of the tax, maintain their consumption levels and replace private saving by saving in the pension plan. Since private and public savings have the same return, they are indifferent to this rearrangement. It is worth noting that this argument presumes that private savings are initially greater than the tax used to finance the pension. If they are not, then equivalence will not apply.

Introducing intergenerational altruism allows the equivalence argument to be extended to pay-as-you-go social security. A pay-as-you-go system can be interpreted as a forced transfer from the young generation to the old. If all members of the old generation were making a positive bequest to their descendants prior to the introduction of the programme, the effects of the programme can be entirely neutralised by the old simply increasing their bequest by exactly the pension they receive. By the definition of a pay-as-you-go system, this increased bequest will exactly match the taxes paid by the young. Therefore, with intergenerational altruism, pay-as-you-go social security will have no effect upon the equilibrium provided the bequest motive is operational prior to the commencement of the programme.

In this context, it should be stressed that intergenerational altruism must manifest itself through each member of generation t having a utility function of the form introduced by Barro (1974)

$$U^t = U(x_t^t, x_t^{t+1}, U^{t+1}),\tag{14.36}$$

where U^{t+1} is the utility level of their descendant. The dependence of U^t upon U^{t+1} provides the linkage that effectively turns the separate generations of the family into a single household. Furthermore, although there may be a bequest motive, bequests may still be zero if the consumer is at a corner solution. For the separable utility function $U(x_t^t) + \sigma^1 U(x_t^{t+1}) + \sigma^2 U^{t+1}$, Weil (1987) shows that the bequest will only be positive if $\sigma^2 > \dfrac{1+n}{1+\tilde{r}}$ where $\tilde{r}$ is the rate of interest in the absence of bequests. If the no-bequest economy is dynamically inefficient then $\tilde{r} < n$ and with discount rate $\sigma^2 < 1$ bequests will never occur.

An alternative specification (used, for example, in Hu (1979)) is to assume that each consumer cares about the size of the bequest, b_t, that they leave to their descendant, rather than their descendant's welfare, so that utility takes the form

$$U^t = U(x_t^t, x_t^{t+1}, b_t).\tag{14.37}$$

With the specification of utility in (14.37), the equivalence result no longer applies. This follows from observing that the introduction of a social security programme that has an initial transfer to generation t will result in standard changes in x_t^t, x_t^{t+1}, b_t via an income effect rather than an increase in b_t exactly equal to the level of the pension. If it is a normal good, the level of the bequest will increase but not to the point that it maintains the welfare of generation $t+1$.

In the presence of intergenerational altruism it is therefore possible for social security programmes to have no effect upon the equilibrium of the economy. Indeed, the discussion above may suggest that this is the typical outcome. However, there are many circumstances in which the Ricardian equivalence result does not apply and, although this pre-empts some of the material of chapter 15, it is worth noting some of these. As already stated the utility function must take the form of (14.36) and the bequest motive must be active for all consumers prior to the introduction of the programme. The existence of bequests in itself is not sufficient; these may simply be left due to uncertainty about the time of death or poor planning. Taxes and benefits must be equal for each household so that if there is a redistributive element to the programme then equivalence will not apply. In addition the empirical evidence already discussed suggests that it does not apply in practice.

Although equivalence may apply in the simple economies used so far if altruistic preferences are introduced, the limits to the result are soon reached when obvious extensions to these economies are made. With respect to the analysis of social security, Ricardian equivalence should therefore be viewed as a theoretical curiosity rather than a result of practical relevance.

4.4 Demographics

The growth rate of the population is an important determinant of the success of a social security programme. A rapidly increasing population will make it easier for the young to provide pensions for the (relatively) smaller number of old. It will also lead to a dilution of the capital stock which makes it more difficult for the pension commitments to be met. This trade-off suggests that there may be a rate of population growth which will maximise the welfare of the representative consumer. Indeed, Samuelson (1975b) claimed to have provided a characterisation of this optimal rate. However, it was shown by Deardorff (1976) that in many reasonable cases Samuelson's conditions actually described the growth rate that minimised welfare. This fact is further clarified in Samuelson (1976).

The connection between the rate of population growth and the optimal level of social security can be investigated by optimising the choice of programme for given n and then varying n; this is the method adopted by Lopez-Garcia (1991). Assuming that each consumer can choose the amount of labour they supply in each period and denoting the level of labour supply by ℓ_t^i, a consumer born in t maximises

$$U^t = U(x_t^t, x_t^{t+1}, 1 - \ell_t^t). \tag{14.38}$$

The social security tax is levied proportionately upon labour income at rate τ so, in the steady state with identical consumers, the budget constraint for the programme is given by

$$\beta = [1+n]\tau w\ell. \tag{14.39}$$

The pension β is assumed to be a constant proportion, ρ, of the net wage so that $\beta = \rho[1-\tau]w\ell$. As a function of the *replacement rate* ρ, the tax supporting the programme is equal to

$$\tau = \frac{\rho}{1+n+\rho}. \tag{14.40}$$

The individual budget constraint is

$$x^1 + \frac{x^2}{1+r} = \frac{[1+n][1+r+\rho]}{[1+r][1+n+\rho]}w\ell = \hat{w}\ell, \tag{14.41}$$

so that maximisation of (14.38) gives consumption demands $x^i = x^i(\hat{w}, r)$, $i = 1$, 2, and labour supply $\ell = \ell(\hat{w}, r)$. Employing the factor price frontier, $w = \varphi(r)$, the equilibrium interest rate is the solution to

$$r = f'\left(\frac{[1-\tau]w\ell - x^1}{[1+n]\ell}\right) = f'\left(\frac{\left[\dfrac{1+n}{1+n+\rho}\right]\varphi(r)\ell(\hat{w}, r) - x^1(\hat{w}, r)}{[1+n]\ell(\hat{w}, r)}\right). \tag{14.42}$$

The solution to (14.42) is denoted $r = r(\rho, n)$.

Substituting into (14.38), the attainable level of utility can be written $U = V(\rho, n)$. Differentiating utility with respect to ρ for fixed n gives

$$\frac{\partial V}{\partial \rho} = \frac{\partial U}{\partial x^2}\frac{[1+n]}{[1+n+\rho]}[n - r(\rho, n)]\left[k\ell\frac{\partial r}{\partial \rho} + \frac{\varphi(r)\ell}{[1+n+\rho]}\right], \tag{14.43}$$

where use has been made of the conditions describing consumer choice. The sign of (14.43) is the same as that of $n - r$ since it can be shown, employing the sufficient condition for stability, that $\dfrac{\partial r}{\partial \rho} > 0$. Hence only if $r(0, n) < n$ will there be an interior, positive solution for ρ. In that case, since the second-order condition can be shown to be negative at $r = n$, the maximising value of ρ satisfies $r(\rho, n) = n$.

Assuming now that an interior solution exists for ρ, with $\rho > 0$, the fact that the optimal social security programme can be employed to maintain the equality of r with n allows (14.42) to be written as

$$n = f'\left(\frac{\left[\dfrac{1+n}{1+n+\rho}\right]\varphi(n)\ell(\varphi(n), n) - x^1(\varphi(n), n)}{[1+n]\ell(\varphi(n), n)}\right). \tag{14.44}$$

Solving (14.44) for ρ, the solution is written $\rho = \rho(n)$. This allows utility to be expressed as $U = V(\rho(n), n)$ and hence

$$\frac{\partial U}{\partial n} = \frac{\partial V(\rho(n), n)}{\partial \rho} \frac{\partial \rho}{\partial n} + \frac{\partial V(\rho(n), n)}{\partial n}. \tag{14.45}$$

However, since ρ is chosen optimally, (14.45) reduces to

$$\frac{\partial U}{\partial n} = \frac{\partial V(\rho(n), n)}{\partial n} = \frac{\partial U}{\partial x^2} \frac{\rho \varphi \ell}{[1 + n + \rho]}. \tag{14.46}$$

Since it has been assumed that $\rho > 0$, (14.46) is always positive so that increasing the rate of population growth will increase welfare. In this case, there is no optimal rate of population growth since the ability of an increasing population to provide a larger pension dominates.

Alternatively, if the optimal replacement rate is negative, utility is always a decreasing function of the rate of population growth. Finally, if a replacement rate of 0 is optimal, so that no social security programme is required for the Golden rule to be obtained, then (14.46) is always zero. It can easily be shown, however, that this may either be minimum, as in Deardorff (1976), or a maximum. The competitive outcome that achieves the Golden rule may therefore be sustained by a rate of population growth that can either maximise or minimise utility, thus being either the best or worst of all worlds.

In conclusion, the relation between the growth rate of the population, the choice of social security programme and the level of utility may take many forms. If there is an optimal social security programme that has a positive pension, then an increase in population growth always raises welfare. The converse holds if the optimal pension is negative. More surprisingly, when it is optimal to have no pension system the rate of population growth that supports such an equilibrium will either maximise or minimise the level of utility. From a policy perspective, there may be benefits to be obtained from rapid population growth as the increasing population can support a more generous social security programme.

5 DETERMINATION AND JUSTIFICATION

There are several justifications for the existence of social security programmes. The optimal programme of section 3 would raise the welfare of all generations that benefited from the attainment of the Golden rule steady state although there may be some losers along the adjustment path (see Flemming 1977). This need not be true of pay-as-you-go systems with their implied intergenerational transfers nor of fully funded systems which may simply replace private saving by public saving. Given these observations, the purpose of this section is to look at various methods of determining the structure of social security programmes and of justifying their existence.

5.1 Voting equilibria

The most obvious mechanism by which the level of social security can be determined is through a system of voting. Although systems of voting differ widely, the literature focuses only upon simple majority voting and the median voter outcome. The rationale for this position is that these are the most tractable analytically and capture the essence of more sophisticated alternatives.

The earliest analysis of these issues is given in Aaron (1966) who shows that since a social security programme with positive benefits always provides a transfer to the old, a median-age voters may find it in their favour to vote for the continued existence of a programme despite its total effect being to reduce the welfare of all households. Browning (1975) considers an economy in which there is no capital market so that the only method of saving is via social security. In such circumstances, majority voting leads to a level of social security in excess of that which maximises lifetime welfare.

A simple result on the outcome of majority voting in an economy with capital markets is obtained by Hu (1979) for the economy of section 4.1. Since population growth is positive, at any point in time the young generation is larger then the old. Combining this observation with the assumption that all consumers are identical, it follows that the programme chosen by majority voting will be that which maximises the lifetime utility of a young consumer. The programme therefore solves

$$\max_{\{x^1, x^2, \alpha, \beta\}} U(x^1, x^2, \alpha), \tag{14.47}$$

subject to the consumer's budget constraint (14.17) and the budget identity of the social security programme (14.22). Assuming that the consumer treats the wage as independent of β when performing the optimisation, the social security programme chosen by majority voting will satisfy

$$[1 + \rho - \alpha\rho]\frac{\partial \tau}{\partial \beta} - \alpha\rho = 0. \tag{14.48}$$

In general, there is no reason to expect that the programme determined by (14.48) will be any more, or any less, generous than the programme arising from (14.27). However, in the special case of labour supply only in the first period of life, so $\alpha = 1$, (14.48) reduces to

$$\frac{\theta}{1-\theta}\frac{r-n}{1+r} = 0, \tag{14.49}$$

so that majority voting will attain the Golden rule.

This analysis is extended by Hu (1982) who considers an economy in which consumers live for three periods. They work in the first two and are retired in the third. The important distinction is that with population growth satisfying the restriction

$$2+n>[1+n]^2,\qquad\qquad\qquad\qquad\qquad (14.50)$$

so that, at any given time, the number of consumers in either the second or third period of their life is greater than the number in their first period, majority voting will always lead to an outcome that is supported by two of the three generations. Furthermore, if there is a possibility that the social security programme determined by voting at time t may be overturned by a re-vote at $t+1$ or later, the possibility of strategic voting arises. That is, a consumer in the early stages of their life may vote for a programme with a low level of tax with the intention later in life of voting for one with higher provision.

Employing this framework Hu (1982) shows that the equilibrium arising from majority voting when consumers are uncertain about the impact of present voting intentions on later outcomes may have an interest rate either above or below that of the Golden rule. This finding indicates that although majority voting need not be efficient, the possibility arises that it may be possible to design a mechanism that implements the Golden rule. The weakness of this framework is that the uncertainty is necessary for a consumer to have an interior solution to their choice of preferred social security tax rate. In the certain case, when no re-voting can occur, they will always choose a tax rate of 1 when the net gain from the programme is positive and zero when it is negative. The uncertainty, however, is introduced in a fairly arbitrary fashion: it is simply assumed that future provision, though uncertain, is increasing in the present level.

An alternative approach to this issue is provided by Boadway and Wildasin (1989) who employ the continuous-time framework described in (14.30)–(14.33) but with $g=0$. The majority-voting assumption results in the equilibrium level of social security being determined by the median voter. To overcome the problem that in the absence of uncertainty this choice would either be a tax rate of 0 or 1, the capital market is assumed imperfect so that consumers face constraints upon borrowing. In addition, it is assumed that voting is infrequent so that when determining their voting intentions each consumer expects the level of social security adopted to remain constant for the remainder of their lifespan. The major findings are that, given an existing level of social security benefits, preferences are single peaked over alternative levels so that the median-voter outcome applies and that when consumers cannot borrow against future benefits, if the existing level of benefits are below the optimal level for the median-age voter, the median-age voter will also be the median voter.

5.2 Altruism

Voluntary intergenerational transfers can arise when consumers have altruistic feelings about other generations. These feelings can extend both to previous generations and to following generations. Some of the consequences of bequests have been discussed in section 4.3; the focus here is primarily upon voluntary gifts from young to old since this is the essence of a pay-as-you-go programme.

Altruism has been represented as a consumption externality by Veall (1986) with the utility of generation t being of the form

$$U^t = U(x_t^t, x_t^{t+1}, x_{t-1}^t). \tag{14.51}$$

In the formulation of (14.51) the consumption of generation t-1 in the second period of life affects the utility of generation t. When the externality effect is positive, it can be interpreted as a form of altruism. The alternative representation of Hansson and Stuart (1989) develops the Buiter (1980) and Carmichael (1982) formulation of altruism and assumes that each consumer alive at time t has the utility function

$$U^t = \left[\frac{U^1(x_{t-1}^{t-1}) + U^2(x_{t-1}^t)}{[1+n][1+\gamma]} \right] + U^1(x_t^t) + U^2(x_t^{t+1})$$

$$+ \sum_{z=t+1}^{\infty} [U^1(x_z^z) + U^2(x_z^{z+1})] \left[\frac{1+n}{1+\sigma} \right]^{z-t}, \tag{14.52}$$

where the first term captures concern for the older generation, with σ the relevant discount rate, and the third term that for following generations with discount rate σ. Although analytical details are rather different, the two formulations provide an essentially identical motive for the introduction of a pay-as-you-go social security programme that, on its introduction, involves an initial transfer to the older generation. Here the approach of Hansson and Stuart will be followed.

Assume that production is subject to a constant coefficient production function so that the wage rate, normalised at 1, and the interest rate, r, are both constant. Two restrictions upon the utility function are adopted. Firstly, $\sigma > n$ so that the infinite sum in (14.52) converges and $\sigma > r$ so that, as noted in 4.3, no consumer desires to leave a bequest. Denoting the gift given by generation t to generation $t-1$ by a_t, the budget constraints in the first and second periods of life are

$$x_t^t = 1 - s_t - a_t, x_t^{t+1} = [1+r]s_t + [1+n]a_{t+1}. \tag{14.53}$$

The gift a_t satisfies the necessary condition

$$\frac{U^{2\prime}(x_{t-1}^t)}{1+\gamma} - U^{1\prime}(x_t^t) \le 0, = 0 \text{ if } a_t > 0, \tag{14.54}$$

where γ is the rate of discounting applied to the older generation's utility in (14.52).

Hansson and Stuart (1989) note that this economy has two steady state equilibria. The first arises when the first part of (14.54) is satisfied with equality and positive gifts are passed between generations. In such a steady state the fact that $\gamma > 0$ implies, from (14.54), that $U^{2\prime}(x_t^{t+1}) > U^{1\prime}(x_t^t)$ so that the marginal utility of consumption when old is greater than when young. This is in contrast to the outcome without altruism in which $U^{2\prime}(x_t^{t+1}) = \rho U^{1\prime}(x_t^t)$, with $\rho < 1$, see

(14.18). This equilibrium is therefore not Pareto optimal since a marginal increase in s_t would raise the utility of generation t by $U^{2\prime}(x_t^{t+1})[1+r] - U^{1\prime}(x_t^t) > 0$. The second steady state equilibrium occurs when (14.54) is an inequality and gifts are zero. If $n \geq r$, then the outcome is not Pareto optimal since an introduction of gifts can raise welfare of all generations. This is not possible if $n < r$.

The structure of a social security programme that is acceptable to the two generations alive at the time of its introduction, say time 0, is constructed by first deriving the optimal programme for the old, generation -1, and the then for the young, generation 0, where the programme takes the form of gifts from young to old $\{a_0, a_1, \ldots\}$ and savings $\{s_0, s_1, \ldots\}$. For generation -1 the optimal programme solves

$$U^{2\prime}(x_{-1}^0) - \frac{U^{1\prime}(x_0^0)}{1+\sigma} \leq 0, = 0 \text{ if } a_0 > 0, \tag{14.55}$$

$$U^{2\prime}(x_{t-1}^t) - \frac{U^{1\prime}(x_t^t)}{1+\sigma} \leq 0, = 0 \text{ if } a_t > 0, t > 0, \tag{14.56}$$

and

$$-U^{1\prime}(x_t^t) + U^{2\prime}(x_t^{t+1})[1+r] \leq 0, = 0 \text{ if } s_t > 0, t > 0. \tag{14.57}$$

The optimal programme for generation 0 also satisfies (14.56) and (14.57) but replaces (14.55) by

$$\frac{U^{2\prime}(x_{-1}^0)}{1+\gamma} - U^{1\prime}(x_0^0) \leq 0, = 0 \text{ if } a_0 > 0. \tag{14.58}$$

The first point to note is that savings must tend to zero. Assume otherwise, then (14.56) and (14.57) imply that

$$U^{1\prime}(x_{t+1}^{t+1}) = \frac{U^{2\prime}(x_t^{t+1})}{1+\sigma} = \frac{U^{1\prime}(x_t^t)[1+\sigma]}{1+r} = \frac{U^{2\prime}(x_{t-1}^t)[1+\sigma]^2}{1+r}. \tag{14.59}$$

From the assumption that $\sigma > r$, (14.59) implies that as $t \to \infty$, $U^{1\prime}(x_t^t) \to \infty$ and $U^{2\prime}(x_{t-1}^t) \to \infty$ or $x_t^t \to 0$ and $x_t^{t+1} \to 0$. The budget constraints (14.52) and (14.53) can then be combined to give

$$s_t = 1 - x_t^t - \frac{x_{t-1}^t}{1+n} + s_{t-1}\frac{1+r}{1+n}. \tag{14.60}$$

Hence $x_t^t \to 0$ and $x_t^{t+1} \to 0$ imply $s_t \to \infty$ contradicting $s_t \leq 1$. Thus for some t $s_t = 0$. Now let $\hat{t}$ be the first period with zero savings. Because savings are positive for all earlier periods, (14.56) and (14.57) imply that $x_{t+1}^{t+1} < x_t^t$ and $x_t^{t+1} < x_{t-1}^t$. From (14.60) it then follows that

$$s_{t-1} - s_t > [s_t - s_{t+1}]\left[\frac{1+n}{1+r}\right], \text{ for } 0 \leq t < \hat{t}. \tag{14.61}$$

As $\hat{t}$ is the first period with $s_t = 0$, $s_{\hat{t}-1} > s_{\hat{t}}$ which implies from (14.61) that $s_t > s_{t+1}$ for all $0 \le t < \hat{t}$. If there were any period after $\hat{t}$ with $s_t > 0$ then the same backward induction argument would contradict $s_{\hat{t}} = 0$.

Contrasting (14.55) and (14.58), it can be seen that generation -1 would prefer that a_0 be larger than the level that would be chosen by generation 0. More importantly, since (14.56) are common to the characterisation of the optimal programme for both generations, given a value of a_0 both generations would agree upon the values of $\{a_1, a_2, \ldots\}$ and $\{s_0, s_1, \ldots\}$ that should constitute the remainder of the programme. Furthermore, (14.56) and (14.57) also capture optimal choices for the older generation in every future time period so that they would always support the continuation of the programme.

That the programme raises the welfare of the introducing generations can be seen by setting a_0 at the level, say $\bar{a}_0$, determined in the equilibrium without social security with further transfers set optimally. Comparison of (14.54) and (14.56) then shows that the equilibrium set of transfers without social security is not optimal for generations -1 and 0 so that they must gain by the introduction of the programme. Their welfare could potentially be raised further by choosing a value of $a_0 \ne \bar{a}_0$. If the solutions of (14.55) and (14.58) both determine a value of a_0 lower than $\bar{a}_0$ then the maximum of the two would form part of an equilibrium programme. The converse holds when $\bar{a}_0$ is less then the solutions to (14.55) and (14.58). In other cases, the level $\bar{a}_0$ will lie in the acceptable range. The move to such an equilibrium social security programme moves the economy to a Pareto optimum. Although the programme raises the welfare of the generations that introduce it, this need not apply to any of the later generations although, as already noted, no generation will seek to change the programme. In particular, if the initial steady state was one without transfers, the introduction of the programme reduces the utility of all generations after a given date. To see this, note that without social security, total lifetime consumption would be $1 + rs_t$ with consumption levels chosen to maximise $U^1(x_t^t) + U^2(x_{t+1}^t)$. With social security savings fall to zero by date $\hat{t}$ so, if $n = 0$, total lifetime consumption after $\hat{t}$ must equal 1 and, from (14.57), this is not chosen to maximise $U^1(x_t^t) + U^2(x_{t+1}^t)$. Generations after $\hat{t}$ must clearly be worse off.

5.3 Myopia

An obvious motivation for the introduction of social security is that consumers do not make appropriate provision for their retirement. This may be because they are myopic and fail to appreciate their later needs, either discounting the future completely or placing a lower weight upon it than would capture their true preferences. Alternatively, consumers may make mistakes in their planning, lack information or simply be irrational. Whatever the reason, empirical evidence (Diamond (1977), Kotlikoff, Spivak and Summers (1982)) does suggest that consumers accrue insufficient savings to cover retirement.

Although the behavioural foundations of myopia differ significantly from those of consistent utility maximisation, the formulation of myopic behaviour of Feldstein (1985) can be incorporated into the analysis developed above by making only minor adjustments. Assume that the preferences of each consumer can be represented by the utility function

$$U^t = U^1(x_t^t) + U^2(x_t^{t+1}),\tag{14.62}$$

but, due to myopia, the consumer chooses their saving decision to maximise

$$U^t = U^1(x_t^t) + \lambda U^2(x_t^{t+1}),\tag{14.63}$$

where $0 \le \lambda \le 1$ captures the degree of myopia. Complete myopia is given by $\lambda = 0$. Each consumer works only during the first period of life and divides post-tax wages between consumption and savings subject to the budget constraint

$$x_t^t = [1 - \tau]w_t - s_t.\tag{14.64}$$

A second aspect of consumers' myopia is that they underestimate the level of benefits received from the social security programme in their retirement. The perceived budget constraint is therefore

$$x_t^{t+1} = [1 + r]s_t + \alpha\beta_{t+1},\tag{14.65}$$

with $\alpha < 1$. It should be clear that the two aspects of myopia have conflicting effects upon the level of savings. Adopting the assumption that $U^1(x_t^t)$ and $U^2(x_t^{t+1})$ are logarithmic, the optimal level of saving is

$$s_t = \frac{\lambda}{1 + \lambda}[1 - \tau]w_t - \frac{\alpha\beta_{t+1}}{[1 + \lambda][1 + r]},\tag{14.66}$$

where it should be noted that low values of λ reduce saving while low values of α increase it. Using the budget constraint for the social security programme, $\beta_t = \tau w_1[1 + n]$, and assuming that the wage grows at rate g, so that $w_{t+1} = w_t[1 + g]$, (14.66) can be written

$$s_t = \frac{\lambda}{1 + \lambda}[1 - \tau]w_t - \frac{\alpha\tau[1 + \gamma]w_t}{[1 + \lambda][1 + r]},\tag{14.67}$$

where $[1 + \gamma] = [1 + n][1 + g]$.

In contrast to the myopia in consumer behaviour, the social security programme is chosen to maximise the social welfare on the basis of true preferences. In year t the total utility of those alive is

$$W_t = [1 + n]^{t+1}\ln([1 - \tau]w_t - s_t) + [1 + n]^t\ln([1 + r]s_{t-1} + \beta_t).\tag{14.68}$$

The optimal social security programme is defined as that which maximises the steady state value of (14.68). When $\alpha = 0$, so that the future pension is entirely discounted, the optimal tax rate is

$$\tau = \frac{[1 + \lambda][1 + \gamma] - \lambda[1 + r][2 + n]}{[1 + \lambda][1 + \gamma][2 + n] - \lambda[1 + r][2 + n]}.\tag{14.69}$$

With complete myopia, $\lambda = 0$ and (14.69) reduces to $\tau[2+n]^{-1}$ with corresponding pension $\beta = \dfrac{[1+n]}{[2+n]} w$. If population growth is zero, the pension is exactly half the wage. It rises above half the wage when population growth is positive. More generally, it can be seen from (14.69) that the tax rate falls, and with it the pension, as λ rises. Hence the less myopic the consumers, the lower is the pension. If the pension is restricted to be non-zero, then $\beta = 0$ if

$$\lambda \geq \frac{[1+\gamma]}{[1+r][2+n]-[1+\gamma]}. \tag{14.70}$$

Therefore, even though myopia may in some cases justify social security, even in this simple framework there is a range of partial myopia described in (14.70) for which social security is not justified. If $\alpha \neq 0$ broadly similar conclusions apply and there remains a significant range of parameter values for which social security is not justified. In addition, it can be shown that the optimal level of pension is decreasing in α.

The main message of this analysis is that myopia is not in itself justification for the introduction of social security. Although myopic consumers will not make sufficient provision for their retirement this is not a sufficient reason for providing a state pension.

This myopia formulation is also used by Feldstein (1987) to assess the means testing of social security. In an economy with a mixture of myopic consumers and fully rational consumers, there is a natural trade-off between providing protection for the myopic who fail to make adequate provision for retirement and reducing the incentive to save of the rational. The argument in favour of means-testing is that it allows an overall reduction in the size of the programme and therefore of the distortion it causes. The reduction in distortion is especially relevant in this situation since those who would not receive benefits after means-testing would not have their savings behaviour affected at all by the existence of the programme.

In an economy that is composed of a mixture of completely myopic ($\lambda = 0$) consumers and fully rational ($\lambda = 1$) ones who, except for the value of λ, have identical preferences and earnings, Feldstein (1987) shows that there is a strong case for means-testing but it is not always superior to a programme of universal benefits. The reason why the universal system may be superior is that means-testing may result in a low level of benefits since, if the benefit is not to be universal by default, it is necessary to provide an incentive for some consumers to continue saving. An upper bound is therefore placed upon means-tested benefits which may be below the level attainable in a universal programme.

5.4 Uncertainty

The motivation for social security in the presence of uncertainty has already been addressed for static economies in chapter 7. It was shown there how social insurance could raise welfare by enabling intragenerational transfers of income. Essentially, the insurance contract reallocated income from the fortunate to the unfortunate. In a dynamic setting a social security programme can also provide intergenerational income transfers as insurance against unfavourable outcomes. This intergenerational insurance aspect of social security clearly has important implications for the design of programmes.

Two forms of uncertainty will be considered in this section. The economies considered up to this point have been characterised by populations that have grown at a steady rate so that the size of each generation has been known with certainty. The first source of uncertainty to be considered arises from randomness in the size of the generation that is born at each date. In this case, social security can play a role in insuring against the risk of being born in a large generation. The second source of uncertainty is introduced via randomness in the production technology. That is, given known inputs, output is determined by a random process. Social security can then act so as to insure those generations faced with unfavourable realisations of the productive shock.

Random population growth and random output both represent forms of aggregate uncertainty that cannot be affected by the actions of individual consumers. In contrast, section 6 will consider individual uncertainty about the length of life. Since the length of life may potentially be affected by decisions taken by consumers, lifetime uncertainty is of a different nature from aggregate uncertainty and requires a separate treatment.

5.4.1 Population uncertainty

To be born into a generation that is large relative to its predecessor and its successor has two disadvantages. When working, the wage received will be low since the labour–capital ratio is high and when retired the return on savings will be low since the capital–labour ratio will be high in the next period. In the absence of social security, large generations will therefore have a relatively lower level of welfare than small generations. These observations are incorporated into the analysis of social security by Smith (1982).

Population uncertainty can be introduced by taking the economy of section 3 but treating the growth rate of population as a random variable. The size of the generation born at t is given by $H_t = [1 + n_t]H_{t-1}$ where n_t is drawn from some known distribution. To simplify the analysis, it is assumed that consumers born at $t-1$ know the value of n_t when making their savings assumption. Two alternative structures for the pay-as-you-go social security programme are considered. In the *fixed tax* system, the level of tax remains constant for all generations but the level of pension received is dependent upon generation size. Alternatively, in a *fixed pension* system it is the level of the tax that is variable.

Under the fixed tax system, a tax rate of τ in period t is equal to a pension of $[1 + n_t]\tau$ for each member of generation $t-1$. The budget constraint of a consumer born in t is therefore

$$x_t^t + \frac{x_t^{t+1}}{1+r_{t+1}} = w_t - \frac{r_{t+1} - n_{t+1}}{1+r_{t+1}} \tau. \tag{14.71}$$

Hence, in a dynamically efficient equilibrium with $r_{t+1} \geq n_{t+1}$ if the interest rate and the wage are unaffected by the introduction of social security, no generation (with the exception of the generation that benefits when the system is first introduced) can be made better-off by the introduction of the fixed tax programme. The same result can also be shown to apply if the wage rate and interest rate do adjust provided consumption is never an inferior good. The reason for this conclusion is simple. With the fixed tax large generations will receive smaller pensions than small generations despite being the poorest.

Under a fixed pension system with the pension fixed at β, a member of generation t will pay a tax of $\dfrac{\beta}{1+n_t}$ so that their budget constraint is

$$x_t^t + \frac{x_t^{t+1}}{1+r_{t+1}} = w_t - \frac{\beta}{1+n_t} + \frac{\beta}{1+r_{t+1}}. \tag{14.72}$$

If the economy is dynamically efficient with $r_{t+1} \geq n_{t+1}$, this does not rule out the possibility that $r_{t+1} < n_t$ which, when the interest rate and the wage rate are constant, will occur when generation t is large. For large generations (14.72) therefore shows that the introduction of a social security programme with a fixed pension may benefit large generations although it will reduce the welfare of small generations. When the wage rate and interest rate are not fixed, the offsetting effects of the reduction in wage rate due to reduced saving and the receipt of the pension leave the outcome ambiguous. However Smith (1982) does provide an example for which expected utility, where the expectation is taken with respect to the distribution of generation size, increases if risk aversion is sufficiently great.

An alternative approach to the insurance role of social security with an uncertain population is discussed by Brandts and de Bartolome (1992). As already noted, if the generation born at t is large, the wage will be low and the return on capital high. Retired consumers therefore gain by the birth of a large generation whilst the large generation loses. The converse occurs when the generation is small. Since, at any time t, the incomes of the young and the old are negatively correlated, there are potentially gains to be obtained from the provision of insurance. To fully exploit these, it must be necessary for transfers to be made from young to old or *vice versa*.

The analysis of Brandts and de Bartolome determines whether the introduction of a *small* programme can be Pareto improving for the existing members of the generation born at 0 and potential members of generation 1. The existence and structure of a Pareto-improving contract is then dependent upon the process by which potential consumers become actual consumers. The interpretation is that there exists a pool of potential consumers who may become members of generation 1 with some probability and the size of generation 1 is determined according to a known distribution function.

Three cases are examined. In the first, the welfare of an unborn worker is taken to be the expected utility in the first period of life if they were born. A Pareto-improving contract will almost always exist in this case although the structure of payments may run in the opposite direction to those that would provide insurance. The second case corresponds to that of Green (1988) and assumes that unborn workers are arranged in a queue with those at the front certain to be born and others further down the line only born if the generation is large. Since those who will only be born if the generation is large care only about the payment they will receive in that state, no contract exists that is Pareto-improving. In the final case, each potential consumer in the pool of unborn consumers is treated symmetrically and has the same probability of being born. In this case, a social insurance contract is always Pareto improving.

5.4.2 Output uncertainty

The interaction between output uncertainty and social security has been analysed by Enders and Lapan (1982) in an economy in which labour is the sole input into production and production is subject to a multiplicative disturbance. Since the form of technology leads to an absence of capital as a store of value, fiat money is introduced to serve this purpose. In consequence, the underlying structure of the economy is distinct from those studied in previous sections.

Given labour supply of ℓ_t from a consumer of generation t, the output of that consumer is given by

$$y_t = \chi_t \ell_t, \tag{14.73}$$

where χ_t is the random disturbance. It is assumed that $\mathcal{E}[\chi_t] = 1$, that $\mathrm{cov}(\chi_t, \chi_{t+i}) = 0$ all i and that the same value of χ_t is realised by all consumers in generation t. With product price p_t, the budget constraint in the first period of life is

$$p_t x_t^t + M_t = p_t \chi_t \ell_t [1 - \tau], \tag{14.74}$$

and in the second period

$$p_{t+1} x_t^{t+1} = M_t + \beta_{t+1} = p_t [\chi_t \ell_t [1 - \tau] - x_t^t]. \tag{14.75}$$

It is assumed that the pension is determined according to the relation

$$\beta_{t+1} = \tau p_{t+1} \chi_{t+1} L_{t+1} \left[\frac{\ell_t}{L_t} \right], \tag{14.76}$$

where L_t denotes aggregate labour supply. This formulation relates the level of pension to work effort in period t. Alternative specifications could equally well be adopted. If each generation is of identical size, the market for the consumption good will clear in period t if

$$\frac{\bar{M}}{p_t} + x_t^t = \chi_t L_t [1 - \tau], \tag{14.77}$$

with $\bar{M}$ total money supply. From (14.77) it can be seen that given x_t^t the market clearing price level is dependent upon the realisation of χ_t.

If there were no uncertainty in the economy, so that $\chi_t = 1$, all t, the stationarity of the economy implies that the price level would be constant over time, and the identical consumers of each generation would each supply the same quantity of labour. Eliminating M_t between (14.74) and (14.75), and using (14.76), it can be seen that the resulting lifetime budget constraint is independent of the parameters of the social security system so that the social security system described has no effect in a certain environment. This conclusion arises because under the assumption of a constant population, the return on social insurance taxes is equal to the return on private saving.

When uncertainty is present, each consumer chooses their labour supply prior to the realisation of χ_t but chooses consumption and savings after χ_t has been realised. Their preferences are represented by the utility function $U(x_t^t, x_t^{t+1}, \ell_t)$.

Denoting the propensity to consumer out of gross income, $\dfrac{x_t^t}{\chi_t \ell_t}$, by ξ, a stationary rational expectations equilibrium for this economy is now defined.

Stationary rational expectations equilibrium

A *stationary rational expectations equilibrium* is a pair of functions $p(\chi), \xi(\chi)$ and a level of labour supply ℓ that satisfy

(i) $[1 - \xi(\chi)]\chi H \ell = \dfrac{\bar{M}}{p(\chi)} + \tau \chi H \ell,$

(ii) $\xi(\chi) = \arg\max_{\{s\}} U\left(\chi \ell s, \mathscr{E}_{\chi^{+1}} \left[\dfrac{p(\chi)\chi \ell [1 - \tau - s]}{p(\chi^{+1})} + \tau \chi^{+1} \ell \right], \ell \right),$

and

(iii) $\ell = \arg\max_{\{s\}} \mathscr{E}_{\chi, \chi^{+1}} \left[U\left(\chi \ell \xi(\chi), \dfrac{p(\chi)\chi s [1 - \tau - \xi(\chi)]}{p(\chi^{+1})} + \tau \chi^{+1} s, s \right) \right],$

where χ is the productivity level in the first period of a consumers life, χ^{+1} the level in the second period and $\mathscr{E}_x$ denotes the expectation taken over the random variable x. Condition (i) captures market clearing, (ii) the choice of consumption to maximise utility taken after χ is realised and (iii) the choice of labour supply made before χ is realised.

To permit an explicit solution a utility function of the CES form

$$U = \left[\frac{1}{\rho} \right] \left[[x_t^t]^\rho + [\lambda x_t^{t+1}]^\rho + [1 - \ell_t]^\rho \right], \quad \rho < 1, \; \rho \neq 0, \tag{14.78}$$

is adopted where $\lambda \le 1$ is the rate of time preference. For $\rho = 0$ this collapses to a log-linear function. The following theorem can then be proved.

Theorem 14.1 (Enders and Lapan)

Two equilibrium solutions to (ii) exist: (a) $\xi^1(\chi)=1-\tau$, (b) $\xi^2(\chi)<1-\tau$. If $\lambda\left[\dfrac{1-\tau}{\tau}\right]^{1-\rho}<1$, *(a) is the unique solution. Furthermore, for equilibria character-*

ised by (b) there is a level of the tax rate $\tau^*=\dfrac{\lambda^{1/1-\rho}}{1+\lambda^{1/1-\rho}}$, *such that a social security*

programme with tax rate τ^* maximises the expected utility of each consumer.

Proof

The solution of the maximisation in (ii) is characterised by

$$[\chi\ell\xi]^{\rho-1}=\lambda\mathscr{E}_{\chi^{+1}}\left[\frac{p(\chi)}{p(\chi^{+1})}\left[\frac{p(\chi)\chi\ell[1-\tau-\xi]+\tau p(\chi^{+1})\chi^{+1}\ell}{p(\chi^{+1})}\right]^{\rho-1}\right], \qquad (14.79)$$

which can be reduced to

$$\chi^{\rho}\xi(\chi)^{\rho-1}[1-\tau-\xi(\chi)]=\lambda\mathscr{E}_{\chi^{+1}}\left[[\chi^{+1}]^{\rho}[1-\tau-\xi(\chi^{+1})][1-\xi(\chi^{+1})]^{\rho-1}\right], \qquad (14.80)$$

by employing (i) and the assumption that all consumers are identical. Solutions (a) and (b) can then be seen by inspection.

Noting that χ and χ^{+1} have the same distribution, for solution (b) (14.80) can be further reduced to

$$\lambda\mathscr{E}\left[\left[\frac{1-\xi(\chi)}{\xi(\chi)}\right]^{\rho-1}\right]=1. \qquad (14.81)$$

Since $\xi^2(\chi)<1-\tau$, the inequality $\lambda\mathscr{E}\left[\left[\dfrac{1-\xi(\chi)}{\xi(\chi)}\right]^{\rho-1}\right]<\lambda\left[\dfrac{1-\tau}{\tau}\right]^{1-\rho}$ must hold in

such an equilibrium. Hence for tax rates such that $\lambda\left[\dfrac{1-\tau}{\tau}\right]^{1-\rho}<1$, (b) cannot be

an equilibrium.

Now let τ^* satisfy $\lambda\left[\dfrac{1-\tau^*}{\tau^*}\right]^{1-\rho}=1$. Then as $\tau\to\tau^*$ from below, $\xi\to1-\tau^*$

with $1-\tau^*=[1+\lambda^{1/1-\rho}]^{-1}$ and $\ell(\tau^*)=[[1+\lambda^{1/1-\rho}]^{-1}[\mathscr{E}(\chi^{\rho})]^{1/\rho-1}+1]^{-1}$. Again employing the observation that χ and χ^{+1} have the same distribution, expected utility can be written

$$\mathscr{E}[U]=\left[\frac{1}{\rho}\right][[1-\ell]^{\rho}+\ell^{\rho}\mathscr{E}[\chi^{\rho}[\xi(\chi)^{\rho}+\lambda[1-\xi(\chi)]^{\rho}]]]. \qquad (14.82)$$

It is clear that this is maximised by $\xi(\tau^*)$ and $\ell(\tau^*)$.

This analysis demonstrates how the existence of a social security programme can raise the level of welfare when the economy is faced by production uncertainty.

Since no social security was required in the equivalent economy with certainty, production uncertainty provides an argument for the provision of social security that does not depend on any form of economic irrationality, such as myopia, or market failure.

6 LIFETIME UNCERTAINTY

The distinguishing feature of uncertainty about the length of life is that it constitutes individual, rather than aggregate, risk. Since the risk is individual, information about the nature of the risk may be held by the individual and be unobservable to the government. Furthermore, individuals may take unobservable actions that affect the nature of the risk. Each of these aspects of individual risk leads to a position of asymmetric information between agents in the economy which can result in the failure of markets to achieve a Pareto-efficient outcome. Such failure provides a further motivation for the introduction of social security.

Consider an economy in which each consumer lives with certainty for one period but with some positive probability less than 1 may die before they enter their second period of life. The payment of tax towards a social security programme can then be viewed as the purchase of an annuity which has a return equal to the pension if the consumer survives into the second period and a return of zero if they do not. The analysis of Sheshinski and Weiss (1981), which is described in more detail below, introduced this perspective of social security and showed how the introduction of such annuities with an actuarially fair return, where none previously existed, could raise welfare.

If all information were public, there is clearly no reason why such annuities could not be provided privately at actuarially fair rates of return. If they were, the introduction of a social security programme with the same structure of returns would have no effect on welfare. To avoid this conclusion, Sheshinski and Weiss (1981) rule out such private annuities while Karni and Zilcha (1986) allow private annuities but assume that they can only be provided at actuarially unfair rates for reasons of resource cost in provision. The individual nature of lifetime uncertainty, however, provides sufficient reasons for not expecting actuarially fair private annuities to be available. If the probability of not surviving into the second period of life differs between consumers and is private information, then the problem of adverse selection may arise. That is, an annuity designed for those who have a low probability of survival will also appeal to those with a high probability. Hence any actuarially fair annuity will entail a loss for its supplier. If individuals can take actions that affect the probability of survival which cannot be observed by the suppliers of annuities then moral hazard will lead to no actuarially fair annuities being offered.

The basic model of uncertain lifetime and the annuity approach to social security are now described. This is followed by an analysis of the consequences of adverse selection and moral hazard for economies with both private annuities and social security.

6.1 Symmetric information

Uncertainty in the length of lifetime is captured by assuming that each consumer lives with certainty for one period of life during which they work and that they then live for a fraction θ, $0 \leq \theta \leq 1$, of the second period during which they are retired. The retirement period θ is distributed randomly across each generation and the distribution is the same for all generations. The value of θ is known neither to a consumer nor to the government but its distribution is known to both.

In addition to the standard form of saving that pays a return of r, a fully funded social security programme is represented as an annuity that pays a return throughout a consumer's retirement. The social security programme is assumed to be actuarially fair so that its return is given by $\dfrac{1+r}{\bar{\theta}}$ where $\bar{\theta} = \mathscr{E}[\theta]$. For later comparison with a pay-as-you-go programme, the optimum social security programme is interpreted as the level of annuity that is chosen by one of the (*ex ante*) identical consumers. Denoting the purchase of annuities by a representative consumer born in t by a_t, a consumer solves the maximisation

$$\max_{\{x_t^t, x_t^{t+1}, a_t, s_t\}} U = U^1(x_t^t) + \mathscr{E}[U^2(x_t^{t+1}, \theta) + V(b_t)], \tag{14.83}$$

subject to the budget constraints

$$x_t^t = w + b_{t-1} - a_t - s_t, \tag{14.84}$$

and

$$b_t = [1+r]s_t + \left[\frac{[1+r]}{\bar{\theta}} a_t - x_t^{t+1}\right]\theta, \tag{14.85}$$

where b_{t-1} is the bequest received, b_t the bequest left and $V(b_t)$ the utility derived from the bequest. The first-order conditions for this maximisation with respect to s_t, a_t and x_t^{t+1} are respectively

$$-U^{1\prime} + [1+r]\mathscr{E}[V'] = 0, \tag{14.86}$$

$$-U^{1\prime} + \frac{[1+r]}{\bar{\theta}}\mathscr{E}[\theta V'] = 0, \tag{14.87}$$

and

$$\mathscr{E}[U_x^2 - \theta V'] = 0. \tag{14.88}$$

From (14.86) and (14.87) it follows that $\mathscr{E}[\theta V'] - \bar{\theta}\mathscr{E}[V'] = 0$, so that $\mathrm{cov}(\theta, V') = 0$ and hence, when $V'' < 0$, b_t is constant for all θ. From the budget constraints (14.84) and (14.85) it then follows that $x_t^{t+1} = \dfrac{1+r}{\bar{\theta}} a_t$ and b_t

$=[1+r]s_t$. Since the consumer chooses the purchase of annuities to maximise welfare, a fully funded system with tax rate τ equal to the value of a_t that arises from the solution to conditions (14.86) to (14.88) will be optimal.

Turning now to a pay-as-you-go system, let the tax paid by generation t be denoted by τ_t so that the benefit received by a member of generation $t-1$ is $\dfrac{\theta \tau_t}{\theta}$.

With this notation, the budget constraints facing a consumer are

$$x_t^t = w + b_{t-1} - \tau_t - s_t,$$ (14.89)

and

$$b_t = [1+r]s_t + \left[\frac{\tau_{t+1}}{\theta} - x_t^{t+1}\right]\theta.$$ (14.90)

To characterise the optimal policy, it is first noted that level of welfare of generation t is now determined by the net bequest, $b_t - \tau_{t+1}$, left to the following generation. The optimal programme then solves

$$\max_{\{x_t^t, x_t^{t+1}, \tau_t, s_t\}} U = U^1(x_t^t) + \mathscr{E}[U^2(x_t^{t+1}, \theta) + V(b_t - \tau_{t+1})],$$ (14.91)

subject to (14.89) and (14.90). The first-order conditions for this maximisation with respect to s_t, τ_t and x_t^{t+1} are respectively

$$- U^{1\prime} + [1+r]\mathscr{E}[V'(b_t - \tau_{t+1})] = 0,$$ (14.92)

$$\mathscr{E}[V'(b_t - \tau_{t+1})][\theta - \bar{\theta}]] = 0,$$ (14.93)

and

$$\mathscr{E}[U_x^2 - \theta V'(b_t - \tau_{t+1})] = 0.$$ (14.94)

The solution to (14.92)–(14.94) satisfies $\tau_{t+1} = x_t^{t+1}\bar{\theta}$ and $b_t = [1+r]s_t$. More importantly, it is clear from inspection of (14.86)–(14.88) and (14.92)–(14.94) that the outcomes under the two social security programmes will involve the same levels of consumption and the bequests will differ by an amount equal to the social security tax. The optimal levels of the two programmes therefore achieve the same real equilibrium and the method of financing, whether fully funded or pay-as-you-go, is irrelevant. In addition, it is clear that the introduction of the social security system raises expected utility.

Sheshinski and Weiss (1981) extend this analysis to show that a decrease in the birth rate increases the optimal level of social security whilst reducing bequests and savings. As to be expected, an increase in life expectancy also increases the optimal level of social security.

6.2 Adverse selection

In the economy described in section 6.1 the optimal allocation achieved by the fully funded social security programme could also be achieved by an actuarially fair privately provided annuity. If such a private annuity were provided, no further welfare improvements could be achieved by the provision of social security. However, the existence of private annuities is not, in itself, sufficient to make the provision of social security redundant. Myopia on the part of consumers, which was discussed in 5.3 and in this context by Feldstein (1990), will result in an inefficient equilibrium as consumers will not purchase sufficient annuities. Enforced purchases through social security could then raise welfare. The same would apply to mistaken assessments of survival probabilities.

A social security programme may also be justified if private annuities are not actuarially fair. The lack of actuarial fairness may arise simply as a result of the resources that are employed in operating the annuities and in the provision of risk premia to underwriters. This aspect of private annuities provides the motivation for the analysis of Karni and Zilcha (1986) which shows that the introduction of social security will improve welfare provided that it offers better terms than private annuities. There is no reason though why the costs of running a public annuity system should be any less than those of a private system so that this motivation for social security is not entirely persuasive.

A second reason why private annuities should not be actuarially fair arises from private information about survival probabilities and the adverse selection problem that arises. Unlike a statutory social security programme, the suppliers of private annuities are subject to competition in the market. As first shown by Rothschild and Stiglitz (1976) in the context of insurance markets, with adverse selection it is possible for the competitive equilibrium to be Pareto inefficient with the equilibrium contract not offering full insurance. The same reasoning was shown by Eckstein, Eichenbaum and Peled (1985) to apply to private annuity markets.

It is now assumed that each generation can be divided into two groups, A and B, with γ type B consumers for each type A. All consumers are endowed with ω units of the single, non-produced consumption good and live for a least one period. Consumers in group i have a probability ρ_i of surviving into the second period of life with $0 < \rho_A < \rho_B < 1$. Assuming that each generation is large, these probabilities are also the proportions of each type that live for a second period. Focusing attention on steady state equilibria only, the utility of a type i consumer is given by

$$U^i = U(x_1^i) + \rho_i U(x_2^i), \tag{14.95}$$

where the survival probability is used to discount second-period utility.

Pareto-efficient allocations for this economy are characterised by solving the optimisation

$$\max_{\{x_1^i, x_2^i, i = A, B\}} \sum_{i=A,B} \mu^i U^i, \ \mu^i \geq 0, \ \sum \mu^i = 1, \tag{14.96}$$

subject to

$$x_1^A + \rho_A x_2^A + \gamma x_1^B + \gamma \rho_B x_2^B = \omega[1 + \gamma]. \tag{14.97}$$

When both $\mu^i > 0$, the solution to the optimisation is characterised by

$$\frac{U'(x_1^A)}{U'(x_2^A)} = \frac{U'(x_1^B)}{U'(x_2^B)}. \tag{14.98}$$

For later comparison, it should be noted that this optimum can be sustained by the provision of two private annuities that have returns of $\dfrac{1}{\rho_A}$ and $\dfrac{1}{\rho_B}$. The first will be purchased by type A consumers and the second by type B. This results in a separating equilibrium with both types of consumers purchasing annuities that are actuarially fair for their group.

Asymmetric information is introduced by assuming that each consumer knows their probability of survival and the population proportions. The government knows the probabilities of survival and the population proportion but cannot infer the survival probability of an individual consumer. An annuity contract is defined as a pair $\{a^v, \zeta^v\}$ where a^v is the number of units of the annuity that must be purchased and ζ^v the return. A consumer purchasing contract $\{a, \zeta\}$ will achieve utility level

$$V^i(a, \zeta) = U(\omega - a) + \rho_i U(\zeta a). \tag{14.99}$$

From (14.99) the gradient of an indifference curve is

$$\frac{dx_1^i}{dx_2^i} = -\rho_i \frac{U'(\zeta a)}{U'(\omega - a)}, \tag{14.100}$$

so that at any level of consumption the gradient of a type B consumer's indifference curve will be steeper than that of a type A. The equilibrium of a competitive market in annuity supply is now determined and shown to be inefficient. The possibility for a social security programme to raise welfare is then discussed.

An equilibrium in the supply of contracts is defined as follows.

Contract equilibrium

An equilibrium is a set of contracts such that:

(i) no contract in the equilibrium set makes a negative profit;
(ii) no contract outside the equilibrium set would make a positive profit if offered.

The properties of the equilibrium are given in theorem 14.2.

Theorem 14.2 (Eckstein, Eichenbaum and Peled)

(i) There can be no pooling equilibrium.
(ii) If an equilibrium exists it is a separating equilibrium in which consumers of type A purchase a contract of the form $\left\{ a_1, \dfrac{1}{\rho_A} \right\}$ and the contract purchased

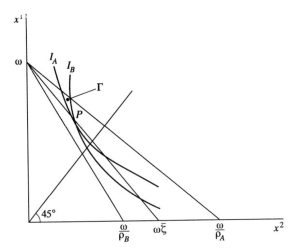

Figure 14.1   Non-existence of pooling equilibrium

$$by\ type\ B\ consumers\ is\ \left\{ \frac{\rho_B}{1+\rho_B}\omega,\ \frac{1}{\rho_B} \right\}.$$

(iii) For sufficiently small values of $\lambda > 0$, there is no equilibrium.

Proof

(i) If a pooling equilibrium were to exist it must satisfy the zero-profit condition $a^A + \gamma a^B = \bar{\zeta}[\rho_A a^A + \rho_B \gamma a^B]$ for the pooling rate of return $\bar{\zeta}$ and a^A, a^B are the purchases of annuities by As and Bs. Since pooling implies $a^A = a^B = a$,

$$\bar{\zeta} = \frac{1+\gamma}{\rho_A + \rho_B \gamma} \cdot \frac{1}{\rho_B} < \bar{\zeta} = \frac{1+\gamma}{\rho_A + \rho_B \gamma} < \frac{1}{\rho_A}.$$ In figure 14.1 a potential pooling equili-

brium contract is shown by P. All other contracts with return $\bar{\zeta}$ must also lie on the line joining ω and $\omega\bar{\zeta}$. The relative slopes of the indifference curves then implies that a contract such as Γ that is preferred to P by group A consumers and makes positive profit always exists regardless of the location of P on the line $\langle \omega, \omega\bar{\zeta} \rangle$.

(ii) It is a condition of equilibrium that each contract offered must make non-negative profits. The contract purchased by type B consumers cannot therefore be more favourable than that which gives full insurance and consumption levels

$$x_1^B = x_2^B = \frac{\omega}{1+\rho_B}$$ nor can the contract offered to type As be preferred by the Bs to

the full insurance contract. Hence if a separating equilibrium exists it must have full insurance for the Bs and the type As being supplied with the contract defined as the solution to

$$\max_{\{a_1\}} U(\omega - a_1) + \rho_A U\left(\frac{a_1}{\rho_A}\right),$$

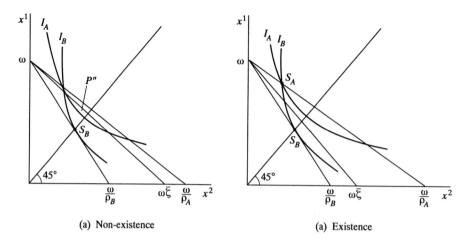

(a) Non-existence　　　　　　　　(a) Existence

Figure 14.2　Separating equilibrium

subject to the restriction that type Bs prefer their full insurance contract

$$[1+\rho_B]U\left(\frac{\omega}{1+\rho_B}\right)\geq U(\omega-a_1)+\rho_B U\left(\frac{a_1}{\rho_A}\right).$$

This proves (ii).

(iii) The potential separating equilibrium of (ii) with type A's contract at S_A and B's at S_B is shown in figure 14.2. This equilibrium will not exist if the line describing actuarially fair contracts is as shown in (a). In that case a contract such as P'' will be preferred by both types and will make a positive profit. This will always be possible for small γ. The separating equilibrium does exist in (b) since no pooling contract can make positive profit. This proves (iii).

Having now characterised the competitive equilibrium, it is possible to consider the effect of introducing social security. The distinction between contracts that can be offered by private firms and social security is that a social security programme can cross-subsidise the provision of annuities to one group with the proceeds from another. If a competitive firm attempted to do this, it would be undercut by another firm that offered a slightly more attractive version of the profit-making contract. To show that circumstances exist in which social security can raise welfare, consider each consumer having to participate in a mandatory programme which involved the purchase of $\bar{a}$ units of annuity with an actuarially fair return $\bar{\rho}=\dfrac{1+\gamma}{\rho_A+\gamma\rho_B}$ based on the population survival probabi- lities. Figure 14.3 shows how the social security programme raises welfare. The forced purchase of annuities with value $\bar{a}$ at the actuarially fair rate leaves at most $\omega-\bar{a}$ to consume in period 1. Beginning at this point on the population fair rate line, the two groups can then purchase annuities along their own fair-return

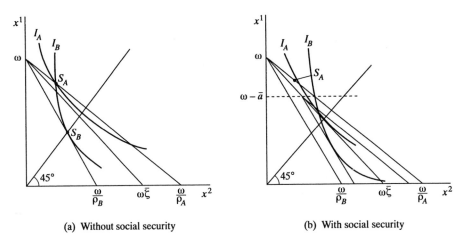

(a) **Without social security**   (b) **With social security**

Figure 14.3   Social security

lines. This modifies the budget constraints from their initial position in (a) to the new position in (b) with a consequent change in the separating equilibrium. The new separating equilibrium is determined by the intersection of the indifference curve of type Bs through the full insurance point with the fair-return line of type As. In (b) this intersection is shown above the initial indifference curve of type As. Therefore in this case social security leads to a Pareto improvement. However, study of the figure will show that this need not be the case.

   The outcome of this analysis is that social security may not always be able to improve upon the equilibrium of the competitive market but, even when it can, it will not lead to a Pareto-efficient outcome. The government is constrained by the same informational limitations as the competitive market and has only the advantage of being able to cross-subsidise between contracts. This is not sufficient to achieve the Pareto-efficient outcome of full insurance for both types. It should also be noted that when the social security programme does lead to a Pareto improvement, the type As would prefer to exchange private annuities for social security whereas the type Bs would prefer the opposite.

   An alternative analysis of the effect of adverse selection is given in Abel (1986a). That analysis is generalised by the inclusion of a bequest motive and private savings. However, only a pooling equilibrium in the provision of private annuities is considered. It is shown that the rate of return on private annuities is below the population (fair) rate and falls when social security, which is fair, is introduced. The effect of social security on the capital stock is ambiguous.

6.3 Moral hazard

Moral hazard can be introduced into the analysis of social security by assuming that consumers can take action which affects their longevity but cannot be observed by firms providing annuities or by the government. This can be incorporated into the framework used above by assuming that the probability of survival is dependent upon the level of consumption of some health-related activity so that $\rho = \rho(e)$. If the consumption raises longevity then $\rho'(e) > 0$ and if it reduces it $\rho'(e) < 0$.

The central reason why the competitive supply of annuities in such an economy is inefficient is that consumers, when choosing their consumption level of e, take account only of the direct cost of the activity. Since the price of a fair annuity is based upon $\rho(e)$, the health-related activity also has an indirect cost via the effect it has upon the price of annuities. A consumer maximising subject to fixed prices does not take this into account. This externality generates an inefficient equilibrium as discussed in chapter 10.

These ideas have been formalised by Davies and Kuhn (1992). They show that the nature of the externality leads to an overinvestment in the health-related activity in the sense that a reduction in investment accompanied by an actuarially fair reduction in the price of annuities would raise welfare. Furthermore, since the government is constrained by the same informational deficiency as private firms, provision of social security at fair returns cannot raise welfare and will reduce it if mandatory purchases are above private purchases. Unlike adverse selection where the government could pool risks when the firms could not, the government has no advantage over firms in the case of moral hazard.

7   CONCLUSIONS

Many aspects of social security have been addressed in this chapter from the design of an optimal programme in the Diamond economy to the interaction of social security and asymmetric information. In terms of broad policy conclusions, the most compelling must be that there are many circumstances in which the introduction of a social security programme can raise welfare and, of those considered above, only myopia involved any irrationality on the part of the agents in the economy.

Without uncertainty, social security could be justified by dynamic inefficiency in the economy even when the retirement decision was made endogenous. More surprisingly, the conflicting effects of an increase in the rate of population growth led to there being several possible relations between it and the level of welfare and, consequently, between the rate of population growth and the structure of social security. With aggregate uncertainty, social security could play a limited redistributive role between fortunate and unfortunate generations. Individual uncertainty introduced asymmetric information and, as the government need have no informational advantage over other agents, it was not always possible for social security to raise welfare. Finally, it should also be noted that voting mechanisms were shown to be an inefficient means of determining the level of social security to be provided since there was no obvious connection between the level they determined and the optimal level.

15

DEBT AND TAXATION

1 INTRODUCTION

In the policy analyses of previous chapters it was invariably assumed that the government revenue requirement was pre-determined and the policy instruments were chosen to maximise welfare given this fixed requirement. The satisfaction of the revenue constraint implicitly prevented the government issuing any debt. In a static setting there is some sense in this procedure since, by its very nature, the static setting prevents a comprehensive analysis of the effects of the borrowing and repayment process. Introducing time and considering the intertemporal maximisation of welfare permits the endogenisation of government debt and allows the determination of its optimal level to become part of the overall policy formulation process. It also allows the interaction between debt and taxation to be explored. The employment of both debt and taxation as instruments of government policy will affect the capital market and, through this, the dynamic evolution of the economy and the eventual steady state.

The content of this chapter will reflect these intertemporal issues. Section 2 is concerned with the effects of the maintenance of a constant stock of debt upon the long-run equilibrium of the economy. Section 3 then analyses the relation between lump-sum taxation and debt and characterises the optimal combination of the two instruments. The focus of section 4 is upon debt neutrality and the circumstances in which this does, and does not, hold. Section 5 of the chapter is more concerned with tax policy than debt and it studies the optimisation of income and interest taxation in an economy with an heterogeneous population. In this case, both intragenerational and intergenerational redistribution are important.

It should be noted that the policy optimisation problems studied in this chapter are complicated by the infinite timespan of the economy. This leads to the maximisation being subject to the infinite set of constraints which describe the evolution of the economy. Two ways of characterising the solutions to such problems are illustrated. The first is based upon the methodology of dynamic programming; in particular the principle of optimality. The second approach reduces the dimensionality of the problem by assuming that the chosen allocations achieve Pareto optimality between generations. This provides a shadow interest rate with which future variables can be discounted.

2 THE EFFECT OF DEBT

The effect of national debt has long been a contentious issue, with the debate stretching back to at least Ricardo (1817). It is also a subject at the heart of policy analysis since the issuing of debt is an important practical policy tool. The conservative perspective upon debt is that it can only be harmful to welfare and that governments should do all they can to minimise borrowing. Alternatively, the philosophy of Keynsianism is that debt is simply another tool of policy and should be employed whenever advantageous. To assess these competing viewpoints, it is clear that a dynamic economy must be analysed as its effects are felt through its issuing, servicing and redemption of debt.

   The existence of debt instruments as an alternative to investment in physical capital as a means of saving for consumers alters the relationship between the level of savings and available capital for the following period. In fact, capital accumulation must be less for any given level of private saving. The taxes required to service debt also have an effect upon the behaviour of consumers and the equilibrium of the economy. Given these observations, the question remains as to whether debt is always harmful to welfare. This section will determine both the positive effects of debt on the long-run equilibrium of the economy and its welfare effects. This is undertaken for both internal and external debt. The analysis is set in the Diamond economy, with a fixed labour supply, and a diagrammatic framework is employed that simplifies the derivation of results.

2.1 External and internal debt

The starting point of the analysis is to distinguish between internal and external debt. This is necessary since they have distinctly different effects upon the stationary equilibrium and the welfare level of consumers.

   External debt is debt owed to agents located abroad, that is the holders of the debt are not resident in the economy that issued the debt. On such debt there is an interest charge that must be paid each period and this must be financed by either further borrowing or by taxation. The important features of such debt are that it is not in competition with physical capital as a savings instrument for the consumers of the issuing economy but its servicing and repayment lead to a flow of resources out of the economy.

   In contrast, *internal debt* is held by residents of the economy in which it is issued. With internal debt the government borrows off its own citizens by providing bonds which compete with private capital. Private savings are divided between the two investment instruments. When there is no uncertainty bonds and capital will be perfect substitutes, so in equilibrium they must pay the same rate of return. The cost of financing internal debt is again met either by further borrowing or by taxation. In contrast to external debt, internal debt does not lead to any resources being transferred away from the economy that issues the debt.

2.2 Effects of debt

The analysis now considers the real effect upon the steady state equilibrium, and the utility level of each consumer, of internal and external debt, starting with external debt. The analytical technique employed, as in Diamond (1965), is to characterise the steady state of the economy as the simultaneous solution to a pair of equations for a fixed stock of debt. The consequence of a change in the level of debt can then be found by determining its effect upon the graphs of these equations.

2.2.1 External debt

It has already been noted that the analysis is conducted for a fixed stock of debt. Before it can be undertaken, it is first necessary to clarify the sense in which the level of debt is fixed since alternative interpretations are possible. If the stock of debt were fixed in absolute terms, it would eventually have no effect upon the economy as population growth took place and the level of debt per capita became asymptotically zero. Therefore, rather than fix the absolute stock of debt, it is assumed that the level of debt per young consumer remains constant and the effect of changes in this ratio are analysed.

Denote the quantity of external debt in period t by D_t^1 and the debt per young consumer ratio, D_t^1/H_t, by d_t^1. If the ratio is to remain constant, then the growth of the absolute stock of debt is governed by

$$D_{t+1}^1 = [1+n]D_t^1, \tag{15.1}$$

where n is the growth rate of the population. The payment of interest upon the debt is financed either by new borrowing or through taxation. With interest rate r_t, the payment of interest upon the debt in period t is

$$r_t D_t^1, \tag{15.2}$$

and new borrowing is

$$n D_t^1. \tag{15.3}$$

The difference between (15.2) and (15.3) given by

$$[r_t - n]D_t^1, \tag{15.4}$$

represents that part of the interest payments that must be financed by taxation.

The tax employed to generate the required revenue is assumed to take the form of a lump-sum tax on the young generation. Given (15.4), the level of this tax for each consumer when young is

$$T_t = [r_t - n]\frac{D_t^1}{H_t} = [r_t - n]d_t^1. \tag{15.5}$$

With this tax payment included, the budget constraint of a consumer born in period t becomes

$$x_t^t + \frac{x_t^{t+1}}{[1 + r_{t+1}]} = w_t - [r_t - n]d_t^1, \tag{15.6}$$

so that *full income*, $\hat{M}_t$, is given by

$$\hat{M}_t = w_t - [r_t - n]d_t^1. \tag{15.7}$$

From the maximisation of the utility function $U = U(x_t^t, x_1^{t+1})$, subject to (15.6), the savings function for a member of generation t is

$$s_t = s_t(\hat{M}_t, r_{t+1}) = w_t - [r_t - n]d_t^1 - x_t^t(\hat{M}_t, r_{t+1}). \tag{15.8}$$

Capital market equilibrium requires that the capital–labour ratio is related to the level of savings by

$$[1 + n]k_{t+1} = s_t(\hat{M}_t, r_{t+1}), \tag{15.9}$$

so that the interest rate satisfies

$$r_{t+1} = f'\left(\frac{s_t(\hat{M}_t, r_{t+1})}{1 + n}\right) = f'\left(\frac{s_t(w_t - [r_t - n]d_t^1, r_{t+1})}{1 + n}\right). \tag{15.10}$$

Given r_t, (15.10) implicitly determines a relationship between w_t and r_{t+1}. This relation describes the locus of pairs of wage rate and interest rate for which capital demand is equal to supply and is denoted by $r_{t+1} = \psi(w_t; r_t, d_t^1)$ and is dependent upon the level of internal debt via the determination of the level of savings.

Profit maximisation by firms occurs when the wage rate satisfies the equality $w_t = f(k_t) - k_t f'(k_t)$ and the interest rate $r_t = f'(k_t)$, where k_t is the capital–labour ratio. Together these imply the factor price frontier (see 14.4.1) $w_t = \phi(r_t)$ with $\phi'(r_t) = -k_t < 0$ and $\phi''(r_t) = -\frac{1}{f''} > 0$. It should be noted that ϕ is independent of the level of debt.

The long-run steady state equilibrium of the economy, with $r_t = r$ all t, occurs when $r = \psi(w:r, d^1)$ and $w = \phi(r)$ are satisfied simultaneously, where d^1 is the constant stock of debt. If an equilibrium exists, the steady state will be stable if the ψ curve is steeper (in absolute value) than the ϕ curve. It is assumed that the ψ curve is downward sloping, that an equilibrium exists (so the curves intersect)

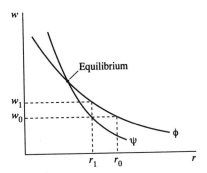

Figure 15.1 Equilibrium and stability

and that the equilibrium is stable and unique. These assumptions give the configuration of figure 15.1 which also shows part of the path of the economy starting from an initial point r_0. It can be seen that, given the assumptions placed on the gradients of the curves, the adjustment process is convergent to the equilibrium at the intersection of the two curves.

To discover the effect of changes in the level of external debt it is only necessary to determine how the change affects the ψ curve. From (15.10) it is evident that the effect will depend upon sgn. $\{r_t - n\}$. If $r_t = n$, so that the Golden rule is achieved, there will be no effect. From differentiating (15.10), holding r_t constant, it can be found that

$$\frac{\partial r_{t+1}}{\partial d^1} = \frac{f''[n - r_t]\dfrac{\partial s_t}{\partial w_t}}{1 + n - f''\dfrac{\partial s_t}{\partial r_{t+1}}}. \tag{15.11}$$

The assumption that the ψ curve is downward sloping restricts the denominator of (15.11) to be positive. The numerator is positive if $r_t > n$ and negative for $r_t < n$. Hence, for given r_t, the ψ curve pivots around the point $r = n$ as the level of external debt increases. This is illustrated in figure 15.2 below.

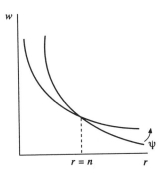

Figure 15.2 Effect of increase in external debt

It is now straight forward to exhibit the effect of an increase in debt upon the long-run equilibrium. In the steady state

$$r = f'\left(\frac{s(w - [r - n]d^1, r)}{1 + n}\right) = f'\left(\frac{s(\phi(r) - [r - n]d^1, r)}{1 + n}\right). \tag{15.12}$$

From differentiating (15.12) the effect of an increase in external debt upon the steady state interest rate is

$$\frac{\partial r}{\partial d^1} = \frac{f''[n - r]\dfrac{\partial s}{\partial w}}{1 + n - f''\dfrac{\partial s}{\partial r} + f'' d^1 \dfrac{\partial s}{\partial w}}. \tag{15.13}$$

The three possible outcomes, which depend upon the sign of $n - r$, are shown in figure 15.3.

In both cases (a) and (c) where $n - r$ is non-zero, the increase in external debt moves the steady state interest rate, determined by the intersection of the curves, further from the Golden rule interest rate. If $r < n$, then the steady state wage rate w rises and if $r > n$, then w falls. When the economy is already at the Golden rule interest rate then the differential increase in debt has no effect.

The effect upon the welfare level of a consumer via changes in the steady state levels of r and w is found by differentiating the utility function, defined following (15.7), taking account of the demand function and using the factor price frontier to eliminate the wage rate. Doing this gives

$$\frac{dU}{dd^1} = -U_1\left[[r - n] + d^1\frac{dr}{dd^1} + \frac{k}{1 + r}[r - n]\frac{dr}{dd^1}\right]. \tag{15.14}$$

The three terms in the brackets on the right-hand side of (15.14) are related to the taxes required to finance the debt, the change in the tax burden due to interest rate changes and the change in factor payments respectively.

Theorem 15.1 summarises the effects of external debt.

Theorem 15.1 (Diamond)
 (i) *If $r > n$, a differential increase in external debt raises r, reduces w and reduces utility;*
 (ii) *If $r < n$, a differential increase in external debt reduces r, raises w and may increase utility;*
 (iii) *If $r = n$, a differential increase in external debt has no effect.*

Proof

 (i) When $r > n$ the first and second bracketed terms of (15.14) are positive. As $\dfrac{dr}{dd^1}$ has the sign of $[r - n]$, the third term is also positive. It is then clear that utility will fall as the level of debt increases.

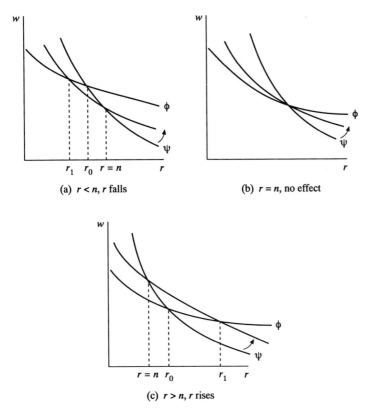

Figure 15.3   Steady state effect

(ii) When $r < n$ the first two terms of (15.14) are negative and the third positive. Hence there are offsetting effects which arise due to r falling, but w rising.

(iii) Obvious from (15.13) and (15.14).

The reasoning behind the conclusions of this theorem is that when $r > n$, the capital stock is too small and the levying of a tax to service the debt has the effect of taking the economy further from the optimal level of capital. The opposite applies when $r < n$ and efficiency is increased by the reduction in the capital stock. This gain has to be offset against the direct loss in welfare due to the imposition of the tax and the net effect may still be a reduction in welfare.

2.2.2 Internal debt

In the case of internal debt, the issue of debt results in the government borrowing from its own citizens. This leads to competition between government debt and physical capital for consumer savings. Internal debt therefore affects the economy both through the taxes required to service the debt and through its effect on the capital market.

Denoting the ratio of internal debt to the number of young consumers in period t by d_t^2, the savings function of a consumer of generation t is now given by

$$s_t = s_t(w_t - [r_t - n]d_t^2, r_{t+1}). \qquad (15.15)$$

In (15.15), the term $[r_t - n]d_t^2$ captures the tax payment required to service the debt. On the supply side of the capital market, there is now both private capital and government bonds. Equilibrium requires that the aggregate level of saving must be equal to the total stock of capital and debt, or

$$S_t \equiv H_t s_t = K_{t+1} + D_{t+1}^2. \qquad (15.16)$$

Expressing (15.16) in terms of quantities per member of generation $t+1$ gives the alternative equilibrium condition

$$\frac{s_t}{1+n} = k_{t+1} + d_t^2. \qquad (15.17)$$

The ψ curve for the case of internal debt is found by substituting from (15.17) into $r_{t+1} = f'(k_{t+1})$ to give

$$r_{t+1} = f'\left(\frac{s_t(w_t - [r_t - n]d_t^2, r_{t+1})}{1+n} - d_t^2\right). \qquad (15.18)$$

It follows from (15.18) that for constant r_t

$$\frac{\partial r_{t+1}}{\partial d_t^2} = \frac{-f''\left[[r_t - n]\dfrac{\partial s_t}{\partial w_t} + 1 + n\right]}{1 + n - f''\dfrac{\partial s_t}{\partial r_{t+1}}}. \qquad (15.19)$$

Assuming that consumption is a normal good, so $0 < \dfrac{\partial s_t}{\partial w_t} < 1$, it follows that $\dfrac{\partial r_{t+1}}{\partial d_t^2} > 0$. An increase in internal debt, holding r_t constant, therefore causes the ψ curve to move out to the right. The effect of this upon the steady state is to lower the wage rate but to increase the interest rate, regardless of the initial position. This is shown in figure 15.4.

The change in utility brought about by the increase in debt can be found by differentiating the utility function to be

$$\frac{dU}{dd^2} = -U_1[r - n]\left[1 + \frac{k + d^2}{1 + r}\frac{dr}{dd^2}\right]. \qquad (15.20)$$

The effects of internal debt are summarised in the following theorem.

Theorem 15.2 (Diamond)

(i) If $r > n$, utility is decreased by a differential increase in internal debt.

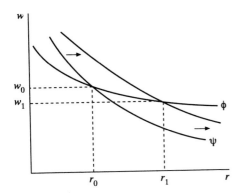

Figure 15.4   Effect of an increase in internal debt

(ii) If $r<n$, utility is increased by extra debt.
(iii) If $r=n$ there is no effect.

Proof

As $\dfrac{dr}{dd^2}>0$, the second bracketed term in (15.20) is positive. The conclusions then follow immediately.

The explanation behind this theorem is that when $r>n$ the increase in debt raises the interest rate and moves the equilibrium further from the optimal point of $r=n$. This must reduce welfare. When $r<n$ the increase in debt causes r to move closer to n. This effect is sufficient to raise welfare despite the competition for savings between government debt and physical capital.

3 OPTIMISATION OF DEBT AND LUMP-SUM

In a static economy with identical consumers, the only role that lump-sum taxation can have is to collect revenue (and, of course, it is the most efficient method of revenue collection). Other than this, there is no role for it to play in raising efficiency or welfare. The same cannot be said in an overlapping generations context since the potential inefficiency of the competitive equilibrium opens up additional avenues by which lump-sum taxation can affect welfare. By varying the timing of taxation over the lifecycle it is possible for lump-sum taxes to affect the savings decisions of consumers and, through this mechanism, the level of the capital stock. This affects the intertemporal evolution of the economy. The employment of lump-sum taxation also makes it possible for the government to achieve intergenerational transfers of income. These observations makes the study of the design of lump-sum taxes a worthwhile exercise.

The purpose of this section is to characterise an optimal lump-sum tax policy for an economy with an homogeneous population of consumers. The homogeneity assumption removes the need to consider intragenerational transfers and focuses attention upon the intergenerational consequences of taxation. It also overcomes some of the objections to the use of lump-sum taxes expressed in chapter 2. Before undertaking this, it is first necessary to determine the relationship between lump-sum taxes and internal debt since there are important interconnections between the two policy instruments.

3.1 Lump-sum taxation and debt

The provision of government debt and the use of lump-sum taxation are both methods of affecting the lifecycle behaviour of consumers. When viewed as such, it is not surprising that there is a significant degree of substitutability between the two instruments. To investigate this substitutability formally, it is assumed that each household in generation t, in a Diamond economy with variable labour supply, is subject to a lump-sum tax of T_t^t in the first period of their life and one of T_t^{t+1} in the second period. Either, or both, of these may be negative. With these taxes, the lifetime budget constraint of a consumer is

$$x_t^t + \frac{x_t^{t+1}}{1+r_{t+1}} = w_t \ell_t - T_t^t - \frac{T_t^{t+1}}{1+r_{t+1}}. \tag{15.21}$$

Using R to denote the level of government revenue to be collected, the government budget constraint is

$$H_t T_t^t + H_{t-1} T_{t-1}^t = R + [1+r_t]D_{t-1} - D_t, \tag{15.22}$$

where D_t is the quantity of debt issued in period t. In per-capita terms the government budget constraint becomes

$$T_t^t + \frac{T_{t-1}^t}{1+n} = \tilde{R} + \frac{[1+r_t]d_{t-1}}{1+n} - d_t, \tag{15.23}$$

with $d_{t-1} = \frac{D_{t-1}}{H_{t-1}}$, $d_t = \frac{D_t}{H_t}$ and $\tilde{R} = \frac{R}{H_t}$. Since the lump-sum tax in the first period of life, T_t^t, affects consumers' savings decisions, the capital market equilibrium condition becomes

$$[1+n]\tilde{k}_{t+1} = w_t \ell_t - T_t^t - x_t^t - d_t, \tag{15.24}$$

where $\tilde{k}_{t+1} = K_{t+1}/H_{t+1}$ is the level of capital per young consumer. It is important to distinguish this from the capital–labour ratio $k_{t+1} = K_{t+1}/H_{t+1}\ell_{t+1}$ since the two are not equal when labour supply is variable.

A *tax policy* is a sequence of lump-sum taxes $\{\dots, T_{t-1}^{t-1}, T_{t-1}^t, T_t^t, T_t^{t+1}, T_{t+1}^{t+1}, \dots\}$ and a *debt policy* is a sequence of government debt issues $\{\dots, d_{t-1}, d_t, d_{t+1}, \dots\}$. Together with the factor price frontier, (15.21), (15.22) and (15.24) describe the equilibrium of the economy for any given tax policy and debt policy.

The following theorem, originally due to Bierwag *et al.* (1969), relates tax policies and debt policies.

Theorem 15.3 (Bierwag, Grove, Khang)

The combined tax policy $\{\ldots, T_{t-1}^{t-1}, T_{t-1}^{t}, T_t^{t}, T_t^{t+1}, T_{t+1}^{t+1}, \ldots\}$ *and debt policy* $\{\ldots, d_{t-1}, d_t, d_{t+1}, \ldots\}$ *lead to the same real equilibria as:*

(i) a tax policy $\{\ldots, \hat{T}_{t-1}^{t-1}, \hat{T}_{t-1}^{t}, \hat{T}_t^{t}, \hat{T}_t^{t+1}, \hat{T}_{t+1}^{t+1}, \ldots\}$ *and no debt, where* $\hat{T}_t^{t} = T_t^{t} + d_t$ *and* $\hat{T}_t^{t+1} = T_t^{t+1} - [1 + r_{t+1}]d_t$;

(ii) a tax policy $\{\ldots, \tilde{T}_{t-1}^{t-1}, 0, \tilde{T}_t^{t}, 0, \tilde{T}_{t+1}^{t+1}, \ldots\}$ *and a debt policy* $\{\ldots, \tilde{d}_{t-1}, \tilde{d}_t, \tilde{d}_{t+1}, \ldots\}$, *where* $\tilde{T}_t^{t} = T_t^{t} + \dfrac{T_t^{t+1}}{1 + r_{t+1}}$ *and* $\tilde{d}_t = d_t - \dfrac{T_t^{t+1}}{1 + r_{t+1}}$;

(iii) a tax policy $\{\ldots, 0, \hat{T}_{t-1}^{t}, \hat{T}_t^{t+1}, \hat{T}_{t+1}^{t+2}, \ldots\}$ *and a debt policy* $\{\ldots, \hat{d}_{t-1}, \hat{d}_t, \hat{d}_{t+1}, \ldots\}$, *where* $\hat{T}_t^{t+1} = [1 + r_{t+1}]T_t^{t} + T_t^{t+1}$ *and* $\hat{d}_t = d_t + T_t^{t}$;

and

(iv) a tax policy $\{\ldots, T_{t-1}, T_t, T_t, T_{t+1}, \ldots\}$ *and a debt policy* $\{\ldots, \breve{d}_{t-1}, \breve{d}_t, \breve{d}_{t+1}, \ldots\}$, *where* $T_t = \left[\dfrac{1 + r_{t+1}}{2 + r_{t+1}}\right]\left[T_t^{t} + \dfrac{T_t^{t+1}}{1 + r_{t+1}}\right]$ *and* $\breve{d}_t = d_t - \dfrac{T_t^{t}}{2 + r_{t+1}} - \dfrac{T_t^{t+1}}{2 + r_{t+1}}$.

Proof

(i) With the tax policy alone the equilibrium conditions become

$$x_t^{t} + \frac{x_t^{t+1}}{1 + r_{t+1}} = w_t \ell_t - \hat{T}_t^{t} - \frac{\hat{T}_t^{t+1}}{1 + r_{t+1}}, \tag{15.25}$$

$$\hat{T}_t^{t} + \frac{\hat{T}_{t-1}^{t}}{1 + n} = \tilde{R}, \tag{15.26}$$

and

$$[1 + n]\tilde{k}_{t+1} = w_t \ell_t - \hat{T}_t^{t} - x_t^{t}. \tag{15.27}$$

Contrasting (15.24) and (15.27) shows that the capital market will be unaffected by the change in policy if $\hat{T}_t^{t} = T_t^{t} + d_t$. Substituting into (15.26) and equating to (15.23) gives $\hat{T}_t^{t+1} = T_t^{t+1} - [1 + r_{t+1}]d_t$. It can also be seen that these changes leave the consumer's budget constraint unaffected. Parts (ii) to (iv) are proved in an identical manner.

The relevance of theorem 15.3 is that it shows that a restricted lump-sum tax policy, either one employing uniform taxes (case (iv)) or one with taxes levied in only one period of life (cases (ii) and (iii)), and an appropriate debt policy is as effective as lump-sum taxes differentiated across the lifecycle. It is arguable that the uniform lump-sum tax policy requires less information than the differentiated policy so that employing a uniform tax can economise on information with no loss in potential welfare. The theorem also shows that in characterising the optimal lump-sum tax policy, any one of the five combinations of tax and debt policies will lead to the same real equilibrium.

3.2 Optimal lump-sum taxation and debt

Theorem 15.3 shows that in order to demonstrate the effect of an optimal lump-sum tax policy it is sufficient to consider only one of the five alternative combinations of lump-sum taxes and debt. The representation chosen here will be to adopt (i) and to set government debt equal to zero in all periods. Once the results are derived, the translation can easily be made to one of the other forms of policy. The technique used to characterise the choice of policy is the principle of optimality of dynamic programming which has been employed in this context by Diamond (1973), Atkinson and Sandmo (1980) and Park (1991).

The aim of the government is assumed to be the maximisation of the discounted sum of utility from period s, in which the maximisation takes place, onwards. With discount rate γ, the social welfare function is that used in chapter 13, section 3.5.2 and is given by

$$\sum_{t=s}^{\infty} \gamma^t V\left(T_t^t + \frac{T_t^{t+1}}{1+r_{t+1}}\right),$$ (15.28)

where $V\left(T_t^t + \dfrac{T_t^{t+1}}{1+r_{t+1}}\right)$ is the indirect utility function of the generation born in t.

It is clear from the budget constraint in (15.21) that it is the discounted sum of lump-sum taxes that determines welfare rather than the individual taxes.

The maximisation is constrained by the behaviour of the household and by production possibilities. The maximisation of utility by each consumer subject to (15.21) determines commodity demands and labour supply of the form

$$x_t^t = x_t^t\left(T_t^t + \frac{T_t^{t+1}}{1+r_{t+1}}\right), \quad x_t^{t+1} = x_t^{t+1}\left(T_t^t + \frac{T_t^{t+1}}{1+r_{t+1}}\right) \text{ and } \ell_t = \ell_t\left(T_t^t + \frac{T_t^{t+1}}{1+r_{t+1}}\right).$$

With a working population of H_t each choosing to undertake ℓ_t hours of employment, output with a capital stock of K_t is given by $F(K_t, H_t \ell_t)$. Assuming that the production function is homogeneous of degree one, output is given in terms of capital per young consumer, $\tilde{k}_t = K_t/H_t$, as $H_t \ell_t f\left(\dfrac{\tilde{k}_t}{\ell_t}\right)$. Output is allocated between consumption, government purchases, R, and savings. With no depreciation, the demand for output equals its supply when

$$F(K_t, H_t \ell_t) + K_t = H_t x_t^t + H_{t-1} x_{t-1}^t + R + H_t s_t.$$ (15.29)

Expressing this equality in terms quantities of per worker (15.29) becomes

$$\ell_t f\left(\frac{\tilde{k}_t}{\ell_t}\right) = x_t^t + \frac{x_{t-1}^t}{1+n} + \tilde{R} + [1+n]k_{t+1} - k_t.$$ (15.30)

The equality of savings in period t to capital in $t+1$ requires that

$$[1+n]\tilde{k}_{t+1} = w_t \ell_t - T_t^t - x_t^t, \tag{15.31}$$

which can be used in (15.30) to give the alternative representation of production possibilities

$$\tilde{k}_t + \ell_t \left[f\left(\frac{\tilde{k}_t}{\ell_t}\right) - w_t \right] - \frac{x_{t-1}^t}{1+n} - \tilde{R} + T_t^t = 0. \tag{15.32}$$

Equation (15.30) can also be solved to express the capital stock of period $t+1$ as a function of variables at t. Doing this gives

$$\tilde{k}_{t+1} = \left[\frac{1}{1+n} \right] \left[\ell_t f\left(\frac{\tilde{k}_t}{\ell_t}\right) - x_t^t - \frac{x_{t-1}^t}{1+n} - \tilde{R} + \tilde{k}_t \right]. \tag{15.33}$$

The optimal choice of lump-sum taxation is now characterised by the use of the maximum principle of dynamic programming. The government enters period s with the capital stock already determined by the savings decision of period $s-1$. In addition, the lump-sum taxes affecting generation $s-1$ are also pre-determined. The maximum welfare that can be achieved from period s onwards is therefore a function of $\tilde{k}_s$ and $T_{s-1}^{s-1} + \dfrac{T_{s-1}^s}{1+r_s}$. This *maximum value function* is denoted $\Psi\left(\tilde{k}_s, T_{s-1}^{s-1} + \dfrac{T_{s-1}^s}{1+r_s}; s \right)$ or just $\Psi(s)$ when the meaning is clear.

From the basic recursive relation of dynamic programming (see Stokey and Lucas with Prescott 1989), the maximum value at s must be equal to the maximised value of period s's indirect utility, constrained by productive feasibility, plus the maximum value attainable in $s+1$ discounted. That is

$$\Psi(s) = \max_{\{T_s^s, T_s^{s+1}\}} \left\{ V(Z_s) + \lambda_s \left[\tilde{k}_s + \ell_s \left[f\left(\frac{\tilde{k}_s}{\ell_s}\right) - w_s \right] \right. \right.$$
$$\left. \left. - \frac{x_{s-1}^s}{1+n} - \tilde{R} + T_s^s \right] + \gamma \Psi(s+1) \right\}, \tag{15.34}$$

where $Z_s = T_s^s + \dfrac{T_s^{s+1}}{1+r_{s+1}}$ and $\Psi(s+1) = \Psi\left(\tilde{k}_{s+1}, T_s^s + \dfrac{T_s^{s+1}}{1+r_{s+1}}, s+1 \right)$.

The necessary conditions for the maximisation in (15.34) with respect to T_s^s and T_s^{s+1} are

$$\frac{\partial V}{\partial Z_s} + \lambda_s \left[\frac{\partial \ell_s}{\partial Z_s} \left[f - w_s - f' \frac{\tilde{k}_s}{\ell_s} \right] - \ell_s \frac{\partial w_s}{\partial Z_s} \right] + \lambda_s + \gamma \frac{\partial \Psi(\tau+1)}{\partial Z_s}$$
$$+ \gamma \frac{\partial \Psi(\tau+1)}{\partial \tilde{k}_{s+1}} \left[\frac{1}{1+n} \right] \left[\frac{\partial \ell_s}{\partial Z_s} \left[f - f' \frac{\tilde{k}_s}{\ell_s} \right] - \frac{\partial x_s^s}{\partial Z_s} \right] = 0, \tag{15.35}$$

and

$$\frac{\partial V}{\partial Z_s} \frac{1}{1+r_{s+1}} + \lambda_s \left[\frac{\partial \ell_s}{\partial Z_s} \left[f - w_s - f' \frac{\tilde{k}_s}{\ell_s} \right] - \ell_s \frac{\partial w_s}{\partial Z_s} \right] \frac{1}{1+r_{s+1}} + \gamma \frac{\partial \Psi(s+1)}{\partial Z_s} \frac{1}{1+r_{s+1}}$$

$$+\gamma \frac{\partial \Psi(\tau+1)}{\partial \tilde{k}_{\tau+1}}\left[\frac{1}{1+n}\right]\left[\frac{\partial \ell_{\tau}}{\partial Z_{\tau}}\left[f-f'\frac{\tilde{k}_{\tau}}{\ell_{\tau}}\right]-\frac{\partial x_{\tau}^{\tau}}{\partial Z_{\tau}}\right]\frac{1}{1+r_{\tau+1}}=0. \qquad (15.36)$$

Comparison of (15.35) and (15.36) shows immediately that $\lambda_s = 0$. The reason for this is that the flexibility in the lump-sum taxes allows T_s^s to be varied whilst keeping Z_s constant. This renders the production constraint ineffective. Conditions (15.35) and (15.36) therefore both reduce to

$$\frac{\partial V}{\partial Z_s}+\gamma\frac{\partial\Psi(s+1)}{\partial Z_s}+\frac{\partial\Psi(s+1)}{\partial k_{s+1}}\left[\frac{\gamma}{1+n}\right]\left[\frac{\partial\ell_s}{\partial Z_s}\left[f-f'\frac{\tilde{k}_s}{\ell_s}\right]-\frac{\partial x_s^s}{\partial Z_s}\right]=0. \qquad (15.37)$$

Differentiating (15.34) with respect to the state variables $\tilde{k}_s$ and Z_{s-1} gives

$$\frac{\partial\Psi(s)}{\partial\tilde{k}_s}=\left[\frac{\gamma}{1+n}\right]\frac{\partial\Psi(s+1)}{\partial\tilde{k}_{s+1}}[1+f'], \qquad (15.38)$$

and

$$\frac{\partial\Psi(s)}{\partial Z_{s-1}}=-\left[\frac{\gamma}{1+n}\right]\frac{\partial\Psi(s+1)}{\partial\tilde{k}_{s+1}}\frac{\partial x_{s-1}^s}{\partial Z_{s-1}}\left[\frac{1}{1+n}\right]. \qquad (15.39)$$

Equations (15.37) to (15.39) provide the characterisation of the optimal policy.

The structure of the optimal policy is easily seen if the move is now made to the steady state. In a steady state $\dfrac{\partial\Psi(s)}{\partial\tilde{k}_s}=\dfrac{\partial\Psi(s+1)}{\partial\tilde{k}_{s+1}}=\dfrac{\partial\Psi}{\partial\tilde{k}}$ so that (15.38) reduces to

$$1+n=\gamma[1+f'], \qquad (15.40)$$

which is the modified Golden rule. Unrestricted lump-sum taxes can therefore take the economy to the modified Golden rule equilibrium, even with variable labour supply, since they cause no distortion on any of the markets. This result should be contrasted to the results on social security in chapter 14, section 4.1 where the pension affected the retirement decision. This effect is absent in the present framework.

In the steady state, (15.39) reduces to

$$\frac{\partial\Psi}{\partial Z}=-\left[\frac{\gamma}{1+n}\right]\frac{\partial x^2}{\partial Z}\frac{\partial\Psi}{\partial\tilde{k}}\left[\frac{1}{1+n}\right], \qquad (15.41)$$

where x^i is the steady state level of consumption in the ith period of life. From the budget constraint (15.21) differentiation with respect to Z shows that in the steady state

$$w\frac{\partial\ell}{\partial Z}\frac{\partial x^1}{\partial Z}=1+\frac{1}{1+r}\frac{\partial x^2}{\partial Z}. \qquad (15.42)$$

Substituting from (15.41) and (15.42) then yields

$$\frac{\partial V}{\partial Z}=\left[\frac{\gamma}{1+n}\right]\frac{\partial\Psi}{\partial\tilde{k}}. \qquad (15.43)$$

Since $\dfrac{\partial V}{\partial Z}$ is the private marginal utility of income, (15.40) and (15.43) show that
the optimal lump-sum tax policy will achieve the modified Golden rule and will
equate the private marginal utility of income to the discounted return of further
investment in capital.

3.3 Summary

This section has detailed the connections between lump-sum tax policy and debt
policy and has shown the equivalence of unrestricted lump-sum tax policies to
combinations of debt and restricted lump-sum taxes. Combined with the
analysis of optimal lump-sum taxes, these results show how the modified
Golden rule equilibrium can be sustained by a number of combinations of policy
instruments.

   In assessing these results, it should be borne in mind that the economy under
consideration was restricted by the assumption of an homogeneous population.
This limits the scope for the worthwhile differentiation of lump-sum taxes, since
consumers are only distinguished by their date of birth, and therefore makes
feasible a policy that achieves the optimal outcome. If there were further degrees
of differentiation of the consumers, for example by endowment of labour, then
lump-sum taxes could be differentiated across the lifecycle and over the
endowment. A debt policy and a uniform lump-sum tax policy would then not
be equivalent to the optimal fully differentiated set of lump-sum taxes. There
would then be less justification for expecting the optimum to be achievable since
this would also require intragenerational redistribution which could not be fully
undertaken with uniform lump-sum taxes. However, as shown by Park (1991),
the modified Golden rule will be satisfied by the correct choice of uniform lump-
sum taxes and debt policy even with a heterogeneous population but other taxes
will be required to supplement them in order to achieve intragenerational
distributional aims. Since, in practice, populations are not homogeneous, this
observation justifies the study of policies that are not equivalent to the set of
optimal lump-sum taxes.

4 DEBT NEUTRALITY

The concept of *debt neutrality*, or *Ricardian equivalence*, can be traced back to
Ricardo (1817). A brief summary of some aspects of debt neutrality relevant for
the analysis of social security has already been given in chapter 14. In this section
the emphasis will be upon proving the basic neutrality result and exploring its
limitations.

   The essence of debt neutrality is that the real economy is unaffected by
whether the government chooses to raise revenue by using taxation or through
the issue of debt. Although the payment of taxes clearly reduces wealth, the issue
of debt would seem to leave the wealth of consumers intact since it simply

displaces private capital from the portfolios of consumers. However, this overlooks the fact that the issue of debt implies future tax liabilities for its servicing and redemption. Discounted back to the present, these future liabilities reduce the present value of wealth by precisely the same amount as the tax payment. Since wealth is identical in both cases, so must be the equilibrium outcome. This simple argument is the foundation of the theory of debt neutrality.

The next subsection will formally demonstrate the neutrality result for two extreme cases. The first considers debt which is redeemed after a single period and the second involves consumers with infinite lives. The second case is intended to motivate the mechanism by which intergenerational altruism generates the neutrality result in the case of finite lives. The main neutrality result is then presented and some extensions and limitations are discussed.

4.1 Two special cases

Debt neutrality will now be demonstrated for two special cases in which the mechanism behind the result is particularly transparent. These follow the simplifying approach of Barro (1974) in which the government gives an equal number of bonds to each of the identical consumers in the economy. If after the receipt of these bonds, the consumers do not perceive their wealth to have increased, then debt neutrality is said to apply.

It is assumed that the gift of debt is a one-off event and that taxation must be used to service the debt and to meet its repayment. When future tax liabilities are taken into account, the present discounted value of wealth becomes

$$\Omega^1 = \Omega^0 + D - DTL, \tag{15.44}$$

where Ω^0 is the consumers wealth before receiving the bonds, Ω^1 the level of wealth after receiving the bonds, D the value of bonds received and DTL the discounted tax liabilities arising due to the issue of the debt. Two different assumptions on the structure of repayment of the debt are now shown to generate the same neutrality conclusion.

Under the first set of assumptions the bond is paid off with interest the year after issue and the same set of consumers is alive in both years. In this case, with interest rate r, the interest and principal paid the year after issue is given by $[1+r]D$. Discounting this back to the present shows that DTL has the value

$$DTL = \frac{[1+r]D}{1+r} = D. \tag{15.45}$$

Substituting from (15.45) into (15.44) shows immediately that the issue of the debt has no net effect upon wealth. This is a consequence of the recipients of the bonds realising that they face the tax liability for its redemption. The receipt of the bond is therefore not treated as an increase in wealth.

The second set of assumptions involve a bond that is never redeemed but on

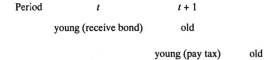

Period t $t+1$

      young (receive bond)   old

           young (pay tax)   old

Figure 15.5   Receipts and payment for one-period debt

which interest is paid in perpetuity and consumers who have infinite lifespans. In this case the discounted tax liabilities must be equal to the discounted value of the stream of interest payments. This gives

$$DTL = \int_0^\infty rDe^{-rt}dt, \tag{15.46}$$

where rD is the tax payment per period. Thus $DTL = D$ and the bond again has no effect upon net wealth.

The special feature of these two cases that makes the neutrality result so transparent is that the consumers who receive the bonds also pay the future taxes used to finance them. In an overlapping generations economy, it would appear at first sight that such a result could only apply in very particular circumstances since the set of living consumers changes each period. The important insight of Barro (1974) was to show how intergenerational altruism could support the neutrality result in general circumstances.

4.2 Intergenerational altruism

The discussion of the examples above emphasised the importance of the recipient of debt financing its servicing and repayment via taxation. In an overlapping generations economy this will in general not occur. For example, figure 15.5 indicates the pattern of receipts and payments if a one-period bond was given to the young of generation t and redeemed through taxes upon generation $t+1$. If the generations were not linked in any way, the gift of debt in this economy would raise the wealth of generation t, reduce that of generation $t+1$ and would have real effects upon the equilibrium.

The linkages between generations that are needed to support the neutrality result in an overlapping generations economy can be introduced by assuming that each consumer gives birth to a number of descendants. If the consumer cares about the welfare of their descendants, so that intergenerational altruism is present, then it is likely that they will choose to leave a bequest. The effect of the debt transfer can then be neutralised by changes in the size of the bequest and, as will be shown below, since the initial size of bequest was optimal it will also be optimal to neutralise the effect of the debt issue. Conversely, it may be the case that a consumer cares about their forebear and reflects this by giving a gift to their forebear. The neutrality result can then be attained by changes in the size of the gift offsetting the debt issue.

To formalise these arguments, consider first the case of concern for descendants. Assume that each consumer has $1+n$ descendants and that the utility of a typical member of generation t is assumed to be dependent upon the utility they derive from consumption and the return from the well-being of their descendants. Adopting an additively separable functional form for simplicity, the utility function can then be written as

$$U(t) = U(x_t^t, x_t^{t+1}) + \frac{U^*(t+1)}{1+\delta},$$
(15.47)

where $U^*(t+1)$ is the welfare level of each descendent and δ is the discount rate. The budget constraints of the consumer, incorporating the taxes required to finance the debt and the bequests given and received, are

$$x_t^t + s_t = w_t - T_t,$$
(15.48)

and

$$x_t^{t+1} + [1+n]b_t = [1+r_{t+1}][s_t + b_{t-1}].$$
(15.49)

These budget constraints embody the assumptions that each consumer in generation t has $1+n$ descendants and leaves a bequest of b_t. Each consumer also receives a bequest of b_{t-1} in the second period of their lives and, since this was actually bequethed in the previous period, it receives interest at the market rate. Lump-sum taxes, T_t, are paid in the first period of life.

The necessary conditions for the optimal choice of consumption and bequest can be derived from (15.47)–(15.49) as

$$\frac{\frac{\partial U}{\partial x_t^t}}{\frac{\partial U}{\partial x_t^{t+1}}} = 1 + r_{t+1},$$
(15.50)

and

$$\frac{\partial U}{\partial x_t^{t+1}} [1+n] \geq \left[\frac{1}{1+\delta}\right] \frac{\partial U^*(t+1)}{\partial b_t},$$
(15.51)

with $b_t = 0$ if (15.51) is a strict inequality. Noting that an increase in the bequest is simply an increase in second-period lump-sum income for the descendants which, after the addition of interest, must be valued at the marginal utility of consumption, it follows that $\dfrac{\partial U^*(t+1)}{\partial b_t} = [1+r_{t+2}] \dfrac{\partial U}{\partial x_{t+1}^{t+2}}$ so (15.51) can be written as

$$\frac{\frac{\partial U}{\partial x_t^{t+1}}}{\frac{\partial U}{\partial x_{t+1}^{t+2}}} \geq \frac{1+r_{t+2}}{[1+\delta][1+n]}. \tag{15.52}$$

Letting D_t be the value of bonds issued in period t the budget constraint of the government in period t is

$$[1+r_t]D_{t-1} = D_t + H_t T_t. \tag{15.53}$$

By defining $d_t = \dfrac{D_t}{H_t}$, (15.53) can be alternatively written

$$[1+r_t]d_{t-1} = [1+n]d_t + [1+n]T_t. \tag{15.54}$$

With bequests, equilibrium in period t satisfies the usual conditions ((13.39) and (13.40)) for the determination of the interest rate and wage rate, and the capital market equilibrium condition

$$s_t + b_{t-1} = [1+n]k_{t+1} + d_t. \tag{15.55}$$

To characterise the steady state, the level of debt and the lump-sum tax rate are held constant at d and T. Substituting from the steady state version of (15.53) and (15.54) into (15.48) and (15.49), the steady state levels of consumption satisfy

$$x^1 = f - kf' - [1+n]k + \left[b - \left[\frac{1+f'}{1+n} \right] d \right], \tag{15.56}$$

and

$$x^2 = [1+n][1+f']k - [1+n]\left[b - \left[\frac{1+f'}{1+n} \right] d \right]. \tag{15.57}$$

The steady state conditions for consumer choice (15.50) and (15.52) reduce to

$$\frac{\frac{\partial U}{\partial x^1}}{\frac{\partial U}{\partial x^2}} = 1 + f', \tag{15.58}$$

and

$$[1+n][1+\delta] \geq 1 + f'. \tag{15.59}$$

From (15.59) the bequest motive will only be operative in the steady state if $[1+n][1+\delta] = 1+f'$. Since $\delta > 0$, this implies that the equilibrium interest rate must be above the growth rate of population so the capital–labour ratio must be below the Golden rule level for bequests to be positive.

It is now possible to prove the first neutrality result.

Theorem 15.4 (Barro)

If the bequest motive is operative, so that bequests are positive both before and after any change in the level of bonds, such a change has no effect upon either the short-run equilibrium or the steady state equilibrium.

Proof

To see that there is no effect upon the steady state equilibrium, it is sufficient to observe that the consumption levels are determined by conditions (15.56) dependent upon the values of k and $b - \left[\dfrac{1+f'}{1+n}\right]d$. It is then clear that any change in d can be offset by a change in b, leaving k and the steady state consumption levels unchanged. Such a change also leaves (15.58) and (15.59) satisfied.

To show that a change in the level of debt is neutral in the short run, consider the government wishing to increase d to $d + \tilde{d}$ starting at time t. It can achieve this by giving each member of generation $t-1$ a quantity $\tilde{d}$ of bonds, which they will sell to generation t, and by selling $\left[\dfrac{n}{1+n}\right]\tilde{d}$ bonds to each member of generation t. To finance the interest payments on the bonds held by generation $t-1$ a tax of $\left[\dfrac{r_t-n}{1+n}\right]\tilde{d}$ is levied on each member of generation t. With these changes, the budget constraint of a member of generation $t-1$ in period t is

$$x_{t-1}^t = [1+r_t][s_{t-1}+b_{t-2}] - [1+n]b_{t-1} + [1+r_t]\tilde{d}. \tag{15.60}$$

and the constraints facing generation t are

$$x_t^t = w_t - T_t - s_t - \left[\frac{r_t-n}{1+n}\right]\tilde{d}, \tag{15.61}$$

and

$$x_t^{t+1} = [1+r_{t+1}][s_t+b_{t-1}] - [1+n]b_t. \tag{15.62}$$

The capital market equilibrium condition becomes

$$s_t + b_{t-1} = [1+n]k_t + d_t + \tilde{d}. \tag{15.63}$$

To show that the change in the level of debt can be neutralised by a changes in the level of bequests, let b_{t-1} be increased by $\left[\dfrac{1+r_t}{1+n}\right]\tilde{d}$ and b_t by $\left[\dfrac{1+r_{t+1}}{1+n}\right]\tilde{d}$ and let s_t fall by $\left[\dfrac{r_t-n}{1+n}\right]\tilde{d}$. Substituting these changes in (15.60) to (15.63) shows that the change in debt is cancelled from the equilibrium conditions and that the levels of consumption remain unchanged. Neutrality therefore applies.

To prove an identical result for the case of concern about forebears, assume that the utility of a consumer in t takes the form

$$U(t) = U(x_t^t, x_t^{t+1}) + \frac{U^*(t-1)}{1+\delta},$$

(15.64)

where $U^*(t-1)$ is the welfare level of the consumer's forebear. Denoting the gift received by a forebear by g_t, the budget constraints are

$$x_t^t + s_t + \left[\frac{1}{1+n}\right] g_t = w_t - T_t,$$

(15.65)

and

$$x_t^{t+1} = [1 + r_{t+1}][s_t] + g_{t+1},$$

(15.66)

where these follow from the observation that each forebear has $[1+n]$ descendants. The necessary conditions for the optimal choice of consumption and gift can be calculated to be

$$\frac{\dfrac{\partial U}{\partial x_t^t}}{\dfrac{\partial U}{\partial x_t^{t+1}}} = 1 + r_{t+1},$$

(15.67)

and

$$\frac{\partial U}{\partial x_t^{t+1}} [1 + r_{t+1}] \geq \left[\frac{1+n}{1+\delta}\right] \frac{\partial U^*(t-1)}{\partial g_t},$$

(15.68)

with $g_t = 0$ if (15.68) is a strict inequality. Exploiting the fact that an increase in gift is equivalent to an increase in lump-sum income, (15.68) can be written as

$$\frac{\partial U^*(t-1)}{\partial g_t} = \frac{\partial U}{\partial x_{t-1}^t}.$$

(15.69)

The steady state levels of consumption satisfy

$$x^1 = f - kf' - [1+n]k - \left[\frac{1}{1+n}\right][g + [1+f']d],$$

(15.70)

and

$$x^2 = [1+n][1+f']k + [g + [1+f']d].$$

(15.71)

and the steady state version of (15.68) is

$$1 + f' \geq \frac{[1+n]}{[1+\delta]}.$$

(15.72)

Gifts can be positive only when (15.72) is an equality which requires the economy to be overcapitalised relative to the Golden rule.

Using these conditions, the second neutrality theorem follows.

Theorem 15.5 (Carmichael)

If the gift motive is operative, so that gifts are positive, both before and after any change in the level of bonds, such a change has no effect upon either the short-run equilibrium or the steady state equilibrium.

Proof

The proof is essentially identical to that of theorem 15.4. In the steady state it is the value of $g+[1+f']d$ that is relevant so that under the conditions of the theorem any change in d can be offset by a change in g. In the short run a change in the level of gifts and savings can also be found that will offset the change in the level of debt.

After the publication of Barro's (1974) demonstration of the neutrality result for economies with bequests, the comments of Feldstein (1976), Buchanan (1976) and Barro's (1976) reply were directed to the discussion of whether the neutrality proposition was applicable when the rate of interest was less than the rate of growth. As shown in theorem 15.5, which is based on Carmichael (1982), neutrality does apply in this latter case if the gift motive, rather than the bequest motive, is operative. This latter result, and the related work of Buiter (1980), has itself been criticised by Burbidge (1983b) for the form of utility function employed. The contention of Burbidge is that consistency of treatment between descendants and forebears places additional restrictions upon the rates of discounting that can be employed. However, as noted in the reply of Buiter and Carmichael (1984), the utility function is constructed as the representation of an underlying preference ordering and if the preference ordering does not restrict discount rates nor should the utility function. Viewed in this way, the discount factors in (15.47) and (15.64) implicitly adjust for the number of descendants and forebears respectively.

Given the importance of an operative bequest motive, it is worth clarifying the conditions under which bequests will be positive. Drazen (1978) provided a partial analysis of this issue but the first substantive result was given in Weil (1987). To demonstrate this result, assume that in the economy with concern for descendants there is no debt and that the utility function is also additively separable in consumption with the form

$$U(t)=U(x_t^t)+\beta U(x_t^{t+1})+\frac{U^*(t-1)}{1+\delta}. \tag{15.73}$$

The steady state equilibrium is then the solution to

$$x^1=f-kf'-[1+n]k+b=w(k)-[1+n]k+b, \tag{15.74}$$

$$x^2 = [1+n][1+f']k - [1+n]b = [1+n][1+r(k)]k - [1+n]b, \tag{15.75}$$

$$U'(x^1) = \beta[1+r(k)]U'(x^2), \tag{15.76}$$

and

$$[1+n][1+\delta] = 1+f' = 1+r(k) \equiv 1+r^*. \tag{15.77}$$

The equality in (15.77) captures the assumption that the bequest motive is operative.

If the optimal level of bequests is zero, (15.76) will be satisfied when evaluated at $b=0$. Otherwise substituting (15.74) and (15.75) into (15.76) then shows that the optimal value of the bequest will satisfy

$$\text{sgn}.\{b\} = \text{sgn}.\{U'(w(k) - [1+n]k) - \beta[1+r^*]U'([1+r^*][1+n]k)\}. \tag{15.78}$$

Now denote the savings function of the equivalent economy without bequest motive (i.e., the solution to $U'(w-s) - \beta[1+r]U'([1+r]s) = 0$) by $s = s(w,r)$. Using this definition, (15.78) is equivalent to

$$\text{sgn}.\{b\} = \text{sgn}.\{[1+n]k - s(w,r)\}. \tag{15.79}$$

Assuming that the identity $[1+n]k - s(w,r) = 0$ has a unique solution $\bar{k}$, which would be the steady state capital–labour ratio in the economy without bequest motive, the following theorem can be proved.

Theorem 15.6 (Weil)

If $s(w,r) - [1+n]k > 0 \forall k \in (0, \bar{k})$ and $s(w,r) - [1+n]k < 0 \forall k > \bar{k}$, then the bequest motive is operative in the steady state if and only if $\dfrac{1}{1+\delta} > \dfrac{1+n}{1+\bar{r}}$, where $\bar{r} = f'(\bar{k})$ is the steady state interest rate of the corresponding economy without bequest motive.

Proof

From (15.79), the bequest will only be positive if $[1+n]k - s(w,r) > 0$. This implies, from the assumptions of the theorem, that the steady state capital stock, k^*, of an economy with an operative bequest motive satisfies $k^* > \bar{k}$. From (15.77), the economy with bequest motive satisfies $\dfrac{1}{1+\delta} = \dfrac{1+n}{1+r^*}$ and, since $k^* > \bar{k}$, $r^* < \bar{r}$. Hence the bequest motive can only be operative when $\dfrac{1}{1+\delta} > \dfrac{1+n}{1+\bar{r}}$.

The assumptions employed in the proof of this theorem regarding the relation of $s(w,r) - [1+n]k$ to $\bar{k}$ to are equivalent to the assumption that the unique steady state of the economy without bequest motive is stable. From the conclusion of the theorem, it can be seen that the bequest motive will be operative provided the discount factor applied to descendants utility is sufficiently great. That is, there must be a sufficient degree of intergenerational concern for bequests to be positive.

This section has shown how bequest and gift motives can extend the two-period lived consumers of the overlapping generations economy into infinitely lived dynasties connected by intergenerational altruism. Once this has been done, it is not surprising that neutrality results which apply for infinitely lived consumers then apply in the overlapping generations framework. It is important to stress that these results rely on changes in the level of bequests or gifts being able to offset changes in the pattern of debt and taxes. If neither of these motives is operative or the level of transfer is small, this may not be possible.

4.3 Generalisations

One aspect of the neutrality results described above that has received attention is the assumption of certainty. Blanchard (1985) has considered the possibility that the lifespan of each consumer may be of random length. The introduction of such uncertainty has the implication that those who benefit from any debt issue will have a probability of less than one of being alive to face any future tax payments. In the analysis of Blanchard each consumer has a constant probability of their life continuing (which gives rise to the description of such an economy as embodying perpetual youth) and the population remains constant as new consumers are born at each point in time to replace those who have died. To prevent unintended bequests, a life insurance market offering insurance at fair terms is assumed to be operational. When there is no bequest motive, neutrality does not hold in such an economy. This analysis is extended by Buiter (1988) to show that a necessary and sufficient condition for debt neutrality to apply in such an economy is that the sum of the probability of death and the growth rate of population is identically zero. This is clearly violated in the Blanchard analysis except when the consumers have a zero probability of death and are therefore infinitely lived.

Although the focus to this point has been upon debt neutrality, an economy with an operative gift or bequest motive is capable of neutralising a broad range of fiscal policies. Since Bernheim and Bagwell (1988) show that almost any policy can be neutralised, the fact that this seems refuted by practice suggests that the economy in which such propositions can be derived is not a successful representation of reality. To attempt to achieve debt neutrality without the neutrality of all policy, Abel and Bernheim (1991) note that changes in the level of debt are often neutralised by exploiting only a few links in the intergenerational chain whereas the neutralisation of other policies requires the exploitation of many links. This observation motivates the introduction of friction into the intergenerational altruism via the derivation of utility from the act of giving, imperfect knowledge of the later generation's preferences and social norms that govern bequests. The first two allow approximate neutrality in the short run but drive the marginal propensity to consume to zero. The third avoids this conclusion but does lead to the conclusion that an exogenous increase in wealth of any one consumer can never be a Pareto improvement. Due to these unpalatable conclusions, the introduction of friction in this way cannot be claimed to be a successful mechanism for retaining debt neutrality whilst eliminating more general neutralities.

Finally, it should be noted again that debt neutrality fails if the gift or bequest motives are not operative. In addition, it can also fail when the change in policy leads to redistribution among consumers with differing marginal propensities to consume. This did not occur in the theorems above since all consumers were identical and the policy affected each equally. It can also occur when lifetimes are uncertain and insurance markets are imperfect (Abel 1986a) and when the tax instruments are not lump sum. As yet, neither empirical evidence (see Bernheim 1987 and Sweeney 1988) nor experimental evidence (Cadsby and Frank 1991) has confirmed or refuted whether neutrality applies in practice.

5 INCOME AND INTEREST TAXATION

In a dynamic economy an income tax leads to the double taxation of savings: once when the income is received and then again when the interest income from savings is received. This fact has often been used to support the contention, for example in Meade (1975), that an expenditure tax which avoids the double taxation would be preferable to an income tax. This view overlooks the fact that it is necessary to establish that the double taxation leads to an inferior outcome. Simply counting the number of instances of distortion is not a sufficient analysis. More relevant for the present discussion is the potential dynamic inefficiency of an overlapping generations economy. If the economy is on a path with excessive capital accumulation then there may be a gain to introducing a distortion into the savings decision that reduces the level of capital. Since interest and income taxes have different effects upon the steady state equilibrium of the economy, the design of the tax system should take advantage of this by combining the two instruments. These issues are now addressed for non-linear taxes on income and interest in an economy with a heterogeneous population.

The optimal combination of income and interest taxation has been approached using two different methods. Atkinson and Sandmo (1980) and Park (1991) employ the dynamic programming method described in section 3. The results of Atkinson and Sandmo are restricted to an economy in which consumers only differ with respect to their date of birth and are otherwise homogeneous. Such a setting does not explore the full potential of the taxes for effecting intragenerational transfers. Although Park considers a heterogeneous population, few concrete results are derived. The alternative approach, developed in Ordover and Phelps (1975, 1979), Ordover (1976), and Phelps and

Riley (1978), is based on the observation that what links generations t and $t+1$ are the capital stock provided by the members of generation t and their claim to consumption in the second period of life. The maximisation of social welfare can then be reduced to a single-period problem by assuming that the welfare of generation t is maximised subject to the constraints that the capital stock provided for generation $t+1$ does not fall below some chosen level and that second-period consumption is not above some fixed level. This alternative approach is now described.

The details of the analyses differ in the objective functions of the government and the manner in which the constraining levels of capital stock and second-period consumption are chosen. Ordover and Phelps (1975), Ordover (1976) and Phelps and Riley (1978) all employ a Rawlsian maxi–min objective for the government whereas Ordover and Phelps (1979) consider a more general Bergson–Samuelson social welfare function. In Ordover and Phelps (1975) the levels of capital stock and second-period consumption were arbitrarily chosen and it was required that they were held constant over time. Although simple, this procedure cannot, in general, maximise any social welfare function satisfying the Pareto criterion (2.49) since opportunities to raise welfare are being missed. Phelps and Riley (1978) showed how the requirement that the capital stock and level of second-period consumption be Pareto optimal in the allocations between generations could be given a simple representation and incorporated into the optimisation. This made possible the general analysis of Ordover and Phelps (1979) which is now described.

The heterogeneous population is introduced by combining the Mirrlees economy of chapter 5 with the Diamond overlapping generations economy. Each consumer lives for two periods, consuming in both but working only in the first period. Within a generation, consumers are differentiated by their level of ability. Denoting the ability level by s, $0 \geq s \geq S, S$ finite, the cumulative distribution of s is given by $\Gamma(s)$ with the normalisation $\Gamma(S)=1$. This normalisation restricts the generations to be of equal size. The corresponding density function is $\gamma(s)$. Writing the consumption levels and labour supply (in hours) of a consumer of ability s born in t as $x_t^t(s), x_t^{t+1}(s)$ and $\ell_t(s)$, the consumption levels and *effective* labour supply per member of generation t are

$$x_t^1(s) = \int_0^S x_t^t(s)\gamma(s)ds, \qquad (15.80)$$

$$x_t^2(s) = \int_0^S x_t^{t+1}(s)\gamma(s)ds, \qquad (15.81)$$

and

$$z_t(s) = \int_0^s s\ell_t(s)\gamma(s)ds. \tag{15.82}$$

The preferences of each consumer are given by the utility function $U = U(x_t^t, x_t^{t+1}, \ell_t)$ and this is maximised subject to the budget constraint

$$x_t^t + \frac{x_t^{t+1}}{1+r_{t+1}} = w_t s\ell_t - T_\ell(w_t s\ell_t) - T_s(x_t^{t+1}). \tag{15.83}$$

In (15.83), $T_\ell(w_t s\ell_t)$ is the income tax function, with w_t the wage rate, and $T_s(x_t^{t+1})$ the tax on second-period consumption. The latter tax is essentially equivalent to a tax on savings. To simplify the analysis by eliminating the need for discounting in the government budget, it is assumed that the tax on second-period consumption is pre-paid in the first period of life.

Given consumer choices $x_t^t(s), x_t^{t+1}(s)$ and $\ell_t(s)$, total differentiation of the utility function with respect to s gives

$$\frac{dU}{ds} = U_{x_t^t} x_t^{t'} + U_{x_t^{t+1}} x_t^{t+1'} + U_{\ell_t} \frac{z_t'}{s} - U_{\ell_t} \frac{z_t}{s^2}. \tag{15.84}$$

Applying the argument of (5.13)–(5.15) that $s' = s$ must minimise $U(s') - U\left(x_t^t(s), x_t^{t+1}(s), \frac{z_t(s)}{s'}\right)$, it follows that

$$U_{x_t^t} x_t^{t'} + U_{x_t^{t+1}} x_t^{t+1'} + U_{\ell_t} \frac{z_t'}{s} = 0, \tag{15.85}$$

and hence that

$$\frac{dU}{ds} = -U_{\ell_t} \frac{z_t}{s^2} \geq 0. \tag{15.86}$$

Equation (15.86) is the first-order condition for self-selection that must constrain the choice of tax functions. The final part of the description of the consumer is to solve the identity $U(s) = U(x_t^t(s), x_t^{t+1}(s), \ell_t(s))$ to write

$$x_t^t(s) = x_t^t(U(s), x_t^{t+1}(s), \ell_t(s)). \tag{15.87}$$

The production function for the economy is given by the constant returns to scale function $F(\tilde{k}_t, z_t)$ where $\tilde{k}_t$ is the level of capital stock per member of the young generation. The identities $w_t = F_z(\tilde{k}_t, z_t)$ and $r_t = F_k(\tilde{k}_t, z_t)$ determine the wage rate and interest rate via optimal choice of factors by firms. The capital stock left to generation $t+1$ is given by

$$\tilde{k}_{t+1} = F(\tilde{k}_t, z_t) + \tilde{k}_t - x_t^1 - x_{t-1}^2. \tag{15.88}$$

The optimisation problem facing the government in period t is to maximise the welfare level of generation t determined by the social welfare function

$$W^t = \int_0^S U(x_t^t(s), x_t^{t+1}(s), \ell_t(s)) \gamma(s) ds, \tag{15.89}$$

subject to the constraints

$$\bar{x}_t^2 \geq \int_0^S x_t^{t+1}(s) \gamma(s) ds, \tag{15.90}$$

$$F(\tilde{k}_t, z_t) + \tilde{k}_t - \int_0^S x_t^t(s) \gamma(s) ds - x_{t-1}^2 \geq \bar{\tilde{k}}_{t+1}, \tag{15.91}$$

and the differential equation (15.86). In (15.90) $\bar{x}_t^2$ is the maximum permissible mean level of second-period consumption to which the members of generation t are entitled and in (15.91) $\bar{\tilde{k}}_{t+1}$ is the minimum level of capital stock they must endow to the next generation. For this maximisation, $x_t^{t+1}(s)$ and $\ell_t(s)$ are the control variables, $U(s)$ is the state variable and $x_t^t(s)$ is determined from (15.87). This formulation leads to the Hamiltonian

$$H(s) = U(s)\gamma(s) + \lambda^t[\bar{x}_t^2 - x_t^{t+1}(s)]\gamma(s)$$
$$+ \rho^t[F(\tilde{k}_t, z_t) + \tilde{k}_t - x_t^t(s) ds - x_{t-1}^2 - \bar{\tilde{k}}_{t+1}]\gamma(s) + \mu^t(s)\left[-\frac{U_\ell \ell_t(s)}{s}\right],$$
$$\tag{15.92}$$

where λ^t and ρ^t are the Lagrange multipliers on the constraints and $\mu^t(s)$ is the co-state variable.

The next step is to exploit the requirement that $\bar{x}_t^2$ and $\bar{\tilde{k}}_{t+1}$ are Pareto optimal to simplify (15.92). It follows from the interpretation of Lagrange multipliers that $\dfrac{\partial W^{t*}}{\partial \bar{x}_t^2} = -\lambda^t > 0$ and $\dfrac{\partial W^{t*}}{\partial \bar{\tilde{k}}_{t+1}} = \rho^t < 0$ where W^{t*} is the maximum value function for the optimisation. From these

$$\left.\frac{\partial \bar{\tilde{k}}_{t+1}}{\partial \bar{x}_t^2}\right|_{W^{t*}} = -\frac{\dfrac{\partial W^{t*}}{\partial \bar{x}_t^2}}{\dfrac{\partial W^{t*}}{\partial \bar{\tilde{k}}_{t+1}}} = \frac{\lambda^t}{\rho^t} > 0. \tag{15.93}$$

Similarly

$$\left.\frac{\partial \tilde{k}_t}{\partial x_{t-1}^2}\right|_{W^{t*}} = -\frac{\dfrac{\partial W^{t*}}{\partial x_{t-1}^2}}{\dfrac{\partial W^{t*}}{\partial \tilde{k}_t}} = \frac{1}{1 + F_k(\tilde{k}_t, z_t)}, \tag{15.94}$$

which, when stepped one period forward, gives

$$\left.\frac{\partial \tilde{k}_{t+1}}{\partial x_t^2}\right|_{W^{t+1*}} = -\frac{\dfrac{\partial W^{t*}}{\partial x_t^2}}{\dfrac{\partial W^{t*}}{\partial \tilde{k}_{t+1}}} = \frac{1}{1 + F_k(\tilde{k}_{t+1}, z_{t+1})}. \tag{15.95}$$

The allocation is Pareto efficient when the gradients given in (15.93) and (15.95) are equal so that the indifference curve of the social welfare function, defined over $\bar{x}_t^2$ and $\tilde{k}_{t+1}$, are tangential for periods t and $t+1$. Therefore, at a point on the locus of Pareto optima

$$\frac{\lambda^t}{\rho^t} = \frac{1}{1 + F_k(\tilde{k}_{t+1}, z_{t+1})}. \tag{15.96}$$

The restriction in (15.96) can be substituted into the Hamiltonian to give the simplified form

$$H(s) = U(s)\gamma(s) + \mu^t(s)\left[-\frac{U_\ell \ell_t(s)}{s}\right]$$

$$+ \rho^t\left[\frac{\bar{x}_t^2 - x_t^{t+1}(s)}{1 + F(\tilde{k}_{t+1}, z_{t+1})} + F(\tilde{k}_t, z_t) + \tilde{k}_t - x_t^t(s)ds - x_{t-1}^2 - \tilde{k}_{t+1}\right]\gamma(s). \tag{15.97}$$

Next define $r_{t+1}^* = F(\tilde{k}_{t+1}, z_{t+1})$ and denote $\varDelta_t^* = \dfrac{\bar{x}_t^2}{1 + r_{t+1}^*} - \tilde{k}_{t+1}$. From the second-period budget constraint of consumers it can be seen that $\varDelta_t^*$ is the market value in period t of one-period bonds sold to consumers of generation t and which will be redeemed in $t+1$. The Hamiltonian can then be written as

$$H(s) = U(s)\gamma(s) + \mu^t(s)\left[-\frac{U_\ell \ell_t(s)}{s}\right]$$

$$+ \rho^t\left[\varDelta_t^* - \frac{x_t^{t+1}(s)}{1 + r_{t+1}^*} + F(\tilde{k}_t, z_t) + \tilde{k}_t - x_t^t(s)ds - x_{t-1}^2\right]\gamma(s). \tag{15.98}$$

Optimising with respect to $x_t^{t+1}(s)$ provides the necessary condition

$$\rho^t\left[-\frac{1}{1 + r_{t+1}^*} - \frac{\partial x_t^t(s)}{\partial x_t^{t+1}(s)}\right]\gamma(s) + \mu^t(s)\left[-\frac{\ell_t}{s}\left[U_{\ell x_t^t}\frac{\partial x_t^t(s)}{\partial x_t^{t+1}(s)} + U_{\ell x_t^{t+1}}\right]\right] = 0, \tag{15.99}$$

for the determination of the tax schedule $T_s(\cdot)$.

From condition (15.99), two theorems can be proved.

Theorem 15.7 (Ordover and Phelps)

The marginal rate of interest income tax, $T_s'(\cdot)$, is zero at $s = M$.

Proof

The transversality condition for the optimisation is that $\mu'(M)=0$. At $s=S$ this reduces (15.99) to

$$\rho'\left[-\frac{1}{1+r^*_{t+1}}-\frac{\partial x^t_t(s)}{\partial x^{t+1}_t(s)}\right]\gamma(s)=0. \tag{15.100}$$

As $\rho'<0$ and $\gamma(s)>0$, (16.73) shows that there is no distortion in choice.

Theorem 15.8 (Ordover and Phelps)

When the utility function is separable between consumption and labour, interest income is tax exempt.

Proof

The separable utility function is written as $U(\Psi(x^t_t,x^{t+1}_t),\ell_t)$. Then

$$U_{\ell x^t_t}\frac{\partial x^t_t}{\partial x^{t+1}_t}+U_{\ell x^{t+1}_t}=U_{\ell\Psi}\Psi_{x^t_t}\frac{\partial x^t_t}{\partial x^{t+1}_t}+U_{\ell\Psi}\Psi_{x^{t+1}_t}$$

$$=-U_{\ell\Psi}\Psi_{x^{t+1}_t}+U_{\ell\Psi}\Psi_{x^{t+1}_t}=0, \tag{15.101}$$

where the second equality follows from using $\dfrac{\partial x^t_t}{\partial x^{t+1}_t}=-\dfrac{\Psi_{x^{t+1}_t}}{\Psi_{x^t_t}}$. Equation

(15.101) implies that $\rho'\left[-\dfrac{1}{1+r^*_{t+1}}-\dfrac{\partial x^t_t(s)}{\partial x^{t+1}_t(s)}\right]\gamma(s)=0$ for all s which proves the

theorem.

The argument behind theorem 15.7 is essentially equivalent to that of theorem 5.6: given the upper-bound upon ability, there is no gain from having the choices of that consumer distorted. Theorem 15.8 is different in nature and shows that the tax on interest income is redundant when the utility function is weakly separable and an optimal income tax is employed. Despite the different effects of the two taxes, there is nothing to be gained by having an interest tax in addition to a non-linear income tax when preferences are separable. Without separability, both taxes will be employed.

6 CONCLUSIONS

The analysis of tax policy in dynamic economies involves consideration of both intragenerational and intertemporal allocations. Compared with the static analysis, there is also a broader range of instruments available since the use of debt becomes a meaningful option. This chapter has attempted to capture these issues and to illustrate alternative methods of analysis.

The effects of debt were demonstrated in an economy without intergenerational altruism. Although an increase in external debt can rarely lead to an increase in welfare, in an overcapitalised economy an increase in internal debt will. The policy relevance of this finding has to be considered in the light of the Ricardian equivalence proposition that changes in debt have no real effect upon the economy. A proof of this proposition was given but it was also argued that it required a particular form of intergenerational altruism and that there were numerous circumstances in which equivalence does not apply.

In dynamically efficient economies with a homogeneous population, the introduction of an income tax or an interest tax simply adds a distortion and reduces welfare. With a heterogeneous population intragenerational distribution also becomes relevant. Despite this, an interest tax is redundant when the utility function is separable and the optimal non-linear income tax is employed.

REFERENCES

Aaron, H. (1966) 'The social insurance paradox', *Canadian Journal of Economics and Political Science*, **32**, 371–4.

(1982) *Economic effects of social security*, Washington: The Brookings Institute.

Abel, A.B. (1986a) 'Capital accumulation and uncertain lifetimes with adverse aelection', *Econometrica*, **54**, 1079–97.

(1986b) 'The failure of Ricardian equivalence under progressive wealth taxation', *Journal of Public Economics*, **30**, 117–28.

Abel, A.B. and B.D. Bernheim (1991) 'Fiscal policy with impure intergenerational altruism', *Econometrica*, **59**, 1687–711.

Abrams, B.A. and M.A. Schmitz (1984) 'The crowding out effect of government transfers on private charitable contributions: cross sectional evidence', *National Tax Journal*, **37**, 563–8.

Ahmad, E. and N.H. Stern (1984) 'The theory of reform and Indian indirect taxes', *Journal of Public Economics*, **25**, 259–98.

Allen, F. (1982) 'Optimal linear income taxation with general equilibrium effects on wages', *Journal of Public Economics*, **17**, 135–43.

Allingham, M.G. and A. Sandmo (1972) 'Income tax evasion: a theoretical analysis', *Journal of Public Economics*, **1**, 323–38.

Andersen, P. (1977) 'Tax evasion and labour supply', *Scandinavian Journal of Economics*, **79**, 375–83.

Anderson, R. and J.G. Ballentine (1976) 'The incidence and excess burden of a profits tax under imperfect competition', *Public Finance*, **31**, 159–76.

Andreoni, J. (1988a) 'Privately provided public goods in a large economy: the limits of altruism', *Journal of Public Economics*, **35**, 57–73.

(1988b) 'Why free ride?', *Journal of Public Economics*, **37**, 291–304.

(1989) 'Giving with impure altruism: applications to charity and Ricardian equivalence', *Journal of Political Economy*, **97**, 1447–58.

(1990) 'Impure altruism and donations to public goods: a theory of warm-glow giving', *Economic Journal*, **100**, 464–77.

Aoki, M. (1971) 'Marshallian external economies and optimal tax-subsidy structure', *Econometrica*, **39**, 35–53.

Arrow, K.J. (1950) 'A difficulty in the concept of social welfare', *Journal of Political Economy*, **58**, 328–46.

(1951a) 'An extension of the basic theorems of welfare economics', in J. Neyman (ed.), *Proceedings of the second Berkeley symposium on mathematical statistics and probability*, Berkeley: University of California Press.

516

(1951b) *Social choice and individual values*, New York: Wiley.

(1963) 'The role of securities in the optimal allocation of risk-bearing', *Review of Economic Studies*, **31**, 91–6.

(1965) *Aspects of the theory of risk-bearing*, Helsinki: Yrjo Jahnssonin Saatio.

(1969) 'The organisation of economic activity: issues pertinent to the choice of market versus non-market allocation' in *The analysis and evaluation of public expenditures: the PPB system*, Washington DC: Joint Economic Committee of the Congress of the United States.

(1970) *Essays in the Theory of risk bearing*, Amsterdam: North-Holland.

Arrow, K.J. and G. Debreu (1954) 'Existence of equilibrium for a competitive economy', *Econometrica*, **22**, 265–90.

Arrow, K.J. and F. Hahn (1971) *General competitive analysis*, San Francisco: Holden Day.

Arrow, K.J. and R.C. Lind (1970) 'Uncertainty and the evaluation of public investment decisions', *American Economic Review*, **60**, 364–78.

Ashenfelter, O. and J. Heckman (1973) 'Estimating labour supply functions', in G.C. Cain and N.W. Watts (eds.), *Income maintenance and labour supply*, Chicago: Rand McNally.

d'Aspremont, C. and L.-A. Gérard-Varet (1979) 'Incentives and incomplete information', *Journal of Public Economics*, **11**, 25–45.

Atkinson, A.B. (1970) 'On the measurement of inequality', *Journal of Economic Theory*, **2**, 244–63.

(1972) 'Maxi-min and optimal income taxation', paper presented at the Budapest meeting of the Economic Society.

(1987) 'On the measurement of poverty', *Econometrica*, **55**, 749–64.

Atkinson, A.B. and A. Sandmo (1980) 'Welfare implications of the taxation of savings', *Economic Journal*, **90**, 529–49.

Atkinson, A.B. and N.H. Stern (1974) 'Pigou, taxation and public goods', *Review of Economic Studies*, **41**, 119–28.

Atkinson, A.B. and J.E. Stiglitz (1972) 'The structure of indirect taxation and economic efficiency', *Journal of Public Economics*, **1**, 97–119.

(1976) 'The design of tax structure: direct versus indirect taxation', *Journal of Public Economics*, **6**, 55–75.

(1980) *Lectures on public economics*, London: McGraw-Hill.

Auerbach, A.J. (1979) 'Wealth maximisation and the cost of capital', *Quarterly Journal of Economics*, **93**, 433–46.

(1983) 'Taxation, corporate financial policy and the cost of capital', *Journal of Economic Literature*, **21**, 905–40.

Auerbach, A.J. and M.A. King (1983) 'Taxation, portfolio choice, and debt-equity ratios: a general equilibrium model', *Quarterly Journal of Economics*, **97**, 587–609.

Aumann, R.J. (1964) 'Markets with a continuum of traders', *Econometrica*, **34**, 1–17.

Averch, H. and L.L. Johnson (1962) 'Behaviour of the firm under regulatory constraint', *American Economic Review*, **52**, 1053–69.

Balasko Y. and K. Shell (1980) 'The overlapping-generations model, I: the case of pure exchange without money', *Journal of Economic Theory*, **23**, 281–306.

(1981) 'The overlapping-generations model, II: the case of pure exchange with money', *Journal of Economic Theory*, **24**, 112–42.

Balasko, Y., D. Cass and K. Shell (1980) 'Existence of competitive equilibrium in a general overlapping-generations model', *Journal of Economic Theory*, **23**, 307–22.

Balcer, Y. (1980) 'Taxation of externalities: direct versus indirect', *Journal of Public Economics*, **13**, 121–9.

Baldry, J.C. (1986) 'Tax evasion is not a gamble', *Economics Letters*, **22**, 333–5.

Ball, M.J. (1973) 'Recent empirical work on the determinants of relative house prices', *Urban Studies*, **10**, 213–33.

Ballentine, J.G. and I. Eris (1975) 'On the general equilibrium analusis of tax incidence', Journal of Political Economy, **83**, 633–44.

Baron, D. (1989) 'The design of regulatory mechanisms and institutions', in R. Schmalansee and R. Willig (eds.), *Handbook of industrial organisation*, Amsterdam: North-Holland.

Barone, E. (1935) 'The ministry of production in the collectivist state', in F.A. von Hayek (ed.), *Collectivist economic planning*, London: Routledge.

Barro, R.J. (1974) 'Are government bonds net wealth?', *Journal of Political Economy*, **82**, 1095–117.

(1976) 'Reply to Feldstein and Buchanan', *Journal of Political Economy*, **84**, 343–9.

Barten. A.P. (1964) 'Family composition, prices and expenditure patterns', in P.E. Hart, G. Mills and J.K. Whitaker (eds.), *Economic analysis for national economic planning*, London: Butterworth.

Baumol, W.J., E.E. Bailey and R.D. Willig (1977) 'Weak invisible hand theorems on the sustainability of multiproduct natural monopoly', *American Economic Review*, **67**, 350–65.

Baumol, W.J. and D.F. Bradford (1970) 'Optimal departures from marginal cost pricing', *American Economic Review*, **60**, 265–83.

Baumol, W.J. and J. Benhabib (1989) 'Chaos: significance, mechanism and economic applications', *Journal of Economic Perspectives*, **3**, 77–105.

Baumol, W.J. and W.E. Oates (1988) *The theory of environmental policy*, Cambridge: Cambridge University Press.

Becker, W., H.-J. Büchner and S. Sleeking (1987) 'The impact of public transfer expenditures on tax evasion', *Journal of Public Economics*, **34**, 243–52.

Beckerman, W. (1979) 'The impact of income maintenance payments on poverty in Britain 1975', *Economic Journal*, **89**, 261–79.

Berge, C. (1963) *Topological spaces*, London: Oliver and Boyd.

Bergson, A. (1938) 'A reformulation of certain aspects of welfare economics', *Quarterly Journal of Economics*, **68**, 233–52.

(1973) 'On monopoly welfare losses', *American Economic Review*, **63**, 853–70.

Bergstrom, T.C. (1976) 'Regulation of externalities', *Journal of Public Economics*, **5**, 131–8.

Bergstrom, T.C. and R.C. Cornes (1983) 'Independence of allocative efficiency from distribution in the theory of public goods', *Econometrica*, **51**, 1753–65.

Bergstrom, T.C., L. Blume and H. Varian (1986) 'On the private provision of public goods', *Journal of Public Economics*, **29**, 25–49.

(1992) 'Uniqueness of Nash equilibrium in private provision of public goods', *Journal of Public Economics*, **49**, 391–2.

Bernheim, B.D. (1987) 'Ricardian equivalence: an evaluation of theory and evidence', *NBER Macro Annual*, 263–304.

Bernheim, B.D. and K. Bagwell (1988) 'Is everything neutral?', *Journal of Political Economy*, **96**, 308–38.

Besley, T. and I. Jewitt (1990) 'Optimal uniform taxation and the structure of consumer preferences', in G.D. Myles (ed.), *Measurement and modelling in economics*, Amsterdam: North-Holland.

Beveridge, W. (1942) 'Social insurance and allied services', Cmd. 6404, London: HMSO.

Bhatia, K.B. (1981) 'Intermediate goods and the incidence of the corporation income tax', *Journal of Public Economics*, **16**, 93–112.

(1982a) 'Intermediate goods and the theory of tax incidence', *Public Finance*, **37**, 318–38.

(1982b) 'Value-added tax and the theory of tax incidence', *Journal of Public Economics*, **19**, 203–23.

(1986) 'Taxes, intermediate goods, and relative prices: the case of variable coefficients', *Journal of Public Economics*, **31**, 197–213.

Bierwag, G. O., M. A. Grove and C. Khang (1969) 'National debt in a neo-classical growth model: comment', *American Economic Review*, **59**, 205–10.

Bigelow, J.P. (1993) 'Inducing efficiency: externalities, missing markets, and the Coase theorem', *International Economic Review*, **34**, 335–46.

Blackorby, C. and D. Donaldson (1978) 'Measures of relative inequality and their meaning in terms of social welfare', *Journal of Economic Theory*, **18**, 59–80.

Blanchard, O.J. (1985) 'Debt, deficits and finite horizons', *Journal of Political Economy*, **93**, 223–47.

Blundell, R. (1992) 'Labour supply and taxation: a survey', *Fiscal Studies*, **13**, 15–40.

Blundell, R. and A. Lewbel (1991) 'The information content of equivalence scales', *Journal of Econometrics*, **50**, 49–68.

Boadway, R.W., M. Marchand and P. Pestieau (1991) 'Optimal linear income taxation in models with occupational choice', *Journal of Public Economics*, **46**, 133–62.

Boadway, R.W. and D.E. Wildasin (1989) 'A median voter model of social security', *International Economic Review*, **30**, 307–28.

Bohm, P. (1971) 'An approach to the problem of estimating the demand for public goods', *Swedish Journal of Economics*, **73**, 55–66.

  (1972) 'Estimating demand for public goods: an experiment', *European Economic Review*, **3**, 55–66.

  (1984) 'Revealing demand for an actual public good', *Journal of Public Economics*, **24**, 135–51.

Boldrin, M. and M. Woodford (1990) 'Equilibrium models displaying endogenous fluctuations and chaos', *Journal of Monetary Economics*, **25**, 189–222.

Bonnisseau, J.-M. (1991) 'Existence of Lindahl equilibria in economies with nonconvex production sets', *Journal of Economic Theory*, **54**, 409–16.

Bordignon, M. (1990) 'Was Kant right? Voluntary provision of public goods under the principle of unconditional commitment', *Economic Notes*, 342–72.

  (1993) 'A fairness approach to income tax evasion', *Journal of Public Economics*, **52**, 345–62.

Bös, D. (1986) *Public enterprise economics*, Amsterdam: North-Holland.

Bourguignon, F. (1979) 'Decomposble income inequality measures', *Econometrica*, **47**, 901–20.

Bradford, D.F. (1981) 'The incidence and allocation effects of a tax on coporate distributions', *Journal of Public Economics*, **15**, 1–22.

Brandts, J. and C.A.M. de Bartolome (1992) 'Population uncertainty, social insurance, and actuarial bias', *Journal of Public Economics*, **47**, 361–80.

Break, G.F. (1957) 'Income taxes and the incentive to work: an empirical study', *American Economic Review*, **47**, 529–49.

Brito, D.L. and W.H. Oakland (1977) 'Some properties of the optimal income tax', *International Economic Review*, **18**, 407–23.

Brookshire, D.S., M.A. Thayer, W. Schulze and R. D'Arge (1982) 'Valuing public goods: a comparison of survey and hedonic approaches', *American Economic Review*, **72**, 165–77.

Brown, C.V. and E. Levin (1974) 'The effects of income taxation on overtime', *Economic Journal*, **84**, 833–48.

Brown, S.J. and D.S. Sibley (1986) *The theory of public utility pricing*, Cambridge: Cambridge University Press.

Browning, E.K. (1975) 'Why the social insurance budget is too large in a democratic society', *Economic Inquiry*, **13**, 373–88.

Buchanan, J.M. (1976) 'Barro on the Ricardian equivalence theorem', *Journal of Political Economy*, **84**, 337–42.

Buchanan, J.M. and M. Kafoglis (1963) 'A note on public goods supply', *American Economic Review*, **53**, 403–14.

Buhmann, B., L. Rainwater, G. Schmaus and T.M. Smeeding (1989) 'Equivalence scales, well-being, inequality, and poverty: sensitivity estimates across ten countries using the Luxembourg income study (LIS) database', *Review of Income and Wealth*, **34**, 115–42.

Buiter, W.H. (1980) 'Crowding out of private capital formation by government borrowing in the presence of intergenerational gifts and bequests', *Greek Economic Review*, **2**, 111–42.

  (1988) 'Death, birth, productivity growth and debt neutrality', *Economic Journal*, **89**, 279–93.

Buiter, W.H. and J. Carmichael (1984) 'Government debt: comment', *American Economic Review*, **74**, 762–5.

Burbidge, J.B. (1983a) 'Social security and savings plans in overlapping-generations models', *Journal of Public Economics*, **21**, 79–92.

(1983b) 'Government debt in an overlapping-generations model with bequests and gifts', *American Economic Review*, **73**, 222–7.

Burtless, G. and J.A. Hausman (1978) 'The effect of taxation on labour supply: evaluating the Gary negative income tax experiment', *Journal of Political Economy*, **86**, 1103–30.

Bush, W.C. and L.S. Mayer (1974) 'Some implications of anarchy for the distribution of property', *Journal of Economic Theory*, **8**, 401–12.

Cadsby, C.B. and M. Frank (1991) 'Experimental tests of Ricardian equivalence', *Economic Inquiry*, **29**, 645–64.

Cagan, P. (1965) *The effects of pension plans on aggregate savings*, New York: National Bureau of Economic Research.

Callan, T. and B. Nolan (1991) 'Concepts of poverty and the poverty line', *Journal of Economic Surveys*, **5**, 243–61.

Carmichael, J. (1982) 'On Barro's theorem of debt neutrality: the irrelevance of net wealth', *American Economic Review*, **72**, 202–13.

Cass, D. and J.E. Stiglitz (1972) 'Risk aversion and wealth effects on portfolios with many assets', *Review of Economic Studies*, **39**, 331–54.

Chamberlin, J. (1974) 'Provision of collective goods as a function of group size', *American Political Science Review*, **68**, 707–16.

(1976) 'A diagrammatic exposition of the logic of collective action', *Public Choice*, **26**, 59–74.

Chen, P. (1990) 'Prices vs. quantities and delegating price authority to a monopolist', *Review of Economic Studies*, **57**, 521–9.

Chipman, J. (1970) 'External economies of scale and competitive equilibrium', *Quarterly Journal of Economics*, **84**, 347–85.

Christiansen, V. (1980) 'Two comments on tax evasion', *Journal of Public Economics*, **13**, 389–93.

(1981) 'Evaluation of public projects under optimal taxation', *Review of Economic Studies*, **48**, 447–57.

(1984) 'Which commodity taxes should supplement the income tax?', *Journal of Public Economics*, **24**, 195–220.

(1988) 'Choice of occupation, tax incidence and piecemeal tax revision', *Scandinavian Journal of Economics*, **90**, 141–59.

(1993) 'A normative analysis of capital income taxes in the presence of aggregate risk', *The Geneva Papers on Risk and Insurance Theory*, **18**, 55–76.

Christiansen, V. and E.S. Jansen (1978) 'Implicit social preferences in the Norwegian system of indirect taxation', *Journal of Public Economics*, **10**, 217–45.

Clarke, E.H. (1971) 'Multipart pricing of public goods', *Public Choice*, **11**, 17–33.

Clotfelter, C.T. (1983) 'Tax evasion and tax rates: an analysis of individual returns', *Review of Economics and Statistics*, **65**, 363–73.

Coase, R.H. (1960) 'The problem of social cost', *Journal of Law and Economics*, **3**, 1–44.

Collet, P. and J. Eckmann (1980) *Iterated maps on the interval as dynamical systems*, Basel: Birkhauser.

Corlett, W.J. and D.C. Hague (1953) 'Complementarity and the excess burden of taxation', *Review of Economic Studies*, **21**, 21–30.

Cornes, R. and T. Sandler (1984a) 'Easy riders, joint production and public goods', *Economic Journal*, **94**, 580–98.

(1984b) 'The theory of public goods: non-Nash behaviour', *Journal of Public Economics*, **23**, 367–79.

(1985) 'The simple analytics of pure public good provision', *Economica*, **52**, 103–16.

Cornwall, R.R. (1977) 'The concept of general equilibrium in a market economy with imperfectly competitive producers', *Metroeconomica*, **29**, 55–72.

Coulter, F.A.E., F.A. Cowell and S.P. Jenkins (1992) 'Differences in needs and assessment of income distributions', *Bulletin of Economic Research*, **44**, 77–124.

Cournot, A.A. (1838) *Recherches sur les principes mathématiques de la théorie des richesses*, Paris: Librairie des Sciences Politiques et Sociales.

Cowell, F.A. (1977) *Measuring inequality*, Oxford: Phillip Allan.

   (1981) 'Taxation and labour supply with risky activities', *Economica*, **48**, 365–79.

   (1985a) 'The economic analysis of tax evasion', *Bulletin of Economic Research*, **37**, 163–93.

   (1985b) 'Tax evasion with labour income', *Journal of Public Economics*, **26**, 19–34.

Cowell, F.A. and J.P.F. Gordon (1988) 'Unwillingness to pay', *Journal of Public Economics*, **36**, 305–21.

Cowell, F.A. and K. Kuga (1981) 'Additivity and the entropy concept: an axiomatic approach to inequality measurement', *Journal of Economic Thoery*, **25**, 131–43.

Cowling, K.G. and D.C. Mueller (1978) 'The social costs of monopoly power', *Economic Journal*, **88**, 727–48.

Cowling, K.G. and M. Waterson (1976) 'Price-cost margins and market structure', *Economica*, **43**, 267–74.

Cramer, J.S. (1969) *Empirical econometrics*, Amsterdam: North-Holland.

Craig, B. and R.G. Batina, (1991), 'The effects of social security in a life cycle family labor supply simulation model', *Journal of Public Economics*, **46**, 199–226.

Crane, S.E. and F. Nourzad (1986) 'Inflation and tax evasion: an empirical analysis', *Review of Economics and Statistics*, **68**, 217–23.

Crawford, V.P. and D.M. Lilien (1981) 'Social security and the retirement decision', *Quarterly Journal of Economics*, **95**, 505–29.

Cremer, H. and F. Gahvari (1993) 'Tax evasion and optimal commodity taxation', *Journal of Public Economics*, **50**, 261–75.

Cremer, H., M. Marchand and P. Pestieau (1990) 'Evading, auditing and taxing', *Journal of Public Economics*, **43**, 67–92.

Cripps, M.W. and G.D. Myles (1989) 'Price normalisations in general equilibrium models of imperfect competition', University of Warwick.

Cross, R. and G.K. Shaw (1982) 'On the economics of tax aversion', *Public Finance*, **37**, 36–47.

Dales, J.H. (1968) *Pollution, property and prices*, Toronto: University of Toronto Press.

Dalton, H. (1920) 'The measurement of the inequality of incomes', *Economic Journal*, **30**, 348–61.

Danziger, S., R. Haveman and R. Plotnick (1981) 'How income transfer programs affect work, savings, and the income distribution: a critical review', *Journal of Economic Literature*, **19**, 975–1028.

Dasgupta, D. and J.-I. Itaya (1992) 'Comparative statics for the private provision of public goods in a conjectural variations model with heterogeneous agents', *Public Finance*, **47**, 17–31.

Dasgupta, P., P. Hammond and E. Maskin (1979) 'The implementation of social choice rules: some general results on incentive compatibility', *Review of Economic Studies*, **46**, 185–216.

   (1980) 'On imperfect information and optimal pollution control', *Review of Economic Studies*, **47**, 857–60.

Dasgupta, P., A. Sen and D. Starret (1973) 'Notes on the measurement of inequality', *Journal of Economic Theory*, **6**, 180–7.

Dasgupta, P. and J.E. Stiglitz (1972) 'On optimal taxation and public production', *Review of Economic Studies*, **39**, 87–103.

Davidson, C. and L.W. Martin (1985) 'General equilibrium tax incidence under imperfect competition: a quantity-setting supergame snalysis', *Journal of Political Economy*, **93**, 1212–23.

Davies, J.B. and P. Kuhn (1992) 'Social security, longevity, and moral hazard', *Journal of*

Public Economics, **49**, 91–106.

Davis, O. and A. Whinston (1962) 'Externalities, welfare and the theory of games', *Journal of Political Economy*, **70**, 241–62.

Deardorff, A.V. (1976) 'The optimum growth rate for population: comment', *International Economic Review*, **17**, 510–14.

Deaton, A.S. (1977) 'Equity, efficiency, and the structure of indirect taxation', *Journal of Public Economics*, **8**, 299–312.

  (1979) 'The distance function in consumer behaviour with applications to index numbers and optimal taxation', *Review of Economic Studies*, **46**, 391–405.

  (1981) 'Optimal taxes and the structure of preferences', *Econometrica*, **49**, 1245–60.

Deaton, A.S. and J. Muellbauer (1986) 'On measuring child costs: with applications to poor countries', *Journal of Political Economy*, **94**, 720–44.

Deaton, A.S., J. Ruiz-Castillo and D. Thomas (1989) 'The influence of household composition on household expenditure: theory and Spanish evidence', *Journal of Political Economy*, **97**, 179–200.

Deaton, A.S. and N.H. Stern (1986) 'Optimally uniform commodity taxes, taste difference and lump-sum grants', *Economics Letters*, **20**, 263–66.

Debreu, G. (1951) 'The coefficient of resource utilisation', *Econometrica*, **19**, 273–92.

  (1954a) 'Representation of a preference oredering by a numerical function', in R.M. Thrall, C.H. Coombs and R.L. Davis (eds.), *Decision processes*, New York: Wiley.

  (1954b) 'Valuation equilibrium and Pareto optimum', *Proceedings of the National Academy of Sciences of the U.S.A.*, **40**, 588–92.

  (1959) *Theory of value*, New York: Wiley.

  (1970) 'Economies with a finite set of equilibria', *Econometrica*, **38**, 387–92.

  (1980) 'Existence of competitive equilibrium', in K.J. Arrow and M.D. Intriligator (eds.), *Handbook of mathematical economics*, Amsterdam: North-Holland.

Debreu, G. and H. Scarf (1963) 'A limit theorem on the core of an economy', *International Economic Review*, **4**, 235–46.

Decoster, A. and E. Schokkaert (1989) 'Equity and efficiency of a reform of Belgian indirect taxes', *Recherches Economiques de Louvain*, **55**, 155–176.

Delipalla, S. and M. Keen (1992) 'The comparison between ad valorem and specific taxation under imperfect competition', *Journal of Public Economics*, **49**, 351–67.

Desai, M. and A. Shah (1988) 'An econometric approach to the measurment of poverty', *Oxford Economic Papers*, **40**, 505–22.

Diamond, P.A. (1965) 'National debt in a neo-classical growth model', *Journal of Political Economy*, **55**, 1126–50.

  (1967) 'The role of the stock market in a general equilibrium model with technological uncertainty', *American Economic Review*, **57**, 759–76.

  (1973a) 'Consumption externalities and imperfect corrective pricing', *Bell Journal of Economics*, **4**, 526–38.

  (1973b) 'Taxation and public production in a growth setting', in J.A. Mirrlees and N.H. Stern (eds.), *Models of economic growth*, London: Macmillan.

  (1975) 'A many-person Ramsey tax rule', *Journal of Public Economics*, **4**, 227–44.

  (1977) 'A framework for social security analysis', *Journal of Public Economics*, **8**, 275–98.

Diamond, P.A., L.J. Helms and J.A. Mirrlees (1980) 'Optimal taxation in a stochastic economy', *Journal of Public Economics*, **14**, 1–29.

Diamond, P.A. and J.A. Mirrlees (1971) 'Optimal taxation and public production 1: Production efficiency and 2: Tax rules', *American Economic Review*, **61**, 8–27 and 261–78.

  (1973) 'Aggregate production with consumption externalities', *Quarterly Journal of Economics*, **87**, 1–24.

  (1986) 'Payroll-tax financed social insurance with variable retirement', *Scandinavian Journal of Economics*, **88**, 25–50.

Diamond, P.A. and J.E. Stiglitz (1974) 'Increases in risk and in risk aversion', *Journal of Economic Theory*, **8**, 337–60.

Dickson, V.A. and W. Yu (1989) 'Welfare losses in Canadian manufacturing under alternaitve oligopoly regimes', *International Journal of Industrial Organisation*, 7, 257–67.

Dierckx, I, C. Matutes and D. Neven (1988) 'Indirect taxation and Cournot equilibrium', *International Journal of Industrial Organisation*, 6, 385–99.

Dierker, H. and B. Grodal (1986) 'Non-existence of Cournot-Walras equilibrium in a general equilibrium model with two oligopolists', in W. Hildenbrand and A. Mas-Collel (eds.), *Contributions to mathematical economics*, Amsterdam: North-Holland.

Dixit, A. (1979) 'Price changes and optimum taxation in a many-consumer economy', *Journal of Public Economics*, 11, 143–57.

Dixit, A.K. (1970) 'On the optimum structure of commodity taxes', *American Economic Review*, 60, 295–301.

Donaldson, D. and J.A. Weymark (1980) 'A single-parameter generalisation of the Gini indices of inequality', *Journal of Economic Theory*, 22, 67–86.

Drazen, A. (1978) 'Government debt, human capital, and bequests in a life-cycle model', *Journal of Political Economy*, 86, 505–16.

Dreze, J.H. (1964) 'Some postwar contributions of French economists to theory and public policy with special emphasis on problems of resource allocation', *American Economic Review*, 54, 1–64.

(1970–1) 'Market allocation under uncertainty', *European Economic Review*, 2, 133–65.

(1974) 'Investment under private ownership: optimality, equilibrium and stability', in J.H. Dreze (ed.), *Allocation under uncertainty: equilibrium and optimality*, New York: Macmillan.

Duffie, D. and H. Sonnenschein (1989) 'Arrow and general equilibrium theory', *Journal of Economic Literature*, 27, 565–98.

Eaton, J. and H.S. Rosen (1980) 'Labor supply, uncertainty, and efficient taxation', *Journal of Public Economics*, 14, 365–74.

Ebert, U. (1992) 'A reexamination of the optimal nonlinear income tax', *Journal of Public Economics*, 49, 47–73.

Ebrahimi, A. and C. J. Heady (1988) 'Tax design and household consumption'. *Economic Journal (Supplement)*, 98, 83–96.

Ebrill, L.P. and S.M. Slutsky (1982) 'Time, congestion and public goods', *Journal of Public Economics*, 17, 307–334.

(1990) 'Production efficiency and optimal pricing in intermediate-good related industries', *International Journal of Industrial Organisation*, 8, 417–42.

Eckstein, Z., M. Eichenbaum and D. Peled (1985) 'Uncertain lifetimes and the welfare enhancing properties of annuity markets and social security', *Journal of Public Economics*, 26, 303–26.

Edgeworth, F.Y. (1925) 'The pure theory of monopoly', in *Papers relating to political economy*, New York: Burt Franklin.

Eeckhoudt, L. and P. Hansen (1982) 'Uncertainty and the partial loss offset provision', *Economics Letters*, 9, 31–5.

Eichhorn, W. (1988) 'On a class of inequality measures', *Social Choice and Welfare*, 5, 171–7.

Enders, W. and H.E. Lapan (1982) 'Social security taxation and intergenerational risk sharing', *International Economic Review*, 23, 647–58.

Engel, E. (1895) 'Die lebenskosten Belgischer arbeiter-familien früher und jetzt', *International Statistical Institute Bulletin*, 9, 1–74.

Feehan, J.P. (1989) 'Pareto-efficiency with three varieties of public input', *Public Finance*, 44, 237–48.

Feige, E.L. (1979) 'How big is the irregular economy?', *Challenge*, 5–13.

(1981) 'The UK's unobserved economy', *Journal of Economic Affairs*, 1, 205–12.

Feige, E.L. and R.T. McGee (1983) 'Sweden's Laffer curve: taxation and the unobserved economy', *Scandinavian Journal of Economics*, 85, 499–519.

Feldstein, M.S. (1973) 'On the optimal progressivity of the income tax', *Journal of Public*

Economics, **2**, 236–376.

(1974) 'Social security, induced retirement and aggregate capital accumulation', *Journal of Political Economy*, **82**, 905–26.

(1976a) 'On the theory of tax reform', *Journal of Public Economics*, **6**, 77–104.

(1976b) 'Perceived wealth in bonds and social security: a comment', *Journal of Political Economy*, **84**, 331–6.

(1985) 'The optimal level of social security benefits', *Quarterly Journal of Economics*, **100**, 303–20.

(1987) 'Should social security benefits be means tested?', *Journal of Political Economy*, **95**, 468–84.

(1990) 'Imperfect annuity markets, unintended bequests, and the optimal age strcture of social security benefits', *Journal of Public Economics*, **41**, 31–43.

Fields, G.S. and J.C.H. Fei (1978) 'On inequality comparisons', *Econometrica*, **46**, 303–16.

Fisher, I. (1930) *The theory of interest*, New York: Macmillan.

Flemming, J.S. (1977) 'Optimal payroll taxes and social security funding', *Journal of Public Economics*, **7**, 329–49.

Fogelman, F., M. Quinzii and R. Guesnerie (1978) 'Dynamic processes for tax reform theory', *Journal of Economic Theory*, **17**, 200–26.

Foley, D.K. (1970) 'Lindahl's solution and the core of an economy with public goods', *Econometrica*, **38**, 66–72.

Foster, J.E. (1983) 'An axiomatic characterisation of the Theil measure of income inequality', *Journal of Economic Theory*, **31**, 105–21.

Foster, J.E., J. Greer and E. Thorbecke (1984) 'A class of decomposable poverty measures', *Econometrica*, **52**, 761–7.

Friedland, N., S. Maital and A. Rutenberg (1978) 'A simulation study of income taxation', *Journal of Public Economics*, **10**, 107–16.

Friedman, J.W. (1977) *Oligopoly and the theory of games*, Amsterdam: North-Holland.

Gabszewicz, J.J. and J.-P. Vial (1972) 'Oligopoly "a la Cournot" in general equilibrium analysis', *Journal of Economic Theory*, **4**, 381–400.

Gale, D. (1955) 'The law of supply and demand', *Mathematica Scandinavica*, **3**, 155–69.

(1973) 'Pure exchange equilibrium of dynamic economic models', *Journal of Economic Theory*, **6**, 12–36.

Gary-Bobo, R.J. (1989) 'Cournot-Walras and locally consistent equilibria', *Journal of Economic Theory*, **49**, 10–32.

Geanakoplos, J.D. and H.M. Polemarchakis (1984) 'Intertemporally separable, overlapping-generations economies', *Journal of Economic Theory*, **34**, 207–15.

Geeroms, H. and H. Wilmots (1985) 'An empirical model of tax evasion and tax avoidance', *Public Finance*, **40**, 190–209.

Gigliotti, G.A. (1984) 'Total utility, overlapping generations and social security', *Economics Letters*, **15**, 169–73.

Gini, C. (1912) *Variabilita mutabilita*, Bologna.

Glazer, A. (1989) 'The social discount rate under majority voting', *Public Finance*, **44**, 384–93.

Gordon, J.P.F. (1989) 'Individual morality and reputation costs as deterrents to tax evasion', *European Economic Review*, **33**, 797–805.

Gorman, W.M. (1959) 'Are social indifference curves convex?', *Quarterly Journal of Economics*, **73**, 485–96.

(1978) 'Tricks with utility functions', Part 1, LSE Econometrics Programme, Discussion Paper No. B1.

Gorman, W.M. and G.D. Myles (1987) 'Characteristics', in *The new Palgrave dictionary of economics*, London: Macmillan.

Grandmont, J.-M. (1985) 'On endogeneous competitive business cycles', *Econometrica*, **53**, 995–1045.

Green, J. (1988) 'Demographics, market failure and social securiy' in S.M. Wachter (ed.), *Social security and private pensions*, Lexington: Lexington Books.

Green, J. and J.-J. Laffont (1977) 'Characterization of satisfactory mechanisms for the revelation of preferences for public goods', *Econometrica*, **45**, 427–38.

(1979) *Incentives in public decision making*, Amsterdam: North-Holland.

Green, J. and E. Sheshinski (1976) 'Direct versus indirect remedies for externalities', *Journal of Political Economy*, **84**, 797–808.

Griliches, Z. (1971) 'Hedonic price indexes for automobiles: an econometric analysis of quality chage', in Z. Griliches (ed.), *Price indexes and quality chage: studies in new methods of measurement*, Cambridge, MA: Harvard University Press.

Grinols, E.L. (1985) 'Public investment and social risk-sharing', *European Economic Review*, **29**, 303–21.

Grossman, S.J. and O.D. Hart (1979) 'A theory of competitive equilibrium in stock market economies', *Econometrica*, **47**, 293–330.

Groves, T. (1973) 'Incentives in teams', *Econometrica*, **41**, 617–31.

Groves, T. and J. Ledyard (1977) 'Optimal allocation of public goods: a solution to the "free rider" problem', *Econometrica*, **45**, 783–809.

Groves, T. and M. Loeb (1975) 'Incentives and public inputs', *Journal of Public Economics*, **4**, 211–26.

Guesnerie, R. (1977) 'On the direction of tax reform', *Journal of Public Economics*, **7**, 179–202.

Guesnerie, R. and J.-J. Laffont (1978) 'Taxing price makers', *Journal of Economic Theory*, **19**, 423–55.

Gutmann, P.M. (1977) 'The subterranean economy', *Financial Analysts Journal*, 26–8.

Hahn, F.H. (1973) 'On optimum taxation', *Journal of Economic Theory*, **6**, 96–106.

(1982) *Money and inflation*, Oxford: Basil Blackwell.

Hansson, I. and C. Stuart (1989) 'Social security as trade among living generations', *American Economic Review*, **79**, 1182–95.

Harberger, A.C. (1954) 'Monopoly and resource allocation', *American Economic Review*, **45**, 77–87.

(1962) 'The incidence of the corporation income tax', *Journal of Political Economy*, **70**, 215–40.

Harris, R.G. and J.G. MacKinnon (1979) 'Computing optimal tax equilibria', *Journal of Public Economics*, **11**, 197–212.

Hart, O.D. (1975a) 'On the optimality of equilibrium when the market structure is incomplete', *Journal of Economic Theory*, **11**, 418–43.

(1975b) 'Some negative results on the existence of comparative statics results in portfolio theory', *Review of Economic Studies*, **42**, 615–21.

(1982) 'A model of imperfect competition with Keynsian features', *Quarterly Journal of Economics*, **97**, 109–38.

(1985) 'Imperfect competition and general equilibrium: an overview of recent work', in K.J. Arrow and S. Honkapohja (eds.), *Frontiers of economics*, Oxford: Basil Blackwell.

Hatta, T. (1986) 'Welfare effects of changing commodity tax rates toward uniformity', *Journal of Public Economics*, **29**, 99–112.

Hausman, D. (1985) 'Taxation and labour supply', in A.J. Auerbach and M. Feldstein (eds.), *Handbook of public economics*, Amsterdam: North-Holland.

Heady, C. and P. Mitra (1980) 'The computation of optimum linear taxation', *Review of Economic Studies*, **47**, 567–85.

Heller, W.P. and D.A. Starrett (1976) 'On the nature of externalities', in S.A.Y. Lin (ed.), *Theory and measurement of economic externalities*, New York: Academic Press.

Hellwig, M.F. (1981) 'Bankruptcy, limited liability, and the Modigliani-Miller theorem', *American Economic Review*, **89**, 155–70.

(1986) 'The optimal linear income tax revisited', *Journal of Public Economics*, **31**, 163–79.

Helpman, E. and E. Sadka (1978) 'The optimal income tax', *Journal of Public Economics*, **9**, 383–93.

Hicks, J.R. (1939) *Value and capital*, Oxford: Clarendon Press.

Hildenbrand, W. and A. Kirman (1988) *Equilibrium analysis*, Amsterdam: North-Holland.

Hirshleifer, J. (1964) 'Efficient allocation of capital in an uncertain world', *American Economic Review*, Papers and Proceedings, **54**, 77–85.

(1966) 'Investment decisions under uncertainty: applications of the state-preference approach', *Quarterly Journal of Economics*, **80**, 252–77.

Holmstrom, B. (1979) 'Groves' scheme on restricted domains', *Econometrica*, **47**, 1137–44.

Houthakker, H.S. (1960) 'Additive preferences', *Econometrica*, **28**, 244–57.

Hu, S.C. (1978) 'On the dynamic behaviour of the consumer and the optimal provision of social security', *Review of Economic Studies*, **45**, 437–45.

(1979) 'Social security, the supply of labor, and capital accumulation', *American Economic Review*, **69**, 274–83.

(1982) 'Social security, majority-voting equilibrium and dynamic efficiency', *International Economic Review*, **23**, 269–87.

Hurwicz, L. (1979a) 'Outcome functions yielding Walrasian and Lindahl allocations at Nash equilibrium points', *Review of Economic Studies*, **46**, 217–25.

(1979b) 'On allocations attainable through Nash equilibria', *Journal of Economic Theory*, **21**, 140–65.

Intriligator, M.D. (1971) *Mathematical optimization and economic theory*, Englewood Cliffs: Prentice Hall.

Ireland, N.J. (1977) 'Ideal prices vs. prices vs. quantities', *Review of Economic Studies*, **44**, 183–6.

(1978) 'Roy's identity and monopoly welfare loss', in D.A. Currie and W. Peters (eds.), *Contempory economic analysis*, London: Croom Helm.

Isaac, R.M., K.F. McCue and C.R. Plott (1985) 'Public goods in an experimental environment', *Journal of Public Economics*, **26**, 51–74.

Isaac, R.M. and J.M. Walker (1988) 'Group size effects in public goods provision: the voluntary contribution mechanism', *Quarterly Journal of Economics*, **102**, 179–99.

Isaac, R.M., J.M. Walker and S.H. Thomas (1984) 'Divergent evidence on free riding: an experimental examination of possible explanations', *Public Choice*, **43**, 113–49.

Isachsen, A.J. and S. Strom (1980) 'The hidden economy: the labour market and tax evasion', *Scandinavian Journal of Economics*, **82**, 304–11.

Jenkins, S.P. (1991) 'The measurement of income inequality', in L. Osberg (ed.), *Economic inequality and poverty: international perspectives*, New York: M.E. Sharpe.

Johansen, L. (1963) 'Some notes on the Lindahl theory of determination of public expenditures', *International Economic Review*, **4**, 346–58.

(1977) 'The theory of public goods: misplaced emphasis?', *Journal of Public Economics*, **7**, 147–52.

Jones, R.W. (1965) 'The structure of simple general equilibrium models', *Journal of Political Economy*, **73**, 557–72.

(1971) 'Distortions in factor markets and the general equilibrim model of production', *Journal of Political Economy*, **79**, 437–59.

Kaizuka, K. (1965) 'Public goods and decentralisation of production', *Review of Economics and Statistics*, **47**, 118–20.

Kanbur, S.M.R. (1980) 'Risk taking and taxation', *Journal of Public Economics*, **15**, 163–84.

Kanbur, S.M.R. and G.D. Myles (1992) 'Policy choice and political constraints', *European Journal of Political Economy*, **8**, 1–29.

Kanbur, S.M.R. and M. Tuomala (1994) 'Inherent inequality and the optimal graduation of marginal tax rates', *Scandinavian Journal of Economics*, **96**, 275–82.

Karni, E. and I. Zilcha (1986) 'Welfare and comparative statics implications of fair social security', *Journal of Public Economics*, **30**, 341–57.

Katona, G. (1964) *Private pensions and individual savings*, Ann Arbor: Survey Research Centre, Institute for Social Research, University of Michigan.

Kay, J.A. (1983) 'A general equilibrium approach to the measurement of monopoly welfare loss', *International Journal of Industrial Organisation*, **1**, 317–31.

Kay, J.A. and M. Keen (1983) 'How should commodities be taxed?', *European Economic Review*, **23**, 339–58.

Kay, J.A. and M.A. King (1990) *The British tax system*, Oxford: Oxford University Press.

Kehoe, T.J. and D.K. Levine (1985) 'Comparative statics and perfect foresight in infinite horizon economies', *Econometrica*, **53**, 433–53.

Kemp, M.C. and Y.-K. Ng (1976) 'On the existence of social welfare functions, social orderings and social decision functions', *Economica*, **43**, 59–66.

Kihlstrom, R.E. and J.-J. Laffont (1983) 'Taxation and risk taking in general equilibrium models with free entry', *Journal of Public Economics*, **21**, 159–81.

Kim, O. and M. Walker (1984) 'The free rider problem: experimental evidence', *Public Choice*, **43**, 3–24.

King, M.A. (1974) Taxation and the cost of capital', *Review of Economic Studies*, **41**, 21–35.

(1975) 'Taxation, corporate financial policy, and the cost of capital', *Journal of Public Economics*, **4**, 271–9.

(1977) *Public policy and the corporation*, London: Chapman and Hall.

Kolm, S.-C. (1969) 'The optimal production of social justice', in J. Margolis and H. Guitton (eds.), *Public economics*, London: Macmillan.

(1973) 'A note on optimum tax evasion', *Journal of Public Economics*, **2**, 265–70.

(1976) 'Unequal inequalities I and II', *Journal of Economic Theory*, **12**, 416–42 and **13**, 82–111.

Konishi, H. (1990) 'Final and intermediate goods taxes in an oligopolistic economy with free entry', *Journal of Public Economics*, **42**, 371–86.

Koopmans, T.C. (1957) *Three essays on the state of economic science*, New York: McGraw-Hill.

Koskella, E. (1983) 'On the shape of tax schedule, the probability of detection, and the penalty schemes as deterrents to tax evasion', *Public Finance*, **38**, 70–80.

Kotlikoff, L.J. (1979) 'Social security and equilibrium capital intensity', *Quarterly Journal of Economics*, **93**, 233–53.

(1989) 'On the contribution of economics to the evaluation and formation of social insurance policy', *American Economic Review*, Papers and Proceedings, **77**, 184–90.

Kotlikoff, L.J., A. Spivak and L.H. Summers (1982) 'The adequacy of savings', *American Economic Review*, **72**, 1056–69.

Laffont, J.-J. (1977) 'More on prices vs. quantities', *Review of Economic Studies*, **44**, 177–82.

(1987) 'Incentives and the allocation of public goods', in A.J. Auerbach and M. Feldstein (eds.), *Handbook of public economics*, Amsterdam: North-Holland.

Laffont, J.-J. and E. Maskin (1982) 'The theory of incentives: an overview', in W. Hildenbrand (ed.), *Advances in economic theory*, Cambridge: Cambridge University Press.

Lambert, P. (1989) *The distribution and redistribution of income: a mathematical analysis*, Oxford: Basil Blackwell.

Lancaster, K.J. (1966) 'A new approach to consumer theory', *Journal of Political Economy*, **74**, 132–57.

Landskroner, Y., J. Paroush and I. Swary (1990) 'Tax evasion and portfolio decisions', *Public Finance*, **45**, 409–22.

Lange, O. (1942) 'The foundations of welfare economics', *Econometrica*, **10**, 215–28.

Layard, P.R.G. and A.A. Walters (1978) *Microeconomic theory*, London: McGraw-Hill.

Lee, M.L. and S.-W. Chao (1988) 'Effects of social security on personal saving', *Economic Letters*, **28**, 365–8.

Lerner, A. (1970) 'On optimal taxes with an untaxable sector', *American Economic Review*, **60**, 284–94.

Lewbel, A. (1989) 'Household equivalence scales and welfare comparisons', *Journal of Public Economics*, **39**, 377–91.

(1991) 'Cost of characteristics indices and household equivalence scales', *European Economic Review*, **35**, 1277–93.

Lewis, G.W. and D.T. Ulph (1988) 'Poverty, inequality and welfare', *Economic Journal*, **98**, 117–31.

Lindahl, E. (1919) *Positive losung, die gerechtigkeit der besteuerung*, Lund, reprinted as 'Just taxation – a positive solution', in R.A. Musgrave and A.T. Peacock (eds.), *Classics in the theory of public finance*, London: Macmillan.

Lipsey, R.G. and K. Lancaster (1956) 'The general theory of second best', *Review of Economic Studies*, **24**, 11–32.

Little, I.M.D. (1950) *A critique of welfare economics*, Oxford: Clarendon Press.

Lockwood, B. (1995) 'Multi-firm regulation without lump-sum taxes', *Journal of Public Economics* (forthcoming).

Lopez-Garcia, M.-A. (1991) 'Population growth and pay-as-you-go social security in an overlapping generations model', *Public Finance*, **46**, 93–110.

Lorenz, M.C. (1905) 'Methods of measuring the concentration of wealth', *Publications of the American Statistical Association*, **9**, 209–19.

Lydall, H.F. (1968) *The structure of earnings*, Oxford: Clarendon Press.

Mailath, G. and A. Postlewaite (1990) 'Asymmetric-information bargaining problems with many agents', *Review of Economic Studies*, **57**, 351–368.

Mangasarian, O.L. (1969) *Nonlinear programming*, New York: McGraw-Hill.

Marrelli, M. (1984) 'On indirect tax evasion', *Journal of Public Economics*, **25**, 181–96.

Marrelli, M. and R. Martina (1988) 'Tax evasion and strategic behaviour of the firms', *Journal of Public Economics*, **37**, 55–69.

Marwell, G. and R.E. Ames (1981) 'Economists free ride, does anyone else?', *Journal of Public Economics*, **15**, 295–310.

Mas-Collel, A. (1980a) *The theory of general economic equilibrium*, Cambridge: Cambridge University Press.

(1980b) 'Efficiency and decentralization in the pure theory of public goods', *Quarterly Journal of Economics*, **84**, 625–41.

Mas-Colell, A. and J. Silvestre (1989) 'Cost share equilibria: a Lindahlian approach', *Journal of Economic Theory*, **47**, 239–56.

McClements, L.D. (1977) 'Equivalence scales for children', *Journal of Public Economics*, **8**, 191–210.

McGuire, M. (1974) 'Group homogeneity and aggregate provision of a pure public good under Cournot behaviour', *Public Choice*, **18**, 107–26.

McKenzie, L. (1955) 'Competitive equilibrium with dependent consumer preferences', in National Bureau of Standards and Department of the Air Force, *The Second Symposium on Linear Programming*, Washington, DC.

McLure, C.E. (1974) 'A diagrammatic exposition of the Harberger model with one immobile factor', *Journal of Political Economy*, **82**, 56–82.

(1975) 'General equilibrium incidence analysis: the Harberger model after ten years', *Journal of Public Economics*, **80**, 56–82.

Meade, J.E. (1952) 'External economies and diseconomies in a competitive situation', *Economic Journal*, **62**, 54–67.

(1975) *The intelligent radical's guide to economic policy*, London: Allen and Unwin.

Meyer, R.A. (1971) 'Externalities as commodities', *Amercian Economic Review*, **61**, 736–40.

de Meza, D. (1982) 'Generalised oligopoly derived demand with an application to tax induced entry', *Bulletin of Economic Research*, **34**, 1–16.

Mieszkowski, P.M. (1967) 'On the theory of tax incidence', *American Economic Review*, **75**, 250–62.

(1969) 'Tax incidence theory: the effects of taxes on the distribution of income', *Journal of Economic Literature*, **7**, 1103–24.

Milleron, J.-C. (1972) 'Theory of value with public goods: a survey article', *Journal of Economic Theory*, **5**, 419–77.

Mirrlees, J.A. (1971) 'An exploration in the theory of optimum income taxation', *Review of Economic Studies*, **38**, 175–208.

(1972) 'On producer taxation', *Review of Economic Studies*, **39**, 105–11.

(1975) 'Optimal commodity taxation in a two-class economy', *Journal of Public Economics*, **4**, 27–33.

(1976) 'Optimal tax theory: a synthesis', *Journal of Public Economics*, **6**, 327–58.

(1986) 'The theory of optimal taxation', in K.J. Arrow and M.D. Intrilligator (eds.), *Handbook of mathematical economics*, Amsterdam: North-Holland.

Modigliani, F. and M.H. Miller (1958) 'The cost of capital, corporation finance and the theory of investment', *American Economic Review*, **48**, 261–97.

Montgomery, W.D. (1972) 'Markets in licenses and efficient pollution control programs', *Journal of Economic Theory*, **5**, 395–418.

Moore, J. and R. Repullo (1988) 'Subgame perfect implementation', *Econometrica*, **56**, 1191–220.

Mork, K.A. (1975) 'Income tax evasion: some empirical evidence', *Public Finance*, **30**, 70–6.

Mossin, J. (1968) 'Taxation and risk-taking: an expected utility approach', *Economica*, **35**, 74–82.

Muellbauer, J. (1974) 'Household composition, Engel curves and welfare comparisons between households', *European Economic Review*, **5**, 103–22.

(1977) 'Testing the Barten model of household composition effects and the cost of children', *Economic Journal*, **87**, 460–87.

Muench, T.J. (1972) 'The core and the Lindahl equilibrium of an economy with public goods: an example', *Journal of Economic Theory*, **4**, 241–55.

Munk, K.J. (1978) 'Optimal taxation and pure profit', *Scandinavian Journal of Economics*, **80**, 1–19.

(1980) 'Optimal taxation with some non-taxable commodities', *Review of Economic Studies*, **47**, 755–65.

Murakami, Y. and T. Negishi (1964) 'A formulation of external economy', *International Economic Review*, **5**, 328–34.

Murty, M.N. and R. Ray (1987) 'Sensitivity of optimal commodity taxes to relaxing leisure/ goods separability and to the wage rate', *Economics Letters*, **24**, 273–7.

Muzondo, T.R. (1978) 'Mixed and pure public goods, user charges and welfare', *Public Finance*, **33**, 314–30.

Myerson, R.B. and M.A. Satterthwaite (1983) 'Efficient mechanisms for bilateral trading', *Journal of Economic Theory*, **29**, 265–81.

Myles, G.D. (1987) 'Tax design in the presence of imperfect competition: an example', *Journal of Public Economics*, **34**, 367–78.

(1989a) 'Ramsey tax rules for economies with imperfect competition', *Journal of Public Economics*, **38**, 95–115.

(1989b) 'Imperfect competition and the taxation of intermediate goods', *Public Finance*, **44**, 62–74.

(1994) 'Welfare loss with intermediate goods', in W. Eichhorn (ed.), *Models and measurement of welfare and inequality*, Berlin: Springer-Verlag.

(1995a) 'Ramsey pricing in imperfectly competitive economies', University of Exeter.

(1995b) 'Imperfect competition and industry-specific input taxes', *Public Finance Quarterly*, **23**, 336–55.

Myles, G.D. and R.A. Naylor (1995a) 'A model of tax evasion with group conformity and social customs', *European Journal of Political Economy* (forthcoming).

(1995b) 'Optimal auditing and social customs', University of Exeter.

Nash, J.F. (1950) 'The bargaining problem', *Econometrica*, **18**, 155–62.

Negishi, T. (1961) 'Monopolistic competition and general equilibrium', *Review of Economic Studies*, **2**, 196–201.

Newbery, D.M. (1970) 'A theorem on the measurement of inequality', Journal of Economic Theory, **2**, 264–6.

(1986) 'On the desirability of input taxes', *Economics Letters*, **20**, 267–70.

Ng, Y.-K. (1985) *Welfare economics*, Basingstoke: MacMillan.

Nicholson, J. (1976) 'Appraisal of different methods of estimating equivalence scales and their results', *Review of Income and Wealth*, **22**, 1–11.

Oakland, W.H. (1972) 'Congestion, public goods and welfare', *Journal of Public Economics*, **1**, 339–57.

(1987) 'Theory of public goods' in A.J. Auerbach and M. Feldstein (eds.), *Handbook of public economics*, Amsterdam: North-Holland.

OECD (1993a) *Economic Survey of the United States*, November.

(1993b) *Economic Survey of Japan*, November.

(1994a) *Economic Outlook*, **55**.

(1994b) *Economic Survey of the United Kingdom*, July.

Ordover, J.A. (1976) 'Distributive justice and optimal taxation of wages and interest in a growing economy', *Journal of Public Economics*, **5**, 139–60.

Ordover, J.A. and E.S. Phelps (1975) 'Linear taxation of wealth and wages for intragenerational lifetime justice: some steady-state cases', *American Economic Review*, **65**, 660–73.

(1979) 'The concept of optimal taxation in the overlapping-generations model of capital and wealth', *Journal of Public Economics*, **12**, 1–26.

Osana, H, (1972) 'Externalities and the basic theorems of welfare economics', *Journal of Economic Theory*, **4**, 401–14.

(1973) 'On the boundedness of an economy with externalities', *Review of Economic Studies*, **40**, 321–31.

Otani, Y. and J. Sicilian (1977) 'Externalities and problems of nonconvexity and overhead costs in welfare economics', *Journal of Economic Theory*, **14**, 239–51.

Pareto, V. (1909) *Manuel d'économie politique*, Paris: Girard and Briere.

Parish, R.M. (1972) 'Economic aspects of pollution control', *Australian Economic Papers*, **11**, 32–43.

Park, N.-H. (1991) 'Steady-state solutions of optimal tax mixes in an overlapping-generations model', *Journal of Public Economics*, **46**, 227–46.

Parks, R.P. (1991) 'Pareto irrelevant externalities', *Journal of Economic Theory*, **54**, 165–79.

Peacock, A. and G.K. Shaw (1982) 'Tax evasion and tax revenue loss', *Public Finance*, **37**, 269–78.

Peck, R.M. (1989) 'Taxation, risk and returns to scale', *Journal of Public Economics*, **40**, 319–30.

Pencavel, J.H. (1979) 'A note on income tax evasion, labor supply, and nonlinear tax schedules', *Journal of Public Economics*, **12**, 115–24.

Pezzey, J. (1992) 'The symmetry between controlling pollution by price and controlling it by quantity', *Canadian Journal of Economics*, **25**, 983–91.

Pfingsten, A. (1986) 'Distributionally-neutral tax changes for different inequality concepts', *Journal of Public Economics*, **30**, 385–93.

Phelps, E.S. and J.G. Riley (1978) 'Rawlsian growth: dynamic programming of capital and wealth for intergeneration "maxmin" justice', *Review of Economic Studies*, **45**, 103–20.

Pigou, A.C. (1920) *The economics of welfare*, New York: Macmillan.

Pissarides, C.A. and G. Weber (1989) 'An expenditure-based estimate of Britain's black economy', *Journal of Public Economics*, **39**, 17–32.

Pollak, R.A. and T.J. Wales (1979) 'Welfare comparisons and equivalence scales', *American Economic Review, Papers and Proceedings*, **69**, 216–21.

Prais, S.J. (1953) 'The estimation of equivalent-adult scales from family budgets', *Economic Journal*, **63**, 791–810.

Prais, S.J. and H.S. Houthakker (1955) *The analysis of family budgets*, Department of Applied Economics Monograph 4, Cambridge: Cambridge University Press.

Pratt, J.W. (1964) 'Risk aversion in the small and in the large', *Econometrica*, **32**, 122–36.

Pyatt, G. (1985) 'An axiomatic approach to the Gini coefficient and the measurement of welfare', *Advances in Econometrics*, **3**, 87–109.

Pye, G. (1972) 'Preferential tax treatment of capital gains, optimal dividend policy, and capital budgeting', *Quarterly Journal of Economics*, **86**, 222–42.

Rader, T. (1972) *The theory of general equilibrium*, New York: Academic Press.

Radner, R. (1982) 'Equilibrium under uncertainty', in K.J. Arrow and M.D. Intrilligator (eds.), *Handbook of mathematical economics*, Amsterdam: North-Holland.

Ramsey, F.P. (1927) 'A contribution to the theory of taxation', *Economic Journal*, **37**, 47–61.

Rao, V.V. (1981) 'Measurement of deprivation and poverty based on the proportion spent on food', *World Development*, **9**, 337–53.

Rapanos, V.T. (1991) 'The incidence of corporate income tax under variable returns to scale: comment', *Public Finance*, **44**, 335–6.

Ray, R. (1986a) 'Sensitivity of "optimal" commodity tax rates to alternative demand functional forms', *Journal of Public Economics*, **31**, 253–68.

  (1986b) 'Redistribution through commodity taxes: the non-linear Engel curve case', *Public Finance*, **41**, 277–84.

Reddaway, W.B. (1970) *Effects of the selective employment tax*, London: HMSO.

Regan, D.H. (1972) 'The problem of social cost revisited', *Journal of Law and Economics*, **15**, 427–37.

Reinganum, J. and L. Wilde (1985) 'Income tax compliance in a principal-agent framework', *Journal of Public Economics*, **26**, 1–18.

  (1986) 'Equilibrium verification and reporting policies in a model of tax compliance', *International Economics Review*, **27**, 739–60.

Revesz, J.T. (1986) 'On some advantages of progressive indirect taxation', *Public Finance*, **41**, 182–99.

Rey, M. (1965) 'Estimating tax evasions: the example of the Italian General Sales Tax', *Public Finance*, **20**, 366–92.

Ricardo, D. (1817) *The principles of political economy and taxation*, London: M. Dent and Sons.

Rob, R. (1982) 'Asymptotic efficiency of the demand revealing mechanism', *Journal of Economic Theory*, **28**, 207–20.

  (1989) 'Pollution claim settlements under private information', *Journal of Economic Theory*, **47**, 307–33.

Robbins, L. (1932) *An essay on the nature and significance of economic science*, London: George Allen and Unwin.

Roberts, D.J. (1973) 'Existence of Lindahl equilibrium with a measure space of consumers', *Journal of Economic Theory*, **6**, 355–81.

  (1974) 'The Lindahl solution for economies with public goods', *Journal of Public Economics*, **3**, 23–42.

Roberts, J. and H. Sonnenschein (1977) 'On the foundations of the theory of monopolistic competition', *Econometrica*, **45**, 101–13.

Roberts, K.W.S. (1980a) 'Possibility theorems with interpersonally comparable welfare levels', *Review of Economic Studies*, **47**, 409–20.

  (1980b) 'Interpersonal comparability and social choice theory', *Review of Economic Studies*, **47**, 421–39.

  (1980c) 'Social choice theory: the single and multi-profile approaches', *Review of Economic Studies*, **47**, 441–50.

  (1980d) 'The limit points of monopolistic competition', *Journal of Economic Theory*, **22**, 256–78.

Roberts, M.J. and M. Spence (1976) 'Effluent charges and licences under uncertainty', *Journal of Public Economics*, **5**, 193–208.

Romer, T. (1976) 'On the progressivity of the utilitarian income tax', *Public Finance*, **31**, 329–40.

Rosen, S. (1974) 'Hedonic prices and implicit markets: product differentiation in pure competition', *Journal of Political Economy*, **82**, 34–55.

Rothbarth, E. (1943) 'Note on a method of determining equivalent income for households of different composition', in C. Madge (ed.), *War-time pattern of savings and expenditure*, Cambridge: Cambridge University Press.

Rothschild, M. and J.E. Stiglitz (1973) 'Some further results on the measurement of inequality', *Journal of Economic Theory*, **6**, 188–204.

(1976) 'Equilibrium in competitive insurance markets: an essay in the economics of incomplete information', *Quarterly Journal of Economics*, **90**, 624–49.

Rowntree, B.S. (1901) *Poverty: a study of town life*, London: Macmillan.

(1941) *Poverty and progress*, London: Longman.

Rowntree, B.S. and G.R. Lavers (1951) *Poverty and the welfare state*, London: Longman.

Rubinstein, A. (1982) 'Perfect equilibrium in a bargaining model', *Econometrica*, **50**, 97–109.

(1985) 'A bargaining model with incomplete information about time preferences', *Econometrica*, **53**, 1151–72.

Sadka, E. (1976) 'On income distribution incentive effects and optimal income taxation', *Review of Economic Studies*, **43**, 261–8.

Samuelson, P.A. (1954) 'The pure theory of public expenditure', *Review of Economics and Statistics*, **36**, 387–9.

(1955) 'Diagrammatic exposition of a pure theory of public expenditure', *Review of Economics and Statistics*, **37**, 350–6.

(1958) 'An exact consumption-loan model of interest with or without the social contrivance of money', *Journal of Political Economy*, **66**, 467–82.

(1964) 'Discussion', *American Economic Review*, Papers and Proceedings, **59**, 93–6.

(1975a) 'Optimum social security in a life-cycle growth model', *International Economic Review*, **16**, 539–44.

(1975b) 'The Optimum Growth Rate for Population', *International Economic Review*, **16**, 531–8.

(1976) 'The optimum growth rate for population: agreement and evaluations', *International Economic Review*, **17**, 516–25.

(1977) 'Reaffirming the existence of "reasonable" Bergson-Samuelson social welfare functions', *Economica*, **44**, 81–8.

(1986) 'Theory of optimal taxation', *Journal of Public Economics*, **30**, 137–43.

Sandmo, A. (1972) 'Discount rates for public investment under uncertainty', *International Economic Review*, **13**, 287–302.

(1973) 'Public goods and the technology of consumption', *Review of Economic Studies*, **49**, 517–28.

(1974) 'A note on the structure of optimal taxation', *American Economic Review*, **64**, 701–6.

(1975) 'Optimal taxation in the presence of externalities', *Swedish Journal of Economics*, **77**, 86–98.

(1977) 'Portfolio theory, asset demand and taxation: comparative statics with many assets', *Review of Economic Studies*, **44**, 369–79.

(1981) 'Income tax evasion, labour supply, and the equity-efficiency tradeoff', *Journal of Public Economics*, **16**, 265–88.

Sargent, T.J. (1979) *Macroeconomic theory*, New York: Academic Press.

Sawhill, I.V. (1988) 'Poverty in the US: why is it so persistent?', *Journal of Economic Literature*, **26**, 1073–119.

Sawyer, M.C. (1980) 'Monopoly welfare loss in the United Kingdom', *Bulletin of Economic Research*, **48**, 331–54.

Scitovsky, T. (1951) 'The state of welfare economics', *American Economic Review*, **41**, 303–15.

Scotchmer, S. (1987) 'Audit classes and tax enforcement policy', *American Economic Review*, **77**, 129–36.

Seade, J. (1977) 'On the shape of optimal tax schedules', *Journal of Public Economics*, **7**, 203–36.

(1980) 'The stability of Cournot revisited', *Journal of Economic Theory*, **23**, 749–52.

(1982) 'On the sign of the optimum marginal income tax', *Review of Economic Studies*, **49**, 637–43.

(1985) 'Profitable cost increases', Warwick Economic Research Paper, No. 260.

Sen, A.K. (1973) *On economic inequality*, Oxford: Oxford University Press.

(1976) 'Poverty: an ordinal approach to measurement', *Econometrica*, **44**, 219–31.

(1977) 'On weights and measures', *Econometrica*, **45**, 1539–72.

(1979) 'Issues in the measurement of poverty', *Scandinavian Journal of Economics*, **81**, 285–307.

(1986) 'Social choice theory', in K.J. Arrow and M.D. Intriligator (eds.) *Handbook of mathematical economics*, Amsterdam: North-Holland.

Seneca, J.J. and M.K. Taussig (1971) 'Family equivalence scales and personal income tax exemptions for children', *Review of Economics and Statistics*, **53**, 253–62.

Shell, K. (1971) 'Notes on the economics of infinity', *Journal of Political Economy*, **79**, 1002–11.

Sheshinski, E. (1972a) 'Relation between a social welfare function and the Gini index of inequality', *Journal of Economic Theory*, **4**, 98–100.

(1972b) 'The optimal linear income tax', *Review of Economic Studies*, **39**, 297–302.

(1978) 'A model of social security and retirement decisions', *Journal of Public Economics*, **10**, 337–60.

Sheshinski, E. and Y. Weiss (1981) 'Uncertainty and optimal social security systems', *Quarterly Journal of Economics*, **96**, 189–206.

Shorrocks, A.F. (1980) 'The class of additively decomposable inequality measures', *Econometrica*, **48**, 613–25.

(1983) 'Ranking income distributions', *Economica*, **50**, 3–17.

(1984) 'Inequality decompositions by population subgroups', *Econometrica*, **52**, 1369–85.

Shoven, J.B. and J. Whalley (1972) 'A general equilibrium calculation of the effects of differential taxation of income from capital in the U.S.', *Journal of Public Economics*, **1**, 281–321.

Simons, H.C. (1938) *Personal income taxation*, Chicago: University of Chicago Press.

Smith, A. (1776) *An enquiry into the nature and causes of the wealth of nations*, London: Metheun.

Smith, A. (1981) 'The informal economy', *Lloyds Bank Review*, 45–61.

Smith, A. (1982), 'Intergenerational transfers as social insurance', *Journal of Public Economics*, **19**, 97–106.

(1983) 'Tax reform and temporary inefficiency', *Journal of Public Economics*, **20**, 265–70.

Spence, M. (1977) 'Nonlinear prices and welfare', *Journal of Public Economics*, **8**, 1–18.

Spicer, M.W. and S.B. Lundstedt (1976) 'Understanding tax evasion', *Public Finance*, **31**, 295–305.

Srinivasan, P.V. (1989) 'Redistributive impact of "optimal" commodity taxes', *Economics Letters*, **30**, 385–8.

Srinivasan, T.N. (1973) 'Tax evasion: a model', *Journal of Public Economics*, **2**, 339–46.

Starret, D.A. (1972) 'Fundamental nonconvexities in the theory of externalitites', *Journal of Economic Theory*, **4**, 180–99.

Stern, N.H. (1976) 'On the specification of models of optimum income taxation', *Journal of Public Economics*, **6**, 123–62.

(1987) 'The effects of taxation, price control and government contracts in oligopoly and monopolistic competition', *Journal of Public Economics*, **32**, 133–58.

Stiglitz, J.E. (1969a) 'The effects of income,wealth, and capital gains taxation on risk-taking', *Quarterly Journal of Economics*, **83**, 262–83.

(1969b) 'A re-examination of the Modigliani-Miller Theorem', *American Economic Review*, **59**, 784–93.

(1973), 'Taxation, corporate financial policy, and the cost of capital', *Journal of Public Economics*, **2**, 1–34.

(1974) 'On the irrelevance of corporate financial policy', *American Economic Review*, **64**, 851–66.

(1976) 'The corporation tax', *Journal of Public Economics*, **5**, 303–11.

Stokey, N.L. and R.E. Lucas with E.C. Prescott (1989) *Recursive methods in economic dynamics*, Cambridge, MA: Harvard University Press.

Stone, R. (1954) 'Linear expenditure systems and demand analysis: an application to the pattern of British demand', *Economic Journal*, **64**, 511–27.

Sugden, R. (1984) 'Reciprocity: the supply of public goods through voluntary contributions', *Economic Journal*, **94**, 772–87.

(1985) 'Consistent conjectures and voluntary contributions to public goods: why the conventional theory does not work', *Journal of Public Economics*, **27**, 117–24.

Svensson, L.G. and J.W. Weibull (1986) 'An upper bound on optimal income taxes', *Journal of Public Economics*, **30**, 165–81.

Sweeney, R.J. (1988) *Wealth effects and monetary theory*, New York: Basil Blackwell.

Taggart, R.A. (1980) 'Taxes and corporate capital structure in an incomplete market', *Journal of Finance*, **35**, 645–59.

Takayama, A. (1985) *Mathematical economics*, Cambridge: Cambridge University Press.

Takayama, N. (1979) 'Poverty, income inequality, and their measures: Professor Sen's axiomatic approach reconsidered', *Econometrica*, **47**, 747–58.

Theil, H. (1967) *Economics and information theory*, Amsterdam: North-Holland.

Thompson, L.H. (1983) 'The social security reform debate', *Journal of Economic Literature*, **21**, 1425–67.

Townsend, P. (1979) *Poverty in the United Kingdom*, London: Penguin.

Tuomala, M. (1985) 'Simplified formulae for optimal linear income taxation', *Scandinavian Journal of Economics*, **87**, 668–72.

(1990) *Optimal income tax and redistribution*, Oxford: Clarendon Press.

US Department of Commerce (1993) *Survey of Current Business*, **73**, September.

Varian, H.R. (1980) 'Redistributive taxation as social insurance', *Journal of Public Economics*, **14**, 49–68.

(1984) 'Price discrimination and social welfare', *American Economic Review*, **75**, 870–5.

(1992) *Microeconomic theory*, New York: Norton.

Veall, M.R. (1986) 'Public pensions as optimal social contracts', *Journal of Public Economics*, **31**, 237–51.

Venables, A.J. (1986) 'Production subsidies, import tariffs and imperfectly competitive trade', in D. Greenaway and P.K.M. Tharakan (eds.), *Imperfect competition and international trade*, Sussex: Wheatsheaf.

Vickrey, W. (1964) 'Discussion', *American Economic Review*, Papers and Proceedings, **59**, 88–92.

Virmani, A. (1989) 'Indirect tax evasion and production efficiency', *Journal of Public Economics*, **39**, 223–37.

von Neumann, J. and O. Morgernstern (1953) *Theory of games and economic behaviour*, Third Edition, Princeton: Princeton University Press.

Walras, L. (1874) *Elements d'économie politique pure*, Lausanne: L. Corbaz. English translation by W. Jaffe (1954), *Elements of pure economics*, London: Allen and Unwin.

Warr, P.G. (1983) 'The private provision of a pure public good is independent of the distribution of income', *Economics Letters*, **13**, 207–11.

Weber, S. and H. Wiesmeth (1991) 'The equivalence of core and cost share equilibria in an economy with public goods', *Journal of Economic Theory*, **54**, 180–97.

Weil, P. (1987) 'Love thy children; reflections on the Barro debt neutrality theorem', *Journal of Monetary Economics*, **19**, 378–91.

Weitzman, M.L. (1974) 'Prices vs. quantities', *Review of Economic Studies*, **41**, 477–91.

Weymark, J.A. (1979a) 'Generalised Gini inequality indices', Discussion paper no. 79–12, Department of Economics, University of British Columbia.

(1979b) 'A reconciliation of recent results in optimal taxation theory', *Journal of Public Economics*, **12**, 171–89.

(1981) 'Undominated directions of tax reform', *Journal of Public Economics*, **16**, 343–69.

Wilson, J.D. (1991a) 'Optimal public good provision in the Ramsey tax model: a generalization', *Economics Letters*, **35**, 57–61.

(1991b) 'Optimal public good provision with limited lump-sum taxation', *American Economic Review*, **81**, 153–66.

Yamada, M. (1990) 'An analysis of optimal taxation with tax evasion', *Public Finance*, **45**, 470–90.

Yitzhaki, S. (1974) 'Income tax evasion: a theoretical analysis', *Journal of Public Economics*, **3**, 201–2.

Yohe, G.W. (1978) 'Towards a general comparison of price controls and quantity controls under uncertainty', *Review of Economic Studies*, **45**, 229–38.

Young, D. (1982) 'Voluntary purchase of public goods', *Public Choice*, **38**, 73–86.

AUTHOR INDEX

SUBJECT INDEX